C-E

ECONOMICS

A Canadian Perspective

ECONOMICS
A Canadian Perspective

James D. Thexton

Toronto
OXFORD UNIVERSITY PRESS

Oxford University Press,
70 Wynford Drive, Don Mills, Ontario M3C 1J9

Oxford   New York
Athens   Auckland   Bangkok   Bombay
Calcutta   Cape Town   Dar es Salaam   Delhi
Florence   Hong Kong   Istanbul   Karachi
Kuala Lumpur   Madras   Madrid   Melbourne
Mexico City   Nairobi   Paris   Singapore
Taipei   Tokyo   Toronto

and associated companies in
Berlin   Ibadan

Oxford is a trademark of Oxford University Press

This book is printed on permanent (acid-free) paper ∞.

Canadian Cataloguing in Publication Data

Thexton, James D., 1930–
    Economics: a Canadian perspective

Includes bibliographical references and index.
ISBN 0-19-540747-4

1. Economics.   2. Canada - Economic conditions.
I. Title.

HB171.5.T54   1992   330   C91-095220-5

Senior editors: Geraldine Kikuta, Anthony Luengo
Project editor: Monica Schwalbe
Design: Marie Bartholomew
Cover and chapter opening illustrations: Jay Belmore
Composition: Trigraph Inc.

Printed and bound in Canada by D.W. Friesen

4 5   99

TO ERIC AND THE MEMORY OF PETER

ACKNOWLEDGEMENTS

The efforts of many people, too many to mention individually, have gone into the production of this book. To them all, I am grateful.

Particularly, I would like to acknowledge the following who reviewed parts of the early drafts of the manuscript. Their comments and suggestions were helpful in the preparation of the final draft. They included Ron Bourdeau, Walkerville Collegiate Institute, Windsor; Don Kennedy, Red River Community College, Winnipeg; Brian B. Lorimer, Lorne Park Secondary School, Mississauga; Steve Officer, London South Secondary School, London; T. L. Seymour, Riverdale Collegiate Institute, Toronto; and Jamie Whitaker, Western Technical Commercial School, Toronto.

Special thanks also to all those at Oxford University Press who were involved in the production of the book—especially Monica Schwalbe for her patient and instructive editing. Only she and I know the extent of her contribution.

J.D. Thexton
Toronto
1992

CONTENTS

Acknowledgements   vi

UNIT ONE   Economics is...   1

CHAPTER ONE   Scarcity and Economics   2
CHAPTER TWO   Economic Systems   20

UNIT TWO   Efficient Use of Resources   43

CHAPTER THREE   Demand and Supply   44
CHAPTER FOUR   Dynamics of the Market   73
CHAPTER FIVE   The Entrepreneur   98
CHAPTER SIX   Business Organization and Finance   115
CHAPTER SEVEN   Production and Costs   140
CHAPTER EIGHT   Perfect Competition   157
CHAPTER NINE   Monopoly   175
CHAPTER TEN   Monopolistic Competition and Oligopoly   189

UNIT THREE   Equitable Distribution of Income   211

CHAPTER ELEVEN   Labour Markets and Labour Unions   212
CHAPTER TWELVE   Rent, Interest, and Profit   245
CHAPTER THIRTEEN   The Role of Government   258
CHAPTER FOURTEEN   Distribution of Income   282

UNIT FOUR   Economic Stability   305

CHAPTER FIFTEEN   Our Economic Scoreboard   306
CHAPTER SIXTEEN   Economic Instability   337
CHAPTER SEVENTEEN   Aggregate Demand and Aggregate Supply   364
CHAPTER EIGHTEEN   Fiscal Policy   376
CHAPTER NINETEEN   Money and Banking   393
CHAPTER TWENTY   Monetary Policy   420

UNIT FIVE   Economic Growth and International Trade   443

CHAPTER TWENTY-ONE   Economic Growth and Productivity   444
CHAPTER TWENTY-TWO   International Trade   472
CHAPTER TWENTY-THREE   Trade and Investment Policy   499

Glossary   525

Bibliography   538

Index   541

Economics is...

It is difficult to pick up a newspaper or turn on the television or radio news without encountering economic facts, interpretations, and opinions. To sort out the economic information that surrounds us, we need some familiarity with the subject of economics, and some understanding of how our economy works.

Economics, essentially, is about making choices. We must make choices in our roles as consumers, producers, and citizens of a society. Some choices are relatively easy, such as what groceries to buy or whether to go to a movie. Others are more difficult—what company to work for or what occupation to pursue, for example. Those decisions we make as members of society through our elected representatives are among the most important and most difficult. Decisions, such as whether we should enter a free trade agreement with the United States and Mexico or whether to impose the Goods and Services Tax, affect the lives and prosperity of all Canadians.

In this first unit, we consider the question "What is economics?" and examine how economists conduct their investigations. We then examine economic systems and how traditional, command, and free market economies have attempted to meet the needs of their citizens. The unit concludes with a consideration of Canada's major economic objectives, which become the basis for the subsequent units of this book.

CHAPTER ONE

Scarcity and Economics

A new car? New clothes? A compact disc? The leather or the wool coat? The concert or the film? We are always facing decisions about what we need, what we want, and what we can afford. But as individuals, we are not the only ones faced with these decisions. Families, too, must decide where to live, whether to buy or rent a home, what food and clothing are needed, how leisure time will be spent, and so on.

Local, provincial, and federal governments are also confronted with the ever-pressing need to make decisions. How can revenue be raised—through an increased deficit or with higher taxes? If higher taxes are chosen, which taxes should be raised and by how much? How should the revenues be spent—on jet fighters, hospitals, garbage disposal, or increased welfare payments?

Objectives

a. Relate needs, wants, and resources to the fundamental problem of economics—scarcity.

b. Distinguish among natural, capital, and human resources and provide examples of each.

c. Reach reasoned decisions using a decision-making model.

d. Explain and apply the concept of opportunity cost.

e. Define economics and demonstrate how it applies the scientific method.

f. Distinguish between positive and normative economics with examples.

g. Recognize and avoid some of the common reasoning errors when analyzing economic data.

h. Understand how the terms law, principle, model, and theory are used in economics.

i. Graph and interpret a production possibilities curve.

j. Demonstrate the relationships among the production possibilities curve, scarcity, choice, and opportunity cost.

Why must we continually make choices? The reason is that while our needs and wants are unlimited, our means to satisfy them—our resources (incomes and savings)—are limited. Since our resources are limited, we must use them in the best way possible, in other words, *economically*. Our continual need to make decisions would be much less pressing, however, if choosing one thing did not mean giving up something else.

Needs and Wants

Needs are the basic human physical requirements necessary to sustain life, such as food, clothing, and shelter. We need enough food of appropriate variety to keep us in good health, and enough clothing and shelter to protect us from the rigours of the weather. These physical needs are constant, though they may vary with our circumstances. The types of food, clothing, and shelter we need in the Arctic differs from that we need in the tropics, for example. Our needs may also be influenced by the values and attitudes of our society. Some communities find horseflesh quite acceptable as food. We do not.

Wants are the desire for goods or services not essential to sustain human life, such as stylish clothing, exotic foods, jewellery, or travel in the tropics. While needs may be relatively simple and physical in nature, wants are more complex and largely psychological. With the developments of science and technology, for example, new products such as computers and compact disc players are developed—and we learn to want things earlier generations never dreamed would exist.

As our income grows, our wants for goods and services grow. **Goods** are the concrete, physical products we manufacture, such as furniture and automobiles. **Services** are the activities we engage in and sell to others, such as medical and retail services. Wants have a high reproduction rate. The desire for a new outfit spawns the desire for a new pair of shoes. The race between wants and income is unending, and income is almost invariably the loser. Wants easily outstrip our capacity to satisfy them.

Resources

What exactly, then, are our resources? Many people on being asked this question would tap their wallets or purses, or perhaps mention their bank balances. For most of us, however, our principal resource is our ability to earn money through our labour. Economists define **resources** as all those elements used in the production of goods and services designed to meet our needs and wants. Resources are divided into three broad categories—natural, human, and capital.

Natural resources (sometimes called land) are all the resources in nature that have value. They include land, minerals, fresh water, and forests, for example.

Human resources (also called labour) are the human efforts (manual and non-manual) used in the production of goods and services. Human resources include not only the labour of farmers and factory workers, but also the services provided by secretaries and scientists, for example. To economists, musicians who perform rock concerts and instructors who give lectures in economics are just as engaged in production as are farmers growing fruit and factory workers manufacturing refrigerators. In considering the human resources of a country, we examine not only the size and health of its population, but also the people's education, skills, and willingness to work.

Capital resources are goods used in the production of other goods or services. Factories, machines, and tools are examples. Capital resources differ from natural resources in that they are made by people. They range from the simple implements used in hunting and fishing—such as fishing rods and bows and arrows—to modern automated production lines. The use of capital resources in production enables us to produce more goods and services than would be the case without them.

Scarcity

An understanding of needs, wants, and resources leads us to the fundamental fact of economics—**scarcity**. A limited amount of resources is available to produce a

□ □ □ □ □ □

Skill Development: Decision Making

It is difficult to think of many decisions that do not in some way involve economics. Economics, in fact, has been described as "the science of choice." A reasoned, step-by-step decision-making process can help to make some difficult decisions less formidable. Let's consider an example.

Natasha is in her final year of high school. She has not yet decided what she will do next year, but she is considering three possibilities: continue her studies at college or university, take a job, or perhaps travel in other countries.

Step 1 Define the problem

What is Natasha's problem? State the problem in a single sentence, preferably in the form of a question. In this case, the problem is quite clear: *What should Natasha do next year?* In some more complex situations, such as labour disputes, just sorting out the basic problem can be difficult. This first step in the decision-making process is, therefore, a very important one.

Step 2 List the possible alternatives

What choices does Natasha have? List her three major options. For example, she could:

1. continue her education at college or university.
2. take a job.
3. spend the year travelling.

Step 3 List the criteria

The reason Natasha has a problem is that no single option stands out as the best. The next step, therefore, is to list all the criteria or standards that can be used to judge the alternatives. To define the criteria, consider the advantages and disadvantages of each option. For example, an advantage of taking a job is that Natasha would earn an income next year. A disadvantage of travelling is that she wouldn't earn money. Income next year, therefore, is one criterion.

List the three or four most important criteria.

1. Cost.   2. Income next year.   3. Income in the future.

Step 4 Use the criteria to evaluate each alternative

On a decision-making grid like that in Figure 1.1:

(a) list the alternatives from Step 2 down the left side of the grid
(b) list the criteria from Step 3 across the top
(c) evaluate each alternative using the criteria and place a plus or a minus sign on the grid, depending on whether or not the alternative fulfills each criterion.

Figure 1.1 Decision-making grid

Problem: What should Natasha do next year?

ALTERNATIVES	CRITERIA		
	COST	INCOME NEXT YEAR	FUTURE INCOME
Continue her education	+	- -	+ + +
Take a job	-	+ +	+ + +
Spend the year travelling	+	- -	- - -

Step 5 Give each criterion a weighting

Weight each criterion according to its importance. For example, income next year may be twice as important as cost (x2), while future income is three times as important as cost (x3). Natasha would, therefore, double the score under income next year and triple it under future income.

Step 6 Make a decision!

The decision-making grid displays your criteria, alternatives, and assessment of each alternative. It provides you with a simple and useful summary for reaching a decision on Natasha's problem. A quick addition of the positives shows that Natasha's best choice, according to her priorities, is to take a job next year.

Clearly, many decision-making problems may be much more complex, but this basic framework of outlining the main alternatives, determining the criteria, weighting them, and then using them to assess each alternative can be applied in almost all cases.

Applications

1. What do you plan to do next year? Consider a number of options and use the six-step decision-making model to find the best option for you.

2. Suppose you have been offered three jobs next year, but you are not sure which one to take. Use the decision-making model to reach a decision.

3. You have decided to continue your education next year, but you are undecided about which institution to attend. Use the decision-making model to make a choice.

4. Apply the decision-making model to a problem you have now or have had in the past. Evaluate how well the decision-making model worked for you.

---

limited number of goods and services to meet relatively unlimited human wants. For much of the world's population, the scarcity of adequate food, clothing, and shelter is painfully apparent. Even in affluent Canada, scarcity is always present. Our wants exceed our ability to satisfy them.

Economists thus make a distinction between economic and free goods. **Economic goods** are those that are scarce. Since not enough of them exist to provide for all wants and needs, we must decide how to use and distribute them. We place an *economic value* on them. **Free goods** are those that exist in sufficient quantities to satisfy everyone's wants. There is no scarcity of them. Drinking water is often regarded as free in Canada, for example, apart from the cost of pumping, piping, and purifying. In many countries including Canada, however, it is sold by the bottle. It is, therefore, an economic good.

▌ Opportunity Cost

Since we have scarcity, a decision to buy one item is a decision to give up another. **Opportunity cost** is the cost of all that is lost from taking one course of action over another. It is the satisfaction that would have been derived from the best alternative use of resources. For example, if I decide to have hamburgers for lunch rather than hot dogs, then the opportunity cost of the hamburgers is the satisfaction lost of consuming hot dogs. The opportunity cost of a holiday on a Caribbean

isle includes both the satisfaction lost from an alternative use of resources, and the earnings relinquished in taking the trip.

Opportunity cost is a fundamental economic concept. Any economic decision must consider not only what is to be gained, but also what is lost or given up.

▌ Economics is . . .

What then is economics? **Economics** is the science that studies human behaviour as a relationship between ends and scarce means which have alternative uses.

Since economics includes so much and is changing so rapidly, you are very likely to come across other definitions. Most definitions, however, cover the same essential points—that resources are scarce relative to wants and that we must, therefore, make choices about what will be produced and how it will be distributed. As an independent field of study, economics is relatively recent—only some two centuries old.

▢ Economics as a Science

It may seem peculiar to define economics as a science. After all, when we think of science we usually think of the study of nature, not the study of people.

However, what characterizes a science is not *what* it studies, but rather *how* it pursues its investigations. Economics, like other social sciences such as sociology

□ □ □ □ □ □

Bitter Harvest: Scarcity and Agricultural Land

Some of the best agricultural land in Canada is disappearing rapidly! Although Canada is the second largest country in the world, most of it is unsuited for agriculture. Only a limited area—about 15 percent—can support farming at all, and the bulk of this is on the Prairies.

The best land is in southern Ontario and British Columbia, where development pressures are the most intense. In recent decades, Canada's prime agricultural land has been disappearing at a rapid clip. Between 1966 and 1986, for instance, about 3000 km² of rural land were converted to urban uses, according to Environment Canada. This is much less than 1 percent of all available agricultural land, but in area it is 30 times larger than the city of Toronto.

The trend has alarmed preservationists who worry that Canada is allowing its best farmlands to be destroyed and that, like many less developed countries, it risks losing the ability to feed itself. "It is vital that a country and a province retain their ability to feed as many people as they can," says Gracia Janes, president of the Preservation of Agricultural Lands Society, a St. Catharines-based farm support group. "We're Third World if we can't supply our own food," she declares.

Canada exports more food than it imports, but it imports large quantities of such tropical products as sugar, coffee, tea, cocoa, and bananas that cannot be grown this far north. It has also become dependent on the United States for much of its fresh fruit and vegetables.

This reliance on foreign food sources is of concern to many. By depending on US food supplies and allowing domestic farmland to be destroyed, Canada is becoming vulnerable to US agricultural problems. As in Canada, the stock of US farmland is being diminished by urbanization. A potential warning of things to come is the long-running drought in California, which has reduced the water supply to the state farm sector. Much of Canada's fresh vegetables comes from California. US agricultural production could be further undermined by the consequences of global warming and the reduction of the Earth's ozone layer.

"One of the reasons advanced for not protecting farmland is that we will always be able to buy the food we need from outside the country," says Patrick Mooney, a professor in the department of plant science at the University of British Columbia in Vancouver. But that thinking may be a fallacy, because Canada could become vulnerable to food shortages. "Good agricultural lands in the mildest regions should be protected," he says.

The land under Ontario cities alone would have the capacity to feed more than 750 000 if it had been maintained for agriculture. The area under all of the country's major urban areas could have fed 1.5 million people.

Farmers, however, are finding it increasingly difficult to make a living and many feel they are forced to sell their land. Clearly, farmers receive much more for land sold to developers than for land sold as farmland. One Niagara farm group pointed out that while land sold for farming brings approximately $40 000 per ha, land sold for property development brings as much as $200 000 per ha. The Regional Municipality of Niagara has some of the toughest land-use policies in Canada, intended to limit development on the prime farming areas, but farmers argue that they cannot compete with US growers and need the right to sell parcels of land to developers to ease their financial plight.

Governments and conservation groups are looking for other solutions. One of these is "conservation easements," by which farmers could sell development rights to their land to governments or conservation groups. The farmers would get much needed cash and a fair return on their land, and the land would be protected from development speculators. Other proposals include preservation laws and land reserves. Land reserves were set up in British Columbia in the 1970s to slow the destruction of farmland, though development has continued on many prime parcels around Vancouver.

SOURCE: Adapted from Martin Mittelstaedt, "Bitter Harvest: There's a subtle blight killing our farmlands," *The Globe and Mail*, April 6, 1991.

Applications
1. Define the problem of scarcity outlined in this article.
2. What are the opportunity costs of:
(a) losing the country's prime agricultural land to development

(b) banning development on the agricultural lands.
3. Explain the proposals put forward to ease the problem. Do you consider the proposals workable? What opportunity costs might they involve?

---

and psychology, has much in common with the natural sciences in that it uses a common approach—the **scientific method**. While there are many different ways of outlining how scientists make their discoveries, we can identify four basic steps in the scientific method—observation, collection, explanation, and verification.

Observation

The starting point is often the tickling of our curiosity by what we observe. We want to know why something happens or what the relationship is between two events. Suppose, for example, we notice that as the price of eggs drops, the number bought increases. We then formulate the question: "What is the relationship between the price of eggs and the quantity sold?"

Collection

Next, we collect information to help answer the question. We could survey provincial and federal departments of agriculture, consumers, and grocery stores to find out what happens to egg purchases as prices vary. Economists would try to measure how much egg purchases vary with each variation in price.

However, the economist's data are far less likely to be precise than those of the natural scientist. Chemists can often control all the factors in an experiment, such as temperature, pressure, humidity, and the purity of their chemicals. They can, therefore, isolate the factors they wish to examine. Economists, by contrast, work in an environment with many more uncontrollable factors that could affect the information they are collecting. Incomes, tastes, and the general health of the economy, for example, are constantly changing. Rigorously controlled experiments are usually impossible in economics. Imagine our reaction if we were to discover that the price of eggs had been raised to $50 a dozen so

that a group of economists could examine the relationship between the price of eggs and the quantity bought!

Explanation

The purpose of observation and collection of data is to reach a valid conclusion. The information we have collected must be organized in a logical way to formulate a possible answer to the original question. The tentative explanation is called a hypothesis.

Defined then, a **hypothesis** is an explanation for the relationship between two or more variables, which can be tested by reference to facts. A **variable** is a factor that can take on different values. The variables in our investigation are price and quantity.

After organizing the information, we could state the hypothesis that as the price of eggs increases, the quantity bought decreases. Similarly, as the price decreases, the quantity bought increases. Economists may also be able to predict by how much the quantity bought will vary with given changes in price.

Verification

The final step in the process is to verify the hypothesis. The hypothesis must account satisfactorily for the facts on which it is based, and more importantly, explain new data or predict events. If the hypothesis does this satisfactorily, then it is frequently called a **theory** or generalization. If the hypothesis is unable to explain new data, then it must be modified or rejected.

Once a theory has been adequately tested and accepted, it can be applied either to explain facts which formerly had been puzzling, or to help predict what is likely to happen in the future. Most economic predictions are statements such as: "If you do x, then y will follow." A prediction based on the theory in our example would be: "If you cut the price of eggs, then more eggs will be purchased."

This four-step process for the development of economic theory, summarized in Figure 1.2, is only one sequence. Other sequences may be just as appropriate. For example, the simple observation of events may lead to the formulation of a hypothesis, and the collection of data may be temporarily side-stepped.

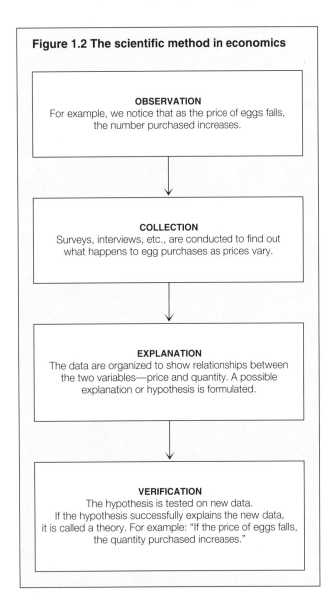

Figure 1.2 The scientific method in economics

OBSERVATION
For example, we notice that as the price of eggs falls, the number purchased increases.

COLLECTION
Surveys, interviews, etc., are conducted to find out what happens to egg purchases as prices vary.

EXPLANATION
The data are organized to show relationships between the two variables—price and quantity. A possible explanation or hypothesis is formulated.

VERIFICATION
The hypothesis is tested on new data. If the hypothesis successfully explains the new data, it is called a theory. For example: "If the price of eggs falls, the quantity purchased increases."

□ Is the Behaviour of People Predictable?

But is the behaviour of people predictable? It may be argued that while in the natural sciences prediction is possible because matter is subject to natural "laws," in the social sciences prediction is impossible because people have free will, and therefore their behaviour is not subject to "laws." A skeptic could point to an individual who always buys a dozen eggs no matter what the price, and say that our generalization is therefore a very imperfect prediction of behaviour.

The point, though, is that while the behaviour of individuals may be unpredictable, that of a large group is predictable. On a hot day more people consume more ice cream and more soft drinks than on a cold day. This statement can be supported by fact. The behaviour of the group is predictable. Whether particular individuals will consume more soft drinks or more ice cream, we don't know. Individual behaviour is unpredictable.

□ Positive and Normative Economics

It is not uncommon, however, to find economists engaged in vigorous dispute. One reason for dispute is that economists have different values, and these value differences play a significant role in public discussion. To understand the debates, it is important to distinguish between positive or analytical statements, and value or normative statements in economics.

Positive (or analytical) economics deals with the analysis of economic facts and the development of theories based on actual observations. It is concerned with two types of statements—descriptive and conditional.

(i) Descriptive statements   These statements describe things as they *are* or *have been*. For example: "Unemployment is at 6 percent." This is a fact.

(ii) Conditional statements   These statements take the form: "If *x* occurs, then *y* will result." For example: "If the federal and provincial governments raise minimum wages, then more people will be unemployed." This statement is a prediction based on the analysis of economic behaviour and can be substantiated or refuted by reference to facts.

Normative (or policy) economics, on the other hand, is concerned with what *should* or *ought to be*. Normative statements cannot be settled solely by reference to facts. They are value judgements, often including the words "should" or "ought to." The goals or policy statements of governments or interest groups are often based on values. An example of a normative statement is: "Government should provide more aid to institutions of higher education." Obviously, this statement is not a fact, but an expression of opinion open to debate.

Laws, Principles, Models, and Theories

In your study of economics, you will come across a number of commonly used terms such as laws, principles, models, and theories. Essentially, they all refer to generalizations about the economic behaviour of institutions and individuals.

The terms "economic laws" and "economic principles" are commonly used in the same way. Thus, phrases such as "the law of supply and demand" and "the principle of supply and demand" express the same generalizations about the relationships between price and quantity demanded and price and quantity supplied, for example. It is important to remember, however, that the laws of economics do not imply the same degree of exactness as the "laws of physics," nor the same legal imperative as the "laws of Canada."

You have certainly come across models before, whether they were models of ships or trains or models of chemical elements or the DNA molecule. In economics, as in other subjects, models are used for teaching and research purposes. Since reality is highly complex and continually changing, models help to explain complex situations by reducing them to their simplest forms. **Economic models** are simplified representations of an economy or part of an economy. They may be expressed verbally, graphically, or mathematically.

An **economic theory** is a generalization or set of generalizations that makes it possible for us to understand and predict economic activity. When predictions about economic behaviour or activity are shown to be in agreement with the facts, we have an economic theory.

Any economic law, principle, model, or theory has three component parts: definitions of the terms used in its explanation; a number of assumptions defining the conditions in which it is applicable; and one or more hypotheses concerning the relationships among the variables it is intended to explain. We have already examined hypotheses. The one component we have not yet examined—assumptions—deserves a closer look.

☐ Assumptions

Jason: "If the price of Chevrolets is reduced by 10 percent, will sales increase?"
Maria: "Yes."

Maria's reply is a common one. Her reply includes a number of assumptions, even though she does not explicitly state them. Any one of a number of factors could nullify the effects of the price cut on the sale of Chevrolets. Maria assumes that the prices of competing automobiles are not reduced significantly—say by 20 percent. She also assumes that the incomes of potential buyers do not decline, for if they did, automobile sales may fall along with them. She assumes that there is no change in tastes that may make the design of the Chevrolet unfashionable and that of its competitors popular, with the consequent impact on sales.

We could go on listing Maria's assumptions, but the point is that anytime we state an economic relationship between two variables, we assume that no other changes are taking place. To understand the relationship, economists must "isolate" it. Only after they establish the relationship will they begin to consider what other changes may affect it. Maria's response could have been, then: "Yes—if we assume no other changes." We would add to our earlier hypothesis: "If we assume no other changes, as the price of eggs increases, the quantity demanded decreases. As the price decreases, the quantity demanded increases." Economists call the phrase "if we assume no other changes" the *ceteris paribus* (other things being equal) assumption.

□ □ □ □ □ □

Skill Development: Economic Reasoning

In examining economic issues, events, and problems, we need to be aware of the common reasoning errors. Let's examine some of these common pitfalls.

Single Causation

Example: The 1990-1991 recession in Canada was caused by the high interest rate policies of the Bank of Canada.

There were many causes of the 1990-1991 recession in Canada, including the slowdown of economic activity in the US, Japan, and the European Economic Community—Canada's main external markets. To assert, therefore, that high interest rates were the sole cause is to oversimplify.

The **single causation fallacy** is the error of believing that a single factor caused an event, when in fact it had many causes.

Cause-and-Effect Fallacy

Example: Day follows night, therefore night (event A) causes day (event B).

It is a fact that day follows night, but this doesn't *necessarily* mean that day causes night. The two events may be purely coincidental, or they may be caused by another factor. In this case, the other factor is the rotation of the earth. The cause-and-effect fallacy is sometimes called either the *post hoc ergo propter hoc* (Latin for *after this, therefore because of this*), or the *post hoc* fallacy.

The **cause-and-effect fallacy** is to believe that because event *x* occurs before event *y*, *x* causes *y*.

Subjectivity   What is A?

A.

B.

What is A?

A.

C.

Is it a bird, antelope, or rabbit? There is, of course, no single correct answer. Each may be correct, depending on the context—whether we see A against the background of B or C. We tend to perceive it as a bird against B, and as an antelope or rabbit against C.

As with these figures, so too with many facts and theories. While theories help us sort our way through the confusion of information we receive everyday, they can distort our vision. We wear a particular set of theoretical spectacles through which we view the world and filter out other perceptions of reality. This helps to explain why, for example, if we live in a country with a capitalist economic system, we may find it difficult to sympathize with other economic systems.

Subjectivity is the perception of observed facts in the light of our own biases and the theories we accept.

Wishful Thinking

Example: "...Given a chance to go forward with the policies of the last eight years, we [in the United States] shall soon...be in sight of the day when poverty will be vanished from this nation."—Herbert Hoover, US president 1928-1932, on the eve of the Great Depression.

This statement is an example of wishful thinking. **Wishful thinking** is seeing what we want to see and believing what we want to believe. Our judgement of an event is clouded by what we hope will happen.

Loaded Terminology

Example: "The Free Trade Agreement was a Tory sell-out of Canadian resources to the United States."

"Sell-out" is used in this statement to sway the readers' attitude toward the federal Conservative government and its trade agreement with the United States. Readers must be aware of authors' possible biases and persuasive techniques.

Loaded terminology is the use of emotionally-loaded terms in an attempt to sway opinion.

Incorrect Use of Terminology

Example: Inflation is caused by rising prices. Therefore, if you stop prices from rising, you cure inflation.

This is an illogical statement. Economists define inflation as a general increase in the level of prices. Inflation *is*, then, generally rising prices. The statement makes as much sense as saying: "Inflation is caused by inflation. Therefore, if you stop inflation, you cure inflation."

It is important to understand economic terms clearly and to use them correctly. Some terms (e.g., investment, profit) have a specific economic meaning that differs from their common usage. If in doubt, consult the glossary in this book or a dictionary of economics.

Personification of a Problem

Example: The Trudeau inflation of the early 1980s.

Complicated problems—such as depression and inflation—are often identified with a prominent person, such as a president or prime minister, as a way of placing the blame on that person. This way of oversimplifying economic and political problems, however, does little to enhance our knowledge or understanding, let alone suggest a solution to the problem.

Personification is the oversimplification of a problem or a situation by identifying it with a prominent person.

The Fallacy of Composition

Example: You are watching your favourite football team in a championship game. Suddenly, your team executes a number of brilliant plays and looks as if it is about to score. To see the game better, you jump to your feet. Standing, you can see the game perfectly—that is, until everyone else stands too. Then, no one can see well.

Individually, you see the game much better when you stand up, but when everyone follows your example, no one has a clear view. So, what may be true for one or a few, may not be true generally.

The **fallacy of composition** states that what is true for an individual or a part is not necessarily true for the whole.

Applications

1. Identify the kind of faulty reasoning displayed in each of the following statements. Give reasons for your conclusions.

(a) Since Victoria, British Columbia has one of the highest death rates in the country, it must be the most unhealthy city in Canada.

(b) The Mulroney recession of 1990-1991.

(c) It is obvious that there was a secret pact to raise the value of the Canadian dollar as part of the Canada-US Free Trade Agreement. You just have to look at the increase in the value of the dollar in the three years after the Free Trade Agreement for the evidence.

(d) The Free Trade Agreement with the United States caused the closure of hundreds of businesses in Canada in 1990 and 1991.

(e) "Prosperity is just around the corner"—a common saying in the 1930s.

(f) If we all get a 10 percent pay increase, we'll all be better off.

(g) Since the rooster crows before dawn, he causes the sun to rise.

(h) The American economy is "absolutely sound" and stocks are "cheap at current prices"—US President Coolidge in the fall of 1928.

(i) "What is good for General Motors is good for the United States"—Charles Wilson, President of General Motors in an appearance in 1953 before the Senate Armed Services Committee.

(j) The cause of unemployment is too many people out of work.

(k) Workers are always trying to do as little work as possible for as much pay as possible.

(l) Are the inside curved lines the same or different?

□ □ □ □ □ □

Skill Development: Graphing

A **graph** is a diagram or illustration that shows how two or more sets of figures are related. In studying economics, it is essential to be able to read and interpret graphs. Much of economics is concerned with relationships between different sets of figures. While these relationships can be described verbally, they can be depicted visually and often more effectively through graphs.

A **co-ordinate graph** consists of two straight lines (called axes or co-ordinates), which intersect at an angle of 90 degrees. The intersection point is called the origin. Figure 1.3 shows a co-ordinate graph. The two co-ordinates divide the space into four quadrants with the positive values of the *x* or horizontal co-ordinate to the right of the origin, and the negative values to the left. The positive values of the *y* or vertical co-ordinate are above the origin, and the negative values below. In the upper right-hand quadrant, the values of both the *x* and *y* co-ordinates are positive. This quadrant is the one used most often in economics.

Plotting Points

Figure 1.4 shows how the following values are plotted on a co-ordinate graph and then joined to form a **curve** .

Point	*x* values	*y* values
A	1	4
B	2	3
C	3	2
D	4	1

Notice we usually refer to a line such as ABCD on the graph as a curve, even though it may be a straight line.

Figure 1.3 A co-ordinate graph

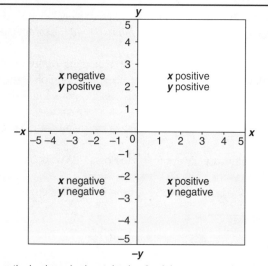

y vertical axis   *x* horizontal axis   **0** origin

Figure 1.4 Plotting points on a co-ordinate graph

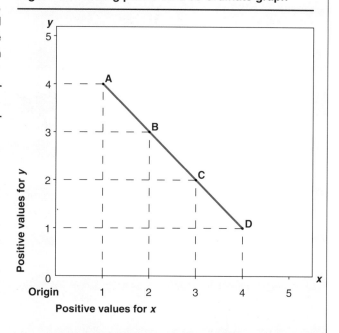

To plot point A, move vertically from 1 on the *x* axis to 4 on the *y* axis. To plot point B, find 2 on the *x* axis and move vertically to 3 on the *y* axis. Follow the same process to plot points C and D. The points are joined to produce a smooth curve (sometimes a straight line).

Production Possibilities Curve

One of the most useful graphs in economics is the **production possibilities curve**. Suppose that on a Caribbean cruise you are shipwrecked alone on an uninhabited, palm-fringed, tropical island. After a few days of exploring the isle, you find that fish and coconuts are the only foods available. You discover, too, that if you devote all the time you have allocated for food production to catching fish, you can catch five fish. But then, of course, you have no time to collect coconuts. You may decide, therefore, to produce fewer fish and more coconuts. A wide range of production possibilities is open to you, from the production of only fish and no coconuts, to the production of some fish and some coconuts, to the production of no fish and only coconuts. We could outline the possibilities in a table, such as Table 1.1.

Table 1.1 Production possibilities on the tropical island

1 POSSIBILITIES	2 COCONUTS	3 FISH
A	0	5
B	5	4
C	9	3
D	12	2
E	14	1
F	15	0

A graph would provide a clearer picture of your options. The basic steps in constructing a graph are:

1. Decide on a title for the graph that clearly and succinctly describes what it illustrates. In this case, it's easy: "Production possibilities on the tropical island."

2. Decide what the graph will measure on each of the two axes and label them.

In economics, by convention, price is always measured along the vertical axis if money is involved, and quantity is always measured along the horizontal axis. The horizontal axis, for example, could measure quantity of goods bought, sold, or produced, or numbers of workers employed. Sometimes time (days, months, or years) is measured along the horizontal axis.

In our production possibilities graph, it does not matter which axis we choose to measure the production of fish or coconuts. In other graphs, though, as we shall see, the decision about what will be measured on which axis is important.

Arbitrarily, we decide to measure the number of coconuts along the horizontal axis and the number of fish along the vertical axis and, of course, we label each axis.

Notice that along the horizontal axis we did not include every number, but instead numbered coconuts by threes. Why?—because it makes the graph easier to read.

Figure 1.5 Production possibilities on the tropical island

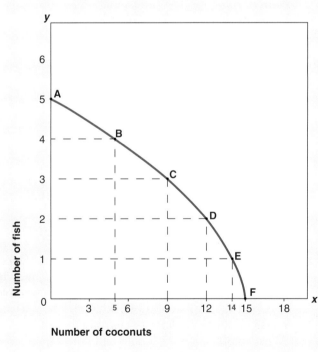

Number of coconuts

3. Plot the points on the graph.

Possibility A is to spend all your time catching fish and no time picking coconuts, so that you produce 5 fish and 0 coconuts. To plot possibility A, then, find 0 on the x axis and go up to 5 on the y axis. To plot possibility B, find 5 on the x axis and then move vertically up the y axis to 4. In the same way, plot C, D, E, and F. The points A, B, C, D, E, and F are joined to form a smooth curve. The curve represents the range of choices for producing food on the island.

Application

1. Using the data in the following table, construct a production possibilities curve.

Table 1.2 Production possibilities

1 POSSIBILITIES	2 GUNS	3 BREAD (IN HUNDREDS OF LOAVES)
A	0	15
B	1	14
C	2	12
D	3	9
E	4	5
F	5	0

Scarcity, Choice, and the Production Possibilities Curve

The nature of the fundamental economic problem—that of unlimited wants exceeding our resources—can be illustrated by a production possibilities curve. As we saw in the Skill Development section on pages 12-14, the production possibilities curve provides us with a simple model of the choices faced by any economy. Let's outline the assumptions behind this simple model.

(i) Two products only   In any economy with literally hundreds of thousands of products, the choices before us are exceedingly complex. To reduce the problem to the very simplest form, we assume that only two goods are produced—say butter and ploughs. Butter symbolizes the production of *consumer goods and services* (those goods and services which directly satisfy people's wants), and ploughs symbolize *capital goods* (those goods used in production to make other goods).

(ii) Full employment   We assume all productive resources are fully employed and producing the maximum output of goods and services.

(iii) Fixed technology   No new methods of produc-

tion are introduced. We are examining the economy over a short period of time.

(iv) Fixed resources   The amount of productive resources (land, labour, and capital) does not change, and the resources can be shifted as desired between the production of butter and ploughs.

☐ Production Possibilities

The production alternatives open to us are outlined in the **production possibilities schedule** shown in Table 1.3. Figure 1.6 shows the production possibilities curve. We can see that a decision to produce more ploughs means of necessity the production of less butter, and *vice versa*. We cannot have our ploughs and eat more butter too. We have to make trade-offs between the two.

If we choose to devote all our productive resources to the manufacture of ploughs (as at alternative A), we will have no butter. This is clearly a very hungry choice! At the other extreme (alternative F), we can choose to produce only butter, and no ploughs. This is a possible choice, but again probably not a desirable one since no ploughs would be available to cultivate the fields.

What combination of ploughs and butter should the society choose? This is a normative or policy question. The production alternative chosen will depend on the needs and values of the society.

Figure 1.6 Production possibilities curve

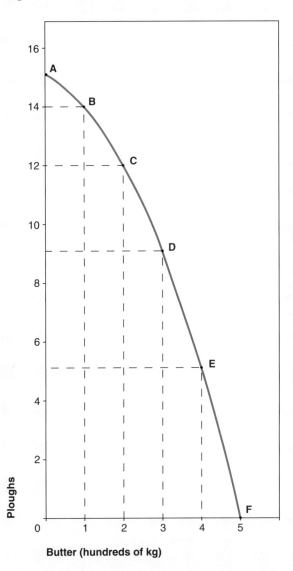

Ploughs (vertical axis)

Butter (hundreds of kg) (horizontal axis)

At A, the economy produces no butter and 15 ploughs. At B, some productive resources are shifted to producing butter (100 kg), so that only 14 instead of 15 ploughs are produced. From A to B, the opportunity cost of 100 kg of butter is 1 plough. Moving from B to F, as the production of butter increases, the production of ploughs decreases. At F, 500 kg of butter are produced, but no ploughs.

Table 1.3 Production possibilities schedule

1 PRODUCTION ALTERNATIVES OR POSSIBILITIES	2 BUTTER (IN HUNDREDS OF KG)	3 PLOUGHS	4 OPPORTUNITY COST OF EACH PLOUGH (THAT IS, THE HUNDREDS OF KG OF BUTTER THAT MUST BE GIVEN UP FOR EACH PLOUGH)
A	0	15	1
B	1	14	2
C	2	12	3
D	3	9	4
E	4	5	5
F	5	0	

☐ The Production Possibilities Curve and Opportunity Costs

The opportunity costs of producing more butter are illustrated by the declining output of ploughs. For example, in moving from alternative A to alternative B, the opportunity cost of 100 kg of butter is 1 plough. As we move from B to C, the opportunity cost of the 100 kg of butter increases to 2 ploughs. Thus, as we move from A to F, increasing numbers of ploughs must be given up to produce each additional 100 kg of butter. This change is in accordance with common sense. As we move from A to B, those resources best able to produce butter (such as more cows) and least able to produce ploughs are used to produce more butter. In other words, available resources are put to their more suitable use. They are used more efficiently.

However, as we move from B to C and on to D, E, and F, resources which are increasingly more suited to produce ploughs are brought into the production of butter, so that by the time we come to F, the opportunity cost of 100 kg of butter is up to 5 ploughs. The use of resources has become increasingly less efficient.

As a result of this increasing opportunity cost, the

production possibilities curve is not a straight line (which would reflect a constant trade-off between butter and ploughs). Rather, it bows outward, as shown in Figure 1.7. As we move from A to B, B to C, C to D, etc., the cost is always 100 kg of butter. But the cost in ploughs measured along the vertical axis from A to R, B to S, etc. is constantly increasing.

□ The Production Possibilities Curve as a Boundary

The production possibilities curve represents a boundary, illustrating the *maximum* potential output of the two goods. Point Z outside the curve, for example, is unattainable. Since our resources are limited and we have assumed that all productive resources are fully employed, points outside the curve are not production possibilities.

In reality, however, we know that not all resources are necessarily fully employed. Part of the labour force may be unemployed, some machines or factories may be idle, or some land may be left uncultivated, for example. Point Y inside the production possibilities boundary (but not on the maximum curve) illustrates this situation. Most societies will have production co-ordinates inside the boundary, but they can aim to reach any point on the curve.

Must the society live within the limitations of the production possiblities curve forever? Remember that we also assumed fixed technology, in other words, no other changes. We examined the production possibilities only over a very short period. Technological advances, such as more efficient machinery, could shift the curve to the right, increasing the maximum potential output.

How then does all this apply to an economy such as Canada's? Obviously, the number of products would be much greater and the production possibilities much more complex, but the basic principle nonetheless applies. Our resources are scarce and we must, therefore, make decisions between producing more of some goods and services and less of others, in an attempt to meet our needs and wants as efficiently as possible. Every society, large or small, must deal with these basic facts.

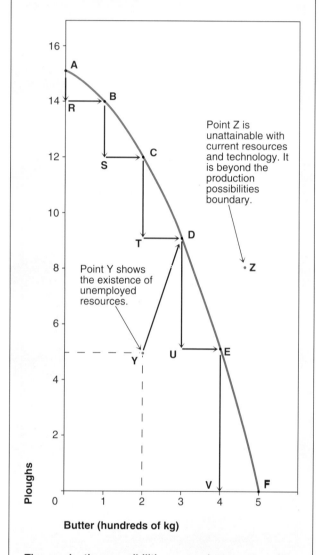

Figure 1.7 Production possibilities curve as a boundary

Point Z is unattainable with current resources and technology. It is beyond the production possibilities boundary.

Point Y shows the existence of unemployed resources.

Ploughs

Butter (hundreds of kg)

The production possibilities curve bows outward as the opportunity cost of butter increases in terms of ploughs. As we move to the right, the horizontal increases are always 100 kg of butter from R to B, S to C, T to D, and so on. The reductions in plough production measured along the vertical axis from A to R, B to S, C to T, and so on continually increase, however, showing the increasing opportunity costs of producing more butter.

□ □ □ □ □ □

Careers in Economics

We've discussed what economics is. But, what do economists do? What are the practical career opportunities for people who have a background in economics? Let's examine some possibilities.

ECONOMIC ANALYST

SIMONS has a challenging opportunity for an individual with cost accounting and economic analysis experience in the resource processing industries. You will participate as a member of a group in the preparation of written proposals and the development of techno-economic feasibility studies and reports.

Responsibilities will include:
- Development of operating cost estimates
- Preparation of pro-forma financial statements
- Analysis of taxation and financial factors
- Calculation of discounted cash flow returns
- Use of computerized financial planning models
- Evaluation of socio-economic benefits
- Comparison of alternate investments using various industrial processes

Qualifications include:
- Strong analytical and communication skills
- At least 5 years experience in the pulp & paper or mechanical wood products industries
- Minimum 3 years experience in market/economic analysis
- Experience in long range planning would be beneficial
- Formal background in accounting

For over 40 years H.A. Simons Ltd. has been providing engineering design and management services to resource processing industries around the world. It is the largest of a group of affiliated consulting engineering companies that has been responsible for a wide variety of projects in over 60 countries.

Simons offers attractive salaries, and a co... package including a retire...

⊕⊕ Public Service Commission of Canada   Commission de la fonction publique du Canada

Senior Economist
Telecommunications

Canadian Radio-Television and Telecommunications Canada Nation Capital Region

We require a specialist in telecommunications to direct the economic analysis of major regulatory issues facing the CRTC. You will be responsible for undertaking specialized economic studies and for providing economic advice concerning all aspects of the Commission's regulation of telecommunications.

To meet your goal, you will identify and analyse economic issues and develop recommendations as to appropriate regulatory responses. These issues will include the extent to which competition should be permitted in existing monopoly markets and the appropriate nature and extent of regulation in a mixed monopoly/competitive environment.

You require at least a master's degree from a recognized university with specialization in economics or an MBA with some economics training. You must also possess substantial relevant experience in the field of telecommunications. Knowledge of English is essential.

We offer a salary ranging from $60,139 to $66,204 commensurate with your qualifications and experience.

Forward your resume and/or application form, quoting reference number
S-8... 0424-145F-(A86), to:
Sy... (613) 996-8001
P... ... of Canada
C...

Closi...
Per...
Priv...
PSC...
Vo...
er...

Business Economist
Montreal

Reporting to the Director, Economics and Business Analysis, CP Limited, you will: monitor economic developments, participate in forecasting macroeconomic, financial and industrial markets conditions, and assist in evaluating pertinent public policy issues, help analyze the business plans, performance and business environments of profit centres, thereby contributing to Canadian Pacific's profit planning and financial reporting process, generally provide thorough and up-to-date expertise to assist all levels of management on a wide range of economic matters affecting Company interests and decisions.

You possess a Master's degree in Economics along with one to three years' relevant experience. Thorough knowledge of micro and macroeconomics theory, familiarity with quantitative methods and graduate courses in Business Cycles, Money and Banking, International Economics, Public Finance or Industrial Organization are essential. A self-motivated individual, you possess good interpersonal skills and an excellent written and verbal command of English.

Salary is competitive and dependent upon qualifications.

Please forward your resume, quoting Project Number 89/08, to:

Supervisor, Management Staffing
Canadian Pacific
P.O. Box 6042, Station "A"
Montreal, Quebec
H3C 3E4

This position is open to all qualified individuals, women, aboriginal peoples, disabled persons and members of visible minorities are specifically encouraged to apply.

⊕ Canadian Pacific

ECONOMIS...

If you are interested in joining our team of market and ... analysts, the Export Development Corporation is offering ... career opportunity as an Economist at our Head Office in Ottawa.

You will be responsible for the assessment of domestic business conditions impacting on Canadian export activity and other aspects of EDC's external environment.

The successful candidate will possess an M.A. in Economics and a minimum of three years experience in the field of economic research and analysis, preferably in the financial services sector.

The Export Development Corporation is a Canadian Crown Corporation that provides insurance, guarantee and financing services to facilitate and develop Canada's export trade.

EDC is an Employment Equity employer which offers competitive salaries coupled with an attractive benefits package.

Qualified candidates are invited to apply by sending a resume no later than May 26, 1989 to:

HUMAN RESOURCES DIVISION
151 O'Connor
4th Floor
Ottawa, Ontario
K1P 5T9

🔷 manitoba hydro
An Affirmative Action Employer

SENIOR ECONOMIC CONSULTANT

MANITOBA HYDRO, A PROVINCIAL CROWN CORPORATION AND MAJOR SUPPLIER OF ELECTRICITY, IS SEEKING A QUALIFIED INDIVIDUAL WITH THE ABILITY TO APPLY AND SUCCESSFULLY PROMOTE STATE-OF-THE-ART TECHNIQUES FOR ECONOMIC ANALYSIS.

Reporting to the Manager, Economic Analysis Department, this individual will:
- Provide specialized expertise in the forecasting of interruptible export rates and related variables through the acquisition of market intelligence and the development of computer models.
- Act as a Project Leader on specified consulting assignments requiring economic analysis.
- Make recommendations suitable for presentation to Executive Management.

Candidates will have a degree in Economics, supplemented by a Master's degree in a quantitative discipline and progressively responsible work experience in a related field. Excellent technical, interpersonal and communications skills are required.

Manitoba Hydro offers generous fringe benefits including a nine (9) day work cycle.

Salary: $46,100 - $60,100 per annum
Closing Date: June 23, 1989
Interested applicants are requested to submit a personal resumé with reference to Competition No. 375 to: Manitoba Hydro
Employment & Placement Dept.
P.O. Box 815
Winnipeg, Manitoba R3C 2P4

Applications

1. (a) Describe the range of jobs available for people with training in economics.

(b) What specific skills and training are required in each job category?

(c) Discuss the various roles economists have in our society.

2. Review other job advertisements for people with economics training in your local newspaper, *The Globe and Mail*, *Financial Post*, or *Financial Times*. What trends can you see in the available job opportunities?

Summary

a. Needs are the basic physical requirements necessary to sustain life. Wants are the desire for goods and services not essential to sustain human life. Resources are all those things used in the production of goods and services designed to meet our needs and wants. Since our wants and needs outstrip our resources, we have scarcity—the fundamental problem of economics.

b. Resources are divided into three main categories. Natural resources are all the resources in nature that have value, such as forests and minerals. Human resources are the manual and non-manual efforts applied to the production of goods and services. Capital resources are the goods, such as machinery and equipment, used in the production of other goods and services.

c. A basic six-step decision-making model involves: 1. defining the problem; 2. determining the alternatives; 3. stating the criteria; 4. evaluating each alternative according to the criteria; 5. weighting the criteria; and 6. making a decision.

d. Opportunity cost is the cost of everything that is lost by taking one course of action over another.

e. Economics is a social science that studies human behaviour as a relationship between ends and scarce means that have alternative uses. It applies the scientific method, which includes four basic steps: observation, collection of data, explanation, and verification.

f. Positive economics is based on facts and describes how an economy actually functions. Normative economics is based on value judgements and describes how things should be (policies and objectives).

g. Some pitfalls to sound economic reasoning in economics are the fallacy of composition, single causation, cause-and-effect fallacy, subjectivity, wishful thinking, loaded terminology, incorrect use of terminology, and personification.

h. The terms law, principle, theory, and model in economics all refer to generalizations about the economic behaviour of people or institutions. Laws and principles do not express the same exactness, however, as in the physical sciences. Models are simplified representations of an economy or part of an economy. An economic theory is a generalization that makes it possible for us to understand and predict economic behaviour.

i. The production possibilities curve is a simple graphical model that outlines the production alternatives of an economy.

j. The production possibilities curve may be seen as a boundary representing the maximum output an economy can achieve with all productive resources fully employed. Economies will produce at some point within or on the curve.

■ Review of Key Terms

Define the following key terms introduced in this chapter and provide examples where appropriate.

needs	economics	economic model
wants	scientific method	positive economics
goods	hypothesis	normative economics
services	natural resources	graph
resources	capital resources	co-ordinate graph
scarcity	human resources	production possibilities
variable	economic goods	curve
theory	free goods	production possibilities
curve	opportunity cost	schedule

■ Application and Analysis

1. "Wants are not unlimited and I can prove it. I had all the bread I wanted to eat at breakfast this morning." Do you agree with this statement? Explain your reasoning.

2. List the resources required to produce wheat. Classify the resources as natural, capital, and human.

3. Complete a chart similar to the example in Figure 1.8 for three decisions you made recently. How was your decision influenced by scarcity?

Figure 1.8 Decisions and opportunity costs

Economic decision (what you actually decided to do or buy)	Choices (the alternatives you considered)	Opportunity cost (your second-best choice)
Put the earnings from my part-time job in a bank account.	(a) Go to a concert. (b) Buy several compact discs. (c) Buy a new sweater and pants.	Buy a new sweater and pants.

4. Decide whether each of the following is a positive or normative statement and explain your answer.

(a) The present rate of inflation is 20 percent.

(b) If the price of apples increases, then more of them will be sold.

(c) The provincial government should control the rents of apartments in major cities.

(d) Dairy farmers receive a fair price for their milk.

(e) Canada has an obligation to provide aid to Bangladesh.

5. "Value judgements have no place in a subject such as economics that purports to be a science." Do you agree with this statement? Give reasons for your answer.

6. Note whether each of the following statements is true (T) or false (F) and explain why briefly.

(a) The cause of unemployment is people out of work.

(b) Excessive government expenditure is the cause of all our economic problems.

(c) The major costs of going to university are the costs of textbooks, tuition, and room and board.

(d) In any economic exchange, one person wins and another loses.

(e) The higher the price, the more useful the good.

(f) Since it seldom occurs, smallpox is scarce in Canada.

Table 1.4 Production possibilities of Country Z

1 PRODUCTION POSSIBILITY	2 GUNS	3 BUTTER (IN HUNDRED TONNES)	4 OPPORTUNITY COST OF EACH GUN
A	0	17	
B	1	16	
C	2	14	
D	3	11	
E	4	6	
F	5	0	

7. (a) Calculate the opportunity cost of each additional gun in Table 1.4.

(b) Graph a production possibilities curve using the data in the table.

(c) Indicate two points, R and S, which are unattainable by Z's economy.

(d) Indicate a point, U, which shows widespread unemployment in Country Z.

(e) Suppose that Country Z goes to war and thus reaches full employment and produces a large quantity of guns. Indicate this new point, X, on your graph.

8. Suppose you have 16 hours a day to divide between study and leisure.

(a) Complete a production possibilities schedule showing your various alternatives.

(b) On a graph, plot the relationship between study and leisure.

(c) Suppose you need 8 hours of leisure each day. Mark this choice, L, on the graph.

(d) Suppose that exams are approaching and you decide you need 12 hours of study a day. Mark this new point, E, on your graph.

(e) What was the opportunity cost of the first hour of leisure?

Economic Systems

The production possibilities curve illustrates that societies—just like individuals—are faced with the ever-present problem of scarcity. Every society must decide how best to meet the needs and wants of its members with its scarce resources.

In this chapter, then, we ask how societies have made decisions about what, how, and for whom to produce in the past, and how they make them today. We examine three different economic systems—the traditional, command, and free market models. These systems are considered first in their pure forms, and then with a view to how they appear in the world today. We then focus on the major characteristics of the Canadian economy. What makes our economy unique and what are our economic objectives? The rest of this book will be concerned with these objectives.

■ The Three Basic Questions

Economists define an **economic system** as the set of laws, institutions, and customs by which a society determines how to use its scarce resources to meet the needs and wants of its members. To establish an economic system, any society—a modern capitalist industrialized nation, a modern socialist industrialized nation, an Amazonian tribe, a medieval monastery—must in some way answer three basic questions: what to produce, how to produce, and for whom to produce.

What to Produce
What goods and services shall our society produce and in what quantities? Should we produce wheat, fish, compact disc players, and computers? If so, how many? How do we choose among the various options and amounts? If we produce these goods and services, what must we give up?

How to Produce
How shall the goods and services be produced—that is, by whom, with what resources, and in what way? Should cabinets be made by skilled craftspeople or by mass production in large automated factories? Should they be made by privately-owned companies or by state-owned corporations? What is the most efficient use of our scarce resources?

For Whom to Produce
For whom shall the goods and services be produced? In other words, how is the society's total output of goods and services to be shared among the people? Is it to be shared equally, or are some to receive more than others? If so, on what basis should such a decision be made?

■ Three Economic Systems

There have been three very different ways to answer these major questions: by tradition, command, and the market. We'll examine these economic systems in their pure or theoretical forms first, and then consider how they appear in the world today.

□ The Traditional Economy

In a **pure traditional economy**, the traditions or past practices of the society provide the answers to the three main questions. People in a traditional economy produce the same goods they produced in the past, in the same ways, and in the same quantities. Skills are passed along within the same family from generation to generation. People receive the same share of the total output as they always received in the past.

Several centuries ago, the traditional economy was the dominant form of economic organization throughout much of the world. People lived in relatively small rural societies. Their needs and wants were relatively simple and could be met by small domestic industries and some trade with nearby communities. People grew much of their own food, built their own homes from local materials, and produced their own clothing and other necessary goods.

Population, industrial, and technological growth, however, have transformed most traditional economies. Today, tradition has the strongest influence in economies of relatively isolated rural communities in the less developed countries.

Advantages and Disadvantages
How are we to assess the traditional economy? In the absence of natural calamities such as drought or flooding, and unnatural ones such as war and rebellion, its supreme virtue is stability and security for its people. All members of the traditional society know their economic roles—what they'll produce, how they'll produce it, and what and how much of the goods and services they'll receive. Members do not have to adapt to change continually.

But while stability and certainty have advantages, they also have serious drawbacks. The traditional economy can stifle economic initiative and innovation, and institutionalize inequalities. In some cases, customs are so unyielding that the society collapses under the weight of its traditions. It is unable to adapt to the changing world around it. The possibilities for growth, change, or improvement in an individual's or the society's economic life are limited. People are compelled to accept their lot in life.

◻ The Pure Command Economy

In a **pure command economy**, the answers to the what, how, and for whom questions are provided by a government or other central authority. The pure command economy is centrally planned. A central authority owns the natural and capital resources and decides how they are to be used, what goods and services are to be produced and by what methods, and how the economic rewards are to be distributed.

While no pure command economy exists, approximately one-third of the world's population has lived with a planned economy (under socialism or communism) in the countries of eastern Europe, China, and the former USSR, for example.

Advantages and Disadvantages

Central planning is a major strength of the command economy. Resources can be focussed on a consistent and logical set of national objectives, such as the development of heavy industry or the provision of social services. The former Soviet Union, for example, was able to industrialize rapidly after the 1917 revolution by concentrating on the production of capital goods, such as machinery and factories. Other nations have emphasized the provision of social services, such as universal education and health care.

But command economies are not without their problems. Many people may not agree with the objectives set by government. They may prefer more consumer goods rather than more steel foundries or nuclear weapons, for example. They may also prefer individual freedom of movement from job to job and place to place, which is not possible in a totally planned economy. Each individual's job and place is carefully set out to fit into the overall economic plan. An individual may be required to study computer programming rather than medicine if the government determines that computer programmers will be in short supply. A worker may be compelled to stay in a particular area if his or her skills are required there. Quotas may be set to regulate the number of particular goods produced and bonuses offered if quotas are met. Without the spur of competition, however, goods and services may

be produced inefficiently, since the easiest way to meet quotas is often to produce low quality goods.

It is also evident that planning an entire economy is a very complex task and the odds of making serious errors are high. Suppose, for example, the plan calls for an increase in the output of leather shoes by 10 percent. What would this involve? Obviously, the supply of leather to the shoe industry needs to be increased. But to increase the supply of leather, the tanning industry must process more leather, more cattle have to be slaughtered to provide the leather, and more cattle have to be raised.

All we have begun to consider is one raw material for one industry. We also need to increase production of all the other materials needed in the leather shoe industry—nails, glue, shoelaces, thread, etc. And how much should the labour force, machinery, and other necessary productive resources be increased? How many more workers are needed and who will train them, etc.? The necessary resources and raw materials also have to be ready at the right time in the production process.

Clearly, then, planning a change in the output of even one simple good—such as leather shoes—is a complex operation. Making similar plans for the tens of thousands of products in a modern economy and co-ordinating these plans to ensure that all will go smoothly is an immensely complex task.

◻ The Pure Market Economy

In a **pure market economy** (sometimes called the free market, free enterprise, or capitalist system), the actions of many individual buyers and sellers operating through a system of prices and markets co-ordinate economic activity. The economy is not centrally planned. Natural and capital resources are privately owned. Individual buyers and sellers, by their actions and decisions in the market, answer the three basic questions.

What will be produced is determined by buyer or consumer demand. Businesses produce the goods and services demanded because they provide the highest profits. Thus, if consumers demand bread, indicated by the amount they buy (their dollar votes in the market), businesses will produce bread because they know they will be able to sell large amounts and make a profit.

The profit motive also plays a role in determining how goods and services will be produced. Consumers demand the lowest prices. Businesses can, therefore, sell the most and secure the highest returns by following the least costly and most efficient methods of production.

The for whom question is answered by the incomes people receive for their contributions to the production process—primarily their labour. The amount they earn determines how much they can spend on goods and services, and thus how much they will receive of the total national output.

Advantages and Disadvantages

The advantages of a pure market system are fairly evident. The goods and services produced are those that consumers want and are willing to buy. Workers are free to move from job to job and place to place and to negotiate their own terms of employment with employers. Business people are free to combine productive resources to produce those goods and services that consumers want in the most efficient manner. Individuals can use their skills and initiative to improve their economic well-being.

The market system is not without its disadvantages, however. Consumer decisions about what is to be produced may be unwise. People may prefer to spend more on alcohol, tobacco, or luxury travel than on schools or hospitals, for example.

Great inequalities of wealth may also arise. Goods and services are not necessarily distributed fairly. They go to those with the most dollars. Some people may engage in wasteful and conspicuous consumption, while other disadvantaged people go cold and hungry. The elderly, ill, those with disabilities, and those whose skills have been rendered obsolete by the advance of technology often receive little income, while those who are able to work and to anticipate and meet consumer demand are rewarded. A market system may, therefore, lead to the concentration of economic (and hence political) power in the hands of a few, who may use this power to enrich themselves at the expense of the rest of the population.

A market system may also be subject to some instability, facing periodic upswings and downturns in economic activity. This instability may cause hardship for many, particularly those who are unemployed as a result of the downturns as businesses go bankrupt or lay off workers.

■ Mixed Economies: Today's Reality

In reality, none of the three pure, or theoretical, types of economic systems exists. In fact, economies are mixed—that is, they contain elements in varying proportions of each of the three theoretical types. Thus, while the Canadian economy is primarily a market system, it contains elements of both the traditional and, more importantly, the command system. We refer to the Canadian economy as a **mixed market economy**. Similarly, while the economy of the former USSR was primarily a command system, it contained elements of both traditional and market systems, and was known as a **mixed command economy**. Today, the economies of many—if not all—of the Soviet republics are moving to incorporate more aspects of the free market model.

▢ Canada: A Mixed Market Economy

How, then, are we to define Canada's mixed market economy? It differs from the pure market model principally in that federal, provincial, and local governments play a significant role.

The Role of Government

Governments not only provide us with a large array of goods and services, but also influence our economic activities through taxes, subsidies, laws, and regulations. Laws protecting property rights, defining legal contracts, and ensuring fair competition, for example, provide the framework within which the Canadian economy operates.

Ownership of productive resources While private ownership of productive resources generally prevails in Canada, there are significant areas of government own-

□ □ □ □ □ □
Economic Thinkers

Adam Smith (1723-1790)

The characteristics and advantages of the free market economy were outlined in the 1700s by Adam Smith, a Scottish professor of moral philosophy. Smith is often called the "father of economics." His two-volume work, entitled *An Inquiry into the Nature and Causes of the Wealth of Nations* (usually referred to as *The Wealth of Nations*), was published in 1776 and was the most influential work on economics published in the eighteenth century.

Many of Smith's ideas developed in response to the rapid economic changes he observed during his lifetime. The Enclosure Movement in Britain divided large tracts of common agricultural land into small individual plots, whose owners began to run their farms for a profit. Inventions, such as spinning and weaving machinery, heralded the emergence of the factory system. A class of land and factory owners, who employed workers in increasingly specialized tasks and ran their enterprises for a profit, gradually developed. Opportunities for individual economic initiative were increasing. At the same time, governments were also taking a firm hand in economic affairs. Merchants and industrialists, however, were feeling increasingly stifled by government regulations and taxes.

A note on Smith's character: Smith was noted for his eccentricity and apparent absent-mindedness. In the 1780s, *"the inhabitants of Edinburgh [Scotland] were regularly treated to the amusing spectacle of their most illustrious citizen, attired in a light-coloured coat, knee breeches, white silk stockings, buckle shoes, flat broad-brimmed beaver hat, and cane, walking down the cobbled street with his eyes fixed on infinity, and his lips moving in silent discourse. Every pace or two he would hesitate as if to change his direction, or even reverse it. . . ."*

SOURCE: THE WORLDLY PHILOSOPHERS © 1953, 1961, 1972, 1987 by Robert L. Heilbroner. © renewed 1981, 1989 by Robert L. Heilbroner. Reprinted by permission of Simon and Schuster.

Self-Interest
Based on his observation of developments around him, Smith came to the conclusion that the major motivating force in our economic life is individual self-interest. If we want food or clothing, we appeal not to the generosity of food producers or clothing makers, but rather to their desire to make a profit. The profit motive is the major impetus to economic growth and prosperity.

Competition
But what would prevent producers from charging unreasonably high prices for their goods—which the pursuit of self-interest would surely dictate? To Smith, the answer was clear. If any clothing maker, for example, sought to charge exorbitantly high prices, no one would buy from her. People would buy from other competing clothing makers whose prices were lower, and she would either have to cut prices or face

bankruptcy. Thus, competition among producers works to control rampant self-interest for the general good.

What was true for the individual clothing maker, was also true for the industry in general. If all clothing makers raised prices to exorbitant levels, producers in other industries would move into the clothing industry to take advantage of the high profits. Soon, however, clothing production would exceed consumer demand and again the producers would be forced to lower prices or go bankrupt. Thus, competitive markets hold self-interest in check.

This control over self-interest comes about automatically in a market economy. It does not require the heavy hand of government in Adam Smith's view. In general, Smith believed that government intervention in the economy was either harmful or useless. He did recognize, however, that government had an important role in four main areas—the provision and administration of law and justice, defence, education, and public works such as streets, canals, and harbours.

Division of Labour
Smith was struck by the enormous increase in wealth that had taken place over the sixteenth and seventeenth centuries in Britain. In his view, one of the principal reasons was the division of labour—the specialization of workers in the production process. The division of labour, Smith believed, occurs naturally out of self-interest, and does not require government direction and control. It is a direct result of the desire to make a profit by using the most efficient means of production.

SMITH IN HIS OWN WORDS

The Motivating Factor of Self-Interest

In civilized society man stands at all times in need of the co-operation and assistance of great multitudes, while his whole life is scarce sufficient to gain the friendship of a few persons. In almost every other race of animals each individual, when it is grown up to maturity, is entirely independent, and in its natural state has occasion for the assistance of no other living creature. But man has almost constant occasion for the help of his brethren, and it is in vain for him to expect it from their benevolence only. He will be more likely to prevail if he can interest their self-love in his favour, and show them that it is for their own advantage to do for him what he requires of them. Whoever offers to another a bargain of any kind, proposes to do this. Give me that which I want, and you shall have this which you want, is the meaning of every such offer; and it is in this matter that we obtain from another the far greater part of those good offices which we stand in need of. It is not from the benevolence of the butcher, the brewer, or the baker, that we expect our dinner, but from their regard to their own interest. We address ourselves, not to their humanity but to their self-love, and never talk to them of our own necessities but of their advantages.

SOURCE: Adam Smith, *An Inquiry into the Nature and Causes of the Wealth of Nations*, edited by Edward Cannan (London: Methuen, 1951), p. 18.

1. Do you agree that self-interest is the main motivator behind our economic actions? Explain.

2. How might self-interest be kept in check in a:
(a) command economy
(b) traditional economy?

"The Invisible Hand"

But the annual revenue of every society is always precisely equal to the exchangeable value of the whole annual produce of its industry, or rather is precisely the same thing with that exchangeable value. As every individual, therefore, endeavours as much as he can both to employ his capital in the support of domestic industry, and so to direct that industry that its produce may be of the greatest value; every individual necessarily labours to render the annual revenue of the society as great as he can. He generally, indeed, neither intends to promote the public interest, nor knows how much he is promoting it. By preferring the support of domestic to that of foreign industry, he intends only his own security; and by directing that industry in such a manner as its produce may be of the greatest value, he intends only his own gain, and he is in this, as in many other cases, led by an invisible hand to promote an end which was no part of his intention. Nor is it always the worse for the society that it was no part of it. By pursuing his own interest he frequently promotes that of the society more effectually than when he really intends to promote it. I have never known much good done by those who affected to trade for the public good. It is an affectation, indeed, not very common among merchants, and very few words need be employed in dissuading them from it.

SOURCE: Adam Smith, *An Inquiry into the Nature and Causes of the Wealth of Nations*, edited by Edward Cannan (London: Methuen, 1951), pp. 477-478.

3. (a) What is the "invisible hand"?
(b) What is the "end which was no part of his intention"?
4. Do you agree with Smith's point of view? Explain.

The Division of Labour—"Pinmaking"

To take an example, therefore, from a very trifling manufacture; but one in which the division of labour has been very often taken notice of, the trade of the pinmaker; a workman not educated to this business (which the division of labour has rendered a distinct trade), nor acquainted with the use of the machinery employed in it (to the invention of which the same division of labour has probably given occasion), could scarce, perhaps, with his utmost industry, make one pin in a day, and certainly could not make twenty. But in the way in which this business is now carried on, not only the whole work is a peculiar trade, but it is divided into a number of branches, of which the greater part are likewise peculiar trades. One man draws out the wire, another straights it, a third cuts it, a fourth points it, a fifth grinds it at the top for receiving the head; to make the head requires two or three distinct operations; to put it on, is a peculiar business, to whiten the pins is another; it is even a trade by itself to put them into the paper; and the important business of making a pin is, in this manner, divided into about eighteen distinct operations, which, in some manufactories, are all performed by distinct hands, though in others the same man will sometimes perform two or three of them. I have seen a small manufactory of this kind where ten men only were employed, and where some of them consequently performed two or three distinct operations. But though they were very poor, and therefore but indifferently accommodated with the necessary machinery, they could, when they exerted themselves, make among them about twelve pounds [5 kg] of pins in a day. There are in a pound [0.5 kg] upwards of four thousand pins of middling size.

SOURCE: Adam Smith, *An Inquiry into the Nature and Causes of the Wealth of Nations*, edited by Edward Cannan (London: Methuen, 1951), pp. 8-9.

5. (a) What does Smith see as the advantages of the division of labour? What are the disadvantages?

(b) How might self-interest have naturally led to the division of labour?

(c) How might it contribute to the concentration of wealth in the hands of a few?

(d) Why is the division of labour important? Give an example in our society and note the advantages and disadvantages.

□ □ □ □ □ □

Economic Thinkers

Karl Marx (1818-1883)

Karl Marx is considered a founder of socialism and communism. Born in Germany, he was forced to flee the country because of his radical views and finally settled in England in 1849. Living almost a century later than Adam Smith, Marx witnessed many of the changes brought about by the Industrial Revolution in Britain. By the year of his death, the United Kingdom had been transformed from an agricultural-commercial society to one in which the dominant mode of production was the steam-powered factory. A rapidly growing working class was increasingly concentrated in squalid cities and subjected to the appalling working conditions of the factories. Child labour

and grinding poverty were the lot of many families. An increasingly powerful class of capitalists was challenging the aristocracy for political power.

Throughout his life, Marx was very influential in international workers' organizations. He believed that workers were being exploited by the capitalist system and sought to unite workers around the world. His most important works were *The Communist Manifesto* (1848), which he wrote in collaboration with his friend Friedrich Engels, and the three-volume *Das Kapital* (1867-1894), only one volume of which appeared in his lifetime.

A Prussian police spy's report on Marx: *As father and husband, Marx, in spite of his wild and restless character, is the gentlest and mildest of men. Marx lives in one of the worst, therefore one of the cheapest, quarters in London. He occupies two rooms...In the whole apartment, there is not one clean and solid piece of furniture.*

SOURCE: David McLellan, *Karl Marx: Early Texts* (Oxford: Blackwell, 1972), p. 129.

Marx's Theory of Labour

Marx's criticism of the capitalist or free market system was based on two related theories: the theory of value and the theory of surplus value. According to Marx, the value of any good is the value of the labour used in its production. He included in this value the amount of labour *directly* used in its production provided by the workers actually working on the good, and the amount of labour *indirectly* involved in production—that is, the amount embodied in the machinery and buildings used in its production. "As values, all commodities are only definite masses of congealed labour-time," he said.

In a capitalist or free market system, however, the capitalist (business owner) receives an amount for the good which is greater than the total of the direct and indirect costs. This additional amount or profit, Marx called the surplus value. The surplus value arises because workers (the proletariat) are forced to sell their labour to the capitalists (the bourgeoisie) and the capitalists pay them less than the labour is worth. Thus the workers in a capitalist system are exploited by the capitalists.

A View of the Capitalist System

According to Marx, the capitalist system contained within it the seeds of its own destruction. As the capitalists strive to accumulate more and more wealth, competition among them increases, many small businesses go bankrupt, and profits generally fall. To squeeze out more and more surplus value, the capitalists cut wages and substitute capital equipment (machinery) for labour, causing the workers to become increasingly "immiserized." Working conditions deteriorate, pay declines, and increasing numbers of workers are unemployed. This "reserve army of the unemployed" ensures that wages will not rise above the minimum survival level, since capitalists can always obtain desperate workers at low wages.

The increasing accumulation of wealth in the hands of fewer and fewer capitalists and the growing concentration of workers in increasingly large factories provides fertile ground for the growing class consciousness of workers. Economic depressions get deeper as workers' consumption declines and production increases. Finally, in a catastrophic depression, the workers rise in violent revolution against the capitalist system. Capitalism collapses and a new economic system—socialism—is established. Under this system, the workers control all land and productive resources. Eventually, all would share equally in the total output and the state would disappear. This final ideal stage of socialism was called communism.

MARX IN HIS OWN WORDS

The Labour Theory of Value

The daily cost of maintenance of labour power [workers' wages], and the daily output of labour power, are two very different things. The former determines the exchange-value of labour power; the latter, its use-value. Though it be true that only half a day's labour is requisite to maintain the worker throughout the twenty-four hours of the day, this does not prevent his working for the whole working day of twelve hours. The value of labour power, and the value which that labour power creates in the labour process, are, therefore, two completely different magnitudes. This difference in the values was what the capitalist had in mind when he bought the labour power. Of course, it was essential that the labour power should have a useful quality, should be able to make yarn, or boots, or what not; for labour must be expended in a useful form if it is to produce value. But the really decisive point was that this commodity, labour power, had the specific use-value of being a source of value, of being able to produce more value than it itself had. That is the specific service which the capitalist expects from labour power.

SOURCE: Karl Marx, *Capital*, Vol. 1, introduced by G.D.H. Cole and translated by Eden and Cedar Paul (London: Dent, 1930), pp. 187- 88.

1. Explain why, according to Marx, it is advantageous for a capitalist to hire workers.
2. (a) Might Marx agree with Adam Smith that self-interest is the major motivator in a capitalist economic system? Why or why not?

(b) What differences are there in the way the two thinkers view self-interest?
3. Do you agree with Marx that capitalists exploit the workers? Explain your position.

The Future of Capitalism

The modern worker. . .instead of rising with the progress of industry, sinks ever deeper beneath the social conditions of his own class. The labourer becomes the pauper, and pauperism increases even more rapidly than population and wealth. It is thus clear that the bourgeoisie is unfit any longer to remain the ruling class in society, and to impose on society as a supreme law the social system of its class. It is unfit to rule because it is unable to assure existence in slavery to its slave [the worker], because it is forced to let him sink into a state in which it must feed him, instead of being fed by him. . .

The essential condition for the existence and rule of the bourgeois class is the accumulation of wealth in private hands, the formation and increase of capital; the essential condition of capital is wage-labour. Wage-labour rests entirely on the competition among the workers. The progress of industry, of which the bourgeoisie is the involuntary and irresistible agent, replaces the isolation of the workers, due to competition, by their revolutionary union through association. With the development of modern industry, therefore, the very ground whereby it has established its system of production and appropriation is cut from under the feet of the bourgeoisie. It produces, above all, its own grave-diggers. Its downfall and the victory of the proletariat are equally inevitable.

SOURCE: Karl Marx and Friedrich Engels, *The Communist Manifesto*. In Raymond Postgate, *Revolution from 1789-1906* (New York: Harper Torchbooks, 1962), pp. 148-49.

4. (a) What does Marx predict will be the future of capitalism?
(b) Outline briefly how he has reached this conclusion.
5. Do you agree with Marx's analysis? Explain why or why not.
6. How would Adam Smith have responded to Marx's views on the struggle of the classes and the future of capitalism?

The Marxist Program
We have already seen the first step in the working class revolution is the raising of the proletariat to the position of ruling class, the victory of Democracy.

The proletariat will use its political power to wrest by degree all capital from the bourgeoisie, to centralise all instruments of production in the hands of the State, i.e., of the proletariat organised as the ruling class, and to increase as rapidly as possible the total mass of productive forces.

This, naturally, cannot be accomplished at first except by despotic inroads on the rights of property and on the bourgeois conditions of production; by measures, therefore, which appear economically insufficient and untenable, but which in the course of the movement outstrip themselves, and are indispensable as means of revolutionizing the whole mode of production.

These measures will naturally be different, in different countries.

Nevertheless, for the most advanced countries, the following will be pretty generally applicable:

*1. Abolition of property in land and confiscation of ground rents to the State.
2. A heavily progressive income tax. [that is, as income increases, an increasing percentage will be taken in taxes]
3. Abolition of inheritance.
4. Confiscation of the property of emigrants and rebels.
5. Centralization of credit in the hands of the State, by means of a national bank with State capital and an exclusive monopoly.
6. Centralization of the means of transport in the hands of the State.
7. Extension of national factories and instruments of production, cultivation and improvement of waste lands in accordance with a general social plan.
8. Obligation of all to labour; organization of industrial armies, especially for agriculture.
9. Combination of agricultural and industrial labour, in order to remove the distinction between town and country.
10. Free public education for all children. Abolition of factory labour for children in its present form. Combination of education with material production, etc.*

In the place of the old bourgeois society, with its classes and class antagonisms, an association appears in which the free development of each is the condition for the free development of all.

SOURCE: Karl Marx and Friedrich Engels, *The Communist Manifesto*. In Raymond Postgate, *Revolution from 1789-1906* (New York: Harper Torchbooks, 1962), pp. 154-55.

7. Briefly summarize the main elements of Marx's program.
8. What key characteristics of the command system can you see in Marx's program?
9. With what parts (if any) of Marx's program do you agree? With what parts (if any) do you disagree? Explain why.
10. Summarize the major similarities and differences between the ideas of Adam Smith and Karl Marx.

---

ership. Municipalities may own land, transit vehicles, and road systems; provincial governments may own hydro-electric, thermal, and nuclear power stations, roads, telephone companies, and natural resources; and the federal government owns railway systems, ships, planes, and vast areas of land, for example.

In the 1980s, the governments of many countries with mixed market economies began to divest themselves of many state-owned industries. In Canada, for example, the federal government completed the sale of Air Canada in 1991 to private individuals. But the municipal, provincial, and federal governments still hold considerable assets. Among many other properties, Canadian provincial and federal governments own over 350 crown corporations. Federal crown corporations, for example, include Atomic Energy Canada, Canadian National Railways, and the Canadian Broadcasting Corporation.

Influence on what is produced   While most decisions about what to produce are made by consumer expenditures, government regulations in some cases restrict the kinds of goods that may be produced. The general production and sale of alcohol and drugs, for example, are regulated by government. Substantial government purchases of such goods as wheat, military goods, and police equipment encourage the production of these goods and thus directly influence what is produced. Government grants, such as those to school boards, colleges, and universities for books and scientific equipment, indirectly influence what is produced. Taxation, by taking money out of the hands of private citizens and corporations and putting it in the hands of government, also influences production. The tax revenues may be used to provide the public goods and services (such as public transport) that private business would not generally provide.

Influence on how goods and services are produced Government regulations affect how goods and services are produced. Laws set basic health standards for food production and protect workers from dangerous working conditions. Government subsidies and favoured tax treatment are used to encourage the installation of pollution control equipment or to aid sectors of the economy, such as small businesses. Through their ownership of crown corporations, governments influence postal distribution, the production and transmission of electricity, broadcasting systems, and many other production processes and services.

Influence on for whom to produce   Although consumers acting through the price system have the greatest impact on who gets how much, government also plays an important role in the distribution of income. As we have seen, the market system may produce inequalities of wealth, and some government programs and policies therefore aim to redistribute incomes. Income taxes are designed to take more from the affluent than from the poor. Some government programs, such as education, police, and fire protection, are made available to all (though they are not really free since we pay for them through our taxes). Other programs may be specifically designed to help the disadvantaged—such

as the poor, sick, unemployed, and elderly—by providing them with an income or with institutional or professional care.

☐ Characteristics of the Canadian System

What, then, are the major characteristics of the Canadian system? We'll consider the part played in our economy by the private ownership of productive resources, self-interest, markets, prices, profit, consumer sovereignty, competition, and government involvement.

Private Ownership of Productive Resources
One of the major characteristics of mixed market economies is private ownership of productive resources. Individuals have the right to buy and sell not only consumer goods, but also natural productive resources such as land and forests, and capital resources such as machines and factories. Ownership of these resources means that individuals have the right to benefit or make a profit from them. They may also hire human resources (labour) to aid in the production process.

In addition, part of the right of private property includes the right to bequeath property to one or more designated individuals or institutions in the event of death.

Self-interest
Self-interest, or the pursuit of our own advantage, is the major motivating force in a market economy because it is essentially an individualistic system. Each unit in the economy attempts to do what is best for itself. Business people respond to the wants of consumers to realize a profit or, at the least, to avoid a loss. Owners of the productive resources engage the resources where they bring the highest returns. Workers move to jobs that offer the highest pay, best benefits, and most agreeable working conditions. Consumers purchase those goods and services that give them the greatest satisfaction at the lowest cost.

Self-interest provides consistency and direction to what would otherwise be a chaotic system. It makes the behaviour of the various groups in a market system predictable.

□ □ □ □ □ □
A Spectrum of Economies

The economies of the world can be placed along a spectrum. At one pole of the spectrum is the pure market economy with completely decentralized decision-making. Individuals operating in the market provide answers to the three main questions. Government's role in the economy is non-existent. At the opposite pole—that of the pure command economy—a central authority provides the answers to the three main questions. Individual economic decision-making is non-existent.

Along the spectrum between the two poles, we can place the economies of the world. Canada, for example, would be close to the pure market end of the spectrum. However, since government involvement in the Canadian economy is significant, it is not at the extreme pure market pole.

Application
1. Where on the spectrum would you place the USA, China, the United Kingdom, and Russia? Justify your decision in each case.

Figure 2.1 A spectrum of economies

Pure command economy	Pure market economy
(also known as communism, socialism, or collectivism)	(also known as pure capitalism, free enterprise, or free market economy)

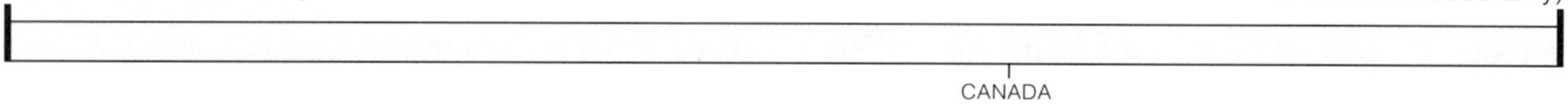

CANADA

- Centralized decision making
- Government answers the three basic questions
- State ownership of productive resources

- Decentralized decision making
- Mechanism of the market answers the questions
- Private ownership of productive resources

Markets

A **market** is a network that keeps buyers and sellers in contact for the purposes of exchanging goods and services and determining prices. Generally, when we think of a market, we think of a place where buyers and sellers meet face to face to exchange goods for money. But direct contact and the exchange of money are not essential. There are many different types of markets in which buyers and sellers interact without direct contact or the exchange of money. The stock market is an example. If you wanted to sell your shares in Collected Moose Swamp Incorporated, you would get in touch with your broker. If I want to buy shares in the same stock I, too, would get in touch with my broker. Representatives of the two brokerage houses meet on the floor of the stock exchange to make the transaction. You and I don't need to meet directly or exchange money.

In Canada, the various markets (interactions between buyers and sellers) operate relatively freely, though with some government control, as we saw earlier. Producers are generally free to supply what they believe meets the demands of consumers and exchange their goods in any number of the various markets.

Prices

Price is the exchange value of goods and services expressed in money terms. One of the functions of the market is to determine the price of a good or service.

Generally, a strong demand but limited supply of a good means a high price, while an abundant supply that exceeds demand means a lower price.

Prices, in turn, provide information and incentives to buyers and sellers. Suppose, for example, that apples are produced in large quantities in Nova Scotia, but very few are grown in Ontario. Prices of apples will fall in Nova Scotia where they are abundant, and rise in Ontario where they are scarce. The higher prices for apples in Ontario will provide Nova Scotia apple sellers with *information* that there are eager buyers in Ontario, and with an *incentive* to ship their apples to Ontario. The system of markets and prices thus works to meet demand automatically.

Profit

Profit is the amount left from the income of a business once all expenses have been paid. It is the reward for those business people who successfully combine resources to produce the goods and services consumers want and will buy. The size of the profits is often directly related to how well the business is able to anticipate and meet the wants of consumers. Profit thus acts as a key incentive in a market economy for the efficient production of goods and services.

Consumer Sovereignty

Consumer sovereignty refers to the dominant role the consumer plays in a market economy by determining what, how, and for whom goods and services are to be produced. Through their dollar votes in competitive markets, consumers tell producers what they want and need. Business people produce those goods and services in demand because they bring the highest profits. Since consumers also demand low prices, producers are encouraged to follow the most efficient production methods. Consumers also determine for whom goods and services are produced through their own labour and initiative, by which they earn their incomes.

Competition

The continuing search by consumers for lowest prices and greatest satisfaction, and by owners of productive resources for highest returns, implies the existence of **competition**. Competition serves to control self-interest. Attempts by individual entrepreneurs in an industry to raise prices to exorbitant levels for larger profits are doomed to failure. Consumers will choose less expensive products. The entrepreneurs will then face two choices—either lower prices and survive, or go bankrupt. Similarly, attempts by all entrepreneurs in an industry to raise prices unreasonably is also destined to failure. Their higher prices and profits will act to attract others into the industry, thereby increasing the competition and forcing prices and profits down once again.

Government Involvement

The final major characteristic of the Canadian mixed market economy is the role of government. As we have seen, governments influence our economy through taxation, expenditures, regulations, and production of goods and services. Governments become involved in the economy in an attempt to rectify some of the failures of the market system. Groups such as people with disabilities, the sick, elderly, and very young, for example, may not receive enough to sustain a reasonable standard of living. Governments, therefore, use their taxation and spending programs to redistribute income in favour of the less fortunate.

☐ Objectives of the Canadian Economy

What objectives do we want our economy to achieve? At various times different individuals and groups have suggested a number of objectives for the economy. One such group is the **Economic Council of Canada (ECC)**, an advisory body established by the federal government in 1963 to study the future prospects of the economy, to advise government about appropriate economic policies, and to inform the Canadian public. The Council reports to parliament through the prime minister. Membership includes a full-time chairperson and two full-time directors (usually professional economists), as well as twenty-five part-time members drawn from different parts of the private sector— business, labour, the farming sector, or the academic community, for example.

In its first annual review published in December 1964, the Council identified five economic goals for

Canada: full employment; a high rate of economic growth; reasonable stability of prices; a viable balance of payments; and an equitable distribution of rising incomes.

This list of goals, however, is far from complete. Some would argue that economic freedom—the right of people to change jobs, own property, move from place to place, and spend income as they wish—is an important objective. Economic security—the freedom from fear that long-term unemployment, illness, or disability will reduce individuals and families to destitution—for some Canadians has become an increasingly important objective. Another important goal is the economic independence of Canada. A frequently expressed fear is that, with the growth of US-owned companies in Canada and with the implementation of the Free Trade Agreement, control of the Canadian economy will increasingly be exercised south of the border. Clearly, the protection of our environment and the reduction of pollution have also become pressing economic objectives.

As all of these goals are key to the Canadian economy, we will spend much of our time in this book examining them. The units of the book are organized around the major goals set out by the ECC with one addition—economic efficiency, which is examined in Unit Two. Unit Three, therefore, discusses the equitable distribution of income. Unit Four covers economic stability, combining the related goals of full employment and reasonable price stability. Unit Five deals with the final two closely related goals of economic growth and a viable balance of payments in international trade. By way of introduction, let's consider these goals together here briefly.

Efficiency

Economic efficiency is the goal of realizing the most effective use of productive resources to yield the greatest benefits. Since economic resources are scarce, it makes obvious sense to use them in a way that yields the highest return. An economy can have full employment and stable prices, but still be performing poorly. Resources may be engaged wastefully or goods may be produced which do not best meet our needs.

The economy should, therefore, strive for both technological and allocative efficiency. **Technological efficiency** is the production of the maximum amount of goods and services with the available resources. **Allocative efficiency** is the production of the best combination of goods and services to meet consumer needs and wants.

Equitable Distribution of Income

Canada has a high standard of living compared with that of many other nations in the world. Nevertheless, there are definite inequalities in the distribution of income. Some individuals and families pass their lives in poverty, while others enjoy life in luxury.

Inequities can be seen not only among individuals and families, but also among the various provinces and regions of the country. On the average, people in the Maritimes have significantly lower incomes than those in the central provinces, for example. Even in affluent provinces, some areas are noticeably poorer than others. Such inequities offend our sense of what is fair and just, and make an equitable distribution of income an important objective.

The goal of an equitable distribution of income does not mean *equal* incomes for all, however, but rather a "fair" distribution of income. There is, of course, considerable vagueness in the phrase "equitable distribution." While we can agree that incomes should be fair or just, when we come to defining "fair" in actual amounts, disagreements begin. Similarly, while we may be able to agree that no one should be poor in Canada, it is difficult to agree on an appropriate definition of poverty and on practical policies and programs to deal with the problem.

Full Employment

Unemployment is an obvious waste. The time lost by unemployed workers is gone forever, as are the goods and services they would have produced. But the costs of unemployment go beyond the lost output of goods and services. Prolonged unemployment erodes human hopes, skills, and feelings of self-worth. There is good reason why many would include full employment as a major goal of the Canadian economy.

The statistic we usually refer to when we talk about employment is the **unemployment rate**—that is, the percentage of the labour force that is unemployed. The **unemployed** are those over the age of fifteen who are actively seeking work and have no employment. Excluded are those who, though not working, are not actively seeking work. Thus full-time high school, college, and university students, retirees, and prison inmates are not considered "unemployed."

Full employment, we would then assume, is 100 percent employment. However, in any healthy economy, people are always moving from one job to another and are, therefore, temporarily unemployed. In Canada, much unemployment is seasonal, reaching a peak in February and March each year and a low in August and September. Thus, if we have an annual unemployment rate of 6 or 7 percent, many economists would agree that that is about as close to full employment as we are likely to get.

Reasonable Stability of Prices

Unemployment was the most serious problem during the Great Depression of the 1930s in Canada. In the 1970s and early 1980s—from about 1972 to 1982—one of the most serious economic problems faced by Canada and many other western countries was inflation. **Inflation** is a general increase in the prices of goods and services over time.

Notice that inflation is a *general increase* in prices. We would not classify an increase in the price of one or a few goods or services as inflation. Only a price increase of many goods and services can cause a rise in the general level of prices and, thus, inflation.

While the losers from widespread unemployment are obvious (the many unemployed), the effects of inflation are more subtle. The winners are the sellers—they receive more for their goods and services. The losers are the buyers—they have to pay more for the goods and services. Unlike unemployment, it is not obvious whether the country as a whole is better or worse off with inflation. Some assert that a low rate of inflation—less than 4 percent per year—is beneficial in that it helps to lower the rate of unemployment and smooth the necessary changes in an economy. Since producers receive more for their goods and services with inflation, they can afford to employ more workers and produce more.

But beyond a moderate amount, inflation can cause havoc in any economy. At 1000 percent inflation per year, money loses its value rapidly and people spend it as fast as they can make it. Germany in the early 1920s experienced the devastating impact of prices rising out of control, a situation known as **hyperinflation**. This economic situation helped undermine German society and bring the Nazis to power. More recently, some Latin American countries have faced soaring inflation rates, which have seriously undermined their economies.

But even a rate of say 10-12 percent can have a serious impact on a society. As prices rise, the real value of money—what the money will actually buy—declines. This means that those on fixed incomes, such as pensioners, have their incomes eroded. As inflation progresses, they can buy less and less. Prices must be kept reasonably stable to maintain the standard of living and the health of the economy.

Economic Growth

Economic growth is the increase over a period of time (usually a year) of a country's or region's output of goods and services. Economic growth is often expressed as annual percentage increases in the output of goods and services, or **Gross Domestic Product (GDP)**. For example, the Canadian economy grew in *real* terms by 2.5 percent in 1989 and by 0.5 percent in 1990. By *real* terms, we mean in terms of the amount of goods and services produced—not simply in money amounts. The dollar value of the goods and services produced increased by 7.3 percent in 1989 and by 3.5 percent in 1990. The difference between the real increase in the GDP and the increase in money terms is accounted for by inflation. After 1989, the real rate of economic growth began to decline—slowing to 0.5 percent in 1990 and to −1.5 percent in 1991 with the recession.

The advantages of economic growth are clear. With increases in the GDP, we have a higher standard of living. More goods and services are produced and our incomes can buy more. Resources can be used to help the poor at home and abroad without lowering Canadian living standards.

But there are disadvantages, also, to economic

□ □ □ □ □ □

Our Economic Issues

The following table shows some of the results of the fifth annual *Maclean's* Decima public opinion poll.

What is the most important issue facing Canada today and in the 1990s?

ISSUES	1985	1986	1987	1988	1989	1990s
Environment	*	*	2	10	18	29
Goods and Services Tax	*	*	*	*	15	5
Inflation/economy	16	12	12	5	10	9
Deficit/government	6	10	10	6	10	8
National unity	*	*	*	*	7	4
Free trade	2	5	26	42	7	5
Abortion	*	*	*	*	6	3
Employment	45	39	20	10	6	6

*not cited by a significant number of poll respondents
SOURCE: Reprinted by permission of *Maclean's*, Maclean Hunter Limited, Jan. 1, 1990.

Applications

1. (a) What do you think are the three most important issues facing Canada in the 1990s? Why?
(b) Do your top three issues agree with those in the *Maclean's* poll? Suggest reasons for any differences.
2. Conduct your own poll. You could list issues for respondents to rank or have them provide their own list. Compare the results with the *Maclean's* Decima poll and discuss the similarities and differences.
3. What do the major issues listed in the *Maclean's* poll indicate about how Canadians view economic conditions in the 1990s?

growth. Increased growth implies, at least in part, increased production of capital goods at the expense of consumer goods. More resources are directed into expanding production facilities, for example, but the increase in consumer goods does not come immediately. Thus, fewer consumer goods are produced initially in the expectation of more in the future.

Another problem associated with increased growth—and one that is becoming the object of growing concern—is the pollution of the environment. Increased production may lead to increased pollution of our atmosphere, water systems, and land. Methods, such as recycling and new pollution controls, must be found to ease the stress on the environment.

Viable Balance of Payments

The **balance of payments** is the summary of all foreign transactions made by Canadians over a period of time. These include purchases and sales of goods and services and all foreign borrowing, lending, and investing.

The payments made to Japanese companies for imported automobiles, for example, are included in our balance of payments. Similarly, the interest paid on loans from banks in other countries and the profits made by companies located in Canada, but owned by people in other countries, are also included.

The payments made by people of other countries to Canadians for the goods and services we sell to them, for the interest on the money loaned to them, and the profits of the Canadian businesses established in them constitute our receipts. The summary of our receipts and our payments make up our balance of payments.

The objective of delivering a viable balance of payments is significant because external trade is of great importance to Canada. Today, between a quarter and a third of Canadians are dependent on trade for their jobs, and the gains from international trade make up a significant portion of our GDP.

□ Assessing the Objectives

In examining the goals of our economy, we have considered some of the problems and compromises associated with them. Let's examine these issues more closely.

(i) Interpretation of goals While we may agree generally on the nature of the goals, there is clearly a problem with how they are to be interpreted. What, for example, is meant by a "reasonable" stability of prices, and what is an "equitable" distribution of rising incomes? How are the numerous politicians and inter-

est groups to reach agreement on definitions and clear policies? The objectives will clearly not be easy to achieve.

(ii) Complementary goals   Some goals may be complementary. That is, the achievement of one goal means another is achieved as well. For example, as we move toward full employment, unemployment diminishes—and unemployment is one of the major causes of an inequitable distribution of income. Thus, as we achieve the goal of full employment, we also tend to diminish inequitable distribution of income. But, are all the goals complementary?

(iii) Conflict among goals   Some goals may conflict with one another. For example, policies designed to encourage full employment and economic growth may lead to inflation and thus the instability of prices.

Policies designed to promote an equitable distribution of income may conflict with the goal of economic efficiency, since higher taxes used to provide the economically disadvantaged with an income may reduce incentives to work and produce. How are conflicts such as these to be resolved? What compromises have to be considered?

(iv) Priority among goals   When conflicts arise among goals, decisions must be made on which are most important. If there is a conflict between full employment and stable prices, we have to decide which one takes priority and what compromises we are willing to accept. Suppose we believe that full employment is more important than price stability. Are we, then, willing to accept high inflation to ensure full employment, or are we willing to trade off some unemployment to gain more price stability?

□ □ □ □ □ □

From Marx to the Market: Economy in Transition

The former Soviet Union was the first country to use the ideas of Karl Marx as a basis for its economic and social system. Marx had not provided a clear blueprint for establishing socialism, but between 1917 and 1933, Vladimir Lenin and his successor Joseph Stalin experimented with three different models. In the early 1930s, Stalin selected the model that remained until the late 1980s. What were the major principles behind the Soviet economy, and why has it undergone such astounding changes?

What to Produce
Until the massive changes in the early 1990s, a key feature of the Soviet economy was state ownership of natural and capital resources, with a few exceptions such as some retail businesses, housing, and plots of land on collective or state-owned farms. Decisions about what to produce were made by the top ranks of government. The state planning commission, Gosplan, had the responsibility of transforming the government's directives into a national economic plan. Ministries under Gosplan directed each

industrial sector and various regional authorities. Five-year plans set the basic framework for allocating resources (How much and what kinds of investment? How much consumption? etc.), and one-year plans outlined the specific directives for ministries, industries, and regions.

Until recently, decisions emphasized the production of defence and capital goods (machinery, factories, etc.). Capital goods accounted for some 35 percent of total output, compared with approximately 25 percent in Canada. Consumer goods, on the other hand, were given low priority.

How to Produce
The government, through its planning bodies—Gosplan and individual ministries—also typically decided what investments and purchases should be made by individual firms. Managers had some jurisdiction over the number and types of workers they could hire. The managers' major goal, however, was to fill their firm's part of the economic

plan, usually expressed in terms of production quotas. Often, the easiest way to meet these quotas was to produce low quality, uniform products.

For Whom to Produce

Decisions about for whom goods and services were to be produced also rested with government. In the past, high priority was placed on the production of capital and military goods. In the 1980s, an increased share of capital investment was directed into agriculture to increase food output, and into the production of consumer goods.

Many goods and services were provided to individuals for free or at low cost. Medical care, for example, was free. State-owned apartments in Moscow were rented at just 13 percent of the average wage. Trips on urban transit systems were provided at nominal prices. By contrast, prices in the free markets and those set by the co-operative enterprises were high, but the quality and availability of goods was much better than in the state stores.

Performance of the Economy

The emphasis on capital and arms production in the Soviet economic plans allowed the nation to withstand a devastating invasion during World War II and to achieve rapid growth and industrialization. The Soviet economy grew at a rate of 7 percent in the 1950s and 5 percent in the 1960s. Growth slowed to a more modest rate in the 1970s and early 1980s.

The slowdown was the result of a number of factors. With the shift in emphasis from the production of capital goods to consumer goods, goals were less well defined. Moreover, industrial growth was spurred by the migration of farm workers to the cities, which clearly could not continue indefinitely.

By the mid 1980s, the Soviet economy began to stagnate. In 1990, for the first time in the post-war era, the Soviet government reported a fall in output. Many incomes continued to rise, however, causing an increase in inflation. Fears of continued price increases and food shor-

tages led people to hoard food. In the first half of 1991, output fell by 10 percent compared with the previous year. Many staples were rationed and the lines at supply centres grew longer.

Problems of the Soviet Economy

Central planning seemed poorly suited to the complexities of a modern economy with changing goals. Some key problems of the economic system included the difficulties of co-ordinating production, a lack of quality control, few incentives for workers, and pollution of the environment.

The production and distribution of goods and services with central planning was seldom efficient. Shortages and gluts of particular goods were not uncommon. Production quotas also placed the emphasis on quantity over quality, and managers had little concern for the demands of consumers. Workers had security in their jobs, but as a result also had little incentive to produce more and better quality goods. With meeting production quotas as the major concern, little attention was paid to the damage done the environment.

Reforms

In this context of a stagnating economy, the Soviet leader Mikhail Gorbachev began a number of programs in 1987 to restructure the economy. This restructuring was called *perestroika*. Gorbachev argued that the central bodies were unable to control the day-to-day activities of every Soviet enterprise. He therefore advocated a reduction in central control in favour of more management autonomy and accountability of enterprises. Financial rewards, he asserted, should reflect more accurately the firms' contribution to the Soviet economy.

Gorbachev's views were embodied in the Law of the State Enterprise of June 30, 1987, which was viewed as the keystone of his reform efforts. Under the terms of the law, enterprises would manage their own affairs and operate under profit and loss accounting. Enterprises that lost money would be bankrupt. In addition, enterprises could free themselves gradually from the production orders of central planners and find their own customers. Thus, Soviet enterprises would move away from central control toward management autonomy in a number of stages.

At the same time, a new law permitted the establishment of private enterprises in twenty-nine consumer goods and services, such as the production of clothing and toys, and car and TV repairs. Private enterprises were permitted in these areas since state industries were ignoring them. By 1989, some 2 million (out of a population of 290 million) people were engaged in private industries.

Gorbachev also encouraged the establishment of private, family, and jointly-owned farms to replace the state collective farms established under Stalin. But Soviet farmers, unlike their Chinese counterparts, did not leap at the opportunity to leave the collective farms.

In 1990, two radical reform plans were announced. The first was the Shatalin "500-day" plan (named after its author, the economist Stanislav Shatalin), which proposed to establish a mixed market economy. Eighty percent of the Soviet economy was to pass into private hands and prices were to be set by the market rather than by state planners. State subsidies to money-losing industries were to be cut off. Credit would be available only through "western-style" banks. The plan was rejected by the legislature of the former Soviet Union, but it was adopted "in principle" by the legislature of the Russian republic by the lop-sided vote of 213 to 2.

The second radical reform plan was the Presidential Plan, which incorporated the basic features of the Shatalin Plan and was adopted by the former Soviet Congress of People's Deputies in 1990. It advocated a market system with substantial government involvement, stating that there "is no alternative to switching to a market system." The plan called for the privatization of productive resources and the reduction of central control, while control by the republics was to increase. An 18- to 24-month transition period to a market economy was envisaged. Various republics instituted their own laws and decrees to encourage the movement toward a market system.

The Rise of the Republics

Continuing economic problems, burgeoning nationalism, and the increasing assertiveness of the republics all combined to destroy the Soviet Union by the end of 1991. Republic after republic declared its independence and in December of 1991, all but Georgia joined a Commonwealth of Independent States originally established by three of the largest republics: Russia, Byelorussia, and Ukraine.

The basic principles of the Commonwealth dealt largely with economic matters. Among the issues agreed on were:

"To carry out co-ordinated, radical economic reforms aimed at creating feasible market mechanisms, transformation of property, and ensuring the freedom of entrepreneurship..."

"To conduct a co-ordinated policy of price liberalization and social protection..."

"To help create joint-stock companies..."

Clearly, the Soviet Union, and the mixed command economic system so characteristic of it since 1928, had collapsed. In a remarkably short time, the basic aims of the 1917 Bolshevik Revolution were reversed.

Applications

1. What key characteristics defined the former Soviet Union as a mixed command economy up to 1985?

2. (a) What problems did the Soviet Union face in the 1980s?

(b) What were some of the major causes of these problems? Explain.

3. Describe the economic reforms proposed in the late 1980s and early 1990s. How effective were they?

4. What are the key economic objectives of the republics in the 1990s?

5. (a) Compare the Canadian economy with the economy of the former Soviet Union (to 1985). Consider the characteristics of the two systems, their objectives, advantages, and disadvantages.

(b) Compare the Canadian economy with the new economic system in Russia.

Summary

a. An economic system is the set of laws, institutions, and customs by which a society determines how to use its scarce resources to meet the needs and wants of its citizens.

b. The three major questions any economy must answer are what, how, and for whom to produce.

c. A traditional economy answers the three major questions by relying on its past practices. Its major advantages are stability and security for its people. Its major disadvantages include limited opportunities for innovation, initiatives, and economic improvement.

In a pure command economy, the three major questions are answered by a government or other central authority, which owns all productive resources. The major advantage of the command system is a central plan that can be focussed on clear, national objectives. Disadvantages include limited individual freedom, a lack of incentives for efficient production, and a large margin for error in the planning of a very complex economy.

In a pure market economy, resources are privately owned and the actions of individual buyers and sellers operating through a system of prices and markets co-ordinate the economy. Advantages include economic freedom, incentives for efficient production, and the production of goods and services consumers want and need. Disadvantages include the inequitable distribution of income, cyclical fluctuations in economic activity, and the possibility of unwise consumer decisions.

d. Adam Smith was one of the earliest proponents of the market system. He believed that the major motivating force in the economy is self-interest, which is kept in check by competition. These forces work automatically in the marketplace and do not require government intervention.

Karl Marx's theories were used as the basis for command economies in many socialist and communist countries. He believed that under a capitalist or free market system, the workers were paid less than the full value of their labour and that they would eventually revolt, creating a more egalitarian distribution of goods and services.

e. The Canadian economy is primarily a market economy but contains elements of a command economy, and is therefore known as a mixed market economy. The economy of the former Soviet Union was an example of a mixed command economy.

f. On a spectrum of economies, the pure market system is at one pole with decentralized decision-making and private ownership of resources, while the pure command economy is at the opposite pole with centralized decision-making and state ownership of resources. The economies of the world can be placed between the two poles.

g. The major characteristics of the Canadian economy include private ownership of productive resources, self-interest, relatively free markets in which prices are determined, the drive for profits, consumer sovereignty, competition, and significant government involvement.

h. The major objectives of the Canadian economy—many set out by the Economic Council of Canada—include economic efficiency, equitable distribution of income, full employment, a reasonable stability of prices, economic growth, and a viable balance of payments.

i. In the 1980s, the mixed command economy of the former Soviet Union faced serious difficulties, including a drop in output, inflation, and shortages. Reforms were instituted to move the economy toward a free market system, and economic reforms were continued by the Commonwealth of Independent States after the dissolution of the Soviet Union.

▮ Review of Key Terms

Define the following key terms introduced in this chapter and provide examples where appropriate.

economic system	competition
traditional economy	Economic Council of
pure command economy	Canada
pure market economy	economic efficiency
mixed market economy	technological efficiency
mixed command economy	allocative efficiency
self-interest	unemployment rate
market	the unemployed
price	inflation
profit	hyperinflation
consumer sovereignty	balance of payments

▮ Application and Analysis

1. Develop an organizer, or use the example given below, to compare the major characteristics of traditional, pure command, and pure market economies.

CHARACTERISTICS		TYPE OF ECONOMY		
		TRADITIONAL	PURE COMMAND	PURE MARKET
How each economy answers the three basic questions	What to produce			
	How to produce			
	For whom to produce			
Ownership of productive resources				
Assessment of each economy	Advantages			
	Disadvantages			

2. (a) Read the following statements and determine whether each one refers to a traditional (T), market (M), or command (C) economic system.

(i) Goods and services are distributed to consumers according to the ways they have been distributed in the past.
(ii) The goods and services are distributed according to a plan.
(iii) Resources are distributed in the same ways that they always have been.
(iv) Consumer purchases ultimately determine the way in which goods and services will be produced.
(v) The motivation for increased productivity is the desire to make a profit.
(vi) Consumer purchases in markets do not act as signals in determining what will be produced.
(vii) Medical and hospital services are provided free of charge.
(viii) Crops are planted in the same way they have been planted in the past.

(b) Read the statements again and decide which basic economic question each statement answers (What, How, or For whom).

3. (a) Suppose you are a member of the central planning committee in a command economy. It becomes clear that your next five-year plan must incorporate the following directives. List five factors that must be considered to fulfill each directive.

(i) The production of woollen sweaters must be increased by one million units.
(ii) 25 000 doctors must graduate over the next five years to maintain the current doctor/patient ratio.
(iii) Wheat production must be increased by planting 10 000 additional hectares.
(iv) 10 000 fewer automobiles will be produced in order to manufacture 5000 additional combines for the wheat farms.

(b) Explain how each of these needs might be met in a free market economy.

4. (a) Classify the following Canadian economists according to whether they work in business, govern-ment, labour unions, journalism, or academic institutions (colleges and universities).

(b) Choose three economists listed below and briefly outline their training and careers.

(i) Dian Cohen
(ii) Marie-Josée Drouin
(iii) Jacques Parizeau
(iv) Melville Watkins
(v) Robert Bourassa
(vi) Allan MacEachen
(vii) Richard Lipsey
(viii) Wendy Dobson
(ix) Gerald Bouey

5. What would you consider to be the three most important objectives for the Canadian economy in the 1990s? Justify your choices.

6. Case Study—The East German Economy (1989)

Guiding his Mercedes taxi cab through early evening traffic, Horst Wachendorf smiles at every exhaust-belching East German Trabant he passes.

Happy as he is at the recent turn of history in his divided city of Berlin, Mr. Wachendorf recognizes that the tiny, glass-fibre *Trabis* sputtering at his side represent more than just East Germany's drive to freedom. They also underline just how far Socialist Germany fell behind its capitalist sibling during a 40-year separation.

"They build a car in the 1950s and that's it for the rest of the century," the West Berlin taxi driver remarks. "Here, every year somebody thinks 'what can we add on, how can we make it better.'"

Indeed, the *Trabi*, the car that grabbed world atten-tion by ferrying tens of thousands of refugees to the West, is a perfect metaphor for East German decline.

Before the Second World War, the complex where Trabant was made in East Germany was part of a four-car consortium that included the forerunner of West Germany's Audi AG. In fact, the Trabant was manufac-tured in Audi's pre-war plant at Zwickau. But while some parts of the consortium stayed put after the war, Audi fled west to its main plant in Ingolstadt, a corporate refugee forced to start anew. Today, its cars can drive rings around the two-stroke, 26-horsepower *Trabis*.

"Simply, Audi was in competition with a lot of auto-mobile companies in West Germany and they had to be good to stay alive, whereas Trabant had no competition," says economist Claus Schnable. "They were given the exclusive right to make cars and there was always demand, no matter what they did."

"They started on the same footing," says Dietrich Beier, chief economist of the Berliner Bank. "That is why socialism is condemned."

The extent of today's economic gap was evident at the inauguration of a new engine plant in Karl Marx Stadt. The cash-strapped East Germans purchased the line from Volkswagen AG—Audi's parent—which agreed to take back 430 000 of the simple, bare-boned engines (no transmission or electronics) in payment.

For Volkswagen, the engine line represented obsolete equipment that cried out for replacement with automated technology. "But for the East Germans, it was a 30-year advance," Volkswagen spokesman Otto Wachs said.

"If you look at the technology of the Trabant and the production methods, it's still at the level of the 1950s."

Just how the East Germans managed to lose so much ground in just four decades is testimony to the colossal shortcomings of Stalinist planning systems. After all, nobody was better at socialism than the Germans, but still they couldn't keep up.

As information begins trickling out—for years, the East German government either fabricated statistics or treated them as state secrets—it is becoming apparent that the country's economy actually had been going nowhere for some time.

"It is conceivable East Germany had zero or negative growth for all of the 1980s," said Christopher Mattheisen, an East European analyst with London-based WEFA Group.

Next door, the driving force of the West German economy throughout the decade was the adoption of new technology, spurred on by heightened competition.

But the East's highly centralized planning system was incapable of making the necessary adjustments.

With East German products such as the Trabant trapped in a time warp, the country's exports fell off sharply. In 1973, 4 percent of machinery production was sold to the West; by 1986, the figure had fallen to under 1 percent.

The East Germans found themselves pushed out of market after market—even the West German one next door—by the newly industrialized countries of Asia.

East Germany's Stalinist formula included 214 central guidelines to enterprises and the organization of industry into 140 unwieldy monopolies called Kombinate.

The East German economy was turned inward. Instead of importing production machinery from, say, the Czechoslovaks, the Kombinate were ordered to manufacture it themselves. Each became a self-contained economy, mini-autarchies within the state autarchy.

Today, East Germany, a country of just 16.5 million, produces its own versions of 80 percent of the goods made in the world. Needless to say, not all things are done well.

This drive for self-sufficiency resulted in poor allocation of precious investment funds. The East Germans spent a fortune, for instance, developing reserves of brown coal.

Whereas many West German homes are heated by clean natural gas imported from the former Soviet Union, East Germany was ruining its environment trying to burn a low-quality fuel that is as likely to freeze on truly cold days as it is to ignite.

The East Germans also poured billions into developing a micro-electronics industry, including a costly exercise at re-inventing the one-megabyte chip.

As a consequence of these wasteful investment policies, East Germany's infrastructure has been badly neglected. Two-thirds of its housing and much of the rail, telephone, and road systems date from the Nazi era.

SOURCE: Adapted from Edward Greenspon, *The Globe and Mail*, December 21, 1989.

(a) How does the case of the Trabant reveal some of the problems with the former East German economy? List these problems.

(b) What advantages does the East German economy have for revitalization?

(c) How is the comparison of the East and West German economies particularly useful?

Efficient Use of Resources

Economic efficiency is the goal of realizing the most effective use of resources to yield the greatest benefits. Of course, the question is how are we to achieve this goal, and how are we to assess whether the many individual producers and consumers in our economy make the best use of resources?

In this unit, therefore, we examine how our economy operates, and how producers and consumers make decisions about the use of resources. We focus first on the forces of supply and demand and how they interact to determine prices and output in individual markets. Then, we turn to entrepreneurs and business organizations to examine their roles. Finally, we consider the various types of market structures affecting the decisions of producers and consumers, and assess the efficiency of each one.

Our focus in this unit and the next is on microeconomic issues. **Microeconomics** examines the role of individual producers and consumers in specific markets. In other words, we put the economy under a *micro*scope to study the workings of its individual parts. In Units Four and Five, we turn to **macroeconomics**—the study of the economy as a whole, including investigations of such questions as the overall level of consumption, investment, government spending, prices, employment, and output. We move from the smaller to the larger picture.

□ □ □ □ □ □

CHAPTER THREE

Demand and Supply

We have all heard the refrain—"it's a matter of supply and demand." The forces of supply and demand are basic to the operation of our economy. Though they are certainly not the answer to all questions, they do help to explain how individual buyers and sellers make decisions in a market. These decisions are in many ways based on common sense. We all know that if tickets for a major concert are in short supply, demand and prices will be high. The band may decide to hold another concert to meet the demand.

Demand and supply thus help to determine how much will be produced, and at what price it will be sold. And remarkably, the forces of supply and demand work automatically in our economy to co-ordinate the exchange of goods and services and determine prices.

Objectives

a. Demonstrate, using a simple circular flow model, the real and money flows between households and businesses through product markets.

b. Define demand and graph a demand schedule.

c. Explain and apply the law of demand, using schedules and graphs.

d. Outline the factors causing changes in demand and graph the effects.

e. Calculate, graph, and apply the price elasticity of demand for products and outline the factors that affect it.

f. Relate the concepts of utility, the law of diminishing utility, and consumer surplus to demand.

g. Define supply and graph a supply schedule.

h. Explain and apply the law of supply, using schedules and graphs.

i. Outline the factors causing a change in supply and graph the effects.

j. Calculate, graph, and apply the price elasticity of supply for products and outline the factors affecting it.

k. Demonstrate the difference between a shift in demand or supply, and a change in quantity demanded or quantity supplied.

A Circular Flow Model of the Economy

Before we examine the forces of demand and supply in more detail, it is helpful to consider how goods, services, and money are exchanged in our market economy. For an overview of our economy, we can examine a simple circular flow model. In other words, we can reduce the economy to its basic parts. Figure 3.1 illustrates this basic model. It shows two main sectors of the economy—the household and business sectors.

The household sector represents the buyer or consumer side of the economy. A **household** is any person or group of persons living together and functioning as an economic unit. A household may be a family, single individual, or group of unrelated individuals. Through

their needs and wants for goods and services and their expenditures (dollar votes), households represent the demand or consumer side of the economy.

The business sector is the producer or seller side of the economy. **Businesses** are economic units involved in the production and distribution of goods and services. They may be very small operations, such as a corner store, or very large enterprises, such as a steel or automobile corporation. Businesses provide households with the goods and services they need and want and thus represent the supply side of the economy.

Between households and businesses are the products markets. Through these markets, households purchase goods and services, and businesses sell them.

Two flows link the sectors. One is the **real flow** of goods and services from businesses through the products markets to households; the other is the **money flow** in the opposite direction from households to businesses as payment for the goods and services they receive.

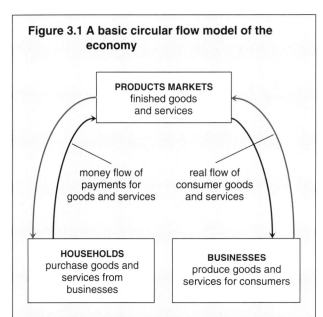

Figure 3.1 A basic circular flow model of the economy

PRODUCTS MARKETS
finished goods
and services

money flow of
payments for
goods and services

real flow of
consumer goods
and services

HOUSEHOLDS
purchase goods and
services from
businesses

BUSINESSES
produce goods and
services for consumers

This model shows the real flow of goods and services from businesses (producers) through the products markets to households (consumers). A money flow moves in the opposite direction from households through the products markets to businesses. This flow represents the payments of households to businesses for the goods and services received. At this point, the model is only a half circle. Later we will see how the flow is completed.

The Nature of Demand

Let's consider the demand side of the economy first. If a blockbuster sale on compact discs were announced tomorrow, we all know that "demand" would be high, and people would buy in large quantities. So what does demand mean? Demand expresses a relationship between price and the quantity of a product purchased. Specifically, **demand** refers to the quantities of a good or service consumers are willing and able to buy at various prices over a period of time.

Notice that this definition specifies *able* as well as willing to buy. Willingness alone has no effect unless it is backed by the ability to buy—that is, the actual dollars and cents that can turn that willingness into a reality. We must not only *want* that compact disc, but also have the *actual money* to go out and buy it.

Notice, too, that demand refers not to one particular quantity and price, but to a series of quantities and their prices over a particular time. In other words, consumers may be willing and able to buy two compact discs a month at $15 each, but this price and quantity alone would not define the demand. In one month, consumers may also be willing and able to buy three discs at $10 each, or one disc at $20 each. Demand includes all of the possible quantities consumers will buy at various prices. Demand, therefore, is generally expressed in a **demand schedule**.

Let's consider a simple example. The demand schedule in Table 3.1 shows the relationship between the price and quantity of orange juice demanded per week by one student. At 50 cents a glass, the student buys 11 glasses per week; at 60 cents a glass, 10 glasses per week, and so on. The information in this schedule can be plotted on a graph as a **demand curve**, shown in Figure 3.2. By convention in economics, price is measured along the vertical axis and quantity along the horizontal axis. The demand curve slopes downward, illustrating clearly that as the price increases, the quantity of orange juice demanded decreases.

☐ The Law of Demand

Our example illustrates the **law of demand**, which states that as the price of a good falls the quantity purchased increases, providing all other things remain the same. Conversely, as the price rises, the quantity purchased decreases. In short, we can say that there is an *inverse relationship* between price and quantity demanded. If price falls, quantity demanded rises and *vice versa*. Price and quantity move in opposite directions. This inverse relationship is illustrated by the downward slope of the demand curve. In fact, the law of demand is often referred to as the law of *downward-sloping* demand.

The law of demand applies to practically all products. For example, if you regularly buy a can of soda a day with your lunch for 90 cents and the price of the soda rose to $1.50, you would probably decide to skip the soda and buy a less expensive drink, as would many other people. The quantity of soda demanded would fall. An exception to the law occurs, however, when the satisfaction enjoyed from a good is dependent on its price. For example, insofar as the satisfaction of owning diamonds is for some people dependent on their having a high price, they will buy fewer diamonds, not more, if the price decreases.

Table 3.1 A student's demand schedule for orange juice over one week

1 PRICE PER GLASS (IN CENTS)	2 QUANTITY DEMANDED PER WEEK (IN GLASSES)	3 POSITION IN FIGURE 3.2
100	4	A
90	6	B
80	8	C
70	9	D
60	10	E
50	11	F

As price increases, the quantity of orange juice demanded decreases, and *vice versa*.

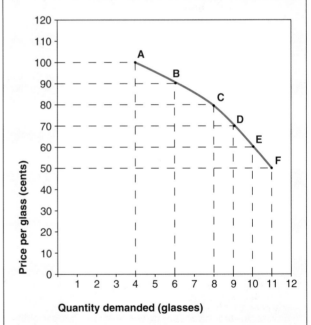

Figure 3.2 A student's demand curve for orange juice over one week

The demand curve (plotted from Table 3.1) slopes down to the right, illustrating clearly that as price increases, quantity demanded decreases, and as price decreases, quantity demanded increases.

☐ Market Demand

So far, we have considered only one buyer's demand for orange juice. In reality, there may be thousands or millions of buyers. What, then, is the relationship between one buyer's demand and the demand of a large number of people in a given market? The answer, as you would expect, is that the market demand is the sum of all individual demand.

To illustrate, let's assume that there are only three buyers of orange juice in the market. Their individual demand schedules are shown in Table 3.2. Figure 3.3 illustrates how the individual demand curves are combined to determine the market demand.

Table 3.2 Market demand schedule for orange juice over one week, three buyers (in glasses)

1 PRICE PER GLASS (IN CENTS)	2 QUANTITY DEMANDED BY BUYER 1		3 QUANTITY DEMANDED BY BUYER 2		4 QUANTITY DEMANDED BY BUYER 3		5 TOTAL DEMANDED PER WEEK	6 POSITION IN FIGURE 3.3
100	4	+	3	+	·2	=	9	U
90	6	+	5	+	4	=	15	V
80	8	+	7	+	5	=	20	W
70	9	+	8	+	6	=	23	X
60	10	+	9	+	7	=	26	Y
50	11	+	10	+	8	=	29	Z

Market demand is the sum of all individual demand.

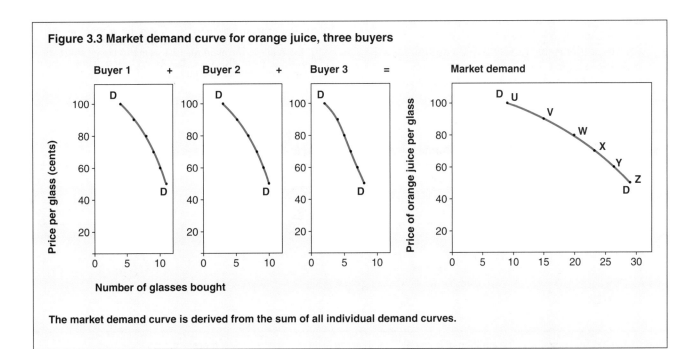

Figure 3.3 Market demand curve for orange juice, three buyers

The market demand curve is derived from the sum of all individual demand curves.

☐ Changes in Demand

We have also assumed that the only factor affecting demand is price. As price changes, quantity demanded changes. But when we stated the law of demand, we added "providing all other things remain the same." And, of course, other things do not remain the same. Demand depends on a number of different factors and a change in any one of these factors can cause a shift in the demand curve. The five major *non-price* determinants of demand are the size of the market, average incomes, the price of related goods, tastes, and expectations.

Size of the Market

How does the size of the market affect demand? Let's return to our market for orange juice. Table 3.3 shows a demand schedule when the size of the market has been increased by the addition of one other buyer, Buyer 4. As a consequence, the total demand at each price level also increases. Whereas formerly (see Table 3.2) the market demand for orange juice was 9 glasses per week at $1.00 a glass, with an increased market, demand also increases to 14 glasses at $1.00 per glass. At a price of 90 cents a glass, demand increases from 15 to 22 glasses, and so on. As demand increases, the demand curve shifts to the right. Figure 3.4 illustrates this shift in the demand curve.

As you would expect, a reduction in the size of the market will have the effect of reducing demand. Sup-

Figure 3.4 An increase in demand for orange juice

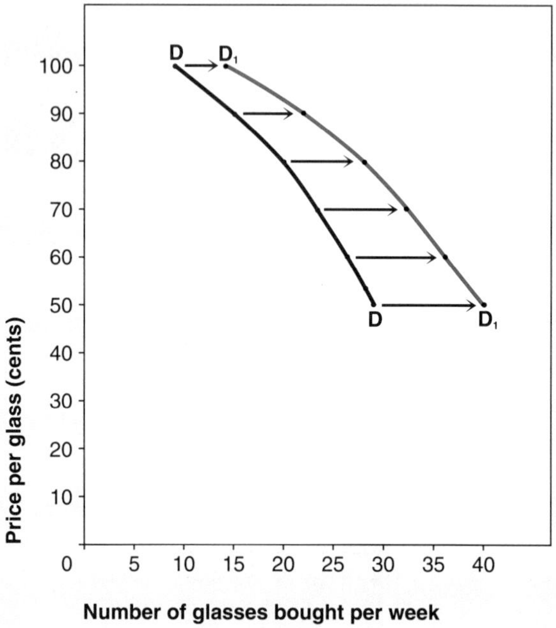

An increase in demand is shown by a shift of the demand curve to the right. With an increase in the size of the market, for example, the demand curve shifts to the right from DD to D₁D₁. At all price levels, the quantity demanded has increased.

Table 3.3 Market demand schedule for orange juice over one week, four buyers (in glasses)

1 PRICE PER GLASS (IN CENTS)	2 QUANTITY DEMANDED BY BUYER 1		3 QUANTITY DEMANDED BY BUYER 2		4 QUANTITY DEMANDED BY BUYER 3		5 QUANTITY DEMANDED BY BUYER 4		6 TOTAL DEMANDED PER WEEK
100	4	+	3	+	2	+	5	=	14
90	6	+	5	+	4	+	7	=	22
80	8	+	7	+	5	+	8	=	28
70	9	+	8	+	6	+	9	=	32
60	10	+	9	+	7	+	10	=	36
50	11	+	10	+	8	+	11	=	40

The market has increased with the addition of Buyer 4. Total demand at each price level has, therefore, also increased.

Figure 3.5 A decrease in demand for orange juice

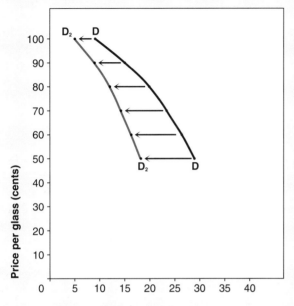

A decrease in demand is shown by a shift of the demand curve to the left. With a decrease in the size of the market, for example, the demand curve shifts from DD to D₂D₂. At all price levels, the quantity demanded has decreased.

Table 3.4 Market demand schedule for orange juice over one week, two buyers (in glasses)

1 PRICE PER GLASS (IN CENTS)	2 QUANTITY DEMANDED BY BUYER 1		3 QUANTITY DEMANDED BY BUYER 2		4 TOTAL DEMANDED PER WEEK
100	3	+	2	=	5
90	5	+	4	=	9
80	7	+	5	=	12
70	8	+	6	=	14
60	9	+	7	=	16
50	10	+	8	=	18

The size of the market has decreased by one buyer. Total demand at each price level has, therefore, also decreased.

pose the market is composed of only two buyers. At each price on the demand schedule, shown in Table 3.4, the quantity demanded is less than before. At $1.00 per glass, only 5 glasses are demanded instead of 9; at 90 cents a glass, only 9 glasses are demanded instead of 15. As demand declines, the demand curve shifts to the left. Figure 3.5 illustrates this shift in the demand curve.

In summary, then, an increase in the size of the market for a product brings an increase in demand, and the demand curve shifts to the right. A decrease in the size of the market means a decrease in demand, and the demand curve shifts to the left.

Average Incomes

Perhaps the most important of the non-price determinants of demand is average income. If the incomes of buyers rise significantly, their consumption of orange juice will likely rise as well because they can afford more. If their incomes fall, their orange juice consumption will also likely fall. The higher our incomes, the more we can afford and the more we are likely to buy.

The demand for most goods will rise with a general increase in incomes. Commodities for which demand varies *directly* (in the same direction) with income are called **superior** or **normal goods**. Steak is one of the most commonly cited examples, since with a rise in incomes, people will buy more steak. Those who have not bought it before will buy it, and those who have bought it previously will buy more—without buying less of any other product.

Commodities for which demand varies *inversely* (in the opposite direction) with income are known as **inferior goods**. Cabbage and potatoes are examples. When incomes rise beyond a certain point, the demand for these goods tends to decline because people switch to "higher grade" food products, such as meat and fruit.

Price and Availability of Related Goods

Substitute or **competing goods** are those that can be interchanged for one another, such as cassette tapes for compact discs, or apple for orange juice. If the price of apple juice rises, it is likely that the demand for a substitute good such as orange juice will increase. Similarly, if the price of apple juice falls, the demand for orange juice will likely decrease since the substitute good is cheaper.

Complementary goods are pairs of goods that "go together" or complement each other in the sense that the consumption of one involves the consumption of the other. Oil and gasoline are examples. If the price of gasoline rises and, as a consequence, you use your car less, your demand for oil will fall. Conversely, if the price of gas falls and you use your car more, your demand for oil will increase.

Tastes

If blue jeans cease to be fashionable and grey woollen pants are "in," then the demand for blue jeans will decrease and the demand for grey woollen pants will increase. The demand curve for blue jeans will shift to the left and that for grey woollen pants will shift to the right. Consumer tastes, often influenced by advertising campaigns, have a definite effect on demand.

Changes in technology may also bring about shifts in demand. The development and consumer acceptance of compact discs, for example, brought a decline in the demand for LPs (long-play records).

Expectations

Expectations for the future also influence consumer demand. If we expect that prices are going to rise in the future, then we are likely to buy now to beat the price increases. On the other hand, if we expect prices to fall in the future, we are likely to postpone our spending. For example, if widely-believed housing experts predict rising home prices in the near future, then prospective homeowners are likely to buy now. Similarly, if it is widely believed that home prices are about to drop significantly, then home seekers are likely to defer their purchases until the prices drop.

Expectations of price increases will shift the demand curve to the right, and expectations of price decreases will shift the demand curve to the left.

■ Price Elasticity of Demand

We saw earlier that as prices change, the quantity of a product demanded also changes. Can we determine just how much the quantity of a product sold can be affected by a price change? **Price elasticity of demand** refers to the responsiveness of quantity demanded to a change in price. Demand may be elastic, inelastic, or of unitary elasticity.

Elastic Demand

Suppose that tomorrow morning Air Canada were to cut the price of air fares to the Caribbean by 25 percent. It's likely that the total amount of money spent on Air Canada Caribbean fares would be greater after the price cut than before. Why? Some people who would have travelled to other parts of the world would likely take advantage of the Air Canada deal and travel to the Caribbean. Others who may not have considered a holiday, or who normally travel with another airline, may also take advantage of the Air Canada deal.

If Air Canada raised its fares to the Caribbean by 25 percent, many people who would have taken its flights there would choose other alternatives—such as flights on other airlines to the Caribbean or flights to other destinations. The total amount of money spent on Air Canada trips in this case would likely fall, even with the 25 percent increase in price. We would call the demand for Air Canada flights **price elastic** because a price cut produces a rise in demand for the service, and a price hike leads to a reduction in demand.

Inelastic Demand

Suppose now that the price of salt increases by 25 percent. Will the price increase have much effect on our purchases of salt? Will the amount of salt we put on our food change significantly? Probably not. Similarly, a decrease in price by the same amount is unlikely to convince us to buy much more salt. Most of us buy the salt we need regardless of the price. The demand for salt is **price inelastic**. It increases little with a price cut and decreases little with a price rise.

Unitary Elasticity of Demand

In some cases, demand for a product may be of **unitary elasticity**—that is, a price increase or decrease will have no effect on total revenue. The loss in revenue due to a reduction in price is exactly balanced by the increase in sales. Conversely, the increase in revenue due to an increase in price is exactly balanced by the reduction in sales.

The elasticity of demand for a product is likely to vary over the demand curve. That is, the demand for a product may be of unitary elasticity at one point, elastic at other points, and inelastic at yet other times, as we will see.

☐ Calculating Elasticity of Demand

One method of calculating the elasticity of demand for a product is outlined in the Skill Development section in this chapter on pages 63-65. Here we'll examine another method of determining whether the demand for a good or service is elastic or not—the total revenue test.

As we have seen, if a decrease in the price of a product brings higher total revenues, then demand for

the product is elastic. If a price decrease lowers total revenue, then demand for the product is inelastic. By calculating total revenue from quantities sold at various price levels, therefore, we can determine the elasticity of a product. Total revenue is calculated as price multiplied by quantity sold (TR = P x Q).

Figure 3.6 shows that the daily demand for Air Canada tickets to the Caribbean is elastic because a reduction in ticket prices from $200 to $150 per ticket brings an overall increase in total revenue. At $200 a ticket, total revenue is $150 000. But at $150 a ticket, total revenue increases to $262 500. Similarly, Figure 3.7 illustrates by the total revenue test, that the demand for salt is inelastic since a reduction in price from $2.00 to $1.50 per kg leads to a fall in total revenue from $3500 to $3000.

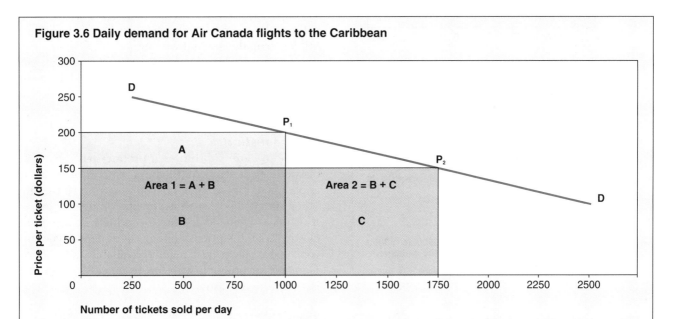

Figure 3.6 Daily demand for Air Canada flights to the Caribbean

At P₁, price is $200 per ticket and the quantity sold is 1000 tickets. Total revenue is indicated as area 1 on the graph. Total Revenue (TR) = Price (P) x Quantity (Q)
= $200 x 1000
= $200 000

When the price is reduced to $150 per ticket at P₂, the number of tickets sold is 1750. Total revenue is indicated as area 2. Total Revenue (TR) = Price (P) x Quantity (Q)
=$150 x 1750
=$262 500

Since total revenue increases from $200 000 to $262 500 with the price cut, the demand for Air Canada flights to the Caribbean is price elastic.

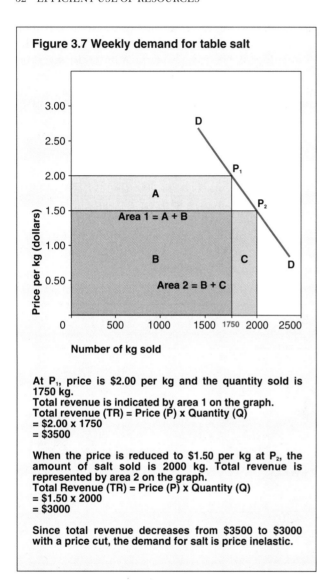

Figure 3.7 Weekly demand for table salt

At P₁, price is $2.00 per kg and the quantity sold is 1750 kg.
Total revenue is indicated by area 1 on the graph.
Total revenue (TR) = Price (P) x Quantity (Q)
= $2.00 x 1750
= $3500

When the price is reduced to $1.50 per kg at P₂, the amount of salt sold is 2000 kg. Total revenue is represented by area 2 on the graph.
Total Revenue (TR) = Price (P) x Quantity (Q)
= $1.50 x 2000
= $3000

Since total revenue decreases from $3500 to $3000 with a price cut, the demand for salt is price inelastic.

■ Factors Affecting Elasticity of Demand

Why is the demand for some goods elastic and others not? Let's examine some of the major reasons.

Amount of Consumers' Budget Spent on the Product

If a good takes only a small amount of consumers' budgets, price changes are unlikely to influence the quantity demanded very much. Reductions in the price of salt or pepper, for example, are unlikely to lead to greater consumption. They comprise so small a portion of our budget that we tend to ignore price changes. Demand for them is inelastic.

For goods and services that comprise a large percentage of consumers' budgets—such as rents for apartments, or purchases of new automobiles—the demand is elastic. Increases in prices for these goods and services will prompt people to look for alternatives. They may look for cheaper accommodation or postpone their purchase of a new automobile. Reductions in prices are likely to encourage purchases.

Luxuries and Necessaries

Goods that are necessaries, such as basic food and clothing, generally have an inelastic demand. We have to buy them whatever the cost because we cannot go without them. Price variations, therefore, have limited influence on the amount we buy.

Luxuries, on the other hand, such as mink coats and sports cars, have an elastic demand. We don't need them, so price changes have a significant influence on the number we buy.

Close Substitutes

The more close substitutes a product has, the more elastic is its demand. With an increase in the price of apple juice, for example, consumers can turn to some other kind of juice, such as tomato, orange, or grapefruit juice. Demand for these products is, therefore, elastic. But if the price of either salt or pepper goes up, consumers have no readily available alternative. Demand for products with few or no close substitutes is, therefore, inelastic.

Time

The longer the period of time under consideration, the more elastic the demand for a product. If the price of gasoline increases, for example, there is little we can do about it immediately. Over time, however, automobile manufacturers can produce more fuel-efficient automobiles and governments can provide more public transport. Alternate sources of energy, such as electricity and propane, can also be explored.

□ □ □ □ □ □

Elasticity of Demand—Some Applications

The elasticity of demand isn't just an abstract concept. It has significant practical applications. Let's consider some examples.

Manufacturing

In the early years of this century, the automobile was considered a luxury "plaything" of the rich. The founder of the Ford Motor Company, Henry Ford, reasoned that he could change that and put the automobile within the reach of the average American. Consequently, he mass produced the Model T and cut prices dramatically. In 1908, the Model T sold for $850. By 1913, it was selling for $500. Ford believed that increased sales would more than make up for the reduction in price and that his total revenue would rise. He was right. The demand for automobiles was *price elastic*. Between 1908 and 1927, some 15 million Model Ts rolled off the assembly lines. Sales and revenues soared. From being a luxury plaything of the rich, the automobile became a near necessity for the average North American.

Agriculture

Farmers are often concerned when the weather is bad for their crops, but paradoxically, they may have just as much cause for concern when the weather is good. Bumper crops for North American farmers have the effect of depressing prices for the crop, so that total revenues actually drop despite increased sales. Consequently, farmers may receive more from a small crop than a large one. Why? The demand for many agricultural products is *price inelastic*.

Sin Taxes

Have you ever noticed that the so-called "sin products," such as cigarettes and alcohol, are the favourite targets of finance ministers when it comes to raising taxes? Why? The reason is, at least in part, that the demand for these products is *price inelastic* and an increase in taxes will bring an increase in government revenues. If government were to raise taxes on products with elastic demand, total revenues could in fact fall.

Health groups, on the other hand, lobby Canadian governments to impose higher taxes on tobacco products because they believe the taxes will discourage smoking. These groups argue that while the demand for tobacco products is price inelastic, a generally accepted rule of thumb is that a 10 percent increase in taxes (and thus prices) translates roughly into a 5 percent reduction in consumption.

The price deterrent works mainly on entry-level smokers, many of whom are teenagers. Demand for cigarettes among teens is *price elastic*. According to the 1991 federal budget, a 10 percent price increase will reduce cigarette consumption among young Canadians by as much as 14 percent. In addition, Canadian studies indicate that relatively few people start smoking after age 20. Thus, heavy taxes on cigarettes and other tobacco products could have a positive impact on the health of Canadians— thanks, in part, to the elasticity of demand.

Applications

1. Suppose Saskatchewan farmers have suffered a severe drought this season, drastically reducing their wheat yields. What effect might this have on the total amount they earn from their crop? Why?

2. Suppose the federal government decides to impose a 20 percent tax on automobile sales in a campaign to reduce pollution from vehicle exhausts. What effect might this tax have on the demand for automobiles? Explain why.

3. Via Rail, the crown corporation that operates passenger rail service in Canada, has set an objective to maximize revenue. A study by Transport Canada indicated that the company could increase revenues substantially by raising fares in the Windsor-Quebec City corridor by at least 20 percent. Via Rail disagreed, arguing that price increases above the rate of inflation would have a very negative effect on the market in the short term. Who do you think is right? Support your point of view with reference to the elasticity of demand.

□ □ □ □ □ □

Elasticity of Demand—A Summary

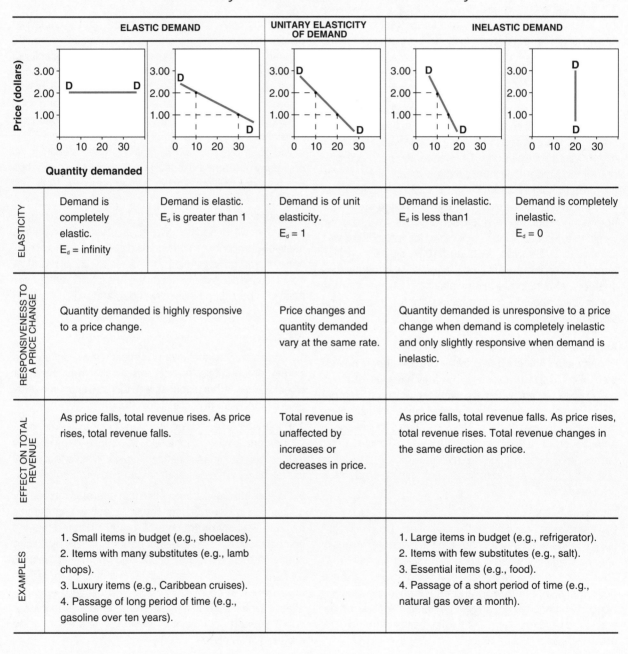

	ELASTIC DEMAND		UNITARY ELASTICITY OF DEMAND	INELASTIC DEMAND	
ELASTICITY	Demand is completely elastic. E_d = infinity	Demand is elastic. E_d is greater than 1	Demand is of unit elasticity. $E_d = 1$	Demand is inelastic. E_d is less than 1	Demand is completely inelastic. $E_d = 0$
RESPONSIVENESS TO A PRICE CHANGE	Quantity demanded is highly responsive to a price change.		Price changes and quantity demanded vary at the same rate.	Quantity demanded is unresponsive to a price change when demand is completely inelastic and only slightly responsive when demand is inelastic.	
EFFECT ON TOTAL REVENUE	As price falls, total revenue rises. As price rises, total revenue falls.		Total revenue is unaffected by increases or decreases in price.	As price falls, total revenue falls. As price rises, total revenue rises. Total revenue changes in the same direction as price.	
EXAMPLES	1. Small items in budget (e.g., shoelaces). 2. Items with many substitutes (e.g., lamb chops). 3. Luxury items (e.g., Caribbean cruises). 4. Passage of long period of time (e.g., gasoline over ten years).			1. Large items in budget (e.g., refrigerator). 2. Items with few substitutes (e.g., salt). 3. Essential items (e.g., food). 4. Passage of a short period of time (e.g., natural gas over a month).	

☐ Effects of the Elasticity of Demand

Price changes on goods and services we buy will have two effects—one on our incomes and one on any substitute goods we may buy.

Income Effect

Suppose we regularly buy compact discs. A reduction in the price of the discs will increase what our incomes can buy—in other words, our *real* incomes are increased. We can buy more discs than before with the same income. Conversely, an increase in the price of compact discs will diminish our real incomes. We can buy less with the same income. The **income effect** is the increase in quantity demanded based on an increase in real incomes. The income effect of a price change will depend on *how much the price is changed* and *what proportion of total expenditure* is made on the goods.

Substitution Effect

The **substitution effect** is the change in the quantity of a good demanded because of a change in price, when the real income effect is eliminated. A reduction in the price of compact discs means that we are likely to buy more compact discs rather than tapes. In other words, we *substitute* compact discs for tapes. With an increase in the price of compact discs, however, we are likely to substitute tapes for compact discs.

The income and substitution effects help to explain the inverse relationship between price and quantity demanded. As prices rise, the income and substitution effects reduce the quantity demanded. As prices fall, these two effects increase the quantity demanded.

■ Utility and Demand

Utility is the pleasure, satisfaction, or usefulness derived from the consumption of a good or service. Utility can't be measured. It is an analytical concept used by economists to describe how consumers divide their limited resources among the goods and services they buy.

How does utility relate to demand? Suppose on a hot day you decide to have a milk shake. You haven't had one in a long time and you enjoy it so much, you decide to have another. How does the utility derived from this second shake compare with that derived from the first? Most likely, the enjoyment is reduced. Suppose you buy a third, fourth, and fifth milk shake. By the time you have a sixth milk shake, you are probably experiencing negative utility or disutility. As we consume more, total utility may increase, but the utility derived from each additional good consumed decreases.

This example illustrates the law of diminishing marginal utility. The **law of diminishing marginal utility** states that each additional unit consumed in any given time yields less utility or satisfaction than the one previously consumed, all other things being equal. Table 3.5 and Figures 3.8 and 3.9 illustrate this law.

Table 3.5 Diminishing marginal utility

1 QUANTITY OF MILK SHAKES CONSUMED	2 TOTAL UTILITY	3 MARGINAL UTILITY
0	0	
1	4	4
2	7	3
3	9	2
4	10	1
5	10	0
6	9	-1

As the number of milk shakes consumed increases, total utility increases until it reaches 10 with the fourth and fifth milk shake. With the consumption of the sixth milk shake, total utility declines to 9. Marginal utility diminishes with each additional milk shake until it reaches -1.

The law of diminishing marginal utility helps explain why the demand curve slopes downward to the right. Since the marginal utility of a good declines as more is consumed, an individual would clearly only be willing to pay less for additional units of a good.

Figure 3.8 Total utility

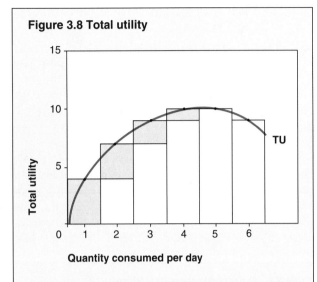

The curve TU illustrates that total utility increases with each additional milk shake up to a maximum of 10, and then declines. Marginal utility, indicated by the shaded areas, clearly declines with each additional milk shake.

Figure 3.9 Marginal utility

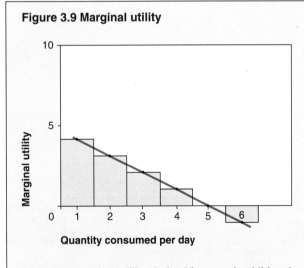

When the marginal utility derived from each additional milk shake is graphed, the curve slopes down to the right. By the sixth shake, it indicates negative utility. The curve illustrates the law of diminishing marginal utility.

◻ Consumer Decisions

A fundamental assumption made by economists is that consumers will try to maximize their total utility. They will distribute their incomes among various goods and services so that the marginal utility derived from each dollar spent is equal. If the last dollar of my income yields three times more utility when I spend it on steak rather than hamburger, I can increase my total utility by buying steak. Increasing my expenditure on steak will lower the marginal utility of the last dollar I spend on steak because of the law of diminishing marginal utility. Similarly, as I decrease my expenditure on hamburger, I increase the marginal utility of my last dollar spent on hamburger.

Eventually, as I go on decreasing my expenditures on hamburger and increasing them on steak, the marginal utilities will have changed so much that both will be equal. At this point, there is no additional utility to be gained in switching from hamburger to steak. If I continued increasing expenditure on steak and decreasing it on hamburger, my marginal utility from the last dollar spent on steak would be less than that from the last dollar spent on hamburger. My total utility would, therefore, be lower.

The **utility maximizing rule** states that total income is spent in such a way that the marginal utility from a dollar spent on one good (e.g., steak) is equal to the marginal utility on every dollar spent on every other good.

◻ Consumer Surplus

The **consumer surplus** is the difference between what an individual is willing to pay for each unit of a good or service and what the individual actually pays (i.e., the market price). Suppose that you bought a small pizza today for $4.00, but since you really like pizza, you would be willing to pay much more for it—perhaps as much as $7.00. The $3.00 you "gain" is the consumer surplus.

Consumer surplus is a result of diminishing marginal utility. For one glass of orange juice, I would be willing to pay $2.00; for the second, $1.50; the third, $1.00; and so on, as shown in Table 3.6. As I consume more

Table 3.6 Consumer surplus on orange juice consumption, one consumer

1 GLASSES OF ORANGE JUICE CONSUMED EACH DAY	2 AMOUNT CONSUMER WOULD PAY TO GET THIS GLASS OF JUICE	3 CONSUMER SURPLUS WHEN MARKET PRICE IS 50 CENTS A GLASS
First	$2.00	$1.50
Second	1.50	1.00
Third	1.00	.50
Fourth	0.50	.00
Fifth	0.25	—
Sixth	0.10	—
Seventh	0.00	—

As the individual consumes successive glasses of orange juice, the amount she would pay for each glass diminishes—thus reflecting the law of diminishing utility. The consumer will continue to buy the orange juice until the amount she would pay to get this glass of juice equals the market price, in this case, at the fourth glass.

Figure 3.10 Consumer surplus of orange juice, per person

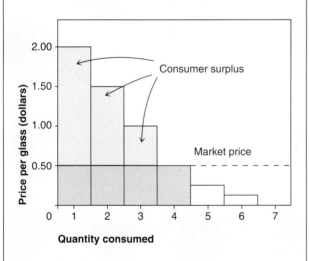

The consumer actually pays the blue shaded area for the four glasses she consumes. The total value of the four glasses to the consumer is the entire shaded area. The consumer surplus is, therefore, the grey shaded area.

and more orange juice, the value I put on each successive glass diminishes.

However, I do not pay a varying price for the orange juice I drink each day. I pay the market price, in this case 50 cents per glass. I would consume four glasses because with that number, the amount I am willing to pay equals the market price. I would not consume a fifth glass because the market price is higher than the amount I am willing to pay. Each glass of orange juice I buy before the fourth glass yields me a surplus. I can gain a maximum surplus of $3.00. Figure 3.10 shows the diminishing consumer surplus graphically. Clearly, as consumer surplus declines, demand declines.

▮ The Nature of Supply

From an examination of demand, we turn to an investigation of supply. Demand focusses on the consumers' or buyers' side of the market; supply focusses on the producers' or sellers' side. The two sides behave in very different ways.

Supply refers to the various amounts of a good or service producers are willing and able to produce and sell at various prices over a particular period of time. Again, since supply refers to a series of quantities and prices, it is expressed in a **supply schedule**, as shown in Table 3.7. As the price of orange juice increases, the quantity supplied also increases. Figure 3.11 is a graph of the schedule, showing the **supply curve**. Notice that it slopes *up to the right*. Consider how it compares with the demand curve we examined earlier.

▢ The Law of Supply

Why does the supply curve slope up to the right, while the demand curve slopes down to the right? Buyers and sellers view prices in different ways. Low prices, for example, encourage buyers to switch from buying other products to buying the low-priced goods. On the other hand, suppliers are discouraged by low prices. They will often move into producing higher priced goods to ensure higher returns.

The opposite occurs with high prices. Buyers tend to switch to lower-priced goods, while sellers tend to

□ □ □ □ □ □

The Paradox of Value

It was seemingly absurd to Adam Smith that water, which is so very useful to us, commands a very low price, while diamonds, which are so unnecessary, command such a high price. This puzzle or seeming contradiction is known as the **paradox of value**.

The answer to the puzzle is in two parts. First, diamonds are so expensive because they are scarce and very difficult to obtain. Water, in most parts of the world, is relatively easy to obtain and abundant. Second, it is not the utility of water as a whole (the total utility) that determines its price, but rather the utility of the marginal or last glass. As we have seen, the utility of the last glass is very, very low.

Application
1. Explain why caviar is very expensive, while bread is inexpensive, referring to the paradox of value.

Table 3.7 Supply schedule for orange juice over one day

1 PRICE PER GLASS (IN CENTS)	2 QUANTITY SUPPLIED PER DAY	3 POSITION ON FIGURE 3.11
100	32	U
90	29	V
80	26	W
70	23	X
60	17	Y
50	10	Z

As the price rises from 50 to 60 cents per glass of orange juice, the quantity supplied increases from 10 to 17 glasses. With each price increase, the quantity supplied also increases.

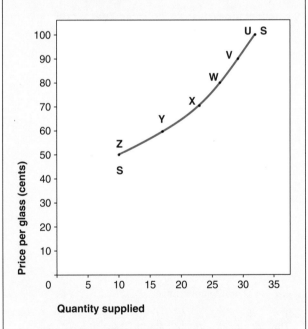

Figure 3.11 Supply curve for orange juice over one day

The supply curve slopes up to the right, illustrating the direct relationship between price and quantity supplied. As price increases, quantity supplied increases and *vice versa.*

produce more of the high-priced good to take advantage of the potential high returns. Thus, while there is an *indirect* or *inverse* relationship between price and quantity demanded (as price rises, quantity demanded falls), there is a *direct* relationship between price and quantity supplied (as price rises, quantity supplied rises). Price and quantity move in the same direction. This relationship is known as the law of supply.

The **law of supply** states that for many goods, the higher their prices, the greater the quantity supplied. Conversely, the lower their prices, the lower the quantity supplied, assuming no other changes.

□ Changes in Supply

As with demand, factors other than price may cause changes in supply. The effect of a change in supply is to shift the entire supply curve. An increase in supply shifts the curve to the right; while a decrease in supply shifts the curve to the left.

Table 3.8 Changes in the daily supply schedule for orange juice (in glasses)

1 PRICE PER GLASS (IN CENTS)	2 ORIGINAL QUANTITY SUPPLIED	3 INCREASE IN SUPPLY	4 DECREASE IN SUPPLY
100	32	37	27
90	29	34	24
80	26	31	21
70	23	28	18
60	17	22	12
50	10	15	5

The first two columns in this table display the same data as in Table 3.7. The final two columns are added to show the effects of an increase and decrease in quantity supplied.

Let's return to our orange juice example outlined earlier. Table 3.8 shows the same prices and quantities outlined in Table 3.7, but adds data showing an increase and a decrease in quantity supplied at each price level. Figure 3.12 shows the effects of an increase in supply on the supply curve—it shifts to the right. Figure 3.13 illustrates the opposite effect. A decrease in the quantity supplied at each price level shifts the entire supply curve to the left.

The principal non-price determinants of shifts in supply are changes in the prices of productive resources, changes in technology, significant shifts in weather conditions (especially for agricultural products), taxes and subsidies, and the prices of related goods and services.

Price of Productive Resources

Changes in the price of one or more productive resources—human, natural, or capital—will shift the supply curve. With a decrease in the price of productive resources, such as cheaper machines, producers will be able and willing to supply larger quantities of goods at each possible price. Supply increases and the supply curve shifts to the right.

With an increase in the price of productive resources, such as an increase in workers' wages, producers will offer less at each possible price. Supply decreases and the supply curve shifts to the left.

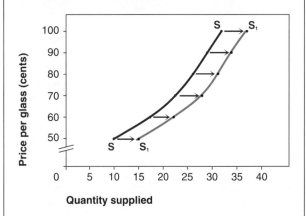

Figure 3.12 An increase in the daily supply of orange juice

With an increase in supply, the entire supply curve shifts to the right from SS (the original curve) to S₁S₁. As price increases, the quantity of orange juice supplied also increases at each price level. Note the two lines // along the *y* axis, which indicate that part of the graph has been omitted.

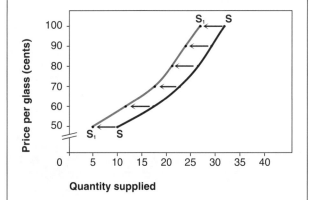

Figure 3.13 A decrease in the daily supply of orange juice

With a decrease in supply, the entire supply curve shifts to the left from SS to S₁S₁. As price falls, the quantity of orange juice supplied at each price level also falls.

□ □ □ □ □ □

Changes in Quantity Demanded or Supplied
vs.
Shifts in Demand or Supply

It is important to recognize a distinction between a change in quantity demanded or quantity supplied, and a shift in demand or supply. A change in quantity demanded or supplied is shown by a movement along a curve, while a shift in demand or supply is represented by a shift of the entire demand or supply curve. What does this mean? Let's consider some examples.

Changes in Quantity Demanded and Movements Along a Curve

As we know, demand expresses a relationship between quantity and price. Changes in quantity demanded are the result of changes in price. As illustrated in Figure 3.14, as the price of a good decreases from A to C, the quantity demanded increases. As price increases from A to B, the quantity demanded decreases. Thus, a change in quantity demanded is shown by a movement *along* the demand curve.

Changes in Demand and Shifts in the Demand Curve

A change in demand occurs when there is a shift or change in the entire demand curve or demand schedule. Shifts in demand may be caused by changes in any of the factors we outlined earlier—including the size of the market, average incomes, prices of related goods, and consumer tastes and expectations.

Suppose an increase in incomes causes an increase in demand for a good. As Figure 3.15 shows, the entire demand curve thus shifts from DD to D_1D_1. Initially, with a price of $10 per unit, 200 units were demanded. With the increase in demand, 300 units are demanded at the price of $10. A decrease in incomes and thus a decrease in demand would shift the entire demand curve to the left to D_2D_2. At the price of $10 per unit, demand thus declines from 200 units to 100 units. A change in demand is, therefore, shown by a shift in the entire demand curve.

Figure 3.14 A change in quantity demanded

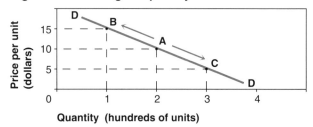

A change in quantity demanded occurs because of a change in price and is shown as a movement along the demand curve. With the demand curve DD and a price of $10 per unit, 200 units are demanded at A. If the price falls to $5 per unit, quantity demanded shifts down along the demand curve to 300 units at C. If price increases to $15 per unit, quantity demanded shifts up along the demand curve to 100 units at B.

Figure 3.15 A change or shift in demand

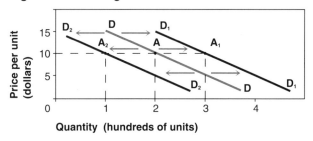

A change in demand occurs because of a change in one or more of the non-price determinants, such as average incomes, and is shown as a shift in the entire demand curve. With the demand curve DD and a price of $10 per unit, 200 units are demanded. If average incomes increase, demand increases and the entire demand curve shifts to the right to D_1D_1. Then, at a price of $10 per unit at A_1, 300 units are demanded. If incomes decreases, the entire demand curve shifts to the left to D_2D_2. At the same price of $10 per unit ($A_2$ on the D_2D_2 curve), 100 units are demanded.

Figure 3.16 A change in quantity supplied

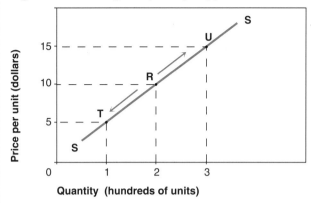

Quantity (hundreds of units)

A change in quantity supplied occurs because of a change in price and is shown as a movement along the supply curve. With the supply curve SS and a price of $10 per unit, 200 units are supplied at R. If the price falls to $5 per unit, quantity supplied shifts down along the supply curve to 100 units at T. If price increases to $15 per unit, quantity supplied shifts up along the supply curve to 300 units at U.

Figure 3.17 A change or shift in supply

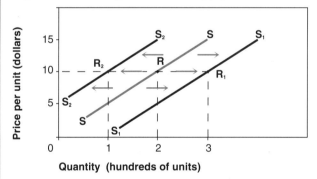

Quantity (hundreds of units)

A shift in supply is caused by a change in one or more of the non-price determinants, such as technology, and is shown as a shift in the entire supply curve to the right or left. With the supply curve SS and a price of $10 per unit, 200 units are supplied at R. If technology advances, supply increases and the supply curve shifts to the right to S_1S_1. At the same price of $10, 300 units are supplied at R_1. If the technology breaks down, supply decreases and the supply curve shifts to the left to S_2S_2. At $10 per unit, only 100 units are supplied at R_2 on the S_2S_2 curve.

Changes in Quantity Supplied and Movements Along the Supply Curve

Changes in quantity supplied are the result of changes in price. As Figure 3.16 shows, as the price of a good supplied decreases from $10 to $5 a unit, the quantity supplied decreases from 200 to 100 units. As the price increases from $10 to $15 a unit, the quantity supplied increases from 200 to 300 units. Thus changes in the quantity supplied involve movements along the supply curve as prices change.

Changes in Supply and Shifts in the Supply Curve

A change or shift in supply occurs when there is a shift in the entire supply curve or supply schedule. A shift in supply can be caused by changes in any of the non-price determinants—including the price of productive resources, technology, weather conditions, taxes and subsidies.

An improvement in agricultural technology, for example, could shift the supply curve from SS to S_1S_1, as shown in Figure 3.17. Thus, before the new technology, 200 units of the good are produced at a price of $10. After the new technology is instituted, 300 units of the good are supplied at $10 per unit. The supply curve shifts to the right. If there is a drought, supply would decrease and the entire supply curve would shift to the left to S_2S_2. At a price of $10 per unit, therefore, only 100 rather than 200 units would be supplied. A change in supply is, therefore, shown by a shift in the entire supply curve.

Applications

1. Suppose the price of a litre of gasoline rises. Construct a graph to illustrate the effect on the quantity of gasoline demanded, showing both the initial situation and the effect of the price change.

2. Construct a graph to illustrate the effect that an increase in the price of apple juice would have on the demand for orange juice.

3. The government announces an increase in the tax on gasoline. Graph the effects of this increase on the supply of gasoline.

4. The price of apple juice has increased substantially due to a blight that has destroyed farmers' crops. Graph the effect of this price change on the supply of apple juice, showing both the situation before the blight and after.

Changes in Technology

Suppose a new fertilizer is developed that increases the yield from every orange tree by a substantial amount and lowers the cost of producing oranges. Orange producers are then able to produce more oranges and provide them at lower prices. Supply increases and the supply curve shifts to the right.

Significant changes in technology include improvements in machinery used in production, new production techniques, new means of transportation, and new ways of combining productive resources, all of which lower the costs of production.

Weather

Weather conditions have an important impact on the production of agricultural goods. A drought, for example, can drastically reduce wheat production (a shift in the supply curve to the left), while excellent growing weather could produce a bumper crop (a shift in the supply curve to the right).

Taxes and Subsidies

Both subsidies and taxes can affect quantities supplied. Subsidies (payments made for the production of a good or service) can lower the prices of goods and services and thus shift the supply curve to the right. Taxes, on the other hand, tend to raise the cost of producing a good or service and thus shift the supply curve to the left.

Prices of Related Goods and Services

A change in the price of one good is likely to shift the supply curve of a second good, when the second good can be produced as an alternative to the first—that is, when both goods use the same factors of production. For example, an increase in the price of wheat may prompt farmers to produce more wheat and less oats. Thus, an increase in the price of wheat can cause a decrease in the supply of oats. Conversely, a decrease in the price of wheat can bring about a shift to the right in the supply of oats. Wheat and oats are substitutes in production, that is, they use the same productive resources.

◼ Price Elasticity of Supply

As we have seen, elasticity of demand describes the responsiveness of *buyers* to changes in price. **Elasticity of supply** describes the responsiveness of *producers* to changes in price. Supply is elastic if suppliers respond strongly to small changes in price by increasing their supply, and inelastic if they respond weakly to significant changes in price.

◻ Factors Affecting the Elasticity of Supply

Factors other than price may also affect the elasticity of supply. The most important factors are time, the possibility and cost of change, and the ease of shifting production.

Time

The most important determinant is the amount of time producers have to respond to price changes in the goods they produce. Generally, the more time available, the easier it is for producers to adjust to price changes. The process of switching resources out of the production of a good whose price has fallen and into the production of a higher-priced good generally takes a considerable period. The more time that is available, the greater the response and the greater the elasticity of supply.

Economists identify three basic response periods.

(i) Immediate supply period   This time period is so short that producers cannot generally change their output and, therefore, cannot react to changes in price or demand for their product. For example, suppose an apple farmer brings her entire crop to market. She must sell the entire crop no matter what the price. She cannot offer more than the entire crop, even if demand is high and the price rises. It will be next year before she will have more apples to sell. Similarly, she cannot afford to sell less than the entire crop because the apples are perishable and any not sold are a total loss.

In the immediate supply period then, supply is fixed or inelastic. Producers cannot vary their output to react to changes in price or demand.

□ □ □ □ □ □

Skill Development: The Calculation of Elasticity

Earlier in this chapter, we outlined the total revenue method of calculating the elasticity of demand. In this section, we'll examine another method that can be used to determine the elasticity of both demand and supply for various products.

A. The Elasticity of Demand

$$\text{Elasticity of Demand} (E_d) = \frac{\%\ \text{change}\ (\Delta)\ \text{in quantity demanded}\ (Q_D)}{\%\ \text{change}\ (\Delta)\ \text{in price}\ (P_D)}$$

$$E_d = \frac{\Delta Q_D}{\Delta P_D}$$

If elasticity is greater than 1, then demand is elastic.
If elasticity is less than 1, then demand is inelastic.
If elasticity is equal to 1, then demand has unit elasticity.

Let's work through an example.

Table 3.9 Demand schedule and elasticity for tea

1 PRICE (IN CENTS PER CUP)	2 QUANTITY DEMANDED (IN CUPS PER DAY)	3 PRICE ELASTICITY OF DEMAND
50	1	
		3.04
40	2	
		1.38
30	3	
		0.73
20	4	
		0.33
10	5	

Suppose the price of tea falls from 50 to 40 cents a cup, and the quantity demanded increases from 1 to 2 cups per day.

Step 1

To calculate the percentage change in the quantity demanded, divide the change in quantity demanded by the *average* of the old and new quantities and multiply by 100.

$$\frac{\Delta Q_D}{\frac{Q_1 + Q_2}{2}} \times 100 = \frac{1}{\frac{1 + 2}{2}} \times 100 = 67\%$$

Δ is the Greek letter delta. (Think of the triangular Δ shape of the delta of a river.) It means "change in" and is calculated as $Q_2 - Q_1$.

Step 2

To calculate the percentage change in price, we use a similar formula.

$$\frac{\Delta P}{\frac{P_1 + P_2}{2}} \times 100 = \frac{-10}{\frac{50 + 40}{2}} \times 100 = -22\%$$

Note that the value of ΔP is negative since the price decreased from 50 to 40 cents a cup. However, we ignore the negative sign.

Step 3

To calculate the elasticity of demand over the range in price from 40 to 50 cents, divide the percentage change in quantity demanded by the percentage change in price.

$$E_d = \frac{\Delta Q_D}{\Delta P_D}\ \frac{67}{-22} = 3.04$$

Since the price elasticity is greater than 1, the demand for tea over the range of 40 to 50 cents is elastic.

We could go through similar calculations to determine the elasticity of demand over each price range outlined in Table 3.9. As the price of tea decreases, the elasticity of demand also decreases. At 20 cents a cup, demand becomes inelastic. Figure 3.18 shows the demand and elasticity of tea graphically.

Figure 3.18 Demand curve and elasticity for tea

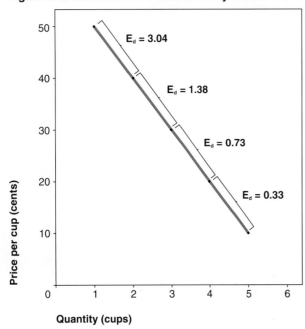

Quantity (cups)

Even though the demand curve has the same slope throughout its length, the elasticity of demand declines as we move down along the demand curve.

B. The Elasticity of Supply

The calculation for the elasticity of supply is similar to that for the elasticity of demand.

$$\text{Elasticity of Supply } (E_s) = \frac{\% \text{ change } (\Delta) \text{ in quantity supplied } (Q_s)}{\% \text{ change } (\Delta) \text{ in price } (P_s)}$$

$$E_s = \frac{\Delta Q_s}{\Delta P_s}$$

If elasticity is greater than 1, supply is elastic.
If elasticity is less than 1, supply is inelastic.
If elasticity is equal to 1, then supply has unit elasticity.

Suppose the price of tea increases from 20 to 30 cents a cup, and the quantity supplied increases from 5 to 10 cups per day.

Table 3.10 Daily supply schedule and elasticity for tea

1 PRICE (IN CENTS PER CUP)	2 QUANTITY SUPPLIED (IN CUPS PER DAY)	3 PRICE ELASTICITY OF SUPPLY
70	40	
60	35	
50	25	
40	15	
30	10	
		1.67
20	5	

Step 1

Calculate the percentage change in the quantity supplied as follows.

$$\frac{\Delta Q}{\frac{Q_1 + Q_2}{2}} \times 100 = \frac{5}{\frac{5 + 10}{2}} \times 100 = 66.7\%$$

Step 2

Calculate the percentage change in price as follows.

$$\frac{\Delta P}{\frac{P_1 + P_2}{2}} = \frac{10}{\frac{20 + 30}{2}} = 40\%$$

Step 3

Calculate the elasticity of supply over the price range of 20 to 30 cents as follows.

$$E_s = \frac{66.7}{40} = 1.67$$

Since the elasticity of supply is greater than 1, the supply of tea over the range of 20 to 30 cents per cup is elastic.

Again, we could use the same formula to calculate the elasticity for tea over each price range outlined in Table 3.10.

Table 3.11 Some actual price elasticities of demand

VERY LOW ELASTICITY (less than 0.5)	LOW ELASTICITY (0.5 to 0.8)	ELASTICITY ABOUT 1.0	HIGH ELASTICITY (1.2 to 1.9)	VERY HIGH ELASTICITY (over 2.0)
Salt	Cigarettes	Beef	Restaurant meals	Foreign travel
Coffee	Alcoholic beverages	Housing	Electricity	Movies
Telephone service	Shoe repairs	China and tableware	Books and maps	Airline travel
Gasoline (in the short run)				
All food (taken as a single good)				

SOURCE: Adapted from Ake Blomqvist *et al*, *Economics*, 3rd ed. (Toronto: McGraw-Hill Ryerson, 1990) and Michael Parkin and Robin Bade, *Economics: Canada in the Global Environment* (Don Mills: Addison Wesley, 1991).

Applications

1. (a) Complete Table 3.10 by calculating the elasticity of supply for tea over each price range from 30 to 70 cents per cup.
(b) Graph the supply curve and indicate the various elasticities over the price ranges on the curve. Note at what points tea is elastic, inelastic, or of unitary elasticity.

2. (a) Select six products listed in Table 3.11 and explain the elasticity of demand for each.
(b) Gasoline in the short run has a very low elasticity. How would its elasticity be likely to vary over the long run? Explain.

(ii) The short-run period In the short run, even though plant (buildings, machinery, etc.) and equipment are fixed, producers can vary output to some extent. They can use their existing plant and equipment more intensively. For example, they can employ more workers or have their workers stay longer hours. The apple farmer's land and equipment are fixed in the immediate supply period, but she can increase her output of apples in the short run by applying more fertilizer or hiring additional workers, for example.

Over the short-term, therefore, supply is more responsive to price changes and thus more elastic than in the immediate period.

(iii) Long-run period Over the long run, firms can make almost all necessary changes. They can enlarge their existing plant and/or buy new equipment. They can also leave the industry and move into producing some other good or provide another service. The apple farmer, for example, can expand or reduce the area she has producing apples, and she can buy or sell new machinery. She may also decide to shift production to some other crop or leave farming altogether. The supply of apples in the long run, therefore, is much more elastic than in the short run.

Figure 3.19 illustrates the effects of these time periods on the supply curve.

Perishability and Cost of Storage

Goods, such as cut flowers and fresh fish, that are expensive to store and spoil quickly must be sold at any price. Supply of these items is, therefore, inelastic. Supply of items that can be more easily and cheaply stored, such as bricks and concrete blocks, are more elastic. They can be withheld from the market until prices are better.

□ □ □ □ □ □

Elasticity of Supply—A Summary

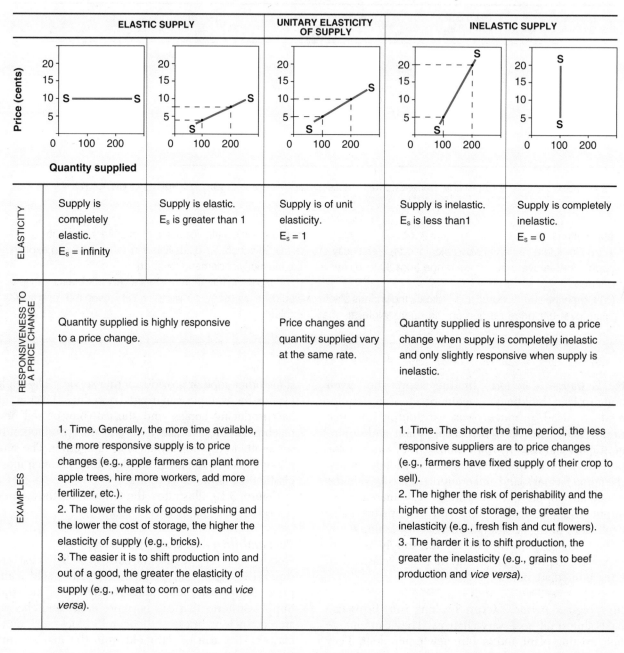

	ELASTIC SUPPLY		UNITARY ELASTICITY OF SUPPLY	INELASTIC SUPPLY	
ELASTICITY	Supply is completely elastic. E_s = infinity	Supply is elastic. E_s is greater than 1	Supply is of unit elasticity. $E_s = 1$	Supply is inelastic. E_s is less than 1	Supply is completely inelastic. $E_s = 0$
RESPONSIVENESS TO A PRICE CHANGE	Quantity supplied is highly responsive to a price change.		Price changes and quantity supplied vary at the same rate.	Quantity supplied is unresponsive to a price change when supply is completely inelastic and only slightly responsive when supply is inelastic.	
EXAMPLES	1. Time. Generally, the more time available, the more responsive supply is to price changes (e.g., apple farmers can plant more apple trees, hire more workers, add more fertilizer, etc.). 2. The lower the risk of goods perishing and the lower the cost of storage, the higher the elasticity of supply (e.g., bricks). 3. The easier it is to shift production into and out of a good, the greater the elasticity of supply (e.g., wheat to corn or oats and *vice versa*).			1. Time. The shorter the time period, the less responsive suppliers are to price changes (e.g., farmers have fixed supply of their crop to sell). 2. The higher the risk of perishability and the higher the cost of storage, the greater the inelasticity (e.g., fresh fish and cut flowers). 3. The harder it is to shift production, the greater the inelasticity (e.g., grains to beef production and *vice versa*).	

Ease of Shifting Production

Can productive resources be easily switched from producing one good to another? If so, the supply of these goods is likely to be elastic. For example, if the price of corn increases, producers of other grains, such as wheat and oats, can switch fairly quickly into corn production. Similarly, if the price of corn falls, farmers can switch from producing corn to wheat or oats fairly easily. The supply curve for wheat is, therefore, relatively elastic.

However, if the price of all grains falls, there are few, if any, substitute activities into which grain farmers can profitably move. The supply of grains is, therefore, more inelastic than the supply of a single grain, such as corn. Other possible activities grain farmers might consider, such as beef, chicken, or dairy farming, would require extensive expenditures and considerable time.

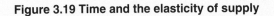

Figure 3.19 Time and the elasticity of supply

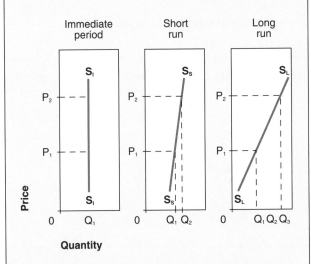

The longer suppliers have, the better they are able to adjust to changes in price. In the immediate period, supply is inelastic. There is no time to adjust to price changes, so price has no effect on supply. In the short run, though plant and equipment are fixed, production can be varied by more intensive use of the existing plant and equipment. Supply is, therefore, more elastic. In the long run, almost any desired changes can be made. Supply is, therefore, even more elastic.

Summary

a. The real (goods and services) and money flows between households and businesses through products markets can be illustrated by a simple circular flow model of the economy. Households (consumers) represent the demand side of the economy, and businesses the supply side.

b. Demand refers to the quantities of a good or service consumers are willing and able to buy at various prices over a period of time. It is represented by a demand schedule and illustrated by a demand curve.

c. The law of demand states that there is an inverse relationship between price and quantity demanded. As the price of a good falls, the quantity demanded increases. As the price of a good rises, the quantity demanded decreases. The typical demand curve, therefore, slopes down to the right.

d. The factors that may cause a shift in demand for a product are the size of the market, the real purchasing value of consumer incomes, the price and availability of related goods, and the tastes and expectations of consumers.

e. Elasticity of demand refers to the responsiveness of the quantity demanded to changes in price. Demand for a good is elastic if a change in price has a significant effect on quantity demanded and a price decrease increases total revenue; inelastic if a change in price has little effect on quantity demanded and a price decrease decreases total revenue; and of unitary elasticity if a change in price has no effect on total revenue.

   Factors affecting the elasticity of demand are the amount of consumers' budgets spent on the product, whether the good is a luxury or necessity, whether the good has close substitutes, and the period of time under consideration.

f. The law of diminishing marginal utility states that the satisfaction or utility gained from the consumption of a good decreases with each additional good consumed. As marginal utility decreases, demand decreases also since consumers generally try to maximize their utility.

Consumer surplus is the difference between what a consumer is willing to pay for a good or service and what he or she actually pays. As consumer surplus declines, demand declines.

g. Supply refers to the various amounts of a good or service producers are willing and able to produce or sell at various prices over a period of time. It is expressed in a supply schedule and illustrated by a supply curve.

h. The law of supply states that there is a direct relationship between price and quantity supplied. As prices rise, quantity supplied also rises. As prices fall, quantity supplied falls. The typical supply curve, therefore, slopes up to the right.

i. Factors that may cause a shift in supply include the price of productive resources, changes in technology, weather conditions (for agricultural products in particular), taxes and subsidies, and prices of related goods and services.

j. Elasticity of supply describes the responsiveness of producers to changes in price. Supply is elastic if a change in price has a signficant effect on quantity supplied and inelastic if a change in price has little effect on quantity supplied.

Factors affecting elasticity of supply include time, perishability and the cost of storage, and the ease of shifting production.

k. A change in demand or supply is caused by any one or more of the non-price determinants and is illustrated by a shift in the entire demand or supply curve to the right or left. A change in quantity demanded or supplied is caused by a change in price and is shown as a movement along the demand or supply curve.

Review of Key Terms

Define the following key terms introduced in this chapter and provide examples where appropriate.

microeconomics
macroeconomics
household
business
real flow
money flow
circular flow model
demand
demand schedule
demand curve
law of demand
superior goods
inferior goods
substitute goods
complementary goods

price elasticity of demand
income effect
substitution effect
utility
law of diminishing marginal utility
paradox of value
consumer surplus
utility maximizing rule
supply
supply schedule
supply curve
law of supply
price elasticity of supply

Application and Analysis

Table 3.12 A daily demand schedule for hamburgers

1 PRICE (IN DOLLARS)	2 QUANTITY DEMANDED
2.00	20
1.80	40
1.60	70
1.40	100
1.20	120
1.00	130

1. (a) Graph the demand curve for hamburgers based on the data in Table 3.12 above and label it DD.

(b) Provide the graph with a title, and label the axes and origin.

2. Devise your own hypothetical demand schedule for a good or service you buy. Plot the demand curve (DD) on a graph and label the graph fully.

3. What effect will each of the following have on the demand for audiotapes? Indicate whether the quantity demanded will increase or decrease, and whether the demand curve will shift to the right or left.

(a) The price of compact discs drops by 10 percent.

(b) Average incomes of teenagers increase by 15 percent.

(c) The price of tape recorders drops by 10 percent.

(d) The teenage population drops by 15 percent.

(e) In six months, the price of tapes is expected to fall by 20 percent.

4. What is the relative price elasticity of demand for the following goods?

(a) clothing

(b) skirts

(c) silk shirts

(d) designer silk shirts

5. Read the following quotations. What (if anything) can you conclude about the price elasticity of demand in each case? Explain your answers.

(a) The freezing weather in Florida's citrus belt will reduce this year's previously predicted bumper crop. . . but, ironically, it will ease the worries of growers who feared they would lose money because of the surplus.

(b) Transit ridership always drops when transit fares increase, but overall revenue nevertheless rises.

(c) The 10 percent increase in postal rates led this municipal utilities commission to deliver its bills by hand.

(d) Without my morning coffee, I can't start my day. Coffee is an essential.

6. For which of the following goods and services is the demand likely to be inelastic? Explain why.

(a) made-to-measure skirts

(b) a Buick Skylark automobile

(c) a Canadian Airline ticket to Hawaii

(d) electricity

(e) bread

(f) designer jeans

(g) milk

(h) salt

(i) pork chops

(j) diesel oil

(k) an electric stove

Table 3.13 Daily demand for hamburgers

1 PRICE (IN DOLLARS)	2 QUANTITY DEMANDED (IN UNITS)	3 TOTAL REVENUE (IN DOLLARS)	4 ELASTICITY
2.00	20	40.00	—
1.80	40	72.00	Elastic
1.60	70		
1.40	100		
1.20	120		
1.00	130		

7. (a) Complete the total revenue and elasticity columns in Table 3.13 above.

(b) For the hypothetical demand schedule you devised in question 2, complete total revenue and elasticity columns.

8. Suppose you have become the business manager of a hockey team. The team owners show you the following graph (Figure 3.20 on page 70) and ask you to tell them at what ticket price they would maximize their revenue. They ask you briefly to explain how you reach your conclusion. The hockey arena has a total of 600 seats.

9. Suppose that after working for the hockey team for some time, you find that the demand curve has shifted to the right.

(a) What evidence would indicate that the demand curve has shifted? Explain.

(b) Draw a graph to show the shift in the demand curve.

(c) Explain the possible reasons for a shift to the left and to the right in the demand curve.

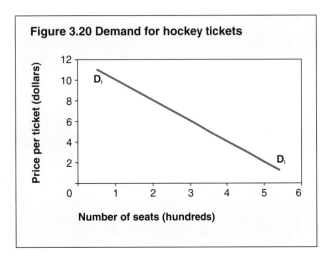

Figure 3.20 Demand for hockey tickets

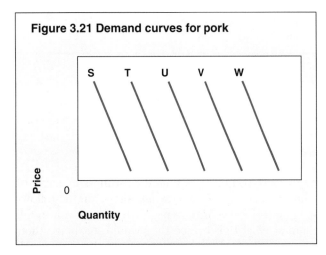

Figure 3.21 Demand curves for pork

10. Classify the following pairs of goods as complementary (C), substitute (S), or independent (I).

(a) beef, pork

(b) butter, margarine

(c) bread, butter

(d) gum, shoes

(e) telephones, taxis

(f) potatoes, strawberry jam

(g) pens, writing paper

11. (a) You are a producer of pork. Read the following newspaper headlines and decide in each case if the event described will cause a change in the demand for pork. If you think there will be a change, decide whether it will be an increase or decrease and identify the appropriate curve in Figure 3.21. Assume that curve U is the original demand curve.

Do not move more than one curve at a time, even if you think there will be a significant increase or decrease in demand. If you are at W and the next headline suggests an increase, you have made a mistake!

(i)   Price of pork to rise in June
(ii) Canadian government warns that eating pork can be hazardous to your health
(iii) Real incomes of Canadians rise for fourth month in a row
(iv) Canadians adopt a new fad: the chickenburger
(v)   With liberalized immigration policies, Canada's population rises dramatically
(vi) Beef prices drop
(vii) Water levels in the Great Lakes reach seasonal levels

(b) Listed below are a number of reasons for changes in demand. Match the changes listed to the appropriate headline above. Some changes may be matched to more than one headline and some headlines may have no match.

(i)   a change in average incomes
(ii) a change in the size of the market
(iii) a change in the price of substitutes
(iv) a change in expectations
(v)   a change in tastes

12. (a) Graph a supply curve for hamburgers based on the schedule in Table 3.14 and label it SS.

(b) Provide the graph with a title and label the axes and origin.

13. Develop a hypothetical supply schedule for a good or service you buy. Plot the corresponding supply curve on a graph.

Table 3.14 Daily supply schedule for hamburgers

1 PRICE (IN DOLLARS)	2 QUANTITY SUPPLIED (IN UNITS)
2.00	200
1.80	150
1.60	120
1.40	100
1.20	70
1.00	40

Table 3.15 Daily supply schedule for hamburgers

1 PRICE (IN DOLLARS)	2 QUANTITY SUPPLIED PERIOD 1	3 QUANTITY SUPPLIED PERIOD 2	4 QUANTITY SUPPLIED PERIOD 3
2.00	200	220	180
1.80	150	170	130
1.60	120	140	100
1.40	100	120	80
1.20	70	90	50
1.00	40	60	20

14. (a) Graph the three supply curves based on the supply schedule in Table 3.15 above and label the curves S_1S_1, S_2S_2, and S_3S_3.

(b) Suggest reasons why the supply curve S_1S_1 might shift:

(i) to S_2S_2, and
(ii) to S_3S_3.

15. What effect will each of the following have on the supply of hot dogs? Indicate whether the quantity supplied will increase or decrease, and whether the supply curve will shift to the right or left.

(a) The price of hot dogs increases by 20 percent.

(b) A new hot dog machine enables restaurant workers to produce hot dogs in half the time.

(c) A tax is levied on sales of hot dogs.

(d) Government decides to subsidize the sale of hot dogs.

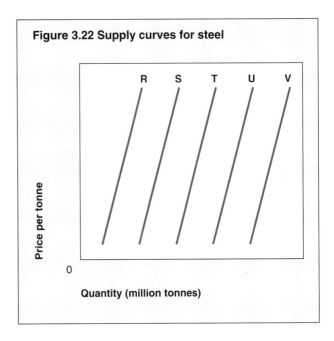

Figure 3.22 Supply curves for steel

16. (a) You are a steel producer. Read the following newspaper headlines and decide in each case if the event described will cause a change in the supply of steel. If you decide there will be a change, indicate whether it will be an increase or decrease and identify the appropriate curve in Figure 3.22. Assume curve T is the original supply curve.

Do not move more than one curve at a time, even if you think there will be a significant increase or decrease. If you are at V and the next headline suggests an increase, you have made a mistake!

(i) Steel workers and steel companies reach an agreement to increase wages by 10 percent
(ii) New steel furnaces increase efficiency of steel mills

(iii) Steel workers strike will begin at midnight tonight

(iv) Price of iron ore falls

(v) Canada's second largest steel producer goes bankrupt and closes down its operations

(vi) Buyers prefer steel fenders to those made of aluminium

(vii) Government introduces a subsidy for aluminium plants installing anti-pollution equipment

(b)   Listed below are a number of reasons for a change in supply. Match the changes listed to the headlines above. Some changes may be matched to more than one headline, and some headlines may have no match.

(i)   a change in technology

(ii) a change in the price of factors of production

(iii) a change in the weather

(iv) government taxes and subsidies

(v) a change in the production of related goods

17. Describe the shift in the demand or supply curve that would produce each of the following results—assuming that only one of the two curves has shifted.

(a)   The price of microcomputers has fallen over the last few years and the quantity bought has risen considerably.

(b)   Hotel prices in Acapulco, Mexico are much lower in July than in February.

(c)   Jeans are "in," so sales of preppie clothes have declined.

(d)   As the Canadian standard of living has increased over past decades, sales of high-priced European cars have increased.

(e)   The failure of Brazil's coffee crop is expected to raise the price of tea.

(f)   The development of the sugar beet as a major source of sugar has lowered land rents on islands producing sugar cane.

CHAPTER FOUR

Dynamics of the Market

Objectives

a. Define a perfectly competitive market.

b. Explain and assess the importance of prices in competitive markets.

c. Demonstrate how the market or equilibrium price and quantity are determined by the interaction of supply and demand using graphs and schedules.

d. Use graphs and schedules to show how shifts in demand and supply affect equilibrium price and quantity.

e. Demonstrate how the elasticity of demand affects equilibrium price and quantity.

f. Demonstrate how the elasticity of supply affects equilibrium price and quantity.

g. Analyze an economic event using a four-question framework.

h. Explain and assess the main ideas of Alfred Marshall, as they relate to supply, demand, market equilibrium, and value.

i. Assess the main advantages and disadvantages of the market system based on the analysis in this chapter.

j. Demonstrate how governments intervene in the market to control prices by instituting floor prices, ceiling prices, and quotas.

As we saw in Chapter 2, markets are central to the operation of our economy. It is through the workings of markets that the three major economic questions—what to produce, how to produce, and for whom to produce—are answered. A **market** is an institution or mechanism that brings together buyers and sellers for the purpose of making an exchange, and establishes the price of the goods or services to be exchanged.

It is important to remember that markets are not tied to any particular physical location and do not require direct contact between buyers and sellers. Exchanges can be made by telephone, fax, mail, or on the floor of the stock exchange. The "market" for a particular good may include buyers and sellers dispersed the world over. In this chapter, we bring together the forces of supply and demand we examined in the last chapter and consider how the decisions of buyers and sellers in competitive markets work to establish prices and co-ordinate economic activity automatically.

▮ Perfect Competitive Market

Some markets have only one seller, others have thousands. In Canada, for example, telephone services in any one town or city are supplied by only one company, as are electricity and natural gas. For many agricultural products, on the other hand, sellers may be numerous. Similarly, the number of buyers of certain kinds of products may be few (e.g., purchasers of steel rail lines) or many (e.g., buyers of food). When buyers or sellers are few, they can, individually, have a significant impact on price. When they are many, they can exercise little individual control over price. In this case, prices are determined by the forces of supply and demand.

A market with many buyers and sellers, and in which no individual buyer or seller is able to influence price, is known as a **perfectly competitive market**. Our focus in this chapter is on competitive markets.

▮ Importance of Prices

Prices are a key factor in competitive markets. They bring order to the seeming chaos of the market system by performing two important and related functions— they provide *information* and *incentives*. High prices, for example, indicate that a particular good is in short supply, and thus provide an incentive for suppliers to increase production and for buyers to withhold their purchases. Low prices, on the other hand, indicate that a particular good is in abundant supply, and provide incentives for suppliers to cut back production and for buyers to increase purchases.

Prices also have an important rationing function. They provide a means of comparing the value of various goods and services, and of allocating goods and services among those wishing to acquire them.

▮ Price Determination by Supply and Demand

How do supply and demand interact to determine prices? The first three columns in Table 4.1 bring together the supply and demand schedules for orange juice we examined in Chapter 3. The demand and supply curves are combined in Figure 4.1.

From Table 4.1, we can see that as price falls, the quantity of orange juice demanded increases and the quantity supplied decreases. But at 70 cents per glass, the quantity supplied and the quantity demanded are both equal at 23. The price at which quantity demanded equals quantity supplied is known as the **equilibrium price**. The quantity at which supply and demand are equal is the **equilibrium quantity**. The equilibrium price and quantity are illustrated in Figure 4.1 by point E, where the demand and supply curves intersect. Orange juice will be sold at 70 cents a glass, assuming no other changes, since at that price supply meets demand. Consumers are getting what they want and producers are selling what they are willing and able to supply.

To understand how this price is determined, consider what happens when the price is above 70 cents, say at $1.00 a glass. At that price, 32 glasses of orange juice are supplied but only 9 are demanded, so that there is an **excess supply** or **surplus** of 23 (32 - 9) glasses of orange juice a day. This surplus is indicated in Figure 4.2 as AU.

The imbalance between supply and demand puts pressure on the price to change. A surplus puts a downward pressure on the price. Sellers will cut prices to get rid of their surplus. Prices will start to fall, from $1.00 to 90 cents and 80 cents. With each reduction in price, the surplus diminishes. When the price reaches 70 cents a glass, quantity demanded and quantity supplied are equal at 23—or, to put it another way, supply and demand are in equilibrium. Buyers purchase 23 glasses and sellers sell the same amount. There is no pressure on the price to change.

Now let's consider what happens when the price is below 70 cents, at 50 cents a glass. At this price, 29 glasses are demanded and only 10 are supplied, creat-

Table 4.1 Daily supply and demand schedules for orange juice and the equilibrium price

1 PRICE PER GLASS (IN CENTS)	2 QUANTITY SUPPLIED (IN GLASSES)	3 QUANTITY DEMANDED (IN GLASSES)	4 EXCESS DEMAND (SHORTAGE −) OR EXCESS SUPPLY (SURPLUS +)	5 PRESSURE ON PRICE	6 DIRECTION OF PRESSURE ON PRICE
100	32	9	+23	Downwards	
90	29	15	+14	Downwards	↓
80	26	20	+6	Downwards	
70	23	23	0	None	Equilibrium
60	17	26	−9	Upwards	
50	10	29	−19	Upwards	↑

As the price of orange juice falls, the quantity demanded increases and the quantity supplied decreases. As long as there is an imbalance between the quantity demanded and the quantity supplied, there is pressure on the price to change. Only at 70 cents per glass—the equilibrium price—is there no pressure for the price to change because the quantity demanded and the quantity supplied are equal at 23 glasses.

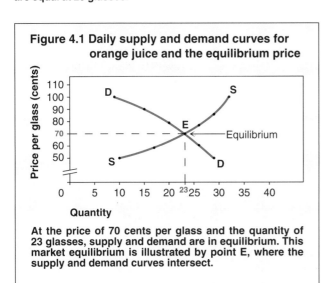

Figure 4.1 Daily supply and demand curves for orange juice and the equilibrium price

At the price of 70 cents per glass and the quantity of 23 glasses, supply and demand are in equilibrium. This market equilibrium is illustrated by point E, where the supply and demand curves intersect.

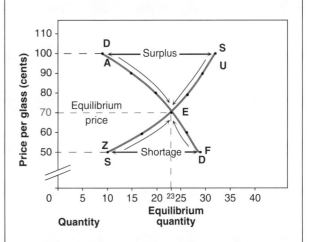

Figure 4.2 A surplus, shortage, and the equilibrium price

The equilibrium price is at point E, 70 cents, where the supply and demand curves intersect and where quantity demanded equals quantity supplied. If the price is higher, at 100 cents, the market has a surplus indicated by AU. The unsold supply puts a downward pressure on the price until it reaches equilibrium at 70 cents once again. If the price is below equilibrium, at 50 cents, the market has a shortage indicated by ZF. Competition among buyers for the limited supply puts an upward pressure on price until it reaches equilibrium at 70 cents with 23 glasses supplied and demanded once again.

ing a **shortage** or **excess demand** of 19 (29 - 10) glasses. This shortage is shown in Figure 4.2 as ZF.

As buyers compete for the limited supply, the price will rise and go on rising until it reaches 70 cents a glass. At that price, we no longer have a shortage since supply and demand are in equilibrium. Again the interaction of buyers and sellers, or the operation of the market, puts pressure on the price to change when there is an imbalance. This time, with a shortage, the pressure is in an upward direction.

□ Shifts in Supply and Demand and the Market Equilibrium

Will the price always stay at 70 cents a glass? Remember that we assumed no other changes. But as we saw earlier, many factors can cause shifts in supply and demand, and these will in turn upset the market equilibrium.

Shifts in Demand

Let's start by examining shifts in demand.

(a) Decrease in demand   Suppose the price of apple juice goes down significantly and many buyers switch from orange juice to the now cheaper alternative. The decrease in demand for orange juice, with a shift in the demand curve to the left, causes a surplus. As the quantity demanded falls, suppliers reduce production and the price falls. Thus the equilibrium price, where quantity demanded equals quantity supplied, also falls. This situation is summarized graphically in Figure 4.3. As the demand curve shifts to the left from DD to D_1D_1, the equilibrium price and quantity shift from E to E_1.

(b) Increase in demand   Suppose, on the other hand, that average family incomes increase and the demand for orange juice increases, causing a shortage. With the increased demand, and the shift in the demand curve to the right, suppliers are encouraged to increase the quantity supplied and buyers, competing for the limited supply, bid up the price. Thus, the equilibrium price and quantity also rise. This situation is summarized in Figure 4.4. As the demand curve shifts to the right from DD to D_2D_2, the equilibrium price and quantity also shift from E to E_2.

All of the factors that may shift the demand curve—average incomes, the size of the market, tastes, prices of competing goods, and consumer expectations—may, therefore, also affect the market equilibrium. A change that increases demand raises the equilibrium quantity and the equilibrium price, while any change that decreases demand lowers the equilibrium quantity and the equilibrium price.

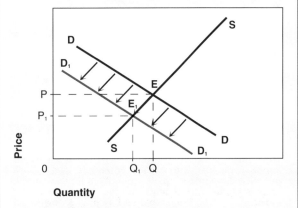

Figure 4.3 Effects of a decrease in demand

With a decrease in demand, the demand curve shifts to the left from DD to D_1D_1 and the quantity demanded decreases from 0Q to $0Q_1$. The market has a surplus and competition among sellers consequently forces the price down from 0P to $0P_1$. The equilibrium point, therefore, also shifts down from E to E_1.

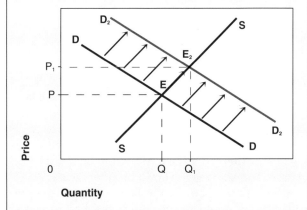

Figure 4.4 Effects of an increase in demand

With an increase in demand, the demand curve shifts to the right from DD to D_2D_2 and the quantity demanded increases from 0Q to $0Q_1$. The market is faced with a shortage and competition among buyers for the limited supply consequently forces prices up from 0P to $0P_1$. A new equilibrium is reached at E_2.

Shifts in Supply

Just as shifts in demand affect equilibrium price and quantity, so too, do shifts in supply.

(a) Decrease in supply   A severe frost in Florida could cause a decrease in the supply of orange juice on the market and a shift in the supply curve to the left. Since the quantity demanded then exceeds the quantity supplied, the market has a shortage. As buyers compete for the available orange juice, the price goes up. It continues to rise until quantity supplied again equals quantity demanded at a new equilibrium. This situation is illustrated in Figure 4.5. As the supply curve shifts to the left from SS to S_1S_1, the equilibrium price and quantity also shift from E to E_1.

(b) Increase in supply   Favourable weather in Florida, on the other hand, may bring a surplus of orange juice and a shift in the supply curve to the right. Since the quantity supplied then exceeds the quantity demanded, competition among suppliers to sell the excess orange juice will push prices down. A new equilibrium is reached when quantity supplied again meets quantity demanded. Figure 4.6 shows this situation. As the supply curve shifts to the right from SS to S_2S_2, the equilibrium price and quantity also shift from E to E_2.

Thus, the factors that may shift the supply curve—changes in technology, weather conditions, taxes and subsidies, and the prices of productive resources and related goods—also have an effect on the market equilibrium. A decreased supply increases the equilibrium price and reduces the equilibrium quantity, while an increased supply decreases the equilibrium price and increases the equilibrium quantity.

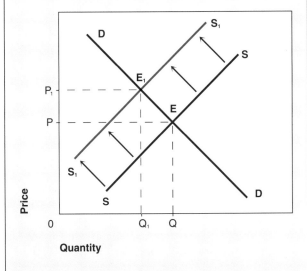

Figure 4.5 Effects of a decrease in supply

With a decrease in supply and a shift in the supply curve to the left from SS to S_1S_1, the market has a shortage. Quantity demanded exceeds quantity supplied. Competition among buyers will push the price up from 0P to $0P_1$, and quantity supplied shifts down from 0Q to $0Q_1$. A new equilibrium is established at E_1, where the quantity demanded and the quantity supplied are again equal.

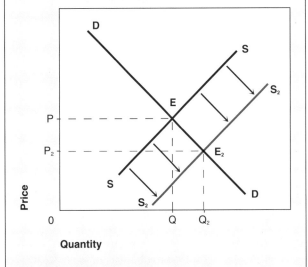

Figure 4.6 Effects of an increase in supply

With an increase in supply and a shift in the supply curve to the right from SS to S_2S_2, the market has a surplus. Competition among sellers forces the price down from 0P to $0P_2$, and quantity supplied increases from 0Q to $0Q_2$. The equilibrium point, where quantity supplied and quantity demanded are equal, thus shifts from E to E_2.

□ □ □ □ □ □

The Case of the Pocket Calculator

In 1970 at high schools, colleges, and universities, it was not uncommon to see students wearing a sort of holster attached to their belts. The holster carried a slide rule—a handy tool for making calculations of all sorts. Just five years later, the slide rule had disappeared and was replaced by the electronic pocket calculator. Today, pocket calculators are in use everywhere—in stores, offices, homes, and classrooms. How did the electronic calculator overtake the market so quickly?

Phase 1
In 1970, Sharp Electronics introduces the first electronic calculator. It is developed for business use and sells at $395 per unit.

Phase 2
By 1971, the first pocket calculators aimed at the domestic market are introduced, priced at $239 each. At this stage, only a few companies are making pocket calculators.

Phase 3
Many more firms begin to produce pocket calculators for the North American market—at one point as many as forty. Prices fall.

Phase 4
Costs of production fall. In the late 1980s, chips for mini-computers are one-twentieth the price they were in 1970. Mass production techniques lower the assembly time of electronic calculators from 30 minutes to 5 minutes. As a result, the price of pocket calculators falls. Today, we can buy a pocket calculator for less than CDN $20. This decline in price is especially remarkable when we compare other 1970 prices in Canada with those today. In 1970, the price of a hamburger and soft drink was less than 40 cents; a litre of gasoline was 11 cents; a North American-produced sedan about $3000; and a stamp for first class mail 6 cents.

SOURCE: Stanley L. Brue /Donald R. Wentworth, ECONOMIC SCENES: Theory in Today's World, 5e, © 1992, pp. 60-62. Adapted by permission of Prentice-Hall, Englewood Cliffs, New Jersey.

Applications
1. Draw supply and demand curves to illustrate the changes in the pocket calculator market for each phase outlined above.
2. What factors caused the changes in supply and demand? Explain.
3. Suggest other products that have gone through similar phases.

Elasticity and the Market Equilibrium

We have already examined elasticity—the responsiveness of buyers and sellers to changes in price. Now let's examine how elasticity affects the market equilibrium.

□ Elasticity of Demand

Inelastic Demand
Suppose the supply of an inelastic good, such as salt, increases in a given market. The supply curve shifts to the right and the price falls. But buyers are unwilling to purchase much more salt, even at a substantially lower price. After all, we can consume only so much salt. The demand for salt is inelastic. As illustrated in Figure 4.7, the equilibrium price falls considerably from $0P$ to $0P_1$, but the equilibrium quantity increases only slightly from $0Q$ to $0Q_1$. The equilibrium point, therefore, shifts down along the demand curve from E to E_1 as shown.

If the supply of salt were to decrease, the supply curve would shift to the left (to S_2S_2) and the price of salt would rise (to $0P_2$). But again, since the demand for salt is inelastic, equilibrium quantity is little changed

(0Q$_2$), though the equilibrium price rises substantially. Buyers are unwilling or unable to do without salt, so their demand changes little despite the large price increase.

Thus, for goods with an inelastic demand, the quantity demanded changes little with a change in supply, but price falls considerably with an increase in supply and rises considerably with a decrease in supply.

Elastic Demand

How do changes in the supply of goods and services with an elastic demand affect the market equilibrium? Suppose the number of available airline flights increases in a given market. As shown in Figure 4.8, the supply curve would shift to the right from SS to S$_1$S$_1$, and price would drop from 0P to 0P$_1$. However, while the equilibrium price changes much less than with inelastic demand, the equilibrium quantity changes

much more. At the lower prices, buyers are more willing and able to buy airline tickets. Demand for them is elastic.

If the supply of airline tickets were to decrease, the supply curve would shift to the left to S$_2$S$_2$, and price would rise to 0P$_2$. But, as shown in Figure 4.8, equilibrium quantity is greatly reduced, while the reduction in equilibrium price is small. Buyers can turn to other means of transportation or decide not to travel at all.

The effect of changes in supply on equilibrium quantity thus depends to a considerable extent on the elasticity of demand. The greater the elasticity, the greater the effect. Conversely, the lower the elasticity, the smaller the effect. The impact of changes in supply on equilibrium price also depends on the elasticity of demand. The more inelastic the demand, the greater the price changes. The more elastic the demand, the smaller the price changes.

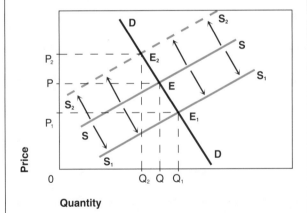

Figure 4.7 Inelastic demand and changes in supply

If the supply of a good with an inelastic demand increases, the supply curve shifts to the right from SS to S$_1$S$_1$. While price falls significantly from 0P to 0P$_1$, the equilibrium quantity increases only slightly from 0Q to 0Q$_1$.

If the supply of a good with an inelastic demand decreases and the supply curve shifts to S$_2$S$_2$, price increases substantially to 0P$_2$ but equilibrium quantity decreases only slightly to 0Q$_2$.

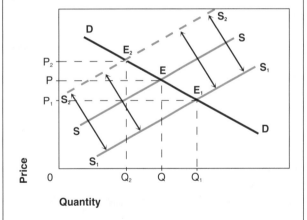

Figure 4.8 Elastic demand and changes in supply

An increase in the supply of a good with elastic demand shifts the supply curve from SS to S$_1$S$_1$. The equilibrium quantity increases from 0Q to 0Q$_1$, and the price decreases from 0P to 0P$_1$. Thus the equilibrium quantity increase is larger and the equilibrium price decrease is smaller than with inelastic demand.

With a decrease in supply from SS to S$_2$S$_2$, the equilibrium quantity decreases considerably from 0Q to 0Q$_2$, while the equilibrium price increases only slightly from 0P to 0P$_2$.

□ □ □ □ □ □

Economic Thinkers

Alfred Marshall (1842-1924)

Alfred Marshall was one of the most influential economists of the late nineteenth and early twentieth centuries. His major achievement was in the development and refinement of microeconomic theory. He helped forge many of the tools we have outlined in this and earlier chapters, including supply, demand, equilibrium, elasticity, and their graphical representations. Marshall also broke new ground in examining the influence of time on value. In addition to being an outstanding economist, he was the teacher of a whole generation of economists. His most brilliant student—John Maynard Keynes—was to revolutionize economic thinking in the 1930s. Marshall's most significant work was *Principles of Economics*, published in 1890.

During Marshall's lifetime, the British economy underwent significant changes. Marshall's youth was passed in the confident optimism of the mid-Victorian era when British industry was supreme in the world. But by the 1870s, Germany and the United States began to rival Britain's industrial power. From 1873 to 1896, Britain experienced a depression; prices and profits fell. A number of surveys of living standards in British cities revealed that while the standard of living had increased since the beginning of the century, there was still widespread squalor and destitution. About one-third of the population lived in poverty. Though the economy saw a return to prosperity before World War I in 1914, the war brought death and destruction on a hitherto unimagined scale. All of these events profoundly influenced Marshall's ideas.

". . .[T]o look at Alfred Marshall's portrait is to see the. . .teacher: white mustache, white wispy hair, kind bright eyes—an eminently professional countenance. . .Marshall. . .was prominently the product of a university. Although he voyaged to America and even across America to San Francisco, his life, his point of view—and inevitably his economics—smacked of the quietude and refinement of the Cambridge [England] setting."

SOURCE: THE WORLDLY PHILOSOPHERS, © 1953, 1961, 1972, 1987 by Robert L. Heilbroner. © renewed 1981, 1989 by Robert L. Heilbroner. Reprinted by permission of Simon and Schuster.

Marshall's Definition of Economics

Marshall defined economics as "the study of mankind in the ordinary business of life; it examines that part of individual and social action which is most closely connected with the attainment and the use of the material requisites of well-being." Economics is a science which differs from physics and chemistry principally in that it is concerned with the "ever changing and subtle forces of human nature." For Marshall, the object of economics is intensely practical: "to contribute to the solution of social problems."

Equilibrium, Value, and Supply and Demand

Marshall's major contribution to economics was in his examination of value.

In Marshall's view, many of the chief problems of economics could be traced to a balance between the forces of supply and demand. By demand, Marshall means a schedule of demand prices of potential buyers. Supply means a schedule of prices of potential suppliers. Value is determined by an equilibrium between supply and demand, which can be represented graphically. His well-known analogy presents his position: we can think of it as an arch. The keystone is value or price, and the two sides are supply and demand.

The Element of Time

In working out equilibrium, time is a key element. In the short run, supply is fixed. Over the long run, however, supply can be varied. More mines or factories can be opened or closed, for example. Hence, in the short run, demand has the greatest influence on price. In the long run, as supply can be varied independent of demand, supply has the greatest influence on price. At no time, however, can supply or demand be eliminated from the determination of price.

In Marshall's famous analogy, demand and supply are similar to the two blades of a pair of scissors. It is just as useless to ask which blade—the upper or the lower—does the cutting as to ask whether supply or demand alone determines price. However, while both blades do the cutting, one is active and the other is passive. In the short run, the demand blade is active and the supply blade passive. In the long run, the supply blade is active and the demand blade passive.

MARSHALL IN HIS OWN WORDS

Markets and Time

Again, markets vary with regard to the period of time which is allowed to the forces of demand and supply to bring themselves into equilibrium with one another, as well as with regard to the area over which they extend. And this element Time requires more careful attention just now than does that of Space. For the nature of the equilibrium itself, and that of the causes by which it is determined, depend on the length of the period over which the market is taken to extend. We shall find that if the period is short, the supply is limited to the stores [inventory] which happen to be at hand: if the period is longer, the supply will be influenced, more or less, by the cost of producing the commodity in question; and if the period is very long, this cost will in its turn be influenced, more or less, by the cost of producing the labour and the material things required for producing the commodity. These three classes of course merge into one another by imperceptible degrees...

1. Marshall notes that if the period is short, supply is "limited to the stores at hand." Explain this statement.
2. Explain the effect of the cost of production on supply over the short and long runs.

On Equilibrium

When demand and supply are in equilibrium, the amount of the commodity which is being produced in a unit of time may be called the equilibrium-amount, and the price at which it is being sold may be called the equilibrium-price.

Such an equilibrium is stable, that is, the price, if displaced a little from it, will tend to return, as a pendulum oscillates about its lowest point; and it will be found to be a characteristic of stable equilibria that in them the demand price is greater than the supply price for amounts just less than the equilibrium amount, and vice versa.

When demand and supply are in sta-

Pendulum

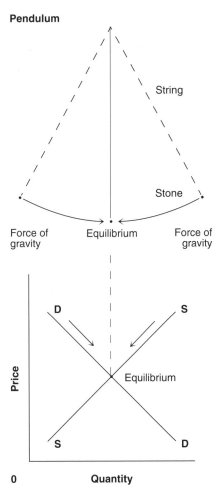

ble equilibrium, if any accident should move the scale of production from its equilibrium position, there will be instantly brought into play forces tending to push it back to that position; just as, if a stone hanging by a string is displaced from its equilibrium position, the force of gravity will at once tend to bring it back to its equilibrium position. The movements of the scale of production about its position of equilibrium will be of a somewhat similar kind.*

3. Referring to the diagram, explain how Marshall's pendulum relates to the supply and demand graph shown. Use the terms supply, demand, equilibrium price, and equilibrium quantity in your answer.

On Value

We might as reasonably dispute whether it is the upper or the under blade of a pair of scissors that cuts a piece of paper, as whether value is governed by utility or cost of production. It is true that when one blade is held still, and the cutting is effected by moving the other, we may say with careless brevity that the cutting is done by the second; but the statement is not strictly accurate, and is to be excused only so long as it claims to be merely a popular and not a strictly scientific account of what happens.

In the same way, when a thing already made has to be sold, the price which people will be willing to pay for it will be governed by their desire to have it, together with the amount they can afford to spend on it. Their desire to have it depends partly on the chance that, if they do not buy it, they will be able to get another thing like it at as low a price: this depends on the causes that govern the supply of it, and this again upon the cost of production. But it may so happen that the stock to be sold is practically fixed. This, for instance, is the case with a fish market, in which the value of fish for the day is governed almost exclusively by the stock on the slabs in relation to the demand: and if a person chooses to take the stock for granted, and say that the price is governed by demand, his brevity may perhaps be excused so long as he does not claim strict accuracy. So again it may be pardonable, but it is not strictly accurate to say that the varying prices which the same rare book fetches, when sold and resold at Christie's auction room, are governed exclusively by demand. . . .

Thus we may conclude that, as a general rule, the shorter the period which we are considering, the greater must be the share of our attention which is given to the influence of demand on value; and the longer the period, the more important will be the influence of cost of production on value. For the influence of changes in cost of production takes as a rule a longer time to work itself out than does the influence of changes in demand. The actual value at any time, the market value as it is often called, is often more influenced by passing events and by causes whose action is fitful and short-lived, than by those which work persistently. But in long periods these fitful and irregular causes in large measure efface one another's influence; so that in the long run persistent causes dominate value completely. Even the most persistent

causes are however liable to change. For the whole structure of production is modified, and the relative costs of production of different things are permanently altered, from one generation to another. . .

4. Using the example of the fish market, explain in your own words how demand and supply together affect the value of a product.

5. (a) What "fitful and short-lived" factors might affect the market value of a product?

(b) What "long-run persistent" causes could "dominate value completely"? How would these supersede the short-run effects?

SOURCE: Excerpts taken from Howard Marshall and Natalie J. Marshall, *The History of Economic Thought: A Book of Readings* (New York: Pitman, 1968), pp. 281-284.

☐ Elasticity of Supply and the Market Equilibrium

The market equilibrium is also affected by the elasticity of supply, which is in turn influenced by time. Let's consider how changes in the supply of a product such as Walkmans affects the market equilibrium over the three main time periods.

(i) The immediate term   In the immediate term, manufacturers do not have time to vary the number of Walkmans they produce. The quantity of Walkmans in stores and warehouses is fixed. Supply is inelastic. Changes in demand result in no change in quantity supplied, but considerable changes in price, as shown in Figure 4.9. An increase in demand from DD to D_1D_1 causes a sharp increase in price from 0P to $0P_1$. A decrease in demand from DD to D_2D_2 causes a sharp decline in price from 0P to $0P_2$.

(ii) The short run   In the short run, we assume that the plant capacity of individual producers is fixed. But they can use their plants more or less intensively by varying the number of workers and the number of hours they work, for example. Thus, they can vary the output of Walkmans in response to a change in demand. Supply is more elastic.

As shown in Figure 4.10, price changes less, and equilibrium quantity changes more than in the immediate market period. An increase in demand from DD to D_1D_1 causes a smaller increase in price from 0P to

0P₁ and a greater increase in the equilibrium quantity from 0Q to 0Q₁ than over the immediate term. A decrease in demand to D₂D₂ leads to a smaller decrease in price to 0P₂, but a greater decrease in the equilibrium quantity to 0Q₂.

(iii) The long run In the long run, firms can make almost all necessary changes in plant and equipment. More firms can begin to manufacture Walkmans or those producing them can move out of the industry. Firms may also change the capacity of their plant and equipment. Supply is even more elastic than in the short run. The equilibrium price changes even less and the equilibrium quantity even more with shifts in demand than in the two shorter time periods.

As shown in Figure 4.11, with an increase in demand from DD to D₁D₁, equilibrium price changes only slightly to 0P₁, but equilibrium quantity changes considerably from 0Q to 0Q₁. A decrease in demand to D₂D₂ again means only a slight decrease in price to 0P₂, but a large decrease in equilibrium quantity to 0Q₂.

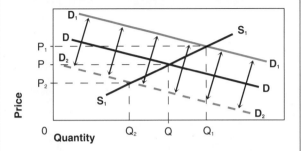

Figure 4.10 Elasticity of supply and shifts in demand — short run

In the short run, supply is more elastic. With an increase in demand from DD to D₁D₁, the equilibrium price increase from 0P to 0P₁ is more moderate than in the immediate term, while the increase in equilibrium quantity from 0Q to 0Q₁ is greater.

With a decrease in demand from DD to D₂D₂, equilibrium price declines more moderately from 0P to 0P₂ than in the immediate term, while the equilibrium quantity decrease from 0Q to 0Q₂ is greater. In the short run, the price change is less and the quantity change is more than in the immediate term.

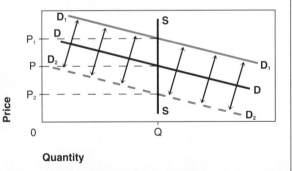

Figure 4.9 Elasticity of supply and shifts in demand — immediate term

In the immediate term, supply is fixed and completely inelastic. An increase in demand from DD to D₁D₁ results in a large increase in equilibrium price from 0P to 0P₁, but no increase in equilibrium quantity.

A decrease in demand from DD to D₂D₂ results in a large decrease in equilibrium price from 0P to 0P₂, and no change in equilibrium quantity.

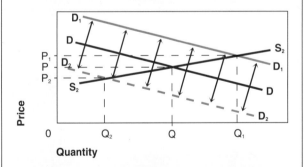

Figure 4.11 Elasticity of supply and shifts in demand — long run

Supply is most elastic in the long run. With an increase in demand from DD to D₁D₁, equilibrium quantity increases considerably from 0Q to 0Q₁. The price rise is moderated even more than in the short run, from 0P to 0P₁.

With a decrease in demand to D₂D₂, the price decrease to 0P₂ is less and the decrease in equilibrium quantity to 0Q₂ is more than in the two shorter time periods.

□ □ □ □ □ □

Skill Development: Analyzing an Economic Event

One of the main reasons for acquiring knowledge and skills in economics is to understand actual events. In this section, we use a basic four-question framework to analyze an economic event you have probably encountered at major concerts—ticket scalping.

Question 1 What is happening?

Among the crowds flocking to rock concerts or major sports events, you may find individuals selling tickets at substantially marked-up prices. They may be offering a $20-ticket at $40 or $50, for example. These individuals have not bought tickets for their own enjoyment and then found unexpectedly that they could not use them. They are ticket scalpers who buy large numbers of tickets at regular prices and then sell them at a substantial mark-up to make a profit. Scalpers get their tickets from various sources: by hiring people to stand in line for them; by purchasing them through the mail; or by buying them from people who have tickets, but cannot attend the event.

Question 2 What economic concepts are involved?

Ticket scalping clearly involves the forces of supply and demand, shortages, and elasticity. The number of concerts a music group gives in any location is limited, as are the number of tickets on sale. Demand, however, is high. There are thus shortages of the concerts and tickets. Supply is limited and inelastic. Demand, on the other hand, is likely to be elastic, since there are many other competing forms of entertainment people may choose to enjoy.

Question 3 Why is it happening?

To understand why scalping takes place, it is helpful to draw a graph depicting the market for concert tickets based on the economic concepts we have identified. We'll assume that tickets for the concert have an official price of $20 each and are all sold out. Tickets are clearly in high demand.

Figure 4.12 illustrates the market for concert tickets. The fixed supply is indicated by the straight vertical curve SS. Demand is shown by the downward-sloping demand curve DD. Since we know that demand exceeds supply, our graph must indicate a shortage of tickets at the price of $20. As we know, high demand will push up the market price. People are willing to pay more than $20 for a ticket. Scalpers, therefore, can expect to sell tickets at prices higher than $20 and make a profit.

Figure 4.12 Market for concert tickets

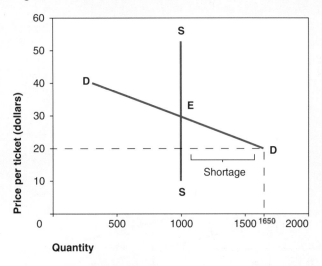

With a fixed supply and a demand that exceeds the supply, there is a shortage of tickets at the $20 price. Scalpers, therefore, can expect that people will be willing to pay more for tickets. With a shortage of 1650 − 1000 = 650 tickets, the equilibrium price will be $30, for example.

Question 4 What are the implications of this event?

Many people feel that ticket scalpers charge unfair prices for tickets and take profits away from the people who actually present the events. Ticket scalping is illegal in a number of jurisdictions in Canada. However, fines are often low—sometimes under $50. Many scalpers seem to regard the fines as simply a cost of doing business.

How could scalping be stopped? One suggestion is to raise fines and enforce the law rigorously against scalpers. The benefits to be gained from scalping would then be reduced and, presumably, fewer people would want to continue scalping. Another approach would be to increase the supply of tickets or decrease the quantity demanded, until supply and demand are in equilibrium. The supply could be increased by offering more concerts, thus shifting the supply curve to the right. The quantity demanded could be decreased by raising the ticket price to the equilibrium price—$30 in Figure 4.12. Alternatively, both price and supply could be increased.

Applications

1. In the late 1980s and early 1990s, with apartment vacancy rates very low in a number of Canadian cities where rent controls were in effect, a few unscrupulous landlords began to charge *key money*. Key money is an under-the-table and illegal fee, over and above the rent, demanded by landlords from prospective and sometimes desperate tenants. It is often disguised as a payment for furniture, drapes, broadloom, or other furnishings in the apartment. Using the four-question model outlined above, analyze this economic situation. Include a graph in your answer.

■ The Case for the Market System

What does all this mean? Essentially, our discussion of the interaction between supply and demand and the determination of equilibrium price and quantity shows how competitive markets are self-regulating, operating without a central decision-making body. Competitive markets co-ordinate economic activity to answer the three major questions (what, how, and for whom to produce), as we saw in Chapter 2. Let's consider the advantages and disadvantages of the market system in some detail, now that we have examined more closely how it operates.

□ Advantages of the Market System

Flexibility and Adaptability
The market system is flexible and adaptable. Consumers can often more readily adjust to changing economic conditions than can a central decision-making authority. If a scarcity of natural gas forces prices up, for example, consumers can adjust in their own ways. One person may respond by lowering the thermostat during the day, another by taking fewer hot showers, and yet another by washing clothes only in cold water. This exercise of choice by consumers is, for many,

preferable to government rationing or regulation of house and hot water temperatures.

Moreover, the shortage of natural gas will raise demand for alternative energy sources and encourage producers to look for new alternatives. Thus, as circumstances change through time, prices change and producers and consumers adjust. The market continually adjusts to changing conditions. Government rationing or regulation schemes are much more difficult to change. For some central body to continually make all of the necessary adjustments needed on a day-by-day basis is clearly a gigantic task.

Self-correction
The market system is self-correcting. Suppose, for example, sports equipment manufacturers misjudge the market and produce too many skates and too few skis. With the surplus of skates, prices would fall and bargain sales on skates would be common. With the shortage of skis, however, prices for skis would rise. The high prices are a signal and an incentive for ski manufacturers to increase production, since with the high prices, increased production means higher profits. The low prices on skates, on the other hand, are a signal for skate manufacturers to cut production. Thus, price signals provide manufacturers of skis and skates with the necessary information and motivation to cor-

rect their mistakes as quickly as possible. These changes take place without a central body directing and controlling events.

A central organization may find it more difficult to correct mistakes. It may not wish to admit the mistake and may be unwilling, or slow, to make the necessary adjustments. The body also may not have any incentive to admit and correct a mistake.

Economic Freedom
The market system provides a high degree of individual freedom and decentralization of power. No one is directed to work in any particular occupation. People are free to choose their own occupations and to move from job to job in search of better pay and benefits. People are also free to decide how they wish to spend their incomes. Individuals and households thus determine how income is allocated in a free market system.

Price Are Kept in Check
In pure competitive markets, competition among producers tends to push down prices to equal costs of production. When prices are significantly above the costs of production, new producers will enter the market to take advantage of the high prices and high prospective profits. As more producers enter the market, supply increases and prices fall closer to the costs of production.

☐ Disadvantages of the Market System

Despite these advantages, the competitive market system has a number of disadvantages.

Inequitable Distribution of Income
As we noted in Chapter 2, the distribution of income in a competitive market system may be inequitable. People earn incomes through their own efforts. But labour, like goods and services, is subject to the forces of supply and demand. While some highly skilled people are in demand and receive high incomes, those with few skills or skills that have become obsolete may be in low demand and may receive very low incomes. Moreover, the elderly, sick, and those with disabilities may receive very little income, while others accumulate great wealth. It is often argued, therefore, that the distribution of income in a market system needs modification. We will examine income distribution in more detail in Unit Three.

Spillovers or Externalities
A **spillover** or **externality** is a side effect of production or consumption, which may affect people (positively or negatively) not directly involved in the production or consumption of the goods or services.

One of the most significant spillovers is the pollution of the environment. Since no one owns the rivers or the air, manufacturers and consumers can and do use them to get rid of garbage. In this way, those downwind or downstream—though not directly involved in producing or consuming the goods—are negatively affected. The market provides no incentive for manufacturers or consumers to limit these harmful side effects. Laws must be instituted to control pollution and protect the environment. Similarly, when a homeowner generates a positive spillover effect by creating a beautiful garden which her neighbours enjoy, she is for the most part considering only her own enjoyment.

Monopoly Markets
We have assumed that a market system always includes fully competitive markets. However, in some cases, one or a few suppliers of a good or service may be able to obtain monopoly power. With monopoly power, competition is restricted or eliminated and producers may raise prices or keep them at high levels by restricting supply. Thus, monopolies may not respond to the demands of the consumer and undermine one of the main principles of the market system. As we will see later, carefully controlled monopolies may be desirable in some industries, but in most countries with modified market economies, laws are instituted to promote competition and control monopoly power.

Free Riders
In some cases, free markets do not work. For example, if I construct and operate a lighthouse on a treacherous, rocky coast, I may provide a very valuable service. But it's unlikely that I will stay in business very long, because there is no way I can ensure the light is seen

□ □ □ □ □ □

Pollution and Externalities

Pollution is a negative externality that results from the production and consumption of goods and services. Whenever we drive a gas-powered vehicle, we pollute the atmosphere and contribute to the greenhouse effect. When Canadian farmers produce food, they use fertilizers and pesticides, some of which runs off to pollute rivers and streams. When thermal power stations produce electricity, they also produce sulphur and nitrogen oxides which result in acid rain. Many other human activities also result in pollution.

Over 30 000 commercial chemicals are in use in Canada and as many as 200 more are introduced every year. These chemicals provide Canadians with substantial benefits and help to raise and maintain our standard of living. But their use and transportation also pose risks to the health of humans, wildlife, and the environment.

In waste management, Canadians have an unenviable record. On average, we produce 2 kg of solid waste per day—more than any other citizens in the world. Even so, less than 10 percent of Canada's solid waste is recycled. Solid waste sites around many Canadian cities are filling rapidly. Attempts to find other dump sites meet with opposition from people who don't want landfill sites in their backyards. Canadian environment ministers have set a goal of reducing the amount of waste generated by 50 percent by the year 2000.

What Do We Face?

Acid Rain Acid rain is caused by emissions of sulphur dioxide and various nitrogen oxides from coal-burning electrical power utilities, base-metal smelting, and vehicles on both sides of the Canada/US border. The oxides are carried by winds and return to the earth as acid rain, snow, fog, or dust. According to Environment Canada, 150 000 lakes have been damaged and more than 14 000 are dead. Fifteen million hectares of forest have received high levels of acid rain. In addition, buildings and monuments have been damaged. Some 80 percent of Canadians live in areas with high levels of acid rain. There is evidence that it contributes to respiratory problems in children.

Global Warming Scientists fear that the earth's atmosphere will warm 1.5 to 4.5°C by the middle of the next century. This may not sound like much until we consider that in the last ice age, the temperature dropped only 5°C. Global warming is said to result from the "greenhouse effect," which is caused by the increasing levels of carbon dioxide in the atmosphere. Since the beginning of the Industrial Revolution in the mid-eighteenth century, carbon dioxide levels in the atmosphere have increased 25 percent and it is estimated they will double in the next 30 to 60 years.

According to Environment Canada, some likely effects of global warming include:
- A rise in sea level, flooding low-lying coastal areas.
- A fall in the water level of the Great Lakes, thus hindering navigation and power generation.
- Drier and hotter conditions on the prairies, extending the growing season and making some northern areas of the prairies more suitable for farming.
- An increase in the vulnerability of forests to fires, thus disrupting the Canadian wood and paper industries.
- The destruction of the Canadian ski industry.

Decay of the Ozone Layer The ozone layer protects the earth from lethal ultraviolet and cosmic rays. Chlorofluorocarbons (CFCs) that drift into the atmosphere, (after use in coolants for refrigerators or air conditioners and in the manufacture of foam insulation among other things), can cause deterioration of the ozone layer. Studies have shown that deterioration of the ozone layer is linked to increased ultraviolet radiation and skin cancer. Discovery of a "hole" in the ozone layer over Antarctica in 1990 caused many to worry that the layer may thin elsewhere too, with the consequent impact on human health.

The Costs

Production and consumption, or the exchange of goods and services, involve two types of costs—private and social costs. Private or internal costs are those incurred by producers for such resources as labour and raw materials, and which are passed on to consumers. They are called internal costs because they are included *within* the transactions between producers and consumers. Social or external costs are those costs which *spill over* to affect others and which are not included in the costs of goods and services to the consumer.

It is to the advantage of businesses to produce goods as cheaply as possible—thus they seek to minimize their internal costs. Given a choice between dumping pollutants into the atmosphere or a river at no cost and paying to have them removed or cleaned up, the profit-maximizing producer will choose the cheaper alternative. As a result, goods are cheaper for consumers, but part of the production costs are passed on to the environ-

ment and thus society at large. Figure 4.13 shows the effects of these externalities.

How to Control It

Voluntary Programs Many households, businesses, and governments participate in voluntary recycling programs. They separate their reuseable garbage which is then sold for recycling. Consumers, businesses, and governments may also choose to buy recycled products or those designed to reduce pollution. Support for environmentally friendly legislation is also important.

Direct Controls Direct controls include laws limiting the amount of pollutants industries may emit and mandates for certain procedures that reduce effluents. Governments have instituted regulations for pollution control equipment on automobiles, and have banned leaded gasoline, DDT,

---

Figure 4.13 Social costs and the allocation of resources

(i) No spillover costs

(ii) With spillover costs

(iii) With spillover benefits

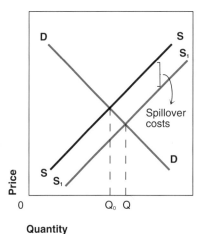
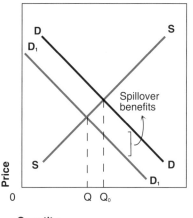

With no spillover costs, the allocation of goods and services is most efficient since all costs and benefits are reflected in the market supply and demand curves.

With spillover costs, producers shift some of their costs to the community. The supply curve shifts from SS to S_1S_1. Equilibrium output is 0Q rather than $0Q_0$ where all costs are internalized. More is produced at lower costs.

With spillover benefits, actual output is less than the optimum because the demand curve shifts from DD to D_1D_1. The market demand curve D_1D_1 underestimates the total benefits. Total output is reduced from $0Q_0$ to 0Q.

and backyard trash fires. Coal-fired power stations are required to install scrubbers that diminish pollutants entering the atmosphere.

There are difficulties with direct controls, however. How do governments decide how much to ban? Producers and labour complain about lost jobs and business. Environmentalists complain that the regulations are too lax. Laws and regulations are also difficult and expensive to monitor on a farm-by-farm and factory-by-factory basis.

Economists argue that regulations are often an inefficient way of controlling pollution. If a government requires a firm to reduce its polluting effluents into a river by 20 000 L a day, for example, it may cost the firm 5 cents a day. How much must society pay? The total is 5 cents x 20 000 L = $1000. Though government achieves the reduction in pollution, society thus still pays.

Taxes on Emissions Taxes on emissions may be a more efficient way of tackling the problem, some economists argue. Metres (similar to gas or water metres) could be installed to measure effluent. Polluters would receive a bill at the end of each month. Thus polluters would pay according to the amount they pollute and they would have an incentive to reduce pollution as far as it is economically feasible.

However, pollution metres do not exist. In fact, it is often only after extensive and expensive laboratory tests that the amount of pollution can be determined. This method may only be feasible for large corporations, therefore, though it has met with some success in the Ruhr valley of Germany. There, taxes on effluents have made it advantageous for firms to extract pollutants from the discharges.

Emission Permits Emission permits may be another option. Governments would decide how much pollution is permissible and then auction permits to bidders. The price would be high if few permits are sold and low if many are sold. The amount of pollution would thus be known, but the idea of "permissible" pollution is politically unattractive.

Thus, while all methods have their advantages and disadvantages, the challenge is to put them into an effective program.

Applications
1. Examine your own behaviour over the next week. In what ways can you reduce the amount of pollution you cause to the environment?
2. Suppose you have been asked to devise a pollution program for your town or province. On which methods discussed above would you place most emphasis? Why? What roles (if any) would the other methods have? Explain.

only by those who pay for my service. There will be **free riders** who don't pay, and they can benefit from my service just as well as those who do pay. Without the prospect of some profits, sellers have no incentive to provide this kind of good or service—called **public** or **social goods and services**. Examples of public goods and services include flood control, national defence, lighthouses, police protection, and the judicial system.

Instability
The market system is subject to periods of upswings and slowdowns. In the mid and late 1980s, for example, the Canadian economy was booming, but in 1990 and 1991, it was in a recession. When the economy did start to recover in 1991, the upturn was slow and weak.

Demand Created by Advertising

While the market may do a good job of meeting the demands of consumers, what can we say in the case of advertising? Producers in fierce competition may use high-powered advertising campaigns to persuade consumers to buy their product. Thus, producers may manipulate consumer tastes and preferences. In this case, the producer and not the consumer is sovereign. Advertising may also create demand for unnecessary or wasteful goods and services. Thus while advertising may provide consumers with the information they need to make wise purchasing decisions, it may also be used to manipulate consumers and increase the profits of producers.

Government Involvement in the Market

Governments may intervene in the market system to control prices when it is felt that the market price may fall too low or rise too high. They may control prices *directly* by setting maximum or minimum prices, or *indirectly* by controlling the supply of products.

☐ Minimum or Floor Prices

A **floor price** is a minimum price below which it is illegal to buy or sell a good or service. The minimum wage is an example. By setting a minimum wage, governments aim to ensure that workers receive a fair wage in line with the cost of living. Without a minimum, if demand for some workers is very low, wages may fall below the cost of living and cause severe hardship. Floor prices are also sometimes set on agricultural products. Particularly good growing conditions may produce a bumper crop, but since the demand for many agricultural products is inelastic, the surplus on the market would cause a drastic drop in prices and farm incomes. Some farmers may, therefore, be driven into bankruptcy.

Floor or minimum prices may be at, below, or above equilibrium. If the floor is at or below equilibrium, it will have no effect. The market will function freely, and supply and demand will balance at equilibrium. A floor price above equilibrium, as shown in Figure 4.14, will result in an excess supply. The effect of the excess will vary, depending on the kind of good or service.

Let's take the minimum wage, for example. Suppose the minimum wage is set above equilibrium at $0P_1$ (say $6.00 an hour), while the equilibrium wage is lower at $0P$ (say $5.25 an hour). The excess supply, Q_1Q_2, is in fact the number of people who are unemployed. The floor price, therefore, sets a higher minimum wage, but may lead to increased unemployment.

Now let's consider a good such as wheat. If the floor price at $0P_1$ is set at say $6.00 per bushel, while the equilibrium price at $0P$ is at $5.25, there will be a surplus of wheat, Q_1Q_2. The surplus will continue to accumulate on farms and in grain elevators as long as the floor price remains above equilibrium. The govern-

ment may buy the surplus, but it will then simply accumulate in government inventories.

Why might governments be willing to accept the consequent unemployment or wheat surplus? The answer is that some people do gain—the farmers who are able to sell their wheat at a price that gives them a greater return, and the workers who are able to sell their labour at a minimum wage higher than the market equilibrium wage.

☐ Price Ceilings

In wartime, and in peacetime during periods of rapidly rising prices, governments have sometimes fixed maximum or ceiling prices for certain essential goods. A **ceiling price** is the maximum legal price that may be charged for a good or service (e.g., rent controls).

As shown in Figure 4.15, with a ceiling price on rents fixed below equilibrium, an excess demand or shortage (Q_1Q_2) results. Normally the market system responds to a shortage with an increase in price, but since this cannot happen with a legal ceiling price, other ways of dealing with the shortage may develop. These include first-come, first-served systems, discrimination among buyers, rationing, and black markets.

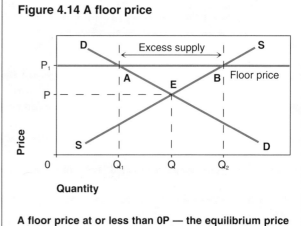

Figure 4.14 A floor price

A floor price at or less than 0P — the equilibrium price — will have no effect since the equilibrium price is either equal to or greater than the minimum legal price. With a floor price above 0P at 0P₁, however, the quantity demanded (0Q₁) is less than the quantity supplied (0Q₂), causing a surplus of Q₁Q₂.

(i) First-come, first-served In this situation, the shortage may cause line-ups at stores which people believe have the good for sale. Line-ups were common outside shops in the former Soviet Union in the late 1980s and early 1990s, for example, when the people faced severe shortages of food and other goods. Those at the front of the line receive the good first. Often, however, supplies of the goods are exhausted long before all those in line are served. Line-ups and short-ages have been common during wars and in countries where price does not function as an effective means of allocating goods and services.

(ii) Discrimination among buyers With price con-trols in effect and a shortage of goods, sellers can discriminate among buyers. They may choose to sell only to "regular customers" or friends, for example.

(iii) Rationing With rationing, government allocates a fixed number of coupons to match the supplies available. To acquire the good, buyers have to surren-der coupons as well as money. This kind of measure is resorted to only when there are extreme shortages (e.g., in wartime).

(iv) Black markets A **black market** is the buying and selling of a good at a price above the ceiling or maximum legal price. When ceiling prices are in effect, some buyers may be willing to pay more than the legal maximum price and some sellers to sell above the ceiling price. Figure 4.15 depicts the extreme and very unlikely situation, in which all buyers are willing to buy and sellers willing to sell at prices above the legal maximum.

☐ Quotas

One method governments use to *indirectly* influence prices is the quota. A **quota** is a restriction placed on the output of a producer. In other words, it is a way of controlling—and in most cases, limiting—the supply of a good. Only those producers given quotas may produce the good.

By limiting supply, quotas push up the price of the product above the free market level, as shown in Figure 4.16. The quota system is widely used to control the prices of agricultural products in Canada. The system has the advantage of avoiding large accumula-tions of unsold products.

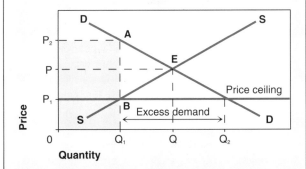

Figure 4.15 A price ceiling and the black market

A ceiling price at $0P_1$, below the equilibrium price of $0P$, causes an excess demand or shortage (Q_1Q_2). Since government has fixed a maximum price, the price may not rise to $0P$ to restore the equilibrium. If all of the goods were sold on the black market, the price would rise to $0P_2$. The black market dealers would receive all of $0Q_1AP_2$, with P_1BAP_2 being the black market profit.

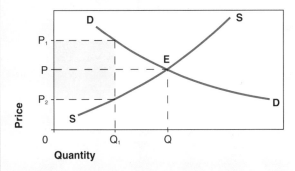

Figure 4.16 The effect of quotas on price

If the market equilibrium is at a quantity of $0Q$ and a price of $0P$, a quota set at $0Q_1$ — below the market equilibrium — will raise the price to $0P_1$. With a supply of $0Q_1$, the price would normally be $0P_2$. Thus, quotas provide producers who have them with additional incomes, represented by the shaded area, and prices can be raised without the accumulation of unsold inventories.

□ □ □ □ □ □

The Case of Canadian Agriculture

Two major economic problems face Canadian agriculture: the long-run tendency of Canadian farm incomes to fall (relative to urban incomes), and the rapid decline in the percentage of the workforce employed in agriculture. From about 3 million people and 40 percent of the population in the early part of this century, the farm population has declined to about 1 million people and less than 5 percent of the population today.

Causes of the Problems

As you might expect, the problems arise from both the demand and supply sides of the market for agricultural products.

1. The Demand Side of the Market The elasticity of demand for food—like that for other essentials—is low. Increases in the real income of Canadians or reductions in the price of food are, therefore, unlikely to translate into increased demand for food products.

The outlook for Canadian food exports—in other words, the demand for Canadian food products in other countries—has also not been encouraging. The formation of the European Common Market and its extensive support for agriculture has changed the Community from a net importer of cereal grains into the world's third largest wheat exporter. Agricultural improvements in less developed countries have also meant that, despite rapidly growing populations, many nations have been able to increase agricultural output considerably.

2. The Supply Side of the Market Since the end of World War II, farm output per worker in Canada has been growing at an average rate of about 5 percent per year. As a result, the supply curve for agricultural products has been shifting steadily to the right.

Moreover, over the short run without government intervention, agricultural supply and prices tend to vary considerably. Farm products are subject to a number of factors beyond farmers' control, such as the weather, which may produce very poor harvests or bumper crops.

Inelastic demand and shifts in supply thus result in wide price fluctuations. Bumper crops drive prices down, while poor harvests push prices up. The costs of farm inputs—such as fertilizer, seed, machinery, and fuel—however, have not varied with the prices of farm crops. Costs of inputs have risen steadily since 1945. Thus, farmers are caught in a squeeze between rising costs and varying revenues—and for many, the result has been bankruptcy.

Government Farm Policy

Government policy to support the agricultural industry has taken two main forms—marketing boards and income support.

Marketing Boards

Marketing boards are organizations of farmers established by government to control the supply and price of agricultural products. Marketing boards have been established in Canada to manage such products as milk, eggs, tobacco, and chicken. They are essentially of two types. One type acts as a marketing agency for producers to sell their products. The other is concerned primarily with controlling prices by controlling supply.

The Canadian Wheat Board is an example of the first type—a marketing agency. A crown corporation established in 1935, it markets the Canadian wheat produced by farmers. The Board provides farmers with an initial payment of about 75 percent of the estimated final price for grain delivered to a licenced elevator. When the wheat is sold, producers receive the full price less the costs of transportation, storage, and administration.

Farmers thus receive a substantial payment early in the growing season and are protected against short-term price fluctuations since they receive the average price for that year. If the Board sells the grain for less than what it paid the farmers, the difference (estimated at between $500 million and $800 million in 1991) is borne by Canadian taxpayers.

Marketing boards that control supplies estimate the size

of the market for the product and then allocate quotas to individual farmers. The farmers sell their produce to the marketing board, which in turn sells it to processors or wholesalers. The marketing board thus acts as a monopoly seller on behalf of the individual farmers. To prevent competition from foreign producers, imports are strictly limited.

Since the marketing boards control the output of farmers, they can successfully limit fluctuations in the prices of farm products. Critics argue, however, that because the boards are controlled by producers, they can use their powers to charge excessive prices. In addition, the quota itself becomes a valuable property. It represents a cost for those who wish to enter farming or expand their operations. Critics also argue that all consumers—rich and poor alike—end up paying higher prices for food. One of the reasons for cross-border shopping in the early 1990s was lower dairy and poultry prices in the US.

Farm Income Support

During the 1980s and early 1990s, Canadian cereal farmers faced tough times. Rising grain outputs in a number of grain-producing countries as they pushed for agricultural self-sufficiency diminished markets and drove down prices. Other nations, in a bid to rid of grain surpluses, began to subsidize grain exports. The result was an international subsidy war in agricultural products between the US and the European Economic Community. Caught in the middle were Canadian grain farmers, who saw prices plummet. In 1991, for example, the world price for wheat was $2.00 per bushel—the lowest price in 20 years.

To assist farmers, the federal government moved to end—or at least scale down—the subsidies through international trade negotiations. Canadian governments also provided farmers with income supplements under a variety of programs. Between 1980 and 1991, the amount was estimated at approximately $12 billion from all levels of government.

Applications

1. (a) Construct a graph to show the general shifts in supply and demand of agricultural products since the end of World War II (that is, over the long run).
(b) What does the graph illustrate about the changes in the general prices of agricultural products?
2. What problems do farmers face over the short term?
3. Construct a second graph to illustrate the effects of marketing boards on the price and supply of agricultural products. Explain the graph.

Summary

a. A market is an institution or mechanism that brings together buyers and sellers to exchange goods and services and establish prices. A perfectly competitive market is one with many buyers and sellers, none of which has control over price. Price is determined by the interaction of supply and demand.

b. Prices are a key factor in competitive markets because they provide information and incentives to buyers and sellers and perform an important rationing function.

c. The equilibrium or market price is the price at which quantity demanded and quantity supplied are equal. It is illustrated graphically as the point where the supply and demand curves intersect.

d. The equilibrium price and quantity change with shifts in supply or demand. An increase in demand raises the equilibrium quantity and the equilibrium price, while a decrease in demand lowers the equilibrium quantity and the price. An increase in supply increases the equilibrium quantity and lowers the price, while a decrease in supply lowers the quantity and raises the price.

e. The elasticity of demand for products also affects equilibrium price and quantity. The more inelastic the demand, the greater the changes in price and the smaller the changes in quantity. Thus, for goods with inelastic demand, quantity demanded varies little with changes in supply, while price falls considerably with increases in supply and rises considerably with decreases in supply.

f. The effects of the elasticity of supply on equilibrium price and quantity vary over time. In the immediate term, supply is completely inelastic, so that there is no change in quantity supplied but considerable change in price. Over the short and long terms, as supply becomes more elastic, the equilibrium quantity supplied changes more and the price changes less.

g. An economic event can be analyzed using the four-question framework: 1. What is happening?; 2. What economic concepts are involved?; 3. Why is it happening?; and 4. What are the implications?

h. One of Alfred Marshall's main contributions to economics was in pointing out that value (price) is determined by an equilibrium between supply and demand and that the market equilibrium varies over time. In the short run, demand is the major determinant, while over the long run, supply is more important.

i. The main advantages of the market system shown in this chapter are flexibility and adaptability, self-correction, economic freedom, and competition that keeps prices in check. The main disadvantages include an inequitable distribution of income, spillover effects, inefficiency in some markets that would be better as monopolies, free riders, and instability.

j. Governments may intervene in the market system to control prices directly by instituting floor and ceiling prices, or indirectly by setting quotas on production.

■ Review of Key Terms

Define the following key terms introduced in this chapter and provide examples where appropriate.

market	free rider
perfectly competitive market	public or social good
	floor price
equilibrium price	ceiling price
equilibrium quantity	black market
excess supply or surplus	quota
excess demand or shortage	marketing board
spillover	

■ Application and Analysis

1. (a) Complete columns 4, 5, and 6 in Table 4.2 on page 95.

(b) Graph the supply and demand curves for hamburgers based on the information in Table 4.2.

(c) What is the equilibrium price and quantity?

(d) Explain why the equilibrium price cannot be:
  (i) $1.80
  (ii) $1.20.

(e) What would happen to the equilibrium quantity and price of hamburgers in each of the following situations? Explain why in each case.
  (i)   the population increases by 10 percent
  (ii) the price of hot dogs falls by 10 percent
  (iii) the wages of workers in hamburger restaurants are increased
  (iv) the price of hamburger buns falls
  (v)   average consumer incomes diminish

2. Suppose that your nearest university has 500 qualified applicants for 100 vacancies in one of its most popular first-year courses. The university is considering which one of the following admission criteria it should use to make its selection:

(a) high school grades

(b) date of application

Table 4.2 Daily supply and demand schedule for hamburgers

1 PRICE (IN DOLLARS)	2 QUANTITY SUPPLIED	3 QUANTITY DEMANDED	4 EXCESSS DEMAND (SHORTAGE –) OR EXCESS SUPPLY (SURPLUS +)	5 PRESSURE ON PRICE	6 DIRECTION OF PRESSURE ON PRICE
2.00	200	20	+180	down	
1.80	150	40			
1.60	120	70			
1.40	100	100			
1.20	70	120			
1.00	40	130			

(c) geographical proximity to the institution

(d) lottery.

It has been shown, however, that by doubling the admission fees to the course, there would be no shortage of space. Compare the relative merits of raising the university fees with each of the four other criteria listed above.

3. Explain why the prices of fresh fruits fall in the summer months (the period when their consumption is highest), while the prices of other summer goods such as water skis and boats go up. Use graphs in your explanation.

4. Platinum is a malleable white metal. Of the 112 t consumed in 1990, almost half was used in the production of automotive catalytic converters to clean exhaust emissions of carbon monoxide and nitrous oxides. Close to another half went into the production of jewellery, almost 90 percent of which is sold in Japan. The remainder was used in the production of consumer products such as glass, plastics, computer chips, and fibre optic cables. Since 1986, however, the market for platinum has undergone a number of significant changes.

Use supply and demand graphs to illustrate each of the following situations in the platinum market. Read through all of the situations before you begin constructing your graphs.

(a) **Situation 1**   Platinum reaches a record high price of US$1000 per troy ounce [31.2 g] in 1986.

(b) **Situation 2**   In 1988, Donald Peters (then chairman of the Ford Motor Company) announces that Ford has developed a catalytic converter which does not use platinum and is cheaper to manufacture than the ones containing platinum.

(c) **Situation 3**   Exports of platinum from the former Soviet Union—a major supplier—increase from 15.5 t in 1989, to 21.7 t in 1990, to 31 t in the first half of 1991.

(d) **Situation 4**   Rumours circulate that the former Soviet Union does not have the large inventories of platinum it was once thought to have.

(e) **Situation 5**   In May 1991, Nissan Motor Company—Japan's second largest automaker—announces it has developed a platinum-free converter costing one-third of the conventional model.

(f) **Situation 6**   In the fall of 1991, strikes and continued labour unrest at the mines of Impala Holdings Ltd. of South Africa—the world's second largest producer of platinum—disrupt supplies of the metal. Platinum closes at $364.40 a troy ounce [31.2 g] on the New York Stock Exchange.

5. Many Canadian towns and cities control the number of taxis in their jurisdictions by restricting the number of taxi licences they issue. Demand for taxi services, however, has continued to increase over recent years with tighter drinking and driving laws, traffic congestion in some downtown areas, and higher automobile and public transit costs. The limited number of licences (and therefore taxis) and the growing demand have pushed the street price of taxi licences up far above the official price charged by the municipalities. In one city, for example, the official licence sells for $5000, while the street market price is about $80 000.

(a) Who are the winners and who are the losers under the system of restricting the number of taxi licences sold?

(b) Two ways of changing the system have been proposed. One is to auction the licences off to the highest bidders, so that the towns and cities receive the full value of the licences. The other is to issue as many licences as people want, thus allowing the market to guide the provision of taxi services. Which option do you believe is best? Support your position.

6. Case Study—Making Canada's Airports Safe

A lack of safety in air-traffic control is being blamed for near collisions at Toronto's Pearson International Airport. This would appear to be a technical or administrative matter but, in reality, the safety problem at Canada's largest airport, like the problem that plagues other major Canadian airports, boils down to economics. It's a matter of supply and demand.

First, the supply. Airline deregulation, with the major opportunities it has provided for lower airfares and hence significant increases in airline travel, has posed no problem for the private sector. Private suppliers have provided more planes, more in-flight meals, more flight attendants, more pilots, more fuel, all the paraphernalia required to respond to the increased demand for air travel.

However, no corresponding expansion has occurred in the supply of airport facilities, and governments don't seem able to solve the problem.

We are told the supply for air-traffic controllers is likely to lag behind the demand by several years. Since airport supply and controller supply seem the two most important ingredients of air safety, the government's failure to provide them would seem crucial to safety problems.

Why such a difference between the response of the private sector and the public sector? The answer is simple: money. When an airline wants to hire more pilots, reservation agents or baggage handlers, or ensure an allocation of fuel, it pays what's required. Financial incentives work. Indeed, the rapid increase in the number of travellers is itself a response to the reduction in the fares charged by the deregulated carriers.

Somewhat paradoxically, while it is true that Toronto's airport has too little space and too few air-traffic controllers, these are the reasons it is said to have safety problems. Rather, safety is in potential jeopardy because economic incentives are being used to ensure that Pearson, as well as our other major airports, will be overcrowded and, therefore, potentially unsafe.

Simply put, airlines are being charged so little to land their planes that there is a guaranteed excess demand for the services of air-traffic controllers.

At the moment, if you drive to Pearson and park overnight, it will cost you $10. If you arrive in a nine-passenger, piston-engine airplane, it will cost you nothing to land and less than the automobile charge to park it. Although they need more airspace and proportionately more air-traffic control service when landing, turbo-prop planes are charged much lower landing fees than a passenger-efficient jumbo jet.

In other words, the structure of fees at our major airports, both for landing and parking, encourage the over-utilization of the facility, compared to the charges in other economic spheres. The structure of fees actually encourages the use of the airport by small planes, which have many other alternative landing sites and carry few passengers, while inhibiting 747s, with their hundreds of passengers, with higher landing fees.

The pricing scheme also has encouraged the hub-and-spoke method of air service: smaller turbo-prop aircraft, like the Dash, are used to provide a connector service to smaller centres. These smaller planes contribute mightily to the current perception of over-utilization.

There is no attempt to spread out the traffic at Canadian airports by charging different fees according to the time of day the plane lands. The United States uses an auctioning system to sell landing times to the highest bidder; Britain has a sliding fee scale that encourages airlines to select less frequently used landing times. At the moment, airlines set their schedules without regard for the cost of landing for the simple reason that the cost doesn't change during the day.

Not surprisingly, while newspapers are filled with stories of crowded airports, travellers who arrive at Toronto or Montreal during the off hours must wonder what all the fuss is about—the corridors are bare and the runways look like well-lit deserts.

If landing rights at major airports were sold on an appropriate, economic basis, the excess demand for landing space—and for the attention of air-traffic controllers—would be much reduced. There would be a tendency for small planes to land elsewhere, or at times when controllers aren't busy with the big planes. Tourists would travel only in off-peak hours, as seat prices then would reflect the much lower cost of landing.

The results would be less apparent at Vancouver's airport, which has only one runway and has already been forced to distribute the load more evenly throughout the day.

Until landing rights are priced sensibly, Canada's major airports will have a crowding problem. Unlike the airports' physical resources and the limited supply of air-traffic controllers, the pricing problem can be solved with the simple stroke of a pen.

SOURCE: Adapted from Michael Walker and Lorna Hoye, "Making Canada's airports safe," *The Globe and Mail*, June 1, 1989. M. Walker and L. Hoye are associated with the Fraser Institute.

(a) According to the article, why has the demand for air travel increased? How has supply not kept up with the demand? What have been the results?

(b) How has the structure of prices caused difficulties at Pearson International Airport? What solutions do the writers of the article suggest for the problem?

(c) Do you agree with the writers' analysis of the problem and their suggested solutions? Explain your point of view.

CHAPTER FIVE

The Entrepreneur

Objectives

a. Define entrepreneurs and explain their major functions and activities in a market economy.

b. Analyze specific case studies to determine the reasons for the entrepreneurs' success and identify the main characteristics of successful entrepreneurs.

c. Develop and evaluate a business plan.

d. Identify the major reasons why businesses fail and analyze case studies of business failures.

e. Outline and assess the three main options available to anyone who wishes to operate a business: starting from scratch, buying an existing business, or buying a franchise.

f. Examine a franchise and consider the major features of franchise arrangements.

g. Assess the major advantages and disadvantages of a franchise arrangement.

h. Develop and evaluate a cash-flow forecast.

We have examined how demand and supply—households and businesses—interact in competitive product markets. Economic activity is coordinated by the decisions of many individual buyers and sellers in the market. In this chapter, we focus on some of these key individual decision-makers—entrepreneurs.

Entrepreneurs are individuals who start their own businesses or who aggressively expand existing ones. They organize natural, human, and capital resources to produce goods and services. Students who establish their own child care, lawn-cutting, wordprocessing, or house-painting businesses are examples of entrepreneurs. So, too, are the local business people who have established their own stores, restaurants, appliance repair services, consulting agencies, and factories.

Some entrepreneurs have been spectacularly successful and are widely known. Steve Jobs and Steve Wozniak, for example, started their own electronics business in Jobs' garage with $1300 while they were still in their twenties. Their Apple Computer Corporation helped make the microcomputer a common appliance in the factory, office, and home. It also made Jobs and Wozniak multimillionaires. Other entrepreneurs fail, and their names are quickly forgotten.

Functions and Activities of Entrepreneurs

Entrepreneurs engage in some key activities in our market economy. They make decisions, organize productive resources, assume risks, innovate, and arrange financing for their businesses. Through all of these activities, they play an important role in co-ordinating economic activity.

(i) Make decisions   Entrepreneurs decide what goods and services to produce, how to produce them, and for whom. They must make key decisions about the design, feasibility, and marketability of their product.

(ii) Organize production   Entrepreneurs bring together productive factors—natural, capital, and human—to produce goods and services. They must determine how best to produce the goods and services, how much to produce, as well as what productive factors are needed and in what amounts. Is specialized machinery required, for example? What specific skills must the workers have, etc.?

(iii) Assume risk   There is no guarantee that entrepreneurs will make a profit or avoid losses. They bear the risks. They must assess the risks against the potential returns and be prepared to deal with problems as they arise.

(iv) Innovate   Entrepreneurs may introduce new products, new technology, or new ways of organizing a business. They often aim to meet new needs, and they must be able to adapt to changing conditions.

(v) Arrange financing   Entrepreneurs must bring together the financial resources necessary to establish their business. They are responsible for determining how much and what types of financing are required, where the financing may be obtained, and how it should be managed.

☐ Some Canadian Entrepreneurs

One of the best ways to learn about entrepreneurs and their businesses is to examine some actual examples. In this next section, you will be analyzing a number of different case studies dealing with Canadian entrepreneurs. As you read the cases, consider the following questions. Use the questions to guide your analysis.

(i) What need did the entrepreneurs identify and what innovative ideas did they put forward to fill that need?
(ii) What skills did they bring to their particular business? If they lacked some key skills, how did they propose to make up for these deficiencies?
(iii) What personal qualities do the entrepreneurs possess that are important to their success?
(iv) What source of financing did the entrepreneurs have? Was it adequate and how was it managed?
(v) How was the good or service marketed? How well did the entrepreneurs assess the size of the market, the competition, production costs, and the price of the product?
(vi) What risks were involved? How were they handled? What key decisions were the entrepreneurs required to make and why were they successful?

Not every case will provide answers to all of these questions. The circumstances surrounding every business are different. But the answers you do find will give you a good idea of what entrepreneurs must consider when they establish a business, and what qualities they need to be successful.

Case Study #1   Peninsula Farms Ltd.

Thirteen years after Sonia Jones started making yogurt from the daily offerings of her cow Daisy, Peninsula Farms Ltd. is milking the yogurt, frozen yogurt, and ice cream market in the Maritimes for $2.5 million in annual sales.

"We just expected to sell the milk to a health food store and we never expected to go beyond that," says Jones, reflecting on a business that started in her kitchen.

Born in England and raised in the US, the Spanish professor and aspiring writer didn't have ambitions to become a yogurt mogul. In 1972, with a freshly minted PhD in hand, she was unable to find a teaching job in New York.

Casting her net wider, she landed a position at Halifax's Dalhousie University. Husband Gordon sold his management consultant firm before the move that turned him into a farmer on the 10-ha property they bought near Lunenburg 90 minutes west of Halifax.

The first commodity they managed was beef cattle. Farming seemed easy until winter came and the cattle had to go in the barn. "That's when we found out what work is all about," Jones says. But it was good preparation for the 16-hour days she would put in producing yogurt and teaching at the university.

At about the same time that two young daughters were added to the family, Daisy was added to the herd. At first milk was given away to neighbours and friends when technical regulations prevented Jones from selling it as originally planned.

But the bother of washing bottles and the lack of a good yogurt in the Maritimes led her to experiment. Using only fresh or fresh-frozen fruit—"I didn't have access to artificial flavours or colouring"—Jones started making what many rate the best yogurt in the market.

From that modest start, Jones soon found herself supplying six health food stores in the Halifax area, earning $150 a week through the extra-curricular sales. Start-up costs were controlled with a unique recycling measure. Six pigs were brought in to feed on the spoiled batches of yogurt.

When some health food stores complained they were losing customers because they couldn't get her product, Jones responded by increasing production. "I had a certain strange sense of responsibility. When people said they needed it for their store, I felt that I couldn't really say no to one, if somebody else had it," Jones says.

Then David Sobey, chairman of Sobeys Inc., the Atlantic provinces' ubiquitous grocery chain, showed interest in adding the product to his dairy shelves. At that time, in 1977, the operation was still based in Jones's kitchen. But Sobey managed to persuade a reluctant Sonia Jones to expand her operation, one cow at a time, to get the milk needed to tackle Sobeys.

The business has outlived Daisy and the kitchen has long since given way to a factory built in 1979, when annual sales were at the $50 000 mark. The 44 employees at the factory now process milk bought from other dairy farms. Looking back, Sobey is surprised by the growth the company has enjoyed. Even Halifax-based Farmers Co-operative Dairy Ltd., with total annual sales of $109 million, acknowledges that Peninsula Farm has about equal market share with them in yogurt. The company also now supplies Save Easy/Superstore (a Weston chain), IGA, and various small local chains.

No longer active in the company on a day-to-day basis, Jones has moved to Halifax to be closer to the teaching job she has maintained since first arriving in Nova Scotia. While her title is chairman and chief executive officer, Jones's primary role is in product development and marketing. Among her projects is the launch of frozen yogurt products. She has also written a book and screenplay about the Peninsula Farm story.

SOURCE: Adapted and updated from Michael Redmond, "Maritimes yogurt queen started with cultured cow," *The Financial Post*, August 23, 1989.

Case Study #2   *Alias Research Inc.*

When the $2-billion Hubble space telescope zeroed in on Saturn, it was a small Toronto animation-software developer that turned billions of bits of scientific data into stunning pictures of a rare storm swirling around the red planet. The US National Aeronautics and Space Administration is using powerful software developed by Alias Research Inc. to transform the Hubble's computer data into meaningful pictures and three-dimensional graphs.

Alias had no such celestial goals when it opened in 1983. Founding president Stephen Bingham simply saw a need for new technology to make video animation easier—and cheaper. As freelance producers, he and Alias co-founder and vice-president Susan McKenna found video-production tools limiting.

In 1983, computer programmer Dave Springer and graphics designer Nigel McGrath accompanied McKenna and Bingham to a computer-graphics trade show in Detroit. Their mission: "If we could find the technology we needed, we'd buy it," says Bingham. "If we couldn't find the technology, we'd make it ourselves." When nothing on the show floor met their needs, the four went off to christen the firm born out of their fruitless visit. "Somebody said, 'What we need is an alias,' and somebody else said, 'Hey, that's a great name.'"

A year and a half later, Alias launched its Alias/1 video animation software. Since then, Alias has updated its flagship product and it produces more than 17 modules that enhance its capabilities.

Alias first made a name for itself in the entertainment industry. Film houses use Alias software to create spinning logos or animated clips for movies. Hollywood's Industrial Light & Magic, a division of director George Lucas's LucasArts, copped an Oscar for special effects using Alias software in the 1989 movie, *The Abyss*. The 1990 Sean Connery blockbuster, *The Hunt for Red October*, used Alias software to create an animated underwater sequence, and the company was involved in creating the special effects seen in *Terminator 2* in 1991.

Alias's early animation triumphs soon led Bingham into industrial design. He realized the potential of this market in 1985. When he strutted his stuff before automotive designers at General Motors, even computer illiterates found they could create on-screen models, cutting design time by up to half. "They immediately bought three systems," says Bingham.

Gradually, Alias convinced industrial designers they could use software instead of pencils, paper, and Plasticine models. Demos usually sell any doubters. Executives at Tokyo's Sony Corp. told Bingham they already had design software. He screened his demo anyway; in minutes, his demonstrator had drawn a 3-D Sony Discman on screen. "They just didn't know this existed," Bingham says. "Sale! Bam! That's how we market."

Sony joins the *Who's Who* of Alias users that includes Boeing, Honda, Kraft, and Reebok. Revenues have rocketed since Alias/1 debuted. In 1985, Alias brought in about $1.2 million; in 1990, when the firm went public, Alias recorded sales of $14.6 million, up from $9 million in 1989. And Alias is preparing to storm the mass market.

SOURCE: Adapted from Cathy Hilborn, "Animation software a designer's dream," *Profit*, March 1991. © 1991 *Profit*, The Magazine for Canadian Entrepreneurs.

Case Study #3 Barrier Technology Inc.

William Kolker credits his decision to buy the licence to a newly developed fire-retardant in 1986 to an unlikely combination of naivete and canny intuition. The licensor sold him on the coating's technical merits and rhymed off dozens of potential construction applications. About three months into the option period, though, Kolker realized how much additional research and development the formula needed. Lured by the prospect of a huge market, he signed a deal anyway.

The licensor's hearty sales pitch turned out to be accurate. A recently inked $15-million agreement with forest-products giant Weyerhaeuser Co. of Tacoma, Wash., will see Kolker's fire retardant laminate bonded to Weyerhaeuser wood and marketed to US building suppliers. But the handsome payoff comes only after Barrier Technology Inc., Kolker's Vancouver company, invested some $2 million and the better part of five years to develop its first commercial product.

Kolker admits he was a licensing greenhorn back in 1985 when business acquaintance Hal Ellis, a chemist and one-time NASA scientist, called him about a ceramic-based fire retardant he'd developed. Ellis had recently sold his formulation to Pyrotite Corp. of Miami. Was Kolker interested in buying the Canadian licence to manufacture it?

Kolker raised $450 000 through private investors in July, 1986, to launch Barrier. Pyrotite Coatings of Canada Inc., the firm's licensing arm, acquired the Canadian rights to manufacture and market the retardant, along with the right to market Pyrotite products worldwide. In return, the Miami licensor received a US$300 000 licensing fee, plus royalties of 15 percent on sales.

Giddy with his acquisition's potential, Kolker visited gypsum, waferboard, and paint companies across Canada—to no avail. The coating set too slowly to be practical in large-scale applications. Worse still, it couldn't meet regulatory standards unless applied in thick layers.

His dreams of rapid market penetration scorched but not extinguished, Kolker took Barrier public on the Vancouver Stock Exchange in September 1987. With shares trading at $1.95, the company raised $2 million to develop a pre-cured form of Pyrotite that met commercial demand. Seven months later, BC Rapid Transit Co. signed a contract for wood panels used in Vancouver's "Skytrain" transit system.

More good news followed. In April, 1989, the American Plywood Association called Kolker to discuss an industry crisis. Through the 1980s, he learned, US builders had relied on chemically impregnated lumber to meet building codes. But the wood began to rot, and now an estimated US$1 billion worth of plywood needed replacement.

Once again Barrier's chemists set to work—this time to improve the laminate's adhesion to plywood. Proof of their success came in September 1990, when Weyerhaeuser signed a tentative four-year deal to purchase, use, and resell Pyrotite laminate in the US, pending final building code approval. Regulatory approval was obtained in May 1991.

Kolker's next move is to broaden his Pyrotite base. He plans to hire more researchers to develop a host of products ranging from electrical cable trays to storage tank liners. Selling that many new products is a tall order, but Bill Kolker thinks he's earned his licence to sell.

SOURCE: Adapted from Jennifer Low, "Playing with fire pays off for Barrier," *Profit*, July/August 1991. © 1991 *Profit*, The Magazine for Canadian Entrepreneurs.

☐ Characteristics of Successful Entrepreneurs

Studies of entrepreneurs have revealed that those who are successful have several characteristics in common. Your analysis of the case studies will have revealed some of these key characteristics. Anyone with adequate financial resources can open a business in Canada, but not everyone is successful. What, therefore, helps make successful entrepreneurs?

☐ ☐ ☐ ☐ ☐

Women Breaking Ground

Studies have shown that women are a growing force in Canadian entrepreneurship. Women are starting new businesses at a rate three times that of men, and now own almost a quarter of all Canadian businesses with paid employees—approximately 200 200 in total in 1990. Most new businesses started by women have been in the business and personal services sectors.

A 1989 survey conducted by the Federal Business Development Bank showed that 40 percent of female entrepreneurs are between the ages of 35 and 44, almost three-quarters have post-secondary education, and over 50 percent are involved in the service sector.

Despite these strides, however, women entrepreneurs still face discrimination—from suppliers, financial institutions, government agencies, and sometimes their own employees—says a report from the Canadian Advisory Council on the Status of Women. The report also notes that 80 percent of women business owners also still earn less than their male counterparts. The Federal Business Development Bank has instituted a program to support women who want to expand their businesses. The trend in the growth of new businesses owned by women is expected to continue.

Applications

1. Why might women be starting new businesses at a faster rate than men?

2. What opportunities does business ownership offer women?

3. Why might women still be facing discrimination in starting their own businesses? How might they counter this discrimination?

(i) Independence   Entrepreneurs often have a desire to be their own boss, to have control of their own businesses. This drive for independence, however, is quite distinct from the characteristics of individuals who cannot accept authority or get along with others. Entrepreneurs are willing to take full responsibility for their businesses and to face the risks, but they also know how to work with others and when to look for help.

(ii) Stamina and good health   Working as an entrepreneur places heavy physical and emotional demands on the individual. In the early years of a business, at least, the entrepreneur has to work long hours for extended periods with little prospect of a vacation. Good health, stamina, and dedication are, therefore, important.

(iii) Self-confidence   Successful entrepreneurs are self-confident. They have a strong belief in their ability to thrive and survive. Self-confidence includes the ability to inspire others—workers, suppliers, and customers—with the value of the business and its products.

(iv) Good leadership   Leadership ability is necessary to motivate, inspire, and work along with employees. Entrepreneurs are often called upon to take the lead in completing sales and dealing with bankers and other creditors.

(v) Experience and knowledge   Entrepreneurs who are knowledgeable about and experienced in their area of business have a decided advantage. Knowledge and experience help them to identify needs, implement new techniques, and gain financing.

(vi) Willingness to take calculated risks   Successful entrepreneurs are willing to take risks. But, they cannot simply gamble—the risks they take must be carefully calculated to achieve their ends. Foolish risks are costly.

(vii) Ability to set realistic goals   Successful entrepreneurs are able to define clearly what it is they wish to accomplish. The goals they set are realistic, and plans to achieve them are carefully laid out.

(viii) Capacity for problem-solving   Entrepreneurs require creative, analytical, and critical thinking skills. They often need to be innovative to survive, and they must be able to step back from problems and analyze them objectively.

Of course, not all entrepreneurs have all of these characteristics and not all are absolutely essential for success. Luck, being at the right place at the right time, and a favourable economic climate are only some of the many other factors that can contribute to success. But entrepreneurs clearly must have many of the above qualities, or find them in others, to be successful. Table 5.1 shows how entrepreneurs rated the factors they feel contributed to their success.

Table 5.1 Factors contributing to business success—a survey

FACTOR	RESPONSE (PERCENT)
Product knowledge	96
Market knowledge	95
Industry knowledge	93
Responsiveness to change	88
Sticking to a mission	77
Devotion and hard work	71
Competitive advantages	70
Commitment to succeed	65
Aggressive marketing	65
Adequate planning	62
Responsiveness to customers	61
Clear market niche	59
Quality product or service	55
Personal selling talent	55
State-of-the-art equipment	54

SOURCE: 150 US independent businesses surveyed in *High Growth Entrepreneurial Ventures 1988.*

Respondents in this survey rated product, market, and industry knowledge as the greatest contributors to success.

□ □ □ □ □ □

Skill Development: Preparing a Business Plan

A **business plan** is a written outline of the management, financing, operating, and marketing plans of a proposed business. Before establishing any enterprise, business people should prepare a carefully considered business plan. An entrepreneur without a business plan is like a sailor without navigational equipment. It is difficult to stay on course without some sense of direction.

Developing a business plan helps entrepreneurs work through and answer the major questions relating to all aspects of their business. It allows them to identify the major strengths and weaknesses of their project, and devise appropriate strategies to deal with any problems. A business plan is also essential for those who wish to attract partners or secure finances from banks or other creditors. Creditors will require a written summary of the proposed business in order to assess its viability.

Let's work through the main components of a business plan using an example of a successful business project established by two students. Rita Ayolu and Michelle Morneau established their business, Cappit, to sell chimney caps door-to-door to homeowners.

Business Plan Components

1. Title Page
A title page helps make the plan look professional. First impressions are often lasting.

Cappit Business Plan	Year One	December 19XX

2. Business Information
This section provides basic information about the business. It should specify the type of business organization—sole proprietorship, partnership, corporation, or co-operative—and note whether or not the business is a franchise. These business organizations are outlined in more detail later in this chapter and in the next chapter. The type of business should also be specified. Entrepreneurs may be engaged in any number of different industries, such as retailing, wholesaling, manufacturing, agriculture, or services.

(a) Business Name: Cappit
Business Address: XXXXXXX
Telephone: XXXXXXXXX

(b) Type of business   Partnership
organization

(c) Is the business a franchise?   Yes____ No X

(d) What kind of business is it?   Retail

3. Company Management
This section should list the names and backgrounds of the company owners/managers, and include the names of any advisors with a brief description of their roles.

Rita Ayolu, owner. High school graduate. Has work experience.
Michelle Morneau, owner. High school graduate. Has work experience.

4. Operating and Marketing Plan
The operating and marketing plan is the heart of the business plan. It outlines how the firm intends to develop, price, sell, and market its product or service.

(a) Product or service. What is the product or service?
Sale of chimney caps. Chimney caps keep animals, birds, leaves and water from getting into the flue and damaging the chimney. The caps have a roof-like plate that covers the flue opening and a wire-net cage underneath. The person installing the caps squeezes together the metal legs that extend down from the cage and slips them inside the flue. The legs spring back to hold the cap firmly in place.

(b) Costs. What does it cost to provide the good or service to the customer? Costs may be expressed (i) by the hour, (ii) by the job, or (iii) by the unit. Include in the estimate labour, inventory, and overhead costs. Knowing how much it costs to provide the good or service to the customer is essential to assess whether the business can make a profit.

VARIABLE COSTS

Labour costs (per unit)

| Installation | $ 4.00 |
| Sales | $10.00 |

People were to be paid $4.00 for each cap they installed and $10.00 for each cap they sold.

Inventory

| Chimney caps (each) | $15.00 |
| Pamphlets and business cards | $ 1.00 |

The major stock of goods they needed to keep were the chimney caps, which they bought for $15.00 each from the manufacturer, as well as pamphlets and business cards.

Other Variable Costs

| (e.g. transportation) | $ 4.00 |

| FIXED COSTS OR OVERHEAD | $ 0.00 |

Fixed costs or overhead include such things as rent and telephone which do not vary with sales. Ayolu and Morneau do not have any overhead costs since both plan to work out of their parents' homes and store materials in their parents' garages.

(c) Price. What is the price each customer will be charged? Price can be shown per unit or per hour. This section should also indicate how the price was determined. It is important to arrive at a reasonable price for the product, based on the estimate of costs and competitors' prices. Too high or too low a price is likely to result in bankruptcy. Entrepreneurs must also allow an amount for their own wages.

Price per cap from manufacturer	$15.00
Cost of installation	$ 4.00
Sales costs	$10.00
Other expenses	$ 4.00
Return to owners (wages, interest, and profit)	$ 3.00
Price per chimney cap installed	$36.00

(d) Customers. What research was conducted to determine the number of potential customers and who they are? Research may include door-to-door, mail, telephone surveys, or interviews with competitors and/or suppliers. It is essential to identify the market for the good or service, and then to focus the sales effort on the best potential customers.

At first, the sales effort was concentrated in a neighbourhood with 15-year-old homes. It was discovered that people with older homes who had had no chimney problems did not see the need for the cap. Sales efforts were, therefore, concentrated in areas with newer homes. Potentially, all homeowners are customers.

(e) Promotion and Advertising. How do you propose to tell potential customers about the business and generate sales? Businesses must have a plan for promoting their product or service. Customers cannot buy a product they do not know anything about.

Door-to-door sales. Sales staff works a particular area together. Fliers are left where no one is home. Business cards and pamphlets are also produced and distributed.

(f) Competition. Who are the competitors? How long have they been in business? What are their strengths and weaknesses? To survive, a new business must be aware of its competitors and be prepared to challenge them, either by offering something they do not have or filling a need they have missed.

No other business in the area sells chimney caps *and* installations door-to-door. Caps are available from local lumber and hardware stores.

(g) Suppliers. Who are the suppliers and what are their terms? A business must have secure and reliable suppliers in place or it will not be able to operate.

Del Metal Works Ltd., Clinton, Ontario. First batch of 100 caps delivered free. Credit granted for the first 100 caps.

(h) Financing. How is the business to be financed? How much will be a personal cash contribution? How much will come from family or friends? How much can be secured by a bank loan? It is necessary to determine how a business will be financed. Without sufficient financial backing, the enterprise will soon founder.

Personal cash contribution—$1500. (From Michelle Morneau's savings). No other funds necessary.

(i) Registration and Insurance. Have the necessary permits and insurance been obtained? Entrepreneurs must check and comply with the laws covering their business in their area of operation. If the necessary documents are not obtained, the business could be shut down. In some municipalities, for example, businesses require a municipal licence. In some provinces, partnerships must be registered with the provincial government.

Licence obtained. Insurance obtained to cover Cappit against theft, damage, and liability.

SOURCE: Adapted from Gerry Blackwell, "Students generate profits like pros," *Small Business*, March 1989, pp. 14-15; and Ministry of Skills Development, *Guidelines and Application For Youth Venture Capital $7,500, Be Your Own Boss* (Toronto: Ministry of Skills Development).

Application

1. Suppose that next summer, instead of taking your usual summer job, you decide that you would like to establish your own business with the help of a few other students. Some of the more obvious examples of businesses established by young entrepreneurs include newspaper or newsletter publishing, wordprocessing, house painting, flier distribution, and tutoring. Choose an idea for a business and develop a business plan including all of the components outlined above.

◻ Why Businesses Fail

According to some estimates, approximately 80 percent of new businesses fail within their first five years of operation. Why do so many businesses fail? Some of the major reasons include personal characteristics of the entrepreneur, inadequate capital, failure to plan sufficiently, poor bookkeeping, excessive inventory, poorly motivated employees, and poor market identification. Let's examine these in a little more detail.

(i) Personal characteristics of the entrepreneur If new entrepreneurs lack some of the key characteristics for success, their chances of failure increase. Unwillingness or inability to work the long hours required, a lack of self-confidence, or an absence of knowledge and experience in the business, for example, will all add to the entrepreneur's difficulties.

(ii) Inadequate capital Many entrepreneurs start their businesses with inadequate capital. They underestimate the costs of day-to-day operations and overlook the fact that many firms do not make a profit in the first (and even second) year of operation. It is essential to plan ahead and ensure that adequate funding is available for the difficult first few years.

(iii) Failure to plan sufficiently Some business people start their businesses without goals or a clear direction. This lack of planning can be fatal. A clear business plan helps the entrepreneur outline a blue-

print for the establishment, operation, and future development of the firm.

(iv) Poor bookkeeping If bookkeeping is poorly done, it is impossible to gauge the financial situation of the firm. Decisions may, therefore, be made with wrong information, and these decisions may lead to bankruptcy.

(v) Excessive inventory While it is essential to have sufficient stock on hand and to take advantage of discounts in volume buying, stock must not sit on shelves or in a warehouse too long. The goods may deteriorate and it is expensive to hold them in inventory, especially when interest rates are high. Unsold stock does not pay the interest on the funds borrowed to purchase the inventory, and if interest rates rise considerably, the firm could lose money. Funds tied up in unsold inventory might also be used more profitably elsewhere.

(vi) Poorly motivated employees We have all had experiences with firms whose employees are rude or indifferent and convince us never to deal with that company again. Poorly motivated—as well as dishonest—employees can cost a company dearly.

(vii) Poor market identification Business people may have a poor perception of the market they are entering. As a result, they may fail to price their good or service appropriately, underestimate the strength of the com-

petition, target the wrong customers, or use ineffective marketing methods.

Business failures, of course, may be the result of a combination of these factors as well as other circumstances. As you examine the following case studies, consider what factors contributed to the failure of the business.

Case Study #4   Myrias Research

The high-technology success story has become something of a cliché. An inspired computer *wunderkind* labours obsessively in a garage to develop a technological breakthrough that leads to fame and fortune.

For a time, Edmonton's Myrias Research Corp. followed the script perfectly. Two university graduates came together in 1982 with a plan to build a mini-supercomputer that would find a profitable niche between desktop PCs and the room-sized mainframes used by scientists. Backed by $500 000 from family and friends, they set to work in an Edmonton basement.

Eight years later, whatever romance surrounded the original notion was gone. Myrias took $30 million in government money with it when it collapsed in 1990, dashing one of Alberta's best hopes to make that province a technological leader.

Accounts of what went wrong vary—the founders say venture capitalists who gained control of the firm didn't understand the machine or its market; management blames a chronic lack of capital for high-tech companies. The benefit of hindsight may point to another conclusion: Myrias took its product to market too soon.

Everyone agrees the task was daunting from the start. Since the mid-1970s, Minneapolis-based Cray Research Inc. has dominated the supercomputer market with machines that use extremely powerful microprocessors or "chips" to solve problems sequentially. Myrias's founders took a different approach. They turned to parallel processing—linking hundreds of microprocessors together and dividing a complex problem among a number of chips to arrive at an answer.

The US Department of Defense was an early believer in parallel processing. Backed by $5.5 million in research contracts, Myrias delivered its prototype to the Pentagon in late 1986. The Department of Defense approved the machine. Myrias's founders wanted to go to the market with a machine that encoded the functions in the hardware (microchips), but the venture capitalists who took over the firm chose to rely on software. They felt the founders' concerns were more academic, and not commercially viable. The $1.5-million SPS-2 the firm took to market in 1988, however, failed. In 1990, Myrias introduced a faster version of the machine, but it was too late.

Management blames chronic funding problems as the root of the problem. Myrias needed another $40 million for a proper sales and marketing campaign, but with public and private sources still waiting for returns on the $40 million already invested, Myrias found the taps had run dry. "It's very, very difficult to start a high-tech company in this country," says Myrias's president. Raising capital in good times is tough enough; the backers say doing it on the brink of the recession was impossible.

A Myrias competitor noted another problem: "You've got to get some early successes to convince customers you're on to a winner...If you miss with your first two shots in this business, you usually don't get a third."

SOURCE: Adapted from Mark Stevenson, "Myrias crashes in rush to market," *Profit*, March 1991. © 1991 *Profit*, The Magazine for Canadian Entrepreneurs.

Case #5   Chatham Run Inc.

In 1986 Steve Cross, the president of Ottawa's Chatham Run Inc., flew to California to cement a relationship with Patagonia Inc., one of North America's top outdoor-clothing suppliers. A close relationship with suppliers was key to what Cross calls his "concept-merchandising" strategy: creating the ideal store environment for full lines from a select number of makers of high-end hiking and climbing gear. No detail went unnoticed: from knowledgeable sales staff down to rustic pine fixtures, Cross says Chatham Run aspired to be "the Ralph Lauren of technical clothing." Concept merchandisers like Esprit and Polo had met with great success in the US, says Cross. His experience as an outdoor enthusiast and retail manager convinced him the time was right to introduce the idea to Canada.

Steady sales growth and a growing list of imitators proved him right. Sales at the downtown Ottawa location were double the industry average in the first year. Buoyed by his early successes, Cross brought in outside investors and spun off what amounted to six new locations in 18 months. Sales continued to climb. But Chatham Run was paddling into troubled waters.

With working capital securing just 10 percent of inventory—well below the retail standard of 50 percent—Chatham Run's future rested on the shaky foundation of supplier credit. Cross's close relationship with Patagonia allowed him long terms of credit, but when a shakeup occurred in 1989, Cross found himself dealing with a new supplier that wasn't willing to base credit terms on anything but the bottom line. Other suppliers tightened their credit terms, too, in early 1990. Cross filed for bankruptcy four months later.

In many ways, the success of Chatham Run's concept created the company's problems. Cross feels the supplier wanted to showcase their concept and so continued to offer favourable credit terms and encourage expansion—until the plug was pulled. The supplier suggests that Cross misinterpreted their intentions. Other observers feel the company expanded too quickly, before it was a solid local success owning its own inventory. One observer noted: "The company suffered from unrealistic expectations. Continually opening one store after another and relying on suppliers to finance us eventually left us nowhere."

SOURCE: Adapted from Catherine Callaghan and Mary Ann Simpkins, "Dream weaver snagged on the bottom line," *Profit*, January/February 1991. © 1991 *Profit*, The Magazine for Canadian Entrepreneurs.

■ Options for Business Operation

Starting a business from scratch is not the only option open to entrepreneurs, however. They may decide to buy an existing business or a franchise. Each has its own risks and opportunities, advantages and disadvantages.

☐ The New Business—"Starting from Scratch"

Starting a new business is the choice of most first-time entrepreneurs. A new business is the most difficult and most risky venture, but also potentially the most personally rewarding. The business is your idea, you organize it, select the location, and hire the workers. You make the decisions. The reward is seeing your own creation grow and prosper. But at the same time, since you have to provide answers to all the questions, it is clearly much more difficult than buying an established business.

Since most businesses start in a very modest way with a small staff and minimum overhead, the owner must clearly understand all aspects of the business, be ready to undertake any task, and work very long hours. The success or failure of the business in large part depends on the knowledge, skill, and just plain hard work of the owner.

☐ Buying an Existing Business

Buying an existing business means that some of the risk and much of the work have been dealt with already. Trained workers, secured suppliers, a business method, and appropriate premises are in place. The business is a functioning entity. Information on past costs and revenues can be obtained from the firm's records. It is possible to step into a fully operational and successful business.

But two important and related questions should be answered before anyone rushes in to buy a business:
1. Why do the owners want to sell?
2. What is the business's true worth?
The owners may wish to sell because they are ill or retiring, but they may also be selling because they see that profits have peaked and the business's prospects for the future are poor. It is important to determine why the business is being sold.

To answer the second question—the worth of the business—it is often best to hire a professional. Though an additional expense, a sound professional assessment of the business can avert disaster.

☐ Buying a Franchise

A **franchise** is a contractual arrangement under which a person or company (the **franchisor**) grants another person or company (the **franchisee**) the right to pro-

Table 5.2 Franchising in Canada
(billions of dollars in sales)

BUSINESS FORMAT	
Food service and hospitality	$ 7.4
Retailing	16.3
Services	3.3
Total	27.0
PRODUCT AND TRADE NAME	
Auto dealers	34.8
Gasoline service stations	11.7
Soft drink bottlers	4.0
Total	50.5
Total franchise industry	77.5

SOURCE: Price Waterhouse Ltd. Franchise Association, 1991.

duce or sell a product or service in a specified area under the franchisor's name.

Franchising has become an integral part of Canadian business. More than 1000 franchisors operate an estimated 50 000 outlets in a whole range of businesses from child care to auto mufflers. In the late 1980s, franchising accounted for over $70 billion in Canadian retail trade. Table 5.2 shows the major areas in which franchises operate in Canada.

While 80 percent of new businesses fail within their first five years, it is estimated that only 20 percent of franchises go under. One major reason is that franchisors are generally well-established companies with management, marketing, and purchasing experience. They provide their franchisees with a proven business formula.

Usually, by terms of the contract, the franchisee pays the franchisor a one-time fee for the franchise, plus a percentage of sales and a payment for advertising. The franchisor generally provides training for the franchisee and his or her personnel; assistance in advertising, financing, and leasing; supply of products or equipment; and use of the franchisor's logos and trademarks. A well-known trademark is a decided advantage when establishing a business.

The franchisees, however, retain some autonomy— the degree of autonomy varies with the franchise—but they must also conform to the terms and conditions outlined in the franchisor's contract. With a franchise, you purchase a "package." As a result, individual freedom and experimentation are limited. When first entering the business and learning about it, the constraints of the contract may not be irksome. But, as the franchisees gain experience, the terms may become confining. The scope for expansion is often limited, unless the franchisee buys additional franchises.

What do franchisors gain from the arrangement? They receive the franchise fee, of course, which may range from a few hundred to a few hundred thousand dollars, and a percentage of the franchise's sales. Since the franchisees finance the establishment of the outlets, the franchisor's returns can grow rapidly. Having independently-minded entrepreneurs run the outlets also frees the franchisor of some management responsibilities and takes advantage of entrepreneurial qualities. But there are drawbacks. Franchisors may not always select suitable franchisees, and making sure all the terms of the contract are followed can be difficult.

Consider the advantages and disadvantages of franchising as you read the following case study.
(i) What are the terms of the franchise contract? In other words, consider the roles and responsibilities of the franchisor and franchisee in the business.
(ii) What are the costs and benefits of franchising to the franchisor and franchisee?
(iii) What makes the business particularly well suited to franchising?
(iv) What qualities of the successful entrepreneur does the franchisor show? Is it advantageous for the franchisee to have the same qualities? Why or why not?
(v) Can you see any problems with the franchise? If so, what are they and how may they be solved?

Case Study #6   Ceiling Doctor International Inc.

"It's not a glamorous business," said Kaaydah Schatten. "It's only a profitable business." Schatten, a Native Canadian, is founder of Ceiling Doctor International Inc., a leading ceiling industrial cleaner. Founded in 1984, the company had established 23 cleaning franchises in Canada and 10 in the US in its first five years—and expansion has continued, reaching into Southeast Asia and the Far East.

Schatten has always been a go-getter. Born on a reserve in Campbell River, BC, the second of six children, she was selling eggs to the "rich" at the age of seven. She noted that the "rich" put their money into real estate. When her family moved to Nanaimo, BC, she applied for a job in a real estate office at the age of twelve. It paid very little, but she typed the offers and learned about mortgages. By seventeen, she was an honours student, working three part-time jobs and heading for success.

Then in 1972, she was thrown through the windshield of a car in an accident. She lost a hip and a lung and spent a year on her back—thinking. Her insurance compensation amounted to $7000, after legal fees. With this, her first real money, she bought a fourplex, improved it, remortgaged it, and bought more property. By the age of twenty-six, she had made her first $5 million on paper. But the federal government cancelled its multiple unit residential building subsidy in 1981, and she lost nearly all she had made. Schatten searched for a business not subject to government policy changes.

Her experiences renovating properties led her to ceiling cleaning. Until 1968, there was no efficient way of cleaning acoustic ceiling tiles. When dirty, they had to be replaced. Schatten looked at several cleaning methods, including then recently developed methods, and decided they could be improved upon. She spent a year mixing chemicals with the help of a local chemist and searching for a suitable high-pressure pump to spray them in a mist.

In 1983, she and her dentist companion moved to Toronto where the bulk of the head office ceilings were. They bought a customer list from a defunct ceiling cleaning firm, and for the first two years, they did all of the cleaning themselves. Then they began to sell franchises.

North American franchises sold for $25 000 each. The fee included ten days' training for the owner, pumping equipment, cleansers, and advertising support. Franchisees paid royalties of 6 percent of sales in Canada and 8 percent of sales in the US. In 1989, half of the franchisees were women, and at least three had as junior partners husbands who had given up jobs worth $50 000 to $60 000 a year.

Schatten sold the master franchise for Japan to Ohkawa Tekko Iron Works Ltd., a leading Japanese steel fabricator, in 1988. Ohkawa also bought franchising rights to Southeast Asia and the rest of the Far East, including China, for $1 million. From modest beginnings, Ceiling Doctor International has grown to be one of the largest ceiling cleaning franchisors in the world.

SOURCE: Adapted from Gordon Donaldson, "Vaulting ambition," *Canadian Business*, January 1989.

□ □ □ □ □ □

Skill Development: Preparing a Cash-Flow Forecast

A **cash-flow forecast**, the second key element in a business plan, is a monthly statement of a firm's projected receipts and expenditures. In other words, it outlines how much a business expects to receive in cash and from whom, and when funds must be spent to pay the bills. With the cash-flow forecast, an entrepreneur can identify when shortages of funds are likely to occur, and not only how much outside funding might be needed, but also when it will be required. The business plan and cash-flow forecast are essential for all business operations, whether new businesses or franchises. Let's work through an example of how to prepare a cash-flow forecast.

George's Grass Grooming

George Grubwinkler, a twenty-year-old student, has decided to establish his own lawn-care business during the months of June, July, and August next summer. George's parents have agreed to loan him the family pickup truck. George makes the following calculations for his cash-flow forecast.

CASH RECEIPTS (MONEY RECEIVED)

(a) Total Sales

George charges a flat rate of $30.00 for cutting the grass and trimming the edges on suburban lots of 15 x 20 m in his neighbourhood. Charges for smaller and larger lots vary on a *pro rata* basis (proportionally). He estimates that he can cut the grass and trim the lawn edges of four lots per day. He intends to work six days per week.

Total sales per day will, therefore, be $30.00 (price per lot) x 4 (number of lots per day) = $120. Total sales per month will be $120 x 26 (days per month)= $3 120.00

	$3 120.00

(b) Loans

George will have a loan from his sister of $500.00.   500.00

(c) Invested Savings

George is investing $500.00 of his savings.   500.00

CASH DISBURSEMENTS (MONEY PAID OUT)

(a) Purchase of Equipment

Lawn edger	$60.00
Miscellaneous (rake, gas and oil containers, etc.)	$100.00
	$160.00

(b) Rental of Equipment

Lawn mower (per month)	$100.00
Pickup truck (per month)	$600.00
	$700.00

(c) Labour Expenses

George will pay himself $40 per day ($40 x 26 days a month) for living expenses.	$1040.00
He will pay a friend $150 to distribute flyers five days a month.	150.00
	$1190.00

(d) Materials

This is the total cost of all materials needed to provide the service, including oil and gas for the truck and lawn mower, and bags for the cut grass.   250.00

(e) Business Licences and Fees

This includes the cost of registering the business and obtaining the necessary permits.   20.00

(f) Advertising

The cost of lawn signs, flyers, and advertisements in the local newspaper.   75.00

(g) Insurance

Premiums for theft, damage, and liability.   200.00

(h) Office Expenses

George operates his business from his room in his home. His office expenses are zero. He does, however, rent an answering machine.   120.00

(i) Other Expenses

Printing of flyers and business cards.	100.00
	$4 525.00

From these calculations, George draws up the following cash-flow forecast.

George's Grass Grooming Cash-Flow Forecast

CASH RECEIPTS

Month	June	July	August	Total
Estimated sales	3 120	3 120	3 120	9 360
Loan from sister	500			500
Other (savings)	500			500
Total	4 120	3 120	3 120	10 360

CASH DISBURSEMENTS

	June	July	August	Total
Purchase of equipment	160			160
Rental of equipment	700	700	700	2 100
Labour expenses	1 190	1 190	1 190	3 570
Materials	250	250	250	750
Business licenses and fees	20	20	20	60
Advertising	75	75	75	225
Insurance	100	100	100	300
Office expenses	40	40	40	120
Other expenses	100	100	100	300
Total	2 635	2 475	2 475	7 585

NET CASH

(i.e., Total Cash Receipts minus Total Cash Disbursements)

Month	June	July	August
Monthly Surplus	1 485	645	645
Monthly Deficit	0	0	0
Cumulative Surplus or (Deficit)	1 485	2 130	2 775

Of course, different businesses will have different kinds of expenditures and different sources of receipts.

Application

1. Develop a monthly cash-flow forecast to complete the business plan you developed in the previous Skill Development section on page 106.

Summary

a. Entrepreneurs are individuals who start their own businesses or who aggressively expand existing ones. They organize natural, capital, and human resources to produce goods and services and assume the risks involved in the business.

b. Studies have shown that successful entrepreneurs share some common characteristics including independence, stamina and good health, self-confidence, leadership abilities, business knowledge, and the abilities to take reasonable risks, set realistic goals, and think creatively and analytically.

c. A business plan is a written outline of the management, financing, operating, and marketing plans of a proposed business. It is essential to secure financing and to ensure that all major questions have been answered.

d. A large percentage of new businesses fail within their first five years. Common reasons are personal difficulties of the entrepreneur, inadequate capital, a failure to plan sufficiently, poor bookkeeping, excessive inventory, poorly motivated employees, and poor market identification.

e. Entrepreneurs have three main options: starting from scratch, buying an existing business, or buying a franchise. Starting from scratch involves the highest degree of risk, but also offers considerable personal satisfaction if successful. The two most important questions to answer before buying an existing business are: 1. Why do the owners want to sell?; and 2. What is the firm's true worth?

f. A franchise is a contractual arrangement under which a person or company (franchisor) grants another person or company (franchisee) the right to produce or sell a product or service in a specified area under the franchisor's name.

g. Advantages for the franchisee include the proven business formula of the franchisor, training programs, advertising assistance, a secure supply of products and equipment, and use of the franchisor's logo or trademark. Disadvantages include limits on individual freedom, innovation, and opportunities for growth.

Advantages for the franchisor are revenues from the franchise fee and royalties, and delegation of management responsibilities to the franchisee. Disadvantages include problems in finding suitable franchisees and difficulties in ensuring that all terms of the contract are met.

h. A cash-flow forecast is a statement of what a business expects to receive in cash and when funds must be spent to pay the bills. It is an important part of a business plan.

▊ Review of Key Terms

Define the following key terms introduced in this chapter and provide examples where appropriate.

entrepreneur   franchisee

business plan   franchisor

franchise   cash-flow forecast

▊ Application and Analysis

1. (a) In groups, develop a questionnaire (10-15 questions) to help people assess whether they have the qualities characteristic of successful entrepreneurs. Keep your questions simple.

(b) When your questionnaire is complete, exchange copies with another group. Fill in the questionnaires individually and evaluate the results. Do you think you could be a successful entrepreneur? How well did the questionnaire help you to assess your qualities?

2. Prepare a short report on a successful entrepreneur in your community. You could conduct interviews, examine promotional material distributed by the company, and check for newspaper articles about the business. Consider the following points in your report:

(a) type of business (retail, consulting, etc.)

(b) management structure

(c) number of employees

(d) how the business fills a need

(e) how the business was started

(f) why the business has been successful.

3. (a) Using an organizer like the one shown below, assess the advantages and disadvantages of starting a new business *vs.* buying a franchise. Add any other criteria you feel are important.

CRITERIA	NEW BUSINESS	FRANCHISE
Risk involved		
Satisfaction for owner		
Opportunities for expansion		
Potential returns		
Degree of independence		
Support available		

(b) Which option would you choose? Explain why.

4. Develop a hypothetical business plan and cash-flow forecast (covering the first three months of the firm) for any one of the case studies in this chapter.

5. Case Study—Ayre's Ltd.
In December 1991, Ayre's Ltd. of St. John's, Newfoundland, announced plans to close most of its stores and liquidate its stock in an attempt to salvage some stores and holdings in St. John's. Ayre's was only one of a number of retail corporations to announce sales or closures in 1991. Others included Dylex (closing Town and Country outlets), Grafton (selling Maher shoe stores), and Henry Birks and Sons (closing some of its jewellery outlets).

Ayre's was founded in 1859. In 1991, it included the J. Michael's chain, Kristy Allan stores, and Berries. Sales at the three divisions totalled about $40 million in 1990 when the corporation broke even, but 1991 was a different story. Despite a restructuring in the spring of 1991 and an injection of $4 million, the situation only got worse. Christmas sales fell far below expectations and the company was forced to make the closings as a result. It owed $15 million to $20 million.

What brought the collapse? According to Ayre's president Miller Ayre, the Goods and Services Tax and cross-border shopping resulted in sales that were "dramatically worse than budgeted for. The consumers' reluctance to spend is clear-cut and massive, particularly when it comes to ladies wear apparel. The recession [1990-1991] is deeper than people are prepared to recognize." According to one retail consultant, "This is the worst period [for retailers] since the Depression." Another consultant described the situation as "largely a battle for survival" among store owners—especially those in the clothing and jewellery sectors.

(a) Outline the factors which led Ayre's to liquidate its three chains.

(b) Explain why each factor had an impact on a retail corporation such as Ayre's.

(c) How is this case of a business "failure" different from the others included in this chapter?

6. Case Study—"Forever Green"
Fil Rosati, Mary Citton, and Steve Morris have invented a new game. It's called "Forever Green." The game will soon be hitting the toy markets and the three inventors hope it will also go over with a pollution-free bang in schools and environmental studies programs.

"Forever Green" has a colourful game board that doesn't exactly lie flat because it's made of recyled materials, and a set of 600 environmental questions aimed at people aged at least 8.

The three inventors—Rosati is a product developer for a manufacturer, Citton is a teacher, and Morris is in marketing—collaborated once before. In 1983, they came up with a children's trivia game called IQ2000, which has sold almost 5 million copies worldwide. It did well enough in Canada, selling 400 000, but it was a particular hit in Germany where it was the top children's game for six years.

Putting a new environmentally sound game together had its harrowing moments. Green chic is a rapidly changing field. Sometimes what was environmentally horrifying at one moment became environmentally correct later, or *vice versa*. The trio were kept scrambling to make sure they wouldn't be printing thousands of game cards with an embarrassing political blunder.

They wrote 2000 questions and threw out more than they kept, weeding out the ones that seemed too difficult, too easy, too ridiculous, or too technical. They then roped in a consultant to winnow them down to 600 by removing questions that were inappropriate or controversial.

Another problem was the varying standards of environmental programs and restrictions across Canada. But the real headaches came when they had to figure out how to manufacture the game without trampling over the principles they were celebrating. They obviously couldn't think of using oil-based inks or varnish.

Forget shrink-wrap. Plastic trays and dividers were an automatic no-no. Even the little coloured player markers had to be made of recycled plastic.

And there was no way to get around it: the game cards and board started out as trees. The more games they sell, the more ex-trees get involved. Morris, Rosati, and Citton tackled the issue by making sure the game is made of recycled material. They also enclose a form in each copy that can be mailed in to have a tree planted in the name of the game-owner, confirmed in a certificate sent back to him or her.

SOURCE: Adapted from Janice Dineen, "Creators of game are green with enthusiasm," *The Toronto Star*, September 24, 1991. Reprinted with permission—the Toronto Star Syndicate.

(a) Evaluate "Forever Green's" chances for success. What factors does the venture have in its favour? What are the drawbacks?

(b) Try to find out whether the game was successful or not and why.

CHAPTER SIX

Business Organization and Finance

Objectives

a. Identify and compare the major forms of business ownership in Canada.

b. Outline the major characteristics of sole proprietorships and partnerships, and assess their main advantages and disadvantages.

c. Define a corporation, outline how it is financed through stocks and bonds, and evaluate it as a form of business organization.

d. Demonstrate how to read stock market quotations and interpret stock market indicators, including the Dow Jones Industrial Average and the TSE 300 Composite Index.

e. Identify the major features of a co-operative and assess its advantages and disadvantages.

f. Prepare and evaluate balance sheets and income statements for a firm.

g. Assess a firm's liquidity and profitability using relevant data and ratios drawn from balance sheets and income statements.

h. Define and identify crown corporations and evaluate their advantages and disadvantages.

One of the first decisions made by entrepreneurs is what form of business organization they should adopt. Canada's modified competitive market economy offers five major options, including the sole proprietorship, partnership, corporation, co-operative, and government enterprise. Each has its own particular advantages, disadvantages, and financing requirements.

In this chapter, we examine each form of business enterprise and consider the role it plays in our economy. We also examine the financial statements and calculations that enable a business owner or buyer to assess the financial position of a firm. How efficiently is it operating? How well is it meeting its objectives? This assessment can be applied to any firm, no matter what its form of business ownership.

□ □ □ □ □

Business Organizations in Canada

Sole Proprietorships

In 1975, Rena Ricardo established a restaurant in Saskatoon with an investment of $50 000. She is the sole owner. With four employees, her net earnings totalled $35 000 last year.**

Raoul Echandi operates his own small electrical appliance repair business from the converted basement of his home. His capital investment in the sole proprietorship totalled $25 000 last year, and his accounting profit was $15 000. Raoul lives in a small Nova Scotia town.**

Partnerships

Abdul Hassan and Lee Wong have owned and operated their home decoration store, Inner Space, in a large suburban mall since 1976. They specialize mainly in the sale of artificial silk flowers, trees, plants, and accessories. Their business, a partnership, had an accounting profit of $47 000 on a capital investment of $76 000 last year.**

Nicola and Raphael Vander Zalm's dairy farm is a partnership established in 1962. Net earnings totalled $70 000 last year on a total capital investment of $475 000. Nicola and Raphael are both owners and operators of this farm in southern Quebec.**

Corporations

Canadian Pacific Limited (CP) was incorporated on February 16, 1881 to build a transcontinental railway linking eastern Canada with British Columbia. The company is involved in rail, ship, and truck transportation, energy, forest products, real estate and hotel operations, telecommunications, and manufacturing. The head office is located in Montreal. CP's assets total more than $20 1/4 billion and its profits in 1990 exceeded $355 million. The company employs over 72 000 workers. Seventy-five percent of the corporation's shares are held by Canadians and ownership is widely distributed.*

The Ford Motor Company of Canada Limited is 100 percent owned by the Ford Motor Company of Dearborn, Michigan, USA. The company makes, assembles, and sells cars, trucks, tractors, and related automotive parts and accessories in Canada, New Zealand, and Australia. Founded in 1911, the firm has its head office in Oakville, Ontario. Total assets exceed $3.6 billion. In 1990, the company sustained a loss of $57 million. Over 28 000 workers are employed by Ford Canada.*

The Bank of Nova Scotia was founded in 1832. Its head office is located in Halifax, Nova Scotia. A variety of banking and financial services are provided by 30 000 employees in the bank's 1017 branches in Canada and 231 branches overseas. The bank is Canada's fourth largest, with assets totalling $87 1/4 billion. Profit in 1990 exceeded $510 million. Ninety-seven percent of the company's shares are held by Canadians and ownership of them is widely distributed.*

Co-operatives

United Grain Growers Limited (UGG) was founded in 1906. The head office is in Winnipeg. The company handles and stores grain produced in western Canada on its own account and for the Canadian Wheat Board. It also processes grain and forage seed, livestock feed and feed supplements, fertilizer, agricultural chemicals, and twine. In addition, the company is engaged in insurance, financial services, magazine and newsletter publication, and pellet manufacturing. Total assets exceeded $380 million in 1990, and net income equalled $690 000. Employees total about 1600. UGG is owned by its members, who may own up to a maximum of 25 shares each and who must be farmers and customers of the company.*

Co-op Fédérée du Québec was founded in 1922. Its head office is located in Montreal. The co-operative processes poultry, other livestock, and dairy products. It also manufactures and distributes feeds, fertilizers, and farm equipment. Assets exceed almost $300 million. Dividends paid to the members totalled $6 3/4 million in 1990. Employees total about 3600. The co-operative is owned by its members.*

Vancity Savings Credit Union was founded in 1946. Its head office is located in Vancouver, British Columbia. The credit union provides retail financial services through its 22 branches in Vancouver, staffed by 728 employees. Total revenue in 1990 was over $267 million, with a net income of almost $6.5 million. The credit union is owned by its members.*

Government Enterprises

Canada Post is a federal crown corporation established in 1981 with its headquarters in Ottawa. It is responsible for the collection, processing, and delivery of as many as 9 billion messages and parcels each year. In 1990, total sales revenue reached almost $3.7 billion and net income almost $150 million. The corporation has approximately 60 000 full-time and part-time employees and $2.5 billion in assets. Sixty percent of its 15 000 retail outlets are operated by private business and 80 percent of total mail volume handled by Canada Post is provided by private business.***

The British Columbia Hydro and Power Authority is a provincial crown corporation engaged in the generation, transmission, and distribution of electricity in British Columbia. The corporation, founded in 1964, has its head office in British Columbia. Its assets total over $9 billion.

Profits reached $160 million in 1990. The authority has almost 5000 workers and is 100 percent owned by the government of British Columbia.*

The Toronto Transit Commission (TTC), founded in 1921, is in the urban commuter transit business. Current capital assets total about $2 billion. The TTC has an operating subsidy of $150 million. The Commission employs nearly 9800 workers and is totally owned by the Municipality of Metropolitan Toronto. The 1991 budget was planned at $671 million with a projected ridership of 450 million.*

* SOURCES: Financial Post, *Survey of Industrials, 1989*, 63rd ed., (Toronto, 1989); Harold W. Blakley *et al.* (eds.), *The Blue Book of Canadian Business 1989* (Toronto: Canadian Newspaper Services International, 1989); Financial Post, *Financial Post 500* (Toronto: Summer 1991).
** Actual or typical examples. With actual examples, the names have been changed to preserve anonymity.
*** SOURCE: Canada Post, *Annual Report 1990-1991*.

Applications

1. Develop an organizer to highlight and compare the major characteristics of the various types of business organizations described above. Your criteria should include the following:
(a) form of ownership
(b) number of employees
(c) amount of assets
(d) length of time in operation
(e) facilities required
(f) type(s) of business (e.g., retailing, financial, diversified, etc.).
2. Summarize the major similarities and differences among the various forms of business ownership.

▪ Forms of Business Enterprise

From the examples given at the beginning of this chapter, you will have some idea of what characterizes the major forms of business enterprise in Canada. Let's examine them more closely.

☐ Sole Proprietorship

A **sole** (or **single**) **proprietorship** is a form of business organization wholly owned by one person. Of the

hundreds of thousands of businesses operating in Canada, most are sole proprietorships. Almost always, the owner operates or manages the business, though there may be several employees. Sole proprietorships predominate in the retail and service industries—boutiques, restaurants, corner stores, service stations, and repair shops are just a few examples. Sole proprietorships are also common among doctors, dentists, lawyers, farmers, mechanics, consultants, land surveyors, and others who offer professional services.

Advantages

The sole proprietorship has many significant advantages, as its popularity affirms. It is relatively easy to establish, flexible in operation, has the owner's personal involvement, allows the owner freedom of action, and is easy to terminate. The legal requirements—that of registering with the local government—are minimal and easily met. Since the single proprietor is the boss, decisions can be made relatively quickly and freely, without the need for agreement among a large number of people. Sole proprietors are generally highly motivated, because the business is their creation. They can take pride in ownership and the profits are theirs—for the most part directly related to the effort and expertise they bring to the business.

Disadvantages

Sole proprietorships are mainly financed from the personal resources of their owners and from what they are able to borrow. Proprietorships are generally restricted in their borrowings because they are subject to **unlimited liability**. That is, if the owner is unable to meet his or her financial obligations, personal assets—such as home and car—as well as business assets can be claimed by creditors. Most sole proprietorships, therefore, are businesses that do not require large initial capital investments.

Lack of continuity is also a disadvantage. If the owner dies or sells the firm, the proprietorship is dissolved. This prospect of impermanence may discourage creditors, who are generally concerned with long-term stability. The sole proprietor may also have no one to rely on when sick or on vacation.

Finally, the sole proprietorship puts a great deal of responsibility on a single individual, the owner-manager. He or she may not have the expertise to handle the wide variety of tasks necessary for the successful operation of the business—such as purchasing, manufacturing, managing, marketing, and bookkeeping. Furthermore, resources may not be available to hire adequate skilled or professional help.

☐ Partnership

A **partnership** is a form of business organization in which two or more individuals enter a business as owners and share the profits and losses. Partnerships are common in service industries, such as small stores and restaurants, and in the professions, such as accounting and law.

The partnership agreement usually specifies what each partner is to contribute to the firm in terms of funds, expertise, and time. It also outlines each partner's share of profits and responsibility for losses, both during the partnership and in the case of its dissolution.

Advantages

Partnerships have some advantages over sole proprietorships. They pool the funds, energies, and talents of two or more individuals. Moreover, with greater personal and business assets, partnerships can borrow more easily from banks and obtain credit from suppliers.

Partners also enjoy the pride of ownership and the satisfaction of being self-employed. The profits (and losses) are theirs. These benefits help ensure a high level of motivation.

Like the proprietorship, the partnership has few legal restrictions. Legal fees are usually incurred in setting up a satisfactory partnership agreement and the partnership must be registered with the provincial government, but other legal requirements are minimal.

Disadvantages

The disadvantages of the partnership are basically similar to those of the proprietorship: unlimited liability, limited capital, and possible lack of continuity.

Partners together are liable for the debts of the business. If one partner fails to pay his or her share, the others are liable to pay it. Partners, too, may be forced to sell personal as well as business assets to pay outstanding partnership debts. Partnerships, however, may include **limited partners** who are not involved in running the firm and whose liabilities extend only to the amount of their financial investment. While a partnership usually has more capital at its disposal than a proprietorship, it has less access to financing than a corporation. Many business operations today need vastly larger amounts of capital than can be obtained from a partnership.

A partnership is dissolved with the death, insolvency, incapacity, or withdrawal of one of the partners. While the partnership may be re-established if the remaining partners buy the withdrawing member's share, uncertainty over the partnership's lifespan is a disadvantage. Successful firms need the assurance of permanence and stability to obtain financing and retain skilled employees.

In a partnership, decisions are likely to be more time-consuming than in a proprietorship, since more people must be consulted. In addition, disputes may arise and if serious, they could impair the operation of the business.

☐ Corporation

A **corporation** is a form of business organization that has a legal existence of its own, separate from that of those who created or own it. Corporations include many of the large firms people are familiar with, such as Air Canada, Canadian Pacific, Bell Canada, Alcan Aluminium, and Shell Canada, to name only a few.

What does the separate legal identity of the corporation mean? Corporations are created by the granting of a federal or provincial charter, which gives them the right to engage in specific activities. If business is to be conducted in a single province only, then incorporation under provincial law is sufficient. Federal incorporation, though more expensive, is appropriate when the corporation expects to do business in several provinces.

Once legally established, the corporation can sue and be sued, enter into contracts, own property, and contract debts in the same way as any adult human being. It can generally incur obligations and these obligations are the legal responsibility of the corporation, but not of its owners. The owners of corporations are known as **shareholders**. A firm may have only a few shareholders or thousands, each owning a part of the company's assets. When a corporation has many shareholders, ownership is generally described as "widely distributed" or "widely held."

Corporation shareholders have the advantage of limited liability. **Limited liability** means that the risk of the corporation's owners is restricted to the amount they have invested in the business. If the corporation is bankrupt, creditors cannot claim the shareholders'

other possessions, such as houses, cars, or personal savings. Thus, the risks of investing in a corporation are much diminished, as compared with a proprietorship or partnership. The corporation can also tap a much wider pool of capital.

Limited liability applies not only to large corporations, such as Air Canada, whose shares are traded publicly on the stock market, but also to firms which are privately owned by a few individuals. These private companies' shares are not offered to the general public. In the past, quite a number of small businesses have been limited private corporations.

When a shareholder dies or wishes to get out of the business, the corporation is not dissolved. The shares can be easily and readily transferred to others, while the corporation carries on its existence.

Table 6.1 on page 120 shows the top 30 corporations in Canada, ranked by total sales.

Financing the Corporate Expansion

Corporations can obtain funds for expansion in the same way as proprietorships and partnerships, that is, by borrowing from banks or by retaining profits to reinvest in the business. But a corporation has other options. It can issue bonds, stocks or shares, and other securities.

(i) Common stocks or shares **Common stocks** or **shares** represent part ownership of a corporation's capital. The ownership of 2 percent of the common stock entitles the owner to 2 percent of the issued dividends (profits), 2 percent of the vote at annual meetings, and 2 percent of net assets if the corporation closes down. Shares in publicly-traded corporations can usually be sold easily. There is, however, no guarantee that the stockholder will receive the original price of the stock when it is sold, or any return from it. Stock prices (as well as dividends) tend to vary significantly over time.

(ii) Preferred shares **Preferred** (or **preference**) **shares** are shares in a company that entitle the owner to a fixed return on investment before profits are distributed to common shareholders. Preferred shareholders are part owners of the company, but give up the right to vote at annual shareholders' meetings for the

Table 6.1 Canada's top 30 corporations in sales, 1990

SALES RANK 1990	1989	COMPANY (ACTIVITY)	SALES ($000)	NET INCOME ($000)	ASSETS ($000)	EMPLOYEES (NUMBER)	% SALES (US OFFSHORE)		OWNERSHIP
1	1	General Motors Canada (autos)	18 458 171	45 526	5 960 991	42 555	64	—	General Motors Detroit MI (100%)
2	2	BCE (telecommunications)	18 373 000	1 147 000	41 987 000	119 000	28	3	Widely held
3	3	Ford Motor of Canada (autos)	13 706 200	(57 100)	3 564 200	28 000	—	—	Ford Motor Dearborn MI (100%)
4	7	Imperial Oil (oil & gas)	11 226 000	493 000	15 196 000	14 702	5	—	Exxon Irving TX (69.6%)
5	6	George Weston (food processing & stores)	10 856 000	125 000	3 707 000	55 818	21	—	CEO Galen Weston (57%)
6	4	Canadian Pacific (diversified)	10 499 700	16 100	20 223 500	72 200	19	7	Widely held
7	8	Brascan (diversified)	10 275 000	80 300	5 718 200	—	—	—	Edper & Hees Int'l Toronto (49.7%)
8	5	Alcan Aluminium (aluminium producer)	10 217 667	633 572	12 351 775	57 000	33	54	Widely held
9	9	Noranda (integrated forest products)	9 434 000	120 000	14 917 000	56 000	33	35	Brascade Resources Toronto (35.7%)
10	11	Seagram (beverages)	7 148 984	882 101	13 312 172	17 700	45	52	CEO E.& C. Bronfman fam. (34.3%)
11	10	Chrysler Canada (autos)	7 067 000	355 300	2 845 000	13 100	71	—	Chrysler Highland Park MI (92.1%)
12	13	Provigo (food stores)	6 525 700	60 700	1 347 800	14 000	12	0	Unigesco (26%) Empire (25%)
13	12	Ontario Hydro (electric utility)	6 484 000	129 000	39 373 000	26 821	—	—	Province of Ontario (100%)
14	14	Thomson (publishing & travel)	6 258 715	449 218	9 116 814	44 800	36	53	Ken Thomson family Toronto (70%)
15	17	Petro-Canada (oil & gas)	5 873 000	181 000	7 278 000	6 353	0	0	Government of Canada (100%)
16	15	Hydro-Québec (electric utility)	5 822 988	404 000	36 684 097	20 067	52	0	Province of Québec (100%)
17	18	Shell Canada (integrated oil)	5 444 000	312 000	6 163 000	7 136	20	—	Shell Petroleum Netherlands (78.2%)
18	16	John Labatt (brewing, food)	5 274 000	169 000	2 946 000	16 500	36	—	Brascan Toronto (39%)
19	23	Imasco (consumer products)[1]	5 234 000	295 100	5 445 000	27 940	41	0	BAT Industries London UK (40.5%)
20	21	Hudson's Bay (department stores)[2]	4 970 000	158 000	2 401 000	—	0	0	Ken Thomson family Toronto (72.5%)
21	19	NOVA Corp. of Alberta (pipelines & nat. gas)	4 736 000	185 000	7 015 000	10 000	12	7	Widely held
22	24	Oshawa Group (food stores)	4 598 798	60 353	953 832	—	—	—	Wolfe family Toronto (100%)
23	28	IBM Canada (information & technology)	4 578 000	316 000	3 170 000	12 741	0	—	IBM Armonk NY (100%)
24	22	Sears Canada (retail & catalogue)	4 571 100	21 300	3 193 700	48 000	—	—	Sears, Robuck & Co. Chicago IL (62.7%)
25	32	Amoco Canada Petroleum (integrated oil)	4 461 000	(53 000)	6 316 000	4 200	—	—	Amoco Chicago IL (100%)
26	27	Canada Safeway (food stores)	4 317 951	73 918	972 918	29 000	0	0	Safeway Oakland CA (100%)
27	39	Varity (auto parts & machinery)	4 159 759	118 430	3 450 587	18 731	38	57	Widely held
28	25	Canadian Wheat Board (grain marketing)[3]	4 110 944	—	5 611 750	466	—	87	Government of Canada (100%)
29	26	Canadian National Railway (freight)	4 077 800	7 734	7 028 300	39 091	11	0	Government of Canada (100%)
30	31	Air Canada (int'l air carrier)[4]	3 939 000	(74 000)	4 579 000	23 100	17	30	Widely held

1. 1989 figures restated to reflect disposal of US subsidiary People Drug Stores.
2. 1989 figures restated to reflect reduced interest in Markborough Properties.
3. Offshore revenues include revenues generated in the US.
4. Net loss includes En Route operations which have been put up for sale.
SOURCE: *Canadian Business*, June 1991.

fixed return. In the event that the corporation is liquidated, preferred shareholders are entitled to an amount equal to the face value of their shares before any payment is made to common shareholders.

(iii) Corporate bonds   Corporations may sell or issue bonds in order to borrow funds. **Corporate bonds** represent the corporation's debt, which it is obliged to pay at some time in the future whether it makes a profit or not.

Corporate bonds are generally long-term, and may fall due 10, 15, or more years from the date of issue. The bonds are also often sold in large denominations, such as $100 000 or more. In return for buying the bond from the corporation, the buyer receives periodic interest payments—usually at six-month intervals—and the payment of face value (or principal) on the maturity date. The bondholder is therefore the creditor, rather than part-owner, of the corporation and is entitled to receive payment prior to the shareholders on dissolution of the corporation. Generally, bonds (like common and preferred shares) may be sold by the purchaser.

Who Controls the Corporation?
At first glance, it would seem that the corporation is run in the interests of its owners—the shareholders. Since a corporation typically has many shareholders, it follows that not all can be managers. Shareholders, who have one vote for each share they own, elect a board of directors. The directors decide on the general direction of the corporation and hire the senior managers. The senior managers are responsible for translating the general directives of the board into detailed day-to-day decisions.

In practice, however, the operations are not so simple. A corporation may have thousands of shareholders scattered across a wide area, and if you own only a few shares, it may not be worth the time and expense to appear at the annual meeting—even if it is held nearby. What you are most likely to do is to grant management's request for a proxy. A **proxy** is a document signed by a shareholder appointing someone other than the shareholder (often the management of the corporation) the right to vote, according to his or her shares, at the annual or other meetings of the corporation. Management, therefore, is likely to be in control of the corporation's meetings. Dissatisfied shareholders may be able to marshal enough votes to oust management, but this is rare. An easier way to express dissatisfaction is simply to sell your stock.

Does it matter if management controls the corporation? After all, if the interests of management and shareholders are identical, why worry? Both management and shareholders want the corporation to be profitable. Healthy profits mean rising prices for shareholders' stock and security for management jobs.

The interests of management and shareholders, however, may not always coincide. Management may be more interested in conserving their jobs and expanding the size of the corporation, than in raising profits.

Advantages
Many of the advantages and disadvantages of the corporation will be apparent from our description of its characteristics. Advantages include access to large amounts of capital, limited liability for shareholders, relatively easy transfer of ownership, and continuity of existence. The corporation is the best suited to raising large amounts of capital, since it can draw on the resources of thousands of shareholders if it so chooses. Limited liability and the easy transfer of shares also encourage investment. Banks, suppliers, and other creditors may be more disposed than with sole proprietorships or partnerships to grant large amounts of credit based on the corporation's continuity and relative stability. Corporations are, therefore, able to engage in business ventures which require large capital investments, such as mining and forestry, and may in fact engage in diverse activities.

Disadvantages
Disadvantages of the corporation include higher costs, stricter government regulations, and in some cases a lower level of motivation among managers. The costs of establishing a corporation are higher than for any other form of business organization. A fee is required to obtain a provincial or federal charter. Lawyers', accountants', and auditors' fees are also likely to be

higher than for proprietorships and partnerships. Government regulations (for example, to have annual shareholders' meetings and to maintain a set of books specifying shareholders, directors, etc.) are also more onerous for the corporation. In partnerships and proprietorships, the owner-managers are likely to be more highly motivated than the managers of corporations, who are usually paid employees.

□ The Stock Market

The **stock market** is an organized market, at which listed stocks can be bought and sold. The **stock exchange** is a building where stocks of major corporations are bought and sold by traders employed by stockbrokers. A **stockbroker** acts as a representative for buyers or sellers, carrying out their transactions on the stock market.

Prices on the stock market may fluctuate in response to changes in the supply and demand for shares. Factors influencing the price of shares include the current profits of the corporation and its future prospects, the political stability of the country or region, and the economic climate (whether it is a time of prosperity or a recession, for example). Stocks can be bought quickly and easily on the market, thus encouraging individuals and institutions to invest and provide capital for business expansion. Transactions on the exchange are published daily in the newspapers and broadcast on radio and television.

There are stock exchanges in many capital cities and provincial centres around the world. The largest exchanges in terms of value of stocks traded are in New York, Tokyo, and London, England. The first exchanges opened in Canada in the mid-nineteenth century. Today, there are exchanges in Vancouver, Calgary, Winnipeg, Toronto, and Montreal. The Toronto Stock Exchange is the largest, accounting for approximately 76 percent of the total shares traded based on value. Montreal is the second largest Canadian exchange with about 19 percent of total share value, and the Vancouver Stock Exchange is third with about 4 percent of total share value.

□ □ □ □ □ □

Skill Development: Interpreting Stock Market Quotations and Indicators

If you turn to the business section of a newspaper, you will often find a number of pages devoted to stock market tables. Usually, these tables will include statistics from Canadian stock markets (Toronto, Montreal, Winnipeg, Calgary, and Vancouver), the New York Stock Exchange, and some of the overseas markets—perhaps London, Tokyo, and Frankfurt. Knowing how to read the stock market pages is a first step toward making sound investment decisions.

Let's examine stock market quotations for five stocks listed on a Canadian stock exchange (page 123). Underneath the stock market statistics are explanations of the various terms used.

Applications

1. (a) What was the highest price paid for Bank of Montreal stock in the 52-week period?

(b) What was the lowest price paid for Bank of Montreal stock?

2. If you had 100 shares of Alberta Energy, what dividend did you receive?

3. How many MacMillan Bloedel shares were traded on this day?

4. If you bought 1000 shares of Bovar Inc. on this day at the closing price, how much did they cost?

5. Suppose you bought 1000 shares of Bovar Inc. at the

Stock Market Quotations

52-week		Stock	Div	High/ Bid	Low/ Ask	Close/ Last	Change	Vol
High	Low							
22 ¼	15 ⅛	Alberta Energy	.33	$19 ½	19 ¼	19 ½	+ ⅜	148 554
35 ¼	27	Bank of Mtl	2.12	$34 ¾	34 ⅛	34 ⅛	- ⅛	68 487
135	36	Bovar Inc		45	42	44	+ 4	28 889
21 ⅜	16 ⅝	MacMillan Blo	.80	$17 ⅝	17 ¼	17 ¼		42 527
51 ¾	36 ½	Royal Bank	2.32	$51 ¾	51	51 ⅛	+ ⅛	89 291

52-week High and Low The highest and lowest prices paid for the stock during the past 52 weeks. Stocks are listed in dollars with fractions indicating partial dollars (51 ¾ = $51.75, and 36 ½ = $36.50). Stocks less than $5 are listed in cents (135 = $1.35, and 36 = 36 cents).

Stock The name of the company. If necessary, the name of the company is shortened. MacMillan Blo, for example, is the short form for MacMillan Bloedel.

High/Bid The highest price that was paid for this stock that day, or if the stock was not traded that day, the highest price that someone bid (i.e., was willing to pay for the stock that day). Royal Bank's high for the day was $51.75.

Div The annual dividend (in dollars) paid by the company. Royal Bank paid a dividend of $2.32 to its shareholders, for example.

Low/Ask The lowest price paid for the stock on this day. Or, if the stock was not traded on this day, the lowest price someone was asking for the stock this day. Royal Bank's low for the day was $51.00.

Close/Last The price paid for the stock on the last trade of the day. The closing price for Royal Bank stock was $51.125.

Change The change in price between the end of this day's session and the previous day's session. The change in the price of Royal Bank stock was 12 1/2 cents.

Vol The total volume of shares of this corporation traded on this day. Total volume traded for the Royal Bank was 89 291 shares.

highest price in the last 52 weeks and sold them at the lowest price. How much did you lose?

6. Check a local newspaper for recent stock market quotations on the five stocks and compare the figures to those listed here.

7. In groups, select a stock and keep a record of how it fares over a specific period of time. Then analyze the results. If there were significant fluctuations in the price of the stock, try to find out why. In conclusion, note whether you would consider the stock a good investment and explain why or why not.

The Dow Jones Industrial Average

The Dow Jones Industrial Average is the best-known and most widely quoted indicator of the general trend in stock market prices in the United States. The Dow (as it is commonly called) is calculated each day the New York Stock Exchange is open and is published in newspapers and quoted on radio and television. Since 1928, the Dow has been based on the closing prices of 30 blue chip (i.e., safe and stable) US corporations traded on the New York Stock Exchange that theoretically mirror the stock market as a whole. These major corporations include Exxon, General Motors, IBM, McDonald's, Texaco, US Steel, and Woolworth.

These 30 corporations are chosen from sectors considered to be the most representative of the US economy. The list has changed considerably from the 11-stock list originally designed in 1884 by Charles Dow. None of the original 11 stocks is part of today's industrial average.

In 1896, Charles Dow and Eddie Jones established a new industrial index composed of 12 other stocks. One corporation—General Electric Co.—is still on the list. Until 1928, the Dow was, as the full name implies, simply an average of the closing prices of the selected stocks. Since 1928, however, calculations have been adjusted to take into account the effects of dividends and the substitution of new companies for old ones. Thus, the Dow Jones Industrial Average can be used over a period of time to track changes in stock prices on the New York Stock Exchange.

Investors—just like sports fans—enjoy statistics. The following are some of the most significant statistics posted by the Dow Jones Industrial Average.

Figure 6.1 Dow Jones average of industrial stock prices, 1929–1991

The Dow Jones Industrial Average is the most widely quoted stock price indicator. It tracks the weighted average prices of 30 blue chip stocks on the New York Stock Exchange.

SOURCE: Paul Samuelson *et al., Economics*, 6th Canadian ed. (Toronto: McGraw-Hill Ryerson, 1988).

Five biggest daily percentage gains
Oct. 6, 1931 up 14.87 percent
Oct. 20, 1929 up 12.34 percent
Sept. 21, 1932 up 11.32 percent
Oct. 21, 1987 up 10.15 percent
Aug. 3, 1932 up 9.52 percent

Five biggest daily percentage losses
Oct. 19, 1987 down 22.61 percent
Oct. 28, 1929 down 12.82 percent
Oct. 29, 1929 down 11.73 percent
Oct. 6, 1929 down 9.92 percent
Dec. 18, 1899 down 8.72 percent

Figure 6.1 summarizes graphically the changes in the Dow from 1929 to 1991.

Applications

1. Refer to Figure 6.1. Describe the general trend in stock market prices since 1929.

2. (a) During what periods did stock market prices decline the most?

(b) During what periods did stock prices increase the most?

(c) How do the fluctuations in stock prices reflect general economic conditions?

3. Consult the business section of your daily newspaper.

(a) What was the last figure for the Dow Jones Industrial Average?

(b) What was this year's high?

(c) What was this year's low?

(d) What is the recent trend in prices on the New York Stock Exchange? What reasons might there be for this trend?

4. Develop a graph to plot the changes in the Dow over the next month. Describe the trend in the prices and suggest reasons for it.

The TSE 300 Composite Index

THE 300 COMPOSITE INDEX DROPS 10.43 TO 3995.33

Prices rose sharply on the Toronto Stock Exchange, with the TSE 300 Composite Index up 12.56 to 3395.26

In today's trading, the TSE 300 Composite Index fell 8.46 points to close at 3295.56

THE MONTREAL EXCHANGE'S MARKET PORTFOLIO INDEX FELL 3.71 POINTS TO 2042.66

The Vancouver Stock Exchange index fell 3.80 points to 698.12

These headlines are familiar to Canadian television viewers, radio listeners, and newspaper readers. The TSE 300 Composite Index is Canada's leading market indicator, which since its inception on January 3, 1977, tracks approximately three-quarters of the dollar value of all Canadian stock trades. However, the other market indicators referred to in the headlines—the Montreal Market Portfolio Index and the Vancouver Stock Exchange Index—are constructed in roughly the same way and are used for the same purposes.

The TSE is composed of 300 stocks divided into 14 groups and 41 sub-groups. For example, the metals and minerals group includes three sub-groups composed of 28 companies. Companies are given a weighting in the index, which roughly reflects the number of shares. The effect, therefore, of stock price changes of small corporations on the index is tiny compared with that of a large corporation, such as Bell Canada or Alcan. Alcan has a weighting of 3.29 percent; Bell Canada has a weighting of 7.199 percent. The much smaller Maritime Telegraph and Telephone Company has a weighting of 0.15 percent. Small changes in Alcan or Bell Canada stock will clearly have a greater impact on the TSE 300 than large changes in the price of Maritime Telegraph and Telephone stock. Figure 6.2 shows the changes in the TSE 300 Composite Index from 1978 to 1991.

Any one of the indexes we have discussed indicates the performance of a stock on its respective stock market. As the indexes rise and fall, they reflect the general movement of stock prices. The indexes can be used to compare daily, weekly, yearly, or multi-year trends in prices on the market. You can see why the indexes are closely followed by brokers, investment managers, investors, and economists.

Applications

1. Refer to Figure 6.2. Describe the general trend of stock market prices since 1978 on the TSE.

2. During what periods did the stock market index rise and fall the most? Why?

3. Consult the business section of your local newspaper.
(a) Note the latest figure for the TSE 300.
(b) What was this year's high?
(c) What was this year's low?
(d) Describe the recent trend(s) in prices on the TSE 300. What reasons may account for the trend(s)?

4. Develop a graph to plot the changes in the TSE 300 over the next two months. Describe the trend in the prices and try to explain it.

Figure 6.2 TSE 300 Composite Index, 1978–1991

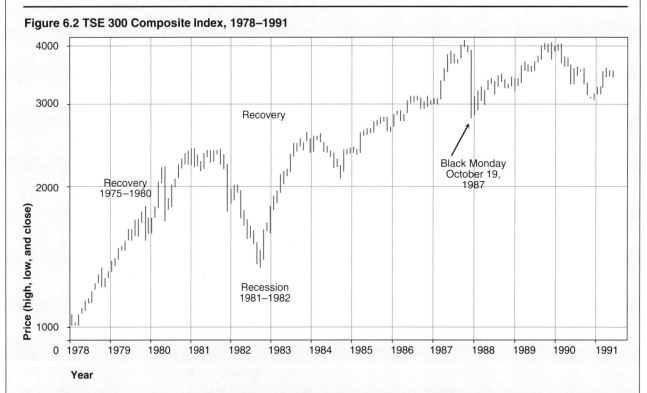

The TSE 300 is the most widely quoted Canadian index of stock market prices. Decreases in the index since 1978 reflect the 1981-82 recession and Black Monday on October 19, 1987. Increases parallel recoveries.

□ Co-operatives

A **co-operative** is a form of business organization jointly owned by a group of people and operated for their mutual benefit. Co-operatives are usually formed by people in the same industry or occupation and are run democratically, with everyone sharing in the profits or surpluses.

The major principles of co-operatives include the following:

(i) Each member has one vote no matter how many shares of the co-operative he or she owns. Control of the co-operative is, therefore, democratic and anyone can join.

(ii) Each member receives a fixed rate of return on each dollar invested. The co-operative is not designed as a means of increasing a person's investment income.

(iii) Surpluses or dividends are paid to members in proportion to the purchases they make in a consumers' co-operative, or the produce they deliver in a produc-

Table 6.2 Canada's largest co-operatives

COMPANY	INDUSTRY	PROFIT ($000)	REVENUE ($000)	ASSETS ($000)	RETURN ON ASSETS	EMPLOYEES	MEMBERS	PROVINCES OF OPERATION
FINANCIAL CO-OPERATIVES								
BC Central Credit Union	Credit Union	6 604	204 730	1 732 986	0.67	206	111	BC
Caisse Centrale Desjardins	Credit Union	54 017	523 301	4 073 490	1.63	150	na	PQ
Co-operative Trust Co. of Can.	Trust Company	1 868	107 197	931 435	0.32	231	4	not PQ
Co-operators General Insurance	Prop'ty & Cas'ty Ins.	17 455	917 730	1 476 410	1.55	2 905	35	All
Co-operators Group	Prop'ty & Cas'ty Ins.	3 612	117 306	84 827	13.28	5 182	35	All
Co-operators Life Insurance	Insurance	1 682	238 691	802 979	0.60	na	35	All
Credit Union Central (Sask.)	Credit Union	19 288	235 924	1 973 766	1.13	354	581 676	SK
Credit Union Central of Ont.	Credit Union	3 343	167 037	1 257 354	0.34	194	na	ON
Cumis Group	Insurance	-2 889	134 778	343 561	-0.88	688	17	All
L'Assurance-Vie Desjardins	Insurance	19 212	724 848	2 617 682	1.09	950	na	PQ
Pacific Coast Savings CU	Credit Union	6 792	98 357	770 681	0.98	500	75 000	BC
Richmond Savings Credit Union	Credit Union	4 222	98 313	800 408	0.72	331	44 559	BC
NON-FINANCIAL CO-OPERATIVES								
Agropur Co-operative Agro-Al.	Agriculture	6 060	498 002	185 171	4.74	1 600	4 620	PQ
Alberta Wheat Pool	Agriculture	5 912	1 222 656	436 045	6.41	1 629	60 000	AB
Calgary Co-operative Assoc.	Retailing	22 315	518 253	115 410	23.99	3 640	302 000	AB
Co-op Atlantic	Retailing	-3 551	425 210	80 992	8.28	1 000	na	NB, NS, PE
CSP Foods	Food Products	3 256	198 036	85 148	2.90	430	0	All
Federated Co-operatives	Wholesale	91 015	1 579 385	635 336	15.92	2 000	750 000	ON, W. Can.
Lilydale Co-operative	Agriculture	5 487	230 056	62 726	14.19	1 450	1 200	AB
Saskatchewan Wheat Pool	Agriculture	35 340	1 949 069	756 288	8.34	2 601	87 000	SK
United Co-operatives of Ont.	Wholesale	-12 942	524 317	176 721	-0.25	1 822	49 200	ON
United Farmers of Alta. Co-op.	Wholesale	13 404	360 704	132 164	10.62	609	94 000	AB

SOURCE: *Globe and Mail, Report on Business Magazine*, July 1991.

ers' co-operative. That is, dividends are distributed on a patronage basis, reflecting how much business the member brings to the co-operative.

Co-operatives have played a significant role in the political and economic life of Canada. The first successful consumers' co-operative was a store established in Stellarton, Nova Scotia in the early 1860s. Later, the Antigonish movement encouraged the development of producers' co-operatives among Maritime fishermen. In the Prairie provinces, co-operatives have been established by grain farmers. These producers' co-operatives have allowed farmers and fishermen, for example, more control over their own affairs. They all have a say in what is to be done with the savings of the operation, they can plan for difficult times, and they are able to take advantage of volume buying in supplies.

Co-operatives have also gained influence in the financial sector through co-operative insurance and trust companies, caisses populaires, and credit unions. These are most common in Quebec, Ontario, and Saskatchewan. Members make deposits, which can then be loaned out to other members who are in need.

Table 6.2 on page 127 shows the major financial and non-financial co-operatives in Canada.

Advantages

Some of the major strengths of co-operatives come from the principles on which they are founded. Democratic control, co-operation rather than competition, and the patronage dividend rather than profits are attractive to many people, making them loyal members. Co-ops can gain for their members the advantages of better prices from large-scale buying and selling.

Disadvantages

Despite some clear advantages, co-operatives have difficulty remaining competitive with private businesses. Their democratic structure makes it hard for them to hire and work with aggressive managers without becoming a commercial operation. The growth of some co-operatives has been limited because they are unable to issue shares or bonds like corporations, and therefore may have difficulty raising capital.

□ □ □ □ □ □

Skill Development: Assessing Financial Statements

For anyone involved in business—owners, managers, or investors—it is essential to understand and assess financial statements. Without financial statements, it is impossible to know how well a company is performing or to evaluate its future prospects. Would you invest in a firm without this basic information?

The two most important financial statements for investors are the balance sheet and the income or profit/loss statement. The **balance sheet** provides a picture of the company's financial status *at a particular point in time*— usually at the close of business on December 31st, the last day of the year. It includes a statement of the firm's assets, liabilities or debts, and shareholders' equity. The **income statement** records the *flow* of a company's earnings and expenditures *over a period of time*, such as a year.

The Balance Sheet

If the only thing you own is a car worth $8000 on which you owe $5000, then you have $8000 in **assets**, $5000 in **debits** (or **liabilities**), and the value of your ownership in the car (your **net worth** or **equity**) is $3000. We can present your situation this way:

Assets	= Liabilities	+ Net worth
What you own:	What you owe:	The value of your
the $8000 car	$5000 debt	ownership:
		$3000 equity

Notice that the two sides of the equation must balance— hence the term *balance sheet*. This same fundamental equation holds true for corporations and all other businesses. The *net worth* of the corporation—the amount the shareholders actually own—equals the total assets minus the total liabilities of the company.

On a balance sheet, assets are shown on the left-hand side and liabilities and net worth on the right-hand side of the page. Let's examine a simple balance sheet for a hypothetical firm which produces computer games, Electron Computer Games Inc.

Electron Computer Games Inc.   Balance Sheet   December 31, 1993

The balance sheet shows the company's financial position on a particular date, December 31, 1993. Everything is put in a common unit—Canadian dollars. Note that the totals of the left- and right-hand sides of the balance sheet are equal—they balance. The two sides must balance because all of the firm's assets must belong to the owners (the net worth) or be owed to the creditors (liabilities).

I Assets include all that the firm owns or is owed. The assets are valued at their historical costs—that is, the costs at the time of purchase, not at the time of the statement. Buildings and equipment are valued at their purchase price minus depreciation (their reduction in value over time due to wear or obsolescence). Assets are categorized as either current or fixed.

Current assets include cash and anything that can be turned into cash within a year, such as bonds and inventories (of product, raw materials, or parts, etc.).

Fixed assets include land, buildings, machinery, trucks, etc., with an allowance for depreciation.

ASSETS	
Current Assets	
Item 1. Cash	$10 000
Item 2. Inventory	40 000
Fixed Assets	
Item 3. Equipment	80 000
Item 4. Buildings	50 000
	————
Item 5. Total assets	
(Items 1+2+3+4)	180 000

LIABILITIES AND NET WORTH	
Liabilities	
Item 6. Current liabilities	
Accounts payable	$10 000
Notes payable	20 000
Item 7. Long-term liabilities	
Bonds payable	50 000
Item 8. **Net Worth**	
(Item 5 minus items 6 and 7)	
Shareholders' equity:	
Common stock	100 000
Total liabilities and net worth	180 000

II Liabilities are all the debts of the firm and include current as well as long-term liabilities.

Current liabilities (accounts payable) include debts for goods and services purchased and to be paid for within the current year.

Notes payable are promissory notes payable to banks or finance companies.

Long-term liabilities are debts payable over longer periods than a year, such as corporate bonds.

Bonds payable are long-term loans for 15 years at 10 percent interest.

III Net Worth is the amount shareholders' actually own. It is equal to total assets minus total liabilities.

Shareholders' equity is the interest of the shareholders in a company if all liabilities were paid off. In this case, then, it is the residual amount which balances our equation: Assets = Liabilities + Net Worth.

The Income Statement

Suppose that a year passes and Electron Computer Games Inc. continues its production of computer games. To show what happened during the year, we turn to the income statement. This statement reports **sales revenues**, **total expenses**, and **net income** (profit or loss) for the year 1994. We can see that:

Net income = Total revenue - Total expenses (or total costs)

Thus, sales revenues of $120 000, costs of operations at $90 000, and interest costs of $5000 left a net income before taxes of $25 000. Corporation income taxes totalled $7000, leaving a net income after taxes of $18 000, of which $6000 was paid in dividends and $12 000 was retained earnings.

Assessing Profitability and Liquidity

We have examined what the balance sheet and income statement reveal about the corporation. Now let's examine how we can use this information to assess the corporation's ability to pay its debts (its liquidity), and to generate profits (its profitability). Two important tools in this assessment are ratios and trend studies.

(a) Ratios

Various ratios can be used to examine financial statements. A ratio is a relationship between two numbers, in which a number is usually related to one. Thus, if there are

---

Electron Computer Games Inc.   Income Statement for the year ending December 31, 1994

Sales revenue is the total amount received from Electron's sales of its computer games over the year.

Cost of operations includes all costs incurred in the company's operations.

Labour services include payments in wages, salaries, and other workers' benefits, such as hospital insurance.

Materials covers payments to outside suppliers for such items as computer discs and paper.

Depreciation is the accounting charge for the decline in value of fixed assets. Electron, like other corporations, has buildings and equipment that through time wear out and become obsolete. Hence, rather than charge the full cost to the cost of operations in the year the buildings or equipment are "replaced," accountants include an amount by which they decline annually.

Item 9. Sales revenue		$120 000
Item 10. Less cost of operations		90 000
(a) Labour services	$50 000	
(b) Materials	20 000	
(c) Depreciation	10 000	
(d) Other operating costs	10 000	
Item 11. Less interest costs		5 000
		————
Item 12. Net income (profits) before taxes (Item 9 minus 10 & 11)		25 000
Item 13. Less corporation income taxes		7 000
		————
Item 14. Net income (profit) after taxes (Item 12 minus 13)		18 000
(a) Dividends	6 000	
(b) Retained earnings	12 000	

Other operating costs are costs not included elsewhere, such as those for research and development, rent, and utilities (e.g., water and hydro).

Interest costs include the costs of money borrowed from bankers and finance companies.

Net income before taxes is the total of sales revenue (income) minus all costs before taxes are deducted.

Corporation income taxes are the taxes on income that corporations (like individuals) must pay annually.

Net income after taxes is, of course, the total income after taxes have been paid—in other words, the total profits. Part of the profits is paid as dividends to shareholders and part is retained by the corporation to finance future expansion (retained earnings).

60 females in your economics course and only 40 males, the ratio of females to males is 1.5 to 1, or 1.5:1.

(b) Trend studies

Ratios for one year have limited value. However, when compared with other ratios—such as ratios for the company over a number of years or with other companies in the same industry—they become very useful. They can then show trends over time and give a more comprehensive picture of the firm's performance. Are profits generally increasing or decreasing? How well is the company performing in relation to other firms in the industry?

Let's examine some of the most commonly used ratios, referring again to the financial statements of Electron Computer Games Inc.

A. Balance Sheet Ratios

The following ratios are calculated from the figures in the balance sheet.

1. Working capital ratio (or current ratio)

This ratio is used as a measure of a corporation's liquidity, or its ability to pay its debts and thus avoid bankruptcy. It shows how much the value of current assets exceeds the value of current liabilities.

$$\text{Working capital ratio} = \frac{\text{Current assets}}{\text{Current liabilities}}$$

$$\text{Example:} \quad \frac{\text{Item 1 + Item 2}}{\text{Item 6}} = \frac{\$50\,000}{\$30\,000} = \frac{1.67}{1} \text{ or } 1.67{:}1$$

Electron Computer Games Inc., therefore, has $1.67 in current assets (cash and its equivalent) to pay every $1.00 of liabilities (debts).

Assessment: How good is this ratio? It depends on the type of business, the rate of inventory turnover, and the firm's credit position. A ratio of 1.67 to 1 is quite good for computer firms like Electron. Notice that if two firms have the same working capital ratio, one may be in a much better position than the other if it has more cash in its current assets. Cash is the most liquid asset and can be used immediately to pay debts.

If the ratio of 1.67 to 1 is quite good, does it follow that

16.7 to 1 is ten times better? The answer is probably no— especially if maintained over a long period of time. It could indicate an undue accumulation of inventory. A large amount of inventory cannot be quickly converted to cash, may be costly to maintain, and may indicate that production and sales are poorly co-ordinated.

2. Quick ratio (or acid test)

The quick ratio is a more stringent test of a firm's ability to pay its debts. It concentrates on quick assets, those that can be readily converted to cash. Inventory is, therefore, deducted from current assets, since it often cannot be quickly converted to cash.

$$\text{Quick ratio} = \frac{\text{Current assets - Inventories}}{\text{Current liabilities}}$$

$$\text{Example:} \quad \frac{\text{Item 1 + Item 2 - Item 2}}{\text{Item 6}}$$

$$= \frac{\$50\,000 - \$40\,000}{\$30\,000} = 0.33{:}1$$

Thus, the company has 33 cents of quick assets for every $1.00 in current liabilities.

Assessment : Again, while there is no hard-and-fast rule, 1:1 is generally considered a good ratio. Companies like Electron, however, may be in a good position despite a much lower ratio, if their inventory is current and their rate of inventory turnover is high. This is because a current inventory with a high rate of turnover is seen as the equivalent of cash.

B. Income Statement Ratios

We will examine one important ratio calculated from the income statement.

1. Net (after-tax) profit margin ratio

This ratio measures the firm's profitability or ability to make a profit. It is useful for comparing the company's performance year-to-year and for comparing the performances of various companies in the same industry.

Net profit margin $= \dfrac{\text{Net income}}{\text{Net sales}} \times 100$

Example: $\dfrac{\text{Item 14}}{\text{Item 9}} \times 100 = \dfrac{\$18\ 000}{\$120\ 000} \times 100 = 15$ percent

The profit margin ratio, therefore, is 15:1. On every $1.00 of sales, the company earns 15 cents in profit after taxes.

Assessment : This ratio summarizes the performance of the firm over the specific time period of one year. By comparing profit margins over a number of years or with other companies in the industry, managers can identify trends and gauge how well the company is performing over longer periods.

C. Combined Ratios

Some ratios are calculated from figures in both the balance sheet and income statement, and are therefore known as combined ratios. They show analysts how well the company's assets are being used.

1. Earnings per common share

This ratio is one of the most widely used and easily understood. It is especially relevant to shareholders and is also commonly reported in the press.

$\dfrac{\text{Earnings per}}{\text{common share}} = \dfrac{\text{Net income}}{\text{Number of common shares outstanding}}$

(we will assume that there are 10 000 shares)

Example: $\dfrac{\text{Item 14}}{10\ 000} = \dfrac{\$18\ 000}{10\ 000} = 1.80{:}1$
common shares

Thus, shareholders earn $1.80 per share.

Assessment : From this ratio, shareholders can assess how profitable their holding in the company is. They can determine whether they are likely to receive a dividend and how much it might be. This ratio can be used to make year-by-year comparisons of share profitability.

D. Value Ratios

Ratios in this group provide measures of the stock market's rating of the corporation. We will examine one of the most widely-quoted ratios.

1. Price-earnings ratio (or PE multiple)

The PE multiple expresses the relationship between market price and earnings per share in one figure. Comparisons can then be made over time and among corporations. PE ratios are calculated only for common stock.

$\text{PE multiple} = \dfrac{\text{Current market price of common share}}{\text{Earnings per share}}$
(in latest 12-month period)

Example: We'll assume that the current price of Electron's common stock is $22.50. Its earnings per share have already been calculated as $1.80.

$\text{PE multiple} = \dfrac{22.50}{1.80} = 12.50{:}1$ or 12.50 times

The market price is, therefore, 12.5 times the earnings on each share.

Assessment: To compare PE ratios between companies' common stock, the corporations must be comparable— that is, in the same industry. A bank's PE ratio should be compared with that of other banks, food stores with other food stores, and so on. The ratio is particularly useful since it summarizes investors' evaluation of a company. A low PE multiple for a particular stock may indicate a good buying opportunity for investors, for example.

Applications

1. Complete the following balance sheet for Electron Computer Games Inc.

2. Complete the following income statement for Electron Computer Games Inc.

3. For 1996, calculate the following for Electron Computer Games Inc.
(a) working capital ratio
(b) quick ratio
(c) net profit margin

Electron Computer Games Inc.
Balance Sheet   December 31, 1996

ASSETS		LIABILITIES AND NET WORTH	
Current Assets		**Current Liabilities**	
Cash	$20 000	Accounts payable	$30 000
Inventory	100 000	Notes payable	50 000
Fixed Assets			
Equipment	240 000	**Long-term liabilities**	
Buildings	120 000	Bonds payable	50 000
Total Assets		**Net Worth**	
		Shareholders' equity:	
		Common stock	
		Total liabilities	
		and net worth	_____
		Approved on behalf of the Board.	
		_____ Director	
		_____ Director	

Electron Computer Games Inc.
Income Statement for the year ending December 31, 1996

Sales revenue		$250 000
Less cost of operations		170 000
(a) Labour services	110 000	
(b) Materials	25 000	
(c) Depreciation	20 000	
(d) Other operating costs	15 000	
Less interest costs		10 000
Net income before taxes		70 000
Corporate income taxes		25 000
Net income after taxes		
(a) Dividends		
(b) Retained earnings		10 000

(d) earnings per common share (assume that the number of common shares is still 10 000)

(e) PE multiple (assume that the stock market price for Electron shares is $40.25).

4. Use the five ratios to compare the liquidity and profitability of Electron Computer Games Inc. in 1993 and 1996. Write a short assessment report showing how you reached your conclusions.

☐ Government Enterprises

While most goods and services are produced by privately-owned businesses in Canada, government enterprises provide services through various levels of government without charge, or through crown corporations.

Examples of government services provided at no *direct* cost (though we pay for them through our taxes) include defence, primary and secondary school education, and police and fire protection. Some services, such as post-secondary education, are offered at substantially subsidized costs. These government services will be covered more fully in Chapter 13.

Crown corporations are independent legal bodies, but unlike private corporations, their shares (or capital stocks) are owned by government rather than private individuals. Crown corporations enable governments to provide goods and services without their activities being subject to day-to-day politics.

The two major types of crown corporations are those that draw their revenue from government budgets, and those that are expected to draw substantial revenues from the sale of their goods and services.

The first operate mainly in a supervisory or administrative role. At the federal level, such corporations include the Atomic Energy Control Board, the Unemployment Insurance Commission, and the National Research Council. The second type of crown corporation is responsible to a provincial legislature or the

Figure 6.3 Types of business enterprises—a summary

	SINGLE PROPRIETORSHIP	PARTNERSHIP	CORPORATION	CO-OPERATIVE	CROWN CORPORATION
OWNERSHIP	Owned by one person.	Owned by two or more people.	Often owned by many shareholders.	Owned by many members.	Owned by government.
SIZE	Small. Limited capital. Few workers.	More capital and workers than a sole proprietorship.	May be very large. Greater capital resources and more workers than proprietorships and partnerships.	May be large.	May be large. Considerable capital resources.
AGE	Short life.	Short life.	Very long life.	Long life. First ones founded in nineteenth century.	Long life. Founded in twentieth century.
EXAMPLES	Taxi firms, professions, farms, home repair and maintenance, stores, restaurants.	Same as sole proprietorship.	Manufacturing and service industries, some very diversified.	Agriculture, retail trade, credit unions, insurance companies.	Service industries which have monopoly elements (e.g., provision of electricity, urban transport, telephone).
ADVANTAGES	Easy to establish and easy to terminate. Flexible in operation. Has owner's personal involvement and high motivation. Decisions quickly and easily made.	Wider pool of talent and capital resources than single proprietor. Relatively easy to establish. Has personal involvement of owners and high motivation.	Has separate legal existence. Unlimited life. Access to unlimited capital. Limited liability.	Democratic control. Co-operation rather than competition. Patronage dividends. May achieve lower prices for members.	May provide services which cannot effectively be provided by private corporations. Not bound to make a profit.
DISADVANTAGES	Limited capital and human resources. Unlimited liability. Lack of continuity.	Less capital and resources than corporations. Unlimited liability. Possible lack of continuity.	Expensive to establish and operate. Stricter government regulations. Managers may be less motivated than owners of sole proprietorships or partnerships.	Difficulty in competing with private business. May have difficulties raising capital.	May be less efficient than private business. Political pressure may influence decisions.

Table 6.3 Largest crown corporations in Canada, 1991

REVENUE RANK	COMPANY	BUSINESS	REVENUE ($000)	RETURN ON CAPITAL PERCENT	RETURN ON CAPITAL RANK	PROFIT ($000)	ASSETS ($000)	EMPLOYEES
FEDERAL								
1	Petro-Canada	Oils	5 873 000	13.32	2	181 000	7 278 000	6 468
2	Canadian National Railway	Transport	4 023 016	0.10	11	7 734	7 028 268	37 255
3	Canada Post Corp.	Communications	3 756 093	9.25	4	148 800	2 507 784	60 324
4	Via Rail Canada	Transport	1 013 368	0.10	12	-32	938 117	7 004
5	Canada Mortgage and Housing	Development	818 230	8.66	6	11 204	9 056 782	2 976
6	Export Development Corp.	Finance	642 323	7.91	7	6 303	7 040 195	490
7	Royal Canadian Mint	Manufacturing	606 162	15.74	1	10 412	107 803	737
8	Farm Credit Corp.	Finance	428 186	9.52	3	-2 689	3 816 719	810
9	Federal Business Devel. Bank	Finance	402 136	9.23	5	10 260	2 822 187	1 150
10	Canadian Broadcasting Corp.	Broadcasting	352 973	-16.97	15	-103 578	941 007	10 512
PROVINCIAL								
1	Ontario Hydro	Utility	6 600 000	5.72	28	129 000	39 373 000	36 474
2	Hydro-Québec	Utility	5 974 000	8.50	22	404 000	36 684 000	18 933
3	Caisse de Dépôt et Placement	Finance	2 802 000	7.87	25	2 726 000	36 245 000	275
4	BC Hydro and Power	Utility	2 053 000	14.06	7	160 000	9 049 000	5 761
5	Insurance Corp. of BC	Insurance	1 745 032	9.60	18	17 190	2 886 651	3 500
6	Alberta Heritage Savings	Finance	1 253 786	9.03	20	1 244 438	12 286 574	0
7	NB Electric Power Comm.	Utility	1 012 998	12.13	14	26 178	2 836 551	3 100
8	Alberta Treasury Branches	Banks	842 767	na	na	9 146	6 871 829	3 119
9	Manitoba Hydro-Electric Board	Utility	835 644	10.71	16	24 197	4 694 539	4 307

SOURCE: *Globe and Mail, Report on Business Magazine*, July 1991.   na = not available

federal parliament. Examples include provincial hydro-electric commissions (such as BC Hydro), liquor boards (such as the Liquor Control Board of Quebec), and telephone companies (such as Alberta Government Telephones). At the federal level, some of the best known are Canada Post and Canadian National Railways. Municipalities may also own semi-autonomous enterprises, which provide services such as public transit, water, and sewage services.

Table 6.3 lists the largest federal and provincial crown corporations in Canada in 1991.

Advantages and Disadvantages

Government plays an important role in a modified market economy. It provides goods or services that cannot be produced at a profit (e.g., national defence) and undertakes a number of regulatory tasks to ensure that private enterprises operate in the best interests of the community. Whether certain services, such as telephone, are best provided by crown or private corporations is an open question, with different provinces arriving at different solutions. Telephone services in Ontario and Quebec, for example, are provided by private corporations, whereas in Saskatchewan they are provided by the provincial crown corporation Sasktel. At various times and in various situations, all three major Canadian political parties have supported government takeover of individual firms or industries.

Canadians often feel that crown corporations are by their very nature inefficient—and Canada Post is often given as the prime example. However, in the 1980s, Canada Post was able to move from posting substantial deficits to a small surplus, though it should be noted this was only with significant increases in rates for various services. One comparative study of privately-owned Canadian Pacific and the crown corporation

Canadian National found that while productivity in the 1950s for CP was 14 percent better than its rival, after deregulation in the 1960s the productivity gap between them vanished. The authors of the study, however, suggest that public ownership may not be less productive by its very nature than private business. The determinant of efficiency may be the amount of competition.

Figure 6.4 compares the degree of private and public ownership of industries in ten countries. Note the types of industries most frequently under public ownership and consider why these industries would be publicly owned.

Figure 6.4 Public enterprise in ten countries

Legend:
- ALL OR NEARLY ALL PRIVATELY OWNED
- 25% PUBLICLY OWNED
- 50% PUBLICLY OWNED
- 75% PUBLICLY OWNED
- ALL OR NEARLY ALL

	AUSTRALIA	AUSTRIA	BELGIUM	BRAZIL	BRITAIN[1]	CANADA[2]	FRANCE	GERMANY	HOLLAND	INDIA	ITALY	JAPAN	MEXICO	SOUTH KOREA	SPAIN	SWEDEN	SWITZERLAND	UNITED STATES
POSTS																		
TELECOMMUNICATIONS																		
ELECTRICITY																		
GAS																		
OIL PRODUCTION			na				na		na	na	na	na		na	na	na	na	
COAL									na		na					na	na	
RAILWAYS																		
AIRLINES																		
MOTOR INDUSTRY																		
STEEL																		
SHIPBUILDING	na	na															na	

SOURCE: Report of the Royal Commission on the Economic Union and Development Prospects for Canada, vol. 2 (Ottawa: Ministry of Supply and Services Canada). Quoted in Paul A. Samuelson *et al.*, *Economics*, 6th Canadian ed. (Toronto: McGraw-Hill Ryerson, 1988).

1. Since the chart was prepared, Britain has privatized British Airways.
2. Since the chart was prepared, Canada has privatized Air Canada.
na = not available

Summary

a. The main business organizations in Canada are sole proprietorships, partnerships, corporations, co-operatives, and government enterprises.

b. Sole proprietorships are relatively small businesses wholly owned by one person, while partnerships are owned by two or more people. Both forms of organization are common in the retail and service industries and in various professions. Advantages are that they are relatively easy to establish, flexible in operation, and have the owners' personal involvement and high motivation. Disadvantages are relatively limited human and capital resources, a lack of continuity, and unlimited liability, which means that owners' personal assets can be claimed for outstanding business debts.

c. The corporation has a legal existence separate from its creators and is owned by a number of shareholders. Advantages include access to large amounts of capital and human resources, continuity of existence, and limited liability for shareholders (they are liable only for the amount of their investment). Disadvantages include high costs, more government regulations as compared to sole proprietorships and partnerships, and the possibility that managers will be less motivated than owners of their own firms.

d. Corporation shares or stocks can be bought and sold on the stock market. The most widely used indicators of trends in stock market prices are the Dow Jones Industrial Average in the United States and the TSE 300 Composite Index in Canada.

e. A co-operative is a form of business organization jointly owned by a group of people and operated for their mutual benefit. Surpluses or dividends are distributed to members on a patronage basis, that is, according to how much business they bring to the co-operative. Advantages are democratic control, co-operation rather than competition, patronage dividends, and lower prices for members. Disadvantages include difficulties in obtaining financing and competing with the private sector.

f. Two financial statements essential for assessing the liquidity and profitability of a business are the balance sheet and the income statement. The balance sheet shows the firm's financial status at a particular point in time, usually at year end December 31. The income statement records the flow of earnings and expenditures over a period of time, usually one year.

g. The working capital ratio, quick ratio, net profit margin ratio, earnings per common share, and price-earnings ratio, along with data from the balance sheet and income statement, can be used to assess the health of a firm.

h. Government enterprises include the services offered through the various levels of government, such as defence and education, and crown corporations, such as Canada Post.

◼ Review of Key Terms

Define the following key terms introduced in this chapter and provide examples where appropriate.

sole proprietorship
unlimited liability
partnership
limited partners
corporation
limited liability

common stocks or shares
preferred shares
corporate bonds
proxy
stock market
stock exchange

stockbroker
balance sheet
income statement
assets
liabilities
net worth

depreciation
co-operative
crown corporation

■ Application and Analysis

1. Which form of business organization would be most appropriate in each of the following cases? Explain why.

(a) a two-person accounting firm

(b) a corner convenience store

(c) a summer business to distribute flyers door-to-door

(d) a chain of restaurants

(e) a regional airline

(f) a bank

2. Identify the form of business organization described in each of the following situations.

(a) You establish your own house painting business with $5000 of your savings.

(b) Rudi and Denise establish their own word processing firm. Each contributes $10 000 and they agree to share the profits equally.

(c) You believe that the price of gasoline is too high in your area. At a community meeting, it is agreed that members will pay $100 each to form an association which will provide gasoline at cost to all members. A community gasoline station is established with the contributions, and community members are employed to run the station.

(d) You are a computer genius who has developed a new microcomputer that can out-perform all existing models and be produced at a fraction of the cost. With two friends, you obtain a charter from the federal government to establish a firm that will produce and sell your computer. To raise the capital you need, you sell 1000 shares at $100 each. You and your friends manage the business and hire 20 employees.

3. The HB Company and the XY Company both have $1 million in capital. The capital was raised as follows:

HB Company—100 000 common shares at $10 per share

XY Company—25 000 common shares at $10 per share
5 000 preferred 10-percent shares at $50 each
$500 000 worth of 12-percent bonds

During the first three years of operation, each company had the same amount to distribute to its shareholders and bondholders:

First year $85 000
Second year $135 000
Third year $185 000

(a) Calculate the dividend payable by each company on each share in each year.

(b) Suppose you anticipate a period of rising prices and profits. Which security would you buy? Why?

(c) If interest rates rise, what will happen to the market price of the bonds?

4. You have decided to invest $10 000 in a Canadian corporation for which shares are traded on a Canadian stock exchange. Before buying any shares, decide on your objectives. Do you want to conserve your $10 000 above all, maximize income from your investment, or acquire capital gains? Once you have decided on your goals, select a few corporations for examination.

To help you decide which corporations to investigate, ask knowledgeable friends and relatives, check the financial section of your local newspaper, or consult the financial sections of the *Globe and Mail*, *Financial Post*, *Financial Times*, or *Canadian Business* magazine for suggestions. Alternatively, you may know of a local corporation that appears to be prosperous and well-managed. Once you have narrowed down your choice to a few corporations:

(a) Examine the corporation's annual reports over the last few years. Check the balance sheets and income statements and calculate some of the key ratios outlined in the Skill Development section on pages 128-

133 in this chapter to assess the firm's profitability, liquidity, and value of shares. Identify the trends in profits and share prices. Annual reports are usually available from your local library or may be obtained by writing to the corporation.

(b) Consult the *Financial Post Corporation Service Cards: Index of Publicly-Held Canadian Companies* for a brief summary of the company's operations.

(c) Contact a stockbroker for his or her views on the firm and to obtain a copy of the stock analysis.

Decide which company's shares you will buy and write a brief report explaining your decision.

5. Over the next month, graph the changes in *either* the TSE 300 Composite Index *or* the Dow Jones Industrial Average. Account for changes in the index.

6. In the 1980s, the federal Conservative government privatized (sold to private interests) a number of crown corporations, including Canadair, de Havilland Aircraft, Teleglobe Canada, and Air Canada. In 1990, the federal government announced a plan to sell Petro-Canada. Some provincial governments also privatized industries. Alberta privatized Pacific Western Airlines in 1983 and Quebec sold Soquem (which held various Quebec mines) and Raffinerie de Sucre de Quebec (a sugar refinery) in 1985. Quebecair Ltd. was sold the following year. Ontario, Saskatchewan, and British Columbia have also privatized industries.

The movement toward increased privatization of crown corporations has sparked heated debate. The arguments for privatization include the following:

(1) Governments should not interfere in the market.
(2) The sale of crown corporations can help to reduce the federal or provincial deficit.
(3) In some cases, the corporations themselves were being outperformed by their competitors and had

major debts.
(4) Private firms should not be subject to competition from publicly-subsidized crown corporations.
(5) By their very nature—because they are government-owned, subject to political interference, and protected from the rigours of the market—crown corporations are generally less efficient than private businesses.

Arguments against privatization include:

(1) Governments must protect and control certain strategic industries. Petro-Canada, for example, was established in 1975 during the oil crisis in the Middle East to increase Canadian ownership in the oil industry. Cultural industries, such as the CBC, should be protected from domination by foreign interests.
(2) Governments must intervene in the market to provide some essential services that private interests would not provide because they could not make sufficient profits. These include public transportation and public utilities such as water services and electricity.
(3) Government ownership of some industries, such as telephone and utilities, is preferable to regulation of these services. If the companies were not owned by government, prices could be substantially higher for consumers and government may have to set regulations to control prices.
(4) Crown corporations are not necessarily less efficient than private enterprises. Some studies have shown that efficiency may be related more directly to the amount of competition in the industry than to government ownership.

(a) What do you think? Should the process of privatization continue? Should crown corporations such as Canadian National Railways or the CBC be privatized? Defend your position.
(b) Do you agree that Petro-Canada should be privatized? Why or why not?

CHAPTER SEVEN

Production and Costs

Objectives

a. Outline and evaluate the profit-maximizing assumption as it is applied to firms.

b. Demonstrate the relationship between a firm's inputs and output with reference to total, average, and marginal product.

c. Recall the law of diminishing returns and apply it in a new context.

d. Distinguish between explicit and implicit costs and demonstrate the difference in how accountants and economists calculate profit.

e. Calculate, graph, and show the relationships among total fixed cost, total variable cost, and total cost over the short run.

f. Calculate, graph, and show the relationships among average fixed cost, average variable cost, average total cost, and marginal cost over the short run for a firm.

g. Graph and apply the long-run average total cost curve.

h. Explain and apply the economies of scale and the diseconomies of scale.

In the previous two chapters, we focussed on business people and firms—the supply side of the market. One of the most significant facts that came out of our discussion was that it is not easy to ensure the survival of a business firm. Business operation is a constant balancing act. One of the key factors in this balancing act is *costs*. A clear knowledge of costs is essential for the survival of a firm.

In this chapter, we examine how firms make decisions about how much to produce based on costs. If a firm continually plugs in more resources, does this guarantee increased production and increased profits? If not, why? What basic tools do firms use to calculate their optimum level of output?

The Profit-Maximizing Assumption

Why is any firm in business? Most people would immediately answer—to make a profit. Economists generally assume that businesses strive to earn the highest profits possible. This is a very useful assumption. It is the basis on which we can predict business behaviour. It tells us what decisions businesses will make in terms of what, how, and for whom they will produce. In other words, based on the profit-maximizing assumption, we can determine the quantity of resources firms will purchase, how many and what types of workers they will employ, and how they will determine their production output, for example.

But is maximum profit always the objective of all businesses? The answer, clearly, is no. Some businesses are run as non-profit enterprises, which aim to earn only enough revenue to cover costs. Many day-care operations in Canada are run as non-profit organizations, for example. Other businesses that do aim to make a profit may also offer scholarships, support for the arts, or employee day-care services which add to their costs, but do not earn revenue. These programs support the objectives of good customer or employee relations, stability, and long-term growth, for example. While it may be argued that even these objectives are tied to the desire for future profits, many firms recognize a need to invest in their employees and in society.

Economic conditions may affect business objectives, however. In tough economic times or when a firm faces bankruptcy, it will be more likely to seek immediate profits (or, at least, minimize losses), than when times are prosperous and revenues are high.

Profit, therefore, is not the only business objective. However, no business can ignore the need to make a profit. The survival of the firm depends on making profits and avoiding losses. If a firm is faced with a choice between option one which looks profitable, and option two which doesn't, which one will it choose? The answer is option one most likely—perhaps not always, but most of the time, and sufficiently often to make our profit-maximizing assumption a useful guide to business behaviour.

The Production Function

The **production function** refers to the relationship between a firm's inputs (or factors of production) and its output. Does an increase in inputs always ensure an increase in output? Let's investigate by considering a hypothetical firm—Petra's Pizza Parlour.

Petra's parlour is a take-out pizza outlet producing only one product—75-cm pizzas with pepperoni, pineapple, and anchovies. Petra's pizzas are excellent and she has a prime location, within a block of a university residence and a community college. Petra, therefore, finds that she can sell as many pizzas as she can make. At first, she hires one worker who is able to produce and sell 30 pizzas a day. Knowing that she can sell more, Petra hires a second worker. Each worker is then able to specialize in particular tasks. One takes the orders and cash, boxes the hot pizzas, and gives them to the customer; the other specializes in preparing and baking the pizzas. As a result of this elementary division of labour, Petra's total daily output increases to 70 pizzas. Since she can still sell as many pizzas as she can make, she goes on hiring additional workers until she has 11 employees and is producing 295 pizzas a day.

The workers (and the additional ingredients, toppings, etc.) Petra uses as she increases production are **variable resources**. They change as output changes. In other words, she needs more of them as she increases production. Her store and equipment or "plant" (ovens, cash register, etc.) are **fixed resources**. They do not change as output increases.

☐ Total, Marginal, and Average Product

Table 7.1 summarizes the changes in output as Petra increases the number of workers (amount of a variable resource) in her store. Column 2 shows that as more workers are hired, the total number of pizzas produced, or the **total product**, also increases. Column 3 indicates the additional output attributable to each new worker. The additional output that comes from each addition of a variable resource (such as labour) is known as the **marginal product**. The marginal product is calculated by the following formula.

$$\text{Marginal product (MP)} = \frac{\text{Change } (\Delta) \text{ in quantity produced (Q)}}{\text{Change } (\Delta) \text{ in the variable factor of production (N)}}$$

$$MP = \frac{\Delta Q}{\Delta N}$$

Thus, referring to Table 7.1, as the quantity produced increases from 30 to 70 pizzas with the addition of a second worker:

$$MP = \frac{70 - 30}{2 - 1} = 40.$$

The second worker, therefore, accounts for 40 additional pizzas.

At first, the marginal output increases. One worker is able to produce 30 pizzas a day. With two workers, output increases to 70 pizzas, as the one extra worker accounts for an additional 40 pizzas. With three work-

Table 7.1 Total, marginal, and average product for Petra's Pizza Parlour

1 NUMBER OF WORKERS (OR UNITS OF A VARIABLE FACTOR OF PRODUCTION) (N)	2 TOTAL QUANTITY PRODUCED (Q) OR TOTAL PRODUCT	3 NUMBER OF PIZZAS PRODUCED BY EACH ADDITIONAL WORKER OR MARGINAL PRODUCT (MP) $MP = \frac{\Delta Q}{\Delta N}$		4 AVERAGE NUMBER OF PIZZAS PRODUCED BY EACH WORKER OR AVERAGE PRODUCT (AP) $AP = \frac{Q}{N}$
0	0			
1	30	30	INCREASING RETURNS OR	30
2	70	40	INCREASING MARGINAL	35
3	120	50	PRODUCT	40
4	180	60		45
5	220	40		44
6	250	30		41.7
7	270	20	DECREASING RETURNS OR DECREASING	38.6
8	280	10	MARGINAL PRODUCT	35
9	288	8		32
10	293	5		29.3
11	295	2		26.8

The output of pizzas changes as the amount of the variable factor of production (labour) is increased. Column 2 shows that as the amount of labour is increased, total output increases. Column 3 indicates that marginal production at first increases (increasing returns or increasing marginal product), but after the fourth worker, it declines (decreasing returns or diminishing marginal product). Column 4 shows that the average number of pizzas produced per worker also at first increases, but after four workers declines.

ers, the extra worker accounts for 50 additional pizzas. The fourth worker accounts for 60 additional pizzas.

The marginal product for Petra's Pizza Parlour rises at an increasing rate up to four workers. After four workers, however, it decreases—declining from 40 pizzas with the fifth worker to 2 pizzas with the eleventh.

Column 4 in Table 7.1 shows the average product. The **average product** is the total product per worker (or per unit of the variable factor).

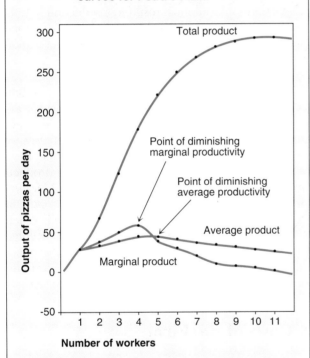

Figure 7.1 Total, average, and marginal product curves for Petra's Pizza

This figure shows the information in Table 7.1 graphically. **The marginal product curve rises up to four workers and then declines, reflecting the law of diminishing returns. The marginal product curve crosses the average product curve at the point where average production is at a maximum. This is the point of maximum efficiency, where the four workers together make the best use of the plant and equipment. The total product curve continues to rise as long as the marginal product is greater than zero.**

$$\text{Average product (AP)} = \frac{\text{Total product (Q)}}{\text{Number of workers (N)}}$$

$$AP = \frac{Q}{N}$$

We can see from column 4 that the average product also increases with each new worker up to the fourth worker. Then, it begins to decline.

Figure 7.1 shows the information in Table 7.1 graphically.

☐ The Law of Diminishing Returns

Petra has come face-to-face with the law of diminishing returns (also called the law of diminishing marginal product). The **law of diminishing returns** states that as additional units of a variable resource (in Petra's case, labour) are added to a fixed resource (in this case, capital, plant, and equipment), beyond some point the marginal product attributable to each additional unit of the variable resource will decline. Figure 7.1 illustrates this situation. The marginal product curve rises up to four workers and then declines as diminishing returns take effect.

Petra's experience is a common one. Toiling alone, one worker has to prepare the dough, knead and cut it, add the fixings, bake and box the pizza, and serve the customers. The worker wastes considerable time switching from one job to another. With one worker, the plant (pizza parlour) and equipment (pizza ovens, etc.) are under-utilized. With the addition of more workers, equipment is used more efficiently. Workers are able to specialize in a single task and time is not wasted switching jobs.

Thus, as more workers are added to an under-staffed pizza take-out, the marginal product of each additional worker rises. But this cannot continue forever. After a certain point, as still more workers are added (in this case after four workers), they will start to get in each other's way. They will have to wait to use the cash register and the ovens, for example. Efficiency decreases and though total product continues to rise, the marginal product of each additional worker declines. Figure 7.2 illustrates the relationship between total and marginal product.

The law of diminishing returns holds true in the production of all goods, including agricultural products. Suppose, for example, a farmer adds successive amounts of fertilizer (the variable resource) to 100 ha of land (the fixed resource) sowed with wheat. Beyond some point, the marginal product of wheat attributable to each addition of fertilizer will decline. If this were not the case, the world's demand for wheat could be met by applying sufficient fertilizer to this single farm of 100 ha!

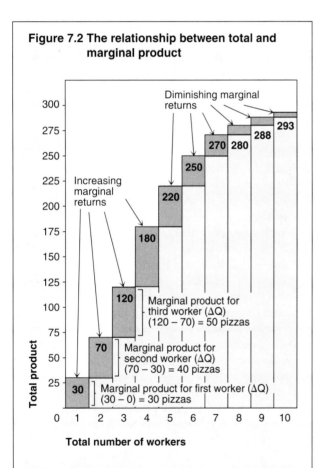

Figure 7.2 The relationship between total and marginal product

With a fixed plant size and amount of machinery, marginal product increases initially as more workers are added, but after four workers declines because of the law of diminishing returns. Total product increases with additional workers as long as the marginal product is greater than zero.

☐ Relationships Among Marginal, Total, and Average Product

Some basic relationships between marginal product and total product and marginal product and average product become clear.

(*i*) *Marginal product and total product* As long as the marginal product is positive, the total product must be increasing. A positive marginal product for each additional unit of the factor employed results in an addition to total product. Similarly, when the marginal product is negative, the total product must be decreasing. A negative marginal product for each additional unit of the factor employed must result in a reduction in total product. When the marginal product is zero, the total product will neither rise nor fall. Total product is then at its maximum.

(*ii*) *Marginal product and average product* When marginal product is greater than average product, average product will rise. Table 7.1 and Figure 7.1 showed, for example, that as the marginal product increases up to the addition of 4 workers, the average product rose. When marginal product is less than average product, on the other hand, average product will fall. Marginal product fell with the addition of the fifth worker in Figure 7.1, and thus average product also fell. When marginal product is equal to average product, average product will neither rise nor fall. The marginal product curve cuts the average product curve at its maximum point. In Figure 7.1, this is after the fourth worker.

Costs of the Firm

Business people are interested not only in how output changes with additional amounts of productive resources, but also how *costs* change with changes in output. Costs are, after all, a major determinant of profit. This relationship between costs and output is known as the **cost function**. First, let's consider what we mean by costs. We will look at costs from two points of view—that of the accountant and that of the economist.

☐ Explicit and Implicit Costs

What economists mean by cost is not the same as what accountants or, for that matter, what most people mean by cost. Let's look at an example. Suppose you own and manage a business in which you have invested $25 000. Your firm's costs, as viewed by accountants and economists, are shown in Table 7.2.

From an accountant's point of view, it looks as though you are doing well. With total revenue at $100 000 and explicit costs (or cash expenditures) totalling $60 000, you have an accounting profit of $40 000. **Explicit costs** are a firm's direct (or out-of-pocket) expenditures on such things as labour, rent, materials, transportation, and electricity.

From an economist's perspective, however, the pic-ture is not as rosy. In addition to the cash expenditures or explicit costs of labour, materials, and rent, etc., economists include other hidden or implicit costs. **Implicit costs** are estimated payments for resources that the firm already owns. Examples include the owner's salary and interest on money the owner has invested in the firm.

If instead of managing your firm, for example, you could have been employed elsewhere at a salary of $25 000, economists take this hidden cost into account to provide a clearer indication of your firm's operating costs. Second, since you not only manage the firm but have invested $25 000 in it, a cost is allowed for the interest you could have earned on your investment. Assuming an interest rate of 10 percent, you could have earned $2500 a year in interest. Economists also

---

Table 7.2 Costs and profits, as seen by accountants and economists

A. Accountants' Perspective

Total revenue		$100 000
Costs (cash expenditures)		
Labour	$10 000	
Materials	40 000	
Rent	10 000	
	$60 000	$ 60 000
Accounting profit		$ 40 000

B. Economists' Perspective

Total revenue		$100 000
Explicit costs (cash expenditures)		
Labour	$10 000	
Materials	40 000	
Rent	10 000	
Implicit (or hidden) costs		
Owner's salary	$25 000	
Interest	2 500	
Normal profit	1 500	
	$89 000	$ 89 000
Economic profit		$ 11 000

Economic profit is less than accounting profit because the economist deducts both explicit and implicit costs from total revenue. The accountant deducts only explicit costs in the calculation of profit.

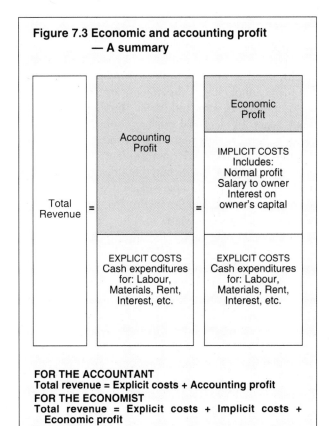

Figure 7.3 Economic and accounting profit — A summary

FOR THE ACCOUNTANT
Total revenue = Explicit costs + Accounting profit
FOR THE ECONOMIST
Total revenue = Explicit costs + Implicit costs + Economic profit

include a cost for assuming the risks and responsibilities of running the business. If this cost, known as **minimum** or **normal profit**, were not taken into account, entrepreneurs would have no incentive to remain in business.

In Table 7.2, we have assumed a minimum or normal profit of $1500. Thus, when we have deducted both the explicit (total $60 000) and implicit (total $29 000) costs from total revenue ($100 000), we are left with an economic profit of $11 000. Figure 7.3 summarizes the differences between how economists and accountants view costs and profit. Throughout this book, we will follow the economists' conception of costs and profit.

☐ Short-Run Costs

Economists also make a distinction between costs incurred over the short run and the long run. Let's consider short-run costs first.

The short run is *not* defined as a specific number of weeks, months, or years. It is the time period in which the firm cannot change the amount or type of its plant or equipment. In some industries, the short run may be many years. In electrical power generation, for example, it generally takes years to construct a new nuclear, thermo-, or hydro-electric power plant. A pizza restaurant, on the other hand, may be able to install additional pizza ovens in the space of a few weeks. Similarly, it may be much easier for a firm to expand than to contract. Restaurant owners may find it more difficult to decrease the size of their restaurants (e.g., by renting a part of them to someone else), than to expand by taking over a neighbouring store.

In the short run, therefore, since plant and equipment are fixed, their costs for the firm are also fixed. However, since variable resources such as labour and raw materials may change, their costs for the firm over the short run are also variable. Costs in the short run thus fall into three main categories:

1. Fixed, variable, and total costs
2. Average (per unit) fixed, variable, and total costs
3. Marginal costs, or the extra costs of producing one more unit.

1. Fixed, Variable, and Total Costs

(i) Total fixed costs (TFC) or overhead costs   **Total fixed costs** are those costs that do not change *in total* with changes in output. They include the costs of insurance, rent, depreciation on capital equipment, interest on debt, and management salaries.

In the case of Petra's Pizza Parlour, they include the depreciation of her equipment, such as her pizza ovens; the interest on money she borrowed to start the business; and rental payments on her store. We assume that her fixed costs are $200 a day, as shown in column 3 of Table 7.3. Petra still has to pay rent, interest, insurance, and depreciation whether she produces no pizzas or 280 pizzas a day. The curve for total fixed cost (TFC), shown in Figure 7.4, is therefore a straight line at $200.

(ii) Total variable costs (TVC)   **Total variable costs** are those costs that vary directly as output varies—that

Table 7.3 Fixed, variable, and total costs for Petra's Pizza Parlour (in dollars)

1 NUMBER OF WORKERS	2 TOTAL OUTPUT (Q) (IN UNITS)	3 TOTAL FIXED COST (TFC)	4 TOTAL VARIABLE COST (TVC)	5 TOTAL COST (TC) TC = TFC + TVC
0	0	200	0	200
1	30	200	80	280
2	70	200	170	370
3	120	200	270	470
4	180	200	380	580
5	220	200	470	670
6	250	200	550	750
7	270	200	620	820
8	280	200	680	880
9	288	200	738	938
10	293	200	793	993

Fixed costs remain unchanged at $200 no matter what the level of output. These costs are incurred even if output is zero. Variable costs rise as the firm increases output. Total cost is the sum of fixed and variable costs. At an output of 30 pizzas, for example, fixed costs are $200 and variable costs are $80 for a total cost of $280. Total costs thus also rise as output increases.

is, as output increases, total variable costs also increase, and as output decreases, total variable costs also decrease. Examples of variable costs include materials, fuel, power, and labour.

For Petra, variable costs would include her workers' wages; the costs of materials for making the pizzas; and the costs of electricity for lighting and running the cash register, ovens, etc. To increase output, she must hire more workers, buy more materials, and use more electrical power. Consequently, her variable costs increase as she produces more pizzas, as shown in column 4 of Table 7.3 and in Figure 7.4. To decrease output, she would hire fewer workers, buy less materials, and use less electrical power. Hence, her variable costs would decrease.

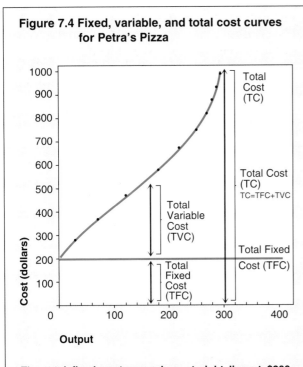

Figure 7.4 Fixed, variable, and total cost curves for Petra's Pizza

The total fixed cost curve is a straight line at $200, since these costs remain constant no matter what the output. The total variable cost rises as output increases. The total cost curve also rises with increases in output, since it represents the sum of fixed and variable costs.

(iii) Total cost (TC) **Total cost** is the sum of fixed and variable costs. Since fixed costs remain unchanged in the short run, total costs increase as variable costs increase. This is shown in column 5 of Table 7.3 and illustrated by the rising total cost curve in Figure 7.4.

For example, if Petra's Pizza Parlour has a total output of 180 pizzas a day, total fixed cost is $200 and total variable cost is $380, giving a total cost of $580. With total output at 250 pizzas, total fixed costs are the same at $200, total variable costs have increased to $550, and thus total costs have also increased to $750.

2. Average (or per unit) Costs

Producers are interested not only in total costs, but also in average or per unit costs. Average costs can be compared to the price of a good or service to give an indication of profit. If average cost exceeds price per unit, the firm is operating at a loss. On the other hand, if average cost is less than price per unit, the firm is making a profit. Let's examine how average fixed cost, average variable cost, and average total cost are determined.

(i) Average fixed cost (AFC) **Average fixed cost** is calculated by dividing total fixed cost (TFC) by output (Q), as shown in column 6 of Table 7.4. That is:

$$\text{Average fixed cost (AFC)} = \frac{\text{Total fixed cost (TFC)}}{\text{Total output (Q)}}$$

$$AFC = \frac{TFC}{Q}$$

Since total fixed cost is constant, dividing it by the quantity produced gives a steadily falling average fixed cost curve as production increases. This is illustrated in Figure 7.5. Thus, as more pizzas are produced and sold, average fixed costs decline.

(ii) Average variable cost (AVC) **Average variable cost** is calculated by dividing total variable cost (TVC) by output (Q). That is:

$$\text{Average variable cost (AVC)} = \frac{\text{Total variable cost (TVC)}}{\text{Total output (Q)}}$$

$$AVC = \frac{TVC}{Q}$$

As shown in Figure 7.5, the AVC curve declines until it reaches a minimum and then rises, producing a U-shape. The AVC curve has this shape because of the law of diminishing returns. At low levels of output, the firm is under-staffed, production is inefficient, and consequently variable costs per unit are high. As more workers are employed, output increases, greater specialization of labour is possible, and capital resources are put to optimum use. Production is more efficient. Variable costs per unit, therefore, decline. But as more and more employees are added, the firm becomes over-staffed, marginal productivity per worker falls, and average variable costs rise.

(iii) Average total cost (ATC)   **Average total cost** is calculated by adding average variable cost and average fixed cost at each level of output, or by dividing total cost by output. That is:

(a) Average total cost (ATC) = Average fixed cost (AFC) + Average variable cost (AVC)

ATC = AFC + AVC

For example, referring to Table 7.4, at an output of 70 pizzas:

ATC = \$2.86 (AFC) + \$2.43 (AVC)
      = \$5.29

(b) Average total cost (ATC) = $\dfrac{\text{Total cost (TC)}}{\text{Total output (Q)}}$

$$\text{ATC} = \frac{\text{TC}}{\text{Q}}$$

For example, at an output of 70 pizzas:

$$\text{ATC} = \frac{\$370\ (\text{TC})}{70\ (\text{Q})}$$
$$= \$5.29$$

Graphically, the average total cost curve is found by adding vertically the average fixed cost and the average variable cost curves, as shown in Figure 7.5.

The output level at which the ATC curve is at a minimum is called the firm's **capacity** or **optimum**

Table 7.4 Total, average, and marginal costs for Petra's Pizza Parlour (in dollars)

1 NUMBER OF WORKERS	2 TOTAL OUTPUT (Q) (IN UNITS)	3 TOTAL FIXED COST (TFC)	4 TOTAL VARIABLE COST (TVC)	5 TOTAL COST (TC) TC = TFC + TVC	6 AVERAGE FIXED COST (AFC) AFC = $\frac{TFC}{Q}$	7 AVERAGE VARIABLE COST (AVC) AVC = $\frac{TVC}{Q}$	8 AVERAGE TOTAL COST (ATC) ATC = $\frac{TC}{Q}$	9 MARGINAL COST (MC) MC = $\frac{\Delta TC}{\Delta Q}$
0	0	200	0	200	—	—	—	—
1	30	200	80	280	6.66	2.66	9.33	2.67
2	70	200	170	370	2.86	2.43	5.29	2.25
3	120	200	270	470	1.66	2.25	3.92	2.00
4	180	200	380	580	1.11	2.11	3.22	1.83
5	220	200	470	670	0.91	2.14	3.05	2.25
6	250	200	550	750	0.80	2.20	3.00	2.67
7	270	200	620	820	0.74	2.30	3.04	3.50
8	280	200	680	880	0.71	2.43	3.14	6.00
9	288	200	738	938	0.69	2.56	3.26	7.25
10	293	200	793	993	0.68	2.71	3.39	11.00

Columns 1 through 5 are reproduced from Table 7.3. Column 6 shows that average fixed costs decline as output increases. Average variable costs (column 7) at first decrease as output increases and then rise as diminishing returns take effect. Average total costs (column 8) also at first decline and then rise with increases in output due to diminishing returns. Marginal cost or the cost of each additional unit of output (column 9) follows a similar pattern.

rate of output, shown as point M in Figure 7.5. This is the point of highest efficiency. Operating above or below capacity increases average total costs. The average total cost curve is, therefore, also U-shaped.

3. Marginal Cost

Marginal cost is the extra or additional cost of producing one more unit of output. That is:

$$\text{Marginal cost (MC)} = \frac{\text{Change in } (\Delta) \text{ total cost (TC)}}{\text{Change in } (\Delta) \text{ quantity (Q)}}$$

$$MC = \frac{\Delta TC}{\Delta Q}$$

For example, referring to column 5 in Table 7.4, we see that it costs $80 ($280 - $200) to increase production from 0 to 30 pizzas. Marginal cost—the cost of producing an additional unit, shown in column 9—is, therefore:

$$\frac{\Delta TC}{\Delta Q} = \frac{280 - 200}{30 - 0} = \frac{80}{30} = \$2.67$$

With an increase in production from 30 to 70 pizzas per day:

$$\text{Marginal cost} = \frac{370 - 280}{70 - 30} = \frac{90}{40} = \$2.25$$

With an increase in production from 70 to 120 pizzas per day:

$$\text{Marginal cost} = \frac{470 - 370}{120 - 70} = \frac{100}{50} = \$2.00$$

As production increases, marginal costs at first fall. However, from Figure 7.5, we can see that the marginal cost curve reaches a minimum and then begins to rise. The marginal cost curve is thus also U-shaped, reflecting diminishing returns. What does this mean? Initially, as the marginal product increases with additions of a variable resource (labour, for example) at a constant cost, marginal costs fall. After some point, however, diminishing returns set in, the marginal product falls, and consequently marginal costs increase.

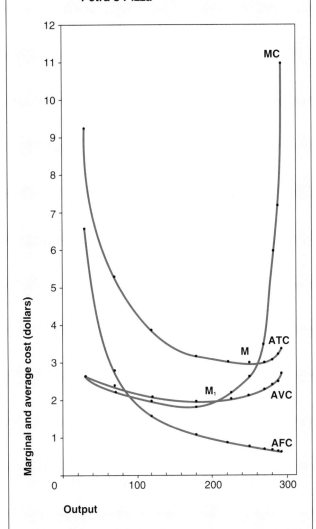

Figure 7.5 Marginal and average cost curves for Petra's Pizza

The MC curve cuts both the AVC and ATC curves at their lowest points (M₁ and M respectively). This is no coincidence, because whenever the marginal (or additional) cost is less than the average variable cost, the average variable cost must fall. Conversely, whenever marginal cost is greater than average variable cost, average variable cost must rise. The same is true for average total cost. Whenever marginal cost is less than average total cost, average total cost must fall and whenever marginal cost is greater than average total cost, average total cost must rise.

□ □ □ □ □ □

Typical Shapes of Total, Average, and Marginal Cost Curves

Figure 7.6 Total cost curves

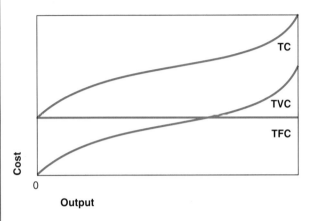

Total fixed cost does not change with output. Total cost and total variable cost rise with increases in output, first at a relatively fast rate and then at a slower rate.

Figure 7.7 Marginal and average cost curves

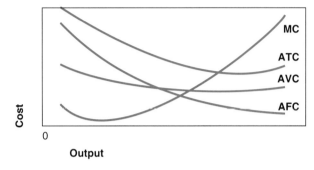

The marginal and average cost curves are calculated from the total cost curves in Figure 7.6. Average fixed cost declines as output increases. Average variable cost and average total cost fall and then rise as output increases. Marginal cost also falls and then rises with increases in output. The MC curve cuts the AVC and ATC curves at their minimum points.

□ Relationships among Marginal Cost, Average Variable Cost, and Average Total Cost

The marginal cost curve crosses both the average variable and average total cost curves at their minimum points, as shown in Figure 7.5. It is clear why. If the marginal cost is less than average total cost, then the average total cost will fall. Similarly, if the marginal cost is less than the average variable cost, the average variable cost will fall. The converse is also true. If marginal cost is greater than either average total or average variable cost, then average total or average variable cost will rise. If the marginal and average costs are equal, the average costs reach a minimum. They cease to fall and are poised to rise.

For Petra, if she produces at the point where her average total cost curve intersects her marginal cost curve, she is producing at her firm's optimum rate of output. If she produces any more or any less, her average total costs will increase.

Average total cost also gives Petra a measure of profitability. If her average total costs are less than the average price of her pizzas, then she will make a profit. The greater the difference, the greater the profit from each pizza. If her average total cost is greater than the price of a pizza, Petra will sustain a loss.

□ Long-Run Costs

So far, we have dealt with the short run—the period in which plant and equipment are fixed. Now we turn to the long run—the period in which *all factors are variable*. In the long run, the firm can change not only the amount of labour and raw materials it uses (variable resources), but also its plant size and the amount and type of equipment it uses (fixed resources). The number of firms in the industry may also vary, as some new firms start production and others shut down. Petra, for example, cannot only hire more workers and buy more dough and other materials, she might also move to a larger store and buy new computerized cash registers. She may also find that she has competition, since a new pizza outlet could move into the area, attracted by the large market.

Since in the long run all costs are variable, the difference between total fixed and variable costs is no longer significant. The appropriate cost concept over the long run is, therefore, total cost. The long-run alternatives faced by the firm can be seen in terms of average total cost in a series of short-run situations. This series of short-run average total cost curves (SATC$_1$, SATC$_2$, etc.) can be strung together to form a long-run average total cost curve, as shown in Figure 7.8. Only four of what could be a very large number of SATC curves are shown in this example.

Each successive SATC curve represents the investment of increasing amounts of capital in plant and equipment. In the long run, a firm is free to select any quantity of capital investment. The LATC curve indicates the amount of capital needed to produce a given number of units per day and the cost per unit. Clearly,

it is in the firm's best interests to choose the capital and quantity that yields the lowest cost per unit.

Suppose a firm decides that it wants to produce 240 units per day. It can produce them with the small plant represented by SATC$_1$, with the larger plant represented by SATC$_2$, or with the yet larger plant represented by SATC$_3$. Which will it select? Clearly, it will choose the plant represented by SATC$_2$, because the average cost per unit is $3.10, rather than $3.45 as it is on SATC$_1$, and $4.10 as it is on SATC$_3$. To produce 400 units, it would select the amount of capital represented by SATC$_3$, keeping its cost per unit to a minimum at $2.50.

Points below the LATC cannot be attained with the current inputs and technology. Points above the LATC curve can be chosen, but the most efficient points lie along the LATC curve. It is the relevant curve when a firm is engaged in long-run planning and is free to select any quantity of capital investment.

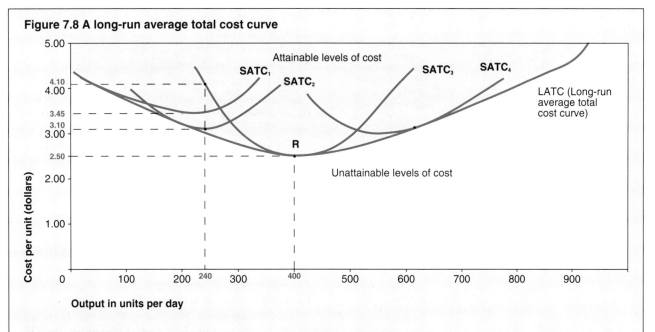

Figure 7.8 A long-run average total cost curve

SATC curves are the short-run average total cost curves that can be achieved with varying amounts of capital (1, 2, 3, 4). LATC is the long-run average total cost curve that encloses all the SATC curves. The LATC curve is U-shaped. At first, average total costs decline due to increasing returns to scale. Then, the curve flattens out as returns are constant. Finally, it starts to rise with decreasing returns to scale and as average total costs increase.

Figure 7.9 A summary of cost concepts

COST CONCEPT	DEFINITION OR CALCULATION	SHAPE OF THE CURVE
TOTAL COSTS		
Total Fixed Cost (TFC)	Also called sunk cost or overhead. Total fixed costs are those costs which do not vary with output (e.g., rent of land and insurance).	Remains unchanged at all levels of output. TFC curve is a straight line parallel to the horizontal axis.
Total Variable Cost (TVC)	Total variable costs (e.g., labour and material costs) increase as output increases.	TVC curve slopes up to the right.
Total Cost (TC)	Total cost is the sum of total fixed cost (TFC) and total variable cost (TVC); that is, TC = TFC + TVC.	TC curve slopes up to the right.
AVERAGE COSTS		
Average Fixed Cost (AFC)	$AFC = \dfrac{\text{Total fixed cost (TFC)}}{\text{Output (Q)}}$	AFC curve falls as output increases.
Average Variable Cost (AVC)	$AVC = \dfrac{\text{Total variable cost (TVC)}}{\text{Output (Q)}}$	AVC curve initially falls, then reaches a minimum and rises. AVC curve is U-shaped due to the law of diminishing returns.
Average Total Cost (ATC)	ATC = Average fixed cost (AFC) + Average variable cost (AVC) OR $ATC = \dfrac{\text{Total cost (TC)}}{\text{Output (Q)}}$	Due to the law of diminishing returns, the ATC curve is U-shaped.
MARGINAL COST		
Marginal Cost (MC)	Marginal cost is the additional cost of producing one more unit of output. $MC = \dfrac{\text{Change } \Delta \text{ in total cost}}{\text{Change } \Delta \text{ in output (Q)}}$	Due to law of diminishing returns, the marginal cost curve is U-shaped. The MC curve cuts the AVC and ATC curves at their minimum points.

☐ Economies of Scale

Economies of scale occur when an increase in inputs results in a more than proportional increase in output. Conversely, **diseconomies of scale** occur when an increase in inputs brings a less than proportional increase in output. Unlike the law of diminishing returns (where only one factor is varied), economies of scale result from varying all factors of production (that is, a firm's full-scale of operations).

Economies of Scale or Increasing Returns to Scale

Increasing returns may occur as a result of changes in four major areas: technical, managerial, financial, and marketing. Technical economies of scale can be achieved by developments such as mass production, which makes increased specialization of labour and machinery possible. Managerial economies can be achieved through the use of more specialized managers supervising more workers. Financial economies may be realized if a firm is able to borrow larger amounts of money at lower rates, or receives a significant discount for buying a large volume of materials. Marketing economies may be achieved through effective advertising campaigns or an increased sales force. All of these changes require large initial expenditures or increased inputs, but may result in proportionally higher outputs.

In Figure 7.8, for example, the LATC curve declines to point R, reflecting increasing economies of scale. Increased inputs result in greater output and lower costs per unit.

Diseconomies of Scale or Decreasing Returns to Scale

Beyond some point (R in Figure 7.8), the LATC curve begins to rise, reflecting the diseconomies of scale. The increased inputs no longer result in proportional increases in output and, therefore, costs per unit rise. Why? Management may become unwieldy as additional levels are added and decision-making may, therefore, become more remote from those who actually carry out the decisions. The effectiveness of advertising or sales campaigns may wane over time. Interest rates may rise, causing financial diseconomies. The advantages of specialization and more efficient production methods may peak. Increased production after that peak will result in inefficiencies and higher average total costs.

If we return to our example of Petra's Pizza Parlour then, we can see that by increasing her inputs of labour and materials, she achieves economies of scale. Printing and distributing a number of flyers and buying a computerized cash register may also increase her returns. But at some point, the effectiveness of these additional inputs will peak and further inputs will cost her more than she receives in extra returns. At that point, she will experience diseconomies of scale. Clearly, firms must be aware of their point of optimum capacity if they are to maximize profit and avoid losses.

Summary

a. Though not the only objective of businesses, making a profit is essential and economists, therefore, assume that firms will attempt to achieve the highest profits possible. This profit-maximizing assumption is a useful guide to business behaviour.

b. The production function refers to the relationship between a firm's inputs and its output. As more units of a variable factor of production are added, total product increases, marginal product (the additional output attributable to each addition of a variable resource) increases at first and then declines, and average product also at first increases and then declines.

c. The changes in marginal and average product reflect the law of diminishing returns. As additional units of a variable resource are added to a fixed resource, at some point the marginal product attributable to each additional unit of the variable resource will decline.

d. The cost function of a firm refers to the relationship between costs and output. Explicit costs are the out-of-pocket cash expenditures incurred by a firm in hiring workers, buying materials, renting a building, and paying interest on borrowed money, for example. Implicit costs are hidden costs paid for resources the business already owns, including a salary to the owner, interest on capital invested in the firm, and a normal profit.

For the accountant, profit equals total revenue minus explicit costs. For the economist, profit equals total revenue minus implicit and explicit costs.

e. In the short run, total fixed costs remain constant at all levels of output. Total variable costs vary directly as output varies. Total cost is the sum of total fixed costs and total variable costs, and therefore also varies directly with output.

f. Average fixed cost declines with increases in output. Average variable cost and average total cost at first decline with increases in output, and then after a certain point increase—though not together. Changes in average variable and average total cost reflect the law of diminishing returns. The AVC and ATC curves are U-shaped.

The marginal cost curve falls at first and then rises, cutting the average variable and average total cost curves at their minimum points. The U-shape of the marginal cost curve also reflects the law of diminishing returns. The firm's optimum rate of output is the point at which the marginal cost curve intersects the average total cost curve.

g. The long-run average total cost curve encloses all the short-run average total cost curves, since in the long-run all costs are variable. A firm will choose the capital investment and quantity that yields the lowest cost per unit.

h. Economies of scale occur when an increase in inputs results in a more than proportional increase in output. Diseconomies of scale occur when an increase in inputs brings a less than proportional increase in output.

▌ Review of Key Terms

Define the following key terms introduced in this chapter and provide examples where appropriate.

production function	total fixed cost
variable resources	total variable cost
fixed resources	total cost
total product	average fixed cost
marginal product	average variable cost
average product	average total cost
law of diminishing returns	optimum rate of output
cost function	marginal cost
explicit costs	economies of scale
implicit costs	diseconomies of scale
normal profit	

▌ Application and Analysis

1. Table 7.5 shows the variations in output at Wendy's Whimburgers (a new fast-food restaurant) per day as she hires more workers.

(a) Complete Table 7.5 by filling in the marginal and average product columns.

(b) On a graph, plot the marginal product and the average product curves.

(c) Label the maximum point on the average product curve M. Compare the values of the average product and the marginal product at this point.

(d) Over what range of inputs does Wendy's achieve:
  (i)   increasing returns
  (ii) diminishing returns?
  Explain.

2. Outline the explicit and implicit costs of going to college or university.

3. Shashi Sharmak has a small submarine sandwich stand. He hires two part-time helpers for $24 000 a year each and pays an annual rent of $10 000 for his stand. The food and other materials he needs cost him

Table 7.5 Total, marginal, and average production per day at Wendy's Whimburgers

1 WORKERS (OR UNITS OF A VARIABLE FACTOR OF PRODUCTION) (N)	2 NUMBER OF WHIMBURGERS OR QUANTITY PRODUCED (Q)	3 ADDITIONAL WHIMBURGERS PRODUCED BY EACH ADDITIONAL WORKER OR MARGINAL PRODUCT (MP) $MP = \frac{\Delta Q}{\Delta N}$	4 AVERAGE NUMBER OF WHIMBURGERS PRODUCED PER WORKER OR AVERAGE PRODUCT (AP) $AP = \frac{Q}{N}$
0	0		
1	20		
2	75		
3	180		
4	300		
5	400		
6	470		
7	520		
8	530		
9	535		

$50 000 a year. Shashi has invested $20 000 of his own money in the firm—money that could earn him $2000 a year in interest. He has been offered $25 000 a year by another submarine sandwich firm to work full-time. He estimates that his skills as an entrepreneur are worth $5000 a year. His total annual revenue is $110 000 a year.

Calculate the following for Shashi Sharmak's business:

(a) explicit costs   (c) accounting profit
(b) implicit costs   (d) economic profit

4. Indicate which of the following are short-run (SR) and which are long-run (LR) adjustments.

(a) Chrysler Canada lays off 1000 workers.

(b) GM Canada installs a fully-automated paint shop in its Oshawa plant.

(c) Grain farmers cut back on the amount of fertilizer they will use this year.

Table 7.6 Total, average, and marginal costs for Mei Ling Wong Chairs Ltd. (in dollars)

1 TOTAL OUTPUT (Q) (IN UNITS)	2 TOTAL FIXED COST (TFC)	3 TOTAL VARIABLE COST (TVC)	4 TOTAL COST (TC) TC = TFC + TVC	5 AVERAGE FIXED COST (AFC) $AFC = \frac{TFC}{Q}$	6 AVERAGE VARIABLE COST (AVC) $AVC = \frac{TVC}{Q}$	7 AVERAGE TOTAL COST (ATC) ATC = AFC + AVC OR $\frac{TC}{Q}$	8 MARGINAL COST (MC) $MC = \frac{\Delta TC}{\Delta Q}$
0		0					
1		45					
2		85					
3		120					
4		150					
5		185					
6		225					
7		270					
8		325					
9		390					
10		465					

Table 7.7 Short-run average cost schedules and long-run average cost schedule for the production of shirts per day (in dollars)

	PLANT A		PLANT B		PLANT C			
1 QUANTITY (Q) (IN UNITS)	2 AVERAGE COST (AC)	3 QUANTITY (Q) (IN UNITS)	4 AVERAGE COST (AC)	5 QUANTITY (Q) (IN UNITS)	6 AVERAGE COST (AC)	7 QUANTITY (Q) (IN UNITS)	8 LONG-RUN AVERAGE COST (LRAC)
---	---	---	---	---	---	---	---
20	25	20	35	20	45	20	
30	22	30	30	30	40	30	
40	20	40	25	40	30	40	
50	23	50	20	50	25	50	
60	25	60	15	60	20	60	
70	40	70	20	70	15	70	
80	50	80	25	80	10	80	
90	70	90	35	90	15	90	
100	90	100	50	100	25	100	

(d) Canada Post decreases the amount of overtime its inside employees work.

(e) Hydro-Québec builds more hydro-electric generating plants at James Bay.

5. Assume that Mei Ling Wong Chairs Ltd. has fixed costs of $100 and variable costs as outlined in Table 7.6 on page 155.

(a) Complete Table 7.6.

(b) Graph the total fixed cost, total variable cost, and total cost curves.

(c) How does the law of diminishing returns influence the shape of the total variable cost and total cost curves?

(d) Graph the average fixed cost, average variable cost, average total cost, and marginal cost curves.

Explain why the marginal cost curve cuts the average variable cost and average total cost curves at their minimum points.

6. Table 7.7 on page 155 shows short-run average cost schedules for the daily production of shirts using three different plant sizes.

(a) For what range of output should the firm use:
   (i)   plant A
   (ii) plant B
   (iii) plant C?

(b) From the data given in Table 7.7, complete the firm's long-run average cost schedule in column 8.

CHAPTER EIGHT

Perfect Competition

We have examined production costs, but clearly they represent only part of a firm's financial picture. To complete the picture, we must also consider revenues or income. Production decisions are based on both costs *and* revenues, and revenues are in turn affected by the type of market structure in which the firm operates. Economies may include more than one market structure. In Canada, for example, market structures include perfect competition—which we have been considering—as well as monopoly, oligopoly, and monopolistic competition.

In this chapter, we briefly outline the four major market structures, and then focus on how the firm in perfect competition makes its production decisions. In the next two chapters, we examine the other three market structures.

Objectives

a. Compare the characteristics of the major market structures: monopoly, monopolistic competition, oligopoly, and perfect competition.

b. Outline the major conditions that must be fulfilled for perfect competition.

c. Calculate and graph the average, total, and marginal revenues for a firm under perfect competition.

d. Demonstrate, using schedules and graphs, two ways of determining profit maximization for a firm: the total revenue-total cost approach and the MR = MC rule.

e. Determine when a firm under perfect competition would operate at the break-even point and when it would shut down.

f. Examine the long-run equilibrium of the perfectly competitive firm.

g. Explain why and under what conditions perfect competition provides an efficient use of productive resources.

■ Market Structures

The various market structures can be characterized by the number of firms in the market, the degree of competition, the type of product or service offered, and the individual firm's control over price.

□ Pure Monopoly

Pure monopoly is a market structure with only one producer of a good or service, for which there are no close substitutes and many buyers. Electric power is usually provided by a single supplier in a given area, for example. Other examples of the goods and services provided by monopolies in Canada include natural gas, telephone services, and urban transportation.

As the sole supplier in a given area, a monopolist has considerable control over price—in other words, it is a "price-maker." It has no competition from either other firms or other close (substitute) products or services. Significant barriers prevent other firms from entering the industry. We will examine these barriers in more detail in the next chapter. Along a spectrum of markets, pure monopoly represents one polar position, as shown in Figure 8.1.

□ Oligopoly

Oligopoly is a market structure in which a few large firms provide most of the goods or services. Imperial Oil, Shell, and Petro-Canada, for example, provide most of the gasoline Canadians use. Other examples include the small number of firms that produce steel and automobiles in Canada. Oligopolistic industries form a major part of the Canadian economy.

Since there are only a few firms in the industry, each one has a significant influence on the price of its product and provides a large share of the output. All will, therefore, take notice of the prices and policies of their rivals. They will compete to a degree. In some cases, the firms may agree to control price and output. The Organization of Petroleum Exporting Countries (OPEC), for example, agreed to limit oil production in order to raise prices and increase profits in the 1970s

and again in the late 1980s. Such agreements are illegal in Canada, however. Along a spectrum of markets, oligopoly is next to pure monopoly.

□ Monopolistic Competition

Monopolistic competition is a market situation in which a large number of sellers provide similar, *but not identical* products. Different hamburger restaurants, for example, offer a similar, but not identical hamburger. This market structure differs from pure monopoly in that the large number of sellers and the differentiated products mean that competition does exist, though it is limited. Each firm provides only a small share of the total output, and hence each is relatively unaffected by the price and output decisions of the others.

However, since each firm's product is slightly different from that of its competitors, it does have some ability to adjust its price. It can raise its price somewhat, but not so much that consumers will turn to other products. It may also lower its price, but not so much that it sustains a loss. With the large number of firms, it also follows that the barriers to entry are not significant. Along the spectrum of markets, monopolistic competition is next to pure competition.

Figure 8.1 A spectrum of markets

| PURE OR PERFECT COMPETITION | MONOPOLISTIC COMPETITION | OLIGOPOLY | PURE MONOPOLY |

Decreasing competition ⟶

Fewer firms ⟶

Increasing control over price ⟶

As we move from perfect competition to pure monopoly along the spectrum of markets, the number of firms decreases, the degree of competition diminishes, and the control over price increases.

☐ Perfect Competition

Perfect competition is a market structure in which there are many firms (buyers and sellers), with no one firm able to influence price and all offering an identical product or service. The stock market and agricultural markets (without government intervention) are examples. One farmer's wheat of a particular grade, for example, is virtually indistinguishable from another's.

As we saw in Chapter 4, it is the interaction of supply and demand that determines price in a perfectly competitive market. Since individual firms have no control over the market price, they are known as "price-takers." They must deal with the prevailing market price at all times. No barriers exist under perfect competition to prevent firms from entering or leaving the industry. Perfect competition is, therefore, the most competitive market structure. On the market spectrum, it is at the opposite pole to pure monopoly.

Thus, for perfect competition to exist, the following conditions must be fulfilled:

(i) Many buyers and sellers The industry must be made up of many buyers and sellers, so that the possibility of agreements among firms to fix prices or restrict output does not exist.

(ii) Small individual output Each firm's output is small in relation to the total output of the good or service, so that the firm's behaviour has no effect on price.

(iii) Identical product All firms produce an identical product, so that buyers have no reason to buy from one firm rather than another. Competition is, thus, at a maximum.

(iv) Full information All buyers and sellers have complete information about the market, products, and prices.

(v) Mobile resources Productive resources are completely mobile. Workers, for example, are free to move into or out of the industry. Firms also face no barriers to entering or leaving the industry.

These five conditions rarely exist—if at all—in reality. Some industries in Canada, particularly agricultural industries such as wheat or egg production, do satisfy the second and third conditions, but marketing boards and price support programs mean that the first and last conditions are not met. Marketing boards and price support programs influence prices and the movement of resources.

Consumer product and retail markets also do not fit these criteria, since the products are not identical (e.g., dresses). If they are (e.g., milk), consumers may not value them identically. Milk at the grocery store 2 km away, for example, is not identical to the milk at the convenience store a block away. The buyer will prefer the milk that is easier to get.

Why Study the Model of Perfect Competition?

It might reasonably be asked—why bother examining the perfect competition model if it exists only rarely, if at all? There are two main reasons:

(i) As we introduce features which differ from the pure market model, the separate effects of each one can be examined.

(ii) Perfect competition generally leads to the most efficient use of resources. It can, therefore, be used as a measure for assessing other market structures.

Suppose you own a firm in a market under perfect competition. Thus, you are unable to influence the price of your product since its price is determined by the market, and there are no barriers to firms entering or leaving the industry. At the market price, you can sell as many of your products as you can make—that is, the demand for your product is perfectly elastic. By restricting output, you cannot raise the price and you have no need to cut your price in order to increase sales. If, for example, the market price is $30, Your Firm (let's call it that) will be able to sell its total output at $30 a unit. The demand schedule for Your Firm is shown in Table 8.1.

By a perfectly elastic demand for your product, remember that we do not mean a perfectly elastic *market* demand. While the demand for an individual firm's products may be perfectly elastic as shown in Figure 8.2, the market demand may be inelastic as between d_1 and d_2 in Figure 8.3. In a perfectly competit-

Figure 8.2 Demand curve for a firm's product under perfect competition

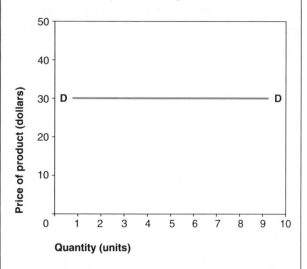

The demand curve for Your Firm under perfect competition illustrates that demand for your product is perfectly elastic. Your Firm sells its entire output at the market price.

Figure 8.3 Total market demand curve

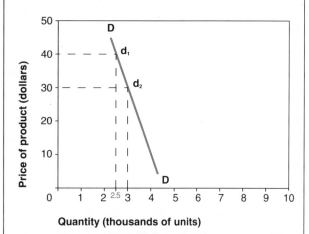

While the demand for an individual firm's product under perfect competition is elastic, the market demand may be inelastic—as between d_1 and d_2.

Table 8.1 Demand schedule for Your Firm's product under perfect competition

1 PRODUCT PRICE PER UNIT (IN DOLLARS)	2 QUANTITY DEMANDED (IN UNITS)
30	1
30	2
30	3
30	4
30	5
30	6
30	7
30	8
30	9
30	10

The demand schedule for a firm under perfect competition shows that the firm has no influence over price. It must accept the market price of $30 at all levels of output. Demand for the product is perfectly elastic, since price has no effect on the quantity demanded.

ive market with many sellers, individual firms make such a small contribution to total output that they have no effect on total market demand or supply. Individually, they can sell all they can make at the constant market price.

▮ Revenues

As a firm in a perfectly competitive market, therefore, you cannot influence price. However, you must decide on a level of output. At what output can you maximize your profits? To answer this question, you must examine the firm's costs and revenues. **Sales revenue** is the money received by the firm in exchange for its products. As with costs, firms must consider their average, total, and marginal revenues.

☐ Average, Total, and Marginal Revenues

Average Revenue (AR)
The demand schedule in Table 8.1 is also a revenue schedule. This relationship is shown in Table 8.2.

Prices to the buyer in Table 8.1 (column 1) are at the same time revenue per unit (or average revenue) to the seller (column 1 in Table 8.2). To show that the buyer pays $30 a unit is also to show that the seller received $30 a unit. Average revenue and price are the same amount considered from two different perspectives—that of the seller (average revenue) and that of the buyer (price).

Specifically, **average revenue** (AR) is the total revenue (TR) from the sale of a product divided by the quantity sold (Q). That is:

$$\text{Average revenue (AR)} = \frac{\text{Total revenue (TR)}}{\text{Quantity sold (Q)}}$$

$$AR = \frac{TR}{Q}$$

For a perfectly competitive firm, average revenue is the same as price.

Total Revenue (TR)

Total revenue is the total receipts from the sale of a product. It is equal to price (P) times quantity sold (Q). That is:

Total revenue (TR) = Price (P) x Quantity sold (Q)
$$TR = P \times Q$$

For Your Firm, total revenue increases by a constant amount—$30—for each additional good sold, as shown in column 3 of Table 8.2. For a perfectly competitive firm, total revenue increases in proportion to quantity sold.

Marginal Revenue (MR)

Marginal revenue is the change in a firm's total revenue that results from the sale of one additional unit. Marginal revenue is calculated in a similar way to marginal cost. It is determined by dividing the increase in total revenue by the increase in units sold. That is:

$$\frac{\text{Marginal revenue (MR)}}{} = \frac{\text{Increase } (\Delta) \text{ in total revenue (TR)}}{\text{Increase } (\Delta) \text{ in quantity demanded or sold (Q)}}$$

$$MR = \frac{\Delta TR}{\Delta Q}$$

Table 8.2 Demand and revenue schedules for a perfectly competitive firm

DEMAND		REVENUE	
1 PRODUCT PRICE (P) OR AVERAGE REVENUE (AR) (IN DOLLARS) $AR = \frac{TR}{Q}$	2 QUANTITY DEMANDED OR SOLD (Q) (IN UNITS)	3 TOTAL REVENUE (TR) (IN DOLLARS) TR = P × Q	4 MARGINAL REVENUE (MR) (IN DOLLARS) $MR = \frac{\Delta TR}{\Delta Q}$
30	0	0	
30	1	30	30
30	2	60	30
30	3	90	30
30	4	120	30
30	5	150	30
30	6	180	30
30	7	210	30
30	8	240	30
30	9	270	30
30	10	300	30

For a firm in a perfectly competitive industry, price is perfectly elastic (column 1). Average revenue is, therefore, the same as price. Total revenue (column 3) increases in proportion to quantity sold. Marginal revenue (column 4) remains unchanged at $30 because total revenue increases by $30 with each unit sold. For the firm in a perfectly competitive industry, price, average revenue, and marginal revenue are all equal.

From column 4 in Table 8.2, we can see that marginal revenue is constant at $30. That is, the addition to total revenue of each additional unit sold is always $30, since price remains constant at $30. Under perfect competition, Your Firm can sell additional units without having to lower its price.

As shown in Figure 8.4, the demand, average revenue, and marginal revenue curves for firms in perfectly competitive markets are thus the same.

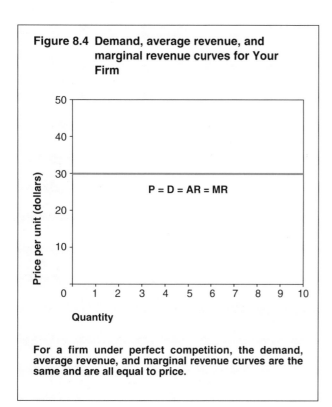

Figure 8.4 Demand, average revenue, and marginal revenue curves for Your Firm

For a firm under perfect competition, the demand, average revenue, and marginal revenue curves are the same and are all equal to price.

▉ Short-Run Output Decisions

How, then, does a firm make its production decisions? In the short run, the competitive firm seeks to maximize its profits by varying its output through changes in variable inputs (labour, raw materials, etc.). It attempts to maximize the difference between total revenue and

total costs, which of course is profit—providing that total revenue exceeds total cost.

We can determine the most profitable output in two ways—either by comparing total revenue and total cost, or by comparing marginal revenue and marginal cost. Both approaches can be used to determine maximum profit for perfectly competitive and non-competitive firms alike.

☐ Total Revenue-Total Cost Approach

The **total revenue-total cost approach** holds that a firm maximizes profit when total revenue exceeds total cost. Table 8.3 shows that total revenue (column 7) is greater than total cost (column 4) at all outputs between 5 and 9 units for Your Firm. Consequently, at these outputs, Your Firm makes a profit (column 8). Which output will the profit-maximizing firm select? Profits are maximized at 7 and 8 units of output at $65. We assume no fractional units. At these outputs, the difference between total revenue and total cost is at a maximum. Economists assume that when there are two levels of output at which profit is maximized, the firm will produce the greater amount—in this case, 8 units.

Figure 8.5 on page 164 displays the profit situation of Your Firm graphically. The total revenue curve is a straight line sloping up to the right because each extra unit adds a constant amount ($30) to total revenue. The total cost curve reflects the law of diminishing returns. At first, total costs increase at a diminishing rate as output increases, since fixed productive resources are being used more and more efficiently. However, after some point, total costs begin to rise at an ever-increasing rate because of the increasingly inefficient use of resources. Two break-even points are shown in Figure 8.5, at outputs of approximately 4 and 10 units. A **break-even point** is an output at which total revenue equals total cost. At this output, the firm has neither a profit nor a loss.

When producing 4 units or less, Your Firm incurs a loss. Just beyond 4 units, where total revenue equals total costs, you break even. At outputs between 5 and 9 units, you make a profit. At just less than 10 units, you break even again, and if you produce more than 10 units, Your Firm again incurs a loss.

Table 8.3 Costs, revenues, and profit for Your Firm (in dollars)

1 TOTAL OUTPUT (Q) (IN UNITS)	2 FIXED COST (FC) FC = 35	3 VARIABLE COST (VC)	4 TOTAL COST (TC) TC = FC + VC	5 AVERAGE TOTAL COST (ATC) ATC = $\frac{TC}{Q}$	6 MARGINAL COST (MC) MC = $\frac{\Delta TC}{\Delta Q}$	7 TOTAL REVENUE (TR) TR = P × Q	8 TOTAL PROFIT (+) OR LOSS (−) TP = TR − TC	9 MARGINAL REVENUE MR = $\frac{\Delta TR}{\Delta Q}$
0	35	0	35	—		0	−35	30
1	35	30	65	65	30	30	−35	30
2	35	55	90	45	25	60	−30	30
3	35	75	110	37	20	90	−20	30
4	35	90	125	32	15	120	− 5	30
5	35	100	135	27	10	150	+15	30
6	35	105	140	24	5	180	+40	30
7	35	110	145	21	5	210	+65	30
8	35	140	175	22	30	240	+65	30
9	35	200	235	26	60	270	+35	30
10	35	270	305	31	70	300	− 5	30

Columns 1, 7, and 9 are taken from Table 8.2. Column 2 shows that fixed costs total $35 and remain unchanged no matter what the output. Variable costs (column 3) increase as output increases at first at a diminishing rate up to 7 units and then at an increasing rate, reflecting the law of diminishing returns. Total costs, average total cost, and marginal cost also reflect the law of diminishing returns. Total profit or loss (column 8) is calculated by deducting total costs from total revenue. For a perfectly competitive firm, marginal revenue = average revenue = the price of $30 a unit. Profit is maximized at an output of 8 units, where marginal revenue = marginal cost = $30.

☐ MR = MC Rule

A second way of determining profit-maximizing output is by comparing marginal costs and marginal revenues. The **MR = MC rule** states that where marginal revenue equals marginal cost, total profit is maximized. In Table 8.3, marginal revenue (column 9) and marginal cost (column 6) are equal at an output of 8 units. Profit is maximized at this output.

Why does the MR = MC rule hold true? At outputs where marginal cost is less than marginal revenue, in other words, where the cost of producing the additional unit is less than the revenue that can be obtained from it, the firm can profit from producing the extra unit. This fact is shown in Table 8.4 and illustrated graphically in Figure 8.6.

At an output of 6 units, for example, marginal cost is $5 a unit and marginal revenue is $30 a unit. Marginal revenue is, therefore, $25 a unit more than marginal cost. The firm can make $25 in extra profit by produc-

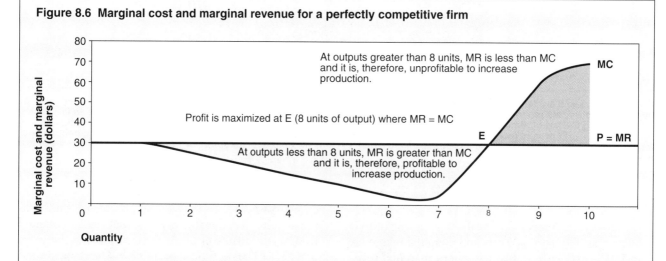

Figure 8.5 Total revenue, total cost, and profit for a perfectly competitive firm

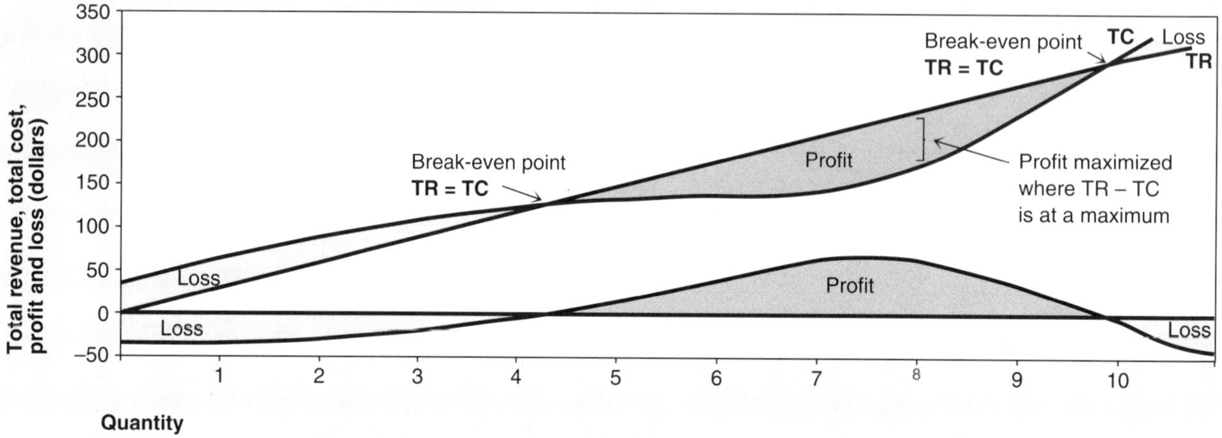

The total revenue curve is a straight line sloping up to the right because each additional unit adds a constant amount ($30) to total revenue. The total cost curve intersects the total revenue curve at two points—at outputs of approximately 4 and 10 units. Between these two break-even points, the firm makes a profit. At an output of 8 units where TR − TC is at a maximum, the firm makes its maximum profit of $65.

Figure 8.6 Marginal cost and marginal revenue for a perfectly competitive firm

The marginal revenue curve (which equals price at $30) is a straight line indicating that the perfectly competitive firm does not have to cut prices in order to sell additional units of output. The marginal cost curve cuts the marginal revenue curve at an output of 8 units, shown as point E, where profit is maximized. Both the total revenue-total cost approach (Figure 8.5) and the MR=MC rule illustrated in this graph indicate the same profit-maximizing output.

ing the additional unit. It will, therefore, be to Your Firm's advantage to produce more goods until MR = MC. As long as MR is greater than MC, the firm can make extra or additional profits by increasing output. When MR = MC at an output of 8 units, no more *extra* profits can be made. Profit has reached the maximum.

At outputs where marginal cost is greater than marginal revenue, profits will be increased if production is reduced until MR = MC. For example, if output is at 9 units, then marginal cost at $60 is greater than marginal

revenue at $30 a unit. Your Firm can increase its profits by cutting back production to the point where MR = MC.

At the point where price = MR = MC, the firm is in **short-run equilibrium**, illustrated by point E in Figure 8.6. At this point, profits are maximized and the firm has no incentive to produce more or less in these circumstances.

Average profit or loss can be calculated by deducting the average total cost from average revenue at each

Table 8.4 Costs, revenues, and profit for Your Firm (in dollars)

1 TOTAL OUTPUT (Q) (IN UNITS)	2 FIXED COST (FC)	3 VARIABLE COST (VC)	4 TOTAL COST (TC)	5 AVERAGE FIXED COST (AFC) $AFC = \frac{FC}{Q}$	6 AVERAGE VARIABLE COST (AVC) $AVC = \frac{VC}{Q}$	7 AVERAGE TOTAL COST (ATC) ATC = AFC + AVC (ROUNDED)	8 MARGINAL COST (MC) $MC = \frac{\Delta TC}{\Delta Q}$	9 AVERAGE REVENUE, MARGINAL REVENUE, AND PRICE AR = MR = P	10 PROFIT (+) OR LOSS (−) PROFIT = Q(AR − ATC)	
0	35	0	35	—	—	—	—	0	−35	
1	35	30	65	35.0	30.0	65	30	30	−35	
2	35	55	90	17.5	27.5	45	25	30	−30	
3	35	75	110	11.7	25.0	36.7	20	30	−20	MR > MC
4	35	90	125	8.8	22.5	31.3	15	30	−5	
5	35	100	135	7.0	20.0	27	10	30	15	
6	35	105	140	5.8	17.5	23.3	5	30	40	
7	35	110	145	5.0	15.7	20.7	5	30	65	
8	35	140	175	4.4	17.5	21.9	30	30	65	MR = MC
9	35	200	235	3.9	22.2	26.1	60	30	35	MR < MC
10	35	270	305	3.5	27.0	30.5	70	30	−5	

Columns 1 through 4 and 7 are reproduced from Table 8.3. Average fixed cost (column 5) declines as output increases. Average variable cost (column 6) at first declines as output increases and then rises, reflecting the law of diminishing returns. Average total cost (column 7) follows a similar pattern. Marginal cost (column 8) is less than marginal revenue (column 9) at outputs between 2 and 6 units. The firm can, therefore, benefit from producing the extra units. Profit (column 10) is maximized at 8 units of output where MR = MC.

level of output. Total profit or loss can be determined by multiplying the difference between average revenue (price) and average total cost by the output; that is, TP = Q(AR - ATC). Profit is always maximized at the point where marginal cost equals marginal revenue.

Figure 8.7 summarizes the firm's profit situation. The marginal cost curve intersects the D = AR = MR = P curve at E. Profit per unit at E is the difference between average revenue and average total cost; that is $Q_1E - Q_1F$ ($30 − $21.9), or EF ($8.10). Total profit is depicted by the rectangle $EFP_1 P$ ($8.10 × $8 = $65).

Changes in Profit Levels of Your Firm

But will Your Firm continue to make these economic profits? The answer is no. Since other firms can easily enter the market, the economic profits will attract competitors. As a number of other firms enter the industry, supply will increase and the supply curve will shift to the right. As a result, the market price will fall as shown in Figure 8.8.

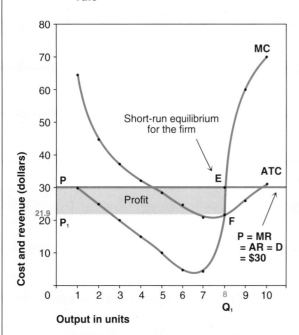

Figure 8.7 Profit determination by the MR = MC rule

Output in units

These curves are plotted from the data in Table 8.4. Total profit is maximized at point E, where the marginal cost curve intersects the marginal revenue curve and where output is 8 units and price is $30 per unit. Profit for each unit is the difference between average revenue and average costs, that is, between Q_1E and Q_1F. Total profit is represented by the total rectangle EFP_1P. When the firm is maximizing its profits at MC = MR = P, it has no incentive to change its output. It is in short-run equilibrium.

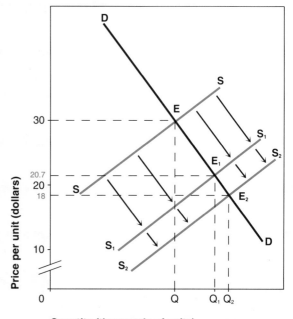

Figure 8.8 Shifts in the industry supply curve with increased competition

Quantity (thousands of units)

The economic profits made by Your Firm attract other firms into the industry, shifting the supply curve to the right from SS to S_1S_1. Price thus falls from $30 per unit to $20.70 per unit and quantity demanded and supplied increases to $0Q_1$. As more firms enter the industry, the supply curve shifts further to the right to S_2S_2. Price falls further to $18.00 per unit and quantity demanded and supplied increases to $0Q_2$.

☐ The Break-Even Point

Suppose the price falls to $20.70 per unit. What will Your Firm do? Table 8.5 summarizes the total costs, revenues, and profits or losses at the new price. As we can see, Your Firm will sustain a loss of $9 if it continues with an output of 8 units. It will, therefore, reduce production to 7 units where it just breaks even. At that point, it has no profits or losses. Thus, the effect of increasing competition is to decrease profits and cut prices.

☐ The Shut-Down Point

Suppose that competition continues to increase and, as a result, price continues to fall until it reaches $18 per unit. From Table 8.6, we can see that with an output of 7 units, Your Firm incurs a loss of $19. If you increase output to 8 units, your losses increase to $31. If you decrease your output to 6 units, your losses also increase, this time to $32.

What, then, should Your Firm do? It looks as though it should shut down and try to cut its losses to a minimum. However, even if Your Firm closes down, it will sustain a loss because you must still pay your fixed costs of $35 for such things as interest on borrowed money, insurance on buildings and machinery, etc.

Therefore, shutting down means Your Firm will take a loss of $35. Staying in business with an output of 7 units means that the loss would be $19—$16 less. It makes more sense for Your Firm to stay in business, therefore, at least in the short run. At an output of 7 units, total revenue is $126, $16 more than your total variable costs of $110.

It follows that as long as total revenue is greater than total variable costs, it is to your advantage to stay in business. If, on the other hand, total revenue is less than total variable costs, then total losses will equal the difference between total revenue and total costs (fixed and variable costs). It then makes sense to shut down,

Table 8.5 Break-even analysis

1 OUTPUT (IN UNITS)	2 TOTAL COST (TC) (IN DOLLARS)	3 TOTAL REVENUE (TR) (IN DOLLARS ROUNDED)	4 PROFIT (+) OR LOSS (−) (IN DOLLARS)
0	35	0	−35
1	65	21	−44
2	90	42	−48
3	110	62	−48
4	125	83	−42
5	135	104	−31
6	140	124	−16
7	145	145	0
8	175	166	−9
9	235	186	−49
10	305	207	−98

Output (column 1) and total cost (column 2) are taken from Table 8.4. Total revenue (column 3) is calculated using the new price of $20.70 per unit. With the fall in price, total revenue at the former profit-maximizing output of 8 units declines from ($30 × 8) $240 to ($20.70 × 8) $166. Instead of a profit of $65, Your Firm sustains a loss of $9. The firm will, therefore, cut production to 7 units where total cost equals total revenue at $145 and the firm breaks even.

Table 8.6 Shut-down point analysis

1 OUTPUT (IN UNITS)	2 TOTAL COST (TC)	3 TOTAL REVENUE (TR)	4 PROFIT (+) OR LOSS (−)	5 TOTAL VARIABLE COST (TVC)	6 FIXED COST (FC)
0	35	0	−35	0	35
1	65	18	−47	30	35
2	90	36	−54	55	35
3	110	54	−56	75	35
4	125	72	−53	90	35
5	135	90	−45	100	35
6	140	108	−32	105	35
7	145	126	−19	110	35
8	175	144	−31	140	35
9	235	162	−73	200	35
10	305	180	−125	270	35

Columns 1, 2, 4-6 are reproduced from Table 8.4. Total revenue (column 3) is calculated using the new price of $18 per unit. Even though Your Firm is incurring a loss at an output of 7 units, the $19 loss is $16 less than the $35 loss it would sustain if it shut down. As long as the firm can continue to cover its variable costs, it is advantageous to stay in business. When total revenue is less than total variable cost, the firm should shut down.

Figure 8.9 Competitive output determination in the short run—a summary

Question	#1 Total revenue – total cost approach	#2 Marginal revenue = marginal cost approach
What quantity should be produced for maximum profits?	Produce to the point at which the difference between total revenue and total cost is at a maximum.	Produce to the point at which marginal revenue (or price) equals marginal cost (MR = MC).
When will production result in an economic profit?	When total revenue is greater than total cost. If total revenue is less than total cost, the firm suffers a loss.	When price is greater than average total cost (ATC). If price is less than ATC, the firm suffers a loss.
Under what circumstances should the firm produce?	1. When TR > TC. 2. When TC > TR by an amount less than fixed costs.	When price is equal to or greater than minimum average variable costs.

---

because total losses will equal only fixed costs. The **shut-down point** is the price below which the firm cannot cover its variable costs—in other words, where variable costs are equal to total revenue.

Long-Run Equilibrium

As we have seen, firms in perfectly competitive markets may make healthy economic profits in the short run, but they cannot continue to make these profits over the long run. The economic profits will draw other firms into the industry. As a result, supply will increase, prices consequently will decrease, and profits will fall. Some firms will experience losses as price falls below their average total costs. In the long run, these firms will leave the industry. As they leave, supply will decrease and prices will start to rise again. Firms which were suffering a loss, will then break even. The long-run tendency in a perfectly competitive market is for firms to meet their minimum average total costs—that is, break even.

Since entry into the industry is easy, firms cannot continue to make economic profits in the long run. The **long-run equilibrium** is achieved only when price, marginal cost, marginal revenue, and average cost are all equal.

Efficiency

How can we assess the benefits of perfect competition then? In other words, do firms under perfect competition achieve the goal of economic efficiency? Economic efficiency requires full employment of resources. If workers are unemployed and factories or machinery are left idle, then potential output is lost. More goods and services could be produced and people could enjoy a higher standard of living.

However, even when all resources are employed, they may not be employed efficiently. Resources may be used inefficiently in two main ways.

(i) Failure to use the least costly methods of production For example, a firm that produces 10 000 pairs of jeans at a cost of $150 000 when the jeans could be produced at a cost of $100 000 is obviously using resources inefficiently. If the jeans were produced efficiently, $50 000 of resources could be transferred to other uses.

(ii) Failure to allocate resources effectively To take an extreme example, suppose so many pairs of socks were produced that they are given away. Obviously, far more are produced than are needed or demanded by consumers. The marginal utility of socks (the satisfaction that

can be gained by production of one more pair) is zero. Suppose, however, that shirts are in short supply and prices are high. Shirts have a high marginal utility. The utility of all consumers could be increased by reducing the production of socks and increasing the production of shirts. No one loses from the reduction in sock production, and some gain by the increase in shirt production.

Efficiency occurs, therefore, at the point where raising one consumer's utility means lowering that of another. Conversely, inefficiency occurs at the point where it is possible to raise one consumer's utility by lowering another's utility.

□ The Competitive Price System and Efficiency

Subject to certain conditions which we'll review later, economists agree that a perfectly competitive market structure will provide for an efficient use of productive resources. This means that the goods consumers want will be produced (allocative efficiency) at the lowest price possible (productive efficiency).

Productive Efficiency
Productive efficiency occurs when output is produced at the lowest attainable cost; that is, when price equals average total cost (P = ATC).

As we have seen, in the long run the firm in a perfectly competitive market is forced to produce at the point of minimum average total cost. The firm must use the best available technology to keep costs per unit down and thus make a profit. The consumer benefits since the firm charges the lowest price, consistent with minimum average total cost. This situation is illustrated in Figure 8.10.

Under perfect competition, therefore, firms are forced to use the least costly methods of production. Theoretically, they achieve productive efficiency.

Allocative Efficiency
Allocative efficiency occurs when resources are allocated in accordance with consumer preferences. It is the point at which price (or marginal revenue) equals marginal cost (P = MR = MC).

Over the long run, firms under perfect competition will continue to produce to the point where marginal revenue (or price) equals marginal cost (MR = MC). To produce beyond this point would mean less than maxi-

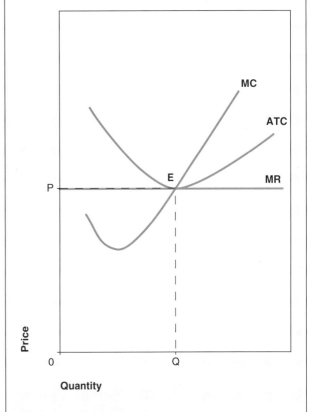

Figure 8.10 The long-run equilibrium of a perfectly competitive firm

In the long run, equilibrium is the point at which "everything is equal" — P (or MR) = MC = minimum ATC. The equality of price and minimum average total cost means that the firm is using the most efficient production techniques, charging the lowest price (P), and producing the highest output (Q) consistent with its production techniques. Equality of price and marginal cost shows that resources are being allocated effectively; that is according to consumer demand.

mum profits for the firm and an over-allocation of resources to its production.

Suppose the marginal cost of producing jeans is $30 and the price of a pair is $20. This means that the value consumers or households place on jeans is $20, but the cost of the resources used in producing them is $30. Price does not equal marginal cost. Resources could be allocated more efficiently if fewer jeans were produced and the resources were diverted to production of other more highly valued goods. By producing one fewer pair of jeans, we give up what consumers value at $20 and gain a value of $30.

If the price of jeans were $40 and the marginal cost of production $30, the production of one more pair of jeans would increase net output by $10. Consumers would gain a pair of jeans valued at $40 for the expenditure of only $30 in resources. Again, price does not equal marginal cost. The value of what is gained does not equal the value of what is lost. The allocation of resources is inefficient.

Under perfect competition, however, firms will produce to the point where price equals marginal cost. Thus, over the long run, resources are allocated efficiently under perfect competition.

□ Limitations on Efficiency

Earlier in this chapter, we mentioned that perfect competition tends toward the efficient use of resources and that it can, therefore, be used as a standard for assessing other market structures. While this is true, note that we have not claimed that perfect competition results in an optimum level of social welfare. As we have seen in earlier chapters, the distribution of income is not necessarily equitable under a perfectly competitive market structure. The efficiency of perfectly competitive markets also has other limitations.

(i) Externalities   Our conclusion that the perfectly competitive market brings about an efficient allocation of resources assumes no spillover costs (or benefits) from the production or consumption of the goods and services. For example, suppose that in the process of

producing jeans, firms dump pollutants into the atmosphere. The firms' supply curves do not include this cost of production. As a result, the jeans are sold at a lower price and more are produced, but their costs fail to include the value members of society place on clean air.

(ii) Productive efficiency and perfect competition may be incompatible   In some industries, such as the production of automobiles and steel, firms must be very large to achieve economies of scale. Perfect competition is then incompatible with efficient production. Efficiency is increased when only one or a few firms produce the goods or services.

(iii) New production techniques may not be introduced   If perfectly competitive firms do not introduce new production techniques as rapidly as do firms in other market structures, then costs will be higher. Over the long run, costs under perfect competition would be higher than those under other market structures.

Thus, while perfectly competitive firms do tend toward efficiency, there are drawbacks. As we will see later, governments may intervene in the market to counter some of these disadvantages.

Summary

a. Pure monopoly is a market structure with only one producer which has considerable control over price. Monopolistic competition is a market situation with many firms which produce a differentiated product and have a small degree of control over price (e.g., hamburger restaurants and hair stylists). In oligopolistic markets, a few firms provide a large share of the output and have significant control over price (e.g., steel and automobile industries in Canada). Perfect competition is a market structure with many buyers and sellers none of which has any control over price (e.g., stock market).

b. The major conditions necessary for perfect competition include: many buyers and sellers, small outputs from individual firms, production of an identical product, full information, mobile resources, no barriers to entry, and no control over price by any individual firm.

c. Sales revenue is the money a firm receives in exchange for its product. For a perfectly competitive firm which has no control over price and faces a perfectly elastic demand curve, demand, price, average revenue, and marginal revenue are all equal (D = AR = MR = P).

d. Profit is maximized in the short run where the difference between total revenue and total cost is at a maximum, and where marginal revenue equals marginal cost (MR = MC).

e. A firm is operating at the break-even point when total costs equal total revenues. At this point, the firm makes neither a profit nor a loss. The shut-down point is the point at which the firm can no longer cover its variable costs, that is, where total revenues equal total variable costs.

f. The long-run equilibrium of the perfectly competitive firm is the point at which price, marginal cost, marginal revenue, and average cost are all equal.

g. The perfectly competitive market will provide an efficient use of productive resources. Productive efficiency is ensured because price is equal in the long run to minimum average total cost (P = ATC). Allocative efficiency is achieved because price (which represents the benefits consumers gain from a product) equals marginal cost (P = MC).

Disadvantages of perfect competition include an inequitable distribution of goods and services, a failure to account for spillover costs and benefits, productive inefficiency in industries that require large economies of scale, and higher costs if new production techniques are not adopted as rapidly as in other market structures.

■ Review of Key Terms

Define the following key terms introduced in this chapter and provide examples where appropriate.

pure monopoly
monopolistic competition
oligopoly
perfect competition
sales revenue
average revenue
total revenue
marginal revenue
total revenue-total cost approach

MR = MC rule
break-even point
short-run equilibrium
shut-down point
long-run equilibrium
efficiency
productive efficiency
allocative efficiency

■ Application and Analysis

Table 8.7 Demand schedule for a product

1 PRICE PER UNIT (IN DOLLARS)	2 QUANTITY DEMANDED (IN UNITS)
3	0
3	1
3	2
3	3
3	4
3	5
3	6

1. (a) Calculate the total revenue, average revenue, and marginal revenue of sales based on the demand schedule shown in Table 8.7.

(b) What can you conclude about the structure of the industry in which this firm operates? Explain.

(c) Graph the demand, total revenue, and marginal revenue curves for this product.

(d) Why do the marginal revenue, average revenue, and demand curves coincide?

Table 8.8 Output, costs, and revenues for a perfectly competitive firm (in dollars)

1 OUTPUT (Q) (IN UNITS)	2 TOTAL FIXED COST (TFC)	3 TOTAL VARIABLE COST (TVC)	4 TOTAL COST (TC) TC = TFC + TVC	5 AVERAGE FIXED COST (AFC) $AFC = \frac{TFC}{Q}$	6 AVERAGE VARIABLE COST (AVC) $AVC = \frac{TVC}{Q}$	7 AVERAGE TOTAL COST (ATC) $ATC = \frac{TC}{Q}$	8 MARGINAL COST (MC) $MC = \frac{\Delta TC}{\Delta Q}$	9 MARGINAL REVENUE (MR) $MR = \frac{\Delta TR}{\Delta Q}$	10 TOTAL REVENUE (TR)	11 TOTAL PROFIT (+) OR LOSS (−) PROFIT = TR − TC
0	200	0	200	O	O	O	O			0
1		30	230	200	30	230	230			80
2		40	240	100	20	200	206			160
3		55	255	75	22	170	170			240
4		100	300	50	25	160	160			320
5		170	370	40	20	150	150			400
6		280	480	4065	15	140	140			480
7		380	580		18 / 7	100 / 90				560

2. (a) Complete the above table.

(b) Use the data in the table to graph the following:

(i) average fixed cost, average variable cost, average total cost, and marginal cost curves

(ii) total revenue and total cost curves indicating the break-even points and the output which yields maximum profit

(iii) marginal cost and marginal revenue curves indicating the level of output at which these two curves intersect.

3. Table 8.9 provides information on costs and revenues for a perfectly competitive firm. The price of the product is $25.

(a) Complete the table.

(b) At what level of output is profit maximized? Explain.

(c) Graph the total revenue and total cost curves. Indicate the break-even points and the output at which profit is maximized.

(d) Graph the marginal revenue and marginal cost curves. Label the point at which the two curves intersect.

Table 8.9 Costs and revenues for a perfectly competitive firm (in dollars)

	REVENUES			COSTS	
QUANTITY (IN UNITS)	TOTAL REVENUE	MARGINAL REVENUE	TOTAL COST	MARGINAL COST	PROFIT
0			20		
1			40		
2			50		
3			70		
4			92		
5			120		
6			150		
7			182		

4. Refer to Figure 8.11.

(a) At what output will Fred's Firm maximize its profit?

(b) What is Fred's maximum profit?

(c) Assume that Fred's is a typical firm. What changes will take place:

(i) in the price, and

(ii) in the output of the product?

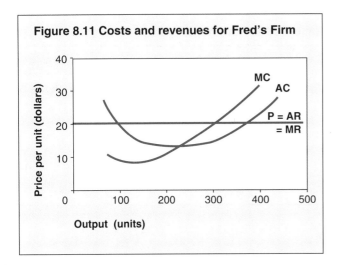

Figure 8.11 Costs and revenues for Fred's Firm

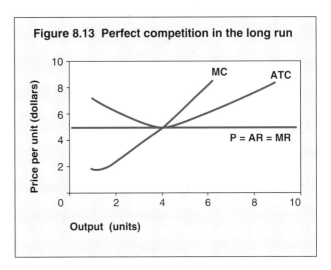

Figure 8.13 Perfect competition in the long run

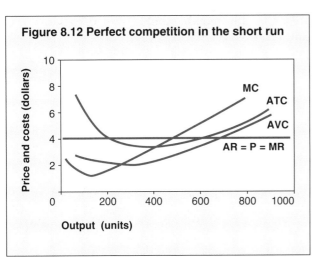

Figure 8.12 Perfect competition in the short run

(f) At what output is total profit maximized?

(g) At the profit maximizing output, what is the:
   (i)   marginal cost
   (ii) marginal revenue
   (iii) cost per unit
   (iv) price per unit
   (v) profit?

(h) In the long run, what will happen to this perfectly competitive firm?

6. (a) Identify the demand curve in Figure 8.13.

(b) If output is at 3 units, what is the price of the product?

(c) What is the average revenue (AR) with output at 3 units?

(d) At what level of output is the average total cost (ATC) curve at a minimum?

(e) With the level of output at 4 units, what is:
   (i)   total revenue
   (ii) total cost
   (iii) total profit?

(f) At what level of output is profit maximized?

(g) At the profit-maximizing output, what is the:
   (i)   price

5. (a) Identify the demand curve in Figure 8.12.

(b) What is the price at an output of 300 units?

(c) What is the marginal revenue at an output of 300 units?

(d) At what output is ATC at a minimum?

(e) At the minimum ATC, what is the:
   (i) price   (iii) total revenue
   (ii) total cost (iv) total profit?

(ii) average revenue   (iv) average cost

(iii) marginal revenue   (v) marginal cost?

(h) What is the:

(i) profit per unit   (ii) total profit?

7. Suppose you have decided to spend a month studying in Europe next summer and you want to determine if it will be worth your while to rent your trailer while you are away. You list your costs as in Table 8.10.

(a) Calculate your total average fixed and variable costs.

(b) What is your break-even point?

(c) What is your shut-down point?

(d) If Isabel offers you $90 to rent the trailer for the month, would it be to your financial advantage to accept her offer? Explain.

(e) If the only offer you receive is $110 to rent the trailer for the month, would it be to your financial advantage to accept it? Explain.

Table 8.10 Monthly trailer costs

AVERAGE MONTHLY FIXED COSTS		AVERAGE MONTHLY VARIABLE COSTS	
Bank interest	$40	Insurance (when used)	$30
Interest foregone on down payment	20	Additional wear on tires, body, etc. when trailer is used	50
Depreciation	50		
Other fixed costs (taxes, licences, etc.)	40	Maintenance	10
		All other variable costs	10

CHAPTER NINE

Monopoly

Objectives

a. Recall and explain the major features of pure monopoly.

b. Outline the major barriers that allow monopolies to exist.

c. Calculate, graph, and apply demand, cost, and revenue schedules for the pure monopolist.

d. Calculate and graph the profit-maximizing output of the monopolist using the total revenue-total cost and the marginal revenue = marginal cost approaches.

e. Compare the efficiency of perfect competition and pure monopoly.

f. Analyze the behaviour of a monopolistic firm and determine how it reacts to changing market conditions.

g. Explain the practice of price discrimination as applied by monopolies.

We have seen that in a perfectly competitive market, the firm—which is one of very many—has no control over the price of its product and faces an infinitely elastic demand curve at the market price. Now we turn to examine the opposite pole of the market spectrum—pure monopoly. We defined a **pure monopoly** as a market structure with only one producer of a good or service, for which there are no close substitutes and many buyers. Examples include telephone, natural gas, electricity, and urban transit services.

Most goods and services produced by firms generally regarded as monopolies, however, do have some substitutes. A letter, telegram, or fax may substitute to some extent for a telephone call, for example. Heating oil, wood, and electricity may be substitutes for natural gas, and taxis or private cars are alternatives to urban transit. However, these substitutes are generally not close or competitive enough to seriously undermine the monopolist's ability to influence price by controlling output. In the broadest sense, all goods and services are in competition with each other for the consumer's dollar.

In this chapter, we examine why monopolies exist, how they make their production decisions, and how efficient they are as compared with the perfectly competitive firm.

■ Why Do Monopolies Exist?

For monopolies to exist, other firms must be prevented from entering the industry. What, then, are these barriers? What conditions are necessary for monopolies to exist?

Ownership of Essential Raw Materials or Patents

Clearly, firms that control an essential raw material or technique can effectively prevent other firms from entering the industry. The Aluminium Company of America, for example, retained a monopoly before World War II by controlling the sources of bauxite, the major raw material in the production of aluminium. Similarly, Inco once controlled about 90 percent of the world's supply of nickel, though it no longer holds this position.

Firms that have invented a new technique or product may obtain a **patent**, giving them exclusive ownership of the technique for up to 20 years in Canada. Without knowledge of the technique, other firms obviously cannot produce the good. Ownership of essential raw materials or patents is most common in manufacturing industries.

Legal Monopolies

Governments may grant companies a **legal monopoly**—or a franchise—to provide a product or service within a particular area. In some localities, for example, one taxi firm may be given the exclusive right to service a local airport. Prior to 1984, it was illegal for private firms to compete with Canada Post in the delivery of mail. Provincial liquor control boards typically have a monopoly to supply wines and spirits within a province.

Natural Monopolies

Some industries, in which competition is impractical and inefficient, may develop as natural monopolies. Many of the services provided by public utilities—such as natural gas, electricity, water, telephone, and urban transportation—fall into this category. **Natural monopolies** occur when a single firm can supply the entire market with lower average total costs, and thus a lower price, than can two or more firms.

Natural monopolies result from the economies of scale. They typically occur in industries with very high fixed costs (or overhead) relative to variable costs. The high initial (fixed) costs of constructing telephone exchanges and running lines through communities, for example, compared to the low cost of adding additional telephone subscribers means that average variable cost falls continuously over an extended range of output. Thus, one firm can supply the market at a lower price than can two or more firms. Consider the unnecessary cost and inconvenience of having three competing phone companies in your locality: three sets of phone lines, three identical phone books, etc. Clearly, such competition would be wasteful and inefficient.

While monopolies are the "natural" market structure in such cases, governments often intervene to regulate the industries. Governments will attempt to ensure that prices are not raised excessively, or that quantities produced are not limited unduly.

Combinations and Collusion

Two or more firms may attempt to eliminate competition and thus establish a monopoly by merging, or by colluding to raise prices and/or limit output. A **merger** is the joining or combination of two or more firms into a single firm. **Collusion** is a covert agreement between firms to reduce or eliminate competition and/or control output. The collusion may be informal, such as by verbal agreement. It may also be formal, such as by the firms' agreement to establish their own marketing organization.

Such monopolies may be difficult to maintain, since high prices and profits are likely to attract competitors into the industry. Collusion to eliminate or even restrict competition may also be illegal, as it is in Canada.

□ □ □ □ □ □

Bitter Sweet!–The Case of the Aspartame Monopoly in Canada

In 1981, the task of losing weight became a little easier for Canadians. In that year, aspartame made its appearance on grocery store shelves. Aspartame is a low-calorie artificial sweetener used in diet foods, chewing gum, mints, and diet soft drinks. It is 200 times sweeter than sugar.

Aspartame was invented by an Illinois-based pharmaceutical company owned by a US multinational chemical corporation. Aspartame was patented in Canada in 1971 and is marketed by a Canadian subsidiary of the corporation. The company thus had a monopoly in Canada because it owned the patent to produce aspartame and had the exclusive right to sell it in Canada. Despite the 1971 patent, extensive testing by Canadian food and drug authorities delayed the appearance of the product on the market until 1981.

The patent was due to expire in 1987. The corporation applied to have the patent extended for five years. It had only been able to take advantage of the patent for seven years (since the product went to market in 1981). The bid failed, however, as consumer groups, trade organizations, and potential competitors lobbied strongly against it. With the expiry of the patent, other companies announced plans to manufacture and/or sell aspartame in Canada.

By 1990, however, despite intense marketing efforts, a Japanese-controlled Canadian company had managed to gain only 3 percent of the Canadian aspartame market. The US corporation had maintained its hold on 95 percent of the market. Complaints brought the case to the attention of Canada's Competition Tribunal. The Tribunal ruled that the US corporation could no longer sign new contracts or enforce existing agreements that made it the exclusive supplier of aspartame to companies in Canada. The US corporation was also prohibited from paying its purchasers for using its logo in advertising or on food packaging.

The bitter sweetener wars became even more heated in the fall of 1991 with the announcement that Health and Welfare Canada had approved the use of a new low-calorie sweetener, called sucralose, after 15 years of intensive testing. Sucralose is 600 times sweeter than sugar, from which it is derived. It can be used in a wider variety of products than aspartame, including baked goods, since it does not break down under heat. It also claims to be more resistant to chemical attack, so that it may be more suitable for acidic drinks than aspartame.

Two other low-calorie sweeteners are on the market. Saccharin is a non-proprietory sweetener that has been in use for about 80 years. Its disadvantage is that it leaves an unpleasant after taste. Acesulfame-K is another patented sweetener that apparently does not taste as much like sugar as aspartame or sucralose.

Other sweeteners are being developed by chemical companies lured by the large profits and expanding world market. The world market—80 percent in the US—was about $1 billion a year in 1991 and growing rapidly. The Canadian market is about $25 million a year (1991 figure). However, entry costs are high. To develop a new sweetener for the world market was estimated to cost more than $400 million in 1991. In addition, a considerable amount of time is required for testing before the product can be sold to customers, even if a patent is granted early on.

Applications

1. Why was the US corporation granted a patent on aspartame in Canada?

2. Why did the extension bid on the patent fail? Do you agree that it should not have been extended? Explain why or why not.

3. What are the barriers to entry in the low-calorie sweetener market?

4. (a) What do you expect will happen to the price of low-calorie sweeteners in the future?

(b) What kind of market structure do you think will evolve in the low-calorie sweetener industry over time? Explain why.

∎ The Monopolist's Demand Curve

We saw that for the firm under perfect competition, demand is perfectly elastic. The individual firm's actions—either to increase or decrease its output—have no effect on price because the firm is only one of very many in the industry.

For the monopolist, the situation is radically different. Since the firm is the only one in the industry, the firm's demand curve and the market demand curve are one and the same—as shown in Figure 9.1. The monopolist's demand curve slopes down to the right. This means that the monopolist can sell more of the product only by lowering the price. The demand for the monopolist's product is typically much more elastic than the demand for the perfectly competitive firm's product. By varying output, the monopolist can control price. It is a "price-maker," rather than a "price-taker."

But the monopolist's control is not unlimited. Let's consider an example. Suppose Marco is the sole hairstylist in an isolated Newfoundland town. He is a monopolist. As shown by the demand curve in Figure 9.1, he can choose to sell either 7 haircuts an hour at $6.00 each, or set the price at $8.00 and sell 5 haircuts an hour. He has control over price *or* quantity, but not both. He cannot choose to sell 7 haircuts an hour at $8.00 each. Demand imposes limits on his freedom.

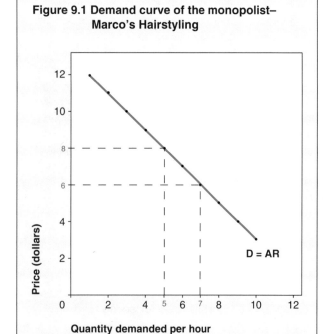

Figure 9.1 Demand curve of the monopolist– Marco's Hairstyling

The monopolist faces a downward-sloping demand curve. It can set either price or quantity, but not both. The firm can set the price at $8.00 and sell 5 products, or set the quantity at 7 and sell the product at $6.00 each. It cannot sell 7 products at $8.00 each. Since the firm and the industry are one and the same in a monopoly, the market demand curve is also the firm's average revenue curve (D = AR).

Table 9.1 Demand and revenues of the monopolist— Marco's Hairstyling

1 QUANTITY DEMANDED (Q) (IN UNITS)	2 PRICE (P) AND AVERAGE REVENUE (AR) (IN DOLLARS)	3 TOTAL REVENUE (TR) TR = P × Q (IN DOLLARS)	4 MARGINAL REVENUE (MR) MR = $\frac{\Delta TR}{\Delta Q}$ (IN DOLLARS)
1	12	12	
2	11	22	10
3	10	30	8
4	9	36	6
5	8	40	4
6	7	42	2
7	6	42	0
8	5	40	-2
9	4	36	-4
10	3	30	-6

For the monopolist, price equals average revenue (column 2). Total revenue (column 3) rises as output increases up to between 6 and 7 units and then declines. Marginal revenue (column 4) declines as output increases at a faster rate than average revenue or price.

The Monopolist's Revenue Curves

What does this demand curve mean for the monopolist's revenues?

Average Revenue

Since the firm and the industry in monopoly are one and the same, the market demand curve for the product is also the firm's average revenue curve. Price is equal to average revenue. As the $D = AR = P$ curve slopes down to the right, the revenue on each unit sold declines as output increases. To raise average revenue, the monopolist must decrease sales.

Total Revenue

From Chapter 8, we know that total revenue equals price times quantity $(TR = P \times Q)$. For the monopolist, total revenue at first rises as output increases, but after a certain point declines. From Table 9.1, we can see that Marco can sell one haircut per hour at $12. His total revenue at that price is, therefore, $12 $(P \times Q)$. If he lowers his price to $11, he can sell 2 haircuts an hour for a total revenue of $22. Total revenue reaches a maximum between 6 and 7 units of output and then declines.

Marginal Revenue

Marginal revenue is the change in the total revenue of the firm that results from the sale of one additional

Table 9.2 Costs, revenues, and profit of the monopolist—Marco's Hairstyling (in dollars)

1 QUANTITY (Q) (IN UNITS)	2 PRICE (P)	3 TOTAL COST (TC) $TC = P \times Q$	4 AVERAGE TOTAL COST (ATC) $ATC = \frac{TC}{Q}$	5 MARGINAL COST (MC) $MC = \frac{\Delta TC}{\Delta Q}$	6 TOTAL REVENUE (TR) $TR = P \times Q$	7 MARGINAL REVENUE (MR) $MR = \frac{\Delta TR}{\Delta Q}$	8 PROFIT (+) OR LOSS (−) $PROFIT = TR - TC$
1	12	13	13		12		-1
2	11	20	10	7	22	10	+2
3	10	26	8.7	6	30	8	+4
4	9	31	7.8	5	36	6	+5
5	8	34	6.8	3	40	4	+6
6	7	36	6.00	2	42	2	+6
7	6	39	5.6	3	42	0	+3
8	5	44	5.5	5	40	-2	-4
9	4	51	5.7	7	36	-4	-15
10	3	70	7.0	19	30	-6	-40

Profit for the monopolist is maximized where TR − TC is at a maximum and where MR = MC, that is, between 5 and 6 units of output. Economists assume the firm will produce the higher output. Marco's Hairstyling will, therefore, do 6 haircuts an hour at $7 per cut.

unit. As shown in Table 9.1, total revenue for 1 unit is $12 and for 2 units is $22. Marginal revenue between 1 and 2 units is, therefore, $10.

$$MR = \frac{\Delta TR}{\Delta Q} = \frac{\$22 - 12}{2 - 1} = \$10$$

Marginal revenue between 2 and 3 units is $8, between 3 and 4 units is $6, and so on. It declines as output increases.

For the monopolist, marginal revenue is less than average revenue or price. For example, between outputs of 1 and 2 units, and 2 and 3 units, average revenue for the monopolist falls from $12 to $11, while marginal revenue falls from $10 to $8.

Why does marginal revenue fall more rapidly than average revenue? Marco receives the full price of $11 for the second haircut he sells, but in order to coax the last buyer into buying that second haircut, he had to cut his price from $12 to $10. In cutting the price to sell this last unit, he has to lower the price for the first unit as well. The extra revenue (MR) from the sale of the last unit is, therefore, less than the price or average revenue. This fact has a significant impact on the monopolist's profit-maximizing decisions.

■ Profit Maximization

As with perfect competition, the monopolist can determine maximum profit by the total revenue-total cost approach or the MR = MC rule.

Total Revenue-Total Cost Approach
Table 9.2 on page 179 outlines the costs and revenues for Marco's Hairstyling. Columns 3 and 6 show that the difference between total revenue and total cost is at a maximum at outputs of 5 and 6 units. Profit at these outputs is $6. When profits are maximized at two different outputs, economists assume that firms produce the higher output. We assume Marco will, therefore, choose to do 6 haircuts an hour at $7 per cut. Figure 9.2 illustrates the profit-maximizing output graphically.

MR = MC Rule
Under perfect competition, the firm's marginal revenue curve is the same as the average revenue (price)

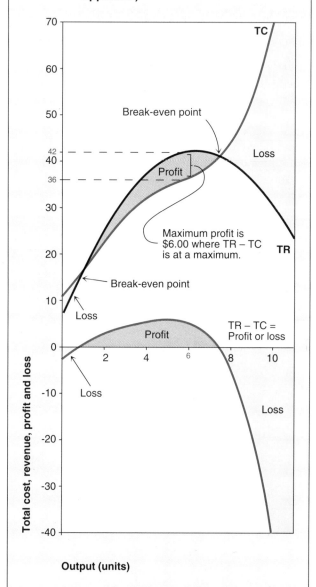

Figure 9.2 The monopolist's maximum profit output (total revenue – total cost approach)

At an output of 6 units, profit (TR – TC) is at a maximum of $6.00. Two break-even points are shown on the graph — at 1.5 and 7.5 units of output where TR = TC. At these two points, profit is zero.

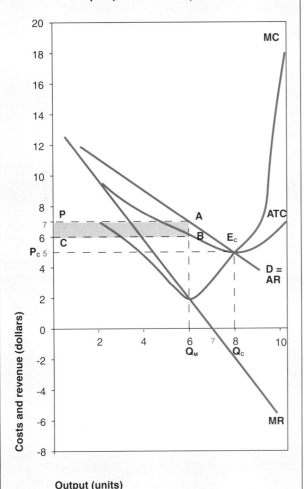

Figure 9.3 The monopolist's maximum profit output (MR = MC rule)

Output (units)

Profit is maximized where MC = MR, that is, at 6 haircuts per hour. From the D = AR curve, we can see that the price per haircut at that output is $7. From the ATC curve, we can see that the average cost is $6. Average revenue, therefore, exceeds average cost by $1. Profit per haircut or average profit is therefore $1 and total profit is $6. The rectangle PABC represents the monopolist's profit. The perfectly competitive firm, however, would sell 8 haircuts (0Q_c) at a price of $5 per cut (0P_c) over the long run. The monopolist, therefore, offers a smaller quantity (0Q_M) at a higher price (0P) than the perfectly competitive firm with the same costs.

and demand curves. This is not the case for the monopolist, since the monopolist can increase sales only by reducing prices. Marco can sell more haircuts only by cutting the price. As shown in Table 9.2, marginal revenue for the third haircut sold is the revenue or price for the third cut ($10) minus the reduction on the other two cuts sold ($1 each)—that is, $8. The marginal revenue curve is, therefore, below the average revenue (price) or demand curve, as shown in Figure 9.3.

Maximum profit for the monopolist is at the point where the marginal revenue and marginal cost curves intersect. For Marco's Hairstyling, this is at an output of 6 haircuts per hour. At that output, average total cost is $6 per haircut and average revenue is $7. Profit per unit is $1 and total profit is $6. The monopolist's profit is shown graphically by the rectangle PABC.

■ Economic Impact of Monopoly

How do perfect competition and monopoly compare in terms of efficiency? In our examination of perfect competition, we reached the conclusion that subject to certain conditions, perfect competition results in productive and allocative efficiency. In the long run, productive efficiency is achieved because firms are forced by the intense competition to operate at the level of output where price equals minimum average total cost. Allocative efficiency is achieved where price equals marginal cost. In Figure 9.3, this means that in the long-run equilibrium, the perfectly competitive firm would sell 8 haircuts (0Q_c) at a price of $5 (Q_cE_c).

Under pure monopoly, *given the same costs*, the situation is less advantageous to society. As we have seen, the monopolist maximizes profits by producing 6 units (0Q_M) at a price of $7 (0P) a unit. The monopolist, therefore, will offer a smaller amount at a higher price. Under perfect competition, 2 more units are sold at a price $2 lower. Since new firms cannot enter the monopoly industry, the monopolist's profits are secure. Under monopoly, price is higher than marginal cost and output is lower than minimum average total cost. From society's point of view, therefore, insufficient amounts are produced at excessively high prices.

□ □ □ □ □ □

De Beers—A Sparkling Example of Monopoly Behaviour

De Beers Consolidated Mines Ltd. is one of the world's strongest monopolies. It produces a sizable portion of all rough diamonds in the world from its own mines and buys nearly all the diamonds produced by other mines. The South African company then markets the combined world output of rough stones through its wholly-owned Central Selling Organization (CSO), based in London. Smaller producers of diamonds willingly sell their gemstones to De Beers because a competitive price war would ruin them, and De Beers pays a top price.

De Beers can afford to pay a high price for rough stones because it receives even higher prices when it sells them to buyers, who cut and finish them into gemstones. Through the CSO, De Beers maintains high prices for rough diamonds by controlling the number of stones placed on the market. When demand is increasing rapidly, the company releases the surplus diamonds in its stockpile. This supply juggling is not a simple activity, for there are more than 2000 varieties of diamonds.

De Beer's strategy is to control the supply of diamonds so that prices rise, slowly, yet steadily. The firm desires to market its stones, and those of its producer-clients in an orderly, controlled, and profitable manner. But several major occurrences in past decades threatened the price structure of diamonds and De Beers's orderly market control. The way in which the firm responded to each threat provides a lesson in monopoly behaviour.

The first major problem threatening De Beers occurred in the first half-decade of the 1970s. Recall that De Beers maintains its monopoly position by agreeing to purchase the uncut diamonds from all the mines in the world and then marketing them through its single CSO. This working arrangement operated smoothly until the world's mines began producing an increasing number of *small* stones (those less than 0.25 carats). That placed De Beers in the position of buying more small stones per year than it could sell at its current prices. If it placed the surplus stones on the market, the price of the small diamonds would fall, and this might produce unfortunate ramifications for the prices of diamonds in general.

De Beers's solution to this threat was to reduce the flow of small diamonds to the market. This left De Beers with a large inventory of small stones. De Beers's executives then devised a strategy to increase the demand for small diamonds, so that the surplus stones could be eased onto the market without reducing their price. De Beers began a campaign to get the public to "think small." An advertising campaign was used to entice the public to buy small diamonds clustered into brooches, pendants, rings, and other jewellery. . . .Other ads attempted to establish a new tradition similar to the giving of engagement rings. The ads encouraged older married people to give their spouses an "eternity ring" as a symbol of continuing affection and appreciation. The eternity ring, to no surprise, consisted of a band containing many *small* diamonds. This campaign succeeded brilliantly and the price charged by De Beers for small sparklers rose throughout the 1970s.

Several interacting circumstances posed a far greater threat to the De Beers's diamond monopoly in the late 1970s and 1980s.

1. A major recession in the United States and several other industrial nations in 1981 and 1982 reduced demand for polished diamonds and placed tremendous downward pressure on De Beers's price structure for uncut stones.

2. The former Soviet Union began to offer many more *polished* diamonds for sale in the world market to gain foreign currency to buy needed grain and finance troops in Afghanistan.

3. Investors and speculators in large diamonds reacted to the falling price of the polished stones by unloading their hoarded diamonds, hoping to get out of the market before prices dropped further.

4. Lower inflation rates in the industrialized countries during the 1980s reduced the demand for commodities such as diamonds, which people earlier were buying as a way to maintain purchasing power. The price of a "one-carat D-flawless brilliant" investment diamond fell precipitously from $60 000 in 1980 to $6000 in 1985!

5. De Beers's new Jwaneng mines in Botswana began production and added tremendously to De Beers's stock of large uncut diamonds.

6. Zaire, the world's biggest producer of diamonds, withdrew from the CSO and began marketing its rough stones directly.

7. The gigantic Ashton Argyle mine in Western Australia began production, adding an estimated 40 percent to the world's diamond output in 1985.

De Beers's reactions to these events were swift and decisive. It negotiated an agreement with the Australians to market nearly all of the gemstone-quality rough diamonds produced from the new Ashton Argyle mine. It reduced production in its famed Premier mine in South Africa and laid off nearly 500 workers. It closed its Koffiefontein and Lesotho mines completely and cut 1982 production by over 2 million carats. De Beers casually reminded its CSO cartel members that an Israeli attempt to break the CSO's grip in 1977 and 1978 nearly broke the Israeli diamond-cutting industry instead. It "enticed" Zaire back into the CSO. Zaire's output consisted mainly of low-priced, industrial-grade diamonds called *boart*. When Zaire left the cartel, De Beers "met the competition" by unloading boart from its large inventory. Boart prices fell 67 percent over a two-year period, and Zaire decided to rejoin the CSO. Finally, the company initiated a multimillion-dollar advertising campaign to promote large diamonds, hoping to prop up the demand for stones at the top end of the price structure.

De Beers did not reduce its prices on rough-cut stones! To maintain its carefully constructed monopoly and its price structure, it stockpiled vast quantities of stones. For example, in 1981 alone, it withheld $1.3 billion in diamonds from the market. In that year, sales from its CSO fell nearly 50 percent and profits declined by nearly the same amount, but the CSO and its price structure were still intact. De Beers's rate of return on equity in this "bad" year was 20 percent.

In "good" years, De Beers's profits equal 60 percent of revenues and rates of return on equity are above 30 percent. Competitive firms would be pleased to duplicate De Beers's bad years. De Beers is a "price-maker" through its control over supply, not a "price-taker."

SOURCE: Stanley L. Brue/Donald R. Wentworth, ECONOMIC SCENES: Theory in Today's World, 5e, © 1992, pp. 92, 94. Adapted by permission of Prentice-Hall, Englewood Cliffs, New Jersey.

Applications

1. Why was De Beers able to maintain a monopoly on diamonds before the threats in the 1970s and 1980s?

2. What threat to its position did De Beers face in the 1970s? How did it deal with the problem?

3. Outline the threats De Beers faced in the 1980s. How did it counter these threats?

4. Do you think De Beers's actions were "fair?" Explain why or why not.

5. Suggest what might happen to the price and supply of diamonds on the world market if De Beers's monopoly were broken and the industry became open to many buyers and sellers.

☐ Non-Identical Costs

Our conclusion that monopoly is less advantageous to consumers than perfect competition is based on the assumption that costs are the same in both market situations. Clearly, however, this is not necessarily the case. Several competing companies supplying telephone services in an area would have much higher costs than a single large supplier. The opposite may be true in other situations. What factors, then, are likely to result in varying costs for purely competitive firms and monopolies?

(i) Economies of scale Consumer demand for a product may not be sufficient to support a large number of companies producing at an output which allows them all to realize the economies of scale. In this case, the firm must be monopolistic to produce at low unit cost.

For example, as we saw earlier, economies of scale are especially important in public utility industries, such as natural gas and electricity. The costs of entering these industries are so high that only very large firms can produce enough and service a large enough area to ensure sufficient returns. Costs for small competitive firms would be much higher.

(ii) Inefficiency Many people contend that, with the lack of competition, monopolists are more likely to allow costs to rise and service and productivity to fall than are competitive firms. In this case, the average total cost curve of the monopolist may be higher than that of the competitive firm and thus prices to the consumer would rise.

(iii) Invention and technological growth Which has the greater ability and incentive to develop new products and improve production techniques to reduce costs—the monopoly or the competitive firm? Competitive firms are keen to adopt improved production techniques, since their very survival depends on efficiency. However, they may have little incentive to develop new products and techniques when their competitors can quickly imitate them. The rewards for the innovating firm may be limited.

Monopolists are more likely to have the resources to innovate, but will they? The answer is maybe. Monopolies do not have the spur of competition to encourage

innovation. On the other hand, they are aware that advances in technology bring lower costs and, hence, higher profits. The development of technology may also help monopolists preserve their exclusive position.

■ Price Discrimination

So far, we have assumed that monopolists sell their products at a standard price to everyone. However, in certain circumstances, monopolists may vary their prices to different consumers—though the costs of production are unchanged. This practice is known as **price discrimination**. Regular adult transit fares, for example, are frequently higher than those for students and/or senior citizens on urban transit systems.

By charging two different prices for two different groups, the monopolist is able to increase profits. Suppose, for example, I am willing to pay $500 for a return air flight between Winnipeg and Vancouver, while you are willing to pay only $250. If the airline can get me (and others like me) to pay $500 while you pay only $250, it can increase profits.

However, if I know that you are getting the trip for half price, I will try to get the trip for $250 as well. The airline must be able to identify separate markets for its services and keep them separate. It must be impossible for you to sell your flight to me. For price discrimination to work, each group of buyers should have different elasticities of demand. Groups of people like you, who are only willing to buy airline tickets at lower prices, will have a higher elasticity of demand for airline trips than people like me, who are still willing to buy at higher prices.

Bus companies can set adult fares higher than student fares because adult demand is more inelastic, that is, less sensitive to changes in price. The adult market and the student market are kept separate by student ID cards and different coloured tickets.

Price discrimination may also occur between countries. For example, a Canadian product may be sold abroad at a lower price than in Canada. This practice is called "dumping" and is usually prohibited when the product is sold in competition with a domestic product because it may lead to unemployment at home.

Summary

a. A pure monopoly is a market structure with only one producer of a good or service, for which there are no close substitutes and many buyers.

b. The main barriers to entry that allow monopolies to exist include: ownership of patents or essential raw materials, the government grant of a legal monopoly or franchise, economies of scale that produce a natural monopoly, and mergers or collusion to raise prices and/or restrict output.

c. Since the firm and the industry are one and the same in a monopoly, the demand curve for the monopolist is the same as the market demand curve and the average revenue curve (price). The D = AR = P curve for the monopolist slopes down to the right, indicating that the monopolist can sell more only by decreasing price. The monopolist is a "price-maker."

d. As under perfect competition, profit for the monopolist is maximized where the difference between total revenue and total cost is at a maximum and where marginal revenue = marginal cost. The monopolist's marginal revenue curve, however, is not the same as its average revenue curve (price). Marginal revenue decreases more rapidly with increases in output than does average revenue.

e. With the same costs, the monopolist will produce a smaller output at a higher price than the perfectly competitive firm. Costs for monopolies and perfectly competitive firms are not necessarily equal, however. Costs may differ as a result of: economies of scale, inefficiencies, and differences in willingness and ability to apply new production techniques and develop new products.

f. De Beers is an example of an international monopoly that has successfully maintained its monopoly position through such actions as creating it own marketing organization, controlling the supply of diamonds, and advertising campaigns.

g. Monopolists may adopt price discrimination—the practice of charging different prices to customers for similar goods or services produced at similar cost. Regular adult transit fares are generally more expensive than student or senior citizen fares, for example. The groups have different elasticities of demand and are kept separate by ID cards and different coloured tickets.

▌ Review of Key Terms

Define the following key terms introduced in this chapter and provide examples where appropriate.

pure monopoly   merger
patent   collusion
legal monopoly   price discrimination
natural monopoly

▌ Application and Analysis

1. Note which of the following are monopolies in Canada and describe the type of monopoly (legal, natural, etc.) where applicable.

(a) Alberta Government Telephones

(b) a taxi firm with a licence to operate in the city of Halifax

(c) Canada Post

(d) a manufacturer of fine textiles

(e) Hydro-Québec

(f) an air courier which has the government licence to service select communities in the Far North

2. (a) Complete Table 9.3 on page 186.

(b) Graph the demand curve for the monopolist and label it D = AR.

(c) Graph the marginal revenue curve and label it MR.

Table 9.3 Demand, total and marginal revenue for a pure monopolist (in dollars)

	DEMAND		REVENUE
1 QUANTITY (Q) (IN UNITS)	2 PRICE (P) P = AR	3 TOTAL REVENUE (TR) TR = P × Q	4 MARGINAL REVENUE (MR) $MR = \frac{\Delta TR}{\Delta Q}$
1	18	18	
2	16	32	+14
3	14	42	+10
4	12		
5	10		
6	8		
7	6		
8	4		
9	2		
10	0		

3. (a) Complete Table 9.4 below.

(b) Graph and label the marginal cost, average cost, marginal revenue, and demand curves.

(c) At what output does the monopolist maximize profit?

(d) At the profit-maximizing output, what is:

   (i)   marginal cost per unit

   (ii) marginal revenue per unit

   (iii) average total cost

   (iv) price

   (v)   average profit

   (vi) total profit?

4. Based on the data in Table 9.4, graph the total revenue, total cost, and profit curves. At what output is profit maximized?

Table 9.4 Revenues, costs, and profit of a pure monopolist (in dollars)

1 QUANTITY (Q) (IN UNITS)	2 PRICE (P)	3 TOTAL REVENUE (TR) TR = P × Q	4 TOTAL COST (TC)	5 TOTAL PROFIT (TP) TP = TR – TC	6 MARGINAL REVENUE (MR) $MR = \frac{\Delta TR}{\Delta Q}$	7 MARGINAL COST (MC) $MC = \frac{\Delta TC}{\Delta Q}$
0		0	14.5	-14.5		
1	18	18	17.5	+0.5	+18	3
2	16	32	20	+12	+14	2.5
3	14		22			
4	12		25			
5	10		30			
6	8		37			
7	6		46			
8	4		57			

5. Case Study—The Rise and Fall of a Monopoly

The following extract describes what happened in the United States just after 1945 when the first ballpoint pens began to appear on the market. As you read, consider why the Reynolds International Pen Company made large profits from ballpoint pens—as high as $500 000 a month—and why after 1951 their manufacture was "only ordinarily profitable."

In 1945, Milton Reynolds developed a new type of pen that wrote with a ball bearing rather than a conventional nib. He formed the Reynolds International Pen Company, capitalized at $26 000, and began production on October 6, 1945.

The Reynolds pen was introduced with a good deal of fanfare by Gimbels [a New York department store], which guaranteed that the pen would write for two years with refilling. The price was set at $12.50 (the maximum price allowed by the wartime Office of Price Administration). Gimbels sold 10 000 pens on October 29, 1945, the first day they were on sale. In the early stages of production, the cost of production was estimated to be around $0.80 per pen.

The Reynolds International Pen Company quickly expanded production. By early 1946, it employed more than 800 people in its factory and was producing 30 000 pens per day. By March 1946, it had $3 million in the bank.

Macy's, Gimbels' traditional rival, introduced an imported ballpoint pen from South America. Its price was $19.98 (production costs unknown).

The heavy sales quickly elicited a response from other pen manufacturers. Eversharp introduced its first model in April, priced at $15. In July 1946, *Fortune* magazine reported that Sheaffer was planning to put out a pen at $15, and Eversharp announced its plan to produce a "retractable" model priced at $25. Reynolds introduced a new model, but kept the price at $12.50. Costs were estimated at $0.60 per pen.

The first signs of trouble emerged. The Ball Point Pen Company of Hollywood put a $9.95 model on the market, and a manufacturer named David Kahn announced plans to introduce a pen selling for less than $3. *Fortune* reported fears of an impending price war

in view of the growing number of manufacturers and the low cost of production. In October, Reynolds introduced a new model, priced at $3.85, that cost about $0.30 to produce.

By Christmas 1946, approximately 100 manufacturers were in production, some of them selling pens for as little as $2.98. By February 1947, Gimbels was selling a ballpoint pen made by the Continental Pen Company for $0.98. Reynolds introduced a new model priced to sell at $1.69, but Gimbels sold it for $0.88 in a price war with Macy's. Reynolds felt betrayed by Gimbels.

Reynolds introduced a new model listed at $0.98. By this time, ballpoint pens had become economy rather than luxury items, but they were still highly profitable.

In mid-1948, ballpoint pens were selling for as little as $0.39 and costing about $0.10 to produce. In 1951, prices of $0.25 were common. Within six years, the power of the monopoly was gone forever. Ever since then, the market has been saturated with a wide variety of models and prices of pens ranging from $0.19 up. Their manufacture is only ordinarily profitable.

SOURCE: Excerpted from Economics 5/ed. by Richard Lipsey *et al.* Copyright ©1978 by Richard Lipsey, Purvis, and Steiner. Reprinted by permission of HarperCollins Publishers.

(a) What characteristics defined Milton Reynolds's production of ballpoint pens as a monopoly?

(b) What was the cost of production and the selling price of the first Reynolds ballpoint pens?

(c) Why was there such a wide disparity between cost and price at first?

(d) Since 1945, what has happened to the price of ballpoint pens? Explain why.

(e) How was Reynolds International Pen Company's monopoly broken?

(f) Suppose Reynolds had been able to keep other firms out of the ballpoint pen business. What difference would it have made? Why?

(g) Suggest another product with a similar price history to that of the ballpoint pen. Did the industry begin as a monopoly? Explain what happened.

6. Individually or in groups, research a monopoly in your province and prepare a short report. Some topics you might consider include:

(a) history of the firm

(b) nature of the monopoly

(c) ownership

(d) number of employees

(e) total sales over the past few years

(f) profits over the past few years

(g) how the monopoly's power is maintained

(h) why this market structure may be appropriate in this industry. Sources of information could include:

(i)   recent annual reports

(ii) *Financial Post Corporation Service Cards: Index of Publicly-Held Canadian Companies*

(iii) library vertical files

(iv) the public relations department of the firm.

7. Debate the following issue: "Resolved that monopolies are inefficient and, therefore, should be abolished."

CHAPTER TEN

Monopolistic Competition and Oligopoly

Objectives

a. Outline four major characteristics of monopolistically competitive markets.

b. Examine and graph the demand, cost, and revenue curves for a monopolistically competitive firm.

c. Demonstrate, using graphs, the short-run and long-run profit-maximizing output of the monopolistically competitive firm.

d. Demonstrate how monopolistically competitive firms attempt to improve their long-run profit position through non-price competition.

e. Compare monopolistic competition and perfect competition in terms of efficiency.

f. Explain and analyze the main characteristics of oligopoly markets.

g. Analyze why oligopoly price theory is less precise than that of the other market structures.

h. Demonstrate why oligopoly prices are "sticky" and tend to change together with reference to the kinked demand curve, collusion, price leadership, and tacit agreements.

i. Analyze the advantages and disadvantages of imperfect competition.

j. Explain how and why governments regulate monopolies and oligopolies and evaluate the effectiveness of the measures.

In the previous two chapters, we examined the two polar market structures—perfect competition and pure monopoly. These two market structures are the exceptions in the economy, not the rule. Most markets in Canada fall between them. The term **imperfect competition** is used by economists to describe the market structures that are neither perfectly competitive nor purely monopolistic. These include monopolistic competition—imperfect competition among the many—and oligopoly—imperfect competition among the few.

In this chapter, we examine the characteristics and profit-maximizing decisions of the monopolistically competitive and oligopolistic firm. We also consider the efficiency of these market structures as compared with perfect competition.

■ Monopolistic Competition

The term "monopolistic competition" correctly suggests elements of both perfect competition and monopoly. **Monopolistic competition** is a market structure in which many firms sell a differentiated product. The large number of firms means that competition exists, but each firm has an element of monopoly in that its product or service has a unique aspect. Examples of monopolistically competitive industries include the retail trade, clothing industry, and restaurant business.

☐ Characteristics of Monopolistic Competition

Let's examine the characteristics of monopolistically competitive firms in more detail.

Many Firms
Though the number of firms is not as great as in a perfectly competitive market, each firm has only a small market share and, therefore, only limited control over price. This control is not enough to have a major effect on sales of competitors. If one firm manages to increase its sales by say 20 percent, this will have little impact on an industry of 40 or 50 competitors. If one clothing store out of 50 in the city, for example, holds a sale, it will attract more customers and increase its sales, but it will not take away a large number of customers from any one of its rivals. They will still have enough customers to operate.

However, if there are only three or four small hardware stores in a small town, they are oligopolists (as we will see later). If one store offers a sale and a large number of people buy from this store, it will greatly reduce sales of the other stores because they depend on the same small base of customers. Consumers have a choice of only a few firms. Though there may be thousands of hardware stores in the larger region, the actual number the consumer realistically has to choose from is an important factor in determining whether a market is monopolistically competitive or oligopolistic.

Product Differentiation
While purely competitive firms turn out a standardized (or undifferentiated) product, monopolistically competitive firms produce a differentiated product—that is, a product with many variations. For example, many firms produce shirts, but the shirts are differentiated by colour, cut, cloth, and style. Advertising, packaging, and brand names can emphasize the differences. Even if products are physically the same, they can be differentiated in a number of ways. A one-litre bottle of Pepsi in a nearby store is better on a hot day than one in a far-away store. Some people would be willing to pay a little more for the Pepsi in the neighbourhood store. Though the product is the same, the customer *perceives* it as different.

Product differentiation gives individual monopolistic competitors some control over price. Consumers are willing, within narrow limits, to pay more for the goods of particular sellers and can have limited preferences for one over others.

Few Barriers to Entry
It is relatively easy to enter monopolistically competitive industries. Firms and their capital requirements tend to be small. Compared to purely competitive firms, however, there may be additional financial burdens in the form of advertising, packaging, and other ways of differentiating a product from its competitors.

Non-Price Competition
Since products in monopolistic competition are differentiated, competition focusses not only on price, but also on such non-price factors as advertising, brand names, and trade marks. Firms under monopolistic competition place a great importance on these factors to attract loyal customers.

The heated advertising war waged by soft drink companies is an example. Some firms may also offer special services to attract customers. Some pizza chains, for example, will offer two-for-one, free delivery over a large area, or a free drink with a particular order.

☐ Demand, Price, and Output in the Short-Run

The demand curve faced by the monopolistically competitive firm is elastic (downward sloping), because its product has a large number of possible substitutes.

Consumers are sensitive to changes in price since they have many similar products from which to choose. If the monopolistically competitive firm raises its price considerably, therefore, it will lose a significant amount of its sales. Some customers will continue buying from the firm because of its advantageous location in the case of a retail store, for example, or because of loyalty to a particular brand name in the case of a small clothing manufacturer. A price cut, on the other hand, will attract some, but not all of its competitors' customers.

The downward-sloping demand curve means that the monopolistically competitive firm's marginal revenue curve also slopes downward. To increase sales, the firm must cut its price and the extra revenue from each additional unit sold, therefore, decreases as output increases.

The effect of changes in price on total sales will depend on the number of competitors and the degree of product differentiation. The larger the number of competitors and the weaker the product differentiation, the greater the effect on sales of a change in price. The smaller the number of competitors and the greater the product differentiation, the smaller the effect on sales of a change in price. It is clearly in the firm's best interests to differentiate its product as much as possible.

□ Profit Maximization

The firm will maximize its profits (or minimize its losses) in the short run at the output where marginal cost equals marginal revenue. Sound familiar? Figure 10.1 shows that in the short run, the firm makes a profit within the shaded rectangle PACE. Price per unit is higher than average total cost within this area. The firm is in equilibrium at point E.

In the long run, however, this favourable profit situation will not persist. Other firms will be enticed into the industry by the above normal profits. The firm's demand curve will, therefore, shift to the left from DD in Figure 10.1 to D_2D_2 in Figure 10.2. The firm then has a smaller share of the market due to the increased competition and diminishing product differentiation, and economic profits will be eliminated. The

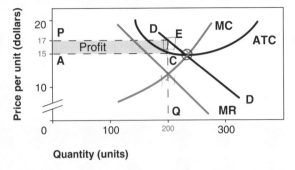

Figure 10.1 Short-run profit maximization and equilibrium under monopolistic competition

The monopolistically competitive firm has a downward-sloping demand curve because its product faces competition from a number of close substitutes. Profit is maximized at the output where MR = MC, in this case 200 units. At that output, average revenue or price at $17 exceeds average total cost at $15. Maximum profit is, therefore, $2. Economic profit is shown by the shaded rectangle PACE.

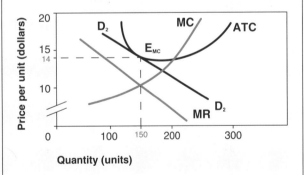

Figure 10.2 Long-run profit maximization and equilibrium under monopolistic competition

Over the long-run, economic profits will attract other firms into the industry. Since the firm then has a smaller share of the market, its demand curve shifts left to D_2D_2 and its economic profit is eliminated. The long-run equilibrium for the firm is at a price of $14 per unit and an output of 150 units — point E_{MC}.

firm will tend to make only a normal profit or break even. Thus, as shown by point E_{MC} in Figure 10.2, the firm reaches long-run equilibrium. Entry and exit into the industry stabilizes.

In practice, however, some firms may continue to make more than a normal profit or take a loss over the long run. Firms may be able to differentiate their product to such an extent that competitors cannot equal them for a long time. A fast-food restaurant may have the only location opposite the main entrance and exit of a college or bus station, for example. A certain brand of footwear or clothing may have developed strong consumer loyalty. On the other hand, some firms may not move out of an industry even though they are incurring economic losses in the long run. A small storekeeper may remain in business because she or he is unwilling or unable to move into another industry.

□ Non-Price Competition

Since the long-run prospect of monopolistically competitive firms is to realize only a normal profit, and since they have only limited control over price, they attempt to gain an advantage through **non-price competition**. As we have seen, three major facets of non-price competition are further product differentiation, product development, and advertising. Let's consider them more closely.

(i) Product differentiation   Product differentiation offers the monopolistically competitive firm some definite advantages. It can build consumer loyalty and thus protect the firm from new competition. It may also convince customers that the product is worth more than its competitors, and the firm will be able to raise its prices. Compared to the standardized product of perfectly competitive firms, differentiated products also better accommodate the tastes and preferences of consumers. The large number of different products and the barrage of advertising information may, however, be so great as to confuse consumers.

(ii) Product development   The drive for product differentiation may, in some cases, lead to product improvement. Monopolistically competitive firms have

the incentive to take advantage of new technology for product improvements, since they may thus gain a larger market share. Consumer demand and the drive toward differentiation has brought us foods processed with less sugar and fat, for example. Some "improvements," however, may be merely superficial, with no real advantage over earlier versions.

(iii) Advertising   Advertising can be used to emphasize the differences between the firm's product and the others in the market, clarify its advantages, promote a high profile among consumers, and develop strong consumer loyalty. In some cases, however, a strong advertising campaign may promote a lesser product over better alternatives.

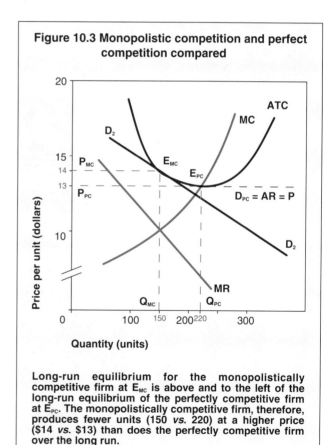

Figure 10.3 Monopolistic competition and perfect competition compared

Long-run equilibrium for the monopolistically competitive firm at E_{MC} is above and to the left of the long-run equilibrium of the perfectly competitive firm at E_{PC}. The monopolistically competitive firm, therefore, produces fewer units (150 *vs.* 220) at a higher price ($14 *vs.* $13) than does the perfectly competitive firm over the long run.

☐ Efficiency in Monopolistically Competitive Markets

As we saw in Chapter 8, perfect competition may be used as a measure of efficiency for other market structures. To achieve productive efficiency, therefore, price must equal minimum average total cost. For allocative efficiency, price must equal marginal cost.

Figure 10.3 provides a comparison of monopolistic and perfect competition. The equilibrium for the monopolistically competitive firm in the long run (E_{MC}) is above and to the left of the long-run equilibrium for the perfectly competitive firm (E_{PC}). The monopolistically competitive firm produces fewer goods (150 units vs. 220 units) at a higher price ($14 vs. $13) than does the perfectly competitive firm. Clearly then, the mono-polistically competitive firm is less efficient than the perfectly competitive one over the long run.

It can be argued that if we were to halve the number of monopolistically competitive firms selling at prices above marginal cost, prices could be cut and efficiency improved. For example, if we were to cut significantly the number of retail stores or small restaurants, or the large variety of shirt or shoe styles, costs and therefore prices could be cut and it seems the customer would be better off.

However, cutting the number of firms also reduces the diversity of products and shopping convenience. Some would argue that the convenience and diversity are well worth the slightly higher prices we have to pay in monopolistically competitive industries.

☐ ☐ ☐ ☐ ☐ ☐
Concentration in Canadian Industry

How much concentration is there in Canadian industry? At first glance, it may appear that a simple count of the number of firms in an industry would provide an answer and indicate where firms fit on the market spectrum. But suppose one industry has five firms controlling an equal share of the entire market and another industry with 21 firms has one firm controlling 80 percent of the market. Evidently, the second industry has a greater concentration despite the larger number of firms. Economists have, therefore, developed concentration ratios. A **concentration ratio** is the percentage of total market sales for the four (or eight) largest firms in the industry.

For example, the four largest firms in Canada provide almost 99 percent of total sales in tobacco products. In construction sales, on the other hand, the four largest firms supply only 2.2 percent of the market.

When considering concentration ratios, it is important to keep the size of the market in mind. The ratios are based on the national market, but the market for a product may in fact be regional or international. The concentration ratios in the cement and newspaper industries, for example, are low, but the market power of firms in these industries is nonetheless considerable. Few Canadian cities have more than two newspapers. Similarly, high transportation costs divide the cement industry into a number of regional markets in which there are typically only a few firms—each with considerable power to influence prices.

The market for the automobile industry, on the other hand, is international. Four firms account for about 90 percent of the cars sold by Canadian producers, but they make up a much smaller proportion of total Canadian car sales. Japanese, German, and South Korean automobile companies make up much of the difference.

As Figure 10.4 shows, concentration ratios vary considerably in Canada. In agriculture, except where government supply management has created legal monopolies, concentration ratios are low—about that of perfect competition. In other industries, such as tobacco and petroleum, ratios are very high. In manufacturing, four firms control about half of sales. In the retail and service industries, especially in large towns, the ratios are low.

Concentration ratios in Canada are higher than those in the US because the market is smaller. However, the Canadian market—especially since the Free Trade Agreement with the US—is much more open to goods produced in other countries than is the US.

Figure 10.4 Share of total sales by four and eight largest firms in selected industries, 1988

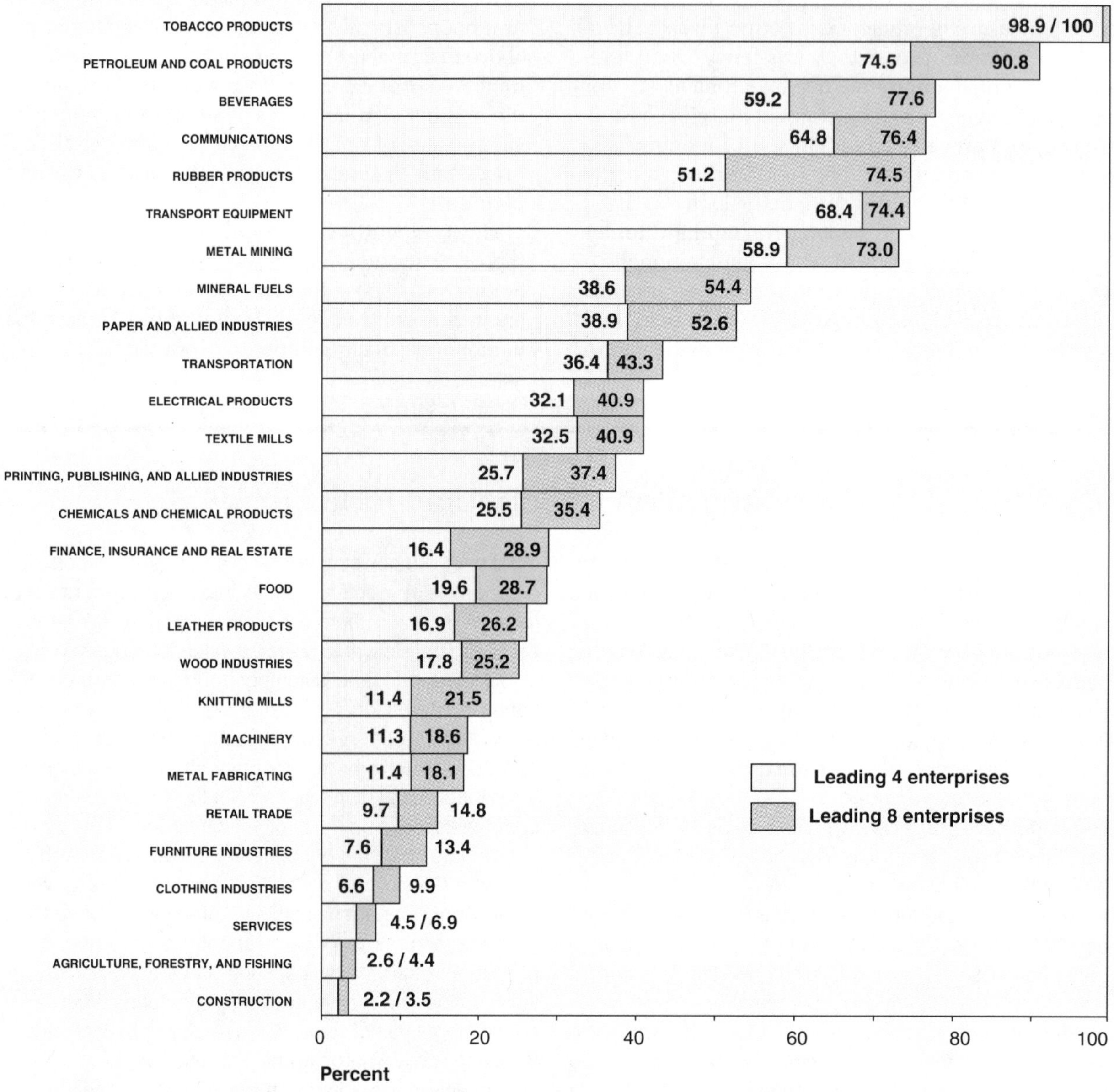

Industry	Leading 4 enterprises	Leading 8 enterprises
TOBACCO PRODUCTS	98.9	100
PETROLEUM AND COAL PRODUCTS	74.5	90.8
BEVERAGES	59.2	77.6
COMMUNICATIONS	64.8	76.4
RUBBER PRODUCTS	51.2	74.5
TRANSPORT EQUIPMENT	68.4	74.4
METAL MINING	58.9	73.0
MINERAL FUELS	38.6	54.4
PAPER AND ALLIED INDUSTRIES	38.9	52.6
TRANSPORTATION	36.4	43.3
ELECTRICAL PRODUCTS	32.1	40.9
TEXTILE MILLS	32.5	40.9
PRINTING, PUBLISHING, AND ALLIED INDUSTRIES	25.7	37.4
CHEMICALS AND CHEMICAL PRODUCTS	25.5	35.4
FINANCE, INSURANCE AND REAL ESTATE	16.4	28.9
FOOD	19.6	28.7
LEATHER PRODUCTS	16.9	26.2
WOOD INDUSTRIES	17.8	25.2
KNITTING MILLS	11.4	21.5
MACHINERY	11.3	18.6
METAL FABRICATING	11.4	18.1
RETAIL TRADE	9.7	14.8
FURNITURE INDUSTRIES	7.6	13.4
CLOTHING INDUSTRIES	6.6	9.9
SERVICES	4.5	6.9
AGRICULTURE, FORESTRY, AND FISHING	2.6	4.4
CONSTRUCTION	2.2	3.5

Percent

The degree of concentration varies widely in Canadian industries from almost 99 percent for the four largest firms in the tobacco industry to 2.2 percent for the four largest firms in construction.

SOURCE: Statistics Canada, Industrial Organization and Finance Division, Corporations Section, *Annual Report: Part 7, Corporations*, October 1991.

■ Oligopoly

Oligopoly is a market structure consisting of a few large firms, so that the actions of any one firm directly affect the decisions of the others. In some industries, firms may manufacture an identical or homogeneous product, such as steel or aluminium. These industries are known as **homogeneous oligopolies**. In other industries, the firms may manufacture a similar but differentiated product, based in part on packaging, styling, etc. Examples are the cigarette, household appliance, and automobile industries. These are known as **differentiated oligopolies** and are most common in industries that sell their products in the retail market (rather than wholesale to other industries).

▢ Characteristics of Oligopolies

The key characteristics of oligopolistic markets are few firms, interdependent pricing, and entry barriers. Let's examine these in more detail.

A Few Large Firms
While there may be more than two or three firms in an oligopolistic industry, a few large firms will be dominant and produce a significant proportion of the total industry output. Canada has a number of small, independent cement producers, for example, but the vast majority of cement is produced by a few large firms. Similarly, while there may be many different taxi firms in a city, if only a few firms have a licence to service a particular area such as the airport, these firms are oligopolistic in that area. The key is not the total number of firms, but the actual number consumers have to choose from in a given area.

Interdependent Pricing
Since only a few firms dominate the industry, each one has some control over price—thus distinguishing the oligopoly from pure competition. However, unlike the monopolist, the oligopolist's control over price is limited. The actions of one oligopolist affect the others in the industry, so that each firm cannot set prices independently. In considering where to set prices, each oligopolist must consider how its rivals will react.

For example, suppose four large firms—W, X, Y, and Z—have approximately one-quarter each of the market for product P. If W cuts its prices, it will gain a larger share of the market. But W's competitors X, Y, and Z, will be directly and adversely affected by W's actions. Their sales and profits will decline unless they react by cutting their prices to match W's, or by cutting them even further below W's prices to start a price war. And, of course, all three firms may not react in the same way. No particular pattern is sure.

Clearly, then, no oligopolist will cut prices without giving careful consideration to the possible ways in which other oligopolists in the same industry may react. Moreover, there is no way of knowing beforehand how oligopolistic competitors will react. The situation faced by the oligopolist is like that faced by the players in a game of poker or chess. There is no way of knowing beforehand how to play your cards or move your chess pieces—it depends on the actions of the other player or players.

This mutual interdependence is unique to oligopoly. In pure competition and monopolistic competition, the number of firms is so great that it is for the most part unnecessary to consider competitors' reactions to one's decisions. For the monopolist, it is unnecessary for the simple reason that there are no competitors.

▢ Why Do Oligopolies Exist?

Why is it that certain industries are composed only or mainly of a few large firms? The reasons are the economies of scale, barriers to entry, and the urge to merge.

Economies of Scale
The economies of scale may be such that it is impossible for more than only a few firms to make a profit in many industries. The costs of establishing an automobile production operation complete with computerized and robotic systems, for example, requires hundreds of millions of dollars. Only large firms can afford these expenditures and produce enough to keep costs down and make an adequate return. Many oligopolistic industries originally included a large number of firms when the level of technology allowed few economies of

scale. However, with technological improvements, economies of scale increased and many firms were forced out of the industry. The number of firms became fewer and fewer.

In the early days of the Canadian automobile industry, for example, there were as many as 80 firms in production. In the twentieth century, mass production techniques and the huge expenditures required to establish a complete assembly line reduced the number of firms, so that today only three firms make 90 percent of the North American-produced automobiles. The steel and petroleum industries went through a similar process.

Barriers to Entry

In addition to the economies of scale, ownership of patents or special licences, control of essential raw materials, and knowledge of production techniques by existing oligopolies also act to bar would-be entrants to the industry. The large expenditures required for non-price competition such as advertising, particularly in the cigarette and cosmetic industries, may also act as a barrier to entry. In addition, consumer loyalty to some products may be very difficult to dislodge, even when a new product offers several advantages.

The Urge to Merge

Firms stand to gain considerably by merging. A merger is the joining or combination of two or more business enterprises into a single enterprise. Mergers may be barriers to competition when they give the merged firm a greater market share, increased control over price, and greater economies of scale. The firm's increased size may also give it the power to demand—and get—lower prices from its suppliers. It can take advantage of discounts on high-volume orders. Some firms may also merge with, or buy out, new competitors that enter the industry.

☐ Price and Output Decisions

In our examination of purely competitive and monopoly markets, we were able to gain a relatively clear idea of how firms in these markets make their pricing and output decisions. These decisions for oligopolies, how-

ever, are less clear-cut. Two factors that make the behaviour of oligopolies more complex are the mutual interdependence of firms and the variety of market situations.

(i) *Mutual interdependence*   As we have seen, with only a few firms in the industry, no firm can predict with certainty how others will react to changes in price. If a firm raises its price, it cannot be sure that others will follow its lead. If it lowers its price to gain sales, it cannot be sure that others will not also lower their prices—thereby negating its advantage. Consequently, the oligopolist does not know the shape of the demand curve it faces.

(ii) *Variety of market situations*   We also saw that oligopolies include industries which may be tightly dominated by two or three firms, or loosely shared by six or seven firms. In addition, oligopolistic industries may produce either standardized or differentiated goods. In some cases, firms may be colluding to control prices and outputs and in other cases not. Clearly, the variety of market situations makes it difficult to fit all oligopolies into a single, all-encompassing pattern of behaviour.

What can we summarize about prices in oligopoly markets then? Two key characteristics are that they tend to be "sticky," and that when one firm changes its price, all firms tend to follow in unison. By "sticky," we mean that prices under oligopoly tend to change much less frequently than under other market structures. In the automobile industry, for example, prices generally are set—often by all firms at once—at the beginning of the model year. They are usually adjusted only occasionally and often almost simultaneously throughout the year. Prices of the 1993 models of all manufacturers, for example, usually drop toward the end of the year once the new 1994 models are available. The firms are, therefore, not at the mercy of a sharp drop in prices as a result of reduced demand. If demand drops, manufacturers will generally cut production rather than price. If they cut price, all firms will likely also have to cut prices and all would lose profits.

Oligopolists, therefore, are "price-seekers." They cannot set prices as monopolists can, and the market does not establish the price for them as under perfect competition. The uncertainty they face means that they must search for an equilibrium price.

How, then, are the remarkably stable prices of oligopolies established? One explanation is the theory of the kinked demand curve.

☐ The Kinked Demand Curve

If there is no collusion or informal agreement among oligopolistic firms, economists explain the price "stickiness" using the model of the **kinked demand curve**.

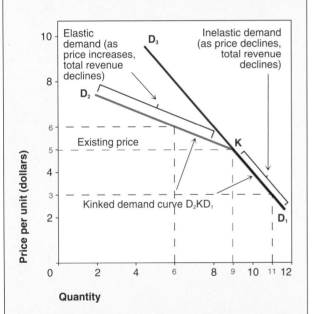

Figure 10.5 The kinked demand curve of the non-collusive, differentiated oligopolist

If the oligopolistic firm lowers its price from $5 to $3 per unit and other firms in the industry follow, then sales may increase but total revenue (price x quantity) falls from $45 to $33. If, however, the firm raises its price from $5 to $6 per unit and other firms do not follow suit, total revenue decreases from $45 to $36. Since total revenue declines when prices are raised or lowered, price will tend to remain fixed at $5 per unit—at the kink, K.

Suppose you are one of four large oligopolistic firms in an industry. Table 10.1 outlines the demand and revenue schedules for your product. Let's assume you are currently selling 9 units at $5 per unit. The demand curve for your product will be kinked, as shown in Figure 10.5, if your competitors behave in the following ways. Economists assume these to be likely reactions.

(i) You cut your prices and your competitors match your price cut   If you cut your prices, your competitors must match your price because they do not want you to take away their customers. For example, suppose you cut your price from $5 to $3. While the number of units you sell increases from 9 to 11, your total revenue (price x quantity) decreases from $45 ($5 x $9) to $33 ($3 x $11) because your competitors have matched your price cut and you cannot sell enough additional units to increase your profits.

(ii) You raise your price and your competitors leave their price unchanged   If you raise your price from $5 to $6 per unit, your competitors see your price increase

Table 10.1 Demand and revenue schedules for the non-collusive, differentiated oligopolist

DEMAND		REVENUE		
1 PRICE (P) (IN DOLLARS)	2 QUANTITY DEMANDED (Q) (IN UNITS)	3 TOTAL REVENUE (TR) (IN DOLLARS)	4 MARGINAL REVENUE (MR) (IN DOLLARS)	5 MARGINAL REVENUE PER UNIT (IN DOLLARS)
7	3	21	—	—
6	6	36	15	5
5	9	45	9	3
4	10	40	-5	-5
3	11	33	-7	-7
2	12	24	-9	-9

The non-collusive, differentiated oligopolist does not gain by a cut in price because competitors will also cut their price to match so that not enough additional units can be sold to increase total revenue. If the oligopolist increases price, competitors will leave their prices unchanged and the higher price will mean fewer sales and thus lower total revenue. The non-collusive, differentiated oligopolist, therefore, faces a kinked demand curve.

as a great opportunity to increase their share of the market at your expense. They, therefore, leave their prices unchanged. As shown in Table 10.1 and Figure 10.5, with a price increase from $5 to $6, quantity demanded decreases from 9 to 6 units. Your total revenue, therefore, decreases from $45 to $36.

To summarize, it seems reasonable to assume that if you cut prices, your competitors follow you. If you raise prices, your competitors stay put. Thus, you face a kinked demand curve.

With this demand curve, what should you do? The most likely answer is to select point K in Figure 10.5, where the kink occurs. In other words, you should stay with the existing price ($5 per unit) and output (9 units). With this strategy, you don't upset your competitors, you keep your share of the market, and you probably maximize profits.

☐ Profit Maximization—The MR = MC Rule

Figure 10.6 confirms that $5 per unit is the price at which profit is maximized. The demand curve for the firm is D_2KD_1, reproduced from Figure 10.5. What is the marginal revenue curve appropriate to this demand curve? For the D_2K section of the demand curve, the corresponding marginal revenue (MR) curve is RS. When we reach the kink at K and move along the demand curve KD_1, the corresponding marginal revenue curve is TU. Due to the sharp differences in elasticity between D_2K and the KD_1 segments of the demand curve, a gap occurs in the MR curve between S and T. We treat this as a vertical section of the MR curve. As we can see, MR = MC at an output of 9 units.

Even with large shifts in marginal cost along the vertical segment of the MR curve, output will remain at 9 units and price at $5 per unit. Thus, price and output are likely to remain stable at the kink.

Problems with the Kinked Demand Curve
The theory of the kinked demand curve does, however, leave some questions unanswered. First, how is the price established to begin with? The kinked curve explains why firms choose the existing price, but not how or why it was originally set. Second, prices in reality are not nearly as inflexible as the theory sug-

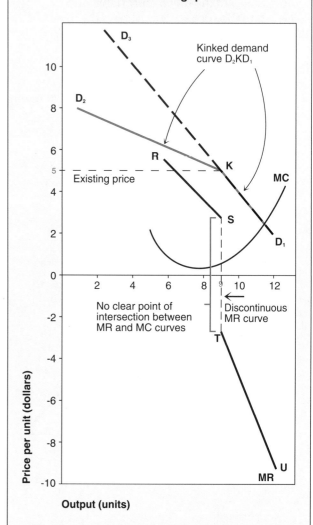

Figure 10.6 Profit maximization by the MR = MC rule for the non-collusive, differentiated oligopolist

Where the demand curve of the oligopolist is kinked—at an output of 9 units—the MR curve is discontinuous (the dotted line). Thus, only a very large increase in costs (and consequent shift in the MR curve) could induce the oligopolist to raise prices. Moreover, no reduction in costs would induce the oligopolist to lower prices, since lower prices mean lower profits. Thus, once set, oligopolistic prices tend to remain stable. Profit is maximized at an output of 9 units and a price of $5 per unit.

gests. Prices of automobiles, for example, do vary. You have probably noticed price increases—and probably more rarely—price decreases from time-to-time. Manufacturers may offer price rebates, lower interest rates on loans, or additional features such as air conditioning, for example—all lowering the set price.

☐ Other Explanations for Oligopolistic Prices

In addition to the theory of the kinked demand curve, the "sticky" prices in oligopolistic industries may be explained by collusion, price leadership, and tacit agreements among firms.

Collusion

The small number of firms, their mutual interdependence, and the barriers to entry in oligopolistic industries are all conducive to collusion. Collusion is an agreement among firms to fix prices or output, or to divide the market. The advantages are clear—the end of uncertainties and higher profits.

What price and output are the collusive oligopolists likely to select? The answer is the same one that the monopolist would choose—the one that maximizes profits where MR = MC. The firms gain monopolistic powers through their collusion.

Collusion may take a number of different forms. One is the cartel. A **cartel** is a formal arrangement between independent firms to fix output or prices or to divide the market geographically, so that each firm is given its own territory. One of the best-known cartels in the world today is OPEC—the Organization of Petroleum Exporting Nations. In the 1970s and early 1980s, the members of OPEC agreed to limit the output of oil and thus raise the price per barrel. Since the member countries account for a large proportion of the world's oil exports, they were able to raise prices considerably.

In other cases, collusion may take the form of an informal verbal agreement. Such agreements are illegal in Canada and the United States, but their informality makes them difficult to identify.

Agreements by oligopolists to raise prices or restrict output tend to be unstable for a number of reasons. In some countries, collusion is illegal. In Canada, for example, Anti-Combines legislation prohibits price-

---

☐ ☐ ☐ ☐ ☐

Collusion

"People of the same trade seldom meet together, even for merriment or diversion, but the conversation ends in a conspiracy against the public, or in some contrivance to raise prices."

Adam Smith, *Wealth of Nations*

A report in a US magazine in 1985 outlined a telephone conversation that took place between two airline executives in 1982. The conversation was taped without the knowledge of one of the executives. The conversation began with the two executives discussing how difficult it was for them both to make a profit when their airlines were flying the same routes and cutting prices. Competition between them was fierce.

During the course of the conversation, one executive suggested that the two airlines both raise their prices together—clearly so that they could both make a healthy profit, rather than continue losing profits by competing against one another on every route. The other executive protested that they should not be discussing prices and indeed colluding to fix prices. He did not follow the other executive's suggestion.

The US government accused the offending executive's airline of attempting to establish an illegal monopolization. The charge was later settled by the executive signing an agreement not to engage in any such activities in the future.

Applications

1. Who would have benefitted if there had been an effective agreement to fix prices? Explain.

2. Who would the losers have been? Explain.

3. Why do governments make price-fixing agreements by competing firms illegal?

fixing agreements. Incentives to cheat on the agreement are also strong. While all firms can benefit together from fixing prices and output, the individual firm can achieve even higher profits by cheating and selling more than the quota. Finally, the greater the number of firms in the industry, the more difficult it is to reach agreements.

The breakdown of a cartel or informal agreement may result in cut-throat competition or price wars. **Cut-throat competition** is the sale of goods at prices below the cost of production in order to drive rivals out of business. During price wars, the firm with the greatest financial resources stands the best chance.

Price Leadership

Price leadership is the practice whereby one firm (the price leader), usually the largest or dominant firm in the industry, initiates price changes knowing that most others will follow suit. In this case, instead of the kinked demand curve, D_2KD_1, we have the "kinkless" curve, D_3KD_1, shown in Figures 10.5 and 10.6.

The curve is kinkless because the uncertainty over prices is eliminated. As the price leader, you will set your price at the point where profit is maximized—where MR = MC. This point is probably close to the profit-maximizing output of the industry, which is why other firms are willing to follow your lead. You can be

□ □ □ □ □ □

The Case of the Flour Bid-Riggers

A routine telephone call and a far from routine response set in motion an investigation that led to the stiffest fines ever imposed under Canadian federal competition law.

The investigation began in 1987 when a procurement manager for the federal Department of Supply and Services called other firms when she received only one offer on a contract for wheat flour distribution as food aid to Third World nations. When the manager heard from one milling executive that it "wasn't the company's turn for the contract," she passed on the information to the Competition Tribunal. As a result, in 1991 three companies pleaded guilty to bid-rigging and were fined $1 million each. Three other firms pleaded guilty to price-fixing and were also fined roughly in proportion to their size with the highest fine at $225 000. Two additional firms were charged in the case.

The charges related to 531 contracts totalling about $500 million between 1975 and 1987 when the bid-rigging took place. Some of the contracts were for food aid to countries suffering from famine such as the Sudan, Chad, and Ethiopia. The export

shipments under the foreign aid contracts of the Canadian International Development Agency were to a variety of other countries including China, Vietnam, Nicaragua, Liberia, and the Philippines.

As part of the bid-rigging scheme, production of wheat flour was monitored by a national milling association, which then allocated the contracts on the basis of each firm's market share. A ceiling price was set by the association, and the company selected to win the bid put in a price just below the ceiling. The other companies bid above the ceiling price or not at all.

Applications

1. What is "bid-rigging?" How was it carried out in this case?

2. Suggest what economic effects the bid-rigging had.

3. According to one official at the Competition Tribunal, bid-rigging is a particularly nefarious form of conspiratorial behaviour. Do you agree? Why or why not?

confident that the other firms in the industry will set the same price you have set.

Many North American oligopolistic industries—such as the coal, cement, glass, and steel industries—have practised price leadership for years. In the automobile industry, for example, the dominant firm (usually General Motors, but sometimes Ford or Chrysler) announces the prices for its new model year and the other firms then follow its lead.

In practice, however, price leadership is not always so clear-cut. An industry may not have only one clear and consistent price leader. One company may take the lead one year and another the next. Some industries may follow a tentative, price-searching, trial-and-error approach. One firm may raise its prices, but if other firms do not follow suit, it may quickly rescind the increase.

Price leaders usually raise prices only occasionally because of the risk involved (other firms may not play "follow-the-leader"). Large price changes are made only when there is a significant change in demand or costs. The price leader may sometimes choose a price that does not maximize the industry's short-run profits. Why? Lower prices (and slightly lower profits) will help dissuade others from entering the industry and will maintain the oligopolistic structure.

Figure 10.7 Markets and their characteristics—a summary

FEATURES	PERFECT COMPETITION	MONOPOLISTIC COMPETITION	HOMOGENEOUS OLIGOPOLY	DIFFERENTIATED OLIGOPOLY	PURE MONOPOLY
NUMBER OF FIRMS	Many	Many	Few	Few	One
TYPE OF PRODUCT	Identical product	Some product differentiation (plus different services and locations)	Standardized product; little or no product differentiation	Differentiated product	One product; no close substitutes
TYPICAL DEMAND CURVE FACING FIRM	Perfectly elastic	Quite elastic	If collusion exists, same as monopoly	Fairly elastic; may be kinked	Elastic
CONTROL OVER PRICE	None; a "price-taker"	A little	Limited by mutual interdependence; considerable with price leadership; a "price-searcher"	Limited by mutual interdependence; considerable with collusion or price leadership; a "price-searcher"	Substantial; a "price-maker," unless price is regulated by government
COMPETITOR REACTION	None	Little	Considerable	Considerable	None
CONDITIONS OF ENTRY	Easy	Easy	Difficult	Difficult	Difficult or impossible
NON-PRICE COMPETITION	None	Some—especially advertising	Some	Extensive	Advertising to increase demand
EXAMPLES	Some agricultural products, stock market	Retail trade, clothing, furniture	Aluminium, steel, cement	Automobiles, cigarettes, computers	Telephone, electrical power, water services

Tacit Agreement

Another way in which oligopolistic firms may reach the same price is by means of a tacit or unspoken agreement. For example, a retailer could guess the price of a product competitors would choose if he or she knew it would be in the range of $9.50 to $10.40. The price would likely be $9.95. Retailers commonly select prices just below the upper dollar range—it is close to $10.00, but looks like $9.00. In some industries, certain prices "make sense." They are logical, and so the firms naturally agree on them without any formal or spoken arrangement.

☐ Non-Price Competition for Oligopolies

Like monopolistically competitive firms, oligopolists also place a great deal of emphasis on non-price competition, including advertising, research and development, and servicing. Often, oligopolists are more willing to engage in non-price competition than in price competition. In a price war, all firms stand to lose profits.

Imperfect Competition and Efficiency

How do firms in oligopolistic markets compare in terms of efficiency with firms under perfect competition—our measuring stick?

As we have seen, oligopolies tend to set prices above the point where marginal revenue equals marginal cost. Thus, prices are higher and output is lower than under perfect competition. It could be argued, therefore, that firms in this market structure make excessive profits. Under perfect competition, price tends to equal marginal cost, to the benefit of the consumer.

When firms are less subject to the rigours of competition, they may be less likely to keep costs low and quality and service high. A less efficient industry may result.

Oligopolistic firms are able to take advantage of economies of scale, however. In some cases, only a few large firms may be able to afford the considerable initial capital expenditures required to enter the industry. High overhead costs mean that the average total cost curve declines over a large amount of output. Prices, therefore, may be above marginal cost, but they may still be much lower than if there were many competing firms in the industry. For example, if there were many steel and automobile companies in Canada, the average cost of producing a tonne of steel or an automobile would probably be much higher. The small firms would be unable to take advantage of the economies of scale over much of their output.

Oligopolies, like monopolies, may have a greater incentive to invest in research and development than do purely competitive or monopolistically competitive firms, because they typically are larger and have more resources to invest. With significant barriers to entry, oligopolies and monopolies are also in a better position to benefit from their investment in product development.

Government Policy Toward Monopoly and Oligopoly

From our examination of the four market structures, it is clear that in two of them—perfect competition and monopolistic competition—individual firms have little or no control over price and output in their industries. Their market power, in other words, is limited. Governments, therefore, have little need or incentive to intervene in these markets to protect consumers.

However, in the other two market structures—monopoly and oligopoly—individual firms do have the power to influence prices and output, and this power may be used to the detriment of consumers. Hence, governments act to regulate these markets and promote the general interest of Canadian consumers.

Government policy toward monopolies and oligopolies falls into three main categories:

(i) Legislation to prevent the reduction of competition.
(ii) Regulation to control or set prices for "natural" monopolies.
(iii) Public ownership of natural monopolies.

□ □ □ □ □ □

A Crack in the Cement Club

Cement in Ontario is about the most expensive in the world. In Toronto, at the beginning of 1991, a tonne of Portland cement powder listed for about $130 (US$110). Just across the border, in New York State, the same goes for US$70. Offshore, it is cheaper still. Given that the main ingredients in cement are limestone and energy, both of which are in bountiful supply in Ontario, the huge price difference points to another powerful market force at work.

Call it an oligopoly. Cement in Ontario, and to a lesser extent in other parts of the nation, is controlled by four players with more than 90 percent of the local business. Concentration is the nature of the cement business itself. Throughout the world, a handful of major players have emerged dominant in the industry, with the French often at the forefront. This is a mature industry, where gradual and expensive improvements in efficiency supplant techno- logical leaps as the major determinant of success. Hence, the barriers to entry are imposing. Building a modern green-field cement powder plant in Canada could cost upwards of $150 million these days.

In Ontario, two different parties have shown intense interest in the local cement price phenomenon. One is an industry veteran and his partner, who is president of one of the country's largest home building companies. Rather than fight the system, the two decided it made much better financial sense to find an external source of cement and sell it within the existing price structure. To do this, they set up their own cement company.

The second party is perhaps even less welcome to the oligopoly: the federal Bureau of Competition Policy. In the spring of 1990, it obtained a search warrant which states that a conspiracy to fix prices and rig bids in the cement and ready-mix concrete industry in the Toronto area existed from May, 1976 to July, 1988. Federal officials obtained this warrant to search the offices of the four major players in the Ontario cement industry, which together dominate the local cement market.

In the booming construction market, with high demand for ready-mix concrete and concrete bricks, an independ- ent operator can easily charge made-in-Ontario prices for cement powder. When things slow down, however, the price of cement powder remains high, but the bottom falls out of the ready-mix concrete market. With only 8 percent of the Toronto concrete market, independents—who do not have their own supplies of cement powder and must pay the high price—are forced into a classic price squeeze.

The operations of the four cement manufacturers include ready-mix concrete distribution and concrete block manufacturing, subsidiaries that generally don't carry the parent company name. They, therefore, control their own supplies of cement powder and are protected against a fall in the market for concrete. In late 1990, for example, price discounting on ready-mix concrete in the Toronto area ranged from $30 to $40 a cubic metre, about 25 percent off the $124.50 list price. Discounts on cement powder, on the other hand, ranged less than 10 percent. Small operators lacking flexibly-priced sources of cement were being squeezed at both ends.

The two new players, therefore, decided to secure their own supply of cement and bypass the big firms. They looked to US and international sources and constructed their own cement terminal on the shores of Lake Ontario near Oshawa.

From the beginning, the new company's strategy was *not* to wage heroic battle against the mammoth cement manufacturers. It called for peaceful co-existence with the major players to reap advantage from the very pricing umbrella provided by the oligopoly. "I don't want to do enough business to make the Big Four want to push me out," says one of the independent company's owners. "I do 100 000 tonnes a year. They do 4.5 million tonnes. What's the point of them cutting the price for all their sales just to get my 100 000 tonnes out of the market?"

The new firm, using its international sources and taking advantage of good shipping rates, however, can land cement in Oshawa for about half the list price in Toronto. So long as the foreign sources are able to provide cement that consistently meets local standards, those numbers are very persuasive.

It may be too good to last. For one thing, the new firm is not the only one to recognize the possibilities. A smaller terminal has started operations in Owen Sound, Ontario, on Georgian Bay. Another question mark is the reaction of the Big Four. For now, they seem to regard the new company as something of a curiosity. "We know it's there," says one general manager of a major firm. "It's a highly integrated market, so there's only so much business it can go after. I can't say it is regarded as a threat, though it could have a minor impact on prices."

Though it remains unspoken, the major players might secretly be relieved by the arrival of new participants, particularly ones obviously not inclined to upset the juicy pricing structure. After all, the federal Bureau of Competition Policy may be more sympathetic to an industry open to all comers than what previously amounted to a closed shop.

SOURCE: Adapted from Dunnery Best, "A crack in the cement club," *Canadian Business*, March 1991.

Applications

1. What characteristics define the cement industry in Ontario as an oligopoly?

2. Why is the industry being investigated by the federal Bureau of Competition Policy?

3. How may small independent firms in the market be squeezed out?

4. How has the new firm discussed in the article attempted to get around the dominance of the Big Four in the industry?

5. (a) What effects does the price and market structure in the industry have on the consumers of cement?
(b) What advantages does it afford the Big Four?

6. Do you believe the Ontario cement industry should continue as an oligopoly? Why or why not? Justify your answer.

☐ Legislation to Prevent the Reduction of Competition

Laws intended to prevent the abuse of power by monopolies and oligopolies were first passed in Canada over a century ago. The old laws were replaced in 1986 by the **Competition Act**. The purpose of the Act is to maintain and encourage competition in Canadian industry. A Competition Tribunal was established under the Act to review any possible violations.

Activities forbidden by the Act include the following:

1. Agreements to fix prices, output, or distribution of goods, or to unduly restrict entry into an industry Firms may, however, exchange statistics and credit information, restrict advertising, and co-operate in research and development, providing that these activities do not limit competition.

2. Mergers and the abuse of dominant position

Mergers that would substantially lessen competition are prohibited. Mergers may be horizontal, vertical, or conglomerate.

A **horizontal merger** is the union of two or more firms in the same industry. The union of Canadian Airlines International Ltd. and Wardair in 1989 is an example. In an attempt to establish itself as Canada's third major air carrier, Wardair cut fares substantially in the 1980s and forced its competitors—Air Canada and Canadian Airlines International Ltd.—to do the same. Wardair failed in its bid, however, and when it looked for a buyer, only Canadian Airlines International Ltd. would agree to purchase the firm. The Competition Tribunal, therefore, accepted the merger, even though it was likely to reduce competition.

A horizontal merger of this kind clearly reduces competition since only two air carriers now have the market share of the original three. However, horizontal mergers may result in significant economies of scale.

A **vertical merger** is the union of a firm with its

□ □ □ □ □ □

Merger! Merger!

Imperial Oil's bid to take over Texaco (Canada) was approved by the federal government's Bureau of Competition Policy in 1989—subject to certain conditions.

Before the merger, the two companies were the second and fourth largest firms selling gasoline in Canada. Imperial Oil had over 3000 service stations, 5 refineries, 32 distribution terminals, and several product pipelines. Texaco had over 2000 service stations, 2 refineries, 21 distribution terminals, and 2 product pipelines. The Bureau of Competition Policy approved the deal provided Imperial Oil sell 543 service stations, one oil refinery, and 14 distribution terminals. Table 10.2 below shows the situation in the industry before divestiture.

Thus, with the approval of the Bureau, only three major oil corporations control over two-thirds of the country's gas stations and refining capacity, rather than four.

While agreeing that Imperial Oil's takeover of Texaco removes a "rigorous and effective competitor" from the Canadian gasoline and home-heating market, the director of the Competitions Bureau asserted that the divestiture agreed to by Imperial would ensure that Canadian motorists would not face price hikes at the pumps due to reduced competition. The director also argued that concentration in the refining sector is "unavoidable if Canada is to obtain the benefits of economies of scale in refining."

Critics of the deal said they would fight it when it went before the Competition Tribunal for final approval. While the Competition Bureau can negotiate with the parties in a merger or takeover to ensure that competition is not diminished, the Competition Tribunal has the final say on whether or not the deal will go through. Critics, such as the Consumers Association of Canada, argued that the deal was unnecessary and dangerous. It gave Imperial Oil too much power in Atlantic Canada, Quebec, and Ontario markets and would result in price hikes at the pump.

The three-member Competition Tribunal in early 1990 refused to approve the deal unless Imperial agreed to sell about 100 more gas stations throughout the country—to bring the total to 638—and agreed to guarantee gasoline supplies to independent retailers, especially in central Canada. In addition, Imperial Oil had to sell all of Texaco Canada's assets in Atlantic Canada.

Imperial accepted all of the provisions for promoting competition suggested by the Competition Tribunal. The deal was given final approval in early 1990.

Table 10.2 The "big three" oil corporations in Canada

CORPORATION	PERCENTAGE OF TOTAL IN THE INDUSTRY	
	GAS STATIONS	REFINING CAPACITY
Imperial	24	27
Petro-Canada	24	22
Shell	18	15

Applications

1. What is the market structure of the gasoline refining and marketing industry in Canada? Explain.

2. Without divestiture, in what ways might the merger be disadvantageous to Canadian consumers and independent gas station operators?

3. How far, in your opinion, does the divestiture negate these disadvantages? Explain your position.

supplier. Stelco, the second largest steel company in Canada, wholly or partly owns companies that supply it with coal and iron ore. The corporation thus secures its supply of essential raw materials and can effectively integrate its operations. Vertical mergers usually do not reduce competition significantly.

A **conglomerate merger** occurs when firms in unrelated industries combine. A conglomerate could include firms from as widely different industries as mining, insurance, and retailing. Conglomerate mergers are less likely to reduce competition substantially than are either vertical or horizontal mergers.

3. Illegal practices A number of trade practices which limit competition are also illegal under the Act. These illegal practices include the following.

(i) Retail sale price maintenance. It is illegal for manufacturers to pressure retailers into selling a product at a price they fix, or for retailers to agree to sell the good at that fixed price.

(ii) Predatory pricing. A firm must not sell a good at a price far less than the cost of production in order to force other firms out of business.

(iii) Price discrimination. A seller may not sell goods at different prices to individuals who are buying similar quantity and quality. Price reductions on bulk purchases or for special events such as clearance sales, however, are legal.

☐ Regulations to Control or Set Prices for Natural Monopolies

As we have seen, in some industries the returns to scale are such that only one firm can operate efficiently. These natural monopolies are common in such industries as electricity and natural gas distribution, telephone services, and rail and bus transportation. If several firms were to compete in any one of these industries, it is likely that costs would rise and the quality of service would decline.

However, monopolies tend to set prices above marginal cost. This is especially true when there are few close substitutes for the firm's product or service. Governments, therefore, control natural monopolies through regulatory agencies.

There are three major regulatory agencies at the federal level. The National Energy Board is responsible for oil and gas pipelines and regulates the export and import of oil and electricity. The Canadian Radio-Television and Telecommunications Commission regulates broadcasting, television, cable television, and telephone rates. The Canadian Transport Commission regulates railway, air, and water transportation.

The most important role of these agencies is to regulate prices. By tradition, the regulated price has been a fair one—that is, it has been set to cover average total costs. Thus, monopoly and oligopoly profits and prices are set at a lower level than would be the case if the industry were unregulated.

☐ Public Ownership of Natural Monopolies

Governments may also control natural monopolies through ownership of the industry. Many of the provincial and municipally-owned corporations in Canada are natural monopolies. Most provinces, for example, own their electrical generation and transmission systems and, in the Prairie provinces, the telephone system. In these industries, government ownership is a substitute for regulation.

Commissions controlling the publicly-owned firms have direct knowledge of costs and can thus set output at break-even levels, or when considered appropriate (e.g., in the case of urban transit), to take a loss.

Summary

a. Four major characteristics of monopolistically competitive markets are many firms, product differentiation, ease of entry, and non-price competition.

b. The monopolistically competitive firm faces a downward-sloping demand curve, so that to increase sales, it must decrease price. The effect of changes in price on total sales depends on the number of competitors and the degree of product differentiation. The larger the number of firms and the weaker the product differentiation, the greater the effect of price changes on sales.

c. In the short run, the monopolistically competitive firm will maximize its profits at the point where marginal cost equals marginal revenue. In the long run, the tendency is for economic profits to be eliminated because above normal profits will attract other firms into the industry. The firm will tend to make only a normal profit or break even in the long run.

d. Monopolistically competitive firms may attempt to improve their long-run equilibrium prospects by non-price competition in the form of product differentiation, product improvement, and advertising.

e. Monopolistically competitive firms are less efficient than perfectly competitive firms. They produce fewer goods at higher cost over the long run. However, the diversity of products and convenience they offer may be worth the higher prices.

f. The major characteristics of oligopoly markets are a few big firms, mutual interdependence in pricing and output decisions, and barriers to entry. Oligopolies may produce a standardized product (homogeneous oligopolies) or a differentiated product (differentiated oligopolies). The three main reasons why certain industries are composed only or mainly of a few large firms are economies of scale, barriers to entry, and the urge to merge.

g. The mutual interdependence of firms and the variety of market situations explain why oligopoly price theory is less clear-cut than that of perfect competition and pure monopoly. Oligopolists are "price-seekers."

h. Prices set by oligopolists tend to be "sticky," and when one firm changes its price, the other firms tend to follow suit. One explanation for this is the theory of the kinked demand curve. Other explanations include collusion, price leadership, and tacit agreements.

i. Disadvantages of imperfect competition as compared with perfectly competitive industries include higher prices and lower output—thus, less efficiency. Two possible advantages are the economies of scale and greater incentives for research and development.

j. Governments regulate oligopolies and monopolies in three ways: by legislation to prevent the reduction of competition; by regulation to control the prices of natural monopolies; and by public ownership of natural monopolies.

■ Review of Key Terms

Define the following key terms introduced in this chapter and provide examples where appropriate.

imperfect competition	cartel
monopolistic competition	cut-throat competition
non-price competition	price leadership
oligopoly	Competition Act
homogeneous oligopolies	horizontal merger
differentiated oligopolies	vertical merger
kinked demand curve	conglomerate merger

■ Application and Analysis

1. Identify the market structure of each of the following industries in Canada.

(a) electric power distribution

(b) automobile manufacturing

(c) toothpaste manufacturing

(d) restaurant operation

(e) steel production

2. Mr Herlock Soames of Baker Street, London, is trying to find out which one of the following suspects is the monopolist. Identify the monopoly from the following statements. What market structure do the other statements describe?

(a) Suspect A. "I sell a product that is exactly the same as that of my many competitors at the market price. I can sell all I want."

(b) Suspect B. "No Sir, Mr Soames, I'm not your monopolist. With huge advertising costs to keep my brand in front of my customers, its tough to break into our market—but a few have made it."

(c) Suspect C. "I'm no monopolist. I've got lots of competition. If I try to raise prices, my competitors rub their hands with glee because they won't change their prices, but they will take my customers. What I do is wait for Gargantua Ltd. to raise its prices, and then I follow them."

(d) Suspect D. "Look here Soames, old trout, I have loads of competitors. New restaurants just like mine are opening all the time, so I have to spend lots of money on advertising, new menus, new recipes, and new decor to convince customers that my place is different and better."

(e) Suspect E. "My industry is virtually impossible to break into and my product is unique."

3. A Spectrum of Competition

PERFECT   PURE
COMPETITION   MONOPOLY

Where on the above spectrum would you place each of the following industries in Canada?

(a) electricity production
(b) telephone services
(c) automobile manufacturing
(d) textile production
(e) retail sales
(f) restaurants
(g) aluminium production
(h) tire manufacturing
(i) mining
(j) wheat production

4. Refer to Figure 10.8. Assuming that the firm wishes to maximize profit, what is:

(a) the profit-maximizing output
(b) price
(c) total revenue
(d) total cost
(e) total profit or loss?

5. (a) Complete Table 10.3.

(b) Graph the demand, total revenue, marginal revenue, and marginal cost curves.

(c) At what price is the demand curve kinked?

(d) Suppose the oligopolist reduces the price per unit to $60. What would happen? Explain.

(e) Assume that all firms in the industry collude. Indicate the new demand curve on your graph and explain its shape.

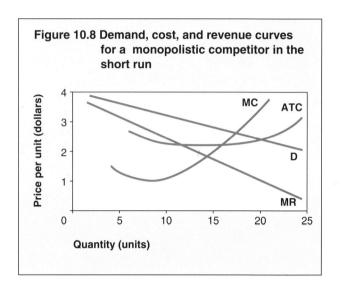

Figure 10.8 Demand, cost, and revenue curves for a monopolistic competitor in the short run

Table 10.3 Demand, costs, and revenues for an oligopolist (in dollars)

DEMAND		REVENUE		COST
1 PRICE PER UNIT	2 QUANTITY DEMANDED (IN UNITS)	3 TOTAL REVENUE	4 MARGINAL REVENUE	5 MARGINAL COST
90	2			25
87	3			27
85	4			30
80	5			33
70	6			40
60	7			50
50	8			70
40	9			100
30	10			140
20	11			190

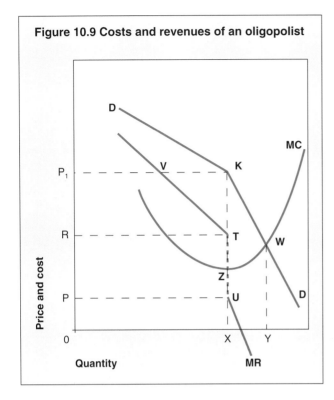

Figure 10.9 Costs and revenues of an oligopolist

6. Refer to Figure 10.9 above.

(a) At what output and price should the oligopolist produce? Explain.

(b) Suppose marginal cost increases by TZ. What changes in price should the oligopolist make? Explain.

7. Suppose Jill Oligopoly is the owner of one of five large firms in an industry.

(a) Why might collusion appear to be in Jill's best economic interest as owner of one of the firms?

(b) What difficulties might she have in reaching an agreement with the other four firms and in making it last?

(c) How would consumers of the product be affected by her actions—assuming she were able to reach an agreement with her competitors? Explain.

(d) What legal problems might Jill have?

8. Debate the following issue: "Resolved that advertising is beneficial from society's point of view."

9. The following is a list of the main divisions and subsidiaries of Canadian Pacific Limited.

Canadian Pacific Limited was incorporated by an act of the dominion parliament on February 16, 1881. Major subsidiaries and divisions include:

CP Rail (a division of Canadian Pacific Limited), which serves all of Canada (except PEI and Newfoundland) with its almost 8000 km of track.

Soo Line Corporation (56 percent owned), a holding company which owns 100 percent of Soo Line Railroad Corporation—a rail and truck freight carrier.

Laidlaw Transportation Ltd. (11 percent owned), a school bus operator and waste service company.

Centennial Shipping Ltd. (100 percent owned), shipping container services.

Canadian Maritime Ltd. (57 percent owned), container shipping services.

Racine Terminal (Montreal) Ltd. (100 percent owned), a shipping container terminal.

Canadian Pacific Express and Transport Ltd. (100 percent owned), trucking and express services.

PanCanadian Petroleum Ltd. (87.1 percent owned), exploration, production, transportation, and wholesale marketing of crude oil, natural gas, and sulphur.

Fording Coal Ltd. (100 percent owned), development and processing of Alberta and British Columbia coal.

Canadian Pacific Forest Products Ltd. (79.7 percent owned), one of the world's largest forest products industries producing pulp, paper, newsprint, and lumber.

Marathon Realty Company Ltd. (100 percent owned), development and ownership of land and buildings—such as shopping centres and office buildings.

Canadian Pacific Hotel Corporation (100 percent owned), owns, leases, and manages Canadian and international hotels.

CNCP Telecommunications (100 percent owned), provides a wide range of communications services—including voice, data, text, and message services across Canada with access to the rest of the world.

AMCA International Ltd. (55.4 percent owned), manufactured products and engineering and construction services.

Syracuse China Corporation (100 percent owned), chinaware.

(a) Outline the types of industries in which Canadian Pacific is involved.

(b) What kind of a merger does Canadian Pacific represent?

(c) What might be the advantages of this kind of merger for the company?

10. Case Study—Motorcycle Firms Guilty of Price Fixing

Five Canadian motorcycle companies and their national industry group have pleaded guilty to collaborating to buoy the price of motorcycles.

The companies pleaded guilty to one count of a 17-count indictment handed down under the federal Competition Act.

An Ontario Supreme Court Justice dismissed the other 16 counts because Crown prosecutors did not provide evidence as part of a plea-bargain agreement.

In addition to the guilty plea, defendants agreed to the Crown's sentencing recommendation of fines totalling $250 000 and a prohibition on future price maintenance.

The indictment states that between April 12 and Nov. 12, 1984, the defendants "did, by agreement or threat, attempt to influence upwards or discourage the reduction" of motorcycle prices offered by dealers at the spring, 1985, trade show in Toronto.

A statement of facts, jointly agreed to by both sides, says the defendants first became concerned about dealers discounting prices during the trade show in 1981.

As a result, exhibitors at the 1983 and 1984 shows were required to display only the manufacturer's suggested list price, and "if an exhibitor failed to follow their rules, he would be removed and not allowed to participate in future shows," the statement said.

The defendants believed the policy "would reduce price discounting at the shows and would result in less price competition in the retail market in the long run."

The rule was dropped prior to the 1985 shows after "consultation" with officials from the Bureau of Competition Policy of the Department of Consumer & Corporate Affairs, the statement said.

The recommended fines will be the largest total fine for a case under the price maintenance provisions of the Competition Act, said the bureau's deputy director of investigations and research.

In an interview from Ottawa, the deputy director declined to reveal who filed the complaint that led to the investigation.

Crown prosecutors declined to say what fines they first proposed, but a source close to the case said initial proposals called for levies of $750 000 for each of the defendants.

SOURCE: Adapted from Colin Languedoc, "Motorcycle firms plead guilty in price probe," *The Financial Post*, October 14, 1989.

(a) In what illegal practice did the five motorcycle companies and their national industry group engage?

(b) How did the defendants expect to benefit from their actions?

(c) What effects would the companies' actions have on consumers?

Equitable Distribution of Income

In Unit One, we examined the three major questions all economies must answer. In Unit Two, we explored two of these questions—*what* goods and services are produced and *how* they are produced. Our focus was on the goal of economic efficiency. In this unit, we consider the third question— *for whom* is the country's output produced, or to put it another way, how are the goods and services shared among the people? Our focus is on the goal of economic equity.

In modern economies, our share of the national output is measured primarily by our incomes. Our incomes are mainly determined by payments for the use of our productive resources. The most obvious of these productive resources is our labour—our own skills, effort, and time. The others are natural and capital resources and entrepreneurial skills. In this unit, we consider what determines the income from these resources.

In Chapter 11, we consider what determines the wages and salaries paid for labour and the effects labour unions have on workers' pay and other benefits. In Chapter 12, we examine what determines the rent of property owners, the interest of capital owners, and the profit of entrepreneurs. Chapter 13 considers the role of government in raising revenue to provide services and payments to households, businesses, and other levels of government. Finally, in Chapter 14, we examine the distribution of income in Canada and consider government programs designed to achieve the goal of economic equity.

▢ ▢ ▢ ▢ ▢ ▢

Labour
Markets
and Labour
Unions

In this chapter and the next, we examine the factors that determine the returns to the owners of the four productive resources—labour, land, capital, and entrepreneurship. In other words, we consider wages, rent, interest, and profit. How are these earnings determined? What factors affect them? What share does each constitute of our total national income? Are these sources of income distributed equitably? These are some of the questions we consider.

Our focus in this chapter is specifically on wages and the labour market. We have examined how prices of goods and services are determined in various markets. As you might expect, the prices of productive resources are determined in a somewhat similar way—by supply and demand.

But, the market for labour and the market for goods differ in one important way—the labour market deals with people, the product market with commodities. If manufacturers abuse the machines they own, it is largely a matter of public indifference. But the abuse of workers is quite another story. Forcing workers to labour long hours in dangerous conditions may lead to strikes, protests, and public outcry. The appalling working conditions suffered by many during the nineteenth century provided the impetus for government regulations and the formation of labour unions to protect workers. Today, in Canada's mixed market economy, government legislation is in place to regulate working conditions and labour unions play a significant role in negotiating with employers on behalf of workers.

In this chapter, therefore, we examine how wages are determined in competitive and imperfectly competitive markets. We then consider the government regulations designed to protect workers and the role of labour unions in the Canadian economy.

The Productive Resources Market and the Circular Flow

Before we examine wages and labour markets in detail, let's consider how the productive resources (land, labour, capital, and entrepreneurship) fit into the overall picture of the economy. In Chapter 3, we saw that real and money flows in the economy can be seen as a circular flow between businesses and households. The goods and services (real flow) produced by businesses are sold through products markets to households, who buy the goods and services for money (money flow).

Now we can add a further dimension to this circular flow model—the **productive resources** or **factors market**, as shown in Figure 11.1. Households are also the owners of all productive resources—land, labour, capital, and entrepreneurial skills. They provide these resources to businesses through the productive resources market, and in return receive income in the form of rent, wages, interest, and profits.

Households, in turn, use this income to buy goods and services they need in the products market. The

productive resources businesses acquire in the factors market are used to produce the goods and services they sell in the products market. Thus, we have the two flows—a money flow between businesses and households and a real flow of goods and services *and productive resources* between businesses and households.

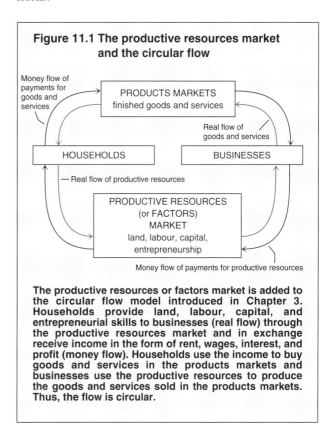

Figure 11.1 The productive resources market and the circular flow

The productive resources or factors market is added to the circular flow model introduced in Chapter 3. Households provide land, labour, capital, and entrepreneurial skills to businesses (real flow) through the productive resources market and in exchange receive income in the form of rent, wages, interest, and profit (money flow). Households use the income to buy goods and services in the products markets and businesses use the productive resources to produce the goods and services sold in the products markets. Thus, the flow is circular.

Wages

Wages or salaries include regular payments and other benefits, such as holidays with pay, paid leave for sickness, and insurance payments to employees for labour services. Wages may be set by the hour, day, week, month, or year, or according to the amount produced. As with goods and services, the forces of demand and supply are important in determining the level of wages and salaries.

■ The Demand for Labour

The demand for labour refers to the number of workers employers are willing and able to employ at various wage rates. While the demand for goods is direct demand, the demand for labour is indirect demand. What does this mean? When you buy a shirt, you buy it because it helps keep you warm and you like its colour, texture, and cut. You gain satisfaction from wearing the shirt. The demand for shirts and other commodities is a direct result of the satisfaction consumers can gain from them and is, therefore, known as **direct demand**.

The demand for the services of the workers who make shirts, however, results from, or is *derived* from, the demand for shirts. The greater the demand for

Table 11.1 Demand for labour by a competitive firm

1 QUANTITY OF LABOUR EMPLOYED PER DAY (Q_L)	2 TOTAL NUMBER OF GOODS PRODUCED PER DAY OR TOTAL PRODUCT (TP)	3 MARGINAL PRODUCT (MP) $MP = \frac{\Delta TP}{\Delta Q_L}$	4 PRICE PER UNIT (P) OR MARGINAL REVENUE (MR) $P = MR = \$10$	5 TOTAL REVENUE (TR) $TR = TP \times P$ (IN DOLLARS)	6 MARGINAL REVENUE PRODUCT (MRP) (IN DOLLARS) $MRP = MP \times P$ OR $MRP = \frac{\Delta TR}{\Delta Q_L}$
0	0		10	0	
1	25	25	10	250	250
2	45	20	10	450	200
3	61	16	10	610	160
4	73	12	10	730	120
5	81	8	10	810	80
6	85	4	10	850	40
7	88	3	10	880	30
8	90	2	10	900	20
9	91	1	10	910	10
10	91	0	10	910	0

As the number of workers increases—other factors of production remaining unchanged—total product increases but at a diminishing rate up to the tenth worker, reflecting the law of diminishing returns. The marginal product of each worker also declines until it reaches zero with the tenth worker. Price remains constant for the competitive firm and equals marginal revenue. As output increases, total revenue (TP x P) increases at the same rate. The marginal revenue product declines steadily to zero with the tenth worker.

shirts, the greater is the demand for workers who produce the shirts. In the same way, the demand for automobile workers is derived from the demand for automobiles. **Derived demand** is the demand for a factor of production that results from the demand for the product it is used to make.

But the demand for labour to produce shirts depends not only on the demand for the shirts, but also on the number of shirts each worker can produce—that is, on the worker's **productivity**.

☐ Competitive Firm's Demand for Labour

In examining the demand for labour, then, we are really dealing with two markets—the product market and the productive resources or labour market. The degree of competition in both markets affects the firm's demand for labour.

Let's start by examining the demand for labour by a firm in a competitive product market and a competitive labour market. By a competitive labour market, we mean one in which no one firm can influence wages and the supply of labour is infinitely elastic (that is, the supply remains the same no matter what the wage rate).

Labour productivity can be shown by the marginal product (MP) of each worker. As we saw with Petra's Pizza Parlour in Chapter 7, after a certain point the marginal product or addition to total output brought about by each additional worker decreases as more workers are employed because of the law of diminishing returns.

Table 11.1 outlines data for a competitive firm. The total number of goods produced per day by one worker is 25 units. The marginal product of the first worker is, therefore, 25 units. With the employment of a second worker, total product increases to 45 units. The amount attributed to the employment of the second worker (that worker's marginal product) is 20 units. The third worker's marginal product declines to 16 units. In this simplified example, diminishing returns set in after the first worker.

What the business person wants to know, however, is the value in dollars of each additional worker's output. After all, the business owner must pay the worker in dollars and wishes to maximize dollar profits. If we know the price of each good, we can calculate the *value* of the additional output produced by each additional or marginal worker—the marginal revenue product. The **marginal revenue product (MRP)** is the addition to the firm's total revenue resulting from each additional worker.

In competitive product markets, the firm faces a perfectly elastic demand curve. No matter how many goods the firm produces, the price remains unchanged. If we assume that the firm's product sells for $10, we can calculate the marginal revenue product for each worker by multiplying the marginal product by the price (which is also the firm's marginal revenue), as shown in column 6 of Table 11.1.

Marginal revenue product (MRP) = Marginal product x Price (or Marginal revenue)
MRP = MP x P or

$$\text{Marginal revenue product} = \frac{\text{Change in } (\Delta) \text{ total revenue (TR)}}{\text{Change in } (\Delta) \text{ number of workers } (Q_L)}$$

$$MRP = \frac{\Delta TR}{\Delta Q_L}$$

The marginal revenue product curve represents the value in dollars of each additional worker's output. It is also the firm's demand curve for labour. For the perfectly competitive firm, therefore, the demand curve for labour slopes down to the right because of the law of diminishing returns or diminishing marginal productivity.

Let's suppose the wage rate is $40 for an eight-hour day. At this rate, the profit-maximizing firm will hire 6 workers as shown in Figure 11.2, since at this point the marginal revenue product is equal to the wage rate. It will not hire 7 workers because the seventh worker would produce only $30 worth of additional output per day, yet must be paid $40. The firm would lose $10 by hiring a seventh worker.

Similarly, profits would be below the maximum if the firm hired fewer than 6 workers (4 workers, for example), since an additional (or fifth) worker would bring $80 in MRP and still be paid only $40.

Thus, if the wage rate is greater than the marginal revenue product of the worker, the profit-maximizing firm will not employ the additional worker. Similarly, if the wage rate is less than the marginal revenue product, the firm will employ the worker. In a competitive market, a firm will hire workers to the point where the wage rate equals the marginal revenue product (W = MRP). This principle is known as the **marginal productivity theory of wages**.

The amount each additional worker adds to the total costs of the firm is called the **marginal resource cost**. In a competitive labour market, since the supply of labour is infinitely elastic at the prevailing wage rate, the marginal resource cost equals the wage rate. To maximize profits, the competitive firm will hire labour to the point where the marginal resource cost (or wage rate) equals the marginal revenue product (W = MRP = MRC).

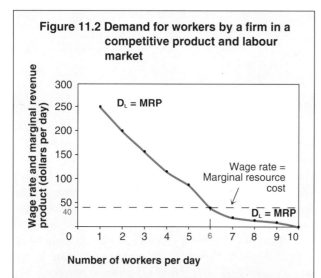

Figure 11.2 Demand for workers by a firm in a competitive product and labour market

Number of workers per day

A firm's demand or marginal revenue product curve for labour (D$_L$ = MRP) in a competitive labour market slopes down to the right because of the diminishing marginal productivity of labour. The firm will hire workers to the point where the wage rate is equal to the marginal revenue product. In this case, with wages at $40 a day, 6 workers will be employed. For a firm in a competitive product and labour market, the marginal resource cost also equals the wage rate and the marginal revenue product.

☐ The Imperfectly Competitive Firm's Demand for Labour

As we noted, the demand for a firm's products under perfect competition remains unchanged no matter what the volume of its sales. Under imperfect competition (monopoly, oligopoly, and monopolistic competition), however, the firm faces a downward-sloping demand curve for its products. If the firm wishes to sell more of its products, it must lower its price.

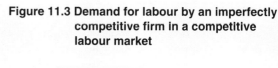
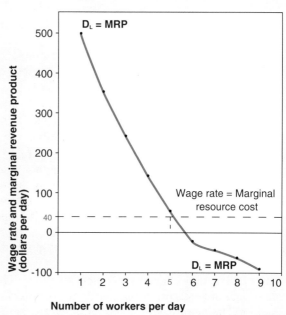

Figure 11.3 Demand for labour by an imperfectly competitive firm in a competitive labour market

Number of workers per day

The imperfectly competitive firm's demand curve for labour is also its marginal revenue product curve. The curve slopes down to the right because of the diminishing marginal productivity of labour. In a competitive labour market, the wage rate remains unchanged no matter how many workers the firm hires. The firm will hire labour to the point where its marginal revenue product equals the wage rate. In this example, with a wage rate of $40 a day, 5 workers will be employed, fewer than the number employed by the competitive firm.

Table 11.2 displays production information similar to that in Table 11.1, but for the firm in imperfectly competitive product markets. While the product price remains the same in Table 11.1 for the firm in a competitive product market, it falls as output increases in Table 11.2 for the firm in an imperfectly competitive product market.

How does this affect the firm's demand for labour, assuming that the labour market is still competitive? The marginal revenue product curve (or the additional revenue resulting from each additional worker) for the imperfectly competitive firm is also its demand curve for labour. As shown in Figure 11.3, the MRP = D_L curve slopes down to the right, but more rapidly than the curve for the competitive firm. Why? While the marginal revenue product of the firm declines as more workers are hired, the price of the firm's product also declines and the marginal revenue product thus falls more quickly.

We can see that at a wage rate of $40 a day, the

Table 11.2 Demand for labour by an imperfectly competitive firm

1 QUANTITY OF LABOUR EMPLOYED PER DAY (Q_L)	2 TOTAL NUMBER OF GOODS PRODUCED PER DAY OR TOTAL PRODUCT (TP)	3 MARGINAL PRODUCT (MP) MP = $\frac{\Delta TP}{\Delta Q_L}$	4 PRICE PER UNIT (P) (IN DOLLARS)	5 TOTAL REVENUE (TR) TR = TP X P (IN DOLLARS)	6 MARGINAL REVENUE PRODUCT (MRP) MRP = $\frac{\Delta TR}{\Delta Q_L}$ (IN DOLLARS)
0	0		0	0	
1	25	25	20	500	500
2	45	20	19	855	355
3	61	16	18	1098	243
4	73	12	17	1241	143
5	81	8	16	1296	55
6	85	4	15	1275	-21
7	88	3	14	1232	-43
8	90	2	13	1170	-62
9	91	1	12	1080	-90
10	91	0			

Columns 1, 2, and 3 are reproduced from Table 11.1. Column 4 shows that price per unit falls as the total number of goods produced each day increases for the imperfectly competitive firm. Total revenue (column 5) rises to a maximum with 5 workers and then declines. Marginal revenue product (column 6), which also represents the demand for labour, declines rapidly as more workers are hired. (Note: For imperfectly competitive firms, MRP cannot be calculated as MP × P.)

imperfectly competitive firm will hire 5 workers. At this point, the marginal revenue product of $55 is greater than the wage rate, so the firm can make a profit. The firm will not hire a sixth worker because the wage rate of $40 a day is greater than the marginal revenue product of -$21.

As we saw in Chapters 9 and 10, the imperfectly competitive firm produces less than the perfectly competitive firm in the same situation. Since the imperfectly competitive firm produces less, it requires fewer resources—in other words, it employs fewer workers.

☐ Market Demand for Labour

The marginal revenue product or demand curves for labour we have examined represent an individual firm's demand (under perfect or imperfect competition) for a particular type of worker in a competitive labour market—a computer software developer's demand for programmers, for example. How, then, do we determine the market demand curve? In Chapter 3, we derived the market demand curve for glasses of orange juice by adding the demand curves of all individual buyers. The market demand curve for labour can be derived in a similar though not identical way—by combining all the individual demand (or MRP) curves for a particular type of worker. As you would expect, the market demand curve for labour slopes down to the right—the lower the wage rate, the greater the quantity of labour demanded.

☐ Shifts in the Demand for Labour

We have developed demand curves for labour assuming that only price and quantity change and that all other factors remain unchanged. But, of course, other factors do not remain unchanged. Why, then, might the demand (or MRP) curve for labour shift? Three major reasons are a shift in the demand for the good the worker produces, a change in the productivity of the worker, and a change in the price of other productive resources.

Demand for the Worker's Product
Since the demand for labour is derived from the demand for the final product, a shift in the demand curve for the product means a corresponding shift in the demand curve for workers involved in its production. An increase in the demand for new houses, for example, means an increase in the demand for workers involved in new home construction. Conversely, a decrease in the demand for new houses would bring a decrease in the demand for housing construction workers.

Worker Productivity
Changes in worker productivity will shift the marginal revenue product curve of labour and, therefore, the demand curve for labour. The relationship between shifts in labour productivity and shifts in demand is a direct one—in other words, they shift in the same direction. An increase in productivity means an increase in demand for the worker, and a decrease in productivity means a decrease in demand for the worker. Improved plant organization, more efficient machinery, additional investments of fixed factors of production (land and capital) for each worker, and additional training, all increase marginal productivity and, therefore, shift the marginal revenue product and demand curves for labour to the right (increasing demand). Poor management, inefficient plant organization, rundown machinery, and lack of training, on the other hand, decrease worker productivity and shift the marginal revenue product and demand curves for labour to the left (decreasing demand).

Price of Other Productive Resources
If other factors of production, such as machinery, are used as substitutes for labour, changes in their price will significantly affect the demand for labour. For example, if the price of robots used on automobile assembly lines is reduced, the demand for assembly line workers will decrease and the demand curve will shift to the left. Changes in the price of production inputs that are complements to labour will also affect the demand for labour. Lower prices for gasoline will likely increase the demand for taxis and thus for taxi drivers. Higher prices for gasoline, on the other hand, would likely decrease the demand for taxis and thus taxi drivers. You can probably think of several other examples.

Elasticity of Demand for Labour

The price elasticity of demand for consumer products (introduced in Chapter 3) indicates how consumers respond to changes in price by varying the quantity they are willing and able to buy. The price elasticity of demand for labour is similar. The more elastic the demand for labour, the more likely are employers to respond to wage changes by varying the number of workers they hire.

Factors Affecting Elasticity of Demand for Labour

As we would expect, some of the factors that influence the elasticity of demand for consumer products are similar to those affecting the elasticity of demand for labour. Factors influencing the elasticity of demand for labour include the elasticity of demand for the consumer product that labour produces, the existence of close substitutes for a particular kind of labour, and the relative significance of labour in the total costs of the firm. A fourth factor affecting the elasticity of demand for labour is the rate at which marginal productivity is declining.

Elasticity of Demand for the Workers' Product
Generally, the more elastic the demand for a consumer product, the more elastic is the demand for the labour that produces it. Since the demand for Caribbean cruises in winter is highly elastic, for example, a small reduction in the price of the cruises will result in a large increase in the number sold—and thus a large increase in the number of workers hired to work on the cruise ships. A change in the price of a product that has an inelastic demand (e.g., salt), on the other hand, will have little effect on the demand for the workers who produce it.

Relative Importance of Labour in Total Costs
If labour makes up a small percentage of the firm's total costs (e.g., jumbo jet pilots' wages), even a large increase in wages is likely to have little effect on the quantity of labour employed. This is because a large increase in wages will have little impact on the price of the product (jet flights). If labour constitutes a large proportion of total costs (e.g., wages of serving staff in an expensive restaurant), however, even a small increase in wages will increase the price of the product significantly, and thus reduce the number of workers employed.

Close Substitutes for the Labour
If there are close substitutes for a particular kind of labour, then the demand for the labour is likely to be elastic. Automatic tellers, industrial robots, and wordprocessors, for example, are potential substitutes for human tellers, assembly line workers, and typists respectively. If the wage rates of these workers increase, or if the costs of the substitutes decrease, it may be to the employers' advantage to replace at least some of the workers with the capital equipment. The demand for these workers, therefore, could drop significantly.

Rate of Marginal Revenue Product Decline
When the marginal productivity of labour declines rapidly, the demand for labour is likely to be inelastic. Employers will be unwilling to hire more workers when the workers will contribute little to total profits. Large decreases in wages may, therefore, mean only small increases in the number of workers employed.

Practical Applications

A knowledge of the elasticity of demand for labour is useful in practice. When the federal and provincial governments consider changes in legal minimum wages, for example, they know that if they increase the minimum wage significantly while the demand for labour is elastic, significant numbers of workers may be laid off. Thus, while some workers earning a minimum wage keep their jobs and benefit with an improved wage, other workers may lose their jobs. The total effect, therefore, may be negative.

Similarly, in collective bargaining negotiations between labour unions and employers, the elasticity of demand for labour plays a significant role. If the demand for labour is highly elastic, a settlement involving a large wage increase may lead to significant layoffs.

With an inelastic demand for labour, on the other hand, unions can bargain for large wage increases confident that such settlements will have little impact on the employment of their members.

Market Supply of Labour

By the supply of labour, we mean the total number of hours or days workers are able and willing to work at various wage rates. All other things being equal, the market supply curve for workers will slope up to the right—like the supply curve for consumer goods. Why? If wage rates for a particular occupation are low, relatively few workers will be willing to work in this labour market since they can receive higher wages elsewhere. However, if the wage rate rises, more workers will be willing to move into the industry. Thus, the higher the wage rate, the greater will be the quantity of labour supplied. The lower the wage rate, the smaller will be the quantity of labour supplied.

Some obvious factors affecting the supply of labour include the size of the workforce, pay and other benefits, the length of the work week, and the age at which people enter the workforce or retire from it. Other less obvious factors affecting the labour supply include unemployment and welfare payments, which by providing an income for those who are not working may act as a disincentive to work. High income tax rates may also act as a disincentive. On the other hand, the changing role of women in society has increased their participation in the workforce and thus increased the supply of labour.

Wage Determination

From an examination of the demand and supply for labour, we can turn to consider how wages are determined in labour markets. We'll consider wage determination in both competitive and imperfectly competitive labour markets.

Wage Determination in Competitive Labour Markets

The competitive market for labour has three main characteristics:

(i) there are many workers with the same skill supplying a particular kind of labour

(ii) many firms demand the various types of labour and compete to hire the workers

(iii) there is no collusion among workers or employers to fix prices.

The equilibrium wage and quantity of labour employed, therefore, is determined by the interaction of supply and demand. For the individual firm under perfect competition, the wage rate is fixed. Since it is only one of many firms hiring the labour, its actions have no impact on the wage rate. It is a "wage-taker." The firm's supply curve for labour is perfectly elastic, since the wage rate will not change no matter how many workers the firm employs. The firm will find it profitable to hire labour to the point where the marginal resource cost (or wage rate) is equal to the

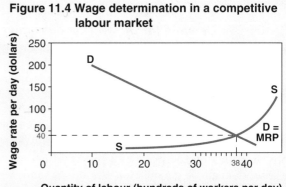

Figure 11.4 Wage determination in a competitive labour market

Wage rate per day (dollars)

Quantity of labour (hundreds of workers per day)

In a competitive labour market, the equilibrium wage rate and quantity of labour demanded is the point at which the supply and demand curves intersect. The market supply curve is more elastic than that for the individual firm since workers can move out of or into the industry as the wage rate changes. At the equilibrium wage of $40 per day, 3800 workers will be hired in this market.

marginal revenue product (or demand).

Figure 11.4 shows the *market* equilibrium wage and quantity of labour employed. At the market wage of $40 per day, 3800 workers will be employed. The market demand curve is derived from the individual firms' demand curves. The market supply curve, however, is more elastic than that for the individual firm. It slopes up to the right. Why? If a particular job has comparatively low wage rates, few workers will be willing to work in this labour market. However, if the wage rate for the job rises, more workers will be willing to take the jobs. Conversely, if the wage rate falls, more workers will leave the job and look for another position that offers higher wages. Thus, the higher the wage rate, the greater is the quantity of labour supplied. The lower the wage rate, the smaller is the quantity supplied.

☐ Shifts in the Supply and Demand for Labour

Shifts in the supply and demand for labour in competitive markets affect the equilibrium wage and quantity of labour employed, just as they do the equilibrium price and quantity of any product. As shown in Figure 11.5, an increase in demand and a shift in the demand curve to the right causes an increase in the equilibrium quantity and wage. A decrease in demand and a shift in the demand curve to the left causes a decrease in the equilibrium quantity and wage.

Figure 11.6 shows the effects of shifts in supply. With an increase in supply from SS to S_1S_1, the equilibrium wage decreases and the quantity employed increases. With a decrease in supply to S_2S_2, the equilibrium wage increases and the quantity employed decreases.

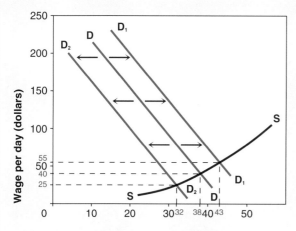

Figure 11.5 Shifts in the demand for labour

With the original demand curve DD and a wage rate of $40 per day, 3800 days of labour are demanded and supplied. If demand increases to D_1D_1, the equilibrium quantity of labour increases to 4300 days and the equilibrium wage rises to $55 a day. If demand decreases to D_2D_2, the equilibrium quantity decreases to 3200 days of labour and the equilibrium wage falls to $25 a day. Thus, an increase in demand for labour brings an increase in the equilibrium wage and quantity of labour employed and *vice versa*.

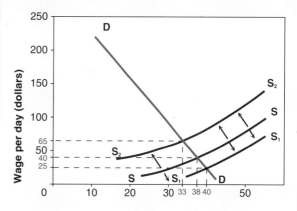

Figure 11.6 Shifts in the supply of labour

With the original supply curve SS and a wage rate of $40 per day, 3800 days of labour are demanded and supplied. If supply increases to S_1S_1, the equilibrium quantity of labour increases to 4000 days and the equilibrium wage falls to $25 a day. If supply decreases to S_2S_2, the equilibrium quantity decreases to 3300 days and the equilibrium wage increases to $65 a day. Thus, an increase in supply means an increase in the equilibrium quantity of labour employed, but a decrease in the wage rate. A decrease in supply means a decrease in the equilibrium quantity and an increase in the wage rate.

☐ Wage Determination in Imperfectly Competitive Labour Markets

Imperfectly competitive labour markets arise when there are few buyers or sellers of labour or both. To illustrate wage determination under imperfect competition, we'll focus on one particular market situation—the monopsony. A **monopsony** is a market situation with only one buyer of a good or service. A monopsony employer, therefore, would have monopoly power in hiring workers. The firm's employment constitutes a significant proportion of the total employment for that type of worker, and workers cannot easily move into other kinds of work or to other locations.

Examples of monopsony in Canada—where one firm is the major employer in a community, for example—include mining towns in northern Ontario, Quebec, and British Columbia; pulp and paper producing communities in British Columbia, Quebec, New Brunswick, Newfoundland and Labrador, and northern Ontario; and small towns with textile mills in eastern Ontario and the Eastern Townships of Quebec.

In these cases, the employer's decision to hire more or less of a particular type of labour will have a significant impact on the wage rate (though labour unions act to limit the market power of monopsonists, as we will see later in this chapter). To employ more workers, the monopsonist has to pay a higher wage rate.

To take a simple example, let's suppose there is only one employer for a particular type of labour. The industry supply curve for labour and the individual firm's supply curve for labour are, therefore, one and the same. As shown in Figure 11.7, the marginal resource cost curve (or the cost of hiring each additional worker) is above and to the left of the supply curve. Why? Since the firm must pay higher wages to employ each additional worker, it must pay those higher wages to all other workers as well. To preserve worker morale, it cannot pay the marginal worker $10 an hour and pay all other workers only $9 an hour. It must pay all workers equally.

The marginal resource cost curve must exceed the supply curve by an amount necessary to provide the new higher wage of the marginal worker to all other workers. The marginal resource cost, therefore,

exceeds the wage rate. It does not equal the wage rate, as in perfectly competitive labour markets.

The profit-maximizing monopsonist will hire workers to the point where the marginal resource cost equals the marginal revenue product. In Figure 11.7, this is at point F. The quantity of labour hired is $0Q_M$ and the wage rate is $0W_M$. In perfectly competitive labour markets, the quantity employed would be greater at $0Q_{PC}$ and the wage rate would be higher at $0W_{PC}$.

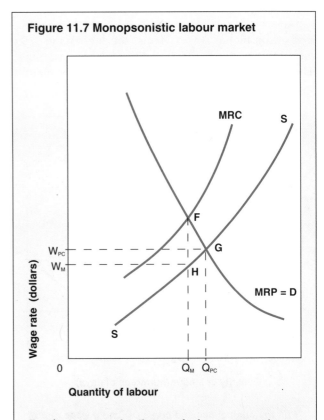

Figure 11.7 Monopsonistic labour market

For the monopsonist, the marginal resource cost curve (MRC) is above and to the left of the supply curve for labour (SS). The equilibrium quantity employed is represented by point F, where the MRC and MRP = D curves intersect and where profit is maximized. The monopsonist will, therefore, hire $0Q_M$ workers at a wage of $0W_M$. In perfectly competitive labour markets, the firm would hire more workers ($0Q_{PC}$) at a higher wage ($0W_{PC}$).

□ □ □ □ □ □

Baseball and Hockey Salaries—An Example of Monopsony Power

In the United States, as a result of a Supreme Court decision, major league baseball is exempt from restrictions on monopolies. This exemption allowed baseball team owners to operate like a monopsonistic cartel until some changes were instituted in 1976.

Before the changes, a "reserve clause" in the contracts of baseball players prohibited them from signing a contract with any other team unless the owner's rights to the player were sold to that team. As a result, though they were still paid high salaries, players were paid less than what they would have been paid had a competitive labour market been allowed. According to one estimate, players receiving a salary of $42 000 in 1969, for example, would have received a salary of $300 000 in a competitive market. Each team was, therefore, a monopoly buyer of its players' services.

In 1976, the Baseball Players' Association began negotiating an agreement whereby players would become "free agents" (they could sell their services to any team) after their fifth season. Thus the reserve clause would be eliminated and the labour market would become more competitive.

Figure 11.8 shows how the salaries of players who became free agents were affected in 1976. Their salaries increased substantially. By 1980, the average player's salary had doubled in real terms. By 1987, average baseball salaries reached US $410 000—far from the US $42 000 (US $130 000 in 1987 dollars) in 1969.

Restrictions on the freedom of players to sell their services to any team also exist in other sports leagues. An example in the National Hockey League is the new player draft. The club that selects or "drafts" a new player has the sole right to sign a contract with that player. A "reserve clause" extends this sole right to a second year. If a player refuses to sign a contract with the team—as Eric Lindros did in 1991 when drafted by the Quebec Nordiques—the player is effectively banned from playing in the NHL for a year unless the team that drafted him is willing to trade the player to another team.

Applications

1. What effect would the restrictions on a drafted player in the NHL have on that player's salary?

2. Who benefits from the restrictions? Explain.

3. Do you think the restrictions should be lifted? Why or why not? What effect might free competition for all players have on salaries in the NHL?

Figure 11.8 Effect of monopsony power on baseball salaries

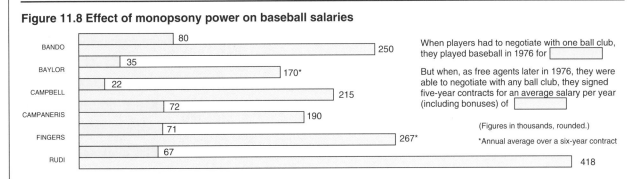

SOURCE: Ake Blomqvist, Paul Wonnacott and Ronald Wonnacott, *Economics,* 3rd Can. ed. (Toronto: McGraw-Hill Ryerson, 1990), p. 712.

▮ Labour Markets

Labour markets play a very important role in our economy. They allocate labour to various occupations according to the demand of employers—which is finally determined by the demand of consumers. In response to an increased demand for computers, for example, the demand for workers producing computers increases, wages increase, more workers are attracted into the industry, and thus output increases—the result desired by consumers.

Since there are as many labour markets as there are kinds of labour, however, wage rates may vary significantly from one occupation to another and from one region to another, even in the same country. If the demand for nurses decreases while the supply remains unchanged, nurses' wages will fall (or at least not rise as rapidly as would otherwise be the case). At the same time, however, the demand for surgeons may rise, bringing an increase in their salaries. Thus, the markets for nurses and surgeons may differ significantly, even though they are both in the health care industry.

When we view the labour market as a whole, then, we can see that it is made up of many different, largely *non-competing groups*. Dentists form one group, carpenters another, computer programmers yet another, and so on. In the short run, an individual's ability to move from one group to another is limited, and that is why the groups are "non-competing." Over time, some movement is possible. Economists, for example, may become college instructors and typists may become wordprocessors. But in the long run, many groups will be non-competing. It is unlikely that many economists will become brain surgeons even with considerable financial incentives, for example. Only when workers can easily switch from one occupation to another are pay scales between them likely to be similar.

▯ Wage Differentials

We are all aware of the great variations in pay received by Canadians—from the millions of dollars paid to star athletes to the minimum wage received by part-time student and migrant workers. The significant barriers to movement among occupations are key factors in these income differentials. Why, then, don't all doctors become surgeons or labourers become plumbers? What are these barriers?

Education, Training, and Experience
The many years of demanding and expensive education and training required for some skilled and professional occupations constitute significant barriers to entry. Compared with unskilled workers, therefore, their numbers in most cases will be smaller and their pay higher. The supply of physicists, doctors, and lawyers, for example, is more limited than that of general labourers and their salary rates are much higher. In some professions, such as teaching and medicine, government regulations prohibit individuals from practising unless they have certain minimum qualifications.

Geographic Immobility
Geographic immobility, the inability or unwillingness of people to move from one location to another, also represents a barrier. A worker may be reluctant to leave family, friends, and familiar surroundings, even for a higher-paying job. Others may not be able to afford a move. Some areas may have difficulty attracting workers. Not everyone, for example, would be willing to work in the far north, even though wages there may be very high to attract workers.

Lack of Knowledge
Inadequate knowledge of available jobs, skill requirements, and wage rates may also inhibit worker mobility. To counter this problem, the federal government has established more than 450 employment centres across the country to provide information and counselling services.

Discrimination
Discrimination against workers based on their sex, ethnic origin, religion, marital status, or some other characteristic not only restricts mobility, but also has other serious social repercussions. Discrimination depresses the demand for the groups discriminated against and puts downward pressure on their incomes. Women and ethnic minorities, for example, have strug-

gled with discrimination in the labour force, which has essentially barred them from entering what were considered "prestigious" occupations. Though the situation is changing and governments have instituted equal pay legislation, discrimination has not been eliminated and significant wage differentials continue to exist.

☐ Is Total Wage Equity Reasonable?

If all these barriers to the free movement of workers were eliminated, would all wages be equal? The answer is that while there would probably be greater equality than there is today, significant wage differentials would still exist. The kinds of abilities needed to be a surgeon or a star musician are possessed by relatively few people, so that these skills are always likely to be highly valued. Some occupations—such as those of police officers, fire fighters, and highrise construction workers—are dangerous; others, such as garbage collection, are unpleasant; still others, such as nursing, involve shiftwork and bear heavy responsibilities. As a result, these workers will likely continue to command higher wages than those in safer, pleasanter, and less demanding positions.

■ The Labour Force

The **labour force** in Canada is that part of the population 15 years of age and over, which is both willing and able to work for a wage or salary. It includes both the employed and unemployed.

To determine the size of the labour force in Canada, we start with the population aged 15 and over and subtract from it those not in the labour market. These people include students, homemakers, the retired, and those unable or unwilling to work. In 1991, with a population over age 15 of 20.7 million and 6.6 million people not in the labour market, the labour force totalled 14.1 million people. Another way of calculating the labour force is to add the number employed (12.7 million in 1991) to the number unemployed (1.4 million in 1991).

☐ Growth of the Labour Force

Canada's labour force has shown remarkable growth since the end of World War II—from 4.5 million in 1945 to 14.1 million in 1991. Much of this growth has been due to the natural increase in population, immigration, and increasing participation rates (particularly of women). The **participation rate** is the percentage of the population that is in the workforce.

In line with the trend in other industrialized countries, Canada's natural population growth has slowed since the 1950s. In 1954, the growth rate was 28.5 live births per thousand. By 1990, it had declined to 14.9 live births per thousand. Immigration has also declined relative to the size of the population. It reached a postwar high in 1957 of 282 000 (17 per thousand population), but was down to 190 000 (8 per thousand population) in 1990, and this figure was higher than any in the 1980s. Growth of the labour force averaged over 3

Table 11.3 Growth in the Canadian labour force, 1945-1991

1 YEAR	2 LABOUR FORCE (IN THOUSANDS)	3 RATE OF ANNUAL CHANGE (PERCENT)
1945	4 520	-0.6
1950	5 198	2.1
1955	5 568	2.4
1960	6 411	2.7
1965	7 179	4.1
1970	8 395	2.5
1975	9 974	3.5
1980	11 573	3.0
1985	12 532	1.8
1990	13 681	1.0
1991 (June)	14 081	1.0

SOURCE: Statistics Canada, *The Labour Force* and *Canadian Economic Observer*, March 1991; *Bank of Canada Review*, July 1991.

The Canadian labour force has grown substantially since 1945 with the increases in population, immigration, and participation rates (particularly of women). Growth rates were highest in the late 1960s and 1970s as the baby boomers entered the workforce, but slowed in the 1980s and early 1990s.

percent in the 1970s as members of the post-war baby boom entered the job market, but then slowed considerably in the 1980s and 1990s.

A significant factor in the continuing growth of the labour force, however, is the increasing participation rate of women. In 1946, the female participation rate was 24.7 percent. By mid-1990, it had more than doubled to 58.6 percent. From comprising less than 22 percent of the labour force in 1950, women comprised approximately 45 percent of the labour force in 1991. Male participation rates have declined marginally as more males retired early. Table 11.3 summarizes the growth in the labour force from 1945 to 1991, and Figure 11.9 shows participation rates by age and sex from 1966 to 1991.

□ Recent Trends in the Canadian Labour Force

Another significant development of the 1980s and early 1990s is the aging of the population. The average age of the workforce increased more than a full year from 35.5 years in 1979 to 36.6 years at the beginning of the 1990s.

Perhaps more striking is the anticipated future growth in the number of senior citizens (those aged 65 and older). In the 1966 census, senior citizens totalled 1.5 million or 8 percent of the population. By 1986, they totalled 2.7 million and 11 percent of the population. By the year 2000, seniors are expected to number about 4 million; by 2021, 6 million; and by 2031, 7.5

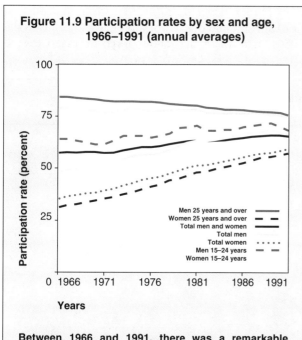

Figure 11.9 Participation rates by sex and age, 1966–1991 (annual averages)

Between 1966 and 1991, there was a remarkable increase in the participation rate of women both over 25 years of age and between 15 and 24 years. Over the same period, participation rates of males between 15 and 24 increased, but those of men over 25 declined. Total participation rates for both men and women show the steady growth of labour force participation since 1966.

SOURCE: Statistics Canada, *Canadian Economic Observer*, Historical Supplement 1990/91 and August 1991.

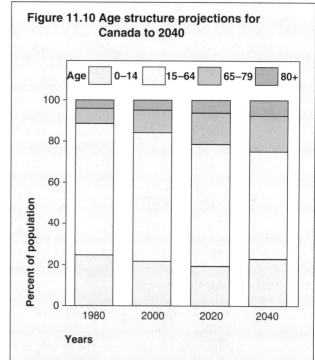

Figure 11.10 Age structure projections for Canada to 2040

The percentage of the Canadian population over age 65 is expected to increase continuously and rapidly to 2040, while the working age proportion of the population (15–64 years) is expected to decline considerably over the same period.

SOURCE: Statistics Canada, *Canadian Economic Observer*, August 1991, p. 34.

□ □ □ □ □ □

Women in the Workforce

Women's participation in the Canadian labour force has increased remarkably since the 1950s. This increasing participation has been due to a number of factors. Perceptions of women's roles in society have changed, for example. Women are acquiring higher education and more specialized skills. The job market has also changed with the expansion of the service sector where requirements of physical strength for jobs are less important.

How far, then, have women come toward breaking the traditional barriers in the workforce? What obstacles still remain in their way? The following figures will give you some insights.

Figure 11.11 Employment of men and women by occupation, 1982 and 1991

	1982		1991	
	WOMEN	MEN	WOMEN	MEN
CLERICAL	79.0	21.0	80.3	19.7
SERVICES	54.5	45.5	55.6	46.4
SALES	39.8	60.2	47.1	52.9
MEDICINE AND HEALTH	85.1	14.9	80.1	19.9
TEACHING	64.3	35.7	62.8	37.2
MANAGERIAL, ADMINISTRATIVE	29.2	70.8	40.0	60.0
PRODUCT FABRICATING, ASSEMBLING, AND REPAIRING	21.2	78.8	19.2	80.8
AGRICULTURE	19.5	80.5	28.7	71.3
SOCIAL SCIENCES	47.5	52.5	61.6	38.4
PROCESSING AND MACHINING	14.1	85.9	23.7	76.3
ARTISTIC AND RECREATIONAL	34.5	65.5	42.2	57.8
NATURAL SCIENCES	14.7	85.3	16.8	83.2
MATERIALS HANDLING	19.5	80.5	20.0	80.0
OTHER CRAFTS AND EQUIPMENT OPERATING	19.5	80.5	20.0	80.0
TRANSPORT EQUIPMENT OPERATING	6.0	94.0	7.0	93.0
CONSTRUCTION TRADES	1.4	98.6	2.0	98.0
RELIGION	15.0	85.0	22.6	77.4
TOTAL	41.3	58.7	44.6	55.4
Percent of jobs	0 50 100		0 50 100	

SOURCE: *Labour Force Annual Averages*, 1981–1988, Statistics Canada, Cat. 71–529, and *Labour Force*, July 1991.

Table 11.4 Leading occupations of women in the United States, 1890, 1940, and 1990

	1890	1940	1990
1	Servant	Servant	Secretary
2	Agricultural labourer	Stenographer, secretary	Cashier
3	Dressmaker	Teacher	Bookkeeper
4	Teacher	Clerical worker	Registered nurse
5	Farmer, planter	Sales worker	Nursing aide, orderly
6	Laundress	Factory worker (apparel)	Elementary school teacher
7	Seamstress	Bookkeeper, accountant, cashier	Waitress
8	Cotton-mill operative	Waitress	Sales worker
9	Housekeeper, steward	Housekeeper	Child care worker
10	Clerk, cashier	Nurse	Cook

SOURCE: *Fortune*, September 23, 1991, p. 10.

Applications

1. Summarize the major similarities and differences between the major occupations of men and women shown in Figure 11.11. Suggest reasons for your findings.

2. Compare the percentages of women in the various occupations between 1982 and 1991. What trends are evident? What do they indicate?

3. What obstacles may women still be facing?

4. Refer to Table 11.4. Between which years did the most significant changes occur in US women's occupations?

5. Compare the list for 1990 with Canadian women's occupations in 1982 and 1991 outlined in Figure 11.11. What are the major similarities and differences? What do they indicate?

million. Figure 11.10 shows the age structure projections for Canada to 2040.

As the proportion of seniors in the population grows, the working age proportion of the population will decline. In 1990, for example, the ratio of non-working age to working age people was 47 for every 100. By the middle of the next century, this dependency ratio is expected to reach 68 for every 100.

The aging population will shift the demand for various goods and services. Aging baby boomers— once called "yuppies" and then "grumpies" or grown-up, mature, professionals by demographers—have already had a significant impact on the goods being produced. Miniature Oreo Cookies were introduced to give baby boomers the taste of their youth without adding to the midriffs, for example. "Relaxed fit" jeans have met with marketing success, and while sales of running shoes have been flat, sales of walking shoes have quintupled. The aging population will also create an increasing demand for health care services (espe-

cially geriatric care) and place a greater tax burden on the working population. Consideration may be given to raising the retirement age above 65 and easing restrictions on young immigrants to increase the working population.

Not only has the labour force gotten older, however, it has also become more educated. In 1979, 10 percent of the workforce had a degree and 29 percent had some post-secondary education, while 17 percent had less than a Grade 9 education. By 1990, more than 15 percent had a degree, 42 percent had some post-secondary education, and only 9 percent had less than Grade 9. These trends are expected to continue into the twenty-first century.

☐ Employment Trends

One of the most far-reaching changes in the Canadian labour market since 1951 is the rise in the proportion of

□ □ □ □ □ □

Jobs in the 1990s—"What's Hot and What's Not?"

Which jobs will be most in demand through the 1990s and into the next century? Which are on the decline? The following list will give you some insights.

Applications

1. What characteristics do the "hot" jobs have in common? What do they indicate about how our economy is changing?

2. What do the fastest growing jobs suggest about social and economic trends in the future?

3. What do the declining jobs indicate about how our economy is changing?

4. In which groups are wages likely to be rising? Explain why.

HOT JOBS IN THE '90S	FASTEST GROWING JOBS IN THE '90S	JOBS IN FASTEST DECLINE IN THE '90S
1 Environmental engineer (creates practical solutions for cleaning up the world)	1 Respiratory therapist	1 Tobacco processor
2 International marketer (because Canadian companies must expand their markets or perish)	2 Systems analyst	2 Typist
3 Issues manager (spots hot issues for companies and governments before they cause trouble and helps manage crises when they occur)	3 Child-care worker	3 Weaver
	4 Electronic data processing equipment operator	4 Fisherman
4 Adult educator (because training will be continual)	5 Occupational therapist	5 Sewing machine operator
	6 Dental hygienist	6 Hospital orderly
5 Process technologist (because being an efficient producer is more important than inventing new products)	7 Chef/cook	7 Statistical clerk
	8 Speech therapist	8 Office machine operator
6 Civil engineer (to rebuild roads, bridges, hospitals, and the rest of the disintegrating infrastructure)	9 Physiotherapist	9 Farmer
	10 Optometrist	10 Radio and TV repair services

NOTE: These figures are projections by Employment and Immigration Canada based on consultation with industry groups.

SOURCE: Reproduced with the permission of Employment and Immigration Canada and Supply and Services Canada, 1992.

Canadians working in the service sector—from 43.9 percent in 1951 to 72.2 percent in 1990. Within the goods-producing sector, the proportion has declined just as dramatically—from 56.1 percent to 27.8 percent over the same period. As shown in Table 11.5, only the construction industry has about kept its proportion of the workforce. Agriculture's share has declined most significantly, while service sector growth has been most evident in public administration and community, business, and personal services.

Table 11.5 Employment trends in Canada, 1951-1990

| | PERCENT OF LABOUR FORCE EMPLOYED | | | | |
	1951	1961	1971	1981	1990
Agriculture	18.4	11.2	6.3	4.4	3.4
Non-agricultural primary industries	4.4	3.0	2.7	2.9	2.3
Manufacturing	26.5	24.0	21.8	19.3	15.9
Construction	6.8	6.2	6.0	5.9	6.2
TOTAL GOODS-PRODUCING SECTOR	**56.1**	**44.5**	**36.9**	**32.5**	**27.8**
Transportation, storage, communication, and utilities	8.8	9.3	8.7	8.3	7.6
Trade	14.1	16.9	16.5	17.1	17.8
Finance, insurance, real estate	3.0	3.9	4.9	5.4	6.0
Community, business and personal services, and public administration	18.0	25.3	33.0	36.7	40.8
TOTAL SERVICE SECTOR	**43.9**	**55.5**	**63.1**	**67.5**	**72.2**
TOTAL ALL INDUSTRIES	100.0	100.0	100.0	100.0	100.0

SOURCE: Statistics Canada, *The Labour Force: Labour Force Annual Averages*, 1951-1988 and 1990.

While the proportion of Canadians working in the goods-producing sector has declined, the proportion in the service sector has increased dramatically—particularly in community, business and personal services, and public administration.

Canadian Labour Legislation

By the terms of the Constitution Act of 1867, provincial governments were granted exclusive rights to legislate in the areas of "property and civil rights." Since contracts between workers and employers fall under this clause, most labour legislation originates in the provinces. Federal government powers are restricted mainly to industries that are interprovincial, national, or international in scope such as banking, interprovincial trade, air transportation, and shipping.

By the 1940s, the rights of workers to organize unions and bargain collectively with employers were generally recognized and incorporated into law. Today, every province has a labour relations act outlining procedures to be followed in the certification of unions and in the collective bargaining process.

Federal and provincial governments also have legislation governing hours of work, public holidays, annual vacations, and discrimination against women and minorities in the workforce. All provinces have minimum wage laws. Federal and provincial legislation also outlines compensation for workers and their dependants in the case of industrial diseases or accidents. These payments are made from a fund levied on employers.

Labour Unions

A **labour union** is a certified organization of workers that negotiates with employers on matters of pay, benefits, working conditions, and other issues. The Canadian Union of Public Employees and the United Steelworkers of America are two of the largest unions with members in Canada. One of the main reasons workers join unions is to increase their bargaining power with employers through collective action. A strong organization can have more clout than a single individual, particularly in a large company or industry.

Labour unions can influence wage rates either by restricting the supply of workers or by increasing the demand for their members' services. Some types of unions have a greater impact on wage rates than others.

The two major types of unions in Canada are craft and industrial unions. An **industrial union** is a recognized organization of many different kinds of workers—including skilled, semi-skilled, and unskilled—usually all employed in the same industry. The National Automobile, Aerospace, and Agricultural Implement Workers Union of Canada is an example. A **craft union** is a recognized association of workers practising a particular trade or craft, such as the United Brotherhood of Carpenters and Joiners of America.

Craft unions are better able to control the supply of labour than are industrial unions because they can enforce a **closed shop**. A closed shop is a term in an agreement between a union and the management of a firm specifying that only union members may be employed. Closed shops thus limit the supply of labour available to the firm and help ensure the demand for the union members' services. Craft unions can also

institute high initiation fees for admission to the union and insist on specific educational admission requirements or long apprenticeship terms. They may also pressure governments to restrict working hours and immigration of workers in the trade and institute programs of early retirement. Industrial unions, since they include many different kinds of workers in various occupations, cannot as easily insist on long apprenticeship programs and educational entrance requirements. Figure 11.12 shows the effect craft unions can have on wages by limiting the supply of workers.

Both craft and industrial unions attempt to increase the demand for labour by increasing the demand for the products made by their members. They can pressure governments to impose taxes and/or quotas on competing imported goods, thus raising the price of their domestic product. They may also lobby governments to buy only Canadian and union-made products and push for advertising that goods are "union made," in the belief that Canadians will prefer these goods.

☐ Collective Bargaining

Collective bargaining is the process of negotiation between representatives of a union and management, the object of which is to establish terms and conditions of employment acceptable to both sides. The most dramatic and publicized instances of collective bargaining are the last-minute marathon sessions held in hotel conference rooms, when agreements are reached at unearthly hours. Generally, however, negotiations begin well before the expiry date of a contract, though the process may take several months.

If the workers are not yet unionized and do not have a contract with management, the first step for the union is certification as the legal representative of the workers. For certification, the union petitions the provincial Labour Relations Board or, if under federal jurisdiction, the Canada Labour Relations Board, for the right to hold an election among the workers. A secret ballot is held, and if the union receives the support of a majority, it becomes the certified legal bargaining agent for the workers. It can then negotiate the first and subsequent contracts with management, as long as it continues to have the workers' support.

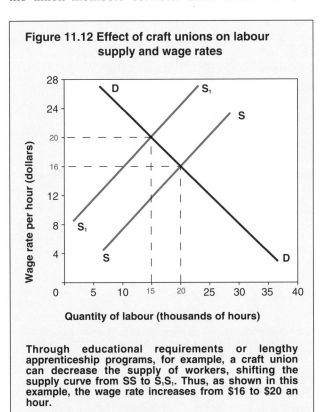

Figure 11.12 Effect of craft unions on labour supply and wage rates

Quantity of labour (thousands of hours)

Wage rate per hour (dollars)

Through educational requirements or lengthy apprenticeship programs, for example, a craft union can decrease the supply of workers, shifting the supply curve from SS to S_1S_1. Thus, as shown in this example, the wage rate increases from $16 to $20 an hour.

Workers can vote to decertify a union if they feel it is not adequately representing their concerns.

In more than 95 percent of the cases, contracts are arrived at by discussion—though issues are sometimes hotly debated by the two sides. The union presents its terms, management offers its proposals, and bargaining continues with further proposals and counter-proposals until an agreement is reached. The major issues discussed in the process include the following.

(i) Wages   The agreement will state the rate of pay for the jobs of all workers covered by the contract.

(ii) COLA clauses   Agreements may include *Cost of Living Allowance* clauses, specifying that wages are to be increased with increases in the cost of living.

(iii) Hours of work   The length of the work day is outlined, as are rates of pay for overtime and holiday pay.

(iv) Fringe benefits   Agreement on benefits including holiday pay, medical, dental and pension benefits, education leave, etc., would be specified in the contract.

(v) Working conditions   Negotiations may also cover safety conditions on the job, recreation facilities, heating, ventilation, etc.

(vi) Grievance procedures   The process for settling alleged breaches of the contract is also clearly outlined.

(vii) Seniority systems   Seniority systems are instituted to protect the jobs of workers who have been with the firm for the longest time. When there are layoffs, a last-in first-out system is used.

(viii) Union security   In addition to protecting and enhancing the working lives of its members, the union is concerned with its own security. It, therefore, seeks to enrol in its ranks all workers in its potential jurisdiction. The union may negotiate to establish either a closed shop, in which only union members may be employed, or a **union shop**, which requires that all new employees become members of the union within a short time—usually a month. The closed and union shops are both preferred by the union to the **open shop**, whereby union membership is voluntary. The **compulsory check-off** of union dues from the union member's pay cheque may also be instituted.

(ix) Term of the contract   Contracts typically run for a term of one, two, or three years. The term is specified during the collective bargaining process.

□ □ □ □ □ □

Collective Bargaining in Verse

We wheedled and threatened and blustered,
We ranted and wrangled and roared;
We chided and fretted, we scoffed and we petted,
We snickered and wept and implored;
We groveled and swore and demanded,
We spurned and we fawned and we brayed,
We trampled on data, we tossed ultimata,
We grumped and we stamped and inveighed;
We whimpered and simpered and shouted,
Pretended, defended, and doubted;
We smiled and we jested, reviled and protested,
Debated, orated, and shouted;
We fumed and we sneered and we whined,
We flattered, cajoled, and maligned,
Consented, revoked, and declined . . .
And finally the contract we signed!

SOURCE: Anonymous, quoted by Henry Mayer in "Should Politics Make Mediators Expendable?" *Labour Law Journal*, 4, No. 5 (copyright May 1953 by Commerce Clearing House, Inc.), p. 317.

Application

1. Does the poem provide a good description of the collective bargaining process? Why or why not?

☐ Settlement of Disputes and Other Actions

If union and management are unable to reach an agreement, federal and provincial governments may call in an outside **mediator** or **conciliator** (frequently a judge) to resolve the issues in the dispute. However, neither side is obliged to accept the conciliator's recommendations. If conciliation attempts break down, a dispute may be submitted to an **arbitrator**. In this case, both sides must accept the arbitrator's ruling. When an agreement is reached, it must be ratified or approved by a vote of union members.

Unions and management seek to accomplish most of their objectives in regular negotiations. However, when negotiations break down and conciliation does not work, both sides may resort to other forms of action. Unions may turn to a strike or boycott; management to a lockout, for example. Each side is aware that such actions can be taken and, in negotiations, must assess the other side's willingness and ability to effect them.

Strikes

A **strike** is the temporary withholding of labour services by a union to compel management into modifying its collective bargaining position. A strike can be a very effective action. However, to be successful, the union executive must have the support of the members and sufficient financial resources to maintain the strike for an extended period. During a strike, the employer is not obligated to pay the striking workers' wages. The union generally has a fund from which to draw strike pay for the workers, but it is considerably less than their normal full wage. The union may also attempt to gain the support of other unions and the general public in order to strengthen its position.

Some unions may choose to institute a **rotating strike**, whereby workers in various parts of a corporation or industry go on strike in turn. In this way, the union can cause considerable disruption, while limiting the cost in lost pay to workers and strike pay it must provide.

Canadian postal workers and air traffic controllers have used rotating strikes in the past to pressure management. Rotating strikes have been effective for air traffic controllers since a full strike would likely bring the rapid enactment by parliament of back-to-work legislation because of the serious danger the strike could pose to air travellers.

Workers may cause further disruption during a strike by **picketing** around the entrance of the struck firm. Employees who are not on strike and workers from other firms making deliveries may be reluctant to cross the picket lines. If they refuse to cross the lines, the union can extend the impact of the strike beyond that caused by the absence of its members.

Work-to-Rule

Instead of going on strike, workers may **work-to-rule.** In this action, workers perform their duties strictly within the bounds of their job descriptions, without shortcuts they may have found and without any additional effort. Teachers under work-to-rule, for example, would work only the regular school day and refuse to participate in extra-curricular activities or mark tests and prepare lessons after school hours.

Boycotts

A **boycott** organized by a union is an action encouraging consumers not to buy the firm's products and workers of other companies not to handle its products. If successful, a boycott can bring additional pressure on the firm to reach an agreement with the union. Members of the United Farm Workers of California and its Canadian supporters, for example, have organized boycotts in Canadian supermarkets to pressure grape and lettuce growers to bargain with the union.

Lockouts

A **lockout** is the temporary closing of a plant or business "locking out" workers. It is the employer's equivalent of a strike. By law, a lockout cannot be enforced unless conciliation has failed. Management may also attempt to keep the plant in operation despite the strike. Replacement workers or strike-breakers (called "scabs" by the strikers) may be hired while the union is on strike. If management can continue to keep the plant operating, its position in the negotiations is considerably stronger.

□ □ □ □ □ □

Skill Development: Clarifying a Normative Economic Issue

Some issues in economics are normative—that is, they are concerned with what should or ought to be rather than what is. Normative issues can be difficult to sort out. Let's consider a sample issue and one approach to clarifying it. The issue is concerned with whether certain groups of workers, such as nurses, should have the right to strike. We'll begin by considering a specific strike action by Manitoba nurses in 1991.

Manitoba Nurses Strike Over Wages

WINNIPEG (CP)—If you break your nose in Manitoba, don't go to a hospital. It's likely not serious enough for treatment with more than 10 000 nurses on strike to back demands for higher wages.

Most of the almost 90 unionized hospitals, nursing homes, and other health-care facilities hit by the strike have deals with nurses to provide emergency services. Even those that don't are receiving similar consideration.

But that doesn't mean every patient who walks into an emergency room is going to be treated. "Things are going as smoothly as we could hope right now," said Dr Neil Swirsky, director of emergency services at St. Boniface General Hospital, as he filled in on the admitting desk. "There're certain patients they won't look after because they've got relatively minor problems—possible broken nose, lacerated scalp, a sore eye, skin rash, those types of things," he said.

"The people that they are looking after? There's a person that came in with chest pains, a possible heart attack, an overdose." The rest are advised to see their doctors.

Despite temperatures hovering around minus 30°C, nurses kept their promise to start picketing hospitals at 7 a.m. after the breakdown of negotiations the night before.

The main issue is wages. Nurses want a hike of 27 percent over two years. Manitoba Health Organizations Inc., on behalf of the province and the unionized hospitals, is offering about 20 percent over three years. There is room for tinkering and other issues such as a pay equity plan in effect at the largest hospitals to complicate matters, but the Health Minister suggested there is no more money available for nurses.

"This is an offer that over three years is going to add some $62 million to nursing salaries in the province of Manitoba," he said. "We think it's very generous." He said it would leave Manitoba nurses roughly in the middle of the pack as far as wages in Canada. Nurses say only those in Prince Edward Island and Quebec now make less than Manitoba's starting wage of $14.10 an hour.

The Health Minister refused to discuss the possibility of back-to-work legislation. "I'm hopeful that both sides will reach a settlement."

To prepare for a strike, Winnipeg's largest hospitals have closed hundreds of beds, cancelled elective surgery, and started admitting only emergency patients. Lydia Harris, assistant head nurse of emergency at St. Boniface, said she didn't like being on strike, but felt the nurses had no option. "We don't want to be out here," she said. "They forced us to be out here and we'll be out here until we get a fair settlement."

Harris, a nurse for 25 years and 13 of those at St. Boniface, said it'll be tough living on strike pay, but nurses can't afford not to strike.

SOURCE: The Canadian Press, June, 1991.

What are the normative issues involved? There are a number of them stemming from the most immediate one of whether the Manitoba nurses should have the right to strike.

1. Should Manitoba nurses have the right to strike in this instance?
2. Should nurses have the right to strike?
3. Should public sector workers have the right to strike?
4. Which workers (if any) should have the right to strike?

Before we begin to consider these issues, some basic questions need to be answered.

Legal Questions

One question we might ask is: "Do the nurses have the legal right to strike?" The answer in this case is yes.

Definitional Questions

Some key terms or phrases may cause confusion because their meanings are not clear. In this case, two terms at least are of great importance.

(i) *Emergency services* In the Manitoba nurses strike, possible heart attacks and overdoses are classified as emergencies and attended by the nurses, while broken noses are not. Obviously, there are a considerable number of injuries and ailments between possible heart attacks and broken noses that are not clearly defined. What are emergencies and what are not?

(ii) *Essential services* While we may agree that workers providing an essential service should not go on strike, the difficulty comes in defining exactly what is or is not an essential service. Do nurses provide an essential service? Do police officers? Do postal workers?

Factual Questions

What additional facts are necessary to help clarify the arguments on either side of the issue? In this case, we might decide, for example, that a knowledge of the final settlement achieved would be useful. To find out, we could examine subsequent news reports or *Canadian News Facts 1991*. We could also contact the Manitoba Nurses Union and Manitoba Health Organizations Inc. for more information. In fact, the Manitoba nurses accepted a two-year contract giving registered nurses a 14-percent pay increase and nursing assistants an 11-percent increase.

Suppose we have settled all of the legal, definitional, and factual questions and are now ready to tackle the normative issues. Let's examine the first issue: "Should Manitoba nurses have the right to strike in this instance?" To clarify the issue, we will outline the arguments on both sides.

The "YES" Side's Arguments	The "NO" Side's Responses	The "NO" Side's Arguments	The "YES" Side's Responses
Manitoba nurses have the legal right to strike. Presumably, the people of Manitoba acting through the legislature thought that the nurses should have the right to strike.	The simple fact that something is legal doesn't mean that it should be done. It may be legal for me to sell my neighbour my garden hose for $500 when her house is on fire—but it isn't ethical.	Lives will be in jeopardy— especially in those cases where people need surgery or treatment for cancer, for example.	The patients whose surgery is delayed can wait or they can get treatment out of the province.
Hospitals and other health care centres have arranged with the striking nurses to provide emergency services. Those really needing care are, therefore, looked after. Others can see their doctors.	Some people who are suffering and are denied the emergency services may have difficulties seeing their doctor—especially on weekends or in the evenings. They will not be adequately cared for.	Nurses, because they work for a government agency, have excessive power to exact high wages. Government agencies are subject to political pressures.	A comparison of the nurses' wages to those of comparable professionals would refute this contention.
Wages of Manitoba nurses are among the lowest in the country. They deserve a better increase than their employer has offered.	The offered pay increase will boost the nurses' wages to the Canadian average.	Nurses claim they are professionals and professionals don't strike. The labour dispute could be settled by arbitration without harming or alarming the people of Manitoba.	But nurses, like other professionals, need the right to strike to protect themselves against exploitation and unfair wages.

Now that the issue has been more clearly outlined, what do you think?

Application

1. Select another group of public sector workers (e.g., police officers, food inspectors, teachers) and use the approach outlined above to determine whether they should have the right to strike. Then, debate the issue. Alternatively, you could focus on another normative issue.

Court Injunctions

Management may seek a court injunction to prevent striking employees from intimidating workers crossing the picket line or damaging the firm's property, should such incidents occur.

☐ Impact of Strikes and Lockouts

Strikes and lockouts are, in fact, relatively rare. Strikes, especially prolonged ones, can have very adverse effects on a business, sometimes even forcing it into bankruptcy. For workers, a long strike may cause finan-

cial hardship and for the general public, life may be considerably disrupted.

Since strikes and lockouts are such newsworthy events, however, it may come as a surprise that the amount of labour time lost as a result of these actions in Canada is quite minimal. Only in the mid-1970s was the percentage of estimated working time lost above 0.5 percent, as shown in Figure 11.13. For the 30 years between 1960 and 1990, the average percentage of estimated working time lost was between 0.2 and 0.3— that is, between two and three days per thousand days worked.

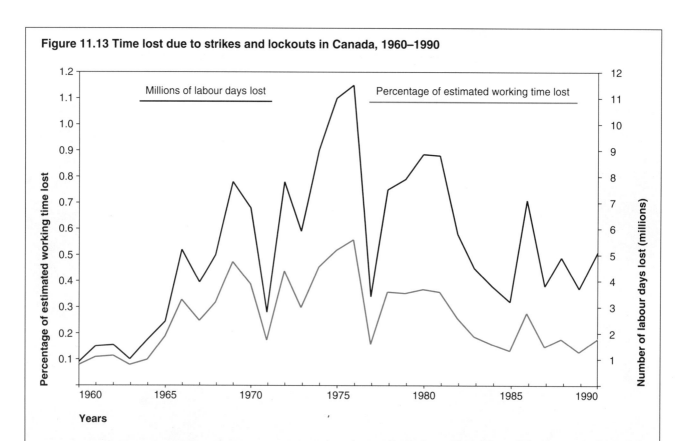

Figure 11.13 Time lost due to strikes and lockouts in Canada, 1960–1990

Time lost due to strikes and lockouts in Canada is relatively minimal. Only in the mid-1970s was the percentage of estimated working time lost over 0.5 percent. Between 1960 and 1990, only between two and three days per thousand labour days were lost, on average.

SOURCE: *Labour Canada, Strikes and Lockouts in Canada 1978, 1983, 1985; Yearbook of Labour Statistics*, International Labour Office, Geneva, 1991.

Labour Unions in Canada

Labour unions have existed in Canada for over 150 years. The first unions were established in the craft industries (printers, shoemakers, carpenters, for example). Their common skill gave them a shared interest and the means to resist the anti-union pressures of their employers. In the 1930s, following the growth of the steel and automobile industries, industrial unions developed.

Union membership since the beginning of the century has grown erratically. During World War I and immediately afterwards, growth was rapid, but declined during the depressed 1930s. The rapid industrial expansion during and after World War II encouraged another surge of growth in union membership. Union membership had passed a million by 1951, two million by 1967, and three million less than ten years later. By 1990, labour union membership had surpassed four million. While total membership increased steadily, however, membership as a percentage of the non-agricultural workforce peaked in 1977-78 at 38.4 percent. Since then, the percentage has declined. Figure 11.14 shows the growth in total union membership, in the number of non-agricultural paid workers, and in the total labour force from 1971 to 1990.

Growth in the late 1960s and in the 1970s was largely due to changes in government legislation giving public sector unions increased power in collective bargaining and the right to strike. Today, three of Canada's largest unions represent public servants. The reduced increases in membership since the late 1970s may be the result of rapid growth in the service sector of the economy, which is not widely unionized. Unions are most common in the manufacturing, construction, communications, transportation, utilities, logging, mining, and public administration sectors. Figure 11.15 on page 238 shows the 15 largest unions in Canada in 1990 by membership.

Structure of Labour Unions in Canada

Labour unions in Canada are organized on four levels—local, national, international, and federations of unions.

Local Unions
A local union is a union that is entirely a local organization. Though there are more than 200 of them in Canada, they account for only a small percentage of total union membership.

Union Locals
The union local is the local branch of a national or international union. In industrial unions, the union local usually constitutes a single plant. In craft unions, it generally covers a geographic area, since union

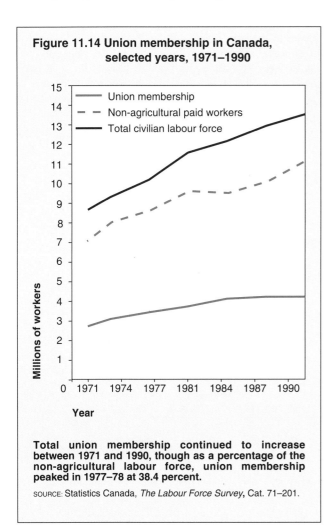

Figure 11.14 Union membership in Canada, selected years, 1971–1990

- Union membership
- Non-agricultural paid workers
- Total civilian labour force

Millions of workers / Year

Total union membership continued to increase between 1971 and 1990, though as a percentage of the non-agricultural labour force, union membership peaked in 1977–78 at 38.4 percent.

SOURCE: Statistics Canada, *The Labour Force Survey*, Cat. 71–201.

members often move from site to site within an area. To members, the local branch is the most familiar part of the union. They elect the executive from among the workers in the local and pay their fees to the local executive. The local signs the contract with management outlining wages and working conditions and is always involved in the collective bargaining process.

National Unions

National unions are made up of many union locals or branches located only in Canada. One of the best known examples is Canada's largest union, the Canadian Union of Public Employees.

International Unions

International unions have a large membership and many locals in Canada, but the bulk of their members and their headquarters are located in the United States. Examples are the United Steelworkers of America and the United Food and Commercial Workers International Union.

In the late 1970s, approximately half of Canadian unions were members of international unions. Since then the proportion has declined, so that now only about two-fifths (representing one-quarter of Cana-

dian unionists) are members of international unions. One notable event in this trend toward the Canadianization of unions was the separation of the Canadian branch from the International United Automobile Workers union in 1985 to form the National Automobile, Aerospace, and Agricultural Implement Workers Union of Canada, often called simply the "Canadian Automobile Workers Union."

Both national and international unions offer expertise and support to locals in contract negotiations, organize recruitment programs, publish union newspapers, and pressure governments on labour issues.

Federations

Federations or central labour organizations are "unions of unions." Their members are unions. The central labour organization probably best known to Canadians is the Canadian Labour Congress (CLC). The CLC is an umbrella organization made up of and financed by international, national, and local unions. The Canadian Union of Public Employees and the United Steelworkers of America, for example, are both members of the CLC. More than half of the total union membership in Canada is associated with the CLC.

The Quebec-based Confederation of National Trade

Figure 11.15 Fifteen largest unions in Canada, 1990 (millions of members)

CANADIAN UNION OF PUBLIC EMPLOYEES	376.9
NATIONAL UNION OF PROVINCIAL GOVERNMENT EMPLOYEES	301.2
UNITED FOOD AND COMMERCIAL WORKERS INTERNATIONAL UNION	170.0
NATIONAL AUTOMOBILE, AEROSPACE AND AGRICULTURAL IMPLEMENT WORKERS UNION OF CANADA	167.4
PUBLIC SERVICE ALLIANCE OF CANADA	162.7
UNITED STEELWORKERS OF AMERICA	160.0
INTERNATIONAL BROTHERHOOD OF TEAMSTERS, CHAUFFEURS, WAREHOUSEMEN AND HELPERS OF AMERICA	100.0
SOCIAL AFFAIRS FEDERATION INC.	94.6
SCHOOL BOARDS TEACHERS' FEDERATION	75.0
SERVICE EMPLOYEES INTERNATIONAL UNION	75.0
CANADIAN PAPERWORKERS UNION	69.0
INTERNATIONAL BROTHERHOOD OF ELECTRICAL WORKERS	64.5
UNITED BROTHERHOOD OF CARPENTERS AND JOINERS OF AMERICA	62.0
INTERNATIONAL ASSOCIATION OF MACHINISTS AND AEROSPACE WORKERS	59.6
LABOURER'S INTERNATIONAL UNION OF NORTH AMERICA	57.2

0   100   200   300   400   500

Two public service unions, the Canadian Union of Public Employees and the National Union of Provincial Government Employees, are Canada's largest unions with over 300 million members.

Unions (CNTU) and the Canadian Federation of Labour (CFL) are two other central organizations, each with about 5 percent of total membership. Other smaller central organizations, the Centrale des unions démocratiques (CSD) and the Confederation of Canadian Unions (CCU), have about 3 percent of union membership.

The role of union federations is largely a political one. They lobby provincial and federal governments to pass legislation favourable to unions. In the past, for example, they pressured governments to enact unemployment and health insurance legislation and laws covering pensions. They also lobbied against the Free Trade Agreement with the United States and the Goods and Services Tax. Central labour organizations may also act to resolve disputes among unions.

The federations have no real power over their affiliated unions, however. They can lead only by persuasion. The strongest action they can take is to expel an offending union in a policy dispute, but for many, this poses little threat. The Teamsters Union, for example, was relatively unaffected by its expulsion from the CLC and operates now as an independent union. The federations do not play a significant role in collective bargaining with management or in organizing strikes.

The structure of labour union organization in Canada is illustrated in Figure 11.16. Independent unions are those which do not belong to national or international unions, or any union federations.

■ Impact of Unions: An Assessment

What impact have unions had on wages in Canada? We can divide this question into two parts—what impact have they had on the wages of their members and what impact have they had on wages in general? From our earlier examination of how unions can influence wages by limiting the supply of their members' services, we can conclude that unions can indeed raise wages. A comparison of workers' wages in unionized and non-unionized industries also shows that non-unionized workers, on average, are paid 10 to 15 percent less than unionized workers. In industries where unions can control supply and entry—as in the construction trades—wages are likely to be highest. In industries where union control is weakest (e.g., hotel workers), the union's power to raise wages is less evident.

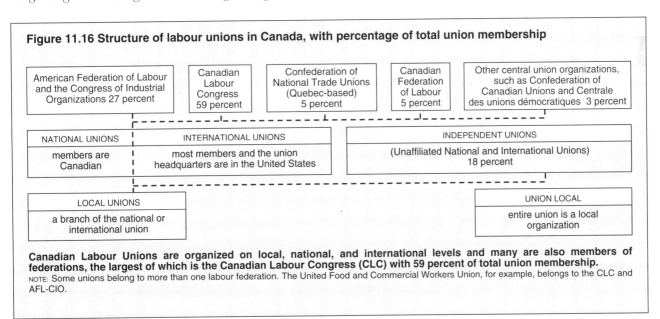

Figure 11.16 Structure of labour unions in Canada, with percentage of total union membership

| American Federation of Labour and the Congress of Industrial Organizations 27 percent | Canadian Labour Congress 59 percent | Confederation of National Trade Unions (Quebec-based) 5 percent | Canadian Federation of Labour 5 percent | Other central union organizations, such as Confederation of Canadian Unions and Centrale des unions démocratiques 3 percent |

NATIONAL UNIONS	INTERNATIONAL UNIONS	INDEPENDENT UNIONS
members are Canadian	most members and the union headquarters are in the United States	(Unaffiliated National and International Unions) 18 percent

LOCAL UNIONS	UNION LOCAL
a branch of the national or international union	entire union is a local organization

Canadian Labour Unions are organized on local, national, and international levels and many are also members of federations, the largest of which is the Canadian Labour Congress (CLC) with 59 percent of total union membership.
NOTE: Some unions belong to more than one labour federation. The United Food and Commercial Workers Union, for example, belongs to the CLC and AFL-CIO.

Summary

a. In addition to the real and money flows between businesses and households through the products markets, productive resources flow from households to businesses through the productive resources market (real flow). In exchange, households receive wages, rent, interest, and profit (money flow).

b. The demand for labour is derived from the demand for the goods and services the labour produces and depends on the labour's productivity shown by the marginal product and, in dollar terms, by the marginal revenue product.

c. The profit-maximizing firm in competitive labour markets has no influence over wage rates. The firm's demand curve for labour is also its marginal revenue product curve, which slopes down to the right because of diminishing returns. The firm will hire labour to the point where the marginal revenue product (= demand) is equal to the wage rate and marginal resource cost.

d. The marginal revenue product curve of the imperfectly competitive firm in a competitive labour market (which is also its demand curve) also slopes down to the right. Since imperfectly competitive firms generally produce less at a higher price than perfectly competitive firms with the same resources, the imperfectly competitive firm will hire fewer workers at the same wage rate.

e. Factors that may shift the demand for labour include a shift in the demand for the labour's product, a change in the productivity of the workers, and a change in the price of other productive resources.

f. The elasticity of demand for labour is influenced by the elasticity of demand for the labour's product, the number of close substitutes for the labour, the relative importance of the labour in the firm's total costs, and the rate at which the marginal revenue product is declining.

g. The equilibrium wage and quantity of labour employed for the competitive firm in a competitive labour market is the point where the supply and demand curves for labour intersect—that is, where the marginal revenue product equals the wage rate. For a monopsonist (a market situation where there is only one buyer of a product), the wage rate is lower and the quantity employed smaller.

h. Income differentials among various groups are in part the result of barriers to movement among occupations. These barriers include education, training, and experience required; geographic immobility; lack of knowledge about opportunities and wage rates; and discrimination. Even if these barriers to movement were eliminated, pay differences would still exist because of the special abilities and skills required for some occupations, and the degree of danger, unpleasantness, and responsibility in some jobs.

i. The size of the Canadian labour force has increased significantly since the 1950s, though growth has slowed in recent decades. Recent trends affecting the labour force include decreased natural population growth and immigration; increasing female participation rates; the general aging of the population; increasing educational levels; and significant increases in the proportion of workers in the service industries paralleled by a decline in the proportion of workers in the goods-producing sector.

j. Labour unions can influence the wage rates of their members by limiting the supply of their members' services through closed shops, high initiation fees, long apprenticeship periods, and pressuring governments to limit immigration of workers and working hours. They may also attempt to increase the demand for their members' services by lobbying governments to buy only union-made products and to impose restrictions on competitive imports. Studies have shown that on average, wages of unionized workers are higher than those of non-unionized workers, but unions do not seem to have increased labour's share of the national income.

   Collective bargaining is the process by which unions and management attempt to reach a mutually acceptable agreement on such issues as wages, hours of work, cost of living clauses, fringe benefits, working conditions, grievance procedures, seniority systems, terms of contracts, and union security.

Review of Key Terms

Define the following key terms introduced in this chapter and provide examples where appropriate.

productive resources
   market
wages
direct demand
derived demand
productivity of labour
marginal revenue product
   (MRP)
marginal productivity
   theory of wages
marginal resource cost
   (MRC)
monopsony
labour force
participation rate
labour union

industrial union
craft union
closed shop
collective bargaining
union shop
open shop
compulsory check-off
conciliation or mediation
arbitration
strike
rotating strike
picketing
work-to-rule
boycott
lockout

Application and Analysis

1. You are the economic consultant for the Super Slick Ski Company—a Canadian company that produces specially designed ski boards for Canadian winter conditions. Your studies of the firm's ski board plant have provided the data outlined in Table 11.6. You also know that Super Slick can sell as many ski boards as it can make at $20 a board and can hire as many skilled workers as it likes at a wage of $120 per day.

(a) Complete Table 11.6.

(b) Referring to Table 11.6, decide how many workers Super Slick should employ. Explain your reasoning.

(c) Suppose the demand for Super Slick's ski boards diminishes, so that the price falls to $18 per board. How many workers should the company then employ? Explain.

2. Suppose Super Slick becomes a ski board monopolist and can charge more than $20 for a ski board.

Table 11.6 Ski board production at Super Slick

1 NUMBER OF WORKERS EMPLOYED (Q_L)	2 NUMBER OF SKI BOARDS PRODUCED PER DAY (Q)	3 MARGINAL PRODUCT (MP)	4 PRICE PER SKI BOARD (P) (IN DOLLARS)	5 TOTAL REVENUE (TR) $TR = P \times Q$ (IN DOLLARS)	6 MARGINAL REVENUE PRODUCT (MRP) $MRP = MP \times P$ (IN DOLLARS)
0	0	0	20	0	—
1	10	10	20	200	200
2	25	15	20	500	300
3	35	10	20	700	200
4	42	7	20	840	140
5	48	6	20	960	120
6	50	2	20	1000	40

The firm can still hire workers in a competitive labour market, however. Table 11.7 outlines the same information as that in Table 11.6, but reflecting the new circumstances.

Table 11.7 Super Slick—all alone and loving it

1 NUMBER OF WORKERS EMPLOYED (Q_L)	2 NUMBER OF SKI BOARDS PRODUCED PER DAY (Q)	3 MARGINAL PRODUCT (MP)	4 PRICE PER SKI BOARD (P) (IN DOLLARS)	5 TOTAL REVENUE (TR) $TR = P \times Q$ (IN DOLLARS)	6 MARGINAL REVENUE PRODUCT (MRP) (IN DOLLARS)
0	0	0	0		
1	10	10	50	500	500
2	25	15	40	1000	500
3	35	10	35	1225	225
4	42	7	30	1260	35
5	48	6	20	960	-300
6	50	2	10	500	-460

(a) Complete Table 11.7 (columns 3, 5, and 6).

(b) Why does the price of the ski boards fall in this example, whereas the price remained unchanged in Table 11.6?

(c) If Super Slick can hire labour at $120 a day, how many workers should it hire? Use a graph to explain why.

3. State the effect each of the following situations will have on the demand for labour in the automobile industry and on workers' wages. Explain why in each case.

(a) the demand for mini vans increases

(b) a new high-tech robotic process for painting automobiles is introduced

(c) the price of gasoline decreases significantly

(d) the economy goes into a severe recession and people buy fewer automobiles

(e) the automobile workers' union negotiates a high wage increase

(f) labour productivity increases considerably

4. (a) Referring to the supply and demand schedule for plumbers in a Canadian city shown in Table 11.8, graph the supply and demand curves.

(b) Explain why the demand curve slopes down to the right.

(c) Explain why the supply curve slopes up to the right.

(d) What is the equilibrium wage? How many workers will be hired at this wage?

(e) What factors are likely to cause shifts in the demand for plumbers?

(f) On your graph, indicate a decrease in the demand for plumbers. What effect will this change have on the wage rate?

5. Which one of each of the following pairs of unions probably has more power in collective bargaining? Explain your answer.

(a) a union of police officers *or* a union of office clerks

(b) a union of Montreal transit workers *or* a union of paper makers

(c) a union of postal workers *or* a union of university professors

Table 11.8 Demand and supply schedule for plumbers

1 HOURS OF LABOUR DEMANDED PER WEEK	2 WAGE (DOLLARS PER HOUR)	3 HOURS OF LABOUR SUPPLIED PER WEEK
10 000	19.00	6 000
9 000	20.00	7 000
8 000	21.00	8 000
7 000	22.00	9 000
6 000	23.00	10 000

6. Issue—The Minimum Wage: Raise or Erase?
How can we raise the incomes of the poor? For some, the answer is simple—legislate a minimum wage below which it is illegal to employ workers. This seemingly simple solution, however, involves more than is at

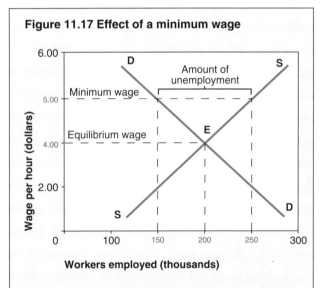

Figure 11.17 Effect of a minimum wage

At the equilibrium wage of $4.00 an hour, 200 000 workers are employed. With a minimum wage set at $5.00 an hour, only 150 000 workers are employed. Thus, with the higher wage rate, 50 000 less workers are employed. The total number of workers unemployed is 100 000 at the wage rate of $5.00 an hour. While the minimum wage reduces the number who are employed by 50 000, it increases the wage rate from $4.00 to $5.00 an hour.

first evident and, as you might imagine, is subject to controversy.

The federal and all provincial governments have enacted minimum wage legislation in Canada. Table 11.9 shows the rates that were in effect in 1991.

While a minimum wage ensures that wages do not fall too low and that all workers receive a basic wage, it can also have less favourable effects. Figure 11.17 illustrates an example. A minimum wage set above the market equilibrium means higher unemployment. Thus, while some workers who keep their jobs gain by the higher pay, others lose because they do not get jobs or are laid off because of the higher wages.

Table 11.9 Minimum wage rates across Canada in effect in 1991

JURISDICTION	EXPERIENCED ADULT WORKERS	YOUNG WORKERS AND STUDENTS
Federal	$4.00	Employees under 17 $4.00
Alberta	4.50	Employees under 18 attending school 4.00
British Columbia	5.00	Employees 17 and under 4.50
Manitoba	5.00	Employees under 18 5.00
New Brunswick	5.00	
Newfoundland	4.75	
Nova Scotia	5.00	Employees 14 to 18 4.55
Ontario	6.00	Students/under 18 employed for not more than 28 hrs. a week or during a school holiday 5.55
Prince Edward Island	4.75	Employees under 18 4.35
Quebec	5.55	
Saskatchewan	5.00	
Northwest Territories	7.00	Employees under 16 6.00
Yukon	6.24	

SOURCE: Labour Canada.
NOTE: Many provinces have excluded groups (e.g., agricultural workers) or have lower minimums for particular groups, such as hunting and fishing guides and those who receive tips or serve liquor.

About one million—or 12 percent—of the total Canadian workforce worked at or near the minimum wage in the 1980s. Studies by Statistics Canada have revealed that 40 percent of minimum wage earners were under 19; 24 percent aged 20 to 24; and 36 percent aged 25 to 69. The typical minimum wage worker is 24 or under, working in the food services industry, and is more commonly found in Atlantic Canada than the Prairies. Many of the minimum wage earners are part-time workers and students—in Ontario, for example, about half the total were students. Women are almost twice as likely to be minimum wage earners than men.

The Case Against

Critics of the minimum wage argue that it is not in the best interests of workers. With higher wages, it is clearly advantageous for employers to hire fewer workers. Increased labour costs may also result in some firms being forced out of business. The effect is that some low-wage workers, which the minimum wage was designed to help, are unemployed. It is argued that it is better for workers to be employed at a wage of $4.50 an hour than unemployed with the minimum wage at $5.00 an hour.

Which workers are most likely to lose their jobs or not get jobs if the minimum wage is raised significantly? The answer often is teens and others who lack skills and work experience. Studies have found that minimum wage legislation does cause unemployment, especially among those aged 16 to 19. It has been calculated that the youth unemployment rate increases from 1 to 3 percent for every 10 percent increase in the minimum wage. For those aged 20 to 24, increases in the minimum wage also have an adverse though less pronounced effect on employment.

Since teenage unemployment rates tend to be twice as high as those of adults, economists have urged the adoption of a "two-tier system," with a lower minimum wage for teens than for adults. Most provinces have followed this suggestion.

As a percentage of the poverty line, minimum wage incomes have fallen drastically. The National Council on Welfare has calculated that the gap between the poverty line and the minimum wage income ranges from about $1500 to over $5000 for a single, full-time worker. In the late 1980s and early 1990s, to reach the poverty line for a family with two children and one adult, the minimum wage would have had to be approximately doubled. Thus, at prevailing levels, the minimum wage fails to lift workers' incomes above the poverty line. In addition, because increases in the minimum wage are likely to have a ripple effect on other wages in the economy, their impact will likely add to inflation.

The Case For

Advocates of the minimum wage point out that its critics have made the unrealistic assumption that labour markets are competitive. In fact, they argue, many are non-competitive. In some cases—e.g., when there is a large firm in a small town—there may be a monopsony buyer of certain types of labour. The legal minimum wage may then have no harmful effects on employment. Moreover, few minimum wage workers are members of a labour union. In the 1980s, for example, less than 4 percent belonged to a union. Since unions cannot help these workers, government should.

The imposition of a minimum wage may actually raise the productivity of labour and thus shift the demand curve to the right, eliminating any unemployment effects. The minimum wage may also have a shock effect on management—forcing them to use workers more efficiently and thus raising their productivity.

It is often assumed that there are two groups of workers with the imposition of the minimum wage—the winners (those who retain their jobs) and the losers (those who are laid off). It is, however, often difficult to distinguish between the two groups. Minimum wage jobs frequently have a high labour turnover rate. Thus, individuals may be part-time winners when they are employed and part-time losers when they are unemployed.

Indeed, minimum wage legislation benefits all workers. It has the effect of raising the wages not only of the lowest paid workers, but also of those with wages above the minimum. Since union wage structures have differences between the various categories of skills, an increase in the pay of the lowest paid workers will also raise the pay of the other groups.

What is your opinion? Should the minimum wage be raised or erased? Explain your point of view.

CHAPTER TWELVE

Rent, Interest, and Profit

Objectives

a. Define rent in the economic sense and demonstrate how it is determined in particular markets.

b. Outline the factors affecting rent.

c. Examine two views of interest—that of the consumer and that of the business owner—and demonstrate how interest rates are determined.

d. Outline and assess the factors affecting interest rates.

e. Recall and apply in a new context, the economist's and accountant's views of profit.

f. Analyze the theories of David Ricardo on rent, wages, interest, and profit and compare his ideas with those of other economists.

g. Assess the proportion of total domestic income attributed to wages, rent, interest, and profit.

We have examined wages—that share of the national income that goes to the productive factor of labour. Now we turn to examine the share of the national income that goes to the other three factors of production—land, capital, and entrepreneurship. Our focus in this chapter is on rent, interest, and profit. The economic meaning of these terms, however, is not always the same as that in common usage.

In this chapter, we will examine exactly what these terms mean in the economic sense and how these sources of income are determined. We'll consider what factors affect them and what share of our national income they constitute. Many of the principles determining wages also apply to the other productive factors.

▮ Rent

For most of us, the term "rent" has a fairly general meaning. It is the amount we pay to an owner for the use over a period of time of an apartment, house, car, tool, or other commodity. Or, if we are the owner, it is the amount we receive. For business people, rent has a similar meaning—the amount paid or received for the use of a store, factory, or machine, etc.

But if we examine this common meaning of "rent" more carefully, we can see that it actually includes a variety of different payments. For example, the rent on an apartment includes payments for the wages of the apartment superintendent and other staff, interest payments on the capital invested in the building, payments for the use of utilities such as hydro and water, and an element of profit for the owner.

For economists, this common meaning of the term is not specific enough. In the pure economic sense, **rent** is defined as the payment made for (or the income earned from) productive resources for which the supply is fixed and completely price inelastic.

Land is the best example of such a productive resource. Will Rogers, the American humourist, once advised: "Buy land—they ain't making any more of the stuff." In general, he was correct. While we may increase the amount of land in production by draining swamps (such as the Holland Marsh in southern Ontario), reclaiming it from the sea (such as much of the Netherlands), or decreasing the amount lost due to erosion, these improvements are seen as increases in capital rather than land. The characteristic that makes land different from the three other productive resources is that, in total, it is fixed in amount. The total supply of land is, therefore, price inelastic. It cannot be increased by increases in price or diminished by decreases in price.

▱ Determination of Rent

As with any other price in competitive markets, rent is determined by the interaction of supply and demand. Rent is the competitive price at which the quantity of land demanded and supplied is equal.

The total supply, as we have said, is fixed. What about the demand? The same factors that affect the demand for labour, or indeed for any other productive resource, also affect the demand for land. These include the productivity of the land, the price of other resources used with the land, and the price of the products grown on the land. The more productive the land, the greater the demand. The cheaper the capital and labour resources used with the land, the greater the demand for the land. The higher the price of the products grown on the land, the greater is the demand for the land, and *vice versa*.

Figure 12.1 shows supply and demand curves for land. The supply curve, SS, is a straight line since the total supply of land is fixed and completely price inelastic. As with other commodities, the demand curve slopes down to the right. With demand at DD, the

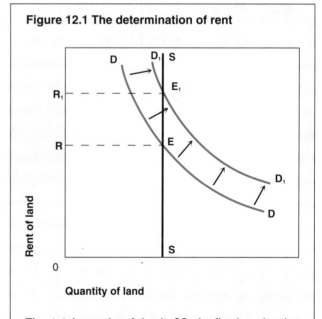

Figure 12.1 The determination of rent

The total supply of land, SS, is fixed and price inelastic. The quantity supplied does not vary with price. With demand at DD, the land will be rented for 0R. If the demand for land increases from DD to D₁D₁, then the rent increases from 0R to 0R₁. The equilibrium point moves from E to E₁. In spite of the increase in price, the quantity of land supplied remains unchanged.

□ □ □ □ □ □

A Single Tax on Land?

In the late nineteenth century, an American newspaper owner and publicist named Henry George spurred a powerful political movement based on the idea of a single tax. He advocated that nothing but rent should be taxed.

What brought him to this idea? He believed that since land (without buildings or other improvements) as defined by economists is a gift of nature, it should be public property. It costs nothing to produce (it is simply there) and we obtain it originally through inheritance or historical accident. George hesitated to suggest nationalization or confiscation of land, but he believed he could achieve the same purpose through a tax which would appropriate for public use all increases in the value of land.

George noticed that as the population of the United States grew and the demand for land increased, landlords enjoyed higher rents. The increased value occurred simply because the total supply of land is inelastic. Landowners do not need to engage in any effort to increase the value of their land—they can simply sit back and collect higher rents as the population grows. George reasoned that since rents rose because of the increase in population, the money belonged to the community as a whole and should be taxed away from the landowners to be used for the general public.

Henry George's argument is based not only on equity—what is right or just—but also on the grounds that the tax would not interfere with the use of resources. Most taxes affect the way in which we use our productive resources. A tax on buildings may cause people to look for, and possibly invest in, something else. A tax on wage income may reduce the incentive to work. People may decide to work less overtime or even withdraw from the workforce if they feel too much of their income will simply be taken in taxes.

A tax on rents need not have such effects. If rents are taxed at 75 percent, what can landowners do? The supply of land cannot be reduced. To remove the land from production would only mean lost rental income for landowners.

In Henry George's view, the amount received from the single tax on land would be so great that all other taxes could be abolished. Freed from the heavy burden of taxes on their consumption and production, workers would enjoy full employment and rising wages.

Applications

1. What are the disadvantages of Henry George's single tax?

2. Should such a single tax be implemented in Canada? Why or why not?

equilibrium point is at E, where the supply and demand curves intersect. Land, therefore, will be rented for 0R.

If demand increases from DD to D_1D_1, the rent increases from 0R to $0R_1$, but the quantity of land supplied remains unchanged. If the rent falls below the equilibrium, then more land will be demanded than can be supplied and the market will have a shortage. Competition among renters will bid up the rent. If the rent were to go above equilibrium, competition among landowners would force it down to the equilibrium point.

When the demand for land increases and the demand curve shifts to the right, a new equilibrium is established at E_1. Even though the rent is more at E_1, the quantity of land supplied remains unchanged.

□ Factors Affecting Rent

So far, we have assumed that all land is the same, but clearly this is not the case. In fact, land varies greatly in productivity due largely to differences in soil fertility, climate, location, and quality, quantity, and kind of mineral deposits or other natural resources on the land.

Thus, for example, the fertile soils of the Quebec lowlands are in greater demand and will command a higher rent than the less productive land of the Canadian Shield. Similarly, land located close to workers and potential customers in the centre of a Canadian city will command a higher rent than that in a more remote location.

Secondly, while the total supply of land is inelastic, the supply of land for a particular purpose is elastic because the various uses to which land can be put may be shifted. If the price of land begins to rise, for example, more land around a large city may be shifted from open space or agricultural purposes to industrial uses. The supply curve for industrial land thus slopes up to the right. Though the total supply of land is inelastic, the supply of land for a specific purpose is elastic and can be increased with an increase in price.

Figures 12.2 and 12.3 illustrate how factors, such as the varying quality of the land and the price of products grown on the land, can affect the rent. Just as with labour and wage rates, the competitive firm will rent land to the point where the marginal revenue product equals the marginal resource cost (or rent).

□ Economic Rent and Salaries

Economists also apply the concept of economic rent to factors of production other than land. "Rocket" Ismail may appear to have little in common with plots of land, but the theory of rent helps to explain his earnings as well. "Rocket" Ismail is the only person with his particular football talents. His services are a unique input with a fixed supply—just like land.

We can divide the "Rocket's" earnings into two parts. The first is the minimum payment necessary for the "Rocket" to play. In other words, we consider the opportunity cost of his playing professional football—what he could earn in the next most financially advantageous occupation. We'll assume the "Rocket" could earn $50 000 a year in his next most financially advantageous occupation.

The second part of the "Rocket's" earnings is the payment for his exceptional talent. This expenditure corresponds to the economic rent on the most fertile or advantageously located land. In 1991, "Rocket" Ismail

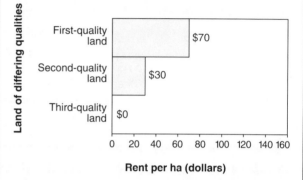

Figure 12.2 Rents for differing qualities of land with wheat at $4.00 per bushel

With wheat at $4.00 a bushel, the productivity of the third-quality land is so low that farmers cultivating it are just able to cover their costs of labour, seed, fertilizer, machinery, etc. The rent on this land, therefore, is nothing. The first-quality land is so fertile that after paying for all the other productive factors, $70 per ha is left over. Rent, therefore, is $70 per ha. Rent on the second-quality land is $40 per ha.

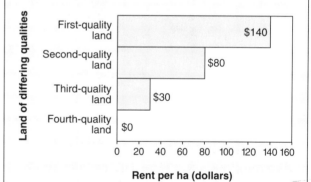

Figure 12.3 Rents of differing qualities of land with wheat at $6.00 per bushel

If the price of wheat rises to $6.00 per bushel due to an increase in population and thus demand, for example, some fourth-quality land is brought into production. Third-quality land, on which formerly no rent was paid, now yields $30 per ha. Similarly, the rent paid on second- and first-quality land increases to $80 and $140 per ha respectively.

signed a four-year contract with the Toronto Argonauts for $16 million. With a salary of $4 million a year and an opportunity cost of $50 000, the rent portion of his salary is $3 950 000. Superstars receive such high incomes because their employers judge their gate receipts will increase by more than the star's salary. Others with exceptional talents, such as film stars, also earn economic rent.

▋ Interest

Interest is the payment made to (or the income earned by) a lender for the use of money over a period of time. If you have ever deposited money in an interest-earning bank account, you loaned the bank money and, in return, you were paid interest for its use. Similarly, if you have ever borrowed money from a bank, you will have paid a price—interest—for the use of the money.

☐ Two Views of Interest

We can look at interest from two different points of view—that of the consumer who is considering the purchase of a good or service, and that of the business owner who is contemplating an investment in capital equipment.

Consumer's Perspective

Let's consider the consumer's perspective first. Suppose you have decided to buy a car. If you are like many Canadians, you will not have enough ready money to pay for it. So what will you do? You can wait, save, and then buy the car when you have enough money, or you can borrow the money and buy the car. In the latter case, you are willing to pay interest in return for the immediate use of the car. Many Canadians buy goods and services—such as airline flights, holiday tours, stoves, fridges, and homes—using borrowed money and paying interest on it.

Suppose you borrow $100 for the car today and you agree to pay $100 plus $15 a year until you pay off the loan. That $15 is the interest (cost or price) you pay for the use of the total amount borrowed (the principal).

Instead of being quoted as an amount—$15, in this case—interest is usually stated as a percentage per year because it is easier to make comparisons on the costs of loans using a standard percentage. The interest paid to depositors by banks, trust companies, and credit unions is also quoted as a percentage per year.

The interest rate—what consumers pay to borrow money—influences the amount they borrow. The higher the interest rate, the less they will borrow. The lower the interest rate, the more they will borrow.

Business Perspective

What about the business owner's point of view? Business owners also borrow money or financial capital. Business capital is of two types—**financial** (or money) **capital** and **real capital** (the tangible assets of the firm, such as buildings and machinery, etc.). Financial and real capital are closely related since the main purpose for raising money capital is to invest in real capital.

Let's assume that a business owner buys a machine for $100 000. For simplicity's sake, we'll assume that the machine is only useful for two years. In other words, it depreciates completely over two years. Depreciation, as we saw in Chapter 6, is the loss in value of capital equipment due to wear and obsolescence. Businesses must include the cost of depreciation in their assessment of a particular investment's profitability. One way is to deduct a constant amount each year, in this case half the amount the first year and half the second.

Suppose the machine is expected to generate enough sales to cover the costs of new materials, labour, etc., and still leave an additional $70 000 a year. The initial investment of $100 000 can then be paid off at the end of two years, leaving a return of $20 000 each year. Thus, the rate of return on the investment is 20 percent.

Just as the demand for labour depends on its productivity, so too does the demand for loans to invest in capital equipment depend on the expected rate of return from that equipment—that is, on the marginal efficiency of investment. The **marginal efficiency of investment (MEI)** is defined as the expected rate of return on marginal or additional investment.

We can envisage a range of investments with different rates of return starting at 20 percent. As the rate declines, the investment becomes less and less attractive. If we plot these investment opportunities in order, starting with the most profitable, we will have the marginal efficiency of investment curve shown in Figure 12.4. This is also the demand curve for investment loans, since demand rises or falls with the potential return on investment.

If the interest rate is at 10 percent, then Q dollars in loans will be invested. On investment opportunities to the left of Q—at A,B,C,D, etc.—firms can make a profit because the marginal efficiency of investment exceeds the rate of interest. Firms will be unwilling to invest in the opportunities to the right of Q—at T, for example—because the rate of return is less than the cost of borrowing money. Profit-maximizing firms, therefore, will invest to the point where the marginal efficiency of investment equals the interest rate.

Factors determining the demand for loans from businesses include the expected rate of return, the demand for the product the investment is used to produce, the price of substitute resources, and the firm's expectations for the future. Since investment in capital is long-term, the firm's view of future economic conditions will influence its investment decisions.

☐ Determination of Interest Rates

As you would expect, interest rates are determined by the supply and demand for funds.

Demand for Loans

As we have seen, the demand for loans comes from consumers and businesses. Governments also borrow money to finance particular projects—such as roads, school buildings, and sewers—and to finance budget deficits. The demand curve for loans is downward-sloping and price elastic. As the price of loans—the interest rate—falls, the demand for loans increases. At lower interest rates, investment opportunities for businesses will be more profitable. For consumers, cheaper loans in effect mean lower prices for goods they use the loans to buy—mainly "big-ticket" items such as automobiles and household appliances. Higher interest rates, on the other hand, mean a decreased demand for loans.

Supply of Loans

Householders, businesses, governments, banks, and financial institutions provide the supply of loans. How price elastic, or sensitive to changes in interest rates, is the supply of loans, however? This question is subject to debate. Some economists believe the supply is inelastic. Banks, as we will see in the next unit, however, can "create" money to loan to customers. In Chapter 19, we will see that the total supply of money in the economy is controlled by the Bank of Canada.

Interest rates—just like other prices in our eco-

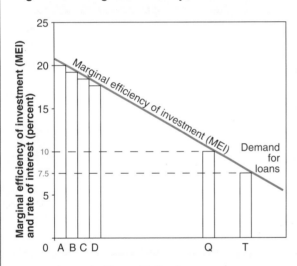

Figure 12.4 Marginal efficiency of investment

Amount of loans (dollars)

The investment opportunities are ranked from those giving the highest rate of return at A (20 percent) to those giving lower rates of return to the right, as at B, C, D, and so on. The resulting MEI curve is also the demand curve for loans. If the interest rate is 10 percent, businesses will demand Q loans—the point where the marginal efficiency of investment equals the interest rate. At points to the right of Q, such as T, the marginal efficiency of investment is below the interest rate. Businesses will not invest in these opportunities (unless the interest rate falls to 7.5 percent) because they would incur losses.

nomy—also have an important rationing function. Higher rates discourage some uses of capital, since capital will be used only in the most remunerative ways.

☐ Factors Influencing Interest Rates

So far, we have assumed that at any one time, there is only one interest rate. In fact, there are many different rates: the bank savings rate, the mortgage rate, and the rate charged on credit cards, to mention just three. What factors cause these differences in rates?

Time to Maturity of the Loan
In general, the shorter the period of the loan, the lower the interest rate. For example, one-year guaranteed investment certificates of banks or trust companies usually have lower rates than five-year certificates. Lenders prefer shorter time periods because they get their money back more quickly, and there is less chance that changes in economic conditions or the borrower's circumstances could affect the repayment of the loan. Long-term lenders are less able, for example, to adjust their interest rates up on a loan should economic conditions change.

Risk
The varying degrees of risk on loans affect the rate of interest. Clearly, the greater the risk of not being repaid, the higher the interest rate the lender will charge. Federal government five-year bonds will have a lower rate of interest (since the risk of defaulting on the loan is very low) than that of the Consolidated Moose Pasture Gold Corporation, which no one has ever heard of.

Size of the Loan
With two loans of the same duration and comparable risk, the larger is likely to have a lower interest rate. Since the administration costs of the two are likely to be approximately the same, the lender may be willing to accept a slightly lower rate on the larger loan.

Anticipated Rate of Inflation
Generally, the higher the anticipated rate of inflation, the higher the rate of interest lenders would expect to cover the possible losses in the money's purchasing power. For example, suppose you loaned a friend $100 for a year. If during that year prices rose by 5 percent, your $100 would buy 5 percent less in goods and services than a year earlier. You would, therefore, expect an interest rate 5 percent higher than if there were no inflation. The **real interest rate** is the marginal rate minus the general increase in prices (inflation). If the interest rate on your loan to your friend was 12 percent, the real rate would be 7 percent (12 - 5).

▊ Profits

We have examined wages, rent, and interest. Now we turn to examine the fourth category of income—profit. **Profit** is the return to the entrepreneur for his or her role in the production of goods and services after all other costs have been covered. In return for the risk of losing money, time, and effort, the entrepreneur receives a profit as payment. Profits are also a reward for innovation, either the introduction of new products or new ways of producing and distributing existing products.

Profits are calculated as the difference between total revenue and total costs. As we saw in Chapter 7, however, the economist's definition of profit differs from that of the accountant. In total costs, accountants include only *explicit costs*—that is, payments made by the firm to outsiders. Economists also include *implicit costs*—payments to those resources owned by the firm. These implicit costs include wages paid to the business owner, interest on any capital the owner may have invested in the firm, and rental costs on any land owned or used by the business. Economic profits are what remain after all opportunity costs—implicit as well as explicit—have been subtracted from total revenue.

The characteristics of entrepreneurs and the factors that can affect the level of profits for businesses have been covered in earlier chapters. They include the personal characteristics and hard work of the entrepreneur, the costs of productive inputs, the type of market structure in which the firm operates, the demand for the firm's product, and the general economic climate.

□ □ □ □ □ □

Economic Thinkers

David Ricardo (1772-1823)

David Ricardo was born in London into a Jewish family in 1772 and became a prominent figure in British politics and economic thought. In 1799, he began to study economics after reading Adam Smith's *Wealth of Nations*. He wrote a number of pamphlets on the economic issues of his day and in 1817 published his most important work—*The Principles of Political Economy and Taxation*.

Immense changes were taking place during Ricardo's lifetime. After being fairly stable for centuries, the population of Britain began to rise rapidly during the eighteenth century. It became increasingly difficult for the farms to feed the growing population. The situation was aggravated by the Revolutionary and Napoleonic wars with France between 1793 and 1815. During this period, the price of wheat (and thus also bread) rose sharply and many people faced starvation. At the same time, factories were developing rapidly in the cities, drawing an immense influx of workers from the countryside. Many workers in the cities lived in crowded, squalid tenements. All of these developments represent the context in which Ricardo formed his views.

One view of Ricardo: *With his earnest and brilliant expositions, which ignored the toss of events and concentrated on the basic structure of society "as if he had dropped from another planet," Ricardo became known as the man who educated Commons. Even his radicalism—he was a strong supporter of freedom of speech and assembly, and an opponent of Parliamentary corruption and Catholic persecution—did not detract from the veneration in which he was held.*

SOURCE: THE WORLDLY PHILOSOPHERS, Copyright © 1953, 1961, 1972, 1987 by Robert Heilbroner. © renewed 1981, 1989 by Robert L. Heilbroner. Reprinted by permission of Simon & Schuster.

Distribution of Income

For Ricardo, the principle or problem of economics was "to determine the laws which regulate distribution"—that is, how the domestic income is divided among rent, profit, interest, and wages.

Ricardo defined rent as "that portion of the produce of the earth which is paid to the landlord for the use of the original and indestructible powers of the soil." Suppose one landlord's fields are fertile and with ten workers and a fixed amount of machinery, she can grow 200 bushels of wheat. A neighbouring landowner's fields are less fertile, so that with the same amount of labour and equipment, he can produce only 100 bushels of wheat. Since both landowners will pay the same amount for labour and equipment (Ricardo assumes competition), the first landowner will be able to produce wheat at a much lower price.

Rent arises from the difference in this cost of production on the two different qualities of land, according to Ricardo.

If the price of grain is high enough to warrant the cultivation of the inferior soils, then the growing of grain on the more fertile land will be very profitable. Suppose wheat sells for $5.00 a bushel and costs $5.00 a bushel to produce on the poorer land and $2.50 a bushel to produce on the best land. Both landlords will sell the grain at the same price—$5.00 a bushel—but the owner of the better land will take as her rent the $2.50 difference in the costs of production on the two qualities of land. Rent, therefore, is determined by the cost of production on the land.

Wages

For Ricardo, there are two prices of labour—a market and a natural price. The natural price—which is the long-run wage—is just high enough for a couple to be able to raise two children. In other words, it is a subsistence wage. The market price or short-run wage is the price which is really paid for labour based on supply and demand. When the market price is above the natural price, the population will increase since the workers are better off and can afford larger families. But with the increasing population, poorer land will be brought into production and the price of food will rise.

Competition among the increasing numbers of workers will force down wages. Similarly, if the market wage is below the natural wage, the condition of workers is wretched and their numbers will be reduced. With the decrease in the supply of workers, wages rise.

Conflict Between Workers and Capitalists

As population increases, more and more land of poorer quality is brought into production. Grain prices, therefore, rise and along with them the rents of the landlords. Money wages also tend to rise to equal the increase in the price of food. Real wages, however, remain unchanged.

How are profits affected by the cultivation of the poorer soils? The share of the landlords increases in both real and money terms. The share of the workers cannot drop below the subsistence level for any long period of time. Therefore, the share of the capitalists must decline.

Ricardo's view of the future was gloomy. Only the landlords stood to gain. All that workers could look forward to was a subsistence wage in the long run. Wages above that level would inevitably result in more children, therefore more workers, more competition, and, of course, lower wages. The capitalists, despite efforts and savings, could only look forward to higher wages and lower profits. Meanwhile, all the landlords had to do was sit back and count their rising rents.

RICARDO IN HIS OWN WORDS

On Rent

Rent is that portion of the produce of the earth which is paid to the landlord for the use of the original and indestructible powers of the soil. It is often, however, confounded with the interest and profit of capital, and, in popular language, the term is applied to whatever is annually paid by a farmer to his landlord.

On the first settling of a country in which there is an abundance of rich and fertile land, a very small proportion of which is required to be cultivated for the support of the actual population, or indeed can be cultivated with the capital which the population can command, there will be no rent; for no one would pay for the use of land when there was an abundant quantity not yet appropriated, and, therefore, at the disposal of whosoever might choose to cultivate it.

On the common principles of supply and demand, no rent could be paid for such land, for the reason stated why nothing is given for the use of air and water or for any other of the gifts of nature which exist in boundless quantity. . . . If all land had the same properties, if it were unlimited in quantity and uniform in quality, no charge could be made for its use, unless where it possessed peculiar advantages of situation. It is only, then, because land is not unlimited in quantity and uniform in quality, and because, in the progress of population, land of an inferior quality, or less advantageously situated, is called into cultivation, that rent is ever paid for the use of it. When, in the progress of society, land of the second degree of fertility is taken into cultivation, rent immediately commences on that of the first quality, and the amount of that rent will depend on the difference in the quality of these two portions of land.

When land of the third quality is taken into cultivation, rent immediately commences on the second, and it is regulated as before by the difference in their productive powers. At the same time, the rent of the first quality will rise, for that must always be above the rent of the second by the difference between the produce which they yield with a given quantity of capital and labour. With every step in the progress of population, which shall oblige a country to have recourse to land of a worse quality to enable it to raise its supply of food, rent, on all the more fertile land, will rise.

1. In what ways is Ricardo's use of the term "rent' different from the common usage today?
2. In Ricardo's view, is the high price of agricultural products due to high rent or *vice versa* ? Explain.
3. How convincing is Ricardo's explanation of the development of rents? Explain.

On Wages

Labour, like all other things which are purchased and sold, and which may be increased or diminished in quantity, has its natural and its market price. The natural price of labour is that price which is necessary to enable the labourers, one with another, to subsist and to perpetuate their race, without either increase or diminution.

The power of the labourer to support himself, and the family which may be necessary to keep up the number of labourers, does not depend on the quantity of money which he may receive for wages, but on the quantity of food, necessaries, and conveniences that become essential to him from habit which that money will purchase. The natural price of labour, therefore, depends on the price of the food, necessaries, and conveniences required for the support of the labourer and his family. With a rise in the price of food and necessaries, the natural price of labour will rise; with the fall in their price, the natural price of labour will fall.

The market price of labour is the price which is really paid for it, from the natural operation of the proportion of the supply to the demand; labour is dear when it is scarce and cheap when it is plentiful. However much the market price of labour may deviate from its natural price, it has, like commodities, a tendency to conform to it.

It is when the market price of labour exceeds its natural price that the condition of the labourer is flourishing and happy, that he has it in his power to command a greater proportion of the necessaries and enjoyments of life, and therefore to rear a healthy and numerous family. When, however, by the encouragement which high wages give to the increase of population, the number of labourers is increased, wages again fall to their natural price, and indeed from a reaction sometimes fall below it.

When the market price of labour is below its natural price, the condition of the labourers is most wretched: then poverty deprives them of those comforts which custom renders absolute necessaries. It is only after their privations have reduced their number, or the demand for labour has increased, that the market price of labour will rise to its natural price, and that the labourer will have the moderate comforts which the natural rate of wages will afford.

Notwithstanding the tendency of wages to conform to their natural rate, their market rate may, in an improving society, for an indefinite period, be constantly above it; for no sooner may the impulse which an increased capital gives to a new demand for labour be obeyed, than another increase of capital may produce the same effect; and thus, if the increase of capital be gradual and constant, the demand for labour may give a continued stimulus to an increase of people.

SOURCE: Extracts from Ricardo's *The Principles of Political Economy and Taxation* reprinted from Marshall and Marshall, *The History of Economic Thought: A Book of Readings* (New York: Pitman, 1968), pp. 105, 106-7, 110, 116-117.

4. What is the "natural price" of labour?
5. Why might wages depart from the natural price?
6. What effects might the demand for labour have on the growth or decline of the population?
7. Have Ricardo's predictions about the future been fulfilled?
8. Many people see a close connection between the economic thought of David Ricardo and Karl Marx. Do you see a connection? Explain.

▮ Total Domestic Income

What share does each of the productive resources contribute to Canada's total national income, then? **Domestic income** is the sum of incomes earned from the total volume of goods and services produced in Canada in one year. Unfortunately, Statistics Canada does not collect data in a way that would show precisely how much of our domestic income comes from each factor of production. The categories shown in Figure 12.5 are the closest approximation, taken from the national accounts. The following are the main categories in the accounts.

(i) Wages and salaries   In addition to the sum of all wages and salaries earned by Canadians, this category includes any additional income, bonuses, or fringe benefits paid during the year. It is calculated as gross pay—that is, pay without deductions for taxes, union dues, etc. Military pay and allowances are also included. This category increased from 55 percent of total domestic income in 1926 to 60 percent in the 1930s and 1940s, and has remained fairly stable at around 70 percent since the 1950s.

(ii) Corporation profits   Total corporation profits are calculated *before* taxes are deducted. This category's share of total domestic income has varied from a high

of 14.8 percent in 1950 to a low of 8.7 percent in 1990. As we would expect, profits make up a smaller proportion of domestic income during depressions (1930s) and recessions (1990).

(iii) Interest and rent   This category is labelled as interest and miscellaneous investment income in the accounts. It includes the returns on investments earned by individuals as well as businesses. The proportion of domestic income constituted by interest and rent remained fairly constant at approximately 3 percent until the 1960s. Since then, it has increased proportionately and absolutely at a rapid rate to 11 percent in 1990. Much of this increase is due to the rising debt level of Canadians and their governments.

(iv) Income of self-employed persons   Included in this category are the incomes of farmers from farm production, of thousands of small unincorporated businesses, and of self-employed professionals—after expenses of operating the business have been deducted. Since the

1920s, the proportion of domestic income from this category has declined continuously from 29 percent in 1926 to 7.6 percent in 1990.

(v) Inventory valuation adjustment   As total inventories vary, the amount of domestic income varies. A year-to-year increase in inventories is counted as an increase in domestic income. A year-to-year decrease is counted as a decrease in domestic income. Inventory is included in corporation profits and is calculated in domestic income since it represents goods produced, though they have not been sold in that year.

Approximately half of self-employed (unincorporated business) incomes may also be included in the wages and salaries category. Thus, as much as 75 percent of Canada's domestic income is in the form of wages and salaries, while only 25 percent is rent, interest, and profit. This may be a surprising statistic, particularly as many people think most income in a "capitalist" economy derives from rent, interest, and profit.

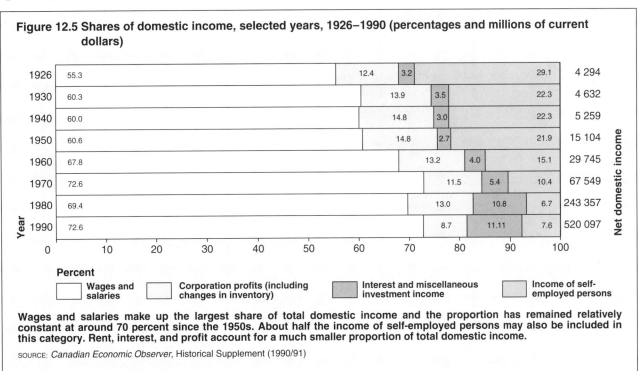

Figure 12.5 Shares of domestic income, selected years, 1926–1990 (percentages and millions of current dollars)

Year	Wages and salaries	Corporation profits (including changes in inventory)	Interest and miscellaneous investment income	Income of self-employed persons	Net domestic income
1926	55.3	12.4	3.2	29.1	4 294
1930	60.3	13.9	3.5	22.3	4 632
1940	60.0	14.8	3.0	22.3	5 259
1950	60.6	14.8	2.7	21.9	15 104
1960	67.8	13.2	4.0	15.1	29 745
1970	72.6	11.5	5.4	10.4	67 549
1980	69.4	13.0	10.8	6.7	243 357
1990	72.6	8.7	11.11	7.6	520 097

Wages and salaries make up the largest share of total domestic income and the proportion has remained relatively constant at around 70 percent since the 1950s. About half the income of self-employed persons may also be included in this category. Rent, interest, and profit account for a much smaller proportion of total domestic income.

SOURCE: *Canadian Economic Observer*, Historical Supplement (1990/91)

Summary

a. Rent, in the economic sense, is the payment made for (or the income earned from) the use of productive resources for which the supply is fixed and completely price inelastic. Land is the best example of such a resource. Rent (or the price for the use of land) is determined by supply and demand. The total supply of land is fixed and price inelastic. The supply of land for a particular purpose, however, is elastic and the supply curve slopes up to the right. The demand curve for land slopes down to the right. Rent is the equilibrium price at the point where the supply and demand curves intersect.

b. Factors affecting rent include the productivity of the land (based on fertility, climate, location, and quality, quantity, and type of natural resources on the land) and the purpose to which it is put.

c. Interest is the payment made to (or the income earned from) a lender for the use of money over a period of time. Interest rates are determined by supply and demand. Demand for loans comes from consumers, businesses, and governments. Consumers borrow money to enjoy the immediate use of goods and services. Business owners borrow money to invest in capital equipment. Their demand for loans depends on the marginal efficiency of investment (the expected return on the investment). Business owners will invest to the point where the marginal efficiency of investment equals the interest rate. The greater the expected return, the greater is the demand for loans. The supply of money for loans is controlled by the Bank of Canada.

d. Factors influencing interest rates include the time to maturity of the loan, the degree of risk involved, the size of the loan, and the anticipated rate of inflation.

e. Profit is the income received by entrepreneurs for their role in the production of goods and services after all costs have been covered. It is the difference between total revenue and total cost. Accountants calculate only explicit costs, while economists include implicit costs.

f. For David Ricardo, the rent of land is the result of differences in the costs of production on the land. Wages are of two types—the natural wage established over the long run (at the subsistence level) and the real wage determined by supply and demand over the short run. Over the long run as the population increases, rents will rise while wages will remain unchanged at subsistence levels and profits will fall. The capitalist's share of the national income, therefore, tends to decline and workers can look forward only to a subsistence wage. Only landlords gain through higher rents over the long run.

g. In Canada, wages and salaries account for almost 75 percent of total domestic income. Rent, interest, and profit make up a much smaller proportion.

▮ Review of Key Terms

Review the following key terms introduced in this chapter and provide examples where appropriate.

rent	marginal efficiency of investment
interest	profit
financial capital	domestic income
real capital	

▮ Application and Analysis

1. Why are rents in city centres usually much higher than those in the suburbs, even though the suburbs are usually growing at a faster rate?

2. Suppose that all the land around Regina is of equal fertility and that it is all used to grow wheat. If the cost of transporting the wheat varies directly with the distance it is transported to Regina—its only market—how would land rents vary in the agricultural area around the city?

3. Why do skyscrapers tend to concentrate in the centres of large cities?

4. Suppose the annual interest rate on a bank loan is 14 percent. Decide whether the interest rates in each of the following cases would be higher or lower and explain why.

(a) a 20-year Manitoba Hydro bond of $20 000

(b) a second mortgage of $10 000 on a residence

(c) a first mortgage of $100 000 on the same residence

(d) a loan of $100 from a local pawn shop

(e) the interest on the unpaid balance of a credit card

5. Suppose you are given the choice of one of each of the following pairs of assets. Given the conditions noted, which would you choose in each case?

(a) an investment that pays $1000 a year for life *or* $10 000 cash when there is no inflation and an interest rate of 2 percent per annum

(b) an investment that pays $2000 a year for life *or* an income of $5000 a year for six years when there is a high inflation rate of 10 percent per annum

(c) shares in a gold mining company that provides an income of $1000 a year *or* Guaranteed Investment Certificates that pay you $1000 in interest when there is an expectation of rising inflation

6. A machine that costs $100 000 is expected to provide a return of $20 000 a year for the next five years, at

which time it will be sold as scrap for $20 000. If the interest rate that the firm has to pay is 10 percent, should it purchase the machine? Explain your answer.

7. Tamil's barber shop employs five barbers and has five chairs. During the week, at the most only four barbers and four chairs are busy. On Saturday, however, all five barbers and chairs are usually occupied. Explain why the cost of providing a haircut on Saturday is greater than on any other day of the week.

8. Suppose the demand for snowmobiles produced by a Quebec manufacturer increases. Explain the effect on each of the following.

(a) the quantity of labour the firm employs in the short run and over the long run

(b) the amount of capital the firm employs in the short run and over the long run

(c) the price of the firm's stock

(d) the dividends paid to shareholders in the company

9. Suppose the increase in the demand for snowmobiles described in question 8 was only temporary and demand has now decreased. Explain the effect on each of the factors, (a) through (d), outlined in question 8.

10. Boeing Aircraft Corporation plans to build a super jumbo jet seating over 600 passengers. Suppose that when it comes into widespread use, it replaces the jumbo jets that seat only 350 passengers.

(a) What kinds of workers are likely to benefit from the new jet's introduction? Why?

(b) What kinds of workers are likely to suffer? Why?

CHAPTER THIRTEEN

The Role of Government

Objectives

a. Outline and assess the major ways in which governments influence the Canadian economy.

b. Examine the major economic functions of governments.

c. Demonstrate government's role in the economy using the circular flow model.

d. Investigate how and why government spending in Canada has increased substantially since Confederation.

e. Compare the level of Canadian government spending with that in other mixed market economies since 1970.

f. Investigate and assess the major components of federal, provincial, and local government spending.

g. Define a tax and distinguish among progressive, proportional, and regressive taxes with examples.

h. Identify and compare direct and indirect taxes.

i. Determine and evaluate the major sources of federal, provincial, and local government revenues, particularly from taxation.

j. Assess the equity, efficiency, and neutrality of the Canadian tax system.

In the previous two chapters, we defined the major components of our total domestic income—wages and salaries, rent, interest, and profits. In this chapter, we begin to examine just how this income is distributed and whether its distribution may be considered "equitable." Governments play a particularly important role in the goal of equitable income distribution. Indeed, in our mixed market economy, governments have a significant effect on many facets of our economic lives.

In this chapter, we briefly review the major functions of governments in our mixed market economy and then focus specifically on governments' role in the distribution of income. We examine the spending and taxing powers of governments—two powers that significantly affect who gets how much.

■ Government and the Market

In our mixed market economy, we expect governments to play a major role. Even a drive to the local supermarket in a foreign car, for example, includes the influences of all levels of government—federal, provincial, and municipal. Provincial traffic laws regulate how we drive and the province charges a licence fee for the car and the driver's permit. Along with the federal government, the province taxes the gasoline used to fuel the automobile. The imported car was also subject to federal trade regulations and customs duties when it entered the country. The taxes we pay to the municipal government are used for the local roads, traffic police, and parking regulations. Government, it seems, is part of even our most routine activities.

☐ Government Actions

Governments influence the market in four main ways: through their expenditures, taxes, regulations, and direction of crown corporations. All of these actions affect *what*, *how*, and *for whom* goods and services are produced.

Expenditures

As we have seen, government purchases of such goods and services as books for elementary schools or equipment for fire fighters influence what will be produced. The allocation of funds for such programs as industrial research affects how goods and services will be produced. Government funds for welfare payments and other social programs influence who receives goods and services.

Taxes

High tax rates on some goods may discourage their production and consumption (cigarettes), thus influencing what will be produced. Low tax rates and/or preferential tax treatment on the depreciation of machinery, may favour a particular form of capital equipment and, therefore, influence how goods and services will be produced. Through personal and corporation income taxes, governments influence who receives how much.

Regulations

Government regulations may prohibit production of some goods and services (narcotics) and promote others (education). Regulations of working conditions affect production methods. Controls on imports may protect jobs and incomes, thus influencing who receives how much.

Direction of Crown Corporations

Through crown corporations, governments provide some goods and services directly, such as rail passenger and telephone services. These corporations thus influence what, how, and for whom the goods and services are produced.

☐ Major Economic Functions of Government

What are the major economic functions of governments? We can sort the many activities of governments into four major functions:
(i) To establish the legal framework of society.
(ii) To encourage the efficient use of economic resources.
(iii) To stabilize the level of macroeconomic activity (that is, to work for the goals of stable prices, full employment, and economic growth).
(iv) To promote the equitable (or fair) distribution of income.

The Legal Framework of Society

Governments set the framework of laws within which economic activity takes place. Governments' function in this case reaches beyond the economy—regulating the many practices of life in human society, such as marriage, divorce, political rights, property ownership, and even traffic regulations. This legal framework established by government is based on the values of the society and on what its members believe to be just. A society in which private ownership of productive resources and the freedom to make profits are rights by law is different from one in which these rights are not instituted, for example. In Canada, governments provide the legal framework for our mixed market economic system.

Efficient Allocation of Resources

In Unit Two, we saw that the market system does not always provide the most efficient allocation of resources. The market allocation of resources may result in market failure. **Market failure** is an imperfection in the price system that results in an inefficient allocation of productive resources. Examples of market failures include public goods, merit goods, externalities, and the breakdown of perfect competition. Governments act to protect Canadians from the consequences of these failures.

(i) Public goods   A **public good** is a good or service that benefits the general public, no matter who pays for it. National defence is an example. Any attempt by one individual to strengthen the army by buying more sophisticated battle tanks will have little direct benefit for that individual. All other Canadians will benefit just as much. Entrepreneurs have little incentive to provide public goods and services since they can derive no direct benefit or return from them. These goods and services, therefore, must be funded collectively, with everyone paying a share. In other words, they must be provided by government. Left to itself, the market system would not provide them. Other examples of public goods and services include police and fire protection and our judicial system.

(ii) Merit goods   **Merit goods** are goods or services that governments consider to be particularly desirable and that they, therefore, support through subsidies and/or regulations. Education is an example of a merit good. Governments encourage education by providing the service at no charge in elementary and secondary schools and by the legal requirement that children attend school.

Similarly, governments may act to discourage the consumption of harmful goods. Governments limit the consumption of dangerous drugs—such as crack cocaine, for example—by making their use and sale illegal. Governments also discourage the consumption of cigarettes by requiring warnings on cigarette packages and by very high taxes.

(iii) Externalities   An **externality** is a beneficial or harmful side effect (or spillover) of production or consumption. Pollution of the air and water, for example, is a negative externality of some industrial production. The costs are borne by the people who depend on and enjoy the clean air and water. A well-kept garden, on the other hand, is a positive externality of gardening, providing pleasure to passers-by and increasing the value of neighbours' homes.

The costs of these externalities are not included in the price of the products, however. The polluters do not bear the costs of the pollution and the neighbours do not pay for the benefits of the well-kept garden. Since the market does not take externalities into account in the price of goods and services, governments may wish to promote positive externalities and discourage negative ones. Governments can intervene to discourage pollution, as we saw in Chapter 4, by passing laws to ban or limit emissions, taxing polluters, subsidizing anti-pollution equipment, or paying for research into anti-pollution methods. Similarly, governments can use their taxing, spending, legal, and regulatory powers to promote positive externalities.

The simple existence of an externality does not mean that government action is warranted, however. Some negative externalities may not be particularly harmful and, therefore, may not warrant government action. In other cases, the private benefits may be enough to encourage positive externalities without government intervention. It is, for example, not usually necessary for governments to encourage people to paint their houses or tend their gardens. The private benefits are usually sufficient to convince owners to do it themselves.

(iv) Breakdown of perfect competition   With the breakdown of competition, producers gain some control over price and may use this monopoly power to the detriment of consumers. In this case, federal and provincial governments act to control monopoly power in two ways. Where efficient production can be attained through competition, the federal government has enacted anti-monopoly legislation to protect and promote competition. Competition is seen as an effective regulator of business activities. Where efficient production cannot be attained through competition—such as in many utility industries, which have large

economies of scale—governments have established commissions to regulate prices and services, or have established crown corporations to provide the services.

Stabilization

Our mixed market economy is subject to periodic upswings and downturns. This instability carries with it the problems of increasing unemployment during recessions and rapidly rising prices or inflation during upswings. Government's role is to help smooth out these ups and downs—to promote stable prices, full employment, and real economic growth. We will examine this role of government more closely in the next two units, Units Four and Five.

Equitable Distribution of Income

We have also noted earlier that the market system does not necessarily provide for an equitable or fair distribution of income. Whether we are rich or poor may depend in large measure on our inheritance. It may

depend on how fortunate we were in owning a plot of well-located or mineral-rich land. Or, it may depend on our having the kinds of skills that just happen to command a high price in the market. Thus, governments have the task of defining what we mean by equity and then developing and implementing programs to ensure that income is distributed equitably. This role of government is our major focus in this chapter and the next.

Government and the Circular Flow

Before we go on to consider in more detail government's role in the distribution of income, let's examine how government fits into the circular flow model of the economy we have developed. As Figure 13.1 shows, government buys goods and services from businesses through the products markets. In return, businesses

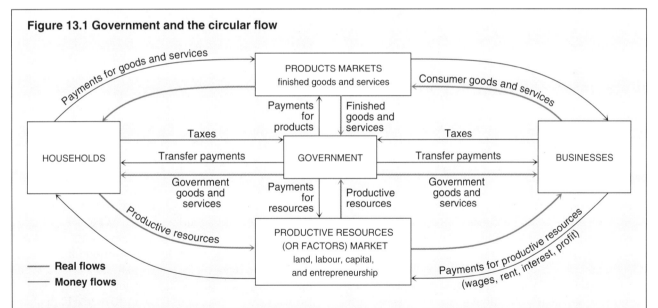

Figure 13.1 Government and the circular flow

Government purchases goods and services from businesses through the products markets and pays businesses in return. It also buys productive resources from households through the productive resources market in return for payments to households. The funds for these government expenditures come from taxes levied on businesses and households. The funds from these taxes are in turn used to provide businesses and households with government services and transfer payments.

receive a flow of payments from government. The real flow of goods and services going from businesses to government is thus matched by a money flow going in the opposite direction from government to businesses.

Governments also purchase productive resources from households through the productive resources or factors market. These productive resources include land, machines, buildings, and labour services, such as those of scientists and secretaries. Payments for these resources flow back from government through the productive resources market to households and represent part of the total income received by households.

Where does the money for these government expenditures on goods and services and productive resources come from? As the diagram shows, taxes levied on businesses and households provide government with the needed funds. Taxes are, therefore, used to buy goods, services, and productive resources from households and businesses and provide them in return with government services (such as roads, schools, and parks) and transfer payments (such as social welfare and unemployment benefits). Some taxes are also used to cover the administration costs of government and keep it functioning.

▮ Government Spending in Canada

Expenditures by all levels of government in Canada—federal, provincial, and local—have increased considerably since Confederation. Before World War I, total government expenditures amounted to approximately 1 percent of our Gross Domestic Product. These expenditures paid for the police and army, some public works (including railroad construction), and the salaries of legislators, public servants, and judges. As late as 1937, total government expenditures did not exceed $1 billion.

During World War II, total government expenditures reached nearly $6 billion—almost 50 percent of our GDP. This percentage fell to about 25 percent in the early 1950s, but since then has grown to almost 45 percent (in 1990). This growth was especially rapid in the two decades between 1965 and 1985. The federal government's expenditures alone increased from $14 million in 1867 to $306 million in 1926 and $159 billion in 1992 (estimated). This represents an increase of more than 11 000 times in 125 years.

What explains this dramatic growth in government spending? Some of the reasons are fairly obvious. Our population has increased more than two and a half times since 1926. With an increased population, we need more government services. Also since 1926, prices have risen more than eight times. In other words, it takes more than $8 today to buy what could be bought with $1 in 1926. We would expect, therefore, that the growth in government expenditures would at least match the increase in the general level of prices. Third, we have been involved in four wars in this century—two of them world wars—and payments for the pensions and debts incurred in these wars have continued to the present. After the major wars, expenditures did not go back to their pre-war levels.

Increases in population and prices and the involvement in war are not enough to explain the huge increase in the percentage of the GDP which is spent by government, and certainly would not explain the large increases since 1926, however. Since the last decade of the nineteenth century, Canadian governments have increased government services beyond the traditional limits of defence, civil protection, and public works. Canadians have also come to expect governments to do more. Consequently, municipal, provincial, and federal governments have begun to supply more health, welfare, and education services. These services include pensions, universal medicare, unemployment insurance, and heavily subsidized post-secondary education.

Figure 13.2 summarizes the growth in total Canadian government spending from 1926 to 1990. Figure 13.3 shows how Canada's increase in government spending compares with that of other nations. In most other mixed market economies like Canada's, the trend has been a general increase in government spending from about 30 percent of GDP in 1970 to a high of just over 40 percent by 1985. Expenditures have since tended to decline. Canadian government expenditures were close to the average of those nations shown in Figure 13.3 in 1979, but by 1989 they exceeded the average.

Figure 13.2 Total government expenditure as a percentage of GDP, 1926-1990

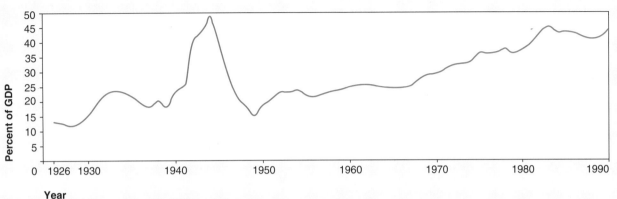

Year

Canadian government spending as a percentage of GDP showed a sharp increase during World War II and after the war did not fall to quite the pre-war levels. Since 1950, the general trend has been a steady increase in government spending with a few exceptions. In the late 1980s and early 1990s, government committed itself to curtailed spending.

SOURCE: Statistics Canada, *Canadian Economic Observer*, Historical Statistical Supplement 1990/91.

Figure 13.3 Comparisons of government spending as a percentage of GDP, selected nations, 1979 and 1989

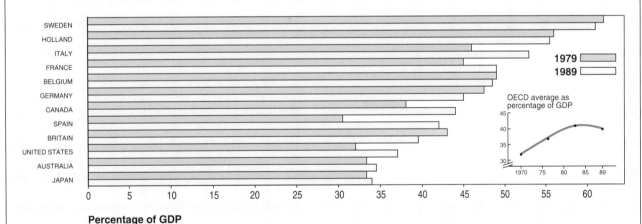

Percentage of GDP

Government spending as a percentage of GDP among mixed market economies in 1979 ranged from a high of approximately 62 percent in Sweden to a low of 30 percent in Spain. Canada was in the middle with expenditures at 38 percent of GDP. By 1989, the range had narrowed with Sweden still the leader at 61 percent and Japan with the lowest expenditure level at 33 percent. By 1989, Canada's government expenditures at 44 percent of GDP exceeded the average.

SOURCE: *The Economist*, March 2, 1991.

☐ Transfer Payments and Purchases

Total expenditures for all levels of government reached some $300 billion in 1990 (45 percent of GDP). The average amount Canadian governments spent per man, woman, and child thus totalled approximately $11 000. These expenditures were of two kinds—for goods and services and for transfer payments.

Expenditures for Goods and Services

Governments purchase a vast array of goods from pencils and tacks to computers, trucks, and tanks. Governments also buy the services of teachers, police officers, meteorologists, and many others. When governments buy computers or the services of meteorologists, they make direct use of the country's productive resources. These resources are not available for any other purpose.

Transfer Payments

Transfer payments are payments made by one level of government to another level of government, individual, or business, for which no good or service is provided in return. Family allowances, federal payments to provincial governments, Canada pension benefits, and unemployment insurance payments are examples.

Federal transfer payments, for example, involve a kind of recycling of money from the general Canadian taxpayer to the hands of needy families, the elderly, and the unemployed. These expenditures do not involve the federal government making direct use of Canadian productive resources. Instead the unemployed, for example, receive their payments from the federal government and decide how they wish to expend the benefits.

▐ How Government Spends

What goods and services do governments provide and which level of government provides what? In other words, how do governments spend or distribute their share of our domestic income?

The powers and responsibilities of the Canadian

federal and provincial governments are set out in the Constitution Act of 1867. By the terms of the Act, the federal government has responsibility for matters that affect the entire country, such as foreign relations, war, international trade and commerce, currency and coinage, and banking. Provincial governments have responsibility for matters of more local importance, such as education, public lands, hospitals, and local works. Both levels of government have responsibility for agriculture and immigration. The powers of municipal governments are determined by the provincial legislatures, but generally cover matters such as local roads, libraries, and building development within their borders.

☐ Federal Expenditures

The federal government is the largest business in Canada by far. It buys more goods, hires more workers, and handles more money than any other organization in the country.

Figure 13.4 shows the major components of federal government spending for selected years between 1981 and 1992. The four main categories of federal expenditures are transfers to persons, transfers to other levels of government, other program expenditures, and the payment of interest on the national debt.

Transfers to Persons

Federal transfers to persons include primarily payments to those over age 65 and unemployment insurance benefits. Also included are family allowances and veterans' benefits. Expenditures for those over 65 have increased steadily since 1981, reflecting the gradual aging of the Canadian population. Increases in benefits were also instituted to keep up with the rate of inflation (the general increase in prices).

Unemployment insurance expenditures, funded by premiums from workers and employers, have also increased significantly since 1981—from $4.5 to $17.2 billion in 1992 (est.). Two rapid increases in expenditures under the scheme between 1981 and 1984 and 1990 and 1992 were mainly the result of recessions and the consequent increases in unemployment.

Family allowances are transfer payments made to

Figure 13.4 Federal government expenditures, selected years, 1981-1992 (est.) (millions of dollars)

	1981	1984	1987	1990	1991	1992 (est.)	
Total	63 170	96 891	116 664	142 703	147 593	157 529	
PUBLIC DEBT	10 658	18 077	26 658	38 820	41 150	43 200	
OTHER PROGRAM EXPENDITURES: DEFENCE	5 063	7 843	9 993	11 452	11 870	12 694	
EXTERNAL AFFAIRS AND AID	1 722	2 638	3 157	3 784	3 585	3 866	
ALL OTHER ORGANIZATIONS	19 461	27 538	29 655	33 666	30 897	33 163	
TRANSFERS TO OTHER LEVELS OF GOVERNMENT	11 467	16 894	19 192	22 772	22 814	21 565	
TRANSFERS TO PERSONS: UNEMPLOYMENT INSURANCE	4 524	9 782	10 444	11 694	13 165	17 200	
OLD AGE SECURITY, GUARANTEED INCOME SUPPLEMENTS, SPOUSE'S ALLOWANCES	7 418	10 406	13 445	16 154	17 502	18 904	
OTHER (FAMILY ALLOWANCE AND VETERANS' BENEFITS)	2 857	3 713	4 120	4 361	4 280	4 461	

Total federal government expenditures more than doubled over the years 1981 to 1992 from $63 170 to $157 529 million. Expenditures on unemployment insurance benefits and the public debt far exceeded the average rate of increase over the period, while spending on family allowances and veterans' benefits grew at a much slower rate than average.

SOURCE: *Public Accounts of Canada* Vol. 1, 1990 and Ministry of Supply and Services, *Estimates: Part I The Government Expenditure Plans 1991-92.*

many Canadian families with children under the age of 18. Expenditures for this program have increased with the increase in population and, to some extent, inflation.

Transfers to Other Levels of Government
These transfer payments provide financial assistance to the provinces and territories for health care services and post-secondary education. Also included are payments to lower income provinces, so that they are able to provide comparable levels of services to their citizens, and the Canada Assistance Plan, by which the federal government shares the cost of the social assistance programs in each province. Since 1981, the amounts paid under the Canada Assistance Plan have tripled.

Total transfer and subsidy payments by the federal government have more than doubled since 1981. As a proportion of total federal expenditures, however, they have remained fairly constant at approximately 40 percent.

Other Program Expenditures
Expenditures on other programs include defence spending, external affairs and aid programs, and funding for other government organizations such as the judicial system and government departments.

The primary aim of defence spending is to deter the use of force against Canada and to defend the country effectively should deterrence fail. Almost half of the $12.7 billion (est.) budget in 1992 went toward salaries and benefits for the approximately 120 000 civilian and military personnel. With the end of the cold war, the government plans to make considerable cuts in total defence expenditures.

Expenditures on external affairs and aid programs are made to implement Canada's foreign policies and assist less developed nations. Since 1981, the spending in this category has almost doubled.

Also included in other program expenditures are expenditures to support an equitable judicial system, maintain law and order, support, facilitate, and co-

□ □ □ □ □ □

John Kenneth Galbraith on Social Balance

John Kenneth Galbraith was born in Iona Station, Ontario, but has spent most of his life in the United States working as a professor of economics and a public official. He has spent many years associated with Harvard University and served as an advisor to several US presidents including John F. Kennedy. Galbraith is also the author of several books, including *The Affluent Society* (1958), *The New Industrial State* (1967), *Economics and the Public Purpose* (1974), *The Age of Uncertainty* (1977), and *The Nature of Mass Poverty* (1979).

In his book, *The Affluent Society*, Galbraith argued that the emphasis on private-sector production had produced private affluence, but public squalor. While goods for private consumption (such as automobiles and televisions) were produced in abundance, those for public use (such as schools, parks, and police protection) were in short supply. Galbraith argued that the real need in society was for the production of public goods. Mass advertising and easy credit ensured the relative production of private goods.

In the following extract, taken from *The Affluent Society*, Galbraith outlines his theory of "social balance." As you read, decide whether you agree with him or not and consider the position you would take.

The line which divides our area of wealth from our area of poverty is roughly that which divides privately produced and marketed goods and services from publicly rendered services. Our wealth in the first is not only a startling contrast with the meagerness of the latter, but our wealth in privately produced goods is, to a marked degree, the cause of crisis in the supply of public services. For we have failed to see the importance, indeed the urgent need, of maintaining a balance between the two.

The disparity between our flow of private and public goods and services is no matter of subjective judgment. On the contrary, it is the source of the most extensive comment which only stops short of the direct contrast being made here. In the years following World War II, the papers of any major city—those of New York were an excellent example—told daily of the shortages and shortcomings in the elementary municipal and metropolitan services. The schools were old and overcrowded. The police force was under-strength and underpaid. The parks and playgrounds were insufficient. Streets and empty lots were filthy, and the sanitation staff was under-equipped. Access to the city by those who work there was uncertain and painful and becoming more so. Internal transportation was overcrowded, unhealthful, and dirty. So was the air. Parking on the streets had to be prohibited, and there was no space elsewhere. . . .

The discussion of the public poverty competed, on the whole successfully, with the stories of ever-increasing opulence in privately produced goods. The Gross National Product was rising. So were retail sales. So was personal income. Labor productivity had also advanced. The automobiles that could not be parked were being produced at an expanded rate. The children. . . disposed to increasingly imaginative forms of delinquency, were admirably equipped with television sets. We had difficulty finding storage space for the great surpluses of food despite a national disposition to obesity. Food was grown and packaged under private auspices. The care and refreshment of the mind, in contrast with the stomach, was principally in the public domain. Our colleges and universities were severely overcrowded and underprovided, and the same was true of the mental hospitals.

The contrast was and remains evident not alone to those who read. The family which takes its mauve and cerise, air-conditioned, power-steered, and power-braked automobile out for a tour passes through cities that are badly paved, made hideous by litter, blighted buildings, billboards, and posts for wires that should long since have been put underground. They pass on into a countryside that has been rendered largely invisible by commercial art. (The goods which the latter advertise have an absolute priority in our value system. Such aesthetic considerations as a view of the countryside accordingly come second. On such matters we are consistent.) They picnic on exquisitely packaged food from a portable icebox by a polluted stream and go on to spend the night at a park which is a menace to public health and morals. Just before dozing off on an air mattress, beneath a nylon tent, amid the stench of decaying refuse, they may reflect vaguely on the curious unevenness of their blessings. Is this, indeed, the American genius?

SOURCE: From THE AFFLUENT SOCIETY 4e by John Kenneth Galbraith. Copyright © 1958, 1969, 1976, 1984 by John Kenneth Galbraith. Reprinted by permission of Houghton Mifflin Co. All rights reserved.

Applications

1. What is Galbraith's theory of social balance?

2. Do you agree with his point of view? Outline why or why not.

3. If you agree there is an imbalance, how could it be alleviated? What costs and benefits would be involved?

---

ordinate the operation of government departments, promote economic development with regard for the environment, and promote the growth and development of Canadian cultural life.

Public Debt

Payments on the public debt are one of the fastest growing components of federal government expenditures. Between 1981 and 1992, payments on the debt quadrupled, making them the largest single element of government spending. Public debt charges are a function of the total debt outstanding and the rate of interest. We will return to examine Canada's public debt in more detail in a later chapter.

☐ Provincial and Territorial Expenditures

As we can see from Figure 13.5, total provincial and territorial expenditures in current dollars increased five-fold between 1975 and 1991—from $28.1 billion to $144.2 billion. Five components dominated expenditures in 1991: health, education, social services, debt charges, and transportation and communications.

Expenditures on health are composed mainly of spending on hospital care and other medical care. Most of the educational expenditures are to help local school boards pay for elementary and secondary education and to provide post-secondary education in universities and colleges. Provincial governments also help pay for a number of social services, such as welfare and daycare centres. The provision of provincial roads and bridges takes about 5 percent of the provincial budget. Debt charges have risen more than eight times from almost $2 billion in 1975 to about $18 billion in 1991.

With the exception of 1979, provincial and territorial governments have run a deficit since 1975.

☐ Local Government Expenditures

Between 1975 and 1990, local government expenditures increased almost four times, from $16 billion to $60 billion. Most local expenditures are in six areas—education, transportation and communications, environment, protection of persons and property, recreation and culture, and debt charges. Of the six areas, the lion's share of expenditures is for education—nearly 40 percent of the total in 1990. Figure 13.6 shows local government expenditures in selected years from 1975 to 1990.

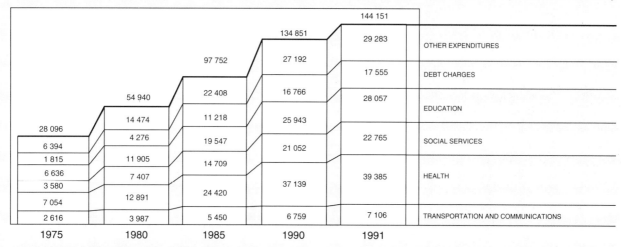

Figure 13.5 Provincial and territorial government expenditures, selected years, 1975-1991 (millions of dollars)

Since 1975, total provincial and territorial government expenditures have increased five-fold. Expenditures are principally in the areas of health, education, and social services.

SOURCE: Statistics Canada.

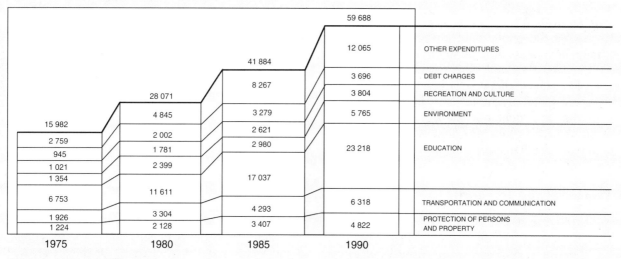

Figure 13.6 Local government expenditures, selected years, 1975-1990 (millions of dollars)

Between 1975 and 1990, local government expenditures increased almost four times. Most local expenditure—almost 40 percent in 1990—is for education.

SOURCE: Statistics Canada.

■ Taxation

So far, we have examined the spending functions of governments. Now we turn to how and where governments obtain the money to spend. Though governments do receive revenue from the sales of goods and services, from investments, by borrowing, and through gifts from citizens, by far the greatest amount of revenue is raised by taxation.

A **tax** is an obligatory payment made by an individual or corporation to government. Taxes are compulsory payments by law. We cannot choose to opt out of paying income taxes this year, for example, and the only way to avoid paying sales taxes is to buy only those goods that are not taxed.

We have a vast array of taxes in Canada. Taxes are imposed on what we earn, what we own, and on what we spend. Some taxes are highly visible, such as income tax and the Goods and Services Tax. Others are hidden, such as excise taxes.

□ Progressivity of Taxes

Taxes levied by governments influence the distribution of income in society. How taxes affect income depends on whether they are progressive, proportional, or regressive.

With a **progressive tax**, the tax rate progresses or increases as income increases. In other words, the more we earn, the more we pay both in total dollars and proportionately. Clearly, the principle behind the progressive tax is to take more from the wealthy and less from the poor. Canadian personal income taxes, for example, are progressive. The greater the taxable income, the greater the proportion paid in taxes. Table 13.1 shows how a progressive tax is levied.

With a **proportional tax**, the tax rate remains unchanged with changes in income. The tax takes a constant percentage no matter what the level of income. As shown in Table 13.1, the proportional tax rate remains at 10 percent, even though income increases. Some people support a single rate income tax, usually suggesting 20 percent. Thus, the same proportion would be deducted from income whether it

Table 13.1 The progressivity of taxes

INCOME	PROGRESSIVE		PROPORTIONAL		REGRESSIVE	
	RATE (PERCENT)	TAX	RATE (PERCENT)	TAX	RATE (PERCENT)	TAX
$1000	10	$ 100	10	$100	10	$100
$2000	15	$ 300	10	$200	9	$180
$3000	20	$ 600	10	$300	8	$240
$4000	25	$1000	10	$400	7	$280
$5000	30	$1500	10	$500	6	$300

With a progressive tax, as income increases the tax rate also increases—in this example, from 10 to 30 percent. With a proportional tax, the tax rate remains unchanged as income increases. With a regressive tax, the rate diminishes (here from 10 to 6 percent) as income increases.

was $20 000 or $200 000. The "one rate fits all" income tax would leave the market distribution of income unaffected.

With a **regressive tax**, the percentage paid in taxes regresses or declines as income increases. Provincial sales taxes, for example, are regressive. As income increases, the percentage paid in provincial sales taxes decreases since the wealthy tend to spend less of their incomes. Regressive taxes thus may increase income inequalities.

□ The Division of Taxing Powers

By the terms of the Constitution Act of 1867, the federal government was given the right to raise money "by any mode or system of taxation." Provincial governments, however, were restricted to *direct* taxation within the province. Municipalities, too, are restricted to *direct* taxes, since these governments have been established by provincial legislatures.

A **direct tax** is one that cannot be transferred or passed on to someone else. Income tax is an example. Everyone must pay the tax on his or her own income. It cannot be paid by anyone else.

An **indirect tax** is one that can be transferred or passed along to someone else. When a Japanese automobile company exports cars to Canada, it simply adds the tariffs—import taxes—to the price of the car and passes the tax along to the buyer, who finally pays it. Examples of indirect taxes are sales and excise taxes and import duties. By agreement with the federal government, the provinces are permitted to impose sales taxes.

☐ Federal Government Revenues

By far, taxes constitute the major source of government revenues. As we have seen, these revenues are then used to provide the services and programs we outlined earlier when we discussed government expenditures. But how much do the governments really take and from whom do they take it? How and where are the taxes levied?

Figure 13.7 shows the five main sources of federal revenue—personal income tax, corporation taxes, unemployment insurance contributions, the sales tax until 1991, and since 1991 the Goods and Services Tax (GST). Personal income taxes account for the largest proportion of federal revenues.

Personal Income Tax

Between 1981 and 1990, the relative proportion of income tax as a share of total federal revenue increased from 41 to 47 percent. This share is expected to increase still further to almost 50 percent by 1993. The tax is paid directly to the federal government.

The amount paid by any individual is arrived at after a series of rather complicated calculations. First, *total income* from all sources—wages, interest, dividends, and capital gains—is calculated. Some types of income, such as capital gains, may qualify for a full or partial tax exemption.

Second, a number of allowable deductions are subtracted from total income to calculate *taxable income*. Examples of allowable deductions include deductions for dependent children and expenses connected with employment (e.g., union dues).

Third, *taxes payable* are calculated from a schedule or table, a small part of which is shown in Table 13.2. If your taxable income in 1990 was $50 000, for example,

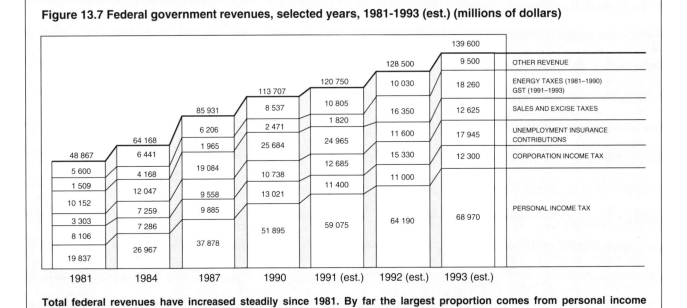

Figure 13.7 Federal government revenues, selected years, 1981-1993 (est.) (millions of dollars)

Total federal revenues have increased steadily since 1981. By far the largest proportion comes from personal income taxes.

SOURCE: Department of Finance, *The Budget, Feb. 26, 1991* and Government of Canada, *Public Accounts of Canada*, Vol. 1, 1990.

we can see using line 2 of Table 13.2 that your federal personal income tax would be:

$4807 + 26 percent of $50 000 – $28 275
= $4807 + 26 percent of $21 725
= $4807 + $5648.50
= $10 455.50

The **marginal tax rate** is the tax that would be paid on an additional dollar of income. In this case, with an income of $50 000, the marginal tax rate is 26 percent. For each additional dollar you earn, you will pay 26 cents in federal income tax.

In 1986, the federal personal income tax schedule contained many more steps than the present one. The marginal rate ranged from 6 to 34 percent. In 1987, the federal finance minister cut the number of tax rates to three, lowered the marginal tax rate for most Canadians, and reduced a number of deductions.

Table 13.2 Federal income tax rates, 1990

TAXABLE INCOME	TAX RATE
line 1 $28 275 or less	17 percent
line 2 $28 275 to $56 549	$4807 plus 26 percent on the next $28 275
line 3 $56 550 or more	$12 158 plus 29 percent on the remaining income

SOURCE: Revenue Canada Taxation.

Corporation Income Taxes

Corporation income taxes provide the second most significant proportion of federal revenues—11.5 percent in 1990. This percentage is down from the proportion in 1981 (16.5 percent), but higher than the 9.6 percent (est.) for 1993.

Corporate income tax is levied on the profits of corporations. In line with the changes in federal personal income tax in the late 1980s, the corporation tax rate was reduced from 50 to 28 percent and the base was broadened.

Unemployment Insurance Contributions

Unemployment insurance contributions totalled almost $11 billion in 1990 and were expected to increase sharply by 1993. Unemployment insurance contributions are made by both employers and employees. The term "insurance" is something of a misnomer since payments do not depend on the risk of unemployment associated with a job. With the same income, construction workers who run a high risk of unemployment and civil servants who have a low risk of unemployment contribute the same amount. Unemployment insurance is, therefore, a tax on income that increases as income increases, but only up to a certain point.

Sales and Excise Taxes

Excise taxes are those taxes levied on specific goods—such as tobacco, beer, gasoline, cosmetics, and liquor. **Sales taxes** are taxes levied as a general percentage on all or most goods sold. General sales taxes and excise taxes tend to be regressive. The poor spend a greater proportion of their income on these taxes than the rich. Sales and excise taxes, however, are relatively easy and convenient to collect.

Excise taxes on such "sin" products as tobacco, alcohol, and gasoline have increased substantially in recent years. Demand for these products is inelastic and high taxes will, therefore, not decrease demand or revenues significantly. Taxes on these products are, therefore, a safe and favoured method of increasing revenues.

Excise taxes and especially sales taxes will provide the government with substantial revenues in the 1990s. However, as we can see from Figure 13.7, revenues from these taxes are expected to fall dramatically in 1991-1992. Why? The reason is simple—the Federal Sales Tax was replaced by the Goods and Services Tax (GST).

The Goods and Services Tax (GST)

The GST replaced the Federal Sales Tax (FST) on January 1, 1991. As a part of the general plan to reform the tax system by lowering rates and broadening the tax base, the federal government proposed to scrap the FST and provincial sales taxes, replacing them with a uniform, nation-wide sales tax. But agreement could not be reached with the provinces. The GST, therefore, replaced only the FST.

Why was the GST imposed? Under the FST, the tax

□ □ □ □ □ □

How Does the GST Work?

Just how the GST works may be a puzzle to many of us. A basic illustration can help to sort out how the tax is levied. Let's consider the stages in the production and sale of a refrigerator. We assume that the mine, the source of the ore in the production process, has no taxable purchases. The GST is set at a uniform rate of 7 percent.

Step 1
The mine sells $100 of ore to the steel maker and charges $7 in GST. Thus, $7 is paid to the federal government in tax.

Step 2
The steel maker, in processing the ore, adds $200 to its value. In selling the $300 of steel, it charges the fridge maker $21 in GST. Since it has paid the mine $7 in tax already, it remits only $21 - $7 = $14 in tax to the federal government.

Step 3
By transforming the steel into a refrigerator, the fridge manufacturer adds $100 of value. The fridge maker then sells the fridge to the retailer for $400 and charges the

retailer $28 in GST. Since the fridge maker has already paid $21 in tax, it remits only $28 - $21 = $7 to the federal government.

Step 4
The fridge retailer puts a mark up of $200 on the fridge when it is sold to the customer. Thus, the price is $600 plus $42 in GST. The retailer deducts what he or she has already paid in tax ($28) and remits the difference ($14) to the federal government. Thus, the federal government receives $7 + $14 + $7 + $14 = $42 in GST, which is the same amount that the consumer pays the fridge retailer.

Figure 13.8 below summarizes the process.

Application
1. Suppose a mine sells ore to a steel manufacturer for $500, the steel manufacturer adds another $500 to the value in production, an auto maker adds $1000 to the value, and the car retailer adds a mark up of $1000. Calculate the GST that would be paid at each stage in the production process and the total finally remitted to the government.

Figure 13.8 How the GST is levied

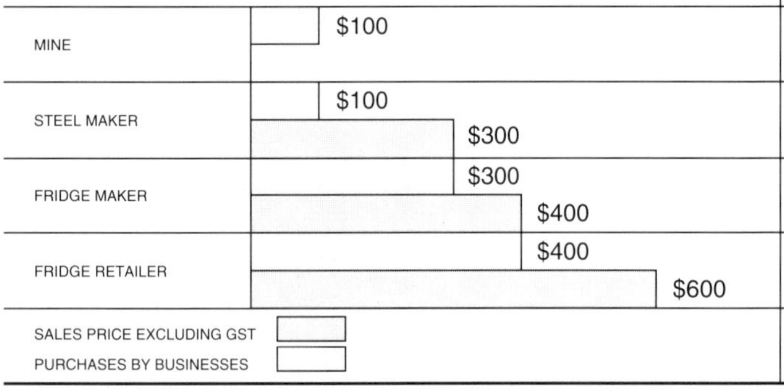

		TAX ON SELLING PRICE	−	TAX CREDIT ON INPUTS	=	NET TAX PAID
MINE	$100	$7	−	0	=	$7
STEEL MAKER	$100 / $300	$21	−	$7	=	$14
FRIDGE MAKER	$300 / $400	$28	−	$21	=	$7
FRIDGE RETAILER	$400 / $600	$42	−	$28	=	$14
SALES PRICE EXCLUDING GST				TOTAL GST TO FEDERAL GOVERNMENT		$42
PURCHASES BY BUSINESSES						

REMEMBER WHEN YOU WERE A KID AND YOUR MOM TOLD YOU THERE WERE NO MONSTERS HIDING UNDER YOUR BED?...

GOODS AND SERVICES TAX

CAM, The Leader-Post, Regina

base was very narrow. Many industries had managed to negotiate special provisions under the FST. The FST was also primarily a manufacturers' tax. Service industries were excluded. In addition, while Canadian export goods were taxed, imported goods were exempt. Thus, Canadian industry was at a competitive disadvantage.

The GST was designed to eliminate these problems. As the name suggests, the tax is levied on both goods *and services*. Since nearly all goods (except some basic food items) and services are taxed, the tax was to have the minimum distorting effects on the allocation of productive resources in the economy.

Under the GST, firms are taxed on the value of their output and allowed a tax credit equal to the tax paid by other firms providing them with inputs. As a product moves from primary producers through processors to wholesalers, the tax is collected. Goods that are produced in Canada for export are tax free, since no tax is levied at that stage and businesses can still claim a credit paid for the taxes on their inputs. Goods manufactured abroad and imported into Canada are subject to the full GST. Thus, Canada's competitiveness is enhanced by the tax. The GST is expected to generate some $18.3 billion in revenue by 1993—13 percent of total federal revenue.

When introduced, the GST was the subject of widespread criticism. Some of the criticism was no doubt due to its visibility—particularly as the FST, which it replaced, was largely invisible. Critics charged, too,

that the tax was regressive. The federal government tried to meet some of this criticism by providing offsetting payments to those with low incomes. Others charged that the GST was a massive "tax grab" by the federal government to allow it to continue its profligate spending activities.

Customs Duties

Customs duties or **tariffs** are taxes imposed on many imported goods by the federal government. A form of indirect taxation, tariffs may be imposed to raise revenues or to protect domestic industry. To the extent, however, that the tariff reduces Canadian purchases of imports, it also reduces government revenues. In 1990, customs duties accounted for about 4 percent of total federal government revenues.

Energy Taxes

Energy taxes are composed mainly of federal government excise taxes on gasoline. In 1990, total federal energy taxes yielded approximately $2.4 billion, or 2 percent of total federal revenues.

Non-Tax Revenue

Non-tax revenue is mainly derived from the earnings of federal crown corporations such as the Bank of Canada and the Canada Mortgage and Housing Corporation, from interest on investments, and from gains made on the purchase and sale of foreign currencies. Total non-tax revenue in 1990 stood at $8.5 billion, or 7.3 percent of total revenues.

☐ Growth in Federal Revenues

Total federal revenues increased substantially every year over the 1981-1990 period, with the exceptions of 1983 and 1984. In these two years, the growth in revenues from a number of taxes slowed or even—in the cases of corporation income taxes, sales taxes, and customs duties—turned negative. Though total revenues continued to grow, they were outstripped in every year by federal government expenditures, as shown in Table 13.3. As a result, the government ran a deficit every year and the total federal debt increased steadily. We shall return to this problem in a later chapter.

Table 13.3 Federal government revenues, expenditures, and deficit, 1981-1990 (millions of dollars)

1 FISCAL YEAR (END MAR. 31)	2 TOTAL REVENUES	3 TOTAL EXPENDITURES	4 BUDGETARY DEFICIT	5 DEFICIT AS PERCENTAGE OF GDP
1981	48 867	63 170	14 303	3.8
1982	60 001	74 873	14 872	4.0
1983	60 705	88 531	27 816	6.9
1984	64 168	96 891	32 723	7.3
1985	70 891	109 222	38 324	8.0
1986	76 833	111 237	34 404	6.8
1987	85 931	116 664	30 733	5.6
1988	97 452	125 535	28 083	4.7
1989	103 981	132 715	28 734	4.4
1990	113 707	142 703	28 966	4.4

SOURCE: Statistics Canada, Public Accounts 1989-90.

In every year between 1981 and 1990, federal government expenditures exceeded revenues, resulting in an annual budgetary deficit. This deficit increased steadily to the mid-1980s, but declined in total dollars and as a percentage of GDP in the late 1980s.

☐ Provincial Government Revenues

Since 1961, provincial revenues have increased rapidly from $3.5 billion in 1961 to $137.4 billion in 1990—30 times in less than 30 years. Figure 13.9 outlines the three major sources of provincial revenues—personal income taxes, indirect taxes, and transfer payments from the federal government.

Personal Income Taxes

Personal income taxes as a share of total provincial revenues have increased both absolutely and proportionately (to about 35 percent of the total in 1990), so that they are now the major source of provincial revenues. All provinces levy a personal income tax and, with the exception of Quebec, it is collected for them by the federal government. The tax is a percentage of the basic federal tax rate ranging from a low of around 43 percent to a high of 60 percent. Alberta, typically, has the lowest provincial tax rate and Newfoundland the highest. The Quebec government levies and collects its own personal income taxes.

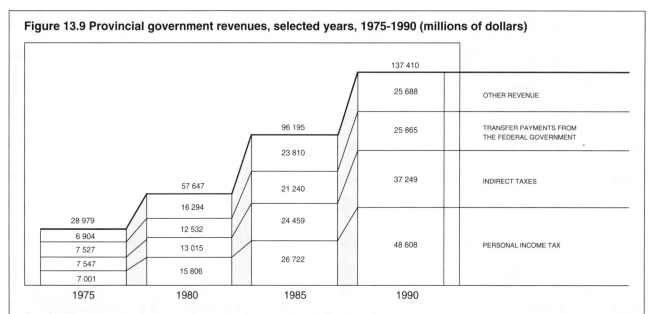

Figure 13.9 Provincial government revenues, selected years, 1975-1990 (millions of dollars)

137 410

25 688 — OTHER REVENUE

25 865 — TRANSFER PAYMENTS FROM THE FEDERAL GOVERNMENT

96 195

23 810

37 249 — INDIRECT TAXES

21 240

57 647

16 294

24 459

28 979

12 532

48 608 — PERSONAL INCOME TAX

6 904

13 015

7 527

26 722

7 547

15 806

7 001

1975   1980   1985   1990

Provincial government revenues have also increased steadily since 1975 with the largest share coming from personal income taxes and indirect taxes, such as sales and excise taxes.

SOURCE: Statistics Canada, *Canadian Economic Observer*, Historical Supplement 1990/91.

Indirect Taxes

Indirect taxes provide the provinces with their second most important source of tax revenue. All provinces, except Alberta, levy a retail sales tax. As a revenue source, this tax has become increasingly important as retail sales increased in the 1970s and 1980s and as the sales tax rates themselves increased. In addition, excise taxes are imposed on specific goods, such as tobacco, alcohol, and gasoline. Taxes are also imposed on the transfer of land and buildings.

Transfer Payments

Transfer payments from the federal government form the third most important source of provincial government revenues. **Equalization payments** are made by the federal government to the "have-not" provinces with a small tax base to ensure that they can "provide reasonably comparable levels of public services without resorting to high levels of taxation." Equalization payments are made with no strings attached. The provinces are not required to give anything in return. Provinces also receive federal grants to help defray the costs of provincial health schemes, post-secondary education, and public assistance programs.

Other Revenue

Other sources of provincial revenue include the corporate income tax, which is collected for most provinces by the federal government (the rate varies with the province); revenues from provincial investments; profits from provincial crown corporations (e.g., liquor boards); and returns from licences and permits.

☐ Local Government Revenue

Since 1961, local government revenue has increased markedly from $2.6 billion to $48.8 billion in 1990—an eighteen-fold increase. The two most important and almost equal components of local government revenue are indirect taxes and provincial transfer payments.

The only substantial source of local government tax revenues—accounting for some 90 percent of revenues from indirect taxes—is the property tax. Land and buildings are assessed for tax purposes at a particu-

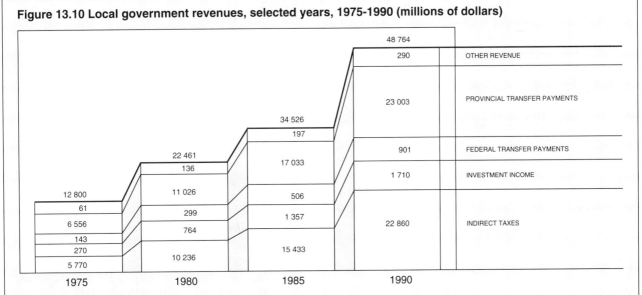

Figure 13.10 Local government revenues, selected years, 1975-1990 (millions of dollars)

Indirect taxes, particularly property taxes, and transfers from provincial governments are the major sources of local government revenues.

SOURCE: Statistics Canada, *Canadian Economic Observer*, Historical Supplement 1990/91.

lar value—say $20 000. The property tax rates are expressed in terms of mills (or thousands) per dollar value of the property. For example, if the rate is set at 65 mills (.065), then for every thousand dollars of assessment, the owner pays 0.065 × 1000 or $65 in property tax. With a property assessment of $20 000, the owner pays 0.065 × $20 000 = $1300 in local property taxes.

Two continuing problems are associated with the property tax. First, since assessments are an estimate, they are frequently challenged. Second, some property owners—pensioners, for example—may find it difficult to pay the tax.

Studies have shown that the proportion of income spent on housing tends to decline with income. Many economists believe, therefore, that the property tax is regressive with income.

Provincial transfer payments provide municipal governments with their other main source of revenue. As municipal government expenditures have been growing rapidly and their only substantial source of revenue is the property tax, transfer payments from the provincial governments have been substantial.

Other sources of local government revenues include transfers from the federal government and income from investments. Figure 13.10 summarizes the major sources of local government revenues.

■ Assessing Our Tax System

How can we assess our tax system, or to put it another way, what criteria can we use to compare one tax system with another? Economists use three criteria to evaluate a tax system—equity, efficiency, and neutrality.

□ Equity

Equity or fairness is easy to agree on in the abstract. We can all say that our taxation system should be just or equitable. The problem comes when we try to assess whether the system is equitable in practice. Two main criteria can be used to assess the equity of a tax system—the ability to pay and the benefits-received principle.

The Ability to Pay

Most people would agree that taxes should, in some way, be related to people's ability to pay. The question is how. Two approaches are horizontal equity and vertical equity.

Horizontal equity means that taxpayers with the same ability to pay should pay the same amount of taxes. The problem is determining what we mean by the same ability to pay. Do two households with the same income—one without children and the other with six—have the same ability to pay taxes? Or, do two individuals with the same income, but one paying substantial union dues and the other none, have the same ability to pay taxes? Our decision in both cases—and we could cite many more—is largely subjective. There are no objective criteria to determine the ability to pay taxes. Canadian governments, however, do take into account the number of dependents, union dues, and a host of other factors in determining the relative ability to pay taxes.

Vertical equity concerns fairness in taxation for people with different incomes. For example, how should the proportion paid in taxes differ for one person earning $1000 a month and another earning $10 000 a month? Again, there are no clear, across-the-board answers. Governments have attempted to achieve some degree of equity by taking into account the expenses of individuals and families and by instituting a progressive personal income tax system designed to take more from high-income earners than low-income earners.

Benefits-Received Principle

The **benefits-received principle** is based on the concept that taxes should be paid in proportion to the benefits received. For example, air travellers pay an excise tax on tickets to help pay for airport security. Taxes on gasoline are paid by those who use the roads and these taxes are used to help pay for road construction and maintenance. Thus, users pay for the benefits they receive.

The "user-pay" principle looks attractive at first

□ □ □ □ □ □

Assessing the GST

Is the GST an equitable tax? Is it efficient and neutral? Should it be reformed? As you read the following article, keep these questions in mind. Consider whether you agree or disagree with the writer's point of view.

GST Should Be Exemption-Free

Don Mazankowski, as the minister of finance, should change the GST to allow no exemptions, not even for basic groceries.

The four criteria economists use in evaluating a tax are efficiency, administration costs, compliance costs, and equity. On each of these grounds, exempting food—or any other item—from the GST constitutes bad policy.

A tax is efficient if it does not lead people to produce or consume one product rather than another simply for a tax advantage. Exempting some items from the tax changes relative prices and, therefore, leads to inefficient patterns of production and consumption.

Though economists rarely downplay the importance of economic efficiency, it seems unlikely that exempting food from the GST leads to a significant reallocation of consumption from other goods to food. After all, people can only eat so much. The argument against exempting food is, therefore, based on the other three criteria.

Exempting food means large administration costs because a distinction is made between non-taxable "basic groceries" and taxable "snack food." In the average grocery store, there are thousands of items and each one must ultimately receive one of these two labels. Such labelling is costly and arbitrary.

Salted peanuts, for example, are snack food, but unsalted ones are basic groceries. A single muffin is a snack, but a package of six is basic groceries. How much salt is required for peanuts to be considered snacks? Why is the crucial number of muffins six, rather than four or 14?

How many civil servants occupy their time with this arbitrary list of taxable and nontaxable foodstuffs? One per item? One per six-pack? Who knows? But any number is a waste of resources.

A second administrative problem is that GST exemptions give individuals the incentive to evade the tax. I don't know if there is truth to the story of the Ottawa dry-cleaner who no longer sells cleaning services but, instead, sells expensive GST-free potatoes and throws dry-cleaning in for free. I don't even know whether such a scheme would be legal, but legality is beside the point. Exemptions to the GST encourage a waste of resources as individuals try to evade it. Furthermore, creative schemes for GST evasion are sure to be followed by a barrage of tax amendments to fill the GST loopholes. More waste.

Exemptions also hike the compliance cost of GST. We have all heard reports of shopkeepers complaining about the complications of calculating the amount of GST to remit to the government. With an ideal GST, which applies to all newly produced goods and services at the same rate, the computation is simple—apply the tax to the difference between sales revenue and non-labour costs.

The numbers for sales revenue and non-labour costs are figures that a firm must, in any event, compute for income tax purposes and for annual reports to shareholders. Thus, with an exemption-free GST, the calculations would, indeed, be trivial. In New Zealand, where an exemption-free GST was introduced in September 1986, accountants have been loudest in favour of the GST.

Things get very messy in a world of GST exemptions, since both revenues and non-labour costs include transactions of some goods which are GST-free and other goods on which the GST is paid. A firm must, therefore, arrive at measures of revenues and non-labour costs that exclude all GST-free items. For a firm which produces several goods from a large number of inputs, even a small number of GST exemptions can make the accountant's job a nightmare.

This is why the GST should be changed to apply to all newly produced goods and services at the same rate, with no exemptions. We would be better off if the dry-cleaner could devote his considerable skills to dry-cleaning rather than tax avoidance, and if the government did not have to match wits with the private sector by filling tax loopholes.

We would be better off if the civil servants now measuring salt content in peanuts were doing something constructive, and if completing a tax form were not an obstacle to running a business.

The alleged benefit of exempting basic groceries is that it makes the tax system more equitable. Since low-income families spend a larger share of their income on food than do high-income families, applying the GST to food appears to impose a heavier burden on the poor than on the rich. This benefit is illusory, however, because it ignores the extra tax revenue that must be raised to offset the tax revenue lost by exempting food.

By applying the GST to all food items, we can make low-income families better off. This is because high-income families spend more on food—in absolute number of dollars—than low-income families. The government should, therefore, broaden the scope of the GST to include food and return the resulting increase in tax revenue equally to all individuals, independent of their income. Since the rich spend more on food than the poor, the poor would be better off as they would receive a payment in excess of their GST payments on groceries.

This would make the GST more progressive, as well as eliminating the significant resource costs discussed above. And it would be simple because the structure is already in place—the existing GST tax credit.

Mazankowski should take a bold first step as the minister of finance. By changing the GST to be exemption-free, he would send a signal to Canada that the finance portfolio is still in capable hands. But if the government continues to ignore the logic of making the GST exemption-free, Canada will have a costly and arbitrary tax. We will all suffer.

SOURCE: Christopher Ragan, "Now's the time to put GST on groceries," *The Financial Post*, May 22, 1991.

Applications

1. Summarize the arguments in favour of imposing the GST on groceries.

2. If the arguments are so strong, why do you think the federal government exempted some groceries?

3. Should the GST be imposed on all food items? Explain your point of view.

4. In terms of the criteria we have discussed for assessing taxes—ability to pay, benefits-received principle, efficiency, and neutrality principle—do you think the GST, as it now stands, is an effective and equitable tax? Explain your position.

glance. After all, why shouldn't those who enjoy a service provided by government pay for it? However, it does have some serious drawbacks. As we have seen, the largest expenditures of the federal government are for social programs—for the elderly, unemployed, and poor—and those who benefit from these programs are in no way able to pay for them. They receive these payments precisely because they are unable to pay. It is also difficult to determine, for many programs, how much each person benefits. For example, by exactly how much does each Canadian benefit from Canadian defence or police expenditures?

□ Efficiency

How efficiently are the taxes collected? Is the tax system viewed as just, so that people do not expend time and energy attempting to evade taxes? Does the system provide government with a predictable income, so that tax rates need not continually be changed? Are the taxes economical, in the sense that the costs of collection are low? Are the taxes relatively simple to understand, so that most people can comprehend how they are levied? Are the taxes as convenient as possible for the taxpayer to pay? Each one of these questions must be addressed to determine the efficiency of a tax system.

□ The Neutrality Principle

The **neutrality principle** affirms that taxes should have a neutral effect on the operation of the market system and on individual decision making. Thus, for example, taxes on income should not dissuade people from working or investing. Corporation taxes should not discourage new enterprises, investment, or expansion. While it is probable that no tax is perfectly neutral, the relative neutrality of taxes should be compared and the most neutral—other things being equal—should be adopted according to the neutrality principle.

We should note, however, that some taxes are intended to be non-neutral. A tax on cigarettes is specifically intended, for example, to dissuade people from smoking. A tax on pollution is levied specifically to discourage pollution. In these cases, the greater the impact on these economic activities, the more effective the tax. While these principles help us assess our tax system and individual taxes, they do not identify the ideal tax or tax system. In taxation, as in many other areas, the Canadian system is a compromise among principles.

Summary

a. Governments influence the operation of the market through their expenditures, taxes, regulations, and direction of crown corporations.

b. The major economic functions of government are to establish the legal framework of society; encourage the efficient use of economic resources; stabilize the level of macroeconomic activity by promoting stable prices, full employment, and economic growth; and promote the equitable distribution of income.

c. Government's role in the economy—as a recipient of productive factors from households and of goods and services from businesses, as a collector of tax payments from both households and businesses, and as a disburser of these payments—can be included in the circular flow model.

d. Since Confederation, government expenditures have increased substantially, reaching almost 45 percent of GDP in 1990. Reasons for this growth in expenditures include the increase in population, higher prices, and the involvement in past wars. More significant, however, is that Canadians have come to expect more of government for health, education, and welfare.

e. The general trend in government spending as a proportion of GDP in mixed market, developed economies has been for expenditures to grow during the 1970s and early 1980s, and to decline since 1986. Canadian government expenditures, however, have risen above the average since 1986.

f. The four main categories of federal government spending are transfers to persons (mainly benefits for those over age 65 and unemployment insurance payments), transfers to provincial governments, public debt charges, and other program expenditures including defence, external affairs, and foreign aid.

The main categories of provincial government expenditures include health care, education, social services, debt charges, and transportation and communications. Local government expenditures are primarily for education, transportation and communications, environment, protection of people and property, recreation and culture, and debt charges.

g. A tax is an obligatory payment made by an individual or corporation to government. Depending on how taxes relate to income, they may be classified as progressive, proportional, or regressive.

h. Taxes that cannot be transferred to others (such as personal income taxes) are called direct taxes. Those that can be transferred (such as import duties) are called indirect taxes. By the terms of the Constitution Act of 1867, the federal government may levy both direct and indirect taxes, but provincial governments may levy only indirect taxes. By agreement with the federal government, provincial governments are permitted to levy sales taxes, however.

i. The federal government's five main sources of revenue are personal income taxes, corporation taxes, unemployment insurance contributions, the Federal Sales Tax up to 1991, and the Goods and Services Tax since 1991.

Provincial government revenues come from three main sources: personal income taxes, indirect taxes, and transfer payments from the federal government. Local government revenues mainly come (almost equally) from two sources—local property taxes and provincial government transfers.

j. Three concepts useful in assessing a tax system are equity (vertical and horizontal), efficiency, and neutrality.

■ Review of Key Terms

Define the following key terms introduced in this chapter and provide examples where appropriate.

market failure
public goods
merit goods
externality
transfer payments
tax
progressive tax
proportional tax
regressive tax
direct tax

indirect tax
marginal tax rate
excise tax
sales tax
customs duty or tariff
equalization payment
horizontal equity
vertical equity
benefits-received principle
neutrality principle

■ Application and Analysis

1. From the following list of goods and services, decide which in your view can best be provided by government (G), private initiative (P), or either—no clear preference (N). Explain your decision in each case.

(a) telephone services
(b) electrical power
(c) groceries
(d) postal services
(e) local transit services
(f) radio services
(g) national defence
(h) police protection
(i) garbage collection
(j) rail transport
(k) television services

2. Which of the following taxes are regressive and which are progressive? Explain why in each case.

(a) tax on beer
(b) local property tax
(c) provincial income tax
(d) provincial sales tax
(e) federal income tax

3. In Canada, each person is entitled to a $100 000 lifetime exemption from capital gains tax. In addition, capital gains income is taxed at three-quarters the rate of employment income. What effect do these two measures probably have on the distribution of income in Canada?

4. (a) Which of the two principles of taxation do you feel is most just—the ability to pay or the benefits-received principle? Why?

(b) Which one do you believe is the easier to implement? Explain.

5. (a) Referring to Table 13.4 below and Table 13.2 on page 271 of this chapter, calculate how much federal income tax you would pay under the 1986 and the 1990 rates if you have a taxable income of:

(i) $25 000   (ii) $60 000.

(b) What are the differences in the amounts paid? Do you think the tax reforms after 1986 were just? Explain.

Table 13.4 Federal income tax rates, 1986

TAXABLE INCOME (DOLLARS)	TAX
1 305 or less	6 percent
1 305	$78 + 16 percent on next $1 306
2 611	287 + 17 percent on next 2 610
5 211	731 + 18 percent on next 2 611
7 832	1 201 + 19 percent on next 5 222
13 054	2 193 + 20 percent on next 5 221
18 275	3 237 + 23 percent on next 5 211
23 496	4 438 + 25 percent on next 13 054
36 550	7 702 + 30 percent on next 26 107
62 657	15 534 + 34 percent on remainder

6. (a) For each of the following examples, determine whether the tax is progressive, regressive, or proportional.

(i) Person 1 earns $100 000 and pays $10 000 in taxes.
Person 2 earns $80 000 and pays $9000 in taxes.
Person 3 earns $20 000 and pays $3000 in taxes.

(ii) Person 1 earns $100 000 and pays $10 000 in taxes.
Person 2 earns $80 000 and pays $8000 in taxes.
Person 3 earns $20 000 and pays $2000 in taxes.

(iii) Person 1 earns $100 000 and pays $30 000 in taxes.
Person 2 earns $80 000 and pays $16 000 in taxes.
Person 3 earns $20 000 and pays $2000 in taxes.

(b) Which type of tax—progressive, proportional, or regressive—do you think is fairest? Why?

7. Some economists have proposed that instead of implementing the GST, the federal government should collect no sales and excise taxes and leave these sources of revenue to the provinces. In return, the provinces should collect no income and corporation taxes, leaving these areas exclusively to the federal government. Outline the arguments for and against this proposal. Where do you stand?

8. Some people have argued that since the provincial and local governments are closer to the people, they should assume more of the powers the federal government now holds. What do you think? List the functions of government that you think can best be performed by the federal government. Explain how you reached your decisions.

9. Consider the following two views of our tax system.

View A Government promotes savings and investments by Canadians by providing the $100 000 lifetime exemption from capital gains income tax, and taxing dividend and other capital gains income at lower rates than employment income. Government also promotes health care research and the arts by allowing tax deductions for contributions. Government encourages home ownership by not taxing capital gains on the sale of one's home. Since these deductions support generally desirable social and economic programs, they do not constitute tax loopholes.

View B The Canadian federal income tax system is a confused hodge podge. The rich get tax breaks on their capital gains and dividend incomes. So, in theory, do the poor—but not in practice. The rich get tax breaks for their contributions to charity and research. Homeowners get tax breaks on their homes. Renters do not. The only way to clear up this mess of exemptions and inequities is to eliminate all deductions and count every dollar of income as being the same. In this way, we will have a fair tax system.

Which point of view (if either) do you feel is right? Explain your position.

10. Does government cost too much? Use the data in this chapter to analyse whether you think government expenditures are excessive. Explain your position.

11. Debate the following: "Resolved that the government which governs least, governs best."

12. Budget Report
Each year, federal and provincial finance ministers present budgets detailing their revenues and expenditures over the past year and their plans for the coming year. For the most recently tabled or to be tabled budget in your area, read the reports in your local newspaper(s) and in magazines such as *Maclean's*, *Saturday Night*, *Canadian Business*, and *Report on Business*. Prepare a written or oral report on the budget, including the following topics:

(a) main revenue sources and amounts

(b) projected future revenues

(c) main expenditures and amounts

(d) projected future expenditures

(e) the budget proposals and the government's explanation for why they have been adopted

(f) assessments of the budget from critics and proponents

(g) your assessment of the budget.

Use graphs, charts, and cartoons to illustrate the report.

13. Analyze the following cartoon. What does it suggest?

ULUSCHAK, Miller Features Syndicate

CHAPTER FOURTEEN

Distribution of Income

How much income inequality exists in Canada and what should be done about it? What is the role of government in income redistribution? Some assert that greater equality of income means increased social harmony and political stability. Others argue that further government attempts to redistribute income may be self-defeating or harmful. Policies to increase taxes on the better-off and distribute the proceeds through government programs to the less well-off are likely to lower incentives of both groups to earn additional income.

How, then, are we to approach the question of economic equity? In this chapter, we examine how much income inequality exists in Canada, why it exists, and the effects of government programs instituted to deal with it.

Objectives

a. Examine recent trends in the distribution of income in Canada.

b. Calculate and use appropriately the mean, median, and mode.

c. Construct and interpret a Lorenz curve to assess the degree of income inequality in Canada and other nations.

d. Examine the reasons for income inequality.

e. Consider the definition of poverty and factors determining the poverty line.

f. Examine the incidence of poverty in Canada.

g. Outline and assess Canadian programs designed to deal with the problem of poverty.

h. Evaluate the effects of transfer payments and taxes on income disparity in Canada.

i. Assess the effectiveness of Canadian welfare programs.

Income Inequality

Canadians receive one of the highest average incomes in the world. In 1990, average GDP per person in Canada was $25 500—comparable to that in the United States and Japan and higher than that in Italy ($22 500), France ($24 200), and the United Kingdom ($19 200). On the average, there is no doubt that Canadians are generally well off.

These average figures, however, hide considerable income inequalities within the country. Most Canadians are aware that some individuals—such as the stars of the sports, entertainment, and business worlds—earn incomes of hundreds of thousands (or even millions) of dollars a year. Raghib "Rocket" Ismail, for example, made headlines when he was signed by the Toronto Argonauts in 1991 for $16 million over four years. Dave Stieb of the Toronto Blue Jays earned an average of $3.25 million per year between 1991 and 1993. Helen Kelesi, ranked twenty-fifth in the world by the Women's Tennis Association in 1990, earned $168 000 in that year.

Not surprisingly, then, the average salaries of professional athletes, particulary baseball and football players, are high. According to the Players' Association, the average salary of the Toronto Blue Jays in 1990 was US $686 326 and that of the Montreal Expos in the same year was US $580 181. Similarly, the average total pay of chief executives in control of large Canadian corporations (those with sales over $300 million) in 1990 was $454 000. The chairman and chief executive officer of Northern Telecom, for example, earned over $2 million in 1990. But each year we also hear of those at the other end of the income scale who are forced to rely on welfare and food banks for necessities. Many others live on a minimum wage in the range of $5 an hour. That there is a considerable degree of income inequality in Canada is undeniable.

Table 14.1 provides some indication of the degree of income inequality. The statistics show that 2.4 percent of Canadian families had incomes less than $10 000 in 1989 and 11.9 percent had incomes between $10 000 and $19 999. At the other end of the scale, a total of 29.1 percent had incomes of over $60 000.

Table 14.1 Percentage distribution of family income groups, 1979-1989 (1989 dollars)

	1979	1980	1981	1982	1983	1984	1985	1986	1987	1988	1989
Under $10 000	4.2	3.4	3.4	3.6	3.9	4.1	3.4	3.1	3.1	2.7	2.4
$10 000 – $19 999	12.4	12.1	12.1	13.3	14.4	14.4	13.7	13.4	12.8	12.3	11.9
20 000 – 29 999	13.2	12.7	13.9	14.5	15.0	14.6	15.0	14.7	14.8	14.4	13.4
30 000 – 39 999	16.2	15.2	16.0	17.1	17.0	16.1	15.8	15.6	15.6	15.8	15.4
40 000 – 49 999	16.5	17.1	16.2	15.5	15.0	15.9	15.3	15.3	15.1	14.1	15.2
50 000 – 59 999	13.1	13.6	13.5	12.3	11.7	12.0	12.2	12.4	12.3	13.1	12.6
60 000 – 74 999	12.3	12.9	12.1	11.5	11.5	11.3	12.0	12.3	12.0	12.5	13.0
75 000 and over	12.1	13.0	12.8	12.2	11.5	11.6	12.5	13.2	14.3	14.9	16.1
Total	100.0	100.0	100.0	100.0	100.0	100.0	100.0	100.0	100.0	100.0	100.0
Average (mean) income	46 104	47 575	46 769	45 617	44 915	44 923	46 036	47 033	47 642	48 498	50 083
Median income	42 362	43 774	42 757	41 034	39 850	40 455	41 201	42 049	42 445	43 241	44 460

SOURCE: Statistics Canada, *Income Distribution by Size in Canada*.

In 1979, 4.2 percent of Canadian families had incomes less than $10 000. By 1989, only 2.4 percent had incomes less than $10 000. At the other end of the scale, the percentage of families with incomes over $75 000 increased by a third, from 12.1 in 1979 to 16.1 in 1989. The percentages of families earning between $10 000 and $74 999 remained roughly unchanged.

Table 14.2 Percentage distribution by income groups of unattached individuals, 1979-1989 (1989 dollars)

	1979	1980	1981	1982	1983	1984	1985	1986	1987	1988	1989
Under $5000	9.4	9.4	7.4	7.8	8.8	8.5	7.7	7.3	7.0	6.1	5.0
$5000 – $7499	12.8	9.2	8.1	7.8	10.0	9.7	9.9	8.7	8.6	9.4	8.1
7500 – 9999	14.3	17.0	16.7	17.5	17.3	14.9	12.1	11.6	11.4	11.9	11.1
10 000 – 14 999	12.3	14.1	15.2	15.7	16.7	17.9	21.2	22.1	21.4	21.0	21.9
15 000 – 19 999	11.3	10.7	11.3	10.7	11.1	11.6	10.9	11.4	11.7	11.9	11.5
20 000 – 29 999	19.9	17.7	18.2	18.4	16.0	17.4	18.3	18.2	18.6	18.1	19.1
30 000 – 39 999	11.2	11.8	12.3	11.3	10.3	10.4	9.9	10.7	11.5	10.9	12.6
40 000 – 49 999	4.6	6.0	5.4	6.0	4.9	5.5	5.3	5.4	5.5	5.8	5.9
50 000 and over	4.3	4.1	5.4	4.8	4.8	4.1	4.7	4.6	4.4	4.8	4.8
Total	100.0	100.0	100.0	100.0	100.0	100.0	100.0	100.0	100.0	100.0	100.0
Average (mean) income	19 628	19 574	20 534	20 437	19 317	19 441	19 994	20 036	20 413	20 590	21 138
Median income	15 570	15 127	16 108	15 534	13 804	14 646	14 711	15 104	15 669	15 721	16 598

SOURCE: Statistics Canada, *Income Distribution by Size in Canada*.

The percentage of unattached individuals earning less than $5000 decreased from 9.4 percent in 1979 to 5.0 percent in 1989. Other categories (except that of $10 000 to $14 999 earners, which showed an increase of almost 10 percent) remained relatively unchanged.

☐ Trends in Income Inequality

If we look for trends in these data, we can see that the percentage of families earning less than $10 000 declined from 4.2 to 2.4 percent between 1979 and 1989 in constant dollar terms; the percentage of those earning between $10 000 and $74 999 remained just about the same; but those earning $75 000 or more increased by about a third—from 12.1 percent to 16.1 percent. Thus, while average family incomes rose between 1979 and 1989 from $46 104 to $50 083, it is probable that the degree of inequality remained unchanged. Comparisons of incomes between 1951 and 1989 show that inequality has remained relatively unchanged between the two dates.

Table 14.2 shows similar data for unattached individuals over the same time period, 1979-1989. The percentage of those in the lowest category, earning under $5000, decreased from 9.4 percent in 1979 to 5.0 percent in 1989. The percentage of those earning $10 000 to $14 999 increased most substantially, from

12.3 percent to 21.9 percent. Other income groups remained relatively unchanged. The percentage of those earning over $50 000 increased by 0.5 percent.

☐ The Lorenz Curve

Another way of displaying income inequality in Canada is shown in Table 14.3 on page 286. Part 1 of the table indicates the share of national income earned by each fifth or quintile (20 percent) of families. Part 2 shows the cumulative income figures, obtained by adding the shares of each fifth to arrive at figures for the first 40, 60, and 80 percent of families. The table indicates that in 1989 the poorest 20 percent of Canadian families received 3.0 percent of total Canadian income before transfers and taxes, while the wealthiest quintile received 42.5 percent of total income. Again, the data indicate that the gap between the highest and lowest income groups is considerable.

The cumulative data can be illustrated by a **Lorenz curve** like that shown in Figure 14.1. If all families

☐ ☐ ☐ ☐ ☐ ☐

Skill Development: On the Average. . .

An **average** is a single number that is typical of a set of numbers. If a friend were to ask you how well you were doing in your economics course this year, you could list all the marks you received on every test, examination, and assignment—a lengthy process! More likely, you would state your average—say 90 percent. This single number summarizes a large number of marks and makes it easier to compare your mark this year with that of previous years and other subjects.

Averages are also used in economics to summarize a number of statistics and make comparisons over time. Average wages, incomes, and unemployment rates, for example, may be compared to gauge how well an economy is performing. If average unemployment rates rise over many months and average incomes decline, it may be time to act.

We should be aware, however, that averages do not give an indication of the range of data from which they are derived. Average incomes in two countries may be the same at $20 000 per year, but while in Country A all incomes may be around $20 000, in Country B there may be large disparities—some people may earn $5000 and others $75 000. These disparities are hidden by the average figure.

Three of the most commonly used averages, or **measures of central tendency** (so called because they are in the middle of a group of numbers), are the mean, mode, and median. It is important to recognize their appropriate uses and their limitations.

The Mean

The **mean** is the sum of a group of scores divided by the total number of scores. For example, suppose Company A has five employees who earn $300, $320, $340, $360, and $380 a week. The mean, therefore, is:

$$\$300 + \$320 + \$340 + \$360 + \$380 = \frac{\$1700}{5} = \$340.$$

The average weekly wage, then, is $340 a week. It is assumed that the values used in calculating the mean are roughly the same. For example, if we added to our list another employee who earned $2000 a week, then the arithmetic mean is in excess of $600. This, as an average or typical number, is misleading since all but one individual earned much less than $600.

The mean is the most widely used of all measures of central tendency and is the one usually meant when we talk about "the average."

The Median

The **median** is the middle number in a range of values that divides the group of numbers into two equal parts—just as a median strip divides a highway in two. The median can be found by inspection—selecting the middle number after arranging them in ascending or descending order—or by the formula:

$$\frac{N + 1}{2}$$ where N = the total number of values.

For example, if we examine the case of Company A with the five employees once again, the median is:

(a) By inspection—$300, $350, $360, $380, $400—therefore, $360, the middle number.

(b) By calculation according to the formula, $\frac{(5 + 1)}{2} = 3$, that is, the third score counting from either end—$360.

If the number of cases is even, then the median is that point above or below which 50 percent of the cases occur. If Company A adds a sixth employee who earns $2000, the median is:

(a) By inspection—$300, $340, $360, $380, $400, $2000—the median is between $360 and $380, thus $370.

(b) By calculation $\frac{6 + 1}{2} = 3.5$, that is, the point halfway between the third and fourth number—$370.

Notice that the median is much less affected by "extreme" numbers (the $2000 per week) than is the mean.

The Mode

The **mode** is the most frequent value of a set of numbers. For example, suppose that Company A hires two more workers (in addition to the six it already has) at salaries of $340 and $280. Since $340 per week is the most frequently occurring value, it is the mode (there are more workers with salaries of $340 than any other value).

The mode is of interest if we want to know such facts as the most usual house price or salary. However, in some cases, the mode can be much less representative of a set of data than the median or the mean. When it is representative, its value approximates that of the mean and the median.

Applications

1. The hourly wages of seven workers of ABC Manufacturing Company are $12, $8, $7, $12, $5, $6, $9. Calculate the following:
(a) the modal hourly wage
(b) the median hourly wage
(c) the mean hourly wage.

2. Suppose that ABC Manufacturing Company hires an additional worker at $13 an hour. Calculate:
(a) the modal hourly wage
(b) the median hourly wage
(c) the mean hourly wage.

3. Five people are sitting together on a park bench—three vagrants, a young unemployed secretary, and a millionairess. The worldly assets of the three vagrants total $6.00 each. The young unemployed secretary's bank account and other assets total $100. The millionairess's total net worth is $15 000 000.
(a) For the assets of these people, calculate the:
 (i) mean
 (ii) mode
 (iii) median.
(b) Which measure of central tendency would you *not* use to describe the wealth of these people? Why?

4. Refer to Table 14.1 on page 283 to answer the following questions.
(a) What trend was apparent in the median income of Canadian families from 1979 to 1989?
(b) In what way did the median income for each of the years 1979 to 1989 differ from the mean income of those years? Suggest reasons why.
(c) Suggest reasons why the mean and the median incomes in 1983 are less than those of the period 1979-1982.
(d) Which one—the mean or the median—is the better indicator of the average income of Canadian families in your view? Explain your answer.

Table 14.3 Income distribution of Canadian families in 1989 before transfers and taxes

PART 1 INCOME DISTRIBUTION		PART 2 CUMULATIVE INCOME DISTRIBUTION		
POPULATION	SHARE OF TOTAL INCOME (PERCENT)	POPULATION	SHARE OF TOTAL INCOME (PERCENT)	POINT IN FIGURE 14.1
Lowest 20 percent	3.0	First 20 percent	3.0	F
Second 20 percent	11.4	First 40 percent	3.0 + 11.4 = 14.4	J
Third 20 percent	18.0	First 60 percent	14.4 + 18.0 = 32.4	K
Fourth 20 percent	25.1	First 80 percent	32.4 + 25.1 = 57.5	L
Highest 20 percent	42.5	Total	57.4 + 42.5 = 100	M

SOURCE: Statistics Canada, *Income after Tax Distributions in Canada*.

While the poorest 20 percent of Canadian families received 3.0 percent of the national income, the wealthiest 20 percent received 42.5 percent of the national income. Again, the data indicate a significant degree of income inequality in the country.

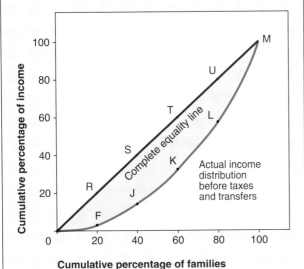

Figure 14.1 Lorenz curve showing family income distribution in Canada before taxes and transfers, 1989

The ideal of complete income equality is depicted by the straight line ORSTUM. Thus, 20 percent of the population would have 20 percent of the income (point R), 40 percent of the population would have 40 percent of the income (point S), and so on. The actual distribution of income in Canada is illustrated by the bowed curve OFJKLM, plotted from the cumulative data in Table 14.3. Point F, for example, shows that the 20 percent of families with the lowest earnings received only 3.0 percent of total income. Point J shows that the 40 percent of families with the lowest incomes received 14.4 percent of total income. The difference between the two curves indicates the degree of income inequality.

SOURCE: Statistics Canada, *Income after Tax Distributions in Canada*, 1989.

received exactly the same income, then the curve would be the straight line ORSTUM. At any point along this line, the percentage of families equals the percentage of the total national income they receive. For example, at point S, 40 percent of families have 40 percent of total national income; at point U, 80 percent of families have 80 percent of national income. This straight line represents the points of complete income equality.

The actual distribution of family income in Canada before taxes and transfers is shown by the curve OFJKLM. This curve is plotted from the cumulative income data in Part 2 of Table 14.3. The degree of inequality is shown by the "bow" in the Lorenz curve, that is, by the difference between the two curves (the shaded area).

However, the degree of family income inequality is not as great as the Lorenz curve suggests, since over a lifetime, family incomes change. Many young families have relatively low incomes, but these increase as the wage earners reach middle age and enter their earning prime. Even when we take lifetime earnings into account, however, inequality in the distribution of family incomes still exists.

☐ What Causes Income Inequality?

Why do we have the degree of income inequality shown in Figure 14.1 and Tables 14.1 and 14.2? As we have seen, the operation of market forces (supply and demand) results in very different incomes for different people. These forces are impersonal, unaffected by any notions of what is a "just" or "equitable" distribution of income. Without government intervention, a capitalist economy is likely to have a high degree of income inequality. Let's consider some of the reasons why.

Ownership of Property

Those who own property or capital—such as stocks, bonds, and real estate—receive an income in the form of rent, interest, and/or profit. Inequalities in the ownership of property result, therefore, in income inequalities.

Data from the mid-1980s show that 25 percent of Canadian families and individuals had a net wealth (the sum of all marketable assets less liabilities) of less than $5000. At the other end of the scale, 5 percent of families and individuals had a net wealth in excess of $300 000. The average net wealth of the 25 percent at the lowest end of the scale was just about zero—since for some in this group, their debts exceeded their assets. The wealthiest 5 percent owned approximately 40 percent of total wealth.

□ □ □ □ □ □

Have We Really Become Wealthier?

Studies have shown that the wealth of Canadians increased significantly over the 1980s. How has our wealth increased and do we really consider ourselves wealthier? Consider these questions as you read the following article.

425 000 Families Now Worth a Million

The average Canadian family's net wealth rocketed by more than 124 percent to about $261 000 from 1983 to the end of [1989], according to a new study. And Canada has 425 000 millionaire families—4.5 percent of all households and twice as many as previously estimated.

But being a millionaire no longer guarantees that you're wealthy. In fact, it's getting downright common.

The details of Canadians' personal wealth are contained in a two-volume report, highlights of which were released by the Toronto accounting firm Ernst & Young (formerly Clarkson Gordon/Woods Gordon). The year-long study concludes Canadians are not only wealthier than was thought, but the wealth is spread around more evenly.

Anyone in Toronto or Vancouver between 55 and 65 who has worked for a company with a pension plan for 20 years or more, bought a house back then in a nice area, and makes between $60 000 and $80 000 a year, probably now has more than $1 million in net assets, the study says.

Home ownership and pension plans have changed the face of wealth in Canada, says Ian Deane, author of the report. "In the past, the really wealthy got their money through business success," he says. "But in the last generation, home ownership became the rule rather than the exception. That created an enormous pool of wealth that is much more broadly distributed."

As the homes are passed down to the next generation, the wealth will become even more widely dispersed, he says, and more families will cross the million dollar threshold. In other parts of the country, many households reached million dollar status by starting a successful company or investing in real estate.

But being a millionaire doesn't mean you're wealthy anymore. "Most people who have $1 million in assets would not consider themselves wealthy," Deane says. "You have to move further up the scale for that."

Fortune magazine concludes that the 1.5 million mere millionaires in the United States can't live the life of the rich unless they have an income of more than $300 000 a year.

The Ernst & Young study counters the widely-held perception that a small group of really wealthy individuals controls a big chunk of Canada's wealth. "Wealth is not concentrated at the upper end any more," Deane says. "It's distributed across the spectrum. That was the biggest surprise to us. We have never seen anything that suggested the average Canadian's net wealth was this high.

On a proportional basis, compared to the United States, Canada has a lot fewer poor people, a lot more in the middle class, and slightly fewer really wealthy people, Deane says. Canadians also save more—putting more money into bank deposits, registered retirement savings plans, and bonds than their American counterparts.

In the United States, the top 1 percent of the population controls 34.5 percent of all personal assets. In Canada, the top 0.2 percent of the population with assets of more than $5 million controls only 12 percent of household wealth, according to the study. But the middle group— 1 million Canadian households with assets of between $500 000 and $5 million—controls 50 percent of the wealth.

The odds of being well off depend largely on where you live. Average household wealth varies widely across the country, from a high of $329 500 in Ontario to a low of $161 600 in Newfoundland.

Researchers have been trying to pin down the country's personal wealth for years. "There is really no way other than asking people of analyzing the wealth of the total population," Deane says. "It's an impossible task for anyone but a government to do."

Statistics Canada last did a survey of consumer finances in 1983, but admits that surveying a couple of thousand people in the country doesn't catch the really wealthy or the really poor. "It's something that's very difficult to get a handle on," says Roger Love, chief of Statistics Canada's income and expenditure section.

Even if they did co-operate, the poor underestimate how much they owe and the rich how much they're worth. Ernst & Young compiled their own data from taxation statistics, census data, surveys, and a wide variety of other sources to come up with a new analysis.

On the whole, everybody's lifestyle is improving, Deane says. Houses and cars are of much better quality now and people travel far more extensively. It now takes two incomes to buy a house instead of one, he says, and that is not likely to change because housing prices always rise to the level where people can barely afford them.

But when young people complain that it's harder for them than it was for their parents, they don't take into account the sacrifices their parents made, he says. "Now people expect to own a house, a car, and take two vacations. It all comes back to the fact that the quality of most people's lifestyles has improved substantially."

The past generation bought homes in Toronto when it was much smaller, he says, and what they thought of as the suburbs is now considered downtown. The same thing will happen to this generation, Deane predicts. The homes they are buying in [the outer suburbs] will be considered downtown in 30 years.

New financial devices such as RRSPs are making it much easier for Canadians to save their money, he says. And as the population ages over the decade, it will save even more, preparing for retirement.

But Ernst & Young conclude that the economic outlook is good. Once the recession [of the early 1990s] ends, unemployment rates will fall to even lower levels than at the height of the '80s boom. More jobs will open up than there will be workers to fill them.

"That's the factor we think will generate a real increase in income," Deane says. "It will be tougher to find people again, so companies will have to pay more."

You might even become a millionaire.

SOURCE: Elaine Carey, "425 000 families now worth a million, report says," *The Toronto Star*, December 15, 1990. Reprinted with permission—The Toronto Star Syndicate.

Applications

1. What factors may account for the broader distribution of wealth, according to the Ernst & Young report?
2. (a) Why would people with $1 million in assets not consider themselves wealthy today?
(b) How has the perception of wealth changed?
3. Explain the difficulties of obtaining an accurate picture of the distribution of personal wealth in Canada.
4. What trends does the report indicate for the future? Do you agree with these views? Explain why or why not.

Differences in Ability

People differ in their mental and physical abilities. Some have the physical abilities to become highly-paid professional athletes. Others have the intellectual abilities to enter such well-paid professions as accountancy, law, and medicine. Thus, differences in mental and physical ability mean that some people are very well paid while others are not.

Differences in Education and Training

Individuals also differ in their education and training. You and I may have the same ability, but if I drop out of high school at age 16 and you go on to finish high school and learn a trade or profession, then you will have a greater capacity to earn a higher income than I. Different investments in human capital will result in income differentials.

Risk and Unpleasantness of Job

Those who are willing to undertake risky or unpleasant jobs are likely to earn more than those in pleasant, safe jobs. A steeplejack, for example, is likely to receive a higher wage to compensate for the physical risk of the job than office workers. Entrepreneurs who introduce a new product or service face the risk of failure and, though many fail, those who are successful may enjoy substantial financial rewards.

Hard Work and Long Hours

People in the same job may earn different incomes because some choose to work longer hours than others. If we both have the same trade or profession, but I spend three afternoons a week playing golf while you work full-time, it will not be surprising if you earn more than I.

Market Power

People who are in a position to influence the prices paid for the goods or services they supply may be able to benefit from this market power with increased incomes. Some labour unions and professional groups have been able to influence the supply of the productive services in their trade or profession, thus boosting the incomes of their members. Similarly, in product markets, owners of firms with some monopoly power are likely to benefit with increased incomes.

Discrimination

Discrimination against groups in society, essentially barring them from certain well-paid trades or professions, has depressed their incomes in some cases for very long periods. In the past, for instance, women were guided into jobs regarded as being typically "female"—such as typist, clerk, nurse, and primary school teacher. These were less well-paid and less prestigious than the typical "male" positions, such as manager, lawyer, doctor, and school principal. Today, despite changes in attitudes, women and minorities continue to experience job discrimination.

Luck

Some differences in income may be due simply to luck, or the lack of it. An individual may win a lottery or just happen to own land on which oil is discovered. Someone else may suffer a crippling accident or a prolonged illness, resulting in substantial losses in earning power. The benefits of good luck and the burdens of bad luck do not affect everyone equally, and they therefore contribute to income inequality.

☐ Is Some Inequality Just?

Evidently, one could argue that some of these reasons for income inequality are just. If I work longer hours, invest more time and money into my education or training, or face greater danger in my job, should I not be paid more than others? On the other hand, discrimination is clearly unjust. Similarly, we could argue that people who do not have the specific abilities or means to enter the highest-paying professions should not be left wanting for what is beyond their control.

While we may be willing to accept some degree of income inequality, therefore, most would agree that there are certain minimum standards below which no one should fall. No one should live in grave poverty and no one should go hungry. Nevertheless, in 1989, poverty was the lot of more than one in eight families and more than one in three individuals living alone. This may be a surprising fact to many of us who think of Canada as an affluent country without a serious poverty problem.

■ Who Are the Poor?

The **poor** are those whose income is inadequate to pay for the basic necessities of life. The problem with this definition, of course, is determining what is meant by "necessities of life." While most people agree these necessities include food, clothing, and shelter, the standards considered acceptable vary. The minimum acceptable standards in developed countries, such as Canada, are considerably higher than those in less developed countries, for example. The definition of poverty is relative and varies the world over.

In Canada, a family is defined as poor if it must spend more than 58.5 percent of its income on the basic necessities of life—food, clothing, and shelter. Studies of family expenditure patterns have shown that the poorer the family, the greater the percentage of income spent on the basic necessities.

This minimum standard of living is generally expressed as a minimum dollar income known as the **poverty line**. The poverty line varies with family size and location of residence. Thus, for a family of five

Table 14.4 The poverty line in Canada, by family size and area of residence, 1989 (in dollars)

SIZE OF FAMILY UNIT	SIZE OF AREA OF RESIDENCE				
	URBAN AREAS (POPULATION)				RURAL AREAS
	500 000 AND OVER	100 000-499 999	30 000-99 999	LESS THAN 30 000	
1 person	12 148	11 537	10 823	10 006	8 983
2 persons	16 027	15 212	14 193	13 168	11 741
3 persons	21 440	20 317	18 988	17 663	15 722
4 persons	24 706	23 481	21 950	20 418	18 175
5 persons	28 790	27 260	25 421	23 685	21 135
6 persons	31 444	29 709	27 770	25 829	20 073
7 or more persons	34 610	32 772	30 628	28 483	25 421

The poverty line is the minimum income required to maintain an acceptable standard of living. This low-income cut off varies with the size of family and area of residence. The larger the family and the larger the town or city of residence, the higher the poverty line.

SOURCE: Statistics Canada, *Income Distribution by Size in Canada*.

living in a rural area, the poverty line in 1989 was $21 135, while for the same size family living in a city of over 500 000 people, the poverty line was $28 790. For a family of two living in a rural area, the poverty line was $11 741, while the same size family living in a large city had a poverty line of $16 027. Since costs in large cities for housing, food, and clothing are higher than those in rural areas, the poverty line in cities is also higher.

Table 14.4 outlines the poverty line in Canada in 1989 by size of family and area of residence.

The poverty line is also adjusted over time to take into account changes in the general level of prices and our concept of what constitutes poverty. A hundred years ago, even after adjustments for inflation, a poverty income of $21 135 for a family of five would have been considered a very good income indeed! Our concept of a minimally acceptable level of income has shifted upward as our standard of living has improved.

☐ The Incidence of Poverty

How widespread is poverty in Canada? Tables 14.5 and 14.6 on the next page provide an indication. As you can see from the tables, poverty is not confined to any one region or province, sex, or age group. Certain groups are more likely to be poor than others, however. The incidence (or likelihood) of poverty is highest among women, the elderly, and those under the age of 24. Unattached individuals are also more likely to be poor than those living in family units. In terms of regions, poverty was least evident in Ontario and most widespread in Atlantic Canada in the 1980s.

The incidence of poverty is also related to the education of the family head or unattached individual. In general, for both families and individuals, the lower the education level, the greater is the incidence of poverty. Table 14.7 shows the relationship between level of education and the incidence of poverty in 1989.

The incidence of poverty generally increased from 1980 to 1984, reflecting the impact of the 1982-83 recession. After 1984, poverty tended to decline as the economy recovered, until by 1989 it had fallen by about one-quarter from the 1980 rate for both families and individuals. In 1989, there were 3 129 000 poor, down by 200 000 from 1988 and by 1 million from the 1983 recession high. The percentage of children living in poverty declined from the decade high of 20 percent in 1984 to 14.6 percent in 1989.

Table 14.5 Incidence of poverty among families in Canada by selected characteristics, 1980, 1984, 1989 (percent)

	1980	1984	1989
TOTAL BY PROVINCE	11.6	13.9	9.6
ATLANTIC PROVINCES	15.4	17.2	11.7
Newfoundland	23.2	21.3	12.8
PEI	10.1	12.1	9.0
Nova Scotia	12.8	14.7	11.4
New Brunswick	13.6	17.9	11.9
QUEBEC	14.7	16.6	11.4
ONTARIO	10.0	10.7	7.0
PRAIRIE PROVINCES	9.8	14.4	11.3
Manitoba	10.9	13.1	11.0
Saskatchewan	10.7	14.8	12.6
Alberta	8.9	14.8	11.0
British Columbia	8.8	14.7	9.7
BY AGE OF HEAD			
24 years and under	19.5	28.6	25.1
25 - 34 years	11.4	17.1	13.0
35 - 44 years	11.0	12.8	9.6
45 - 54 years	9.7	10.8	6.5
55 - 64 years	10.9	12.4	8.2
65 years and over	13.3	11.3	6.2
BY AGE AND SEX OF HEAD			
MALE	8.5	10.6	6.8
Under 65 years	7.9	10.7	7.0
65 years and over	12.9	9.9	5.8
FEMALE	40.5	40.1	32.8
Under 65 years	44.8	43.7	36.9
65 years and over	16.5	21.0	9.6

SOURCE: Statistics Canada, *Income Distribution by Size in Canada*.

The incidence of poverty is higher among families in Atlantic Canada than in any other region, and highest among families with a female head and with a head under age 24.

Table 14.6 Incidence of poverty among unattached individuals in Canada by selected characteristics, 1980, 1984, 1989 (percent)

	1980	1984	1989
TOTAL BY PROVINCE	39.1	37.7	30.5
ATLANTIC PROVINCES	48.2	41.6	34.8
Newfoundland	58.1	43.6	32.0
PEI	57.4	48.3	35.1
Nova Scotia	44.0	37.9	34.7
New Brunswick	47.7	44.8	36.3
QUEBEC	44.4	46.6	41.0
ONTARIO	36.7	43.0	23.5
PRAIRIE PROVINCES	36.1	33.1	30.4
Manitoba	42.4	36.3	30.0
Saskatchewan	44.4	35.9	30.4
Alberta	30.3	30.6	30.7
British Columbia	38.4	35.0	25.2
BY AGE			
24 years and under	41.8	47.3	45.0
25 - 34 years	19.3	21.4	17.6
35 - 44 years	17.6	26.7	20.5
45 - 54 years	28.8	34.2	26.7
55 - 64 years	40.7	43.6	38.0
65 years and over	61.9	49.4	37.5
BY AGE AND SEX			
MALE	29.4	32.1	24.6
Under 65 years	24.4	30.2	24.1
65 years and over	52.8	42.6	26.9
FEMALE	47.3	42.5	35.4
Under 65 years	36.6	36.9	31.7
65 years and over	65.6	51.7	41.0

SOURCE: Statistics Canada, *Income Distribution by Size in Canada*.

The incidence of poverty among unattached individuals is also generally highest for women, for those in Atlantic Canada, and for those under age 24 or over age 65.

Table 14.7 Incidence of poverty according to education level of head for families and unattached individuals, 1989 (percent)

BY EDUCATION OF HEAD	FAMILIES	UNATTACHED INDIVIDUALS
0 - 8 years	25.0	43.5
Some secondary	28.8	21.2
Completed secondary	15.6	13.3
Some post-secondary	8.3	10.8
Post-secondary diploma/ certificate	17.2	14.7
University degree	5.0	5.5

SOURCE: Statistics Canada, *Income Distribution by Size in Canada*.

Poverty is highest among those with the least education.

The Welfare State

A **welfare state** is an industrial capitalist society that seeks to ensure the health, education, and economic prosperity of its citizens by means of government-operated social programs. Canada, along with most other western mixed market economies, is a welfare state. As we saw in the last chapter, Canadian governments spend considerable sums on social welfare programs.

During much of the last century and the first third of this century, there was a widespread belief that individuals and families were responsible for their own well-being. The provision of social services by governments was minimal—with the exception of education.

The traumatic impact of the Depression in the 1930s, however, changed this belief. Canadians began to recognize that the state had an important role to play in ensuring and improving their welfare. Beginning in 1940 with the Unemployment Insurance Act and continuing into the mid-1970s, governments established a welfare state in Canada. Family allowances were instituted. Government spending on primary and secon-

dary education increased rapidly. Programs for the expanded and permanent funding of higher education were introduced.

In the 1960s, the last major blocks in the Canadian welfare state were put in place. Canadians were provided with health insurance. The Canada Pension Plan ensured payments on retirement and the Guaranteed Income Supplement provided help for the needy.

Thus, the Canadian reaction to income inequality, and poverty in particular, is to reduce them by taxation (of which the rich may pay a larger share—as we saw in the last chapter), and by government programs including transfer payments. Transfer payments are all payments made by governments to individuals or families for which no good or service is required in return. They include unemployment insurance benefits, Canada pension benefits, and social welfare payments. Some government programs aim to deal with the causes of poverty; others with its symptoms.

☐ Programs Aimed at the Causes of Poverty

Subsidized education   In Canada, local governments with provincial financial assistance pay for the cost of elementary and secondary school education. Everyone, therefore, has an opportunity to obtain a minimum level of education. Provincial governments also pay approximately 85 percent of the cost of university and community college education. In addition, provinces offer grant and loan programs to assist students from low-income families to meet the costs of post-secondary schooling. In this way, governments help reduce the incidence of poverty by dealing with one of its causes—inadequate investment in human capital.

Promotion of full employment   Government programs to promote full employment help to reduce poverty by keeping people working. In recessions, for example, governments have cut taxes, increased their spending, and lowered interest rates to promote business investment and consumer spending. By stimulating the economy, these actions help to create jobs. We'll examine these programs more closely in the next unit.

□ □ □ □ □ □

Equal Pay For Work of Equal Value?

What does equal pay for work of equal value mean? Why is it being implemented in some areas and what objections have been raised against it?

Kathy Baker is the only secretary at Hamlet Public School in Stratford, Ontario. According to a report in *The Toronto Star*, she received her third and final pay equity increase of 35 cents an hour on January 1, 1990 to bring her wage to $12.87 an hour—about the pay of a janitor with her school board. Kathy Baker is one of those benefitting from Ontario's 1987 Pay Equity Act, which is intended to ensure that women are paid the same as men for work of equal value. She files, types, handles telephone calls from parents and the public, keeps track of attendance records, and looks after scraped knees and elbows. Kathy Baker's job was judged comparable to that of a janitor and her pay was, therefore, raised in three steps to equal that of a janitor.

The following is one way in which pay equity can be implemented.

1. In each organization, job descriptions are prepared through questionnaires given to workers and/or through worker interviews.
2. Using a points system, jobs are rated according to acceptable criteria. Four criteria often used are skill, responsibility, effort, and working conditions.
3. Jobs done mainly by men (60 to 70 percent of workers) are compared with those done mainly by women scoring about the same number of points.
4. Women who are paid less than men in occupations with about the same number of points begin receiving pay increases to equalize the pay levels.

In Manitoba, Prince Edward Island, Quebec, and a number of states in the US, pay equity is being implemented in the government sector only. In Ontario, it is being phased into the private sector as well (firms with more than ten employees) as of January 1, 1993.

But why equal pay for work of equal value legislation? All provinces and the federal government have laws requiring "equal pay for equal work." Women doing the same job as men in the same geographical area must receive the same wage. While the female to male earnings ratio improved considerably since 1971 (when the data were first published) from 58.4 percent to 66 percent in 1989 as shown in Figure 14.2, the ratio has changed little since 1984. Women still receive only about two-thirds the earnings of men.

Figure 14.2 Female to male earnings ratio, 1971-1989 (full-time, full-year)

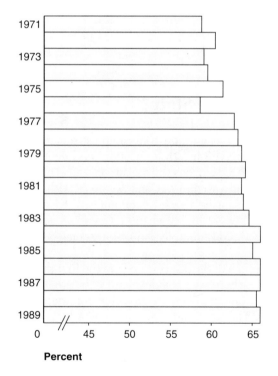

Percent

While the female to male earnings ratio has improved since 1971 from 58.4 to 66 percent by 1989, the ratio changed little after 1984.

SOURCE: Statistics Canada, *Earnings of Men and Women 1971-89*, December 1990.

While women may be receiving equal pay for equal work, they may not be receiving equal pay for work of equal value. In other words, pay differences may still exist for men and women in *different* but comparable jobs. We may have pay equity for men and women within the occupations of wordprocessor and truck driver, but gender pay discrimination may still exist if the majority of wordprocessors are women and this occupation is less well-paid than that of truck driver, which is dominated by men. The answer, therefore, may be to legislate equal pay for jobs of equal worth.

The concept of equal worth has met with a number of objections, however. Comparisons of job values are necessarily subjective. In Minnesota, for example, a registered nurse, chemist, and social worker were ranked as equal. In Iowa, a nurse ranked 30 percent above a social worker, who ranked 10 percent above a chemist.

Others argue that having a board or commission set wage rates disrupts the operation of the market. If pay scales are raised in jobs traditionally regarded as dominated by women, won't more women be attracted to these jobs by the higher pay, thus leading to even more workforce segregation of the sexes? Raising the price of labour will also add to costs of production, thus making Canadian goods more difficult to sell on the world market and increasing inflation. Equal pay legislation, it is also argued, could overprice women's pay and thus contribute to their unemployment.

Economists argue that some of the pay disparities may be due to the particular work cycle of women who have children. Since some women leave the workforce for a period in mid-career to raise children, they have less work experience than men in the same group and thus earn less on average. This may change, however, as fewer women leave the workforce for long periods after they have children and as maternity and paternity leave becomes more acceptable.

A comparison of unmarried male and female earnings in identical occupations, when the men and women were of the same age and had the same work experience and education, showed that the wage difference was between 5 and 10 percent. A Statistics Canada report in 1990 indicated that women aged 15 to 24 earned 82 percent of what comparable men earned. Single women in the same year earned 92 percent of what single men earned. It is argued, therefore, that not all of the pay disparity between men and women is due to gender discrimination.

Applications

1. What do you think? Should we support or reject the concept of equal worth?

2. Should the labour market be left to determine wages and salaries without intervention? Support your point of view.

Reduction of discrimination Governments have acted to reduce discrimination in the workplace against women and minorities. Equal pay for equal work legislation has been passed in all provinces. Legislation requiring equal pay for work of equal value has also been passed by a number of provinces and the federal government. Employment discrimination based on sex, colour, and ethnic origin is illegal.

Worker safety Federal and provincial programs for worker safety aim to reduce the number of job-related injuries and illnesses, thus reducing the loss of income due to disability.

Help for single-parent households Unless affordable daycare is available, many low-income single-parent families are unable to earn enough for themselves and their families. Federally-subsidized daycare is available in many provinces, though the demand still outstrips the supply.

☐ Programs to Alleviate Poverty

Programs to alleviate poverty are of two kinds—social insurance schemes and welfare programs.

Social Insurance Schemes

Social insurance schemes are based on the principle of

universality. **Universality** means that social security payments are paid to everyone—rich or poor, whether needy or not. Examples of universal social insurance programs include the Canada (or Quebec) Pension Plan, unemployment insurance, medical insurance, and (formerly) family allowances.

Even though these universal programs are not specifically directed at the poor, they do help alleviate poverty for many. They provide at least a basic income for those over 65, the unemployed, and those with disabilities who may have no other significant means of income.

(i) Old Age Security pension (OAS)   The OAS is paid to those over age 65 who have been resident in Canada for 40 years after age 18. Those over age 65 who have been resident in Canada for at least ten years after age 18 are eligible for a partial pension. The pension ($354.92 per month in 1991) is the same for all recipients and is adjusted to the cost of living.

(ii) Canada (or Quebec) Pension Plan (CPP or QPP)   The CPP and QPP are financed by contributions from workers and their employers. At retirement, benefits are paid on the basis of a worker's previous earnings and vary with changes in the cost of living. In 1992, maximum retirement benefits were $636.11 per month.

(iii) Family Allowance   The "baby bonus"—as the family allowance is popularly called—was introduced in Canada at the end of World War II. Under the plan, cheques are sent monthly to mothers, single fathers, or guardians with custody of children under the age of 18. In Quebec and Alberta, the amount of the bonus also varies with the age of the children under 18. The amount of the bonus does not change with family income, but the 1992 federal budget set an upper income limit on those eligible for the allowance. In 1991, the amount paid totalled $33.93 per month for each child under 18.

(iv) Unemployment Insurance (UI)   Established in 1940 and greatly expanded in 1971 so that it now covers 90 percent of the labour force, unemployment insurance is one of the most costly single programs of the federal government. Contributions to the scheme are made by workers and employers and are based on the worker's earnings (up to a maximum). Benefits from the plan are also based on earnings. The maximum benefit in 1991 was $408 weekly.

UI was originally intended to provide an income during temporary periods of unemployment. Now, through its provision of benefits after only short periods of employment and through extended benefits to areas of high employment, the plan has changed its original intent.

(v) Health Insurance   All Canadian provinces and territories provide their citizens with health care services at little or no direct cost. For the most part, the cost of health care is financed from the general tax revenue of the province and by transfers from the federal government.

Welfare Programs

In addition to these universal social insurance schemes, governments have instituted a number of welfare programs specifically designed to fight poverty. These programs, therefore, are available only to the poor.

(i) The Guaranteed Income Supplement (GIS)   The GIS is paid to needy people who are recipients of Old Age Security and who have little income beyond it. More than half of those who receive the OAS also receive the GIS. The GIS is indexed (adjusted) to the cost of living. The maximum GIS benefit in 1991 was $421.79 per month for a single individual.

(ii) Canada Assistance Plan (CAP)   For those not covered by any other programs, there is the comprehensive Canada Assistance Plan. This plan aids any needy people—needy mothers with dependent children and people with disabilities, for example. The amount of assistance received depends on the family's or individual's deficit—the difference between their incomes and the cost of their basic needs for food, clothing, and shelter as determined by a social worker. The Canada Assistance Plan is funded by both the federal and provincial governments.

How Effective Are These Programs?

How effective, then, are taxes and transfer payments in reducing income inequality in Canada? Table 14.8 compares income distribution data for families *before* and *after* taxes and transfers.

Table 14.8 Income distribution of Canadian families in 1989, before and after taxes and transfers

POPULATION	CUMULATIVE SHARE BEFORE TRANSFERS AND TAXES	INCOME SHARE (TRANSFERS INCLUDED)	INCOME SHARE AFTER TAXES
First 20 percent	3.0	6.5	7.7
First 40 percent	14.4	19.1	21.3
First 60 percent	32.4	36.9	39.5
First 80 percent	57.5	60.7	63.1
Total	100.0	100.0	100.0

SOURCE: Statistics Canada, *Income after Tax Distributions in Canada*.

Transfers and taxes increase the income shares of the lower quintiles significantly and lower the shares of the upper quintiles.

The effect of transfers and taxes is to raise the income shares of those in the lower quintiles. The impact is especially striking for the lowest 20 percent. Before transfers and taxes, the income share of the lowest quintile was 3.0 percent. After transfers, this share more than doubles to 6.5 percent and after taxes, it increases still further to 7.7 percent.

At the other end of the scale, transfers reduce the income share of the highest quintile from 42.5 percent to 39.3 percent (100 percent − 60.7 percent), while taxes reduce the share even further to 36.9 percent. Thus, the total effect of transfers and taxes is to reduce income inequality by increasing the share of those in the lower quintiles and decreasing the share of those in the higher quintiles. The effect of taxes on the cumulative share is significantly less than that of transfers, however. Figure 14.3 shows the Lorenz curves plotted from these data in Table 14.8.

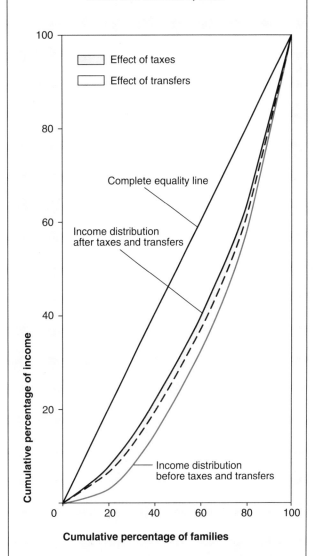

Figure 14.3 Lorenz curve showing family income distribution in Canada before and after taxes and transfers, 1989

This figure is plotted from the data in Table 14.8. A comparison of the Lorenz curves before and after taxes and transfers shows that income inequality is reduced by these means. Taxes, however, are comparatively less effective than transfers.

SOURCE: Statistics Canada, *Income after Tax Distributions in Canada*, 1989.

☐ Trends in Income Distribution

Have income shares changed recently? The answer for the 1980s is very little. If, for example, we compare the after-tax income shares of families in 1980 and 1989 as shown in Table 14.9, we see very little change—despite the fairly common belief that the rich get richer and the poor poorer. Disparities were wider in the middle of the decade with the 1982-83 recession, but by the end of the decade the shares had returned to approximately the 1980 levels.

Table 14.9 After-tax income shares of families, 1980, 1985, 1989 (percents)

POPULATION	1980	1985	1989
First 20 percent	7.2	7.4	7.7
Second 20 percent	13.9	13.3	13.6
Third 20 percent	18.7	18.3	18.2
Fourth 20 percent	23.7	23.8	23.6
Fifth 20 percent	36.5	37.2	37.0

SOURCE: Statistics Canada, *Perspective on Labour and Income*.
The after-tax income share of Canadian families remained relatively unchanged over the 1980s.

☐ ☐ ☐ ☐ ☐ ☐

How Do We Compare?

How does income distribution in Canada compare with that in other nations—particularly the US? The following article provides some insights into the recent trends in the United States.

Middle-Class Blessings: Another View

There are a lot of ways to read statistics—and not all of them show the middle class taking a beating. Americans, in fact, have done about as well as they could reasonably expect for more than a decade now. They have also enjoyed gains, such as a cleaner environment and work benefits, which don't show up in the bare income figures.

Middle-income Americans have actually received a modest increase in their cash pay—a 1 percent annual rise through the 1980s, after adjusting for the broadest index of inflation, the gross national product deflator. Of course, rich Americans have done even better. But any claim that the middle class is doing poorly simply because the rich are doing better is based on jealousy, not facts.

For one thing, the money didn't all go to the rich; much of it went into the environment. Americans have demanded cleaner air and water, purer foods and the removal of toxic wastes, among other measures. The vast investment by business and government in redesigned cars and billion-dollar scrubbers for utility smokestacks may contribute nothing to what is measured as personal income in the United States, but it has improved the quality of life.

An increased chunk of workers' income also goes toward a second social purchase—social security—that has left millions of Americans better off. However grudgingly, Americans have accepted higher payroll taxes to provide a cushion for their parents and for themselves when they retire. Such payments have climbed much more rapidly than inflation. The number of retirees has rocketed ahead, too. Not all of the elderly need the increases; retirees on average now have cash incomes higher than those of working families under the age of 55. Yet working Americans continue to favor a system that provides even the richest retirees with ever larger monthly cheques. Until voters decide this is foolish, they are getting what they ask for.

Fringe benefits also count for a lot. An employee can receive a pay hike in one of two ways: cash or benefits. But even accepting the arguable assessment that cash pay stood still in the 1980s, cash plus total benefits grew as Americans took more vacations and time off, increased their pension coverages and made more trips to the doctor.

Finally, the shrinking family leaves more money to go around. Although household income might have risen slowly, the size of households has slipped from 3.1 persons to 2.6 persons since 1970. That means each member of today's smaller families is getting a bigger piece of the economic pie. In fact, cash income to each

Figure 14.4 Income distribution in the United States

Millions of families are losing the struggle to improve their living standards, as the affluent consume a large share of the nation's wealth.

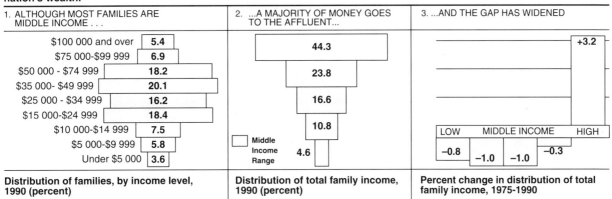

1. ALTHOUGH MOST FAMILIES ARE MIDDLE INCOME . . .	2. ...A MAJORITY OF MONEY GOES TO THE AFFLUENT...	3. ...AND THE GAP HAS WIDENED
$100 000 and over — 5.4 $75 000-$99 999 — 6.9 $50 000 - $74 999 — 18.2 $35 000- $49 999 — 20.1 $25 000 - $34 999 — 16.2 $15 000-$24 999 — 18.4 $10 000-$14 999 — 7.5 $5 000-$9 999 — 5.8 Under $5 000 — 3.6	44.3 23.8 16.6 10.8 □ Middle Income Range 4.6	+3.2 LOW MIDDLE INCOME HIGH −0.8 −1.0 −1.0 −0.3
Distribution of families, by income level, 1990 (percent)	**Distribution of total family income, 1990 (percent)**	**Percent change in distribution of total family income, 1975-1990**

SOURCE: Bureau of the Census.

Figure 14.5 Income inequalities, selected countries

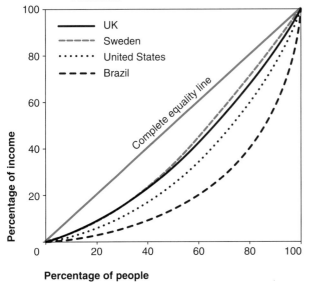

Legend:
— UK
--- Sweden
····· United States
-- - Brazil

Complete equality line

Y-axis: Percentage of income
X-axis: Percentage of people

SOURCE: Paul Samuelson *et al.*, *Economics*, 6th Can. ed. (Toronto: McGraw-Hill Ryerson, 1988), p. 581.

Figure 14.6 Inequalities of wealth, selected countries

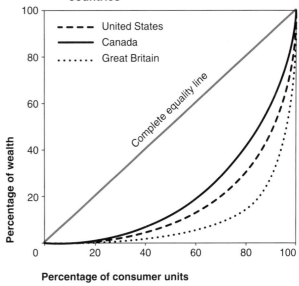

Legend:
-- - United States
— Canada
······ Great Britain

Complete equality line

Y-axis: Percentage of wealth
X-axis: Percentage of consumer units

SOURCE: Paul Samuelson *et al.*, *Economics*, 6th Can. ed. (Toronto: McGraw-Hill Ryerson, 1988), p. 581.

person in the United States has shown a solid increase through the '80s, rising by an average of 1.8 percent a year. This was a third less than increases in the 1960s and 1970s, but still a fairly solid gain given the growth in fringe benefits, social security payments, and environmental spending.

In the first two and a half years of the Bush administration, incomes have grown more slowly than in most of the 1980s. This is probably a momentary glitch rather than a long-term trend. The real victims of the last decade are the poorest 25 percent of American families. By any measure, they have lost real ground in the income sweepstakes to inflation—and also to middle-income groups as well as the run-away rich. These poorest of America's families are trying to raise almost a third of the nation's children. Cry for them. Not for the middle class.

SOURCE: From NEWSWEEK, Nov. 4, 1991. © 1991 Newsweek, Inc. All rights reserved. Reprinted by permission.

Applications

1. (a) In what ways did income distribution in the United States change in the 1980s?

(b) What factors other than personal income does the article suggest should be considered in assessing recent trends?

2. In what ways does income distribution in the US differ from that in Canada?

3. (a) Referring to Figure 14.5 on page 299 and Figure 14.1 on page 287, describe how income inequality in Canada compares with that in Sweden, the United Kingdom, the United States, and Brazil.

(b) Refer to Figure 14.6 on page 299. How does the distribution of wealth in Canada compare with that in the United States and Great Britain?

The Welfare State in the 1980s and 1990s

In the late 1970s and early 1980s, rising unemployment and an aging population brought increasing welfare expenditures. Tax revenues did not keep pace with social expenditures during much of the 1980s. As deficits widened, the federal Conservative government sought ways to cut back on welfare state expenditures. Eligibility standards for unemployment insurance benefits and welfare were tightened. Debate over the principle of pension universality increased and user fees for health care were suggested. Governments sought to de-index pensions and increase taxes on pensioners with high incomes.

Conservatives argue that the modern welfare state has become too heavy a burden for the Canadian economy. Government spending diverts resources from individuals to government and slows economic growth.

Other criticisms levelled against the welfare system include the following.

Disincentives to Work

One frequently stated criticism is that welfare acts as a disincentive to work. Many people on welfare would, in fact, lose money by going to work. If they take part-time work, for example, for each dollar earned they lose a dollar (or more!) from their welfare payments. They are, therefore, better off if they do not work. Only if they are able to find relatively steady full-time work can they gain over the long term. For many who are unskilled or inexperienced, however, finding steady work is not an easy task and so they are caught in what has come to be called the "welfare cycle."

Some argue that unemployment insurance as well, by providing the unemployed with benefits, permits them to seek work at a more leisurely pace than would be the case without the benefits. Unemployment insurance may, in this view, add to the total number of unemployed and the duration of unemployment.

Another related criticism stems from the fact that welfare payments are financed by the taxation of other members of society. Increased taxes may also act as a disincentive to work and investment. If additional income is simply taken away in taxes, people feel little incentive to work harder and earn more.

Administrative Complexities

Critics argue that the administrative complexity of the welfare system has led to growth of an inefficient and expensive bureaucracy. There are so many different agencies, each with its own administration, that it is sometimes difficult to determine which agency an individual or family should approach for help. Some argue that programs also overlap, meaning a costly duplication of resources.

Inequities

Though the system aims for a more equitable distribution of income, it is clear that some who need help do not receive it, while others who may not need it do receive benefits. The system, for example, does little to help the **working poor**—those who work yet whose wages fall below the poverty line. At the same time, individuals who share in family incomes of over $40 000 a year may still receive unemployment insurance benefits if they are temporarily out of work.

Summary

a. Though Canadians enjoy a comparatively high average income, the average figures hide considerable income inequality. Between 1979 and 1989, while family incomes rose, the degree of income inequality changed little.

b. The mean, median, and mode are all averages or measures of central tendency. The mean is the sum of a group of scores divided by the number of scores. The median is the middle number in a range of values that divides the values into two equal parts. The mode is the most frequent value in a set of numbers. These measures must be used appropriately, with their limitations in mind.

c. A Lorenz curve is plotted from income distribution data. The amount of the "bow" in the curve indicates the degree of income inequality.

d. Some of the reasons for income inequality include disparities in the ownership of property and capital, differences in abilities, differences in education and training, degree of risk and unpleasantness of occupations, differences in the number of hours worked, market power, discrimination, and luck.

e. The poor are those who cannot afford the basic necessities of life—that is, adequate food, clothing, and shelter. Definitions of poverty, however, are relative and standards vary the world over. The poverty line is the minimum income required to buy the necessities of life. It changes with changes in prices, family size, degree of urbanization, and our conception of what constitutes poverty.

f. The incidence of poverty in Canada is highest among women, those under the age of 24, the elderly, those with less than a Grade 9 education, and those in the Atlantic provinces. Poverty, however, is not confined to any single region, sex, age, or group.

g. Programs designed to deal with the causes of poverty include subsidized education, measures to promote full employment, laws against discrimination in the workforce, worker safety programs, and aid for low-income, single-parent families. Social insurance programs designed to fight the symptoms of poverty and based on the principle of universality include the Canada (and Quebec) Pension Plan, unemployment insurance, and medical insurance. Welfare programs targeted specifically at poverty include the Guaranteed Income Supplement and the Canada Assistance Plan.

h. Transfers and taxes in Canada lessen the degree of income inequality by increasing the share of the lowest income groups and decreasing that of the highest income groups. Generally, transfers are more effective than taxes in this regard.

i. Canada's welfare programs have been criticized for placing too great a burden on the economy and increasing government deficits, slowing economic growth by diverting money from entrepreneurs to government, causing disincentives to work and investment, creating unnecessary and costly administrative complexity, and not helping those in need, while providing help to those not in need.

■ Review of Key Terms

Define the following key terms introduced in this chapter and provide examples where appropriate.

average
measures of central tendency
mean
median
mode
Lorenz curve

the poor
the poverty line
welfare state
universality
working poor

■ Application and Analysis

1. (a) Using the data in Table 14.10 below, plot on a single graph:

(i) the complete income equality line
(ii) a Lorenz curve of income distribution before taxes and transfers
(iii) a Lorenz curve showing income distribution after taxes and transfers.

(b) What effect did transfers and taxes have on the distribution of income for unattached individuals in 1989?

(c) Compare the Lorenz curves you have drawn with those in Figure 14.3 on page 297 for families.

Table 14.10 Income distribution of unattached individuals, 1989 (percents)

POPULATION	INCOME SHARE BEFORE TRANSFERS	INCOME SHARE WITH TRANSFERS	INCOME AFTER TAXES
Lowest 20 percent	0.1	5.8	6.9
Second 20 percent	5.3	10.5	12.2
Third 20 percent	15.5	15.8	16.7
Fourth 20 percent	27.8	24.7	24.5
Highest 20 percent	51.3	43.3	39.7

ˈ ᴵRCE: Statistics Canada, *Income After Tax Distributions in Canada.*

Summarize the similarities and differences between the two graphs.

2. Marx predicted that the poor would become poorer and the rich richer. David Ricardo believed that landlords would become richer and capitalists poorer. Alfred Marshall's view was that the poor would become less poor and the rich less rich. Which view do recent trends in Canadian income distribution support? Explain.

3. (a) How might the definitions of poverty and the poverty line in Haiti or Ethiopia be different from the definitions used in Canada? Why?

(b) How might you expect the poverty line in Canada to change over the next decade? Explain why.

4. Identify the programs that could provide assistance for the people in each of the following cases:

(a) a single mother with one child and an income of $11 000, living in a rural community

(b) a pensioner with an income totalling less than $500 per month

(c) a student who does not have sufficient funds to attend a university

(d) an auto worker who has been laid off after 15 years and who has no other skills or training

(e) a typist who cannot find steady work, but whose income does not qualify him or her for the Canada Assistance Plan.

5. Though we may not be aware of it, Canada has a number of billionaires. Who are Canada's super rich and how did they make their fortunes? Use your library to find out how one or more of those in the following list acquired their wealth and what companies or enterprises they currently own or control. All of those listed were identified among the world's 202 billionaires in a September 1991 issue of *Fortune* magazine.

(a) Albert, Paul, and Ralph Reichmann—US $12.8 billion

(b) Kenneth R. Thomson—US $6.7 billion

(c) Edgar and Charles R. Bronfman and Phyllis Bronfman Lambert—US $4.1 billion

(d) Kenneth, James, Arthur, and John E. Irving—US $3.7 billion

(e) Garfield and Galen Weston—US $3.6 billion

(f) John, Fredrik, Thor, and George Eaton and family—US $1.7 billion

6. Issue—A Negative Income Tax?

In examining the inefficiencies and inequalities of our present social welfare system, some economists—both left and right of the political spectrum—have concluded that nothing short of fundamental reform is needed. One proposal that meets with considerable support from economists is the negative income tax (NIT) plan. By this plan, our entire welfare system as it currently exists would be scrapped and replaced by a negative income tax. Just as we pay (positive) income taxes when our income rises above a certain level, with the NIT we would be paid a negative income tax when our income falls below a certain level. Thus, our present income tax system would be changed to channel payments to the poor.

The NIT plan has two main components.

(i) A minimum annual income is set for a family of a given size. Let's assume that the minimum is set at $15 000 for a family of two.

(ii) A benefit-loss rate indicates the rate at which benefits are lost as income is earned. We'll assume the benefit-loss rate is 50 percent.

As shown in Table 14.11, as earned income increases from 0 to $5000, the negative income tax decreases

from $15 000 to $12 500 (i.e., $15\,000 - \dfrac{\$5000}{2}$).

Thus, as earned income increases, the negative income tax decreases—but at half the rate.

Total family income, therefore, is $5000 + $12 500 = $17 500. As earned income increases, the negative income tax decreases, until at $30 000, the negative income tax is zero. With an income of $35 000, a family starts to pay a positive income tax.

Total income, however, increases. At the break-even income of $30 000, negative income tax is zero. Beyond $30 000, a positive income tax is paid.

Table 14.11 The negative income tax plan—an illustration (dollars)

PRIVATE EARNINGS	NEGATIVE INCOME TAX	INCOME TAX	TOTAL INCOME AFTER TAX
0	+ 15 000	0	15 000
5 000	+ 12 500	0	17 500
10 000	+ 10 000	0	20 000
15 000	+ 7 500	0	22 500
20 000	+ 5 000	0	25 000
25 000	+ 2 500	0	27 500
30 000	0	0	30 000
35 000	0	-1000	34 000

With the minimum annual income set at $15 000, all families receive that amount even if they have no earnings. With earnings of $5000 and a benefit-loss rate of 50 percent, the negative income tax is $15\,000 - \dfrac{5\,000}{2} = $12\,500.

This example is, of course, but one illustration of the NIT plan. Obviously, the guaranteed annual income can be set at any amount above or below $15 000. Clearly, too, the benefit-loss rate could be above or below the 50 percent in our illustration, or the percentage could be varied at different income levels.

Advantages of the NIT

• The poor have an incentive to continue working. Every dollar the family earns increases its after-tax income.

• The program will streamline the present complex relief programs.

• The NIT can be easily and simply administered by Revenue Canada.

• It is less demeaning to the poor. The minimum level of income is provided as a matter of right—not of charity.

Disadvantages of the NIT
• People may simply take their guaranteed annual income and retire from the workforce.
• The NIT would likely be more expensive than present welfare programs.
• Present programs are tailored to meet the needs of particular groups of people—unemployment insurance for the unemployed, and so on. The NIT does not take specific problems into account.

• Implementation of the NIT requires public support. So far, that political support does not exist.

(a) Debate the resolution: "The NIT should replace our present welfare system." Each side should do further research to expand on the advantages and disadvantages outlined above. Statistics may also be useful to support each position.

(b) Evaluate the debate afterwards. What key issues were raised? How effectively did each side support its position?

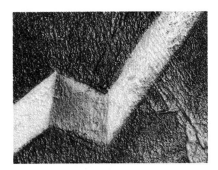

Economic Stability

In Chapter 2, we outlined the goals of the Canadian economy. So far, we have examined two of them—economic efficiency (in Unit Two) and the equitable distribution of income (in Unit Three). In this unit, we turn to economic stability. In other words, how can we achieve stable prices and full employment? Our focus shifts to the macroeconomy.

We begin the unit by examining the various measures used to assess the health of the economy in Chapter 15. Then, in Chapters 16 and 17, we consider the nature and causes of instability in the economy. Why do we have unemployment, inflation, and fluctuations in our total output? Finally, we examine what can be done to combat these fluctuations. We assess various fiscal and monetary policies designed to promote economic stability in the final three chapters of the unit.

□ □ □ □ □ □

CHAPTER FIFTEEN

Our Economic Scoreboard

Objectives

a. Determine how the total output of an economy can be measured.

b. Define Gross Domestic Product (GDP) and examine how it is calculated.

c. Demonstrate the relationship between Gross Domestic Product and Gross National Product.

d. Calculate GDP by the income and expenditure approaches and explain the relationship between the two methods.

e. Investigate other measures of income and spending and indicate the relationships among them.

f. Assess the usefulness of GDP as a measure of our economic welfare.

g. Examine measures of employment and unemployment and assess their value as indicators of economic health.

h. Investigate the incidence of unemployment in Canada.

i. Outline and provide examples of the four major types of unemployment.

j. Define full employment and explain why the full employment unemployment rate has changed over time.

k. Assess the economic and social costs of unemployment.

l. Examine price indexes and assess the Consumer Price Index as a measure of the cost of living.

m. Examine the usefulness and applications of the GDP deflator.

One of the most important questions that arises as we turn to the macro view of the economy is how we are to measure our overall economic performance. Certainly three important indicators are the growth in our total output and how far we have come in meeting the objectives of full employment and stable prices. In other words, we must examine our Gross Domestic Product (GDP), unemployment rate, and inflation rate—three statistics reported regularly in the news and carefully monitored by economists, politicians, business people, and many others. While we recognize the usefulness of these statistics, however, we must also be aware of their limitations.

In this chapter, then, we examine these three major economic indicators and assess their usefulness as measures of our economic well-being.

Measuring Total Product

Measuring the total product of the economy may seem a formidable task, but it is not that much different from how we might measure our own economic performance. If you want to know how you are doing economically, for example, you could calculate your total annual income by adding all that you have earned in wages, rent, interest, and profits over the year. You could then compare your income this year with that of previous years to see how well you are doing.

Similarly, one way of measuring the country's economic performance is to add the incomes of all people in Canada who contribute to the total product and compare this figure with that of previous years. In effect, we are calculating the total income earned from all our productive resources. This method of calculating total product is known as the **income approach**.

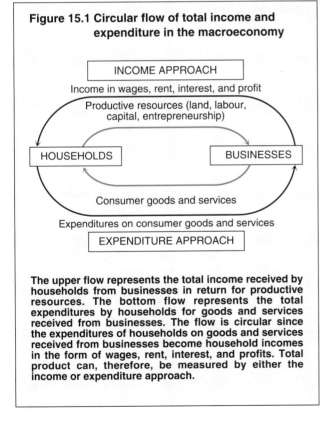

Figure 15.1 Circular flow of total income and expenditure in the macroeconomy

INCOME APPROACH

Income in wages, rent, interest, and profit

Productive resources (land, labour, capital, entrepreneurship)

HOUSEHOLDS   BUSINESSES

Consumer goods and services

Expenditures on consumer goods and services

EXPENDITURE APPROACH

The upper flow represents the total income received by households from businesses in return for productive resources. The bottom flow represents the total expenditures by households for goods and services received from businesses. The flow is circular since the expenditures of households on goods and services received from businesses become household incomes in the form of wages, rent, interest, and profits. Total product can, therefore, be measured by either the income or expenditure approach.

Another way of determining total product would be to calculate the total amount *spent* on all goods and services over the year. In other words, we would be determining the value of all goods and services produced in the country. If a total of $2 billion was spent on automobiles, for example, then automobiles contributed $2 billion to the total product. This method of calculating total output is known as the **expenditure approach**.

Figure 15.1 illustrates these two approaches to measuring total product using the circular flow model of the economy. The flows at the top of the diagram represent the total income received by households (in the form of wages, rent, interest, and profit) for productive resources sold to businesses. The flows at the bottom of the diagram show the total expenditures by households on goods and services produced by businesses. The two flows of income and expenditure will be equal, since expenditures made by households to businesses for goods and services in turn become income for households in return for productive resources sold to businesses. Thus, the flow is circular and total income equals total expenditure.

What Is Gross Domestic Product?

Both the income and expenditure approaches, therefore, will give us the same figure for the country's total product. Economists define the total product or **Gross Domestic Product (GDP)** as the value, at market prices, of all final goods and services produced in Canada over a period of time—usually one year. In 1990, for example, Canada's GDP totalled almost $672 billion. Before we examine in more detail how GDP is calculated, we need to consider what this definition means. Why are market prices used? What are "final goods" and why does the definition specify "produced in Canada?"

Market Prices

The economy produces such a wide variety of goods and services that their total value can only be measured by a common standard—the market price. For example, if an economy produces 2 billion apples and 3 billion oranges in year one, and 3 billion apples and 2 billion oranges in year two, which output is the greater? The answer is—we don't know. We can only reply when we know the price or monetary value of each fruit. If apples have a market value of 15 cents a piece and oranges 10 cents a piece, then we can calculate the total product as follows:

Year 1 $300 million + $300 million = $600 million
Year 2 $450 million + $300 million = $650 million.
Year 2's production, therefore, was greater.

Final Goods

When calculating the GDP, statisticians are careful to avoid **double counting**. The value of each good or service must be counted only once. A distinction is, therefore, made between final and intermediate goods and services. **Final goods** are products that have been bought by the last user and are not for resale or further processing. Goods that are bought for further processing or sale are called **intermediate goods**.

Bread purchased by a consumer, for example, is a final good. It will not be processed further or resold. It is purchased to be consumed as food. The wheat and flour used to make the bread, however, are intermediate goods. Similarly, the service provided by a wholesaler who buys the bread to sell to retailers is an intermediate service.

To avoid calculating the wheat and flour used in bread more than once, therefore, statisticians count only the value-added. The **value-added** is the amount added to the value of a product at each stage of the production process. We saw an example of the value-added approach earlier in our examination of the GST. There, we saw that the 7-percent tax is calculated not on the basis of the final sales price, but on the basis of the value-added at each stage of production.

Table 15.1 illustrates another example. The final sales price of the total bread production sold to consumers is $149 000. This figure over-estimates the actual value of the bread, however, because the original $15 000 value of the wheat is included four times, in the sales price at each stage of production. A wheat farmer sells the wheat to a miller for $15 000, the value

Table 15.1 The value-added in production (thousands of dollars)

	PAYMENTS TO OTHER FIRMS	VALUE-ADDED (PAYMENTS TO RESOURCES)						SALES PRICE
		WAGES	+	RENT AND INTEREST	+	PROFITS	=	
Farmer	0	10	+	3	+	2	= 15	15
Miller	15	8	+	2	+	1	= 11	26
Baker	26	15	+	5	+	2	= 22	48
Retailer	48	5	+	5	+	2	= 12	60
Totals	89	38	+	15	+	7	= 60	149

Value-added equals:
1. Payments to productive resources = 38 000 + 15 000 + 7000 = $60 000
2. Total sales ($149 000) - Total purchases ($89 000) = $60 000
3. Value of the *final* product = $60 000

of the resources needed to produce the wheat. The miller processes the wheat into flour and sells it to a baker for $26 000 (the $15 000 paid to the farmer plus $11 000 paid in wages, rent, profit, etc.), and so on. To avoid counting the wheat each time, therefore, we must calculate only the value-added at each stage.

The total value-added is the sum of all payments made to productive resources in wages, rent, interest, and profit. Alternatively, it can be calculated as the total sales value ($149 000) minus the total value of purchases from other firms ($89 000)—that is, $149 000 - $89 000 = $60 000.

This $60 000 is thus the value of the final product. It is the price paid by the consumer for the productive resources, not the final retail sales value.

Pure financial transactions, such as government and private transfer payments and the sale or purchase of securities, are also not included in the GDP because they do not represent actual current production. Government transfer payments, such as unemployment or welfare benefits, are by definition payments for which no goods or services are provided in return. Private transfer payments, including private scholarships and exchanges of stocks and bonds, involve a transfer of money or financial certificates only. They are not payments for production and are thus not calculated in GDP.

Produced in Canada

Gross Domestic Product is calculated as the total goods and services produced *within* Canada. It differs significantly from another widely quoted measure of total production—Gross National Product. **Gross National Product** measures the value, at market prices, of all final goods and services produced *by all Canadian-owned factors of production*. The essential difference between the two statistics is that GNP measures productive resources that Canadians own, no matter where these resources are located—whether in Canada or any other country. GDP measures the productive resources within Canada, no matter who owns them—Canadians or non-Canadians.

Until mid-1986, when it was replaced by GDP, GNP was the prime measure of Canada's output. Since 1926, when Statistics Canada began making the computations, GDP has always been greater than GNP. This is because a significant portion of the Canadian economy is foreign-owned, while we own a much smaller segment of foreign economies. Table 15.2 shows the relationship between GDP and GNP.

Table 15.2 GDP and GNP compared, 1990 (millions of dollars)

Gross National Product	647 624
SUBTRACT : investment income received from non-residents	– 9 255
ADD : investment income paid to non-residents	+ 33 208
Equals : Gross Domestic Product	671 577

SOURCE: Statistics Canada, *Canadian Economic Observer*, September 1991.

Since a significant portion of our economy is foreign-owned while we own a much smaller portion of foreign economies, GDP has been greater than GNP by 3 to 5 percent every year since 1926 when Statistics Canada began making the calculations. In 1990, GDP was 3.7 percent greater than GNP.

Measuring GDP—Two Approaches

At the beginning of the chapter, we saw how GDP could be calculated using either the income or expenditure approach. Now let's examine how these calculations are made in more detail.

Income Approach

When consumers, businesses, governments, and non-Canadians buy goods or services made in Canada, their expenditures provide income for Canadians. A major component of GDP, therefore, is domestic income from Canadian factors of production. As we saw in Chapter 12, the components of domestic income may be simplified into four categories—wages and salaries, corporation profits before taxes, interest and rent, and incomes of self-employed persons. Other components in the calculation of the income-based GDP include indirect taxes, depreciation, changes in inventories, and a statistical discrepancy. Figure 15.2 on page 310 shows the GDP income-based calculations for 1990.

Wages and Salaries
This category includes not only the total wages and salaries earned by all Canadians during the year, but also any additional income earned in bonuses and fringe benefits. Wages and salaries typically account for the largest proportion of GDP—$377 627 million or 56 percent in 1990.

Corporation Profits
Corporation profits are calculated before taxes and accounted for $45 145 million or 7 percent of GDP in 1990.

Interest and Rent
Interest and rent include the returns on investments in land and capital by both individuals and businesses. In other words, this category includes all income earned from interest on loans and securities, etc., as well as rent on land, buildings, and machinery, and other capital equipment. In 1990, this category totalled $57 940 million or 9 percent of GDP.

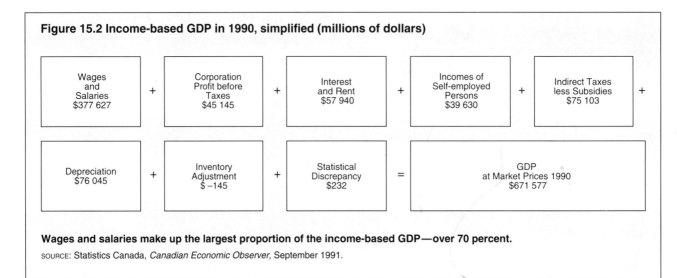

Figure 15.2 Income-based GDP in 1990, simplified (millions of dollars)

| Wages and Salaries $377 627 | + | Corporation Profit before Taxes $45 145 | + | Interest and Rent $57 940 | + | Incomes of Self-employed Persons $39 630 | + | Indirect Taxes less Subsidies $75 103 | + |

| Depreciation $76 045 | + | Inventory Adjustment $ −145 | + | Statistical Discrepancy $232 | = | GDP at Market Prices 1990 $671 577 |

Wages and salaries make up the largest proportion of the income-based GDP—over 70 percent.

SOURCE: Statistics Canada, *Canadian Economic Observer*, September 1991.

Incomes of Self-Employed Persons

Incomes of self-employed persons include the incomes from farm production, small businesses, and self-employed professionals—that is, all unincorporated businesses. Total income in this category in 1990 was $39 630 million (6 percent of GDP).

Indirect Taxes

An indirect tax is a tax that is transferred to others— that is, the tax is not borne by the one who originally pays it. Indirect taxes include essentially all taxes other than income taxes, such as sales, excise, and property taxes. Indirect taxes are treated as a cost of production by businesses and are added to the price of a product. They are, therefore, considered part of the total income derived from productive resources. Subsidies (or grants), on the other hand, are deducted from the costs of production and from prices. They must, therefore, be subtracted from the income of productive resources and are deducted from indirect taxes in the calculation of GDP. In 1990, indirect taxes less subsidies totalled $75 103 million—11 percent of GDP.

Depreciation

Depreciation is an estimate of the loss in value of ~apital goods, such as machinery or buildings, through wear and obsolescence over time. At some point, just to maintain current levels of production, capital goods must be replaced. Depreciation is then a charge against current production, which is not included elsewhere in the calculation of the income-based GDP. In 1990, depreciation totalled $76 045 or approximately 11 percent of GDP.

Changes in Inventory

Inventory is the stock of goods—including raw materials, semi-finished, and finished goods—held for future sale or production by businesses and governments. Inventories include, for example, the wheat that has not been made into flour, the flour that has not been made into bread, and the bread that has not yet been sold to customers. Inventories represent current production. Changes in inventories, therefore, must be calculated into income-based GDP (even though they are not strictly income). In 1990, inventories decreased by $145 million.

Statistical Discrepancy

Inevitably, when the statisticians have finished checking their calculations of GDP using the expenditure and income approaches, they find that the two totals don't quite match. In 1990, for example, they found

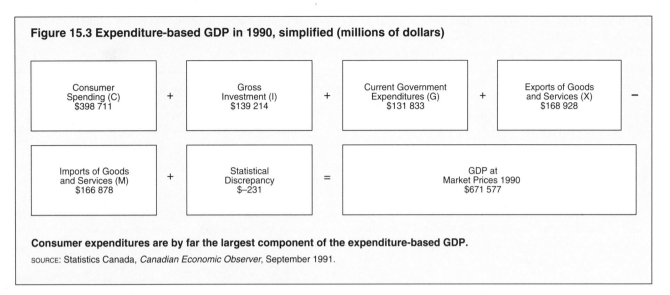

Figure 15.3 Expenditure-based GDP in 1990, simplified (millions of dollars)

Consumer Spending (C) $398 711 + Gross Investment (I) $139 214 + Current Government Expenditures (G) $131 833 + Exports of Goods and Services (X) $168 928 −

Imports of Goods and Services (M) $166 878 + Statistical Discrepancy $−231 = GDP at Market Prices 1990 $671 577

Consumer expenditures are by far the largest component of the expenditure-based GDP.

SOURCE: Statistics Canada, *Canadian Economic Observer*, September 1991.

that the difference between the two figures was $463 million. The discrepancy arises simply because of statistical error. To rectify the situation, the statisticians divide the difference by two and then add half the difference to the lower total (in 1990 the income-based figure) and subtract half the difference from the higher total (in 1990 the expenditure-based figure). Both totals are then the same—$671 577 million—rather than $671 345 and $671 809 million.

□ **Expenditure Approach**

To calculate GDP using the expenditure approach, Statistics Canada totals all spending on final goods and services by the four users of final products: consumers, businesses, governments, and non-Canadians. Figure 15.3 shows the calculations for 1990.

Consumer Spending (C)
All spending by households on goods and services from bread to legal services to automobiles is included in the consumer expenditures category. Household spending typically constitutes the largest proportion of the expenditure-based GDP, totalling 59 percent of GDP and $398 711 million in 1990.

Gross Investment (I)
Gross domestic investment, which totalled $139 214 million in 1990 (21 percent of GDP), consists of the following three components.

(i) Investment by businesses and governments This component includes investment by businesses and governments in fixed capital, such as schools, factories, power plants, and machinery.

(ii) Residential construction Included in this component is the construction of apartment buildings and owner-occupied housing. New homes are considered investments rather than consumer goods because they may be rented for a return.

(iii) Change in the value of inventories Inventories, as we noted earlier, represent current production and changes in inventories, therefore, must be calculated into GDP. Increases or decreases in inventories this year are a result of this year's production and should, therefore, be included in this year's GDP.

Current Government Expenditures on Goods and Services (G)
Government (federal, provincial, and local) expenditures on goods and services for current use include

direct purchases of materials, such as uniforms and paper. Also included are expenditures on labour services, such as those of public servants, soldiers, nurses, and teachers, and expenditures to cover the operations of government services and departments, such as the courts, legislatures, public parks, etc. In 1990, current government expenditures totalled $131 833 million or 20 percent of GDP.

Net Expenditures on Canadian Goods by Non-Canadians (Exports (X) minus Imports (M))

When calculating total expenditures by non-Canadians on Canadian goods and services, imports must be subtracted from exports.

Exports (X) When China buys Canadian wheat, or Americans buy Canadian-made automobiles, these expenditures are added into the calculations of Canada's GDP because the goods and services are produced in Canada. Exports or expenditures by non-Canadians on Canadian goods and services reached $168 928 million in 1990, 25 percent of GDP.

Imports (M) Expenditures on imports are subtracted from exports because imports represent money spent by Canadians on foreign goods and services. To include import expenditures would be to overstate our GDP since personal spending on a German-made automobile, for example, has already been counted in consumer expenditures. Similarly, a firm's expenditures on US-made machinery, for example, are included under investment. Government expenditures on foreign goods, such as Japanese audiotapes, are included under current government expenditures. In 1990, spending on imports totalled $166 878—approximately 25 percent of GDP.

The calculation of the expenditure-based GDP, therefore, may be summarized as follows:

GDP = C + I + G + (X - M)

Table 15.3 summarizes and compares the income- and expenditure-based calculations of GDP for 1990. Note that, as we said earlier, the two figures are the

same once the statistical discrepancy has been calculated, since all expenditures in the economy in turn become income.

Table 15.3 Income- and expenditure-based calculations of GDP for 1990, simplified (millions of dollars)

A. INCOME-BASED GDP		B. EXPENDITURE-BASED GDP	
Wages and salaries	377 627	Consumer expenditures	398 711
Corporation profits		Gross investment	
before taxes	45 145	Fixed capital	97 301
Interest and rent	57 940	Residential construction	45 259
Incomes of self-employed		Inventory adjustment	−3 346
persons	39 630		139 214
Inventory adjustment	−145	Current government	
Indirect taxes		expenditures	131 833
less subsidies	75 103	Exports less imports	2 050
Depreciation	76 045	Statistical discrepancy	−231
Statistical discrepancy	232		
GDP at market prices	671 577	GDP at market prices	671 577

SOURCE: Statistics Canada, *Canadian Economic Observer*, September 1991.

Calculations of GDP by the income and expenditure approaches must produce identical totals, since all expenditures are sources of income in the economy.

Other Measures of Income and Spending

GDP and GNP are not the only measures of income and spending in Canada. Other measures include net domestic income, personal income, personal disposable income, discretionary income, and consumption spending. Figure 15.4 summarizes these various measures and outlines how they are calculated.

Net Domestic Income (NDI)

Net domestic income (NDI) is equal to the income-based GDP minus depreciation, indirect taxes less subsidies, and the statistical discrepancy. These components are deducted because they are not part of the income that goes to owners of productive resources. NDI is the total income earned by Canadian-owned factors of production.

In 1990, wages and salaries accounted for 73 percent of the NDI, while corporate profits constituted 9 percent, interest and rent 11 percent, and incomes of self-employed persons 8 percent. The share of the domestic income going to wages and salaries has remained at about 70 percent for a significant period of time. Corporate profits, however, have varied considerably—falling in recessions and rising in periods of prosperity.

Personal Income (PI)
Personal income (PI) is income received by households—both earned and unearned. Personal income, therefore, excludes corporation income taxes and undistributed corporate profits (or retained earnings) because this income is not received by households. It includes transfer payments—such as pension and unemployment insurance benefits—however, because though unearned, this income is received by households. Personal income, therefore, is equal to NDI minus corporate income taxes and undistributed corporate profits, plus transfer payments.

Personal Disposable Income (PDI)
Once we have paid our personal income taxes, we are free to spend or "dispose" of our personal income as we wish. **Personal disposable income (PDI)**, then, is personal income minus personal income taxes. The basic decision we have to make with our personal disposable income is how much we spend and how much we save.

Discretionary Income
Discretionary income is that part of personal disposable income left after essentials, such as food and clothing, have been paid for. Discretionary income can be saved or spent according to the wishes and tastes of the household.

Consumption Spending
Consumption spending is that part of personal disposable income which is spent. It is, therefore, a major component of the expenditure-based GDP along with investment, government spending, and net exports.

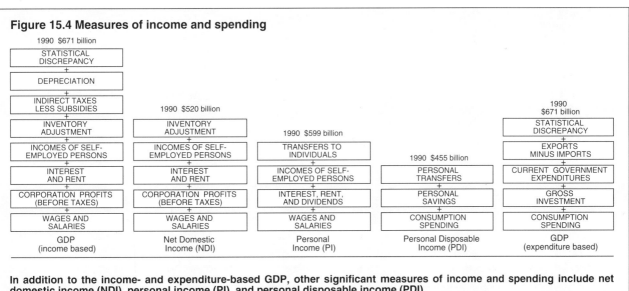

Figure 15.4 Measures of income and spending

In addition to the income- and expenditure-based GDP, other significant measures of income and spending include net domestic income (NDI), personal income (PI), and personal disposable income (PDI).

■ Limitations of GDP

The GDP is a useful measure of economic performance. Large decreases in GDP over a number of years can reflect serious economic problems, as the 30-percent fall during the Depression years of the early 1930s did in Canada. Significant increases, on the other hand, can reflect impressive economic performance—as in West Germany and Japan since 1945.

But, is the GDP a satisfactory measure of our national economic well-being? Does the fact that my total income increased over the past year mean I am better off if I am working longer hours in a thankless job I do not enjoy? A measure of material wealth is not a complete measure of quality of life. Similarly, GDP measures only those goods and services that have an explicit price. It does not include factors such as the quality of the environment, the degree of social harmony, or the amount of leisure time people have—all of which we would consider important to our national well-being.

As a measure of economic well-being, therefore, GDP has a number of limitations. These arise from the nature of the measure itself, from the *inclusion* of elements that make no obvious contribution to our welfare, and from the *exclusion* of elements that *do* make a contribution to our welfare. Let's consider some of these limitations in more detail.

Price Increases

The fact that GDP measures output *at current market prices* can lead to misleading results. Since 1946, the general level of prices has increased every year except 1952 and GDP has increased every year along with it, whether the actual output of goods and services increased or not. For example, in 1982 the GDP increased substantially, yet the actual output of goods and services declined.

Economists, therefore, make a distinction between GDP at market prices or **nominal GDP** and real GDP. **Real GDP** is a measure of actual production. It is calculated by adjusting the money GDP to eliminate the effects of price increases—that is, it is adjusted for inflation. Real GDP is generally a more accurate picture of a nation's economic performance.

Population Increases

If we wished to determine whether Canadians were better off in 1990 than in 1946, we would have to take into account not only the increase in prices, but also the increase in population. If the population increases while GDP does not, people may be worse off. Economists, therefore, calculate the **real GDP per capita**, in other words, the real income per person. They divide the real GDP by the population for that year.

$$\text{Real GDP per capita} = \frac{\text{Real GDP}}{\text{Population}}$$

To answer our question of whether Canadians were better off in 1990 than in 1946, then, we would calculate the following.

In 1946, real GDP per capita was
$$\frac{\$87\ 177 \text{ million}}{12.292 \text{ million}} = \$7092$$

By 1990, real GDP per capita was
$$\frac{\$567\ 541 \text{ million}}{26.603 \text{ million}} = \$21\ 334$$

Over the 44-year period from 1946 to 1990, therefore, real GDP per person increased by about 300 percent.

Calculations of real GDP per capita can put the dilemma of many less developed countries in perspective. In India after 1965, for example, national output grew by approximately 3.5 percent a year, but the population also grew by 2 percent a year. The actual increase in output per person per year, therefore, was only 1.5 percent.

Distribution of Income

Even if we adjust for inflation, an increase in GDP per capita of say 10 percent does not mean that all Canadians are 10 percent better off. It is possible that only a small group in society benefitted from the increase. GDP gives no indication of how our domestic income is distributed, whether equitably or not.

Kinds of Goods Produced

Since GDP measures only the dollar value of output, it makes no distinction between goods that are harmful and those that are beneficial. One hundred cigarettes and an economics text (to give an obvious example of a harmful and a beneficial good!), both selling for $30, are given equal treatment in the GDP.

To take another example, if we have a crime wave in our streets and more is spent on the police, courts, and jails, then our GDP will increase because of the increased expenditures. Similarly, with increased international tensions, our expenditures on armaments will increase and so, too, will the GDP. Yet with the increases in crime and international tensions, we would hardly consider ourselves "better off."

Environmental Pollution

While the GDP adds all the "goods" produced by the economy (such as paper for books and magazines), it does not take into account the "bads" (such as the pollution of rivers, streams, and the atmosphere, which may result from the production of paper). GDP may, therefore, overstate our domestic economic welfare.

Non-Market Goods and Services

Some productive activities are omitted from GDP because they are not sold or marketed for a dollar value. Examples include productive services of homemakers, of the amateur carpenter who repairs her home and the amateur gardener who tends his flowers, and of all volunteer workers. GDP, therefore, excludes some activities that do make a definite contribution to our national welfare.

Leisure

Since the 1920s, the average Canadian work week in manufacturing has decreased by about one quarter. Many people would agree that the increased leisure time increases our quality of life—but GDP takes no account of this. GDP does not measure the well-being resulting from an increase in leisure time.

The Underground Economy

Many economic transactions are not recorded by the statisticians of the GDP. These transactions include illegal activities, such as loan sharking, bootlegging, gambling, and the narcotics trade. Those engaged in these "businesses" prefer to keep their activities hidden for obvious reasons.

The largest part of the underground economy, however, probably comes from "under-the-table" transactions. Lawyers, carpenters, care-givers, waiters, and many others sometimes provide services for cash and do not issue a receipt. These transactions, therefore, are not reported as income at tax time and cannot be traced. They are thus not included in the GDP.

The size of the underground economy in Canada has been estimated by economists at about 14 percent of GDP, without taking barter into account, and it is believed to be growing.

☐ Is There a Better Measure?

Rather than looking at GDP as a definitive measure of well-being, therefore, we should look at it as only one of a number of indicators. The rate of inflation, the rate of employment, life expectancy, and the literacy rate, among others, should also be considered as indicators of national economic well-being. It seems that no one statistic can provide a satisfactory overall measure of our economic welfare.

Some economists have attempted to devise a single, comprehensive measure known as **Net Economic Welfare** or **NEW**. This measure includes not only GDP, but also additions for leisure time and subtractions for urbanization (pollution, overcrowding of cities, etc). Not surprisingly, per person NEW grows at a slower rate than GDP per person. NEW per person, however, actually increased during the Depression of the 1930s, presumably because more people had more leisure time. Though NEW is controversial and may not be a definitive measure, it can help us to keep other priorities such as leisure time in mind.

All statistics, however, have limitations which must be kept in mind. We should be aware of what they include and do not include and how they can be most appropriately used.

□ □ □ □ □ □

Is Our Focus On Total Product Short-Sighted?

David Suzuki is a Canadian writer, television and radio host, and world-renowned geneticist. He is also a leading voice on social and environmental issues. As you read the following article, consider Dr Suzuki's criticisms of GNP (or GDP) as a measure of our economy's "health."

The economy is an overriding political concern at all levels of government. But there is something about our current economic system that is fundamentally flawed and ultimately destructive socially and environmentally.

In part, it's because it is built on the absurd notion of the necessity for constant growth. Cessation of growth is perceived to be catastrophic for the economy, even though we live in a finite world in which endless growth is impossible.

Our economy is made possible by the fact that we, as biological beings, exist on the Earth's productivity. Yet we are told that we need continued economic growth to afford a clean environment. So we rip up the Earth's productive capacity in order to keep on growing, even though this conflicts with the most fundamental rule in economics: You don't spend all of your capital if you want to avoid bankruptcy.

Economists have provided us with various ways to assess the "health" of the economy; for example, the gross national product, which is the total market value of all goods and services in society created in a year.

The GNP is a sacred measure of annual economic growth and positively encourages environmental degradation. A standing old-growth forest, a wild caribou herd, an unused aquifer, a deep-sea vent, or an undammed watershed all have immeasurable ecological value and perform countless "services" in the total planetary biosphere, but do not register on the GNP. Only when people find a way to exploit them for financial returns does the GNP go up.

The GNP is also devoid of assessments of the social and environmental costs associated with the increase in goods and services. Suppose a major fire at a chemical or nuclear plant or pollution from a pulp mill spreads toxic compounds over a vast area and many people become very sick. More nurses, doctors, hospitals, janitors, medicines, etc., will be needed—so the GNP goes up.

If people begin to die as a result of that exposure to toxic substances, then there's greater demand for undertakers, caskets, flowers, air travel for mourners, grave diggers, and lawyers—the GNP rises further. As Ralph Nader has said, "Every time there's a car accident, the GNP goes up."

The GNP is so preposterous that it went up in 1989 because of the Exxon *Valdez* oil spill, the greatest marine disaster in American history. The GNP does not register the quality and quantity of clean air, water, soil, and biological diversity.

And what about the things that don't result in the exchange of money?

The very glue that keeps the social fabric of communities and families intact does not involve money and, therefore, is invisible to the GNP. The person who opts to be a full-time parent fails to register economically, while paid babysitters, nannies, and daycare workers do.

All of the volunteer services performed at many levels of society, including care for the elderly and [those with disabilities] do not register on the GNP.

One of my associates belongs to the Lions Club and spends weeks every year preparing for a road race for quadriplegics. He enjoys it immensely, while providing people with severe disabilities with some excitement and fun. The value to the community of this kind of volunteer work is beyond price, yet it does not contribute to the GNP.

The pre-eminence of the economy and the GNP tears at these hidden social services in developing countries and impels them to pursue cash to service international debt and products of industrial countries.

The role of the GNP in disrupting the social and environmental underpinnings of industrialized nations is illustrated in a story in Adbusters:

"Joe and Mary own a small farm. They are self-reliant,

growing as much of their food as possible and providing for most of their own needs. Their two children chip in and the family has a rich home life. Their family contributes to the health of their community and the nation. . . but they are not good for the nation's business because they consume so little.

"Joe and Mary can't make ends meet, so Joe finds a job in the city. He borrows $13 000 to buy a Toyota and drives [80 km] to work every day. The $13 000 and his yearly gas bill are added to the nation's gross national product.

"Then Mary divorces Joe because she can't handle his bad city moods any more. The $11 000 lawyer's fee for dividing up the farm and assets is added to the nation's GNP. The people who buy the farm develop it into townhouses at $200 000 a pop. This results in a spectacular jump in the GNP.

"A year later, Joe and Mary accidentally meet in a pub and decide to give it another go. They give up their city apartments, sell one of their cars, and renovate a barn in the back of Mary's father's farm. They live frugally, watch their pennies, and grow together as a family again. Guess what? The nation's GNP registers a fall and the economists tell us we're worse off."

You don't have to be an economist to know something's wrong and has to be changed.

SOURCE: David Suzuki, "Our focus on economy short-sighted," *The Toronto Star*, October 13, 1990. Copyright David Suzuki, Southam Syndicate.

Applications

1. (a) List Dr Suzuki's criticisms of the GNP as a measure of the economy's health.

(b) With which criticisms do you agree? With which do you disagree? Explain your point of view.

2. (a) Should the GNP/GDP be scrapped as a measure of economic performance? Explain.

(b) If you believe the GNP/GDP should be scrapped, what would you replace it with? If you think it should be changed, explain how.

■ Employment and Unemployment

We have considered total production as a measure of our economic performance. Now we turn to the issue of full employment. How successful has the Canadian economy been in providing jobs and how is the level of employment measured?

Each month, Statistics Canada conducts a random survey of some 55 000 representative Canadian households to determine who is employed and who is not. Interviewers gather information on all household members of working age, 15 years and over. The **employed** are those who did any work at all—part-time or full-time—during the month, and those who had a job but did not work because of labour disputes, vacations, or illness. In 1990, for example, the total number employed in Canada was 12.6 million.

The **unemployed** include all those without work and who are actively looking and available for work. Also included are individuals who will be starting a new job in the next four weeks or less, or who are on temporary lay off. In 1990, the total number of unemployed was just over one million (1.109 million).

The total **labour force** includes both the employed and the unemployed. In other words, it is the total pool of labour available for work (with the exception of full-time military personnel, inmates of penal institutions, and some others). Those not part of the labour force are full-time students, retirees, and homemakers. In 1990, the Canadian labour force totalled 13.7 million people. When the labour force is expressed as a percentage of the population 15 years and over, it is known as the **participation rate**.

The statistic most commonly quoted and most closely watched, however, is the unemployment rate.

The **unemployment rate** is the percentage of the labour force that is unemployed. It is calculated by the following formula:

$$\text{Unemployment rate} = \frac{\text{Total unemployed}}{\text{Total labour force}} \times 100.$$

For example, in 1990:

$$\frac{1.109 \text{ million}}{13.689 \text{ million}} \times 100 = 8.1 \text{ percent.}$$

Statistics Canada generally publicizes two rates—the actual unemployment rate and the seasonally adjusted rate. The seasonally adjusted rate eliminates seasonal variations (short-term fluctuations), such as the rise in unemployment each winter when farmers, those in the fishing industry, and other seasonal workers are unemployed.

☐ Limitations of Employment Statistics

Just as with GDP, it is important to recognize that the unemployment rate as a measure of our economic performance has limitations.

Few Checks

By definition, the unemployed must be actively seeking work, but it is extremely difficult to check on whether or how seriously all these people are actually looking. For the most part, they are simply asked whether they are looking. Unemployment figures, therefore, are not absolutely accurate.

Underemployment

Those with part-time work are included in the category of the employed, though many may prefer to be working full time. They are, in fact, only partially employed. In 1990, the number of part-time workers totalled 1.9 million. Data are collected on the number of part-time workers who want full-time employment, but the official unemployment rate does not take this distinction into account.

Discouraged Workers

Discouraged workers are those who would like to work, but have stopped looking because they believe no work is available for them. Once they stop looking,

they are no longer considered part of the labour force and are not included among the unemployed. The unemployment rate may, therefore, seriously underestimate the extent of the unemployment problem.

☐ Canada's Employment Record

Despite its weaknesses, the unemployment rate is nevertheless a useful indicator in the assessment of our economic health. By comparing unemployment rates from year to year, we can gain an indication of how effectively our economy is providing jobs for workers. A consistently high rate of unemployment may indicate that the economy is not performing this function adequately and may be in a recession. Unemployment rates for various regions and age groups may also provide an indication of those most likely to suffer from unemployment and thus help governments to devise specific relief programs.

Figure 15.5 shows the average annual unemployment rate in Canada from 1966 to mid-1991. Unemployment has varied as the economy has moved through upswings and slowdowns. Until the 1970s, some variations are evident, but the figures show no clear trend. Since the 1970s, however, average rates have tended to rise. While the average unemployment rate in the 1970s was approximately 7 percent, the average rate rose to over 9 percent in the 1980s. In 1983, the unemployment rate reached its highest point since the Great Depression of the 1930s. The rate declined through the boom of the late 1980s, but rose dramatically once again with the recession of the early 1990s.

☐ Who Are Most Affected?

Unemployment figures by age groups and regions also indicate that not all Canadians are equally affected by unemployment. As shown in Figure 15.6, unemployment rates in Atlantic Canada, Quebec, and British Columbia have consistently been higher than those in Ontario and the Prairie provinces since 1977. Rates in Atlantic Canada are generally the highest in the country. Newfoundland and Labrador has shown especially high rates—exceeding those of every other province

Figure 15.5 Average annual unemployment rates in Canada, 1966-1991

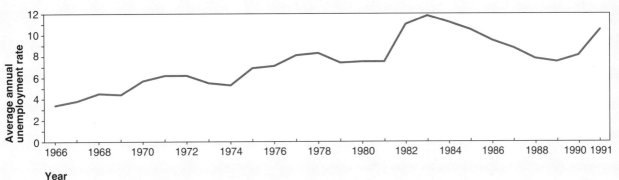

Unemployment rates have varied with the cyclical fluctuations in the economy. Since the 1970s, however, the general trend in the unemployment rate has been upward. Rates averaged at around 7 percent in the 1970s and over 9 percent in the 1980s.

SOURCE: Statistics Canada, *Canadian Economic Observer*, Historical Supplement 1990/91 and September 1991.

Figure 15.6 Unemployment rates by region, 1977-1991 (annual average)

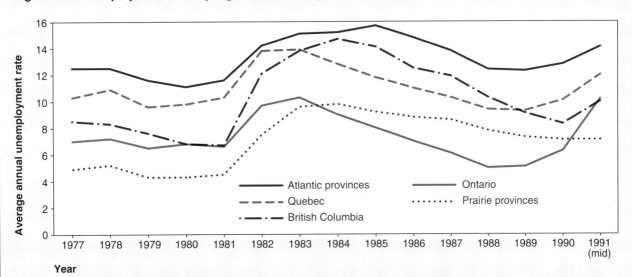

Unemployment rates have been highest in the Atlantic provinces over the period 1977 to 1991, while Ontario and the Prairie provinces generally showed the lowest rates. Rates have also been highest during recessionary periods—1982-83 and 1990-91.

SOURCE: *Bank of Canada Review*, September 1991.

since 1966. In both 1984 and 1985, the rates in this province surpassed 20 percent. More than one in five workers was unemployed. Clearly, some areas of the country carry a greater burden of unemployment than others.

Unemployment rates by age and sex also show wide variations. Figure 15.7 indicates that unemployment rates for those between the ages of 15 and 24 have been consistently higher than for those over age 25. Males between 15 and 24 have a particularly high rate of unemployment, while more women over 25 are unemployed than men. The high rate of unemployment among the 15- to 24-year-olds may be largely due to the fact that many have not yet acquired key job skills and experience. They are, therefore, at a disadvantage.

The prospects for teen employment in Atlantic Canada were especially bleak in the 1980s. In the fall of 1982, the unemployment rate for teens in Newfoundland and Labrador reached 40 percent and very high rates continued into the 1990s.

How do Canadian unemployment rates compare with those of other industrialized nations? Table 15.4 provides some comparisons. As we can see, unemploy-

ment rates in the United States, Germany, and Japan are significantly below those of Canada from 1987 to 1991. France, however, has had rates higher than Canada's, except in 1991.

Table 15.4 Unemployment rates of select industrialized nations, 1987-1991 (annual averages)

	1987	1988	1989	1990	1991 (MAY)
Canada	8.8	7.7	7.5	8.1	10.2
United States	6.1	5.4	5.2	5.5	6.8
United Kingdom	10.3	8.5	7.1	6.9	9.2
France	10.5	10.0	9.4	9.0	9.5
Germany	6.2	6.2	5.6	5.1	4.4 (Apr.)
Japan	2.8	2.5	2.3	2.1	2.1

SOURCE: Statistics Canada, *Canadian Economic Observer*, September 1991.

Unemployment rates in Canada over the years 1987 to 1991 have been higher than those of the United States, Germany, and particularly Japan. France, however, has had rates higher than Canada's, except in 1991.

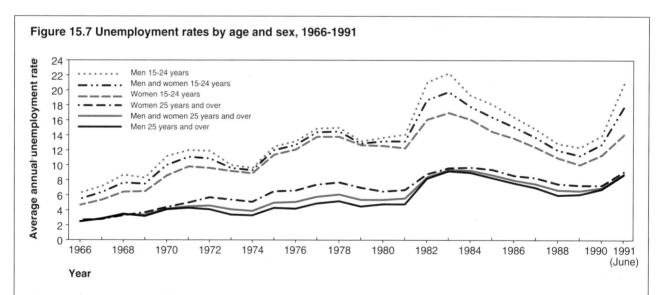

Figure 15.7 Unemployment rates by age and sex, 1966-1991

Legend:
- Men 15-24 years
- Men and women 15-24 years
- Women 15-24 years
- Women 25 years and over
- Men and women 25 years and over
- Men 25 years and over

Over the period 1966 to 1990, unemployment was generally higher among those aged 15 to 24 (particularly males) than among those 25 and over. More women 25 and over were unemployed than men, however.

SOURCE: Statistics Canada, *Canadian Economic Observer*, Historical Supplement 1990/91 and August 1991.

☐ Types of Unemployment

What causes unemployment? Economists have identified four major types of unemployment—frictional, seasonal, structural, and cyclical (or inadequate demand).

Frictional Unemployment

Frictional unemployment refers to the short-term unemployment of those who are "between jobs," or who are just entering or re-entering the labour market. Examples include school graduates looking for their first permanent jobs or workers who have left a position to look for a higher-paying or more suitable one. The term "frictional" describes the fact that the flow of workers from one industry or firm to another is not always perfectly smooth. There are lag times.

Since, in our market economy, employers can dismiss workers and workers are free to change jobs, we will always experience some degree of frictional unemployment. Indeed, it may be considered desirable, since both individuals and the economy benefit when workers are able to move from declining to expanding industries or from unsuitable to more suitable positions. Frictional unemployment may, in fact, increase during periods of economic expansion. Workers are more confident of finding a better job and may be more willing to risk unemployment to gain that position.

Frictional unemployment is generally considered the least serious form of unemployment—providing, of course, that the duration is short. It can be alleviated, however, through unemployment information services and counselling, such as that provided by Canada Employment Centres across the country.

Seasonal Unemployment

Seasonal unemployment occurs as a result of climatic changes, which may leave a significant number of people unemployed for several months each year. In Canada, the construction, lumbering, fishing, farming, and tourism industries are all subject to seasonal fluctuations in employment.

However, the impact of seasonal unemployment is less today than it was in the past. New technologies have been developed to permit construction in winter and a smaller proportion of the workforce is engaged in agriculture and other seasonally-affected primary industries. The increased popularity of winter sports, such as skiing, skating, and snowmobiling, has also helped to balance the large summer demand for workers in the tourism industry.

Structural Unemployment

Structural unemployment occurs when the skills and/or locations of workers do not match those of the jobs available. In Atlantic Canada, for example, many jobs were lost in the late 1980s and early 1990s as fish and other natural resource stocks declined. At the same time, the number of jobs in cities to the west and in occupations such as computer programming increased considerably.

Structural unemployment is particularly serious because it results from structural changes in the economy, such as shifts in demand or changes in production techniques. The increasing use of robots on automobile assembly lines, for example, has meant a decline in the number of unskilled assembly line jobs.

Structural unemployment is also typically long-term. Workers cannot easily and quickly acquire new skills in growing occupations or in expanding locations. They may be reluctant to leave their local communities or to engage in new, sometimes long-term retraining programs (if they are even available) until they have explored all other possibilities.

To combat the problem, governments have established programs to determine and provide information about employment trends. Community colleges have worked together with the business community and labour unions to focus on teaching the emerging skills. Governments have also provided incentives (e.g., low interest loans and preferential tax treatment) to industries that locate in areas struck by structural unemployment.

Cyclical or Inadequate Demand Unemployment

Market economies typically experience periodic upswings and downturns known as business cycles. **Cyclical or inadequate demand unemployment** is caused by the reduction in economic activity during downturns.

It was highest, for example, during the depths of the Great Depression in the 1930s when as much as 20 percent of the Canadian labour force was unemployed. If we examine unemployment rates in the 1980s and early 1990s, we can also see that unemployment was highest during the recession of 1982-83, eased somewhat in the late 1980s, and then rose again with the downturn of 1990-91. The causes and effects of cyclical unemployment will become clearer when we examine the business cycle in the next chapter.

☐ What is Full Employment?

From what we have discovered about the nature of unemployment, is it reasonable to expect 100 percent employment in Canada? Of course, the answer is no. Economists believe that structural, seasonal, and frictional unemployment are to some extent inevitable and even necessary. Cyclical unemployment, however, can be eliminated by stabilizing the downturn and upswing pattern of the business cycle. For economists, then, the goal of **full employment** is achieved when cyclical unemployment is zero or, to put it another way, when unemployment equals the sum of structural, seasonal, and frictional unemployment. Full employment is the lowest possible rate of unemployment.

At full employment, the domestic output that can be produced is called the **potential** or **full-employment output**. However, as we know, the economy does not always operate at its potential and cyclical unemployment is not easily eliminated.

The full employment rate has been adjusted over time. In the 1960s, the Economic Council of Canada suggested that a rate of 3 percent unemployment was reasonable. Full employment would be reached, therefore, with 97 percent of the labour force engaged. This figure was almost attained in 1966. In 1980, the Council revised its figure upward—to 6 percent unemployment. Others have suggested that the realistic full employment unemployment rate has been perhaps as high as 8.5 percent in the past. The consensus seems to be that full employment is reached with a 6 or 7 percent unemployment rate.

Why has the full employment rate changed? First, the structure of the labour force has changed. Teenagers today make up a larger proportion of the labour force and they are more likely to move from job to job than are other workers. Second, improved unemployment insurance and the increasing number of families with more than one wage earner mean that more unemployed workers can afford to take extra time looking for a job. Third, increases in the minimum wage have made some employers reluctant to hire unskilled workers. The basic number of unemployed due to frictional, seasonal, and structural unemployment has, therefore, risen—and so the full employment rate was adjusted.

☐ Costs of Unemployment

There is no doubt that unemployment wreaks severe costs on both the individuals involved and the economy as a whole. These costs are both economic and social.

Economic Costs

Though unemployment insurance benefits help to alleviate some financial hardship for those out of work, individuals and families lose income. The longer the period of unemployment, the greater is the loss of income. The contribution the unemployed would have made to domestic output had they been employed is also lost forever. A GDP that is lower than full potential means that everyone loses. The difference between the potential GDP, which the country could produce at full employment, and the actual GDP is call the **GDP gap**. The GDP gap is, therefore, one measure of the economic costs of unemployment.

As unemployment increases, the GDP gap increases. The widest gap occurred during the Great Depression of the 1930s when approximately 20 percent of the labour force was unemployed. An American economist, Arthur Okun, developed a general law to measure the GDP gap. **Okun's law** is stated as follows:

For every 1 percent that the actual unemployment rate exceeds the full employment rate, there is a 2 percent gap in GDP.

If we take the year 1983 (when the unemployment rate reached 11.8 percent), for example, and assume a full employment rate of 7 percent, then cyclical unemployment equalled 11.8 percent minus 7 percent, or 4.8 percent. In 1983, GDP at 1986 prices totalled $439.448 billion. Using Okun's law, then, we can estimate the GDP gap at:

$$\$439.448 \text{ billion} \times \frac{4.8 \times 2}{100} = \$42.187 \text{ billion.}$$

This is a huge sum—enough to provide every Canadian man, woman, and child with almost $1700 in additional income!

However, as we saw, the cost of unemployment is borne unequally. If we all carried an equal share of the unemployment rate—if, for example, in 1983 we had all been unemployed for about 12 percent of the time—then the burden would not have been so great. However, we have seen that particular groups (those between 15 and 24 years of age and those living in Atlantic Canada) are typically most hard hit. This uneven distribution of the burden makes it difficult for governments to combat the problem, since policies to reduce the national unemployment rate may not alleviate the difficulties experienced in specific regions or by specific groups.

Social Costs

The social and psychological costs of unemployment are even more difficult to combat. Unemployment can result in loss of self-esteem, a decline in job-earning skills, frustration, discouragement, increased family tensions, and social unrest. These costs are not reflected in the economic statistics, but they must be considered in an assessment of our social and economic well-being.

■ Measures of Inflation

The third indicator of economic performance we examine in this chapter is the inflation rate. In other words, we consider how close we have come to achieving the goal of price stability. It is not difficult to understand the importance of this objective when we consider that our incomes may buy much less this year than they did five or ten years ago. **Inflation** is defined as a persistent rise in the general level of prices. The two most frequently quoted measures of inflation are the Consumer Price Index (CPI) and the GDP deflator.

A Simple Price Index

Before we consider these two measures, let's examine how a simple price index is constructed. A **price index** is a number that shows the average percentage change in the prices of a collection of goods and/or services over a period of time.

Suppose we live in a simple economy that produces only one good—gasoline—and we want to construct a price index for our total output. We'll assume that in 1986, the price of gasoline per litre was 30 cents. Today, the price per litre is 75 cents. If we use 1986 as our **base year**—that is, our starting or reference point—then our price index is calculated as follows:

$$\text{Price index} = \frac{\text{Current price}}{\text{Base year price}} \times 100$$

$$= \frac{75}{30} \times 100 = 250.$$

The price index for the current year is, therefore, 250. The price index for the base year (in this case 1986) is always 100, since to calculate it we would be dividing a number by itself and multiplying by a hundred—the result always being one hundred.

To see how useful a price index can be, suppose our gasoline economy produces 100 litres this year, which is the same amount as in 1986. If we compare the output of 1986 with this year's output in current dollars, we will get a distorted picture. In 1986, the total output in dollar terms was 30 cents x 100 litres = $30. This year's output in dollar terms is 75 cents x 100 litres = $75. It appears that total output in 1986 was only two-fifths of this year's—yet in both years the same amount of gasoline was produced.

If, however, we use our simple price index to convert this year's dollar output into 1986 dollars, we have a standard value and a much clearer picture. Our formula is:

$$\frac{\text{Output in current dollars}}{\text{Current price index}} \times 100 = \frac{\text{Cost in constant}}{\text{(1986) dollars}}$$

$$\frac{100 \text{ litres} \times 75 \text{ cents per litre}}{250} \times 100 = \frac{\$75}{250} \times 100 = \$30$$

We can see, therefore, that the real output in the two years is the same but the price of gasoline has risen by 150 percent.

☐ The Consumer Price Index

The **Consumer Price Index (CPI)** measures the average price of goods and services bought by representative urban Canadian households. It is often thought of as the cost of a "basket" of goods and services bought by a typical urban Canadian household. Statistics Canada publishes the CPI monthly, and like our gasoline price index, it is calculated by comparing today's prices of goods and services with the prices of the same goods and services at an earlier date, that is, the base year. The base year is currently 1986.

As the name implies, only *consumer* goods are included in the approximately 400 goods and services surveyed to produce the CPI. Not included are the prices of investment goods, such as machinery and factories, or wholesale goods bought by manufacturers. The survey is carried out in urban centres with populations over 30 000, thus including at least one urban centre in each province.

Not all goods and services in the "basket" can be considered equally, however. A 50-percent increase in the price of salt, for example, is less likely to affect us than a 20-percent increase in the price of housing. Why? Salt figures less prominently than housing in the expenditures of the average household.

Each component of the CPI is, therefore, weighted according to the proportion of a typical household's income spent on it. The CPI thus reflects the relative quantities bought by the average Canadian urban household as well as the average prices paid. Figure 15.8 illustrates the components of the CPI and their weights based on the latest Statistics Canada survey in 1986. Housing, food, and transportation are the largest components.

Table 15.5 shows the percentage increase in CPI categories from 1961 to 1991 (select years) and Figure 15.9 indicates the general trend in the CPI over the same period. The general price level, as measured by the CPI, rose slowly between 1961 and 1971—increasing by only one-fifth. In the next decade, prices more than doubled, with the greatest increase occurring after 1976. In the early years of the 1980s, prices continued to rise rapidly, but increases slowed after 1984.

In general, prices of the CPI's main components kept pace with the increases in the CPI. The most notable exception was the tobacco and alcoholic beverages component, which showed a significant rise, especially in 1991. This increase is largely a result of federal and provincial taxes imposed on these items.

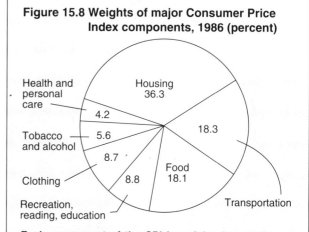

Figure 15.8 Weights of major Consumer Price Index components, 1986 (percent)

Health and personal care

Housing 36.3

4.2

18.3

Tobacco and alcohol — 5.6

8.7

Food 18.1

Clothing

8.8

Recreation, reading, education

Transportation

Each component of the CPI is weighted according to the relative amount typical urban households spend on it. Weights are also attached to individual items within each component (bread in the food component, for example). Housing is the largest component, followed by transportation and food.

SOURCE: Statistics Canada, *Canadian Economic Observer*, September 1991.

Table 15.5 Percentage increase in CPI components, selected years, 1961-1991 (1986 = 100, base year)

	1961	1966	1971	1976	1981	1986	1991 JUNE
Housing	24.3	26.4	33.3	49.2	75.3	100.0	124.5
Transportation	24.0	25.7	31.2	44.7	74.1	100.0	118.5
Food	20.7	24.1	27.2	45.2	78.9	100.0	124.3
Recreation, reading, and education	29.6	32.2	40.2	54.8	76.8	100.0	129.5
Clothing	34.2	38.3	44.0	58.1	84.2	100.0	128.6
Tobacco and alcohol	21.6	23.2	27.8	37.2	58.0	100.0	163.4
Health and personal care	24.0	27.9	34.1	49.3	75.4	100.0	129.0

SOURCE: Statistics Canada, *Canadian Economic Observer*, Historical Statistical Supplement 1990/91 and September 1991.

Prices of the CPI components generally kept pace with the trend in the general CPI except for tobacco and alcoholic beverages, which rose sharply (largely due to tax increases).

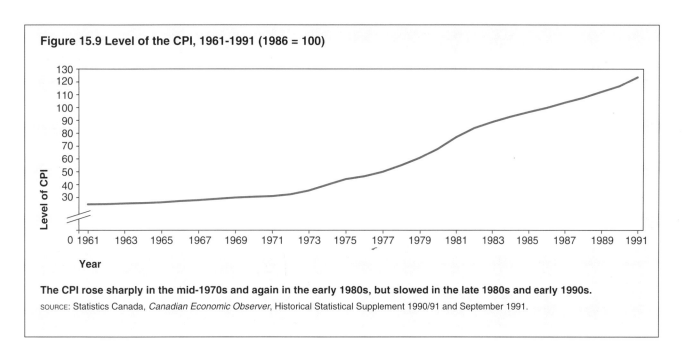

Figure 15.9 Level of the CPI, 1961-1991 (1986 = 100)

The CPI rose sharply in the mid-1970s and again in the early 1980s, but slowed in the late 1980s and early 1990s.

SOURCE: Statistics Canada, *Canadian Economic Observer*, Historical Statistical Supplement 1990/91 and September 1991.

☐ Some Limitations of the CPI

You will have probably already noted some limitations of the CPI. How closely, for example, do your household's expenditures match the proportions shown in Figure 15.8? Let's consider these limitations in more detail.

Individual Cost of Living

The CPI does not measure the cost of living of any one person. Statistics Canada surveys a sample of the population considered representative, but the averages calculated will not apply precisely to any one individual household. A 10-percent increase in the CPI may not affect you greatly, for example, if a large part of the

□ □ □ □ □ □

Constructing a Price Index

How could you construct a price index? It is possible and will give you an accurate picture of just how much the prices of goods and services have changed.

Let's outline a typical, simple example. Suppose we have surveyed the spending habits of students and found that they spend money on just three items—hot dogs, T-shirts, and compact discs. The year in which we have done our survey is the base year—say 1990. Next, we have to determine the prices of the three goods and calculate the average price. Table 15.6 displays the results. As we can see, students spent a total of $100 a month on average.

Two years later in 1992, we survey the prices of the three items again and get the results shown in Table 15.7. We find that, on average, the price of CDs remained unchanged while the prices of T-shirts and hot dogs increased. Our students' budget of 1990 in 1992 prices has increased from $100 to $117, as shown in Table 15.8. Thus, our price index has increased from 100 in the base year 1990 to 117 in 1992. This tells us that the average student's cost of living increased 17 percent over the two years. What cost students $1.00 in 1990 costs them $1.17 in 1992.

Uses of the Price Index

How is this price index useful? One use is that it allows us to make comparisons of costs and incomes over time.

Suppose Jared, a student, has been working at a part-time job for $150 a month since 1990. By 1992, if not earlier, he would have found that his pay doesn't go as far as it did in 1990. The increase in the price index provides Jared with facts he can use to support a case for higher pay from his employer. How much should he ask for, so that his 1992 pay keeps pace with his 1990 earnings?

Table 15.6 Student spending survey, 1990

	AVERAGE PRICE (DOLLARS)	AVERAGE QUANTITY BOUGHT PER MONTH	AVERAGE EXPENDITURE PER MONTH (DOLLARS)
Hot dogs	1.00	60	60.00
T-shirts	10.00	2	20.00
Compact discs	20.00	1	20.00
Total			100.00

Table 15.7 Prices in 1992

	PRICE (DOLLARS)	PERCENTAGE INCREASE SINCE 1990
Hot dogs	1.25	25
T-shirts	11.00	10
Compact discs	20.00	0

Table 15.8 Students' 1990 budget in 1992 prices

60 hot dogs at $1.25	$ 75.00
2 T-shirts at $11.00	$ 22.00
1 compact disc at $20.00	$ 20.00
	$117.00

Table 15.9 College students' budget

	PRICE IN 1986 DOLLARS	AVERAGE QUANTITY BOUGHT PER MONTH IN 1986	PRICE IN 1992 DOLLARS
Hamburgers	1.00	30	2.00
Textbooks	30.00	2	50.00
Jeans	20.00	2	30.00
Sweat shirts	20.00	1	35.00
Movies	5.00	2	7.00
Running shoes	40.00	1	60.00

$$\text{1992 value of base year (1990) pay} = \text{Pay} \times \frac{\text{1992 index}}{100} = \$150 \times \frac{117}{100} = \$175.50$$

The answer is $175.50 a month—a raise of $25.50.

Applications

1. (a) Use the data in Table 15.9 to compute the students' price index for 1992. The base year is 1986. Assume students spend their money on the six items shown.
(b) How might this price index be useful? Explain.

increase comes from higher liquor and tobacco prices, and no one in your household drinks or smokes.

Fixed Weights

As prices change, households vary their spending patterns. Households are likely to shift their expenditures away from relatively high-priced items. When housing prices are exorbitant, for example, more people will delay buying a home. Thus, an index with fixed weights over a number of years is likely to overstate the cost of living.

Changing Consumption Patterns

Over time, commodities in the typical household "shopping basket" change. Computers, microwave ovens, and VCRs, for example, have become common household purchases over just the past few years. The "basket," therefore, may become less representative of current consumption patterns despite periodic revisions.

To help solve some of these problems, Statistics Canada surveys the spending patterns of Canadians twice every ten years and revises the weights. It also periodically sets a new base year to reflect current costs. While the CPI provides a general measure of changing prices, it cannot be considered an accurate measure of living costs for any one household, and cannot always reflect rapidly changing prices and spending patterns.

☐ The GDP Deflator

The **GDP deflator** measures the price changes for all *final* goods and services produced in an economy. The GDP deflator is thus broader than the CPI in that it takes into account not only consumer goods and services, but also investment goods, goods and services bought by government, and imports.

The deflator is used to adjust nominal GDP or GDP in current dollars to real GDP or GDP in constant dollars. Nominal GDP measures the *money* value of output. Since, as we are well aware, prices tend to change, comparing GDP in money terms between two periods is not particularly useful. It is like comparing the height of two people with a measuring rod that is continually shrinking. If, however, we can find out by how much the rod has shrunk when we wish to use it, we can adjust our result.

Similarly, if we wish to compare our economy's output this year with that of last year, we can obtain a more accurate assessment if we know the difference in the value of the dollar between the two years and then adjust this year's estimate accordingly. This adjustment of nominal GDP to real GDP answers one of the weaknesses of the GDP as a measure of our economic well-being—that the value of money by which it is measured varies.

To illustrate the use of the deflator, let's assume that an economy produces only wheels in the amounts and at the prices shown in Table 15.10. A comparison of the GDP for year 1 ($500) and year 3 ($2100) in current dollars greatly overstates the output of year 3 because of the rise in wheel prices. To compare the outputs of the two years more accurately, we need a price index that reflects the overall changes in the price level. By expressing the price index as a decimal (where 100 = 1.00 and 200 = 2.00, etc.) and dividing it into the nominal GDP, we get the real GDP or GDP in constant dollars. The constant dollars are those of the base year, in this case, year 1. We can calculate the price index as follows:

$$\text{Price index} = \frac{\text{Price in any year}}{\text{Price in base year}} \times 100$$

$$\text{Price index for year 2} = \frac{\$20}{\$10} \times 100 = 200 \text{ percent}$$

$$\text{Price index for year 3} = \frac{\$30}{\$10} \times 100 = 300 \text{ percent}$$

Year 1 is the base year and is, therefore, 100 percent.

To convert our GDP for years 2 and 3 from current dollars into constant or year 1 dollars, we calculate the following:

$$\frac{\text{Nominal GDP}}{\text{Price index}} = \text{Real GDP}.$$
$$(\text{expressed as a decimal})$$

For year 2, then, $\frac{\$1200}{2.0} = \$600$.

Real GDP shows the value of each year's output expressed in constant dollars. The outputs of year 1 and 2 are directly comparable when expressed in real terms. Real GDP is, therefore, a better indicator of economic performance than GDP in current dollars.

Now let's consider actual figures from the national accounts. Table 15.11 demonstrates how the GDP deflator is used to adjust nominal GDP for select years between 1971 and 1991 to real GDP. Comparisons of output over these years can then be made more accurately.

With 1986 as the base year, the nominal GDP before 1986 is inflated because prices before 1986 were generally lower than in the base year. After 1986, the nominal GDP is deflated because the general price level is above that of 1986.

Table 15.11 Nominal GDP, real GDP, and the GDP deflator, select years, 1971-1991 (billions of dollars)

1 YEAR	2 NOMINAL OR UNADJUSTED GDP	3 GDP DEFLATOR (1986 = 100)	4 REAL GDP IN 1986 DOLLARS
1971	97.290	33.9	286.991
1976	197.924	53.2	371.688
1981	355.994	80.9	440.127
Base year			
1986	505.666	100.0	505.666
1987	551.597	104.7	526.730
1988	605.147	109.7	551.423
1989	649.102	114.9	564.990
1990	671.577	118.3	567.541
1991 (3rd quarter)	687.220	121.9	563.612

SOURCE: *Bank of Canada Review*, December 1991.

Adjustments with the GDP deflator allow for a more accurate comparison of output levels over the years shown. With 1986 as the base year, the nominal GDP is inflated before 1986 since prices were lower than in 1986. After 1986, the nominal GDP is deflated because prices are generally higher than in 1986.

Table 15.10 The GDP deflator

1 YEAR	2 OUTPUT OF WHEELS	3 PRICE OF WHEELS	4 PRICE INDEX (PERCENT) YEAR 1 = 100	5 NOMINAL GDP OR GDP IN CURRENT DOLLARS (OUTPUT × PRICE)	6 REAL GDP OR GDP IN CONSTANT DOLLARS (NOMINAL GDP ÷ PRICE INDEX AS A DECIMAL)
1	50	$10	100	$ 500	($ 500 ÷ 1.00) = $500
2	60	$20	200	$1200	($1200 ÷ 2.00) = $600
3	70	$30	300	$2100	($2100 ÷ 3.00) = $700

The GDP deflator converts money or nominal GDP into real GDP, which makes output over various years more directly comparable.

□ □ □ □ □ □

Skill Development: Using Economic Statistics

Catherine Harris, a contributing editor for *The Financial Post*, wrote in an article for the *Canadian Economic Observer* :

Statistics are very valuable tools but they can lead you astray if you don't use them properly. It doesn't take a lot of time to check into the margin of error to which particular numbers are subject or to find out the basic concepts behind them. If you don't do so, the conclusions you draw could lead to some bad decisions, to the detriment of your business, job, or even some aspect of your personal life. Statistics are like a car—very useful if used carefully, but likely to cause delays, expense, and all sorts of other problems if not treated with respect.

How should we treat economic statistics? The following are some helpful guidelines based on the article by Catherine Harris.

1. Statistics are estimates.

It is important to remember that statistics are not exact measures. All have margins of error, which must be kept in mind. For example, when Statistics Canada says that GDP was $649 102 million in 1989, what it really means is that it was about $650 billion. And when it reports that the growth in real GDP was 4.3 percent in 1987, what it means is that it was between 4 percent and 4.5 percent.

Margins of error of this magnitude are usually not significant to the users of the data. It's not important whether the economy was growing at 4 percent or 4.5 percent; what is important is that the economy was growing very fast, well above potential (estimated at about 3 percent).

Why does Statistics Canada bother to provide such detailed data when they are just estimates? The precision is necessary to calculate meaningful percentage changes,

establish trends, and examine changes between different components of the economy with accuracy.

2. Rounded figures can be misleading.

Let's consider an example of how using rounded numbers can cause problems. Government capital spending in 1988 was $11 964 million (1981 dollars) *vs.* $11 360 million in 1987. It is certainly appropriate to round these numbers to $12 billion and $11 billion respectively if you're just looking at the level of government investment.

But, if you want to know what the growth rate was between the two years, it would not be a good idea to use rounded numbers. The growth rate is 9.1 percent using rounded numbers and 5.3 percent using unrounded figures. Of course, growth rates must be considered as just estimates too. But a 5.3 percent rise and a 9.1 percent rise don't give the same impression. The correct one is the first because it's based on unrounded numbers—and it should be read as a rise of around 4 to 6 percent.

Using rounded numbers to establish trends presents similar problems, especially for smaller groups or components of the economy. If you rounded the employment levels for Alberta, for example, it would look like there had been no growth from September 1987 to December 1989 because data for each month round to 1.2 million. This gives a totally erroneous impression because there was a strong upward trend during that period. December 1989's employment standing was 6.4 percent above that of September 1987.

3. It is important to find out how accurate figures are.

The bottom line is that analysis of statistics needs to be done with unrounded numbers, but the results—whether levels, percentage changes, trends, or differences between components—should be considered as only approximations.

In determining how much rounding is appropriate for

any given statistic, you need to find out how accurate it is. Accuracy varies widely both between series and within series. In general, the larger the statistic, the more accurate it is. That is, employment figures are more accurate for Canada as a whole than for the provinces, and for the provinces than for cities.

One area where no precise measurement of reliability is possible is the national accounts. That's because it is calculated using a variety of data sources—some direct survey and some estimated by other means. Statistics Canada does, though, give you indications of reliability and guidance in the use of the data.

4. Know exactly what the statistics are measuring.

What statistics measure is very specific. For example, the definition used by Statistics Canada for unemployment is whether someone without a job has looked for work during the past four weeks and is currently available for work. This eliminates discouraged workers and excludes people who don't need to do any kind of job search, even looking at newspaper help-wanted ads, to know if a vacancy occurs—which is the case in many small towns.

As a result, you have to be very careful that the data you're using are in fact a measure of what you think they are. If they aren't, there may well be some other data that are more appropriate.

For instance, if you want to get a handle on the "discouraged worker," you could use an alternative unemployment rate—the rate including persons who have sought work in the past six months but who are not now looking for work because they believe no work is available. In 1989, this rate was 8.2 percent vs. the "official" rate of 7.5 percent. Statistics Canada calculates this rate and seven other alternative unemployment rates on a periodic basis.

A similar caution applies to the Consumer Price Index. We think of the CPI as measuring the average rise in prices in Canada, but in fact it measures the increase in the prices of a specific basket of consumer goods, weighted according to their importance in family expenditure in a specific year. We can use it as a substitute for how much prices of consumer products have risen, but it is only a substitute.

In terms of looking at price changes for individual items in the CPI, it's important to make sure you know exactly what's being priced. The definitions are very precise.

For example, the definition of a sports jacket is single-breasted and tailored for sizes 36-46 regular. It must be made of all wool tweed of good grade, with a fabric weight of 350-400 grams per metre. The lining must be attached by special zig-zag stitch and made of full acetate, rayon, or taffeta. The jacket must be all machine made, with any patterns well matched. Interlinings must be woven and the coat's hem blindstitched. It must also have two welted inside pockets of the same fabric.

Another important point to keep in mind is that Statistics Canada attempts to eliminate price changes attributable to quality change. For example, the increase in the price of cars resulting from the requirement for pollution-emission controls is considered a quality change and thus excluded. The CPI data show a smaller price increase than experienced by the consumer because these quality changes pushed up the cost.

The GDP is another example, since it is a measure of those goods and services for which someone pays and thus excludes all work done by volunteers and home-makers.

5. Statistics may be most useful when combined.

Statistics are much enhanced when used in conjunction with other statistics. This not only provides additional information which is useful in analysis, but it enables you to understand the factors affecting the data you're focusing on.

A very simple example is retail sales. Although not widely reported, Statistics Canada produces retail sales volume figures about a week after the release of retail value figures. But for many analysts, a quick fix on volume is useful immediately. Volumes can be roughly estimated by taking the percentage change in retail sales and subtracting the percentage change in the CPI. (It's best to take the average of the CPI percentage change for the month in question and the following month because retail sales cover the full month, while the CPI is calculated using prices mainly collected during the first two weeks of the month.)

Another useful device is pulling together figures from sectors that have a lot in common. For example, Statistics Canada produces separate output figures for logging, wood industries, and the paper and allied sector. Combining them gives you total output for the forest products sector.

Combining statistics is not always a question of looking at a number of different series. It is equally useful to look at figures which are influencing the series you're examining. For example, unemployment is the difference between the labour force and total employment. As a result, a drop in the unemployment rate does not necessarily mean strong job growth. It could mean that there are fewer people looking for work—which could be an early signal of a slowing economy. It's important to look at what's happened to both employment and the labour force before drawing any conclusions about a change in the unemployment rate.

SOURCE: Adapted from Statistics Canada, *Canadian Economic Observer*, Feb. 1990, pp. 3.19-3.33. Reproduced with the permission of the Minister of Industry, Science and Technology, 1992.

Applications

1. GDP for 1990 in 1986 dollars was given as $567 541. What does this figure really mean?
2. The growth in GDP in 1988 (in 1986 dollars) was given as 4.7 percent. What does this figure really indicate and how does it compare with current estimates of potential output noted by Catherine Harris?
3. (a) "Government current expenditure on goods and services in 1989 and 1990 (real terms) was $110 billion (rounded to the nearest $10 billion). Government leaders are, therefore, to be commended for holding the line on spending."
Actual figures of current government expenditures were $109 075 million in 1989 and $112 430 million in 1990. What mistake did the speaker make?
(b) "The population of Alberta did not change between the first quarter of 1990 and the third quarter of 1991."
Refer to Table 15.12. Why might someone reach this conclusion? What error has been made? What would be a

Table 15.12 Population of Alberta, 1990-1991

1 YEAR AND QUARTER	2 POPULATION (THOUSANDS)	3 POPULATION (MILLIONS)
1990 First quarter	2 450.2	2.5
Second quarter	2 461.1	2.5
Third quarter	2 474.2	2.5
Fourth quarter	2 487.2	2.5
1991 First quarter	2 501.4	2.5
Second quarter	2 513.1	2.5
Third quarter	2 525.2	2.5

more accurate assessment of the change in Alberta's population over the period shown?

(c) Refer to Table 15.13 below. What impression might the rounded numbers give that is not justified by the unrounded numbers?

Table 15.13 Merchandise exports and imports, 1990

	FEBRUARY	MARCH	FEBRUARY	MARCH
	(MILLION DOLLARS)		(BILLION DOLLARS)	
Exports	11 946	12 509	12	13
Imports	11 620	11 492	12	11
Balance	326	1 017	0	2

4. Provide examples of why it is important to know exactly what statistics are measuring with regard to:
(a) the unemployment rate
(b) the Consumer Price Index
(c) GDP.

5. With the increasing labour force participation rates of women, more household chores are being done by others for pay. What effect will this have on the GDP? Explain.

Summary

a. A country's total output can be measured by calculating total incomes earned (income approach) or total expenditures made (expenditure approach) by people in the country. Both calculations will arrive at the same figure since all expenditures become income for the people of the nation.

b. Gross Domestic Product (GDP) is defined as the value, at market prices, of all final goods and services produced in the country over a period of time, usually one year. To calculate the value of final goods only and avoid double counting, statisticians include only the value-added at each stage of production.

c. Gross National Product differs from Gross Domestic Product in that it measures the value, at market prices, of all final goods and services produced by Canadian-owned factors of production. It, therefore, includes production outside Canada. GDP has always been greater than GNP because a significant part of our economy is foreign-owned, while we own a smaller proportion of foreign economies.

d. The income-based GDP is calculated as:
Wages and salaries + Corporation profits before taxes + Interest and rent + Incomes of self-employed persons + Indirect taxes less subsidies + Depreciation + Statistical discrepancy.
The expenditure-based GDP is calculated as:
Consumption expenditures + Domestic investment + Government expenditures on goods and services + Net exports + Statistical discrepancy. That is, expenditure-based GDP = C + I + G + (X - M).

e. Other measures of income and spending include net domestic income (GDP minus depreciation, indirect taxes less subsidies, and the statistical discrepancy), personal income (NDI minus corporate income taxes and undistributed corporate profits plus transfer payments), personal disposable income (PI minus income taxes), discretionary income (PDI minus the cost of essentials), and consumption spending (that part of PDI that is spent).

f. GDP at current prices has several limitations as a measure of our economic well-being. It does not account for price and population increases, the equitable or inequitable distribution of income, the kinds of goods produced whether beneficial or harmful, environmental pollution, non-market goods and services, leisure time, and the underground economy.

g. Statistics Canada regularly gathers data on the size of the labour force, the total employed and unemployed, the total not in the labour force, participation rates, and unemployment rates, among others. The unemployment rate, however, does not include thorough checks, does not measure underemployment, and does not include discouraged workers.

h. In Canada, unemployment is generally highest in the Atlantic provinces and among young adults between 15 and 24 years of age. Rates are also typically higher during economic downturns than during boom periods.

i. The four major types of unemployment are frictional (short-term "between jobs" unemployment), seasonal (due to climatic changes), structural (workers and their skills or locations and the available work do not match), and cyclical (due to the swings of the business cycle).

j. Full employment is reached when cyclical unemployment is zero. The full employment rate of unemployment has increased from about 3 percent in the 1960s to about 6 or 7 percent today because of structural changes in the workforce, improvement in unemployment insurance benefits, minimum wage legislation, and an increase in the number of wage earners per household.

k. The economic costs of unemployment are the lost income of those unemployed and the lost contribution the unemployed would have made to the GDP had they been working. The difference between potential GDP at full employment and actual GDP is called the GDP gap. Social costs are more difficult to measure and include loss of self-esteem, a decline in job-earning skills, frustration, and increased family and social tensions.

l. Inflation is a persistent rise in the general level of prices. One measure of inflation is the Consumer Price Index (CPI), which is based on a survey of 400 goods and services bought by representative urban Canadian households. Each good and service in the survey is weighted according to the amount of the household budget spent on it.

Some limitations of the CPI as a measure of the cost of living are that it does not apply to any individual household and it does not take the changing patterns of household spending into account adequately.

m. The GDP deflator is a broader price index than the CPI since it includes the prices of investment goods, goods and services bought by governments, and imports. The GDP deflator is used to adjust nominal or money GDP to real GDP, making comparisons of GDP over various years more accurate.

◼ Review of Key Terms

Define the following key terms introduced in this chapter and provide examples where appropriate.

income approach
expenditure approach
Gross Domestic Product (GDP)
double counting
final goods
intermediate goods
value-added
Gross National Product (GNP)
inventory
net domestic income (NDI)
personal income (PI)
personal disposable income (PDI)
discretionary income
consumption spending
nominal GDP
real GDP
real GDP per capita
Net Economic Welfare (NEW)
labour force

employed
unemployed
participation rate
unemployment rate
discouraged workers
frictional unemployment
seasonal unemployment
structural unemployment
cyclical unemployment
full employment
GDP gap
Okun's law
inflation
price index
base year
Consumer Price Index (CPI)
GDP deflator

◼ Application and Analysis

1. Which of the following are final products and which are intermediate products? Explain.

(a) wheat bought by a milling company

(b) a loaf of bread bought by a consumer

(c) flour bought by a baker

(d) the last compact discs you bought

(e) the compact discs bought by your local music store

(f) the loaves of bread bought by a restaurant

(g) the gasoline I buy for my car on my way to the cottage

(h) the gasoline used by a truck driver when she delivers bread to your local supermarket

2. For each of the following statements, indicate whether you agree or disagree and why.

(a) Meat bought by a restaurant is a final product, while meat bought by a household is an intermediate product.

(b) Tires bought by a truck owner to be used in a trucking service between Calgary and Edmonton are intermediate goods. Tires I buy for my car, which I use for pleasure trips, are final goods.

(c) The building materials purchased by a building contractor are final goods, while the building materials I buy for my home are intermediate goods.

3. Note whether each of the following activities is included in GDP and explain why or why not.

(a) You sell your used car to a friend.

(b) You buy a new car from a local car dealer.

(c) You buy new clothes worth $200.

(d) You worked for 10 hours cutting the grass on your lot.

(e) You took a flight to Paris, France.

(f) You bought 100 shares of Air Canada stock when the corporation was privatized.

4. Explain the effect of each of the following on:
(i) the size of the GDP
(ii) the well-being of Canadians.

(a) War breaks out in the Persian Gulf and Canadian armed forces are actively involved.

(b) A crime wave sweeps through the major cities of Canada from St. John's, Newfoundland to Victoria, BC.

(c) The industrial work week is lengthened from 35 to 40 hours.

(d) The number of "do-it-yourself" home projects increases, resulting in unemployment for many home renovators.

5. Referring to Table 15.14, calculate the following for 1986 and 1988:

(a) GDP income-based

(b) GDP expenditure-based

(c) domestic income

(d) GNP

(e) net exports of goods and services.

6. Refer to Table 15.15 on page 335. Complete the table by calculating the real GDP per capita for each year (column 5).

Table 15.14 Domestic income and expenditure accounts, 1986 and 1988 (billions of dollars)

	1986	1988
Consumption	297	350
Gross investment	103	133
Current government expenditures	100	112
Exports of goods and services	137	157
Imports of goods and services	133	153
Statistical discrepancy	−1	2
Investment income received from non-residents	7	11
Investment income paid to non-residents	24	29
Wages and salaries	275	326
Corporation profits	45	62
Interest	39	46
Proprietors' net income	31	36
Indirect taxes less subsidies	54	65
Capital cost allowance	60	68
Statistical discrepancy	1	−2

SOURCE: Statistics Canada, *Canadian Economic Observer*, April 1990.

7. The total labour force in Canada in 1989 was 13.503 million. Those not in the labour force totalled 6.637 million, and 1.018 million were unemployed. Calculate the total number employed and the unemployment rate for 1989.

8. What is the labour force status (i.e., employed, unemployed, not in labour force) of each one of the following? Explain why in each case.

(a) a university graduate seeking her first job

(b) a retired autoworker living in Florida who occasionally scans the employment ads in Canadian newspapers

(c) a full-time househusband

(d) an unemployed fisheries worker who has given up looking for work because after three months of trying, he knows that there are no suitable jobs

(e) a mechanical engineer who has left her job to look for a better one

Table 15.15 GDP and population, 1979-1985

1 YEAR	2 POPULATION (THOUSANDS)	3 GDP IN CURRENT DOLLARS (MILLIONS)	4 GDP IN REAL TERMS (1981 = 100) (MILLIONS)	5 REAL GDP PER CAPITA
1979	23 645	276 096	338 362	
1980	23 912	309 891	343 384	
1981	24 221	355 994	355 994	
1982	24 512	374 750	344 082	
1983	24 783	405 425	354 780	
1984	25 021	443 327	374 462	
1985	25 264	476 361	389 324	

SOURCE: *Bank of Canada Review*, July 1987.

(f) a computer operator who has a job, but is too ill to work

9. You are the world-famous detective, M. Hercules Poriot, and you are attempting to solve the case of the seasonally-unemployed worker. Based on the following statements of the five suspects, you must answer these questions:
(i) Who is the seasonally unemployed worker?
(ii) What type of unemployment describes the situation of the others?
(iii) And, of course, like all good detectives, how did you reach your conclusions?

Suspect A I have just graduated from high school and I'm looking for my first job.
Suspect B I left the last job I had as a computer programmer and I'm looking for another job that pays better.
Suspect C I was laid off during the last recession.
Suspect D I was laid off two years ago, but after a year of looking for a job, I've given up. I don't think there are any jobs for me out there.
Suspect E I work on road construction during the summer, but there's little work for me now with snow on the ground.
Suspect F I used to work in the paint shop for an automobile manufacturer, but I became redundant when they replaced us with robotic machinery.

10. Refer to Figure 15.9 on page 325 in this chapter to help you answer the following questions.

(a) In June of 1991, Marcia bought $500 worth of consumer goods. How much would these goods have cost her in June 1986? The CPI in June 1991 was 124.0 and 1986 is the base year.

(b) In 1971, Kai bought $100 worth of consumer goods. What would these goods have cost him in May 1991?

(c) Suppose you started working at Acme Electric January 1, 1990 for a salary of $30 000 a year. Your union's contract with Acme includes a cost of living clause, which means that your pay is fully indexed to the CPI. On January 1, 1991, your pay increases by the amount of the increase in the CPI. How much did your pay increase on January 1, 1991?

(d) Lucien retired at the end of December, 1981 on a fully indexed pension of $25 000. How much would his pension have been at the end of 1985?

11. Refer to Table 15.16 on the next page. Describe how Canada's CPI compares with those of the other nations listed from 1987 to 1991. How may these figures be used as a measure of the economic well-being of Canadians as compared with that of citizens in the other nations?

Table 15.16 Consumer Price Index of select nations, 1987-1991, unadjusted (1985 = 100)

	CANADA	UNITED STATES	UNITED KINGDOM	FRANCE	GERMANY	ITALY	JAPAN
1987	108.7	105.6	107.7	105.9	100.0	110.9	100.7
1988	113.1	109.9	113.0	108.7	101.4	116.5	101.4
1989	118.7	115.2	121.8	112.7	104.2	124.2	103.7
1990	124.4	121.5	133.4	116.5	107.0	131.7	106.9
1991 (May)	131.3	125.7	140.7	119.1	109.5	139.4	110.7

SOURCE: OECD, *Canadian Economic Observer*, September 1991.

12. (a) Complete Table 15.17 by calculating the real GDP in 1986 dollars for 1981 through 1986.

(b)   Describe the changes in each of the following over the period 1981-1986:

(i) nominal GDP
(ii) the rate of inflation
(iii) GDP in constant dollars.

(c)   In which year(s) did real GDP decline?

Table 15.17 GDP, 1981-1986

1 YEAR	2 NOMINAL GDP IN MILLIONS OF CURRENT DOLLARS	3 GDP DEFLATOR (1986 = 100)	4 GDP IN 1986 DOLLARS
1981	355 994	80.9	
1982	374 442	87.9	
1983	405 717	92.3	
1984	444 735	95.2	
1985	477 988	97.6	
1986	505 666	100	

CHAPTER SIXTEEN

Economic Instability

Objectives
- **a.** Trace the fluctuations in the Canadian economy since 1926.
- **b.** Identify and explain the four phases of the business cycle.
- **c.** Analyze the reasons for business fluctuations using the injections-leakages approach.
- **d.** Determine the major components of consumption spending.
- **e.** Examine the components of investment and the major determinants of total investment in the economy.
- **f.** Determine the equilibrium level of income.
- **g.** Consider the theories of John Maynard Keynes concerning consumption, investment, equilibrium, and the role of government in the economy.
- **h.** Investigate the role of government in the balance of injections and leakages.
- **i.** Examine how the foreign trade sector affects the equilibrium of the macroeconomy.
- **j.** Calculate and apply the marginal propensities to consume and save.
- **k.** Examine the equilibrium of the Canadian economy over the 1970s and 1980s.
- **l.** Demonstrate the multiplier effect on investment and consumption.
- **m.** Outline the effects of the accelerator and explain the multiplier-accelerator interaction in the economy.

Canadian history attests to the remarkable economic growth of the country, so that we have today one of the highest standards of living in the world. But our economic growth has not proceeded at a smooth rate. While there have been periods of sustained growth with increasing prosperity and employment, there have also been periods of high unemployment and low or negative growth, as in the early 1930s. We have also experienced a significant rise in the general level of prices, particularly in the period after World War II. And in the 1970s and 1980s, we have at times experienced both inflation and unemployment simultaneously.

In this chapter, we consider the nature of these cyclical fluctuations in our market economy, and why they occur.

Fluctuations in the Canadian Economy

In 1926, the Canadian government began regularly collecting data on the economy. Its records show that the most significant fluctuations in Canadian economic activity took place between 1929 and 1944.

Following the stock market crash of 1929, the Canadian economy (along with the economies of many other countries) collapsed into the Great Depression. Unemployment in Canada reached almost 20 percent and real GDP plunged 30 percent between 1929 and 1933. The economy did not really recover until government began spending large sums of money on the war effort during World War II, thus stimulating economic activity.

Since the end of the war in 1945, however, we have experienced a series of peacetime economic slow-downs in 1951, 1953-54, 1957, 1960-61, 1974-75, 1982, and 1990-91. Table 16.1 summarizes the periods of expansion and contraction in the Canadian economy.

No two contractions or expansions have been exactly alike. Some expansions, like the one between 1983 and 1990, have been long-lived, while others have been short-lived, such as that between 1980 and 1981. Similarly, some contractions have been short and relatively mild like the one in 1980, while others have been long and painful as in 1981-82 and 1990-91.

The Business Cycle

These swings in economic activity are generally referred to as **business cycles**. Some economists, however, prefer the term **business fluctuations** since "cycles" implies an occurrence at regular intervals, which is not accurate as Table 16.1 has shown.

Though business cycles may differ significantly, each cycle generally has four phases: peak, recession, trough, and expansion. These phases are illustrated in Figure 16.1.

Table 16.1 Summary of expansions and contractions in Canadian economic activity, 1951-1991

CONTRACTIONS		EXPANSIONS	
YEARS AND QUARTERS	DURATION IN QUARTERS	YEARS AND QUARTERS	DURATION IN QUARTERS
1951:2 - 1951:4	3	1952:1 - 1953:2	6
1953:3 - 1954:2	4	1954:3 - 1956:4	10
1957:1 - 1957:4	4	1958:1 - 1960:1	9
1960:2 - 1961:1	4	1961:2 - 1974:1	52
1974:2 - 1975:1	4	1975:2 - 1979:4	19
1980:1 - 1980:2	2	1980:3 - 1981:2	4
1981:3 - 1982:4	6	1983:1 - 1990:1	27
1990:2 - 1991:1	4	1991:2 -	

SOURCE: Statistics Canada, *Canadian Economic Observer*, October 1991.

The duration of expansion periods in the Canadian economy has varied considerably from only 4 quarters in 1980-81 to 52 quarters between 1961 and 1974. By comparison, the periods of contraction have been much shorter and more uniform, averaging just over 3 quarters with the longest lasting 6 quarters between 1981 and 1982.

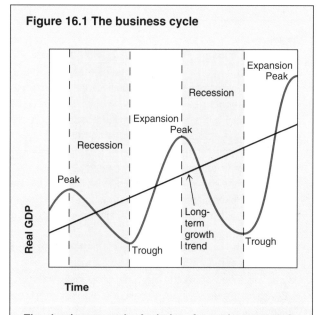

Figure 16.1 The business cycle

The business cycle includes four phases—peak, recession, trough, and expansion. Each phase can differ in duration and severity. Every cycle, however, includes the same phases in the same sequence.

□ □ □ □ □ □

An Analysis of Business Cycles in the 1980s and Early 1990s

If we set out to analyze the business cycles in Canada over the 1980s and early 1990s, where would we begin? Economists examine key indicators to analyze the condition of the economy—including changes in real GDP, employment statistics, bankruptcies, and profit and investment levels. Let's examine some of these indicators.

Figure 16.2   Quarterly percentage change in real GDP, 1980-1991 (seasonally adjusted)

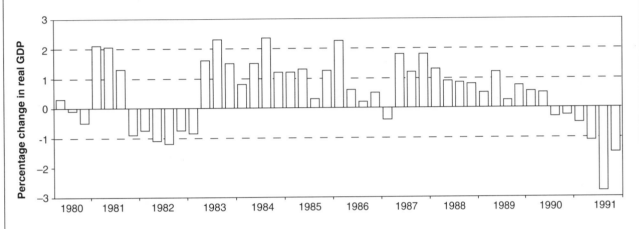

Figure 16.3 Manufacturing capacity utilization rate, 1981-1990

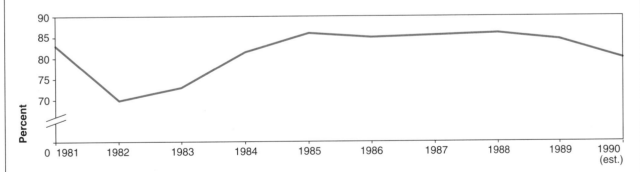

The manufacturing capacity utilization rate is the percentage of potential manufacturing output that is actually produced with existing plant. It indicates the level of economic activity in manufacturing.

SOURCE: Statistics Canada.

Figure 16.4 Business bankruptcies in Canada, 1981-1991

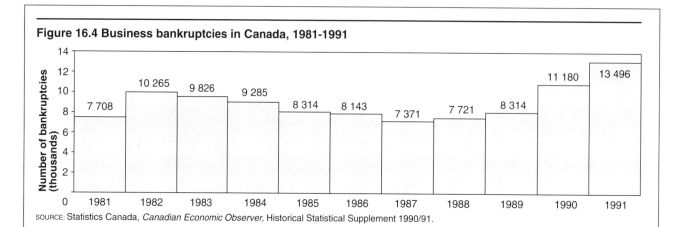

SOURCE: Statistics Canada, *Canadian Economic Observer*, Historical Statistical Supplement 1990/91.

Figure 16.5 Profits as a percentage of GDP, quarterly, 1982-1991

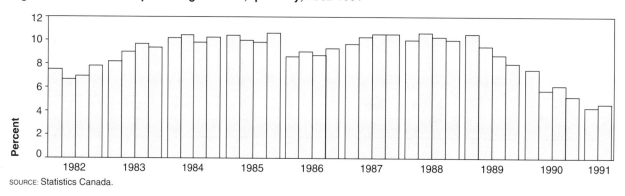

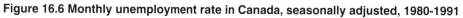

SOURCE: Statistics Canada.

Figure 16.6 Monthly unemployment rate in Canada, seasonally adjusted, 1980-1991

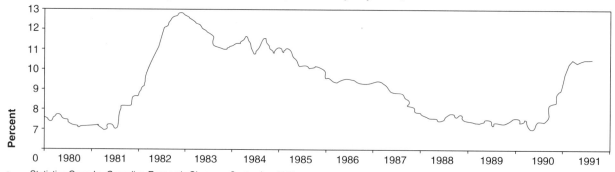

Source: Statistics Canada, *Canadian Economic Observer*, September 1991.

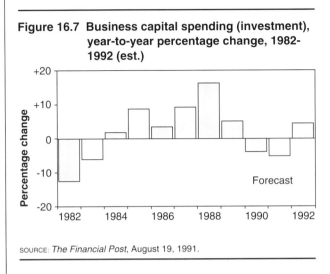

Figure 16.7   Business capital spending (investment), year-to-year percentage change, 1982-1992 (est.)

Percentage change

Forecast

SOURCE: *The Financial Post*, August 19, 1991.

Applications

1. For each figure, determine during which years and quarters the data indicate:

(a) recessions

(b) recoveries.

2. (a) Look for relationships among the figures. Do they indicate upswings and downturns in economic activity during the same periods? Suggest reasons for any discrepancies.

(b) Explain the relationships among the figures. Why might a downturn in manufacturing activity reflect a lower real GDP, for example? Why might higher investment levels be coupled with an upswing? How are unemployment rates and real GDP levels related and what do they indicate about the health of the economy? Analyze these relationships in two or three paragraphs.

Peak

At the **peak** of the business cycle, real Gross Domestic Product is at or very near capacity and the economy reaches or nears full employment. Workers, therefore, can ask for and receive higher wages and businesses can raise prices for their products. The general level of prices, therefore, is likely to be rising. In other words, the economy may be experiencing inflation.

The peak, however, marks the turning point of the cycle toward a recession. In the past, the peak was often characterized by a financial panic—such as the Wall Street stock market collapse known as "Black Tuesday" on October 29, 1929. Recent peaks, however, have been much less dramatic.

Recession

A **recession** occurs when the seasonally adjusted real GDP declines for two or more quarters (three-month periods) in succession. In a recession, businesses cut production, consumer spending decreases, and investment in plant and capital equipment drops significantly. Labour demand also falls and unemployment increases. The rate of increase in the general level of prices for goods and services is likely to slow, and some prices may fall. Stock prices generally decline, business profits drop, and bankruptcies increase. Along with the decrease in the demand for credit, interest rates also fall.

A **depression** is generally defined as a prolonged period of significantly reduced economic activity characterized by widespread unemployment, declining prices, declining output, little capital investment, and many business failures. A depression is both more severe and more prolonged than a recession and can have world-wide repercussions. According to Harry S. Truman, former President of the United States, a recession is when your neighbour is out of work. A depression is when you're out of work. Triggered by the Wall Street stock market collapse of October 1929, the Great Depression of the 1930s was a world-wide catastrophe.

Trough

The **trough** is the low point of the business cycle. Consumption and investment in plant and equipment are at low levels, as are labour demand, prices, profits, and interest rates. Real GDP is significantly below potential output. However, the trough also represents the turning point from recession to expansion.

Expansion

In the **expansion** phase, real GDP begins to grow again as consumption, expenditures, and investment increase. Employment levels also rise toward full employment and there are fewer bankruptcies. Profits and stock prices increase. There is a general feeling of optimism as the economy prospers. However, as employment increases and the economy approaches capacity, prices begin to rise.

☐ The Business Cycle in Canada

Figure 16.8 shows the business cycles in Canada from 1926 to 1991 graphically. Clearly, the most dramatic

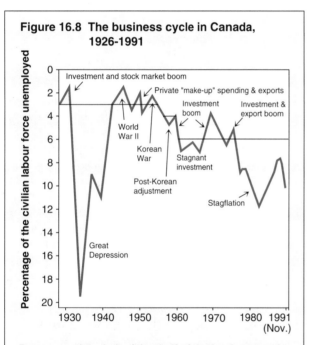

Figure 16.8 The business cycle in Canada, 1926-1991

Booms are the whole rising half of the business cycle. Slumps are the falling half of the cycle. The Great Depression of the 1930s is the most striking downturn in the Canadian economy over the 1926-1991 period. Unemployment reached 20 percent. From 1945-1981, unemployment was generally lower than in the pre-1945 era but reached high levels once again during the recessions of 1981-82 and 1990-91.

SOURCE: R. Campbell McConnell and W. H. Pope, *Economics*, 4th ed. (Toronto: McGraw-Hill Ryerson, 1987), p. 419 and Statistics Canada, *Canadian Economic Observer*.

downturn was that of the Great Depression in the 1930s following the stock market crash in 1929. Over the period 1945 to 1981, despite some fluctuations, unemployment was generally lower than in the pre-1945 years. Since 1981, unemployment rates have generally been higher than those in the previous half century.

▌ Reasons for Business Fluctuations

What causes the fluctuations in the economy? Let's return to our circular flow model of the economy to explain. Our analysis is based mainly on the ideas of John Maynard Keynes from his famous book *The General Theory of Employment, Interest, and Money* and the ideas of his followers. We'll consider two approaches—the injections-leakages approach, and in the next chapter, the aggregate demand-aggregate supply approach.

Let's start with a very simple economy having just two sectors—households and businesses—and only one circular flow between them—that of money. Thus, the real flows of productive resources and of goods and services are excluded, as are the productive resources market and the final products market. Figure 16.9 shows this simple economy.

Suppose that businesses pay households $60 million a year for the use of their productive resources. Households are free to spend all or only some of the $60 million. Note that government and foreign countries are not part of our simple economy, so taxes and foreign trade are not factors.

Let's suppose households spend the whole $60 million during the year. The $60 million will, therefore, flow to the producers, who now have $60 million to pay for the use of productive resources once again. If we were to measure the flow of income in the lower loop and the flow of expenditures in the upper loop, both would equal $60 million a year. As long as the households continue to spend all of their disposable incomes on goods and services, and businesses spend all of their revenues on hiring factors of production from households, total income and total expenditure will remain at $60 million. The simple economy will be in equilibrium.

☐ Spending and Saving

As we know, however, not all households spend all of their incomes on goods and services. Some spend more than they earn, going into debt or dipping into past savings. Others spend less than they earn—they save.

What determines the amount consumers spend? The most important factor is the amount of current disposable income they have. Other factors include expectations of future income, the availability of credit, interest rates, expectations about future price levels, and wealth.

Current Disposable Income

As we have seen, current disposable income is the total income of households after personal income taxes have been deducted. Consumers may spend or save this income as they wish. But clearly, the greater your current disposable income, the greater the amount you are likely to spend on consumer goods and services. Similarly, the greater the disposable income of all Canadians, the greater their total consumption is likely to be. Disposable income grows along with GDP. In general, the greater is the GDP, the greater are disposable income and consumer spending.

Expectations of Future Income

If we expect that our incomes will rise, we are likely to spend more on consumer goods and services than if we anticipate our incomes will fall. Canadians are more likely to spend less and save more of their current incomes during recessions, for example, than during periods of prosperity. Expectations about future income, therefore, affect the total level of consumption in the economy.

Availability of Credit

Credit that is readily available at good rates encourages people to buy goods, especially "big-ticket" items such as household appliances and automobiles. Limited credit and high rates, on the other hand, discourage buying and lower the level of consumption in the economy.

Interest Rates

Changes in interest rates affect the incomes of those who have wealth in the form of stocks and bonds and other assets. High interest rates increase income from bonds and other interest-yielding assets and, therefore, encourage consumption. Low interest rates reduce income from these assets and may reduce consumption.

Interest rates also influence the level of saving in the economy. High rates may encourage increased saving,

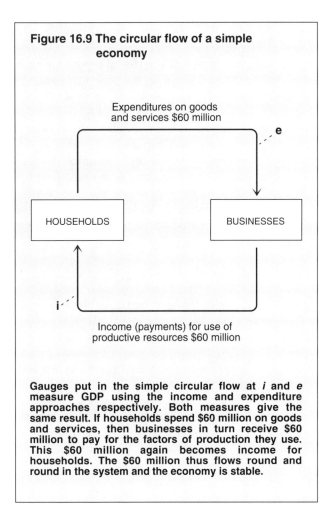

Figure 16.9 The circular flow of a simple economy

Expenditures on goods and services $60 million

e

HOUSEHOLDS

BUSINESSES

i

Income (payments) for use of productive resources $60 million

Gauges put in the simple circular flow at *i* and *e* measure GDP using the income and expenditure approaches respectively. Both measures give the same result. If households spend $60 million on goods and services, then businesses in turn receive $60 million to pay for the factors of production they use. This $60 million again becomes income for households. The $60 million thus flows round and round in the system and the economy is stable.

while low rates may discourage saving. If the interest rates on your bank account, Canada Savings Bond, or Guaranteed Investment Certificate rise significantly, for example, you will probably be tempted to save more money through these securities.

Expectations About Future Price Levels

If people anticipate price increases, they are likely to spend before the prices rise. If they expect price decreases, they are likely to defer their spending. If you are thinking of buying a CD player and it looks like prices will rise in a month's time, for example, you will probably buy it now to take advantage of the lower price. If prices are expected to drop next month, however, you will probably wait until then to make your purchase.

Wealth

It is important to note that wealth and income are not the same. A wealthy person may have little or no income, while a person with a high income may have little wealth if he or she spends all of that income. Suppose two consumers—Devon and Singh—both have incomes of $50 000 a year. Singh, however, has $500 000 in her bank account while Devon has nothing. Who is likely to spend more? The answer is probably Singh. Those with substantial wealth have less need to save from current income. They can use their current income for current spending. Wealth can, therefore, affect the amount of spending from current income.

□ Spending, Saving, and the Circular Flow

Let's return now to the circular flow model. Suppose households plan to save $10 million this year out of their $60 million income and spend the remaining $50 million on goods and services. The $10 million in savings represents a **leakage** from the circular flow— that is, any money taken out of the income-expenditure stream of the economy.

What happens? With households spending only $50 million out of their total income, business inventories will pile up and businesses will be forced to cut back production. Since less is then paid to households for

productive resources than before, the flow of income and expenditure is reduced. Saving thus acts as a drag on domestic production and income.

□ Investment

The level of domestic income will not decline, however, if there is an injection, such as investment, to balance the savings leakage. An **injection** is any expenditure put into the circular flow that raises domestic income. Economists use the term "investment" to mean specifically expenditures on real capital—that is, machinery, equipment, new buildings, residential construction, and inventories. Investments are expenditures not for current, but rather for future consumption. In common usage, investment also includes the purchase of stock certificates or property, but these represent only a transfer of ownership from one person to another, not an increase in productive capacity.

Investment has two main functions in the economy. First, since investment leads to an accumulation of capital in the form of buildings and machinery, etc., it increases the economy's capacity to produce. Second, investment can offset the leakage of savings, and thus may contribute to an increase in national income.

Changes in investment, however, are one of the main causes of fluctuations in the economy. Why? Let's consider the factors.

Volatility of Inventories

Inventories, though a small proportion of total investment, are constantly changing and can, therefore, have a significant effect on the level of investment. The amount of goods held in inventory varies with sales and output. The many factors that may affect the demand and supply of products, therefore, affect the levels of inventory.

Real interest rates also cause fluctuations in inventory. A significant part of the cost of holding inventories is the interest on money borrowed for them. The higher is the real rate of interest, therefore, the higher is the cost of holding inventories and the greater is the incentive to reduce the stocks. The opposite is likewise true.

Shifts in Residential Construction

Residential construction is a major component of total investment. Shifts in residential construction, therefore, will have a significant impact on the level of investment in the economy. Total residential construction investment is related to long-term demographic and social factors such as population increases and household formation.

Over the shorter term, residential construction is affected by income levels and real interest rates. The higher are the levels of income, the more money people have to spend and the greater the demand for homes. Since many homes are bought with substantial mortgages, high real interest rates will discourage home buying while low real interest rates will encourage the purchases. Thus, new residential construction is directly related to rising real incomes and inversely related to real interest rates.

Investment in Plant and Equipment

Three main factors influence the total volume of business investment in new plant and equipment—the rate of return on investments, expectations about the future, and the rate of interest.

(i) Rate of return on investment As we have seen, businesses invest when they expect that the rate of return on their investment will exceed their costs. Since it is reasonable to assume that businesses will invest in the higher-yielding projects first, then as more is invested in an economy, the rate of return on each additional investment is likely to decrease. The expected rate of return on additional or marginal investments is known as the marginal efficiency of investment (MEI). Investment will continue until the MEI equals the rate of interest, that is, the cost of the investment. This relationship is shown in Figure 16.10.

(ii) Expectations about the future Businesses also carefully consider a number of future possibilities before making any investment decisions. These considerations include the future demand for the company's products, the costs of productive factors and raw materials, the amount of competition, the general out-

look for the economy, and government tax and tariff policies.

Businesses are more likely to invest if they expect the demand for their products to rise than if they expect the demand to fall. Similarly, a decrease in the prices of productive resources will do more to encourage investment than a rise in these prices—except where capital may substitute for another factor (such as labour) for which costs are increasing. Expectations of increasing competition will also influence decisions on how much and in what to invest. Investment is generally higher when businesses anticipate a healthy economy than when they expect a recession. Increasing government taxes or tariffs, on the other hand, may act as disincentives to investment. Expectations of increasingly

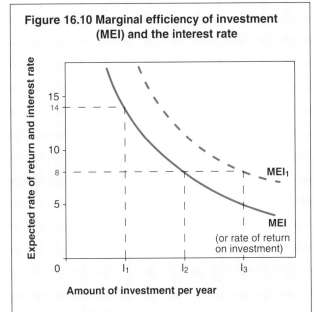

Figure 16.10 Marginal efficiency of investment (MEI) and the interest rate

Amount of investment per year

The expected rate of return or marginal efficiency of investment (MEI) declines as the amount of investment increases since the most profitable investment projects are undertaken first. Investment is expected to continue until the rate of return (MEI) equals the rate of interest. With an interest rate at 14 percent, investment will continue only to I_1. With a lower interest rate, such as 8 percent, investment will continue to I_2. If the MEI curve shifts to MEI_1 due, for example, to an increase in total demand, investment would increase at any interest rate.

heavy taxes on cigarettes, for example, may further reduce consumption and thus discourage investment in tobacco growing and processing.

(iii) The rate of interest   To finance an investment, firms must borrow money and/or take it from retained earnings. If money is borrowed, the business will compare the expected rate of return on the investment with the interest rate. If the expected rate of return is above the interest rate, the firm is likely to invest. If the expected rate of return is below the interest rate, the firm is unlikely to invest.

If the company can finance the proposed investment from retained earnings, it may seem that there is no need to consider the interest rate. However, businesses can earn the market rate of interest on the money if they loan from their retained earnings. The interest a firm could have earned on money reinvested in the firm is as much a cost of investment as interest paid to the bank. The opportunity cost must, therefore, be considered in any investment decisions.

□ Saving, Investment, and the Circular Flow

We can now see that savings do not simply vanish from the circular flow. They can flow back into the system in a number of ways. Businesses may use their retained earnings (which are really enforced savings by shareholders) to finance investments. Personal savings, too, may be used to invest in new homes and thus contribute to real capital.

Other household savings may be placed with financial intermediaries such as banks, trust companies, or insurance companies. Businesses, in turn, may borrow money from these financial intermediaries for investment. Thus, household savings may be channelled back into the circular flow, though it may be some time before the savings are invested.

If savings are used to buy stocks or bonds of existing companies, then they represent a leakage from the flow. However, if the seller of the stocks or bonds chooses to buy goods and services or to make investments in the current period, then the savings make their way back into the circular flow and they do not represent a leakage.

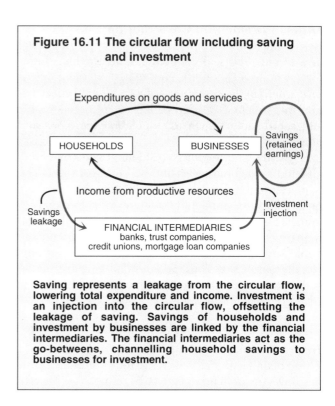

Figure 16.11 The circular flow including saving and investment

Saving represents a leakage from the circular flow, lowering total expenditure and income. Investment is an injection into the circular flow, offsetting the leakage of saving. Savings of households and investment by businesses are linked by the financial intermediaries. The financial intermediaries act as the go-betweens, channelling household savings to businesses for investment.

Households may also choose to hold cash, or "hoard it in a mattress" so to speak. These savings are taken out of the circular flow and do not return until households choose to inject them again by spending them or depositing them with financial intermediaries. Figure 16.11 shows the circular flow of our two-sector economy when savings, investment, and the financial intermediaries are added.

Savings are important, therefore, to finance future investments. But savings must be balanced by a level of spending that will justify the increased production of goods and services the investment will create.

□ Equilibrium Level of Income

At this point, we need to make a distinction between *actual* saving and investment and *planned* saving and investment. As we have seen, actual total expenditures must equal actual total income. In our simple economy, total expenditures consist of consumption and investment expenditures. Thus, GDP = C + I. We have also seen that part of total income is consumed and part is saved. Thus, GDP = C + S. Since expenditures on consumption become an equal amount of income, C = C. The actual saving leakage, therefore, must equal the actual investment injection (that is, actual S = I).

Actual C + I = GDP = C + S
Actual C + I = C + S
Actual I = S

Planned saving and investment, on the other hand, are quite likely to be unequal. Decisions to save are made by households, while decisions to invest are made by businesses. The two sectors have different motivations.

If the amount households and businesses plan to invest equals the amount they plan to save (in our circular flow, $10 million), then the investment injection equals the saving leakage. The economy is at the **equilibrium level of income**.

If intended savings are greater than intended investment, however, expenditure and income will diminish. Conversely, if intended savings are less than intended investment, expenditure and income will increase.

Table 16.2 shows the income, consumption (expenditure), saving, and investment schedules for a simple two-sector economy. The table is based on the assumption that as income increases, savings also increase.

(i) Planned saving is greater than planned investment
With an income of $100 million, households plan to spend $70 million and save $30 million. Businesses plan to invest only $10 million. Since the planned saving leakage is greater than the planned investment injection, sales will decline, inventories will pile up, and businesses will lay off workers. Total income and expenditure will, therefore, decline.

(ii) Planned investment is greater than planned saving
At the other end of the scale, with an income of $30 million, total saving is -$5 million. Householders are borrowing and/or spending from their savings. The

Table 16.2 Income, consumption, saving, and investment schedules (millions of dollars)

1 INCOME	2 CONSUMPTION	3 SAVING	4 INVESTMENT	5 PRESSURE ON INCOME
100	70	30	10	Downward
90	65	25	10	Downward
80	60	20	10	Downward
70	55	15	10	Downward
60	50	10	10	Equilibrium
50	45	5	10	Upward
40	40	0	10	Upward
30	35	-5	10	Upward

With an income of $70 million and above, the amount households plan to save is greater than the amount businesses wish to invest. The saving withdrawal is greater than the investment injection and the pressure on income and expenditure is, therefore, downward. With incomes of $50 million and less, the planned investment injection is greater than the planned saving withdrawal and the pressure on income is, therefore, upward. Only at an income of $60 million are intended saving and investment equal. At this point, the economy is in equilibrium.

total planned investment injection at $10 million exceeds the planned saving withdrawal of -$5 million. Goods will sell quickly, inventories will decline, and businesses will hire more workers. Thus, the pressure on income and expenditure is upward.

(iii) Planned saving and investment are equal Only at an income of $60 million does the economy achieve equilibrium. At this level of income, intended saving and intended investment are equal at $10 million.

But, will the economy stay in equilibrium? Will the investment plans of businesses and the saving plans of households remain in agreement? The answer, as you would expect, is no. The plans of businesses and households depend on different factors, as we have seen, and will be continually changing. When planned saving exceeds planned investment, we can expect that our simple economy will move toward a recession with

□ □ □ □ □ □

Economic Thinkers

John Maynard Keynes
(1883-1946)

John Maynard Keynes is considered one of the most influential economists of the twentieth century. He was born in Cambridge, England in 1883 (the same year Karl Marx died), the son of a professor of economics at Cambridge University. After taking a degree in mathematics, he studied under Alfred Marshall for a year. He spent much of his life in the service of the British government while at the same time teaching economics at Cambridge.

Deeply disturbed by the miseries of the Great Depression in the 1930s, Keynes was highly critical of the prevailing economic theories, which he believed led governments to take no action for economic improvement. In 1935, Keynes wrote to the playwright George Bernard Shaw: "I believe myself to be writing a book on economic theory which will largely revolutionize—not, I suppose at once, but in the course of the next ten years—the way in which the world thinks about economic problems. . . ."

In the view of many economists, Keynes' book, *The General Theory of Employment, Interest, and Money* published in 1936, did indeed revolutionize economic thinking.

One view of Keynes:
[Keynes] had a close circle of friends with whom he met regularly to debate, discuss, and contemplate ideas about society, culture, politics, philosophy, and the arts; this group came to be known as Bloomsbury. Keynes was an active patron of the arts and a supporter of women's suffrage . . . He was a rather plain-looking man but was said to have an effervescent personality; he preferred working in bed each morning, not rising before noon; and he married Lydia Lopokova, a famous Russian ballerina.

SOURCE: From ECONOMICS: OUR AMERICAN ECONOMY by E.L. Schwartz. Copyright © 1990 by Longman Publishing Group.

Classical Theory

Before the 1930s, most economists believed that the economy tended automatically toward full employment. This view was based on **Say's law**—named after J.B. Say, a French economist of the early nineteenth century. According to the law, supply creates its own demand. The production of a good or service automatically creates demand for the good through the income flowing to wage earners, landowners, and other owners of the productive factors. Say's law assumes that total output equals total income and total expenditures, and that all income will be spent on purchasing the economy's output. Economists believed that people would not hoard money when it could be spent on useful goods and services. The economy, therefore, tends toward equilibrium and general overproduction is impossible.

Individual goods and services may be overproduced, but the surplus will automatically push down prices and payments to the owners of the productive factors (wages and profits). If there is a surplus of automobiles, for example, prices and wages will fall and workers may be unemployed. But the workers and entrepreneurs will move into other industries and lower wages may allow firms to recall laid off workers, so that unemployment will eventually disappear. Since individual markets tend toward equilibrium, the macroeconomy also tends toward equilibrium.

Keynes' Theories

The Great Depression of the 1930s, a period of prolonged and severe unemployment and economic stagnation, revealed the weaknesses in Say's law. There were few signs of the automatic correction that supporters of Say's law had expected.

In his book, Keynes argued that it was by no means certain the economy would move toward full employment automatically. Full employment, he believed, was indeed the exception. Governments must actively work to eliminate unemployment by ensuring a level of expenditures that would keep people working and producing.

KEYNES IN HIS OWN WORDS

A *General* Theory

I have called this book The General Theory of Employment, Interest and Money, *placing the emphasis on the prefix* general. *The object of such a title is to contrast the character of my arguments and conclusions with those of the* classical *theory of the subject, upon which I was brought up and which dominates the economic thought, both practical and theoretical, of the governing and academic classes of this generation, as it has for a hundred years past. I shall argue that the postulates of the classical theory are applicable to a special case only and not to the general case, the situation which it assumes being a limiting point of the possible positions of equilibrium. Moreover, the characteristics of the special case assumed by the classical theory happen not to be those of the economic society in which we actually live, with the result that its teaching is misleading and disastrous if we attempt to apply it to the facts of experience.*

1. Why did Keynes emphasize that his theory was a *general* one? What criticisms did he have of the classical economists?

Consumption and Investment

The outline of our theory can be expressed as follows. When employment increases, aggregate [total] real income is increased. The psychology of the community is such that when aggregate real income is increased aggregate consumption is increased, but not by so much as income. Hence employers would make a loss if the whole of the increased employment were to be devoted to satisfying the increased demand for immediate consumption. Thus, to justify any given amount of employment, there must be an amount of current investment sufficient to absorb the excess of total output over what the community chooses to consume when employment is at the given level. For unless there is this amount of investment, the receipts of entrepreneurs will be less than is required to induce them to offer the given amount of employment. It follows, therefore, that, given what we shall call the community's propensity to consume, the equilibrium level of employment, i.e., the level at which there is no inducement to employers as a whole either to expand or to contract employment, will depend on the amount of current investment. The amount of current investment will depend, in turn, on what we shall call the inducement to invest; and the inducement to invest will be found to depend on the relation between the schedule of the marginal efficiency of capital and the complex of rates of interest on loans of various maturities and risks.

2. Why would employers "make a loss" if the whole of the increased employment were devoted to satisfying the increased demand for immediate consumption?

3. What determines:
(a) the equilibrium level of investment
(b) the amount of current investment?

Equilibrium

Thus, given the propensity to consume and the rate of new investment, there will be only one level of employment consistent with equilibrium; since any other level will lead to inequality between the aggregate supply price of output as a whole and its aggregate demand price. This level cannot be greater than full employment. . . But there is no reason in general for expecting it to be equal to full employment. The effective demand associated with full employment is a special case, only realized when the propensity to consume and the inducement to invest stand in a particular relationship to one another. This particular relationship, which corresponds to the assumptions of the classical theory, is in a sense an optimum relationship. But it can only exist when, by accident or design, current investment provides an amount of demand just equal to the excess of the aggregate supply price of the output resulting from full employment over what the community will choose to spend on consumption when it is fully employed.

4. How does Keynes refute Say's law in this extract?

SOURCE: Extracts taken from John Maynard Keynes, *The General Theory of Employment, Interest and Money* (London: Macmillan, 1935), pp. 3, 27-8.

declining total demand, prices, output, and employment. When planned investment exceeds planned saving, the economy will move toward a peak as total demand, prices, output, and employment increase.

However, saving and investment are not the only leakages and injections in the economy. Two other sectors, government and foreign trade, also influence the balance of the circular flow.

□ Government

Government expenditures and revenues from taxation at the federal, provincial, and municipal levels play a major role in the balance of the circular flow.

Government Expenditures (G)
Governments buy goods and services from businesses and hire productive resources from households. These expenditures represent an injection into the economy. Transfer payments, however, are not considered a government expenditure injection. Transfer payments to households (e.g., welfare payments, unemployment insurance benefits, and family allowances) help boost personal disposable income and thus form part of consumption expenditures. Transfer payments to businesses (e.g., subsidies) help boost investment

spending and are thus considered part of investment expenditures.

Taxation (T)
Governments also have the powers of taxation. Some four-fifths of government revenues are derived from taxes levied on households and businesses. Government revenues remove money from the circular flow, thereby reducing the expenditure and income flows. They represent a leakage.

□ Government and the Circular Flow

With the addition of government to the circular flow, we now have two leakages—savings (S) and taxes (T). We also have two injections—investment (I) and government spending (G). Figure 16.12 illustrates the flows. Taxes flow from households and businesses to government. These taxes may, in turn, flow back to businesses in the form of government expenditures on goods and services and transfers to businesses for investment spending. Government tax revenues also flow back to households through payments for productive factors and transfers for consumption spending. Total expenditure in this closed economy (that is, one without foreign trade) is the sum of consumer, investment, and government spending (C + I + G).

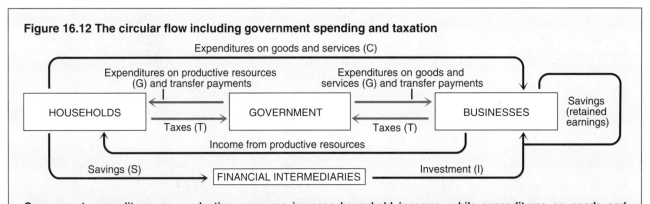

Figure 16.12 The circular flow including government spending and taxation

Government expenditures on productive resources increase household incomes, while expenditures on goods and services increase business incomes. Government expenditures (G) thus represent an injection into the economy, increasing the level of total spending. Taxes (T) paid by households and businesses to government reduce incomes and total spending, and thus represent a leakage from the circular flow. Transfer payments to households and businesses help to increase consumption spending (C) and business investment (I) and are thus not included in government expenditures on resources or goods and services (G).

Let's assume, as before, that our closed economy is in equilibrium at $60 million. The saving leakage equals the investment injection of $10 million. If government expenditures and taxes both equal $20 million, then the economy remains at equilibrium since injections (I + G) equal leakages (S + T). The addition of government, then, does not change the level of national income and expenditure, only their composition. Consumption and investment expenditures are diminished since part of household and business income is taken by government in taxes.

However, as with saving and investment, government revenues and expenditures do not necessarily balance. If government decides to have a budget deficit, then revenues (T) will be less than expenditures (G). If planned saving equals planned investment, then total injections will be greater than total leakages, and the income and expenditure flows will tend to increase.

To achieve economic stability, government may deliberately unbalance its budget. While individual households or businesses may decide to increase or decrease expenditures, they cannot agree collectively as a sector to increase total consumption or investment in order to achieve economic stability. Thus, in the Keynesian analysis, government has a crucial role to play in stabilizing the economy. To increase employment output, and incomes, government may cut taxes and/or increase its expenditures. On the other hand, to "cool off" an overheated economy in which prices are rising, government may reduce its expenditures and/or raise taxes. Thus the income and expenditure flows would diminish. We will examine this role of government in more detail later in the chapter on fiscal policy.

So far then, in our simple model of the economy, income and expenditure flows will remain at equilibrium if total planned injections equal total planned expenditures. We have equilibrium if G + I = S + T. To complete our circular flow model, we need to examine one more sector—foreign trade.

☐ Foreign Trade

When we buy Japanese stereo equipment or when Canadian businesses buy German machinery, the money spent on these imports flows to Japanese and German companies. In our circular flow then, these import expenditures (M) represent a leakage. They reduce the total amont of spending on Canadian goods and services. When Americans buy Canadian cars or Iraqis buy Canadian wheat, these expenditures for our exports (X) represent an injection into the circular flow. They increase spending on Canadian goods.

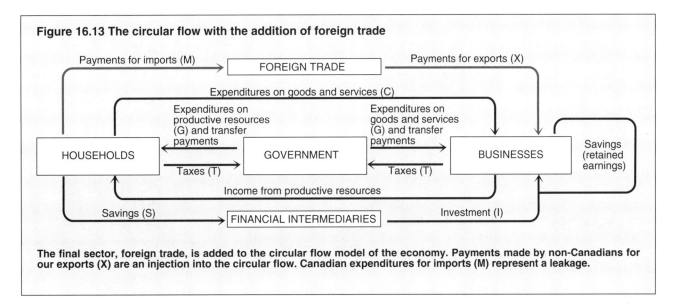

Figure 16.13 The circular flow with the addition of foreign trade

The final sector, foreign trade, is added to the circular flow model of the economy. Payments made by non-Canadians for our exports (X) are an injection into the circular flow. Canadian expenditures for imports (M) represent a leakage.

As with the other sectors of the economy, if injections (X) are greater than leakages (M), then the expenditure and income flows will tend to increase. If injections (X) are less than leakages (M), expenditure and income flows will tend to diminish. If, however, injections (X) equal leakages (M), the flows will have no tendency to change. Figure 16.13 illustrates the flows to and from the foreign trade sector.

Canadian expenditures on exports are largely dependent on the level of total Canadian income. As Canada's GDP increases, imports increase. Canadian governments, however, do have some control over imports. They can limit the quantity of particular imports through quotas or raise the prices of imports through tariffs, for example. Demand for Canadian exports originates outside the country and is, therefore, subject to many external influences. The main factor in the short run is the level of income and expenditures in other trading nations—a factor beyond Canadian control.

The Paradox of Thrift

□ □ □ □ □ □

A paradox is a statement that appears to be false but in fact may be true. The paradox of thrift is the possibility that a community, by attempting to save more (i.e., be more thrifty), may actually save less.

How is this possible? If consumers plan to save more from their current income, they will cut back on their consumption expenditures. If the planned increase in saving is not balanced by planned investment, total expenditures will be reduced. With a reduction in total expenditures, total income and thus total savings are reduced. The community's decision to save more may, therefore, result in its actually saving less.

The paradox of thrift was first noted by John Maynard Keynes.

□ Injections and Leakages—A Summary

Finally, we can see that if total planned injections from all sectors (I + G + X) equal total planned leakages (S + T + M), then the entire economy is in equilibrium. If total planned injections are greater than total planned leakages, total spending and income will tend to increase. If total planned injections are less than total planned leakages, total spending and income will tend to decrease. Figure 16.14 summarizes the effects of injections and leakages on the economy.

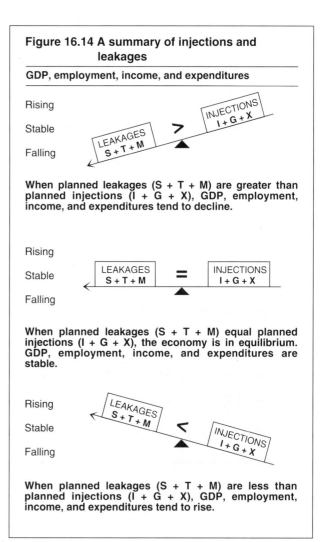

Figure 16.14 A summary of injections and leakages

When planned leakages (S + T + M) are greater than planned injections (I + G + X), GDP, employment, income, and expenditures tend to decline.

When planned leakages (S + T + M) equal planned injections (I + G + X), the economy is in equilibrium. GDP, employment, income, and expenditures are stable.

When planned leakages (S + T + M) are less than planned injections (I + G + X), GDP, employment, income, and expenditures tend to rise.

Equilibrium in the Canadian Economy

Figure 16.15 shows the changes in consumption, investment, government spending, net exports, and GDP in the Canadian economy from 1926 to 1991. As the figure illustrates, changes in consumption expenditures and GDP tend to parallel one another, rising over most of the years shown and declining in the recession years of 1982 and 1991. Current government expenditures have increased consistently from 1950 to 1991. Exports and investment were the most variable. Let's take a closer look at how and why these two elements have most affected the stability of the Canadian economy.

☐ Fluctuations in Exports

Exports are a significant source of instability in the Canadian economy. With almost one-third of our GDP sold in other countries (and approximately 70 percent of that total sold in the US), we are particularly vulnerable to economic fluctuations elsewhere. Our particular vulnerability to fluctuations in the US economy is likely to increase with the implementation of the Canada-US Free Trade Agreement.

An overview of exports since 1971 indicates the ups and downs. Exports in constant dollars fell in 1974, 1975, and again in 1982. In other years, such as 1978 and 1984, exports increased substantially. Since exports constitute such a large proportion of our GDP, these fluctuations have a significant impact on the general stability of the economy.

Fluctuations in Investment

Investment spending is the most variable of all injections and leakages. If we examine total business fixed capital expenditures between 1976 and 1991, we can see that at first, from 1976 to 1978, the annual increase is low—averaging approximately $2 billion a year. Then the average annual increases rise significantly, reaching almost $10 billion between 1980 and 1981.

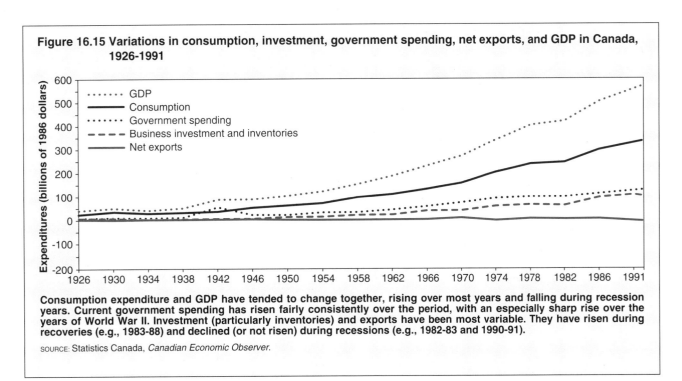

Figure 16.15 Variations in consumption, investment, government spending, net exports, and GDP in Canada, 1926-1991

Consumption expenditure and GDP have tended to change together, rising over most years and falling during recession years. Current government spending has risen fairly consistently over the period, with an especially sharp rise over the years of World War II. Investment (particularly inventories) and exports have been most variable. They have risen during recoveries (e.g., 1983-88) and declined (or not risen) during recessions (e.g., 1982-83 and 1990-91).

SOURCE: Statistics Canada, *Canadian Economic Observer*.

□ □ □ □ □ □

Skill Development: Calculating Marginal Propensities to Consume and Save

The marginal propensities to consume and save are important factors in the determination of Gross Domestic Product. Let's consider how and why.

Marginal Propensity to Consume

As we have seen, as income increases, the level of consumption increases. If your family income has risen over that of last year, for example, the chances are greater that you will buy that car, computer, or CD player you have been considering for some time. The marginal propensity to consume (MPC) measures how much more consumption increases as disposable income increases. Specifically defined, the **marginal propensity to consume (MPC)** is the proportion of any increase in disposable income that a family or a community would spend on additional consumption. It is calculated by the following formula:

$$MPC = \frac{Change\ in\ (\Delta)\ consumption\ (C)}{Change\ in\ (\Delta)\ disposable\ income\ (DI)}$$

The Greek letter Δ (delta) means change in.

Let's consider a specific example. Table 16.3 shows an income, consumption, and saving schedule for a particular family. We can see that as disposable income increases, consumption also increases, though at a slower rate. As the family's income increases from $20 000 to $30 000, for example, its consumption increases from $20 000 to $28 000, that is, by $8000. With the increase in disposable income, $8 out of $10 is used for consumption. The marginal propensity to consume is, therefore:

$$MPC = \frac{\Delta C}{\Delta DI} = \frac{8\ 000}{10\ 000} = \frac{8}{10} = 0.8.$$

We can think of the MPC as that fraction of a dollar increase in disposable income that is consumed. In this case, an increase of $1 in the family's income leads to an increase of 80 cents in consumption. As income increases, however, the marginal propensity to consume decreases.

Marginal Propensity to Save

The marginal propensity to save relates changes in saving to changes in income. Defined, the **marginal propensity to save (MPS)** is the proportion of any increase in disposable income that a household or a community would save. It can be calculated by the following formula:

$$MPS = \frac{Change\ in\ (\Delta)\ saving\ (S)}{Change\ in\ (\Delta)\ disposable\ income\ (DI)}$$

From Table 16.3, we can see that as the family's income increases from $20 000 to $30 000, saving increases from 0 to $2000. The MPS is, therefore:

$$MPS = \frac{\Delta S}{\Delta DI} = \frac{\$2\ 000}{\$10\ 000} = \frac{2}{10} = 0.2.$$

We can think of the MPS as that fraction of a dollar increase in income that is saved. Thus, as the family's income increases from $20 000 to $30 000, for each $1 increase 20 cents are saved. The table also shows that saving increases at a faster rate than consumption as disposable income increases. The marginal propensity to save increases as income increases.

Relationship Between MPC and MPS

As you have probably noticed, MPC + MPS = 1. The reason is that with each dollar of disposable income we receive, we can do only two things—spend or save. Therefore, the fraction we spend (MPC) plus the fraction we save (MPS) must equal one.

MPC and MPS in Canada

Since 1926 (when Statistics Canada began compiling the data), the MPC has tended to remain fairly constant at about .90. However, in the short run, the MPC varies over the business cycle. During recessions, the MPC declines (in 1983 to .83) as consumers become more cautious about spending. Since the MPC varies, so does the MPS. Generally, the MPS is around .10 of personal disposable income, but may rise to .20 during recessions.

Table 16.3 Income, consumption, and saving schedule for a family

1 ANNUAL DISPOSABLE INCOME (DI) (THOUSANDS OF DOLLARS)	2 CONSUMPTION (C) (THOUSANDS OF DOLLARS)	3 MARGINAL PROPENSITY TO CONSUME $MPC = \frac{\Delta C}{\Delta DI}$	4 SAVING (THOUSANDS OF DOLLARS) $S = DI - C$	5 MARGINAL PROPENSITY TO SAVE $MPS = \frac{\Delta S}{\Delta DI}$
20	20		0	
30	28	0.8	2	0.2
40	35	0.7	5	0.3
50	41	0.6	9	0.4
60	46	0.5	14	0.5

As the disposable income of the family increases, consumption increases—though at a slower rate. The marginal propensity to consume thus tends to decrease as income increases—at least initially. Saving, therefore, tends to increase at a faster rate as income increases, initially. The marginal propensity to save increases as income increases. Over the long term in the Canadian economy, however, the MPS has tended to remain quite stable.

Table 16.4 Consumption and saving schedule for an economy (billions of dollars at constant prices)

1 DISPOSABLE INCOME (DI)	2 CONSUMPTION (C)	3 MARGINAL PROPENSITY TO CONSUME (MPC) $MPC = \frac{\Delta C}{\Delta DI}$	4 SAVING (S) $S = DI - C$	5 MARGINAL PROPENSITY TO SAVE (MPS) $MPS = \frac{\Delta S}{\Delta DI}$
200	200			
300	290			
400	370			
500	450			
600	520			

Table 16.5 Canadian personal disposable income, personal expenditure on goods and services, and the marginal propensities to save and consume, selected years (millions of current dollars)

1 YEAR	2 PERSONAL DISPOSABLE INCOME	3 PERSONAL EXPENDITURE ON GOODS AND SERVICES	4 MPC	5 MPS
1926	3 988	3 508		
1930	4 294	4 336		
1940	4 798	4 464		
1950	13 411	12 576		
1960	26 855	25 708		
1970	55 616	51 853		
1980	203 653	172 416		
1990	454 809	398 711		

Applications

1. Complete Table 16.4.

2. Suppose your uncle leaves you an annuity that will pay you $5000 a year for life. Over next year, how much of it do you think you would spend? Calculate:
(a) your MPC   (b) your MPS.

3. (a) Complete Table 16.5.

(b) In 1930, the economy was in a depression. How did the MPC and MPS differ in this year as compared with other years?

(c) In both 1980 and 1990, the economy was in a recession. How did the MPC and MPS differ in these years as compared with earlier years? Explain why.

Between 1982 and 1983, capital spending actually declines with the recession and then gradually increases once again up to the $10 billion year-to-year rise by 1987. In 1990 and 1991, fixed capital expenditures decline for two successive years, thus helping to bring about the recession.

Additions to business inventories form the second and most volatile part of total business investment. In anticipation of strong sales, retailers and wholesalers are willing to buy more finished goods than usual and manufacturers are willing to hold more raw materials. Inventories, therefore, increase rapidly. If sales are expected to be weak, however, retailers, wholesalers, and manufacturers are likely to let their stocks decline, replenishing them only when absolutely necessary. Inventories fluctuated significantly between 1974 and 1975; 1979 and 1980; 1980, 1981, and 1982; and 1989 and 1990. The years of decreases in inventories were years of recession.

☐ The Multiplier Effect

Total investment spending, however, typically accounts for only about one-fifth of GDP and fluctuations in investment lead to only a 2 percent change in GDP. How, then, can such small changes bring about fluctuations in the entire economy? One major reason is the multiplier effect. To explain, let's consider a simple illustration.

Suppose I decide to invest $100 in a new machine to increase output at my factory and I purchase the machine from you. For the moment, we'll assume no taxes and no foreign trade. What would the impact of my investment be on the GDP?

First round   My investment expenditure is an injection of $100 and will thus increase GDP by $100.

Second round   Since I buy the machine from you, your income increases by $100—but you will likely not save all of it. Let's suppose that you decide to spend $80 of it at Gretchen's store. That is, your marginal propensity to consume (MPC) is 0.80 and your marginal propensity to save (MPS) is 0.20. Your expenditure thus adds $80 to the GDP.

Third round   Let's suppose now that Gretchen also has an MPC of 0.80 (and an MPS of 0.20), and she decides to spend $64 of her increased income at another store. She then contributes an additional $64 to the GDP.

Fourth and subsequent rounds   If we assume that everyone else who receives a fraction of the declining expenditure also has an MPC of 0.80, then the process will continue with increasingly smaller expenditures until my original expenditure of $100 has generated additional expenditures of $400. Figure 16.16 illustrates the process.

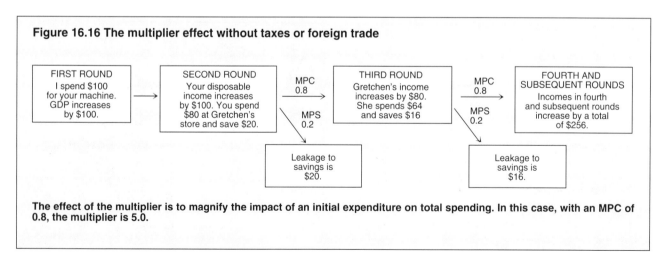

Figure 16.16 The multiplier effect without taxes or foreign trade

FIRST ROUND	SECOND ROUND	MPC 0.8	THIRD ROUND	MPC 0.8	FOURTH AND SUBSEQUENT ROUNDS
I spend $100 for your machine. GDP increases by $100.	Your disposable income increases by $100. You spend $80 at Gretchen's store and save $20.	MPS 0.2 → Leakage to savings is $20.	Gretchen's income increases by $80. She spends $64 and saves $16	MPS 0.2 → Leakage to savings is $16.	Incomes in fourth and subsequent rounds increase by a total of $256.

The effect of the multiplier is to magnify the impact of an initial expenditure on total spending. In this case, with an MPC of 0.8, the multiplier is 5.0.

Table 16.6 The multiplier effect (dollars)

SPENDING	ADDITION TO GDP	CUMULATIVE INCREASE IN GDP
First round 100	100	100
Second round (0.67 X 100) = 67	67	167
Third round (0.67 X 67) = 45	45	212
Fourth round (0.67 X 45) = 30	30	242
Fifth round (0.67 x 30) = 20	20	262
Sixth round (0.67 x 20) = 13 etc.	13	275
Total all rounds	300	300

With an MPC of 0.67, an initial expenditure of $100 generates a $300 addition to the GDP through the respending process.

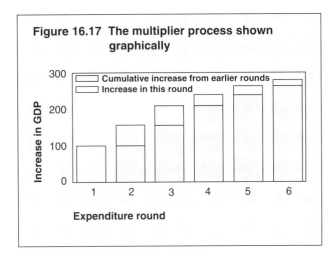

Figure 16.17 The multiplier process shown graphically

The total addition to GDP—including my initial $100—is, therefore, $500. My initial expenditure of $100 was multiplied through the chain of respending to a total expenditure of $500. The multiplier, therefore, is 5.0. Thus, the **multiplier** is the factor by which initial changes in spending change the level of total spending. The size of the multiplier varies with the MPC. If the MPC is 2/3 or 0.67, for example, the effect on total GDP would be as shown in Table 16.6 and Figure 16.17.

With a lower MPC, the multiplier is lower and the effect on total GDP is also less. In general, the greater the MPC, the greater is the multiplier and the greater is the effect on total GDP.

Remember, however, that we assumed no taxes and no foreign trade in our examples. If we incorporate these leakages from the circular flow, the multiplier will be much smaller. Not all of my initial $100 investment expenditure will be yours to spend, for example. Some will be taken in taxes. This tax leakage will occur at each stage of the respending process. In addition, payments for imports represent a significant leakage since between a quarter and a third of the goods and services we buy are imported. Figure 16.18 illustrates the multiplier effect when taxes and foreign trade are considered.

The University of Toronto's Institute for Policy Analysis has estimated that the multiplier in Canada is about 1.87. The Economic Council of Canada estim-

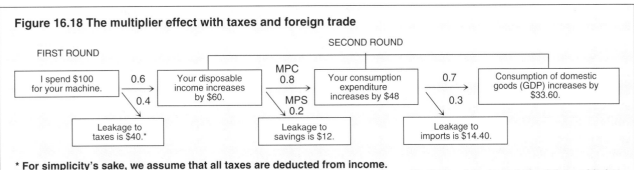

Figure 16.18 The multiplier effect with taxes and foreign trade

* For simplicity's sake, we assume that all taxes are deducted from income.
With the addition of taxes and foreign trade, a total of $33.60 is spent on domestically-produced goods (and thus added to GDP) in the second round, as compared with $80 in the second round of our initial example. The reason is that $40 leaks to taxes and $14.40 leaks outside Canada to pay for imports. These leakages, therefore, lower the multiplier. The cumulative addition to GDP through the respending process is thus also lower.

□ □ □ □ □ □

Skill Development: Calculating the Multiplier

Some basic formulae can be used to calculate the multiplier and thus measure the effects that changes in investment can have on the economy.

A. A Simple Multiplier in an Economy Without Foreign Trade or Taxes

Without trade or taxes, the size of the MPS and the multiplier are closely linked. The smaller is the leakage of the new income to savings, the greater is the multiplier. The multiplier is the reciprocal of the MPS.

$$\text{Multiplier} = \frac{1}{\text{MPS}}$$

Examples:

(a) If the MPS is 0.20, then the multiplier is:

$$\frac{1}{.20} = 5.$$

(b) If the MPS is 0.10, then the multiplier is:

$$\frac{1}{.10} = 10.$$

B. The Multiplier in an Economy With Trade and Taxes

With trade and taxes, we calculate the multiplier by adding the proportion of each additional dollar to income that goes to each one of the three leakages—saving, imports, and taxes. Suppose that the total leakages are 60 percent.

$$\text{Multiplier} = \frac{1}{\text{Savings rate + tax rate + import rate}}$$

$$= \frac{1}{0.6} = 1.67$$

Applications
1. Calculate the multiplier in the following cases:
(a) when an economy without foreign trade or taxes has an MPS of 0.3
(b) when the proportion of each additional dollar that leaks out of the circular flow to taxes is 40 cents, to savings is 10 cents, and to imports is 30 cents.
2. The Canadian economy is more open to foreign trade than is the US economy. On the basis of this fact alone, would you expect the multiplier in the US to be smaller or larger than that in Canada? Explain your reasoning.

---

ates that it is approximately 1.7. An increase in investment spending of $1 million, therefore, would probably increase total expenditures between $1.5 and $2 million.

As you would expect, the multiplier effect can magnify not only increases, but also decreases in investment spending. For example, if investment were cut by $3 billion, with a multiplier of 2.0, total spending would decline by $6 billion. Thus, the multiplier can work in reverse and contribute significantly to recessions and depressions by magnifying the impact of initial spending cuts.

□ The Accelerator

The **accelerator** is the principle by which changes in consumer demand cause magnified changes in the rate of capital investment by businesses, and therefore increased fluctuations in national income. A small increase in consumer demand can cause a disproportionately large increase in the demand for the capital goods to meet that demand and *vice versa*. Thus, while the multiplier shows the effects of an increase in investment on consumer spending, the accelerator shows the converse relationship. Investment that results from increased consumer demand is known as **induced investment**.

To illustrate the accelerator effect, let's consider an example. Table 16.7 outlines the sales and investment figures for a hypothetical firm, Canada Canoe. The firm sells 40 000 fibreglass canoes a year. Each Canada Canoe moulding machine can produce 2000 canoes a

Table 16.7 Sales and investment data for Canada Canoe

1 YEARS	2 YEARLY SALES OF CANOES (THOUSANDS)	3 INVESTMENT MACHINES NEEDED TO MAKE CANOES	4 ADDITIONAL MACHINES NEEDED	5 REPLACEMENT MACHINES	6 TOTAL ADDITIONAL MACHINES OR TOTAL GROSS INVESTMENT	7 PERCENTAGE CHANGE IN INVESTMENT FROM PREVIOUS YEAR	8 PERCENTAGE CHANGE IN CONSUMPTION FROM PREVIOUS YEAR
UNCHANGING SALES							
Year 1	40	20	0	2	2	0	0
Year 2	40	20	0	2	2	0	0
INCREASING SALES							
Year 3	44	22	2	2	4	100	10
Year 4	48	24	2	2	4	0	9
LEVELLING OFF OF SALES							
Year 5	50	25	1	2	3	−25	4
Year 6	50	25	0	2	2	−33	0
DECREASING SALES							
Year 7	46	23	−2	2	0	−100	−8
Year 8	42	21	−2	2	0	0	−9

As demand and thus sales increase, net investment also increases at an accelerated rate.

year and the firm has enough machines to produce the current yearly sales of 40 000 canoes. The firm is, therefore, operating at the full capacity of its moulding machines.

We'll assume each machine lasts 10 years and two machines are replaced each year as they wear out. In years 1 and 2, no additional investment is needed since yearly sales remain unchanged at 40 000 canoes. In year 3, canoe sales increase 10 percent to 44 000. To produce this number, Canada Canoe needs two more machines, for a total of 22. Total gross investment, therefore, rises from 2 to 4 machines—an increase of 100 percent. An increase in sales of only 10 percent, therefore, has a magnified or *accelerated* effect on the demand for investment.

In year 4, sales increase by 9 percent over year 3 to 48 000. To meet this increased demand, 2 more machines are required once again. The increase in total investment, therefore, remains at the same level as the previous year. Between years 4 and 5, sales increase 4

percent to 50 000 canoes. Despite the sales increase, total investment demand decreases from 4 machines in the previous year to 3 in year 5—a decrease of 25 percent.

In years 5 and 6, canoe sales level off. The only investment needed, therefore, is to replace the 2 machines that have worn out. Total investment then falls from 3 to 2 machines—a decline of 33 1/3 percent.

After year 6, sales start to decrease, and in year 7 they fall 8 percent to 46 000. The number of machines now needed falls from 25 to 23. Two machines less are needed so that with the usual two replacement machines, the total number of machines needed falls to zero. Thus, with a drop in sales of only 8 percent, investment falls 100 percent to zero.

In year 8, sales decline 8 percent from 46 000 to 42 000. Total demand for new machines consequently falls to zero. Figure 16.19 shows these effects graphically.

Characteristics of the Accelerator

From our example of the accelerator effect, we can see a number of its major characteristics:

(i) Investment in machinery fluctuates much more than changes in the sales of goods made by the machinery.

(ii) A reduction in the increase of output will cause a reduction in investment (e.g., year 5).

(iii) Total investment may drop precipitously, even though total sales decline only moderately (e.g., year 7).

Since changes in consumer spending can have such exaggerated effects on investment, induced investment is an especially volatile component of total investment. Consumer demand, in fact, has to be rising continuously to simply maintain the level of induced investment. Should it even just level off, induced investment will drop considerably.

Moreover, we have shown the impact of the accelerator on the demand for machinery, but it can have similar effects on the level of any other capital investments as well. With an increase in the dropout rate of teens or a decrease in the birthrate, the construction of new high schools and colleges (or the extension of existing ones) would diminish sharply, for example. Similarly, with an increase in economic activity and the consequent increased shipment of goods, the demand for trucks would rise sharply. Capital goods industries, therefore, are particularly subject to ups and downs in the economy as a whole. A decline in induced investment can also depress consumer spending by the multiplier effect to complicate the problem even further.

☐ The Accelerator-Multiplier Interaction

The multiplier and accelerator thus interact in the economy. For example, increased investment in the machine industry will bring a magnified increase in national income through the multiplier effect. As more is consumed, the industry must increase investment in plant and equipment to meet the demand—thus the action of the accelerator. Increases in investment demand and consumer demand reinforce each other.

At some point, however, the increase in consumer spending slows and brings a decline in investment because of the accelerator. This, in turn, causes a multiplied decrease in national income.

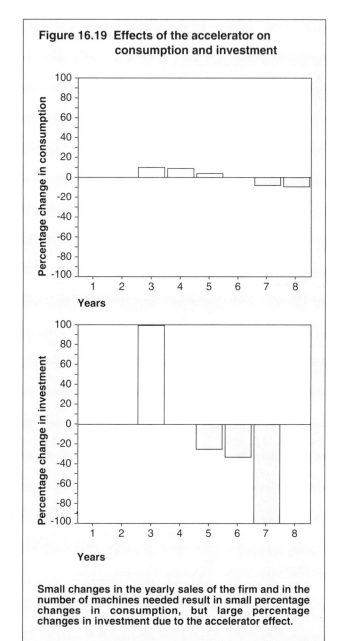

Figure 16.19 Effects of the accelerator on consumption and investment

Small changes in the yearly sales of the firm and in the number of machines needed result in small percentage changes in consumption, but large percentage changes in investment due to the accelerator effect.

Summary

a. Since 1926 (when Statscan began compiling the data), the Canadian economy has gone through a number of expansionary and contractionary periods. No two expansions or contractions, however, have been alike.

b. Periodic swings in economic activity, typically consisting of four phases, are called business cycles. The peak is the high point of the cycle, characterized by a GDP at or near capacity, almost full employment, and rising prices. The recession is a contractionary phase, with declining real GDP for at least two quarters in succession, reduced investment and consumption, unemployment, and little or no increase in prices. The trough is the low point of the cycle with low levels of consumption, investment, labour demand, and prices. The expansionary phase is characterized by a rising real GDP, increasing consumption and investment, growing labour demand, and an accelerated increase in prices.

c. Business cycles occur because of fluctuations in the balance of injections and leakages in the circular flow of the economy. An injection is any expenditure put into the circular flow that increases domestic income (consumption spending, business investment, government spending and transfers, payments for exports). A leakage is any money taken out of the circular flow that reduces domestic income (saving, taxes, payments for imports).

d. The major determinants of consumption spending are current disposable income, expectations for future income, the availability of credit, interest rates, expectations about future price levels, and wealth.

e. The main components of investment are plant and machinery, residential construction, and inventories. The level of investment in the economy is affected by the rate of return on investments, expectations about the future (including the demand for products, costs of productive resources, competition, government tariff and tax policies, and the general economic outlook), and interest rates. Investments, and particularly inventories, are especially volatile and are, therefore, a key source of economic instability.

f. In a closed economy without government, if planned investment equals planned saving, the economy is in equilibrium and stable.

g. John Maynard Keynes challenged the accepted economic theory of his day that capitalist economies always tend toward full employment automatically. He showed that insufficient spending can keep an economy in recession or depression for a long period. According to Keynes, government thus has an important role to play in increasing total spending to bring about full employment.

h. Government expenditures on productive resources and goods and services represent injections into the economy. Taxes, on the other hand, represent leakages.

i. Payments from foreign buyers in exchange for our exports represent injections into the economy, while payments by Canadians for imports represent leakages. In the short run, the amount we spend on imports depends largely on the level of our domestic income (GDP). Governments may also control imports through quotas and tariffs. Canadians have little control over the income received from exports, however, since the demand for our exports originates outside the country.

j. The marginal propensity to consume (MPC) is the proportion of any increase in disposable income that is spent on additional consumption. Generally, as income increases, the MPC decreases, at least initially. Over the long term in Canada, however, the MPC has tended to remain fairly stable.

   The marginal propensity to save (MPS) is the proportion of any increase in disposable income that is saved. Generally, as income increases, the MPS increases. Saving increases at a faster rate than consumption as income increases.

k. Over the period 1926 to 1991 in Canada, fluctuations in spending have been largely due to changes in the level of exports and investment. Significant drops in investment, for example, contributed to the recessions in 1981-82 and 1990-91. Government spending has risen consistently over the period and consumption expenditures in constant dollars increased most years, except in the recession years of 1982 and 1991.

l. Small fluctuations in investment spending can have a significant effect on the GDP because of the multiplier effect. The multiplier is the factor by which initial changes in spending affect the level of total spending. The size of the multiplier varies with the MPC.

m. The accelerator is the principle by which changes in consumer demand cause magnified changes in the rate of capital investment, and thus GDP. The accelerator illustrates that investment spending fluctuates much more than consumer spending.

■ Review of Key Terms

Define the following key terms introduced in this chapter and provide examples where appropriate.

business cycle
peak
recession
depression
trough
expansion
leakage
injection
equilibrium
   level of income

Say's law
marginal propensity to consume
   (MPC)
marginal propensity to save
   (MPS)
paradox of thrift
multiplier
accelerator
induced investment

■ Application and Analysis

1. What effect is each of the following likely to have on the amount of consumer spending? Explain why in each case.

(a) a decrease in income taxes

(b) an increase in the GST from 7 to 10 percent

(c) expectations that the economy will go into a recession in the next six months

(d) expectations that prices will fall in the next three months

(e) a 25-percent fall in stock market prices

2. What effect is each of the following likely to have on the amount of investment? Explain why in each case.

(a) a decline in interest rates

(b) expectations of a coming recession

(c) an increase in the marginal efficiency of investment

3. Refer to Table 16.8 below.

(a) Calculate the total injections.

(b) Calculate the total leakages.

(c) Is the economy in equilibrium? Explain.

Table 16.8 Key economic indicators for a hypothetical economy (billions of dollars)

Gross Domestic Product	100
Consumption expenditures	50
Savings	10
Investment	15
Government expenditures	25
Taxes	20
Exports	30
Imports	25

Table 16.9 Economic data for the economy of Nowhere (billions of dollars)

1 CONSUMPTION	2 SAVING	3 INVESTMENT	4 GOVERNMENT SPENDING	5 TAXES	6 EXPORTS	7 IMPORTS
310	−10	20	30	20	40	5
350	0	20	30	20	40	10
390	10	20	30	20	40	20
430	20	20	30	20	40	20
470	30	20	30	20	40	25
510	40	20	30	20	40	30
550	50	20	30	20	40	35

4. Refer to Table 16.9.

(a) Use columns 1 through 4 to determine the equilibrium GDP for a closed economy without government.

(b) What is the equilibrium GDP for a closed economy with government?

(c) What is the equilibrium GDP for an open economy? Why does this equilibrium GDP differ from that of the closed economy?

(d) Suppose exports drop to zero. What is the new equilibrium GDP of the open economy?

(e) Suppose exports remain unchanged at $20 billion. What is the new equilibrium of the open economy? Explain the relationship between the level of exports and the GDP.

(f) Suppose exports remain unchanged at $40 billion and imports remain unchanged at $10 billion. What is the new equilibrium GDP?

(g) Suppose imports increase to $60 billion. What is the new equilibrium GDP?

(h) What can you infer about the relationship between the GDP and imports? Explain.

5. Explain the effect each of the following would have on GDP.

(a) a decrease in government spending of $100 million with a multiplier of 2

(b) an increase in investment of $500 million with an MPC of 0.6

(c) an increase in taxes of $1 billion with an MPC of 0.8

(d) an increase in savings of $500 million with an MPC of 0.75

6. Complete Table 16.10 below for 10 years. Assume that one machine is needed to produce every 100 refrigerators, that each machine lasts 10 years, and the machines depreciate by 10 percent in each of the 10 years.

Table 16.10 The accelerator process

1 YEAR	2 YEARLY SALES OF REFRIGERATORS	3 NUMBER OF MACHINES NEEDED TO MAKE THE REFRIGERATORS	4 ADDITIONAL MACHINES NEEDED	5 RELACEMENT MACHINES	6 TOTAL ADDITIONAL MACHINES	7 PERCENTAGE CHANGE IN INVESTMENT FROM PREVIOUS YEAR	8 PERCENTAGE CHANGE IN CONSUMPTION FROM PREVIOUS YEAR
1							
2 etc.							

CHAPTER SEVENTEEN

Aggregate Demand and Aggregate Supply

Objectives

a. Outline the components of aggregate demand and explain the shape of the aggregate demand curve.

b. Analyze the factors that may cause a shift in aggregate demand.

c. Define aggregate supply and explain the shape of the aggregate supply curve.

d. Analyze the factors that may cause a shift in aggregate supply.

e. Demonstrate how the equilibrium output and price level are determined by aggregate demand and supply.

f. Determine the relationship between the level of employment and the macroeconomic equilibrium.

g. Outline how shifts in aggregate demand and supply affect the equilibrium.

h. Relate the fluctuations in the Canadian economy from 1971 to 1991 to the levels of aggregate demand and supply.

i. Demonstrate the relationship of the injections-leakages and AS-AD analyses to the business cycle.

In the last chapter, we examined how the macroeconomy may be in equilibrium or disequilibrium using the injections-leakages approach. Now we consider an alternative analysis. In fact, we return to two familiar concepts first introduced in Chapter 3—demand and supply. In Chapter 3, we dealt with demand and supply for specific products in individual (microeconomic) markets and saw how they interact to determine prices and output. Now we apply the concepts to the macroeconomy and determine how *aggregate* supply and demand influence *total* output and *general* price levels. We also consider how injections-leakages, aggregate demand and supply, and business cycles are related—in other words, we complete our examination of the reasons for the business cycle.

Aggregate Demand

Aggregate demand (AD) is the total demand of all consumers, businesses, governments, and foreign buyers for all goods and services produced in an economy. An aggregate demand schedule or curve indicates the various levels of real output that all sectors of the economy are willing and able to demand at various price levels—all other factors being equal.

Aggregate demand (AD) is fundamentally the same concept as GDP we examined in Chapter 15. Both AD and GDP refer to the total expenditures in an economy over a particular time. The one major difference between them is that while GDP refers to *actual* expenditures, AD refers to *actual or planned* expenditures. AD indicates how total expenditures will change with changes in the price level.

What, then, are the components of aggregate demand? They are essentially the same as those that make up GDP—the expenditures of consumers, governments, businesses, and foreign buyers.

The AD Curve

In Chapter 3, we saw that the market demand curve for a particular good or service shows an inverse relationship between price and quantity. As price declines, quantity demanded rises. As the market price of cassette tapes declines, for example, consumers are willing to buy more. They will substitute the lower-priced products (tapes) for the more expensive goods (CDs). Second, as the price of a product falls, the total amount of goods and services that consumer incomes can buy increases, and so consumers can buy more. The market demand curve, therefore, slopes down to the right because of the income and substitution effects.

The aggregate demand curve also slopes down to the right, as shown in Figure 17.1. As the general level of prices declines, the total amount of real output demanded increases. But the reasons for the shape of the aggregate demand curve are not the same as those for the individual market demand curve.

Why? We must remember that aggregate demand is

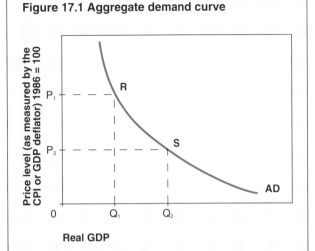

Figure 17.1 Aggregate demand curve

The aggregate demand (AD) curve slopes down to the right. As the general level of prices falls from $0P_1$ to $0P_2$ and we move down along the AD curve from R to S, more goods and services are demanded—$0Q_2$ rather than $0Q_1$. Consumers are able to buy more with their incomes, the demand for money decreases, interest rates decline, more profitable investment opportunities become available for businesses, and domestic products are more competitive with those of foreign countries.

not the sum of all individual product demand, but rather the total demand of the four different sectors of the economy. The explanation for the shape of the AD curve, therefore, depends on the behaviour and components of these sectors, and not on individual product markets. In fact, the AD curve slopes down to the right because of the effects changing general price levels have on consumption, investment, and foreign trade.

Consumption and Investment

If the general price level rises, consumers can buy less with their incomes and the total quantity of goods and services demanded, therefore, declines. Even if increases in wages and salaries keep pace with rising price levels, consumer demand will decline because the money consumers hold in bank accounts, Canada Saving Bonds, and other assets loses value. It can buy less and so consumers will tend to spend less.

At the same time, the demand for money will increase, since consumers and businesses generally need more money for the purchases they wish to make. Interest rates will, therefore, rise and businesses will reduce investment because the potential returns are lower. Consumers will also reduce purchases of items that require borrowed money. Thus, as the general level of prices (inflation) increases, aggregate quantity demanded and real GDP decline.

If the general level of prices declines, the effects occur in reverse. Consumers can then buy more with their incomes and their net wealth (bank deposits, savings bonds, etc.) increases. The demand for borrowed money falls and, consequently, interest rates decline. Businesses, therefore, increase investments in real capital and aggregate demand for real GDP rises.

Foreign Trade

A general increase in prices affects only domestic, not foreign goods and services. Thus, if the prices of Canadian products increase while the prices of imported products remain stable, Canadians and foreign buyers will purchase fewer Canadian products. Aggregate demand will, therefore, fall and with it, real GDP.

Similarly, if prices of Canadian goods and services decline in relation to the prices of imports, Canadian and foreign buyers will purchase more Canadian products and aggregate demand for real GDP increases.

Changing prices, therefore, result in movements *along* the aggregate demand curve. In other words, changes in the general price level affect total quantity demanded. Price level increases result in movements *up* along the AD curve and a reduction in total quantity demanded. Price level decreases result in movements *down* along the AD curve and an increase in total quantity demanded.

☐ Shifts in the AD Curve

As we have seen, real GDP demanded varies as the general price level varies. The effect of price changes on GDP are shown as movements along the AD curve. But, price level is not the only factor that may affect aggregate demand. A change in any one of the four components of aggregate demand (consumption,

investment, government expenditures, and net exports) will shift the entire AD curve to the left or right and thus decrease or increase the demand for real GDP. Let's consider what may cause these shifts.

Changes in Consumer Spending

Suppose consumers decide to curtail spending and increase their savings. Aggregate demand will then decrease and the AD curve will shift to the left, as shown in Figure 17.2. An increase in population, on the other hand, will increase consumer spending and shift the AD curve to the right. Any of the factors that may affect consumer spending, therefore, may also affect aggregate demand.

Changes in Government Spending

If government increases its spending and transfer payments or decreases taxes, aggregate demand will increase and the AD curve will shift to the right. Conversely, a reduction in government spending and

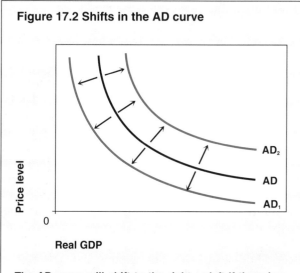

Figure 17.2 Shifts in the AD curve

The AD curve will shift to the right or left if there is a change in one of the components of aggregate demand. If governments increase taxes, for example, aggregate demand will diminish at every price level and the AD curve will shift to the left, as to AD₁. If businesses decide to increase investment expenditures, for example, aggregate demand will increase at every price level and the AD curve will shift to the right, as to AD₂.

transfers or tax increases will decrease aggregate demand and shift the AD curve to the left.

Changes in Business Investment

If future profits are expected to increase, businesses will invest more, thus increasing aggregate demand and shifting the AD curve to the right. An anticipated decrease in future profits will have the opposite effect on aggregate demand. Any of the factors that can affect business investment may shift aggregate demand.

Changes in Foreign Trade

Increases in the value of the Canadian dollar will increase the cost of Canadian goods and thereby make them less attractive to foreign buyers. The AD curve will, therefore, shift to the left. Decreases in the value of the Canadian dollar, on the other hand, will encourage foreign buyers to purchase Canadian goods and thus increase aggregate demand.

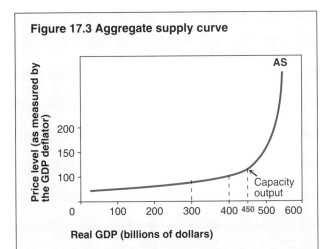

Figure 17.3 Aggregate supply curve

At levels of output less than $400 billion, the AS curve slopes gently upward. The economy is operating well below capacity and resources are available relatively cheaply, so that total real output rises with only minimal increases in the price level. At outputs beyond $400 billion as the economy moves closer to capacity, the AS curve rises more steeply. Shortages of resources may occur and it becomes increasingly expensive to produce more output. Prices, therefore, rise. Finally, at an output of $500 billion, the AS curve becomes vertical. No more can be produced.

■ Aggregate Supply

Aggregate supply (AS) is the total value of all goods and services produced in an economy over a particular period. In other words, aggregate supply is the sum of all final goods and services produced by all domestic firms in an economy. An aggregate supply schedule or curve shows the amounts of real GDP all firms are willing and able to supply at various price levels over a particular period.

The aggregate supply schedule depends primarily on the volume and quality of productive resources used and the level of technology. Aggregate supply is related to GDP, but while real GDP is the actual total product supplied over a particular period, aggregate supply indicates both actual and planned total output all firms would be willing to supply at different price levels.

The AS Curve

Just as the AD curve had a certain similarity to the individual market demand curve, so too does the AS curve have a resemblance to the individual market supply curve. The market supply curve slopes up to the right, indicating a direct relationship between price and quantity supplied. The higher the price, the greater is the quantity supplied. As the price of wheat increases, for example, firms shift out of the production of other grains and into wheat production, thus increasing the supply of wheat.

The aggregate supply curve also slopes up to the right, as shown in Figure 17.3. As the general level of prices rises, total real output also increases. But the AS curve does not slope upward for the same reason as the individual market supply curve. Since we are dealing with total supply, the idea that firms can switch from producing one good or service to another to increase supply does not apply.

What determines the slope of the AS curve, then? At first, the slope of the AS curve is slight, but as output increases, the slope becomes steeper until the curve is vertical. As Figure 17.3 shows, at outputs up to $400 billion, the AS curve slopes gently upward. Since these output levels are well below capacity, resources such as labour and raw materials are still available in significant amounts. Producers are willing and able to increase output with only small increases in price. The costs of resources are relatively low and in the short-run—over a few months or a year—some costs, such as rent and wages, are relatively fixed. Rents of buildings are settled usually for a period of years and labour contracts often for up to two or three years.

As output begins to approach capacity, however, it becomes increasingly expensive to increase production. Productive resources become more scarce and some industries may experience shortages. Consequently, prices of these inputs will increase as businesses bid to obtain them. Firms will also charge higher prices to cover their increasing costs. As output increases further, more shortages will appear and prices will rise higher. The AS curve, therefore, begins to rise more steeply as the economy moves closer to capacity output.

What determines capacity output? The capacity output of an economy is determined by the quantity and quality of the available resources—natural, human, and capital. The more an economy has of these resources and the higher their quality, the greater will be its capacity output.

As we have seen, then, changes in the price level result in movements *along* the AS curve. That is, price level changes cause changes in the total quantity supplied. An increase in the price level increases the total quantity supplied (real GDP) and a decrease in the price level decreases the total quantity supplied (real GDP).

☐ Shifts in AS

Factors other than changes in the price level can cause shifts in the aggregate supply curve. Shifts in AS are known as **supply shocks**. The major causes of supply shocks are changes in the price of inputs, changes in the quantity of productive factors, and changes in productivity.

Price of Inputs
If prices of inputs (such as labour) rise, then the

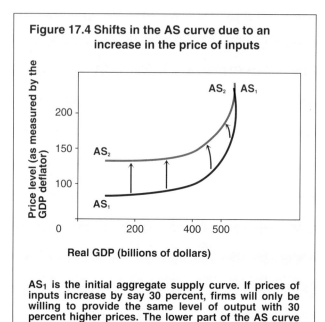

Figure 17.4 Shifts in the AS curve due to an increase in the price of inputs

AS$_1$ is the initial aggregate supply curve. If prices of inputs increase by say 30 percent, firms will only be willing to provide the same level of output with 30 percent higher prices. The lower part of the AS curve thus shifts from AS$_1$ to AS$_2$.

current profitability of firms will be reduced. For any given level of output, therefore, firms' costs increase. They will be willing to provide the same levels of output only at higher prices. As a result, the AS curve shifts to the left, as shown in Figure 17.4. A decrease in the prices of inputs will have the opposite effect and shift the AS curve to the right. The curves converge once output will no longer change no matter what the price.

Quantity of Productive Factors
Changes in the size of the labour force and/or capital stock, for example, will also influence aggregate supply. The larger the labour force or the capital stock, the greater will be the quantity of goods and services supplied. The entire AS curve thus shifts to the right, as shown in Figure 17.5, because capacity output is raised. The greater the quantity of productive resources, the greater is the potential output of the economy. Decreases in the quantity of productive resources will have the opposite effect.

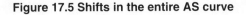

Figure 17.5 Shifts in the entire AS curve

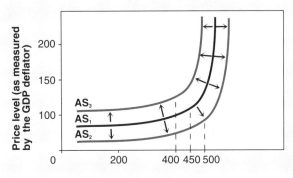

Real GDP (billions of dollars)

An increase in aggregate supply due to increases in the factors of production or productivity shift the entire AS curve to the right from AS₁ to AS₂. Capacity output thus increases from $450 billion to $500 billion. Decreases in the factors of production or productivity shift the entire curve to the left from AS₁ to AS₃ and reduce capacity output to $400 billion.

Figure 17.6 Equilibrium output and price level in the macroeconomy

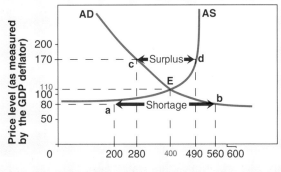

Real GDP (billions of dollars)

The macroeconomy reaches equilibrium at the point where AS equals AD—in this example, at a price level of 110 and a real GDP of $400 billion (point E). If AD exceeds AS, the economy has a shortage. For example, at a price level of 80, aggregate quantity demanded is $560 billion (point b) and aggregate quantity supplied is $200 billion (point a). Firms will raise prices until the price level reaches 110 once again. If AS exceeds AD, the economy has a surplus—such as at a price level of 170, where aggregate quantity demanded is $280 billion (point c) and aggregate quantity supplied is $490 billion (point d). Firms would then lower prices until equilibrium is again reached.

Productivity

Improvements in technology or in the skill level of workers, for example, increase productivity and thus output. Firms can produce more from their existing capital stock. Again, the entire AS curve then shifts to the right and capacity output is increased, as shown in Figure 17.5. Decreases in productivity will have the opposite effect.

▌ Equilibrium Output and Price Level

In markets for individual goods and services, equilibrium is reached at the price where quantity supplied and quantity demanded are equal. As you would expect, in the macroeconomy, equilibrium output and price level are attained where aggregate demand equals aggregate supply—that is, where the two curves intersect. In other words, at equilibrium, the quan-

tity of real GDP demanded and supplied are equal.

How is this equilibrium reached? Suppose the price level is above the point where the AS and AD curves intersect, point E in Figure 17.6. AS then exceeds AD and there is a surplus. Firms would be aware that they could not sell all of their output and they would, therefore, cut their prices. As the price level falls, the aggregate quantity supplied falls. When AS again equals AD, there is equilibrium and firms no longer need to cut prices.

If the price level is below the point where the AS and AD curves intersect, then AD exceeds AS and the economy has a shortage. Competition among buyers for the goods and services will push up prices. Businesses will then raise prices until AD again equals AS.

□ Equilibrium and Employment

When the economy is in equilibrium, do we have full employment? The answer is—possibly, but not necessarily. At equilibrium, we may have unemployment, full employment, or even more than full employment. An economy may fluctuate among these three situations.

Unemployment Equilibrium

Unemployment equilibrium occurs when the macroeconomic equilibrium real GDP is less than capacity real GDP. The gap between equilibrium real GDP and capacity GDP is known as a **recessionary gap**. This situation is shown in Figure 17.7. With a real GDP of $350 billion and a capacity GDP of $450 billion, resources such as labour are unemployed, causing the recessionary gap. The Canadian economy was in this situation during the 1990-91 recession.

Full Employment Equilibrium

Full employment equilibrium occurs when actual real GDP equals capacity GDP, as shown in Figure 17.8. Equilibrium real GDP and capacity GDP both equal $450 billion. All workers (with allowances for the full employment unemployment rate) are employed in the economy. The Canadian economy experienced full employment equilibrium during the boom years of the mid-1980s.

Above Full Employment Equilibrium

The economy is in **above full employment equilibrium** when actual real GDP is greater than capacity GDP. How can this occur? It is possible for employment to be pushed beyond the full employment level. This occurs whenever the unemployment rate falls below the full employment unemployment rate. As we have seen, the full employment unemployment rate in Canada is currently considered to be in the range of 6 to 8 percent. Unemployment may be less than this rate if people who are not in the workforce are enticed into it by abundant vacancies. Workers may also work overtime. Actual GDP may then rise above capacity GDP.

This difference between actual real GDP and capacity GDP is called an **inflationary gap**. As Figure 17.9 illustrates, when actual real GDP is $475 billion and capacity GDP is $450 billion, the inflationary gap is $25 billion. Canada faced an inflationary gap in 1989-90.

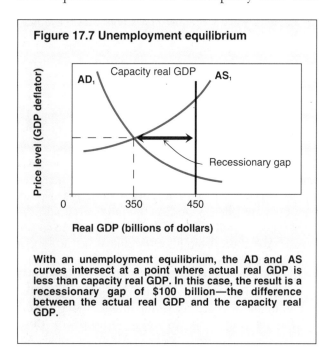

Figure 17.7 Unemployment equilibrium

With an unemployment equilibrium, the AD and AS curves intersect at a point where actual real GDP is less than capacity real GDP. In this case, the result is a recessionary gap of $100 billion—the difference between the actual real GDP and the capacity real GDP.

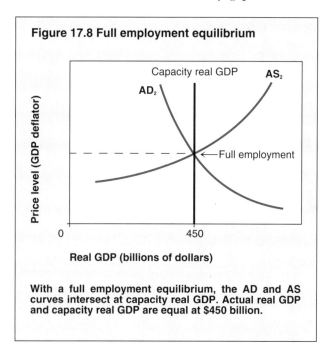

Figure 17.8 Full employment equilibrium

With a full employment equilibrium, the AD and AS curves intersect at capacity real GDP. Actual real GDP and capacity real GDP are equal at $450 billion.

Changes in Aggregate Demand and Equilibrium

A shift in either aggregate demand or aggregate supply will affect the equilibrium levels of real output and prices. As we have seen, shifts in aggregate demand will occur if there are changes in any of its components. Increases in consumption, investment, government spending, or foreign spending on Canadian goods and services will shift the AD curve to the right. Decreases in any of these components will shift the AD curve to the left.

With a shift in the AD curve to the right, total quantity of real GDP demanded and the price level increase. With a shift in the AD curve to the left, total quantity of real GDP demanded and the price level decrease.

Changes in Aggregate Supply and Equilibrium

As we have seen, shifts in aggregate supply or supply shocks occur as a result of changes in three factors—the price of inputs, the quantity of productive factors,

and productivity. Let's assume there is an increase in the price of inputs, which occurred in 1973 when the Organization of Petroleum Exporting Countries (OPEC) decided to restrict the supply of oil on the world market and thus force up prices. The price of oil quadrupled. Production costs for many Canadian firms, therefore, increased and were reflected in higher prices for consumers. The result was a shift in the AS curve to the left, as shown in Figure 17.10. The general level of prices rose and real output decreased.

If the price of oil had decreased, the AS curve would have shifted to the right, resulting in a lower price level and higher real output.

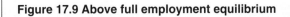

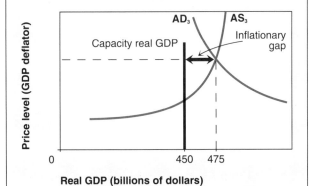

Figure 17.9 Above full employment equilibrium

With above full employment equilibrium, the AD and AS curves intersect at a point where actual real GDP is beyond capacity real GDP. The result is an inflationary gap of $25 billion—the difference between the actual real output and the capacity real output.

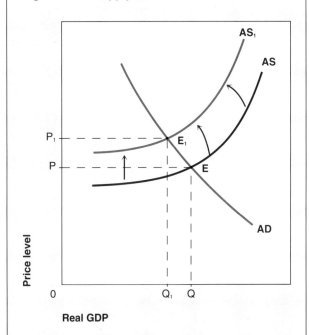

Figure 17.10 Supply shock

A supply shock, such as that created by the quadrupling of oil prices in 1973, shifts the AS curve to the left—as to AS₁. To produce the same level of real GDP, businesses must charge higher prices. The price level, therefore, rises from $0P$ to $0P_1$, and real output declines from $0Q$ to $0Q_1$. A decrease in AS or a supply shock, therefore, causes an increase in the equilibrium price level and a decrease in the equilibrium real GDP. A decrease in AS would have the opposite effects.

□ AS, AD, and Equilibrium in the Canadian Economy

Aggregate demand and supply may also help to explain the fluctuations in the Canadian economy. Let's examine the years 1971 to 1991. To plot the AD and AS curves for 1971, we would show the two curves intersecting at the real GDP ($287 billion) and the GDP deflator or price level (33.9) for that year, as shown in Figure 17.11. Points plotted for all the other years to 1991 indicate three major trends—an increase in real GDP, an increase in the price level, and economic fluctuations.

Increase in Real GDP

As the Canadian population increased over the period 1971-1991, so too did consumption, capital investment, and government spending. New technologies were developed and new resources were discovered. The AS curve, therefore, shifted to the right and real GDP increased, roughly doubling over the 20-year period.

Increase in the Price Level

As Figure 17.11 illustrates, the price level increased more than four-fold from 1971 to 1991. Part of this increase in the price index was due to supply shocks such as increases in the price of inputs—for example, oil price hikes in 1973 and 1974. Prices have also increased steadily as aggregate demand has increased over the years.

Economic Fluctuations

The path of economic development has not been smooth because of fluctuations in aggregate demand and aggregate supply. In the early 1970s, growth was rapid and price increases low. In 1974 and 1975, growth slowed and prices rose rapidly. In the late 1970s, both growth and the price level increased rapidly.

Similar fluctuations were evident in the 1980s. From 1980-82, prices rose quickly but growth rates declined, becoming negative in 1982. As the economy recovered from the 1982 recession, growth was again strong to 1989. Then in 1990 and 1991, development slowed once again as the economy moved into another recession.

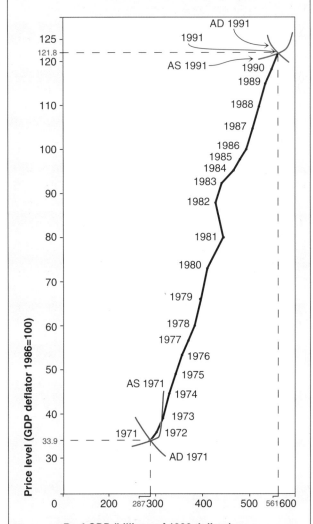

Figure 17.11 AS and AD in the Canadian economy, 1971-1991

Real GDP (billions of 1986 dollars)

Price level (GDP deflator 1986=100)

The real GDP and GDP deflator are plotted for each year from 1971 to 1991. Shifts in AD and AS cause the points to shift from year to year. The shifts show a general increase in real GDP and the price level over the years, as well as periodic fluctuations in the economy.

SOURCE: Statistics Canada, *Canadian Economic Observer*, Historical Supplement 1990/91 and September 1991.

Reconciling Business Cycles, the Injections-Leakages Approach, and the AS-AD Approach

Our investigations in this and the previous chapter have shown that business fluctuations (the instability of prices and employment) are a characteristic of our economy. Our examination of injections and leakages, and of aggregate demand and aggregate supply, identified some of the reasons for this instability. The injections-leakages and AS-AD approaches can both be used to analyze the business cycle. Figure 17.12 summarizes how the injections-leakages and AS-AD analyses help to explain the business cycle.

The next logical question is how we might deal with these instabilities—particularly the problems of inflation and unemployment. This question is the focus of the final three chapters in this unit.

Figure 17.12 Injections-leakages, AS-AD, and the business cycle

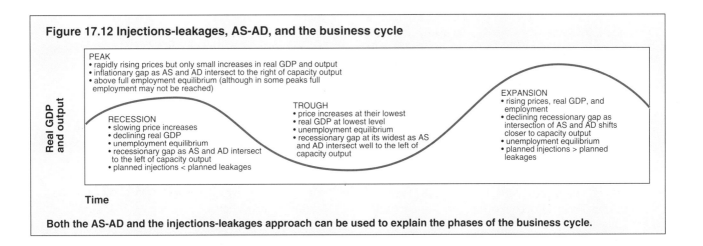

Both the AS-AD and the injections-leakages approach can be used to explain the phases of the business cycle.

Summary

a. Aggregate demand (AD) is the total demand of all consumers, businesses, governments, and foreign buyers for all goods and services produced in an economy. An AD schedule shows the various levels of real GDP all sectors of an economy are willing and able to demand at various price levels, all other factors being equal.

   The AD curve slopes down to the right because as the general price level rises, total demand declines since consumers can buy less with their incomes, businesses reduce investment as potential returns are lower, and the demand for domestic products declines.

b. Aggregate demand will shift with a change in any one of its components—consumption, investment, government expenditures, or foreign trade. A decrease in any of these components will shift the AD curve to the left, thus decreasing real GDP and the price level. An increase in any of these components will shift the AD curve to the right, increasing real GDP and the price level.

c. Aggregate supply (AS) is the total value of all goods and services produced in an economy over a particular period. An AS schedule shows the amounts of real GDP all firms are willing and able to supply at various price levels over a particular period.

The AS curve slopes up to the right. At first the slope of the curve is slight, but it becomes steeper as total supply approaches and exceeds capacity output. The AS curve has this shape because as total output increases, productive resources become increasingly scarce and expensive. As total output increases, therefore, the price level rises.

d. Shifts in aggregate supply are called supply shocks and may occur because of changes in three factors—the price of inputs, the quantity of productive factors, and productivity. An increase in the price of inputs will shift the AS curve to the right, thus increasing the price level at the same level of output. An increase in the other two factors will shift the entire AS curve to the right, increasing the price level and output. A decrease in these factors has the opposite effect on the AS curve.

e. The macroeconomy is in equilibrium when AS = AD. Shown graphically, equilibrium is the point at which the AS and AD curves intersect.

f. An economy in equilibrium does not necessarily have full employment. Full employment equilibrium occurs only when actual real GDP is equal to capacity real GDP. The economy is in unemployment equilibrium when actual real GDP is less than capacity real GDP and in above full employment equilibrium when actual real GDP is greater than capacity real GDP. With unemployment equilibrium, the difference between actual and capacity GDP is known as the recessionary gap. With above full employment equilibrium, the difference is called the inflationary gap.

g. An increase in aggregate demand will raise the equilibrium price level and real GDP. A decrease in AD will have the opposite effect. An increase in aggregate supply will lower the general price level and increase real GDP. A decrease in AS will increase the general price level and reduce real GDP.

h. AS and AD curves for the Canadian economy from 1971-1991, plotted from real GDP and GDP deflator data, show that the period was characterized by a general increase in real GDP and the price level, as well as economic fluctuations.

i. Both the injections-leakages and AS-AD approaches may be used to explain the instability (business cycles) in an economy.

■ Review of Key Terms

Define the following key terms introduced in this chapter and provide examples where appropriate.

aggregate demand (AD)
aggregate supply (AS)
supply shock
unemployment
  equilibrium
recessionary gap
full employment equilibrium
above full employment
  equilibrium
inflationary gap

■ Application and Analysis

1. Refer to Table 17.1.

Table 17.1 AS and AD schedules for a hypothetical economy

1 QUANTITY OF REAL GDP DEMANDED (MILLIONS OF DOLLARS)	2 PRICE LEVEL (GDP DEFLATOR)	3 QUANTITY OF REAL GDP SUPPLIED (MILLIONS OF DOLLARS)
10	130	80
20	125	80
30	120	70
40	115	60
50	110	50
60	105	40
70	100	30
80	95	20
90	90	10
100	85	0

(a) Graph the aggregate demand and aggregate supply curves for the hypothetical economy.

(b) What is the equilibrium price level?

(c) What is the equilibrium level of GDP?

2. Suppose that the quantity of real GDP produced at each price level in Table 17.1 increases by $10 million, while the quantity of real GDP demanded remains unchanged.

(a) Graph the new aggregate supply curve.

(b) What is the new equilibrium price level?

(c) What is the new equilibrium level of GDP?

3. For each of the changes listed below, indicate whether the change will result in a movement along, or a shift in, the aggregate supply or aggregate demand curve. Also indicate what effect, if any, each will have on the price level and real GDP in the short run.

(a) federal income taxes increase

(b) a major increase in investment spending occurs when the economy is in the trough of the business cycle

(c) the price of oil increases four-fold

(d) the price of consumer goods declines

(e) the price of factors of production used by many businesses declines

4. As the principal economic advisor to the Cabinet, you have been asked to answer the following questions about the state of the Canadian economy next year. You must base your predictions on the information in Table 17.2 and support your conclusions.

(a) What will the real GDP be next year?

(b) What will the price level be?

(c) What do you predict the rate of inflation will be?

(d) Will the economy be functioning at, above, or below capacity next year?

Table 17.2 Forecasts for the Canadian economy next year (billions of 1986 dollars)

1 PRICE LEVEL (GDP DEFLATOR) (1986 = 100)	2 REAL GDP DEMANDED	3 REAL GDP SUPPLIED	4 CAPACITY OUTPUT
100	800	350	660
110	750	450	660
120	700	550	660
130	650	650	660
140	600	675	660

This year, the real GDP is $590 billion and the price level is 120.

5. In the fall of 1990, the Canadian economy was in the second and third quarters of a recession. The invasion of Kuwait by Iraq and the consequent UN embargo on oil exports from the two nations sent world prices sharply upward. In Canada, gasoline prices by December had increased almost 20 percent. Prices of other oil products also rose significantly.

(a) What effects would you expect the increase in oil prices to have on aggregate demand and aggregate supply? Explain.

(b) Graph AS and AD curves to show the impact of the price increases.

6. With the eviction of Iraq from Kuwait and the increase in oil output (especially by Saudi Arabia), world oil prices began to fall. In Canada, gasoline prices fell about 25 percent between January and June 1991. Other prices of oil products followed suit.

(a) What effects would you expect the decrease in oil prices to have on aggregate demand and supply, other things being equal? Explain.

(b) Graph AS and AD curves to show the impact of the price decreases.

CHAPTER EIGHTEEN

Fiscal Policy

We have examined business fluctuations in a market economy and considered why they occur. The key question, then, is can we control or avoid them? Certainly, John Maynard Keynes argued that governments can and must.

Since 1945, Canadian governments have accepted that they have an important role to play in stabilizing the economy. By a stable economy, we mean one that reaches *full employment without inflation*. Deliberate actions taken by Canadian governments to smooth the fluctuations of the economy are generally known as **stabilization policy**. Stabilization policy includes both fiscal and monetary policies.

This chapter focusses on fiscal policies. We examine when particular fiscal policies are appropriate and how effective they are.

Objectives

a. Define fiscal policy and determine the appropriate policies to combat a recession and inflation.

b. Analyze, using graphs, the effects of fiscal policies on aggregate demand, output, employment, and the price level.

c. Demonstrate the effects of fiscal policies on the business cycle.

d. Examine and assess the limitations of fiscal policies.

e. Distinguish between discretionary fiscal policies and automatic stabilizers in the economy.

f. Analyze the various budget positions governments may take.

g. Assess Canadian federal government budgets from 1966 to 1991 and their consequences.

h. Assess the federal debt—its growth and the problems associated with it.

i. Examine and assess what is being done to control the federal deficit and reduce the debt.

What Is Fiscal Policy?

Fiscal policy refers to changes in government spending and taxing programs that influence the level of aggregate demand and thus the levels of income, output, prices, and employment. For example, if the economy is sliding into a recession and injections are declining, government may act to increase its expenditures and/or decrease taxes. Thus, total injections increase and leakages decrease. In other words, aggregate demand increases. With this fiscal policy, government acts to slow, stop, or reverse the descent into recession.

Conversely, when the economy is booming and the inflation rate is rising, government can act to curb aggregate demand by cutting the government expenditure injection and raising the taxation leakage. Thus, the aggregate demand curve shifts to the left and the general level of prices falls, diminishing or eliminating inflation.

Government, in its use of fiscal policy, thus leans against the prevailing economic temperature. It acts to "cool off" an economy that is overheating, and "warm up" an economy that is cooling down. Any deliberate government actions to alter spending or taxation policies in order to influence the level of output and employment is **discretionary fiscal policy**. In other words, the policies are at the discretion or desire of the government. We will see later that some fiscal action occurs without the direct action of government.

Let's consider in a little more detail the appropriate discretionary fiscal policy to deal with first a recession (and thus the problem of unemployment) and then inflation.

☐ Policies in a Recession

Suppose the country is experiencing widespread unemployment, but little inflation, and real output is well below capacity. An **expansionary fiscal policy**, one that will stimulate the economy, is appropriate. The government has three choices.

(i) Increase government expenditures and leave tax revenues unchanged   Increased government expenditures, as we have seen, increase injections and shift the aggregate demand curve to the right, thus helping the economy out of a recession. Typically in the past, governments have engaged in public works to achieve this objective, constructing roads, bridges, dams, schools, and other public buildings. Such increases in government expenditures will have a multiplied effect on aggregate demand and thus on national income.

In constructing or upgrading roads, for example, government contractors will hire numerous workers, including heavy equipment operators, truck drivers, labourers, and surveyors. Contractors will also need raw materials, such as gravel, concrete, and asphalt. Gravel, concrete, and asphalt companies will, in turn, require more workers to produce the materials. The disposable incomes of all the employed workers will increase and they will spend more on household appliances, clothing, furniture, etc. The increased spending will stimulate the household appliance, clothing, furniture, and other industries. Thus, the initial government expenditure has a ripple effect throughout the economy.

(ii) Reduce tax revenues and leave government expenditures unchanged   Reductions in personal income taxes increase personal disposable income and thereby consumer spending. Similarly, increased capital cost allowances (tax deductions for depreciation of capital) and lower corporation taxes are likely to encourage investment. Increased corporate investment, like increased government expenditures, will have a ripple effect on the economy, increasing demand for many products and stimulating employment. Tax reductions, while total government expenditures remain unchanged, thus increase injections and raise aggregate demand.

(iii) Increase government expenditures and decrease tax revenues   To raise employment during a recession, government may decide to combine a program of public works—building roads and harbours, for example—with a cut in taxation—personal income tax, for example. In this way, the tax leakage is reduced and the government spending injection is increased. Aggregate demand increases and the aggregate demand curve shifts to the right. Employment, income, and output thus increase.

Effects on the AD Curve and Equilibrium

Figure 18.1 illustrates the effects of these fiscal policies on the aggregate demand curve and economic equilibrium. The AD curve shifts to the right, increasing real output (and thus employment) and moving the economy closer to capacity. The recessionary gap between actual real GDP and capacity GDP is, therefore, reduced. Prices, however, rise slightly.

☐ Policies to Combat Inflation

Suppose, however, the country has achieved full employment, but the level of spending is so high that prices are increasing rapidly. A **contractionary fiscal policy**, one that will check output and spending, is therefore appropriate. Government, once again, has three choices.

(i) Decrease government expenditures and leave tax revenues unchanged   Decreases in government expenditures will decrease total injections and thus lower aggregate demand. People's disposable incomes will be reduced and they will spend less. Business investments will also fall. As a result, real GDP will decline and prices will fall.

(ii) Increase tax revenues and leave government expenditures unchanged   An increase in tax revenues, without offsetting increases in government spending, will increase the leakages from the economy. Once again, people's disposable incomes will be reduced, spending will be curtailed, and business investments will decline. Aggregate demand will, therefore, fall and with it real GDP and prices.

(iii) Increase tax revenues and reduce government expenditures   The government could implement a program combining increased taxes and reduced expenditures to lower aggregate demand, output, and prices.

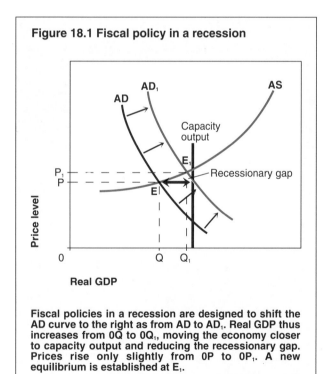

Figure 18.1 Fiscal policy in a recession

Fiscal policies in a recession are designed to shift the AD curve to the right as from AD to AD₁. Real GDP thus increases from 0Q to 0Q₁, moving the economy closer to capacity output and reducing the recessionary gap. Prices rise only slightly from 0P to 0P₁. A new equilibrium is established at E₁.

Figure 18.2 Fiscal policy to combat inflation

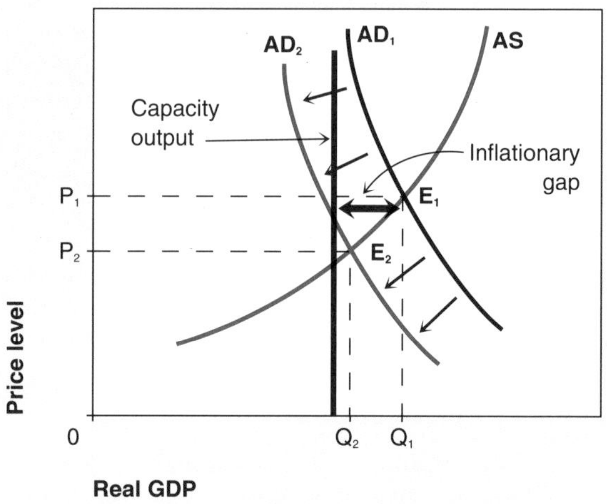

Fiscal policies to combat inflation are designed to shift the AD curve to the left as from AD₁ to AD₂, reducing real GDP from 0Q₁ to 0Q₂ and moving the economy closer to capacity output. The inflationary gap is, therefore, reduced and the price level falls from 0P₁ to 0P₂. A new equilibrium is established at E₂.

Effects on the AD Curve and Equilibrium

Figure 18.2 shows the effects of these fiscal policies to combat inflation on the aggregate demand curve and equilibrium. The aggregate demand curve shifts to the left, decreasing real GDP and moving the economy closer to capacity output. The inflationary gap between actual real GDP and capacity real GDP is, therefore, reduced and the general price level declines.

☐ Effects of Fiscal Policies on the Business Cycle

What effects can these fiscal policies have on the business cycle, then? Figure 18.3 provides an illustration. By reducing aggregate demand through reduced expenditures and/or increased taxes as the expanding economy approaches the peak, government aims to curb the ascent and thus inflation. Similarly, by raising aggregate demand through increased expenditures

and/or reduced taxation during a recession, government aims to check the descent to the trough. The overall effect is a reduction in the fluctuations of the cycle, in other words, a stabilization of the economy.

☐ Limitations of Fiscal Policy

Fiscal policies may appear fairly straightforward and the effects on aggregate demand relatively easy to achieve. However, the question of exactly which policy to implement, at what point, and to what degree is a complex one. The widespread ramifications of a particular policy may be very difficult to predict.

In any attempt to design and implement a suitable fiscal policy, therefore, Canadian governments face a number of significant problems.

Fixed Expenditures

Governments can generally vary only a relatively small amount of their expenditures easily. Many items, such as pensions, salaries, interest on debt, and health and welfare payments, are relatively fixed.

Co-ordination of Policies

It is not always easy to co-ordinate fiscal policies among governments. Government expenditures and taxing powers in Canada are spread among many different levels of government—federal, provincial, and local. It is possible, therefore, that provincial or municipal governments will be following spending and taxing policies different from those of the federal government.

Timing

Fiscal policy action must be carefully timed to be effective, but it is difficult to predict economic conditions even a few months in advance. The difficulty is increased by three delays—or lags—in dealing with an economic problem. First is a **recognition lag**—a delay between the onset of recession or inflation and the recognition of the extent and nature of the problem. Second, once a problem has been recognized by economists, it takes some time to decide what should be done about it. Thus, there is a **decision lag**. The final delay is between the time a policy has been

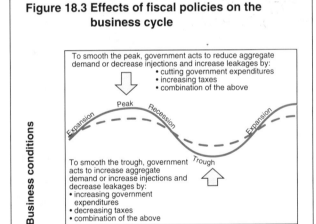

Figure 18.3 Effects of fiscal policies on the business cycle

To smooth the peak, government acts to reduce aggregate demand or decrease injections and increase leakages by:
• cutting government expenditures
• increasing taxes
• combination of the above

To smooth the trough, government acts to increase aggregate demand or increase injections and decrease leakages by:
• increasing government expenditures
• decreasing taxes
• combination of the above

Business conditions

Time

Expansion — Peak — Recession — Trough — Expansion

To smooth the fluctuations of the business cycle, government fiscal policies lean against the prevailing economic trends. Near the peak of expansion, government acts to check the expansion by reducing aggregate demand. As the economy moves into a recession, government acts to check the slowdown by increasing aggregate demand.

approved and the time it takes to have an effect—the **implementation lag**. If government decides, for example, to increase spending on public works, a delay occurs before actual work begins. Plans have to be made, land has to be purchased, contracts have to be drafted and signed, and so on.

Regional Variations in Conditions

Economic conditions may vary greatly in different regions of the country. In 1989 and early 1990, for example, unemployment was low in parts of southern Ontario (less than 6 percent), but at recession levels (above 12 percent) in Atlantic Canada. In this situation, a tax cut to aid Atlantic Canada would likely stoke the fires of inflation in Ontario.

☐ Automatic Stabilizers

Are deliberate government actions always necessary to combat economic fluctuations? The answer is no, not always. Our economy has some **automatic stabilizers**, which act to change government revenues and expenditures and thus to stabilize the economy without any specific action on the part of governments. Unem-

ployment insurance payments, welfare payments, and our progressive personal income tax structure are examples of automatic stabilizers.

How do they work? Welfare assistance and unemployment insurance payments fall as unemployment falls and rise as unemployment rises. Government thus automatically spends less on these programs during peak periods and the reduced expenditures help to slow the economic expansion. Likewise, government expenditures on these programs automatically increase during recessions and help to ease the economic slow-down.

Similarly, as incomes rise, an increasing proportion of our additional income is taken in income taxes. Disposable income, therefore, rises much less rapidly than gross income, placing a check on our spending power and slowing the increase in inflation. Conversely, as disposable income decreases during a recession, a smaller proportion is taken in taxes. Disposable income, therefore, decreases at a much slower rate than gross income, allowing our spending power to stimulate the economy. Thus, our progressive personal income tax structure acts to stabilize incomes and expenditures automatically.

☐ ☐ ☐ ☐ ☐ ☐

Economic Forecasting

If we were able to look into the future and predict economic conditions with some degree of certainty, we might be better able to smooth the peaks and troughs of the business cycle permanently. But to predict the behaviour of many million consumers, tens of thousands of business executives, and the many governments in Canada is both difficult and risky. And just to make the task even more difficult, we have to forecast the economic conditions in our major foreign markets as well. So where do economists start?

Predicting With a Statistical Model

One method of forecasting is based on statistical models. For example, to predict aggregate demand, economists would estimate the future values of each component of aggregate demand—investment, consumption spending, government spending, and net exports. Future investment depends in part on future interest rates and the profit expectations of business executives. Future consumption spending is related to disposable income. Government spending is linked to government expenditure projections. Future exports depend on the prosperity or future GDP of foreign nations. Together, all of these components and interrelationships form a statistical model of the economy that can be used to forecast GDP.

A number of different statistical models have been developed by economists. Two of the best known are the Candide model of the Economic Council of Canada and the Bank of Canada's RDX2 model. Models are limited, however, in that they forecast the future on the foundation of relationships that existed in the past. These relationships may change.

Leading Indicators

Another tool of economic forecasting is the leading indicator. **Leading indicators** are used to predict emerging trends in the business cycle. In other words, they help to predict when changes will take place, whether from trough to recovery or peak to recession, for example.

Leading indicators signal the short-term developments in the economy because they reflect what businesses and consumers have actually begun to produce and spend. Increases or decreases in the number of building permits issued, for example, precede increases and decreases in construction spending. Similarly, changes in orders for goods signal the future level of production.

Statistics Canada's Composite Index of Leading Indicators is one of the most widely quoted leading indicators. The Index encompasses ten components from five sectors of the Canadian economy.

Consumption This component includes furniture and appliance sales, sales of durable goods, and housing expenditures. Consumer spending tends to recover before business spending in an expansion and declines before business spending in a recession. Thus, changes in these three components of the consumption sector should signal changes in the general level of economic activity.

Exports The exports component is based on the US Composite Leading Index. Since trade with the United States comprises approximately 70 percent of our total exports, which in turn account for between one-quarter and one-third of our GDP, changes in the US economy will have a significant impact on the Canadian economy. The US Composite Leading Index reflects changes in the US economy and thus changes in Canadian exports to the US and changes in the Canadian economy as a whole.

Manufacturing The manufacturing component consists of the shipments to inventories of finished goods ratio, new orders for durable goods, and the average work week in manufacturing. Increases in any of these components signal an upturn in manufacturing and thus in the economy. Decreases in any of the components would obviously indicate the opposite effect.

Services The service component is based on one indicator—employment in business and personal services. Included in business services are architectural planning, advertising, job placement, business management, and legal services. Personal services include hotels, restaurants, dry cleaners, and hair salons. These services are considered sensitive indicators of economic change. Architectural and legal services must precede actual construction, for example, and expenditures in hotels and restaurants reflect consumer confidence and the financial health of households.

Finance The finance component is based on the TSE 300 stock price index and the Money Supply (M1). Changes in stock market prices generally signal changes in the economy. Shifts in the money supply cause changes in interest rates and hence shifts in investment and consumer spending on such "big-ticket" items as automobiles and household appliances.

Figure 18.4 on the next page shows the monthly changes in Statistics Canada's Composite Index of Leading Indicators from 1987 to 1991. The Index signalled the coming of the 1990-91 recession some four months before it arrived and indicated its end three months in advance. Studies of the Index by Statistics Canada indicate that it leads the peak of the business cycle by about four months and the trough by one to two months.

Applications

1. Why is Statistics Canada's Composite Index of Leading Indicators based on a composite of indicators from different economic sectors?

2. Why were the particular indicators chosen? Can you suggest others that might also have been used?

3. Research another composite index of leading indicators used for economic forecasting, such as the Royal Bank's Trendicator, and compare it with Statistics Can-

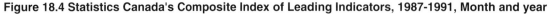

Figure 18.4 Statistics Canada's Composite Index of Leading Indicators, 1987-1991, Month and year

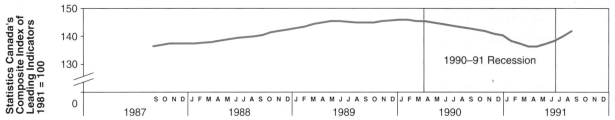

Statistics Canada's Composite Index of Leading Indicators began to decline in December 1989, approximately four months before the 1990-91 recession. It then began to rise in March 1991, signalling the end of the recession in June 1991.

SOURCE: Statistics Canada, *Canadian Economic Observer*, October 1991 and *The Globe and Mail*, November 5, 1991.

ada's Composite Index of Leading Indicators. How do the components of the indexes compare? What similarities and/or differences are there in how the indexes predicted the 1990-91 recession and its end?

4. The Help-wanted Index is another type of leading indicator used by Statistics Canada. It is constructed from help-wanted ads (classified ads only) in 22 major city newspapers from every province in Canada. The number of ads is counted and the total compared with that in the base year (currently 1981). This index is then multiplied by the regional and city 1981 population weights. Since the help-wanted ads signal the hiring intentions of employers, a rise in the index usually foreshadows an increase in economic activity and *vice versa*. The Help-wanted Index typically takes a sharp decline before the onset of a recession, for example.

To construct your own help-wanted index, go through the following steps.

(a) Select one or more community newspapers from your province or region.

(b) From next Saturday's copies of the papers, count the number of classified job ads in each paper. You should be able to find copies of the papers in your library.

(c) Weight the ads from each paper according to the relative population of the urban centre or region. For example, if the population of community A is twice that of community B, weight the ads from community A's newspaper x2, and so on. For example, if there are 100 ads in

community B's paper and 100 ads in community A's paper, the total number of ads would be 100 + (100 x 2) = 300.

(d) To establish this week as your base week, relate the total number of ads to 100 as follows:

$$\frac{100}{\text{Total number of ads}}$$

For example, if the total number of ads is 300, you would have $\dfrac{100}{300}$.

(e) Count the total number of classified job ads in the following Saturday's papers. To establish your index, calculate the following:

$$\frac{100}{\substack{\text{Total number of ads} \\ \text{in previous week}}} \times \text{Total number of ads this week.}$$

For example, if the total number of ads this week is 400,

$$\frac{100}{300} \times 400 = \frac{4}{3} = 133.3.$$

Since your base week is always 100, you can conclude that your index has increased. More jobs were advertised and thus more companies are hiring and you can predict that the employment rate will increase.

(f) Complete similar calculations for subsequent Saturdays. Use your help-wanted index to predict changes in economic conditions in your province or region.

5. What are the limitations of these leading indicators or similar methods of economic forecasting?

Federal Budget Deficits and Surpluses

The use of fiscal policy to stabilize the economy means that at various times governments will intentionally have a budget deficit, a budget surplus, or a balanced budget. Governments may run a **budget deficit**—when expenditures exceed revenues—during recessions to stimulate the economy. Policies for a **budget surplus**—when revenues exceed expenditures—might be implemented to curb inflation. A **balanced budget** is the situation when revenues equal expenditures.

☐ Three Views on Budget Surpluses and Deficits

Economists, however, have differed over how governments should manage their budgets. There are three main schools of thought.

Balance the Budget Yearly

Before the Great Depression and the Keynesian analysis of the economy, it was generally held that government should balance its budget annually. After all, what made sense for prudent individuals and businesses obviously also made sense for governments.

Supporters of this view did not see that to achieve a balanced budget during a recession, taxes and/or government expenditures would have to be raised. Thus, aggregate demand would be reduced, and employment and income would decline further, aggravating the recession.

During an inflationary period, the converse would be true. Tax revenues would rise and if expenditures remained fixed, a budget surplus would result. To balance the budget, the government would have to lower taxes and/or raise expenditures. These policies would increase aggregate demand and thus inflation.

An annually balanced budget would, therefore, magnify the existing problem—whether inflation or unemployment.

Balance the Budget Over the Business Cycle

Those who favour balancing the budget over the business cycle argue that during the expansionary phase, taxes should be increased and/or government expenditures decreased to check inflation, thus producing a budget surplus. During a recession, on the other hand, expenditures should increase faster than tax revenues to stimulate the economy, thus producing a budget deficit. Over the cycle, then, government surpluses would cancel the deficits and the budget would be balanced.

This view seemed logical as long as cycles were of regular duration. However, the economy can sink into prolonged periods of recession and high unemployment (as it did during the Great Depression). Subsequent expansionary periods may be much shorter. Budgets would, therefore, not balance over the long term. As we have seen, the durations of the business cycle's phases are not regular.

Maintain a Surplus or Deficit as the Economy Requires

From the weaknesses in the other two positions came the view that a balanced budget was really of secondary concern. The key point was how the budget could be used to stabilize the economy. The government should run a deficit during recessions and a surplus during expansions, even if the budget may be unbalanced over the long run.

Deficits, thus, were seen to have a cyclical and a structural component. The **cyclical deficit** is that part of the deficit incurred during a recession to stimulate the economy. The **structural deficit** is the amount above the cyclical deficit that would continue to exist even if the economy were at full employment without inflation. While a cyclical deficit may be acceptable, a structural deficit is often considered an indication of financial mismanagement. It represents the government's failure to match its expenditures to its revenues over the long term.

Financing the Deficit

Why is the deficit a problem? The reason is that the deficit must be financed. That is, to make up the difference between its income and expenditures, the government must borrow. It has two main sources of funds.

(i) Debt financing   The government can finance the deficit by selling government bonds on the open market (that is, to the public, chartered banks, insurance companies, and other institutions). Since it is selling bonds to the public, the government must offer an attractive rate. Canada Savings Bonds are the best-known government bonds. Borrowing from the public reduces private spending but government spending increases and so there is little effect on aggregate demand. Its effect is, therefore, not inflationary. It is not the preferred borrowing method when the government wants to stimulate the economy during a recession.

(ii) Money financing   The government may also sell bonds to the Bank of Canada (our central bank). Whatever the government pays the Bank of Canada in interest on these funds returns to the government since the Bank is a crown corporation. Thus, the government actually pays no interest on the loans. Essentially what happens is that in return for the bonds, government deposits at the Bank of Canada are increased and the government can then draw on these newly created deposits for its expenditures. The new government spending increases aggregate demand, but also leads to increases in the price level. Continued financing of a growing deficit in this way will feed inflation.

How do the two methods of financing the deficit compare? Debt financing means that government has to pay interest year by year. These payments are an obligation, which in Canada's case continues to grow. Money financing, on the other hand, means that the government actually pays no interest. It can spend all that it borrows. Money financing thus seems to have the clear advantage, except that it increases inflation. Many fear that governments may increasingly turn to money financing if debts continue to grow, thus damaging the economy with rising inflation.

■ The Federal Debt

Continued large deficits can increase the federal debt as more and more funds must be borrowed—and this is indeed what has happened in Canada. In recent years, the burden and rapid increase of the federal debt has caused alarm in Canada. Let's examine why.

The **federal debt** is the total amount owed by the federal government to households, businesses, and non-Canadians. As Table 18.1 shows, the federal debt has vaulted from just over $27 billion in 1966 to over $400 billion in 1990 (current dollars). This represents an almost 15-fold increase over 15 years. How are these figures significant? As a percentage of GDP, the debt has grown from constituting less than 40 percent of GDP to 80 percent over the same period. In other words, the debt is taking an increasingly larger amount of our national income.

□ □ □ □ □ □
Some Facts About Our Federal Debt

How fast was the debt growing in 1990?
In one hour, by more than $3 million.
In the time it takes to watch a hockey game, by about $10 million.
In one day, by $80 million.

How much do we owe?
In 1981, the debt totalled $12 300 for every household in Canada.
In 1984, it reached $23 100 for every household.
In 1988, it was $34 200 for every household.
In 1990, it was $37 100 for every household.

What are the interest charges?
In 1969, 12 cents of every dollar of federal revenue went to debt interest payments.
In 1981, it was 25 cents.
In 1988, it was 30 cents.
In 1990, it was 32 cents.
And the interest charges continue to grow.

Application
1. What do these trends in the federal debt mean for you?

□ Growth of the Debt

How did the federal debt reach such proportions? To answer this question, we need to examine federal government revenues and expenditures. We'll focus on two periods—1965 to 1975 and 1976 to 1991.

The Period 1965 to 1975

Both revenues and expenditures increased at a rapid rate between 1965 and 1975. Expenditures increased at a rate of about one-third more than the growth in GDP, and while revenues did not grow quite as rapidly, they were not far behind. The government incurred deficits for most of the decade, but compared to deficits in the 1980s, these deficits were small—averaging less than $2 billion a year.

Why did federal government expenditures increase so rapidly? The main reason was a significant increase in the costs of social programs. A number of changes in

Table 18.1 Federal revenues, expenditures, deficits, and debt 1966-67 to 1990-91 (millions of current dollars)

1 YEAR	2 TOTAL REVENUE	3 TOTAL EXPENDITURE	4 SURPLUS/ (DEFICIT)	5 GROSS DEBT	6 DEBT CHARGES
1966-67	9 782	10 076	(294)	27 398	1 180
1967-68	10 798	10 076	(773)	29 435	1 291
1968-69	12 132	12 793	(661)	31 511	1 467
1969-70	14 619	14 248	371	33 751	1 696
1970-71	15 364	16 022	(638)	35 250	1 778
1971-72	17 050	18 375	(1 325)	39 491	2 014
1972-73	19 737	21 101	(1 364)	43 384	2 168
1973-74	23 256	24 804	(1 548)	46 781	2 809
1974-75	30 143	31 496	(1 353)	48 780	3 333
1975-76	32 354	37 464	(5,110)	55 889	3 968
1976-77	35 522	42 086	(6 564)	63 149	5 164
1977-78	35 835	46 254	(10 419)	70 943	5 559
1978-79	38 839	50 687	(11 848)	83 700	7 064
1979-80	45 305	56 863	(11 558)	102 831	8 522
1980-81	53 796	67 829	(14 033)	113 170	10 784
1981-82	67 442	79 381	(11 939)	130 307	15 061
1982-83	68 063	93 766	(25 703)	146 763	16 887
1983-84	71 296	102 961	(31 665)	175 060	18 054
1984-85	78 055	115 039	(36 984)	212 241	22 428
1985-86	83 060	116 911	(33 851)	249 452	25 417
1986-87	90 145	120 826	(30 681)	285 139	26 617
1987-88	103 089	130 720	(27 631)	319 618	29 016
1988-89	109 505	136 334	(26 829)	351 229	33 167
1989-90	118 896	149 320	(30 424)	382 219	39 249
1990-91	127 067	155 502	(28 435)	408 483	41 013

SOURCE: Statistics Canada, *Canadian Economic Observer*, June 1991.

While total federal revenue increased 13 times between 1967 and 1991, it was outpaced by the increase in total expenditures. The annual deficit thus grew from just less than $300 million in 1966 to an average of just less than $30 billion annually in the 1980s and early 1990s. Consequently, the gross debt increased from $27 billion to over $400 billion over the period and debt charges multiplied from $1 billion to over $41 billion.

existing programs increased their costs. Other programs, such as Family Allowance and pension benefits, were indexed to inflation and costs thus increased as inflation increased. Federal contributions to education—especially post-secondary education—also rose. Moreover, new (and expensive) social programs, such as the Canada and Quebec Pension Plans (1965), Canada Assistance Plan (1966), Medicare (1966), and the Guaranteed Income Supplement (1966) were instituted.

As a result, federal social spending rose from about $4 billion (6 percent of GDP) in 1967 to $14 billion (9 percent of GDP) in 1975. Federal spending in other areas also increased significantly, but not at the same rate as spending on social programs. Revenues almost kept pace with expenditures largely due to increases in income taxes.

The federal debt nevertheless rose—almost doubling from $27 billion in 1966 to almost $56 billion in 1975. The growth of the debt and rising interest rates increased annual debt charges from $1 billion to $3 billion over the decade. The debt was not of overwhelming concern at this point because the economy still seemed to be growing at a good rate and it was believed the government would have no problem repaying the debt. From one point of view, the debt seemed to have brought benefits, particularly in the form of the social programs it financed.

The Period 1975 to 1991

Between 1975 and 1991, the debt took on a different complexion. Total federal expenditures and revenues also increased every year, but increases in expenditures quickly outpaced revenue increases. Two of the three major components of government spending largely kept pace with increases in GDP. They were social program spending and other expenditures. The third component, interest on the national debt, grew substantially, however. In current dollar terms, interest on the debt rose from just over $3 billion a year in 1974-75 to over $41 billion a year in 1990-91. As a percentage of GDP, interest charges increased from 2 percent to 6 percent over the same period. The debt was, therefore, proving to be a greater burden on the national income.

As a percentage of GDP, total revenues were roughly equal to expenditures until the 1974-75 recession, when spending rose and revenues plummeted. Figure 18.5 shows revenues and expenditures as a percentage of GDP from 1966 to 1991. The drop in the ratio of revenues to GDP came about mainly because of tax reductions and the transfer of tax revenues to the provinces. Thus, since 1975, annual federal deficits have been high, jumping significantly in the 1982-83 recession as social program spending increased substantially, and remaining in the range of $30 billion to 1991. Figure 18.6 shows federal budget deficits and surpluses from 1966 to 1991, and illustrates graphically the remarkable change over the period 1975 to 1991. With such sustained large deficits, the federal debt jumped to extremely high levels.

□ Real vs. Nominal Deficit and the Debt

The debt must be put in perspective, however—particularly with regard to how it has been affected by inflation. Let's consider an example. Suppose you bought a house for $120 000 when the rate of inflation was 10 percent and the mortgage interest rate was 14 percent. Your downpayment was $20 000 and your mortgage was $100 000. Each year, you pay $14 000 in interest. In the year in which you take the mortgage, you have a deficit. In subsequent years, however, even though the mortgage in money terms remains $100 000, it is reduced by 10 percent a year in real terms because of inflation.

The same kind of reasoning applies to the federal deficit. Suppose, with a balanced budget, the federal government has a debt of $100 billion with an interest rate of 15 percent and an inflation rate of 10 percent. The debt will contribute to neither a surplus nor a deficit in nominal or money terms. In real terms, however, since the value of the debt has been reduced by the rate of inflation—10 percent or $10 billion—the government actually has a surplus of $10 billion.

Similarly, with federal expenditures exceeding revenues by $5 billion, a federal debt of $100 billion, an interest rate of 15 percent, and an inflation rate of 10 percent, the deficit in money terms will be $5 billion. In real terms, however, inflation has reduced the $100-billion debt by 10 percent ($10 billion). In real terms,

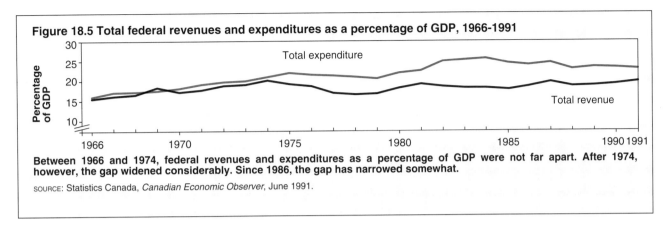

Figure 18.5 Total federal revenues and expenditures as a percentage of GDP, 1966-1991

Between 1966 and 1974, federal revenues and expenditures as a percentage of GDP were not far apart. After 1974, however, the gap widened considerably. Since 1986, the gap has narrowed somewhat.

SOURCE: Statistics Canada, *Canadian Economic Observer*, June 1991.

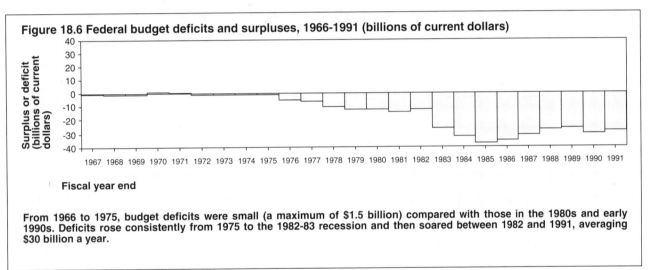

Figure 18.6 Federal budget deficits and surpluses, 1966-1991 (billions of current dollars)

Fiscal year end

From 1966 to 1975, budget deficits were small (a maximum of $1.5 billion) compared with those in the 1980s and early 1990s. Deficits rose consistently from 1975 to the 1982-83 recession and then soared between 1982 and 1991, averaging $30 billion a year.

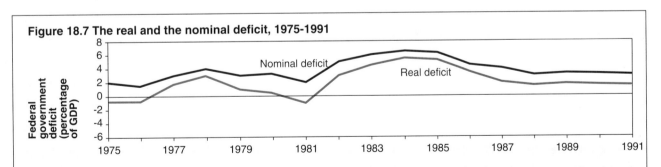

Figure 18.7 The real and the nominal deficit, 1975-1991

The real deficit is determined by subtracting the effects of inflation on interest rates and the deficit. The real deficit is thus lower than the nominal deficit.

then, the government actually has a surplus of $5 billion ($10 billion reduction in debt - $5 billion nominal budget deficit = $5 billion budget surplus in real terms).

How, then, has inflation influenced the deficit in Canada? As we can see from Figure 18.7, while there was a nominal deficit in 1975, there was actually a real surplus. Between 1975 and 1990, while there have been real deficits every year—with the exception of 1981—the real deficits in the 1980s averaged less than 3 percent and had fallen to about 2 percent in 1990. Looking at the debt in real terms changes its complexion significantly. It is not as serious as it would appear at first glance, but it is nevertheless a serious problem. There is a real fear that the government has borrowed beyond its means. Can it repay the debt without seriously cutting expenditures and/or raising taxes?

☐ Problems Associated With the Federal Debt

What problems are associated with the federal debt? They include inequitable income distribution, indebtedness to non-Canadians, a burden on future taxpayers, limitations on fiscal policy, and "crowding out."

Inequitable Income Distribution

It can be argued that since about 90 percent of the federal debt is owed to Canadians (government bondholders), we owe the debt to ourselves. Paying interest on the debt or repaying the debt consists of taxing ourselves or borrowing from ourselves to pay ourselves. It is like taking money out of our pants pockets and putting it into our jacket pockets. We are not actually losing money, just moving it around within the economy. Our total GDP is not reduced.

However, while we all owe the federal debt, only some of us are the federal government's creditors. Most government bondholders are corporations or individuals with above average incomes. Thus, a significant portion of the debt is paid for by people in lower income brackets. One effect of the debt, therefore, is to redistribute income, putting more in the hands of those at the higher levels. The debt works against the objective of an equitable distribution of income.

Indebtedness to Foreign Nationals

As much as one-fifth of government bonds are owned by non-Canadians. This portion of the debt is not internal. Foreign debts reduce our GDP since money leaks out of the Canadian economy to non-Canadians. At the beginning of the 1990s, a significant and growing proportion of our federal debt was owed to non-Canadians.

A Burden on Future Canadian Taxpayers

It is often stated that the debt is a burden on future taxpayers. They will be largely responsible for paying the interest on the debt without sharing in its immediate benefits or having any say in its assumption. It is a case of "taxation without representation."

However, if some or all of the government debt is incurred for long-term social assets—such as schools, roads, or hospitals—then future Canadians will benefit. But if the debt is incurred to pay for current expenditures, such as interest on the debt or unemployment insurance benefits, then no benefits will go to future generations. The only people to gain are those who inherit Canadian government bonds.

Limitations on Fiscal Policy

Continuing large deficits can inhibit governments from implementing key fiscal policies to stabilize the economy. With a large deficit, for example, the government will be reluctant to increase expenditures and cut taxes to battle a recession. Some economists have argued that this was the case during the recession of the early 1990s. The need to reduce the soaring deficit took precedence over the implementation of fiscal policy to pull the economy out of the recession.

Crowding Out

Crowding out refers to the rise in interest rates and the decline in investment caused by increased government borrowing. When the federal government borrows to finance a deficit, the demand for loans increases and interest rates rise. The higher interest rates bring a decrease in capital investment. Thus, the increase in government debt crowds out some capital investment. With lower capital investment, output for future generations is reduced.

Controlling the Deficit

To control the deficit, the government must either raise revenues or reduce spending—or institute some combination of the two. None of these three prospects is particularly popular with Canadians.

(i) Reduce spending   Government attempts to reduce the growth in spending by de-indexing pensions or freezing the pay of public servants, for example, has met with considerable opposition from the groups concerned. In addition, as the population ages, we can expect expenditures on health care and pensions to increase rather than decline.

Many people, therefore, believe that few large cuts in government expenditures are feasible. In their view, the only way to reduce the deficit is to increase revenues.

(ii) Increase revenues   Revenues may be increased by broadening the tax base, increasing taxes, or some combination of the two. The federal government's tax base was broadened with the introduction of the GST, for example. Attempts by governments to raise taxes, however, meet with widespread public opposition and may cause problems in a recession when lower taxes and higher expenditures are the appropriate fiscal policy.

What Is Being Done?

The federal government introduced a plan to reduce the deficit in 1991. By the plan, revenues from the GST were to be funnelled into a special fund used specifically to reduce the deficit. Public servants' salaries were to be frozen for two years and permitted to increase by only 3 percent in the third year. Increases in transfer payments to the provinces were to be limited. The federal government also proposed to legislate ceilings on spending of 3 percent per year for 1992 to 1996.

As a result of these programs, the federal government expects the deficit to fall rapidly, so that by 1996 it will be well below $10 billion.

Summary

a. Fiscal policy refers to changes in government taxing and spending programs that influence real GDP, employment, and the price level. Fiscal policy actions deliberately undertaken by government are known as discretionary fiscal policies and are designed to stabilize the economy.

   During a recession, an expansionary fiscal policy is appropriate. By increasing expenditures, reducing taxes, or some combination of the two, the government can raise aggregate demand and thus combat unemployment by stimulating economic activity. During an expansion, a contractionary fiscal policy is appropriate to combat inflation. By reducing expenditures, raising taxes, or some combination of the two, the government can lower aggregate demand and thus the price level.

b. An expansionary fiscal policy during a recession shifts the AD curve to the right, increasing real GDP and employment by reducing the recessionary gap. A contractionary fiscal policy to combat inflation shifts the AD curve to the left, reducing real GDP to close the inflationary gap and reduce the price level.

c. A contractionary fiscal policy during an inflationary expansion smooths the peak of the business cycle and an expansionary policy during a recession checks the descent into the trough. The overall effect is to reduce the fluctuations of the business cycle and thus stabilize the economy.

d. Fiscal policies are limited by a number of factors: the government can vary only a small amount of its expenditures easily; it can be difficult to co-ordinate fiscal policies among levels of government; there are recognition, decision, and implementation lags before the policies take effect; economic conditions may vary considerably over the country; and forecasting economic conditions is difficult and imprecise.

e. Automatic stabilizers may act, without direct government intervention, to combat unemployment during a recession and inflation during an expansion. These stabilizers include unemployment insurance and welfare benefits, which are automatically reduced during expansionary periods (decreasing spending) and increased during recessionary periods (increasing spending). Canada's progressive personal income tax structure also acts as an automatic stabilizer since it takes more in taxes as disposable income increases and less as disposable income decreases.

f. A government may have a balanced budget, a surplus, or a deficit. Before the Great Depression, some believed the government should balance the budget yearly. Others believed the budget should be balanced over the business cycle, but since the fluctuations are not regular, the budget could not be balanced over the long term. The third position is that governments should maintain a surplus or deficit depending on economic conditions. Large structural deficits, those which are not due to expenditures designed to stimulate the economy during recessions, are to be avoided, however.

g. From 1966 to 1974, the federal government did not incur significantly large budget deficits. After 1974, however, yearly deficits increased consistently. The federal debt has thus risen to unprecedented levels, partly fuelled by growing interest payments.

h. By 1990, the federal debt had reached over $400 billion—an amount equal to about 80 percent of our GDP. The debt has caused serious concern because an increasing proportion is owed to non-Canadians; it works against the goal of an equitable distribution of income; if not used to provide long-term social and economic benefits, it represents a burden on future taxpayers; it hampers the government's ability to implement appropriate fiscal policies during a recession; and it leads to increasing interest rates, crowding out some capital investment.

i. The government introduced a plan to reduce the deficit in 1991 by funnelling revenues from the GST into deficit reduction, freezing public servants' wages for two years and limiting the increase in the third year to 3 percent, limiting transfer payments to the provinces, and legislating spending ceilings to 1996.

▮ Review of Key Terms

Define the following key terms introduced in this chapter and provide examples where appropriate.

stabilization policy
fiscal policy
discretionary fiscal policy
expansionary fiscal policy
contractionary fiscal policy
recognition lag
decision lag
implementation lag
automatic stabilizer

leading indicator
budget deficit
budget surplus
balanced budget
cyclical deficit
structural deficit
federal debt
crowding out

▮ Application and Analysis

1. In a situation of rising inflation, explain the effect each of the following government actions would have on the economy.

(a) a tax cut of $1 billion

(b) a program of public works spending totalling $2 billion

(c) a cut in government spending of $3 billion

(d) an increase in unemployment insurance payments totalling $2 billion

2. Complete Figure 18.8 by indicating whether each federal government action listed is an expansion-

ary or contractionary policy, and whether it is an automatic or discretionary stabilizer.

Figure 18.8 Fiscal actions

FISCAL ACTION	EXPANSIONARY OR CONTRACTIONARY POLICY	AUTOMATIC OR DISCRETIONARY STABILIZER
(a) As a result of the economic recovery, the amount paid in unemployment insurance benefits declines.		
(b) Federal and provincial income taxes are increased.		
(c) As the recession deepens, government expenditures on welfare benefits increase.		
(d) As the economy recovers, the government collects more in income taxes.		
(e) The favourable tax breaks on capital gains are abolished.		

3. Suppose the economy is in the situation shown in Figure 18.9 below.

(a) What budgetary action should the federal government take? Explain.

(b) Copy the graph and indicate the change in the aggregate demand curve that would result from the government's action in (a).

(c) Indicate how the new AD curve would affect the price level and GDP.

(d) Explain why the changes you have shown on your graph occur.

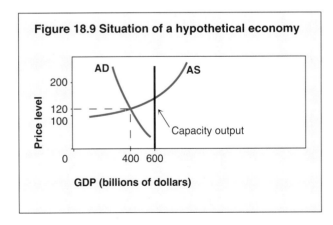

Figure 18.9 Situation of a hypothetical economy

4. Suppose the economy is in the situation shown in Figure 18.10 below.

(a) What budgetary action should the federal government take? Explain.

(b) Copy the graph and indicate the change in the aggregate demand curve that would result from the government's action.

(c) Indicate how the new AD curve would affect the price level and GDP.

(d) Explain why the changes you have shown on your graph occur.

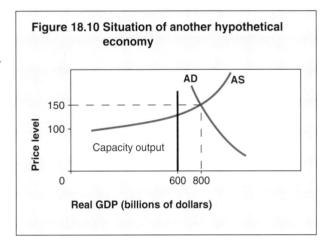

Figure 18.10 Situation of another hypothetical economy

5. Statistics Canada's Composite Index of Leading Indicators is often featured in the media and many public libraries receive the *Canadian Economic Observer*, which contains updates of the Index. Research the current level of Statistics Canada's Composite Index of Leading Indicators. Assess how well the Index has signalled changes in the economy since August 1991.

6. For each situation listed in Figure 18.11 on the next page, indicate the appropriate action. For aggregate demand, taxes, and government spending, indicate an increase or decrease. For the effect on the budget in the final column, indicate whether the budget should move toward a surplus or a deficit.

Figure 18.11 Fiscal action decisions

SITUATION	AGGREGATE DEMAND INCREASE OR DECREASE?	TAXES INCREASE OR DECREASE?	GOVERNMENT SPENDING INCREASE OR DECREASE?	EFFECT ON BUDGET TOWARD SURPLUS OR DEFICIT?
(a) Inflation is running at the high rate of 12 percent and is rising.				
(b) Unemployment is high at 13 percent and is increasing.				
(c) Business investment is falling rapidly and inventories are piling up. Business confidence in the future is at an all-time low.				
(d) Retail sales are expanding at a rapid rate. Inventories are decreasing and investment is increasing. Consumer confidence is high. Economists predict rising inflation.				

Table 18.2 Canadian economic statistics

	THIS QUARTER LAST YEAR	LAST QUARTER	ESTIMATE FOR QUARTER NOW ENDING
Real GDP (annual rate in billions of constant dollars)	343.38	354.40	356.00
Consumer Price Index	140	152	157
Unemployment Rate	6.0	6.1	6.0
Business Fixed Capital Investment (annual rate in billions of dollars)	68.10	76.67	77.20
Business Inventories (annual rate in billions of constant dollars)	1.27	1.30	1.31

7. You are an advisor to the prime minister and you have the statistics in Table 18.2 on the state of the Canadian economy before you.

(a) What is the major economic problem? Explain.

(b) What economic goals are you most interested in achieving?

(c) What fiscal policy actions would be necessary to achieve those goals?

(d) What specific policy actions do you recommend?

8. What, if anything, do you believe should be done about (i) the federal deficit and (ii) the federal debt? Support your point of view.

NOTE: Questions 2 and 6 adapted from the Joint Council on Economic Education, *Master Curriculum Guide in Economics: Teaching Strategies* (New York: JCEE, 1985).

CHAPTER NINETEEN

Money and Banking

Objectives

a. Outline the evolution of money from commodities that had intrinsic value to paper currency and deposit money.

b. Assess the major functions and characteristics of money.

c. Analyze the main factors determining the demand for money and graph the money demand curve.

d. Compare and assess the various definitions of the money supply in Canada and graph the money supply curve.

e. Analyze how the price of money (i.e., the interest rate) is determined in money markets by supply and demand.

f. Outline the components of the banking system in Canada.

g. Demonstrate how money is "created" by banks through demand deposits.

h. Calculate and apply the deposit or money multiplier to determine how the money supply can be increased and decreased.

i. Assess the objectives and functions of the Bank of Canada.

j. Analyze how the Bank of Canada controls the money supply.

We have examined how governments can implement various fiscal policies to help stabilize the economy. Before we go on to consider monetary policies, we need to examine the role of money in an economy and how it can affect economic stability. Money is such an integral part of our economy that we may take its existence for granted—even though we are constantly concerned with obtaining it.

Money bewitches people. They fret for it, and they sweat for it. They devise most ingenious ways to get it, and most ingenious ways to get rid of it. Money is the only commodity that is good for nothing but to be gotten rid of. It will not feed you, clothe you, shelter you, or amuse you unless you spend it or invest it . . . Money is a captivating, circulating, masquerading puzzle.

Source: Federal Reserve Bank of Philadelphia, "Creeping Inflation," *Business Review*, August 1957, p. 3.

◾ The Evolution of Money

In the past, many different commodities considered to have value were used as money, including beaver pelts, cattle, salt, wampum, cloth, corn, knives, and even playing cards. Gold and silver, however, became a standard of value in many societies. The supply of these metals was limited and they were in demand, making them valuable. Both were also easily recognizable and could be divided into small units.

The problem was that traders had to carry the metals in bulk and a set of scales was necessary to weigh the required amounts for every transaction. The invention of coinage some 2500 years ago solved some of these problems. Rulers weighed the metals, minted the coins, and affixed their seal to the coins guaranteeing their weight and quality. Traders could accept the coins "at face value."

Clipping the Coinage

Some unscrupulous citizens, however, began shaving off the edges of the coins but still exchanging them at face value—making a tidy profit. As a result, coins were no longer accepted at face value and people began to insist they be weighed to prove their value. To foil the "clippers," the edges of the coins were milled, so that any tampering would be apparent. Some coins today—dimes and quarters—still have milled edges.

Debasement

Some rulers also found unscrupulous ways to earn a profit. Since they had a monopoly on minting money, they could call in all tarnished coins and issue a bright, new batch—with a base metal mixed in. If a ruler added 1 kg of a base metal to every 9 kg of coins, for example, he or she could mint 11 coins, returning 10 to the citizens and keeping one for his or her own profit.

The result of this debasement was inflation. More money was in circulation chasing the same number of goods, and thus prices rose.

Paper Money

The next step in the evolution of money was paper currency. People often deposited their gold for safe-keeping with goldsmiths, who kept secure safes to harbour the precious metal of their trade. The goldsmiths issued the depositors a receipt. When a depositor wished to buy land, for example, he or she reclaimed the gold from the goldsmith and gave it to the landowner, who most likely returned it to the goldsmith for safekeeping again. It soon became obvious that this onerous and sometimes risky transaction could be more easily accomplished if the buyer could simply give the seller the goldsmith's receipt.

If people generally knew the goldsmith to be reliable, no gold needed to leave the vault. All transactions could be completed through the transfer of receipts. Paper money, when it was first used, thus represented a promise to pay a certain amount of gold or other precious commodity.

Banks evolved as safe places to deposit gold. Receipts issued by banks—or bank notes—were "as good as gold," since they could be converted to gold on demand. Notes issued by privately-owned banks were an important part of the Canadian money supply well into the twentieth century. They were not totally replaced by government-issued bank notes until 1950.

Prior to World War I and again in the 1920s, the currencies of most countries were defined in terms of a specific weight and fineness of gold and could be freely exchanged into gold. This system was known as the gold standard. Some nations used silver in a similar way.

Fractionally-Backed Bank Notes

As people gained confidence in bank notes, they exercised their option of converting the notes to gold less and less. Bankers found that they did not need to keep an ounce of gold for every ounce of gold they had issued in paper currency. For those wishing to withdraw gold, there were usually others wishing to deposit it. Thus, goldsmiths and bankers (many goldsmiths became bankers) could issue more paper money than they had gold in their vaults, and the money could be lent to households and businesses at a profit.

Some imprudent bankers, however, issued too much paper money and found themselves unable to honour their bank notes with gold. Occasionally, as well, the public lost confidence in banks and demanded gold in return for their bank notes, resulting in bankruptcies or bank failures. People were then left with worthless bits of paper.

Fiat Money

Fiat money is money declared by government order (or fiat) to be legal tender. It is not defined in terms of a particular amount of gold or silver and its value is not backed by any precious metal. Its value is simply based on legal declaration. Today, Canadian currency and that of most nations is fiat money.

By 1940, almost all nations had withdrawn people's legal right to convert their bank notes into gold. Paper money is backed by, and convertible into, nothing more than other bank notes. The right to issue bank notes passed from private banks to a central bank that controlled the money supply. Central banks were institutions of a central government.

Deposit Money

Today, we commonly deposit our money with banks. To pay you $100, I can go to my bank, withdraw five $20-bills, give them to you, and you can in turn deposit them in your bank account. To make things even easier, I could write you a cheque for the $100, which you can deposit in your account. No cash then changes hands. All that happens is that $100 is debited from my account and $100 is added to your account.

Is your deposit money? Since you can redeem it in cash and spend it at any time, it is money. Indeed, as we will see, a large part of the total money supply in Canada is in the form of bank deposits of one kind or another.

Money thus evolved from something that had intrinsic value to paper bank notes. Today, bank notes are being replaced by deposit money as we move toward a "cashless society."

◼ What Is Money?

In Canada today, we readily accept little bits of metal (coins) and paper (bank notes and cheques) as money. Though they have little value in themselves, we can exchange them for valuable goods and services. How, then, are we to define money? Essentially, **money** is anything that is generally accepted as a means of payment for goods and services.

Our coins and bank notes are money, then, because we readily accept them as payment from others, and we know that, in turn, we can use them to buy the goods and services we want and need. Secondly, Canadian bank notes and coins are legal tender. By law, they must be accepted as payment for a debt in Canada.

◻ Functions of Money

Money is extremely important in our modern economies. It is the oil that lubricates the wheels and gears of our economy and helps to ensure its smooth running. Money has four principal functions—as a medium of exchange, a measure of value, a store of value, and a standard of deferred payments.

Medium of Exchange

This function of money is the most obvious—money is the generally accepted commodity we use in exchange for all other goods and services. Without money, we would have to rely on a **barter system**, in which goods and services are exchanged for other goods and services. This system is generally awkward and inefficient.

Suppose, for example, you are a shoemaker living in a barter economy and in exchange for your shoes, you want bread. You have to find someone who has a surplus of bread and wants shoes. Finding an individual whose wants coincide with your own—the **double coincidence of wants**—can be time-consuming. The time you spend looking for this individual is time lost that you could spend making shoes (and thereby raising your standard of living). You could not rely on this time-consuming process of exchange to supply all of your needs, so you would have to become more self-sufficient and produce as much as possible yourself. You could not specialize in shoemaking and the society could not take advantage of specialization and mass production. If our society were to turn to a barter system, the result would be a significant drop in our standard of living.

With money, the double coincidence of wants is unnecessary. All the shoemaker has to do is find someone who is willing to exchange money for shoes, and

□ □ □ □ □ □

Common Cents For Canadians?

John Palmer, an economist at the University of Western Ontario, doesn't think pennies make sense for Canadians. Ever since he collected all the pennies he had been throwing into a desk drawer, pasted them in the shape of a heart, and sent them to his wife, he has refused to accept them.

Palmer thinks the penny should be dispatched to the museum along with other outmoded coins. He argues that decades of inflation have made the coin virtually worthless. Pennies cost more to make than they are worth. According to Mike Francis, spokesman for the Royal Canadian Mint, one billion pennies were manufactured in 1989 at a cost of $1.5 billion.

Pennies, Palmer further argues, are economically wasteful. One study in the United States found that it takes an extra three seconds per shopper for check-out clerks to count them out in change. "When you multiply that by all the shopping trips, you're looking at $5 to $6 billion in waste time every year in the US," says Palmer.

What do Canadians think about it? When asked by the Gallup polling organization: "Do you favour or oppose abolishing the one-cent coin?," 36 percent were in favour and 51 percent were opposed. Some of the opposition to the elimination of the penny may be due to the widespread fear that merchants will round up the price of goods and services. Consumers will, therefore, have to pay more.

The mint is considering changes in the coin. The last major change was in 1982 with the introduction of the 12-sided penny, which made it easier for the visually impaired to recognize. To reduce costs, the mint could follow the US lead and make the coin out of a cheaper material—that is, zinc with a copper coating. Zinc, however, is toxic and would be unacceptable because of the danger to children who may swallow the coin. Another possibility is to introduce a two-cent coin.

Applications

1. If you see a penny in the street, do you stop to pick it up? Why or why not?

2. (a) Do you think we should abolish the one-cent coin? Explain.

(b) If you do not think the penny should be abolished, would you suggest any changes to it? Explain.

---

with the money she can buy bread from anyone who is willing to sell. The shoemaker has no need to look for someone who has exactly what she wants and who wants exactly what she has. The use of money, therefore, greatly simplifies exchange and is an essential prerequisite for specialization and mass production.

Measure of Value

Money also provides a common standard by which to gauge the value of diverse goods. Under a barter system, the shoemaker would have to negotiate the value of each pair of shoes against the value of every other good or service she may want in exchange. Would one loaf of bread be worth one pair of shoes or one and a half? What then? Pairs of shoes are not easily divisible and have no generally agreed upon value in terms of other goods.

With money, a unit of currency (such as a dollar) has a generally agreed upon value and is used as the measure of value for all other goods and services. Money is also easily divisible. A compact disc may be $25.50, a car $15 620.99, and so on. With money, the process of exchange, therefore, is made simpler and the value of goods can be more easily measured and compared.

Store of Value

Money is a means of conserving purchasing power for a future occasion. The baker in a barter economy, for example, could not store bread and use it some weeks later in exchange for shoes because the bread would go stale. It is not a good store of value. Money, however, can be used to buy goods and services whenever they are needed. It can be stored more easily and inexpensively than any other good.

Standard of Deferred Payments

Since money can be used as a store of value, it can also be used as a measure of indebtedness or as a standard of deferred payments. Debts can easily be recorded and repaid in money at a future date.

□ Characteristics of Money

From our discussion of money's functions, its basic characteristics will be clear. First, as we have said, to serve as a medium of exchange, money must be generally acceptable. Second, since we often use money in many different places several times a day—at stores, supermarkets, restaurants, and in vending machines, for example—it must be portable and durable. Third, since we need money for small purchases as well as large, money must be easily divisible. It must also be of a recognizable or uniform value, otherwise we would have to weigh and analyze each unit we received. And, of course, money should be difficult to duplicate or counterfeit, otherwise it would be worthless.

Finally, if it is to be a satisfactory store of value and standard of deferred payments, its value must remain fairly stable. Indeed, if the value of money falls rapidly, it will cease to be generally acceptable as a medium of exchange and standard of value. People may resort to a barter system. Germany was caught in just such a situation after World War I when its currency became virtually worthless, and many Latin American countries in the 1980s faced similar situations of soaring inflation.

■ Demand for Money

Like any other commodity, money is affected by supply and demand. While it may be obvious why people demand goods and services, it may not be as obvious why they demand or want to hold money, apart from having it on hand to buy the goods and services needed immediately. Economists have identified three main reasons—the transactions motive, precautionary motive, and speculative motive.

Transactions Motive

The **transactions motive** is the most obvious reason for holding money—to finance immediate purchases. Most of us hold money in pockets, purses, wallets, and chequing accounts to buy groceries, pay the rent, go to movies, etc. In other words, we need money as a medium of exchange.

What determines the size of the transactions balance we hold? Clearly, the greater your income, the more money you are likely to hold—and the more money the firm you work for will hold to pay you. The transactions demand for money thus varies directly with people's incomes. The greater our incomes, the greater is the transactions demand.

Similarly, if our total national income rises, people will tend to demand more money for immediate purchases and thus the transactions demand increases. The transactions demand varies directly with changes in our GDP.

Precautionary Motive

Money is also held by individuals to meet emergencies or deal with unexpected events, such as an illness, accident, or a lay-off from work. Similarly, firms must be prepared for periods of unexpectedly low receipts and/or large expenditures. Thus, there is a **precautionary motive** for holding money.

When incomes are high, people are likely to set aside more money than when their incomes are low. The precautionary demand for money, then, also varies directly with people's incomes—and hence with changes in GDP.

Speculative Motive

The **speculative motive** involves holding money to buy stocks or bonds for profit. If you believe your stocks or bonds are about to fall in value, for example, you are likely to sell the securities and hold your funds in bank deposits until you expect the value of the securities to rise once again. In other words, you are speculating on possible changes in the value of stocks and bonds in order to make money. Your demand for money, therefore, will vary with your expectations about the prices of your securities.

The opportunity cost of holding money is the interest or profits that could be earned from other financial assets. The higher the interest rate, the more that could be earned from the assets and the greater the cost of holding money. Thus, there is an inverse relationship between the speculative demand for money and the interest rate. The higher the interest rate, the smaller will be the quantity of money demanded, and *vice versa*.

☐ The Liquidity Preference

By combining the transactions, precautionary, and speculative demands, we have the total demand for money. Money is the most liquid asset, that is, it can be most readily exchanged for or converted into some other asset or value. People's desire to hold money shows their preference for liquidity. The demand for money, therefore, is known as the **liquidity preference**.

☐ Factors Affecting the Demand for Money

Three main factors influence how much money households and businesses wish to hold—the rate of interest, real GDP, and the price level.

Figure 19.1 illustrates the relationship between the quantity of money demanded and the interest rate. As interest rates decline from I to I_1, the opportunity cost of holding money rises and the quantity of money demanded increases from 0Q to $0Q_1$. As interest rates rise, the opportunity cost of holding money falls and the quantity of money demanded declines. The relationship between interest rates and the demand for money is thus an inverse one.

Changes in real GDP and the price level cause a shift in the demand curve or liquidity preference curve for money. As we have seen, as real GDP varies, real income varies. The higher our real incomes, the more

people will spend and thus the greater the demand for money. The demand curve for money thus shifts to the right from LP to LP_2. The opposite is also true. The lower our real incomes, the less people will spend and the demand for money is reduced. The demand curve for money then shifts to the left from LP to LP_1.

Similarly, if the prices of goods and services you buy increase by say 10 percent, you will need 10 percent more money to finance your expenditures. An increase in the price level will thus shift the demand curve for money to the right. A decrease in the price level will shift the demand curve for money to the left.

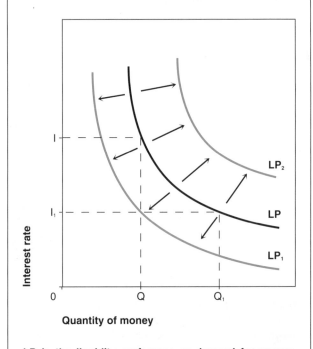

Figure 19.1 Demand for money (or the liquidity preference)

LP is the liquidity preference or demand for money. The quantity of money demanded varies indirectly with the interest rate. As interest rates decline from 0I to $0I_1$, the quantity of money demanded increases from 0Q to $0Q_1$ and *vice versa*. If real GDP or the price level increase, the demand curve for money shifts to the right from LP to LP_2. Conversely, if real GDP or the price level decrease, the demand curve shifts to the left from LP to LP_1.

■ The Money Supply in Canada

From our discussion of the total demand for money, we turn to an examination of the total supply. The **money supply** is the total stock of money available in a country at any particular time. Exactly what is to be included in our definition of the money supply, however, is not a simple matter.

Let's start by considering the various forms of money. For most "small-ticket" items, we pay cash in the form of bank notes and coins, in other words we use **currency**. Currency is obviously money.

However, for some transactions, we might use a cheque. A **cheque** is an order to pay an individual or group a specified sum of money from an account. In the past, most of the money held in banks was in the form of chequing accounts, on which the depositor could, without giving notice, withdraw or transfer money. Since money can be withdrawn *on demand*, chequing accounts are known as **demand deposits**. We can consider these deposits (not the cheques, which are simply notes of authorization for the transfer of funds) as money—that is, these deposits can be used as a medium of exchange.

Other types of deposits cannot be used directly as a medium of exchange. Savings (or notice) and term deposits cannot be used directly to make payments. Cheques cannot be written against them. However, since they can be converted into cash (through withdrawals) or transferred to chequing accounts, they are known as **near money**.

Banks have instituted yet other variations on these accounts. One of these is the daily interest chequable savings account, on which cheques may be drawn (as its name suggests), and on which interest is paid. Interest is not usually paid on true chequing accounts. Another example is the non-personal notice (or savings) account of large businesses, on which banks can require advance notice of withdrawals, but these accounts are connected to chequing accounts to facilitate payments.

But should all of these deposits be included in our definition of the money supply or only some? Economists, in fact, use different definitions.

(i) M1   The narrowest definition of the money supply, known as **M1**, includes only what can be used as a direct medium of exchange—that is, currency outside banks and demand deposits in chartered banks. Currency held in chartered banks is not included because it can only be spent or used for exchange if it is withdrawn or when a cheque is cashed. It is not directly transferable.

M1 was for many years the official definition of the money supply used by the Bank of Canada.

(ii) M1A   In 1982, the Bank of Canada began using an expanded definition of the money supply known as **M1A**. This definition includes daily interest chequable savings accounts and those non-personal savings accounts that are connected to chequing accounts. The Bank recognized that more Canadians were using these accounts just as they had used and were continuing to use chequing accounts—that is, as a source of funds for direct spending.

(iii) M2   **M2** is a broader definition still. It takes into account savings and term deposits—what we have identified as "near money." The argument is that since these deposits can be readily converted into a direct means of exchange, they do affect spending patterns and should be considered part of the country's total money supply.

(iv) M2+   **M2+** is, as its name suggests, broader than M2. It includes M2 plus deposits at institutions other than banks, such as trust and mortgage loan companies, credit unions, and caisses populaires. Since many individuals and businesses use their accounts with these institutions to make payments by cheque, in the view of many economists, these accounts should be considered part of the money supply.

(v) M3   **M3** incorporates M2 as well as foreign currency deposits held in Canada by Canadian residents and large term deposits (over $100 000) held by businesses, often in the form of certificates of deposit (CDs). CDs and foreign currencies are convertible into chequable deposits, though at the risk of a loss.

□ □ □ □ □ □

The Money Supply—A Summary

Definitions

M1 = Currency outside banks + demand deposits inside chartered banks

M1A = M1 + daily interest chequable savings accounts + notice deposits of large corporations

M2 = M1A + non-chequable personal savings accounts + personal fixed term deposits

M2+ = M2 + deposits at trust and mortgage loan companies and deposits and shares at credit unions and caisses populaires

M3 = M2 + foreign currency deposits held in Canada by Canadian residents + large, long-term deposits held by businesses

Components of the Money Supply

Currency Currency includes coins made at the Royal Canadian Mint in Winnipeg and bank notes issued by the Bank of Canada.

Demand deposits Demand deposits are deposits at chartered banks made by individuals, businesses, and governments that can be withdrawn on demand (i.e., without giving notice) by cheque or in cash. These accounts pay little or no interest.

Daily interest chequable savings deposits Cheques may be written on these accounts and withdrawals may generally be made without notice (though the institution may require 30 days notice). Interest is paid on the daily balance.

Non-personal savings or notice deposits These savings accounts of businesses and charitable organizations pay interest and are often connected to chequing accounts. In other words, they may be used to make payments since the chartered banks will transfer funds from them into demand accounts. Depositors may be required to provide notice of withdrawals.

Savings or notice deposits These deposits cannot be used directly to make payments. They are, rather, savings accounts and pay a higher rate of interest than daily interest chequing accounts. Chartered banks have the legal right to require notice of withdrawal (hence the name) from these accounts.

Term deposits These deposits represent funds deposited for a fixed period and they pay a higher interest rate than other deposits. The funds cannot usually be withdrawn before the end of the term without penalty.

Deposits at institutions other than chartered banks Some accounts (such as interest-bearing chequing accounts and non-personal savings deposits) held at trust companies and other financial institutions can be used by individuals and businesses to make payments, just as they are at the chartered banks.

As we have seen, therefore, the money supply can include a whole range of assets that vary in their degree of liquidity—that is, the ease with which they can be converted into a direct means of exchange. Each definition of the money supply has its proponents. Many economists use the M1 or M1A definitions because they include everything that is immediately usable as money. Others feel that near money, included in the M2, M2+, and M3 definitions, has an impact on the economy and should, therefore, be included in any consideration of the money supply.

Figure 19.2 shows the proportion each component—currency, demand deposits, etc.—constitutes in the major definitions of the money supply. You may find it remarkable that currency is the smallest proportion.

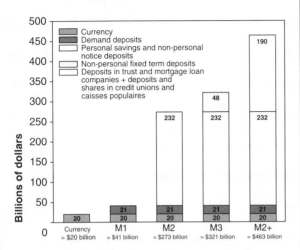

Figure 19.2 Definitions and components of the money supply, July 1991 (seasonally adjusted)

Legend:
- Currency
- Demand deposits
- Personal savings and non-personal notice deposits
- Non-personal fixed term deposits
- Deposits in trust and mortgage loan companies + deposits and shares in credit unions and caisses populaires

Y-axis: Billions of dollars

X-axis (Different definitions of the money supply):
- Currency = $20 billion
- M1 = $41 billion
- M2 = $273 billion
- M3 = $321 billion
- M2+ = $463 billion

Currency is the smallest part of the money supply whether defined as M1, M2, M2+, or M3. The more broadly defined concepts of money—M2, M2+, and M3—constitute a much larger money supply than the narrowly defined M1.

SOURCE: *Bank of Canada Review*, September 1991.

☐ Credit Cards

You will have noticed that in our examination of money, we have not yet mentioned credit cards—even though they are often referred to as "plastic money" and are widely used by Canadians.

In 1990, 23 million people held the two top credit cards (Visa and MasterCard) in Canada, an increase of 100 percent from 11 million in 1980. Total credit card sales in 1990 had reached $37 billion, up from $14 billion in 1985. Canadian adults, however, carry an average of three cards, which is less than the US average of 7.5 cards per adult. According to the *Guinness Book of Records*, the largest collection of valid credit cards is held by Walter Cavanagh of California. "Mr Plastic Fantastic" has 1265 cards—all different—which provide him with US $1.6 million in credit.

According to Tim Wallace, manager of card holder services for the Royal Bank of Canada's Visa operation: "Credit cards started as something people used when they did not have cash. Now they're another payment system—an alternative to cash or cheques." The popularity of credit cards is due to several factors. They are convenient to use, allow the deferral of payments to a later date, allow people to "spread" payments over time, and reduce the risk of using cash. For some

☐ ☐ ☐ ☐ ☐ ☐
Toward a Cashless Society?

Most monetary transactions today take place without the use of cash. Paycheques are deposited and our bank accounts credited electronically. Credit cards are also used widely. The next step? Perhaps the debit card. Richard Thomson, chairman and chief executive officer of the Toronto Dominion Bank, promotes the cashless society as a social virtue. Cash doesn't leave a paper trail to be followed by the police and tax collector. Thus, cash is "the currency of the drug trade and other crimes of the underground economy." Thomson's solution is to make cash more difficult to use and to promote its substitutes—credit

and debit cards and cheques. In addition, the decline in the use of cash should also reduce the targets and incentives, he surmises, "for street crime, muggings, burglaries, and so on."

But just what are debit cards? As you read the following extract, consider the advantages and disadvantages of a debit card compared with a credit card for the consumer.

Will that be cash, credit, or debit?

Consumers across Canada may hear this question more often from retailers in 1993, when a proposed national debit-card network is expected to be in place. A number of pilot projects have been run in cities across the country over the past few years. The biggest of these has been in Ottawa, where nine banks, trust companies, and credit unions have joined with Interac Association, the national network of automated banking machines. The project uses the standard ABM access card, which allows as many as 460 000 eligible users in the Ottawa area to shop and pay by debit card.

A number of stores—from liquor stores to hair salons—have participated in the pilot, which started in 1990, and some have reported that 30 percent of their business was done by debit card. Others, however, have found only 1 percent opt for the payment option.

Whatever the final percentage of users, the participating financial institutions seem reasonably happy about what they've seen. Transaction volumes have increased steadily from the initial 40 000 in October 1990, they say.

"Everything looks positive at this point. The consumers find the service easy to use and there are not too many problems with it," says Barry Kant, manager of point-of-sale development for Royal Bank of Canada, one of the Ottawa pilot project's participants.

The system works something like the one used for the credit card, with one major exception: the consumers have to type in their card's personal identification number on a hand-held terminal to select which account the money is to be withdrawn from to complete the transaction. All is supposed to happen in a matter of seconds.

Peter McKay, manager of electronic funds transfer and point-of-sale products at Bank of Montreal in Toronto, says the pilots represent a huge financial commitment "in the millions of dollars," but he believes over the long haul, the cost will be worth it. For one thing, he says, debit cards will help banks reduce costs associated with processing cheques.

While there's talk of a nationwide network by 1993, some people believe it will be some time before debit cards become as popular as cash or credit. Stores that already accept cash, credit, and cheques may be loath to add another source of payment, says Mel Fruitman, vice-president of the Toronto-based Retail Council of Canada,

a national organization representing major retailers and more than 5000 medium-sized independent merchants.

Gas bars and corner stores—perennial targets for hold-ups—may find them helpful. So might supermarkets, which seldom take credit cards and prefer not to take cheques.

"We think it's a service that, if properly packaged, could be made attractive. But there is still a cost-benefit analysis that has to be done. Whether retailers use [the debit card], and whether they find it useful to them, will depend on how much it costs to provide the service to consumers," Fruitman says.

A related concern is how much the debit-card convenience will cost shoppers. Merchants will have to pay to use the debit-card equipment and consumers will pay an average of about 25 cents a transaction—the financial institutions, after all, want to recover the hundreds of millions of dollars they spent installing the network. Some believe that the cost of installing equipment will be offset by savings on fees charged by financial institutions to process the store's cheques and cash. The cards should also do away with the problem of bounced cheques.

The debit card should also make it harder for people to spend beyond their means. It's also true consumers could spend more than they would if they paid in cash, however. In Ottawa, for example, the Liquor Control Board of Ontario says debit-card transactions are averaging $10 more than cash sales.

SOURCE: Adapted from Bruce Gates, "Debit cards pass test with flying colors," *The Financial Post*, March 28, 1991.

NOTE: The Interac Association announced in 1991 that it would be introducing the debit card to Quebec and British Columbia in 1992, the Prairie provinces in 1993, and Ontario and the Atlantic provinces in 1994.

Applications

1. Compare the advantages and disadvantages of the credit card and the debit card from the point of view of:
(a) the consumer
(b) the retailer
(c) the issuer.

2. Is the debit card money? Explain.

purchases—such as car rentals and purchases made by telephone—credit cards are essential. However, they are not an unmixed blessing. The interest rates charged on balances are relatively high, and since credit cards are so easy to use, some people find it difficult to control their expenditures.

Credit cards, however, are not money. Why not? Suppose I buy a dozen compact discs using my credit card. The bank or other institution that issued the credit card will reimburse the store that sold me the CDs. It is only later that I reimburse the credit card institution, usually by means of a cheque. If I choose to pay in instalments, I will pay an interest charge. My purchase of the CDs is, in fact, not complete until I have paid the credit card bill. Credit cards are a way of postponing payment until a later date. They are not a means of direct payment and are, therefore, not money.

■ The Money Market

By combining the supply and demand for money, we can examine the money market. As shown in Figure 19.3, the money supply is represented by a straight vertical curve, since the total stock of money in the economy is fixed at any one time. The demand for money is represented by the liquidity preference curve we saw earlier. The point at which the demand and supply curves intersect is the interest rate, in other words, the equilibrium price of money in the market.

Shifts in the supply or demand for money will, of course, affect the interest rate. We saw earlier, in Figure 19.1, how changes in GDP or the price level can shift the demand curve for money. We also saw that the relationship between the interest rate and the quantity of money demanded is an inverse one. The lower the interest rate, the greater is the quantity of money demanded and *vice versa*.

While the total supply of money in the economy is fixed at any one time, the Bank of Canada does exercise some control over the money supply, as we will see later in this chapter. The Bank can increase or decrease the total stock of money in the economy. Figure 19.3

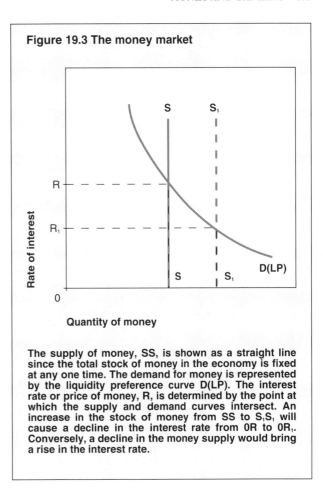

Figure 19.3 The money market

The supply of money, SS, is shown as a straight line since the total stock of money in the economy is fixed at any one time. The demand for money is represented by the liquidity preference curve D(LP). The interest rate or price of money, R, is determined by the point at which the supply and demand curves intersect. An increase in the stock of money from SS to S_1S_1 will cause a decline in the interest rate from 0R to $0R_1$. Conversely, a decline in the money supply would bring a rise in the interest rate.

shows that an increase in the money supply from SS to S_1S_1 causes a reduction in the interest rate. Conversely, a decrease in the money supply leads to an increase in the interest rate. The relationship between the interest rate and the money supply is also an inverse one.

■ The Canadian Banking System

How, then, is the supply of money in the economy controlled? To answer this question, we must examine the Canadian banking system. The chartered banks and the Bank of Canada together form the Canadian banking system. The banking system is an essential component of our larger financial system, which includes what we will later define as near banks, as well as insurance companies, mutual and pension fund brokers, consumer loan companies, sales finance companies, and stock and bond brokers.

We will focus primarily on the banks because they play the most critical role in determining the money supply. The deposits held in Canadian banks make up most of the money supply as defined by M1, M2, M2+, and M3. The chartered banks, as we shall see, are also the ones most affected by the actions of the Bank of Canada.

Under the Constitution Act of 1867, money and banking are federal responsibilities. Each Canadian bank is given a charter by a separate act of parliament, which is why they are called "chartered" banks.

□ Branch Banking

Canada has only eight domestic chartered banks. The five largest—the Royal Bank of Canada, the Canadian Imperial Bank of Commerce, the Bank of Montreal, the Bank of Nova Scotia, and the Toronto Dominion Bank—account for over 90 percent of total Canadian bank assets and each bank has over 1000 branches. A bank branch is simply an outlet at which the bank accepts deposits. In 1980, full banking status was extended to foreign banks under schedules B and C of the Bank Act, so that some 60 banks are permitted to operate in Canada. The Canadian assets of these foreign banks, however, constitute only 16 percent of Canada's total bank assets.

Canada's branch banking system, with only eight banks holding the majority of assets, contrasts with the unit banking system of the United States. There are 15 000 independent banks in the US. Some states have restrictions on the size of banks and, in the past, banking between states was not permitted. Some banks—called national banks—are chartered by the federal government and others—called state banks—are chartered by individual states. The US system is thus much less concentrated than the Canadian banking system.

□ Near Banks

Banks are not the only financial intermediaries in Canada, however. **Financial intermediaries** are all institutions that accept deposits from individuals, businesses, and governments and loan funds to borrowers. They include banks, trust and mortgage loan companies, credit unions, and caisses populaires. Since the functions of trust and mortgage loan companies, credit unions, and caisses populaires are similar to those of the chartered banks, they are often referred to as **near banks**. Table 19.1 shows the top ten banks, credit unions, and trust companies in Canada by total assets in 1990.

Trust companies accept deposits in the form of deposit accounts and guaranteed investment certificates from households and small businesses. They also provide loans to households and businesses, often in the form of mortgages. A **mortgage** is a loan secured by the value of land and buildings. The distinction between the functions of trust companies and chartered banks is becoming increasingly less distinct.

Mortgage loan companies are federally or provincially incorporated companies that borrow money for a period of time to invest in mortgages. They are often associated with banks or trust companies.

Caisses populaires and credit unions are co-operative credit organizations that receive funds by selling shares to and accepting deposits from members. They operate under provincial jurisdiction, unlike the chartered banks which are under federal jurisdiction. Other deposit-accepting institutions include Quebec Savings Banks, Alberta Treasury Branches, and Ontario Savings Banks.

□ Money Creation

To understand how the money supply is regulated, we must first examine how money is created by all those institutions whose deposits circulate as a medium of exchange (that is, banks, trust and mortgage loan companies, credit unions, and caisses populaires). In our discussion of money creation, we will refer to all of these institutions as banks.

We mentioned earlier that only the Bank of Canada

Table 19.1 Top ten banks, trust companies, and credit unions in Canada by total assets, 1990 (thousands of dollars)

BANKS		CREDIT UNIONS			TRUST COMPANIES		
RANK BANK	1990 ASSETS	RANK		1990 ASSETS	RANK		1990 ASSETS
1 Royal Bank of Canada	125 938 027	1	Confederation des caisses populaires Desjardins	42 601 041	1	Royal Trustco Ltd.	40 946 000
2 Canadian Imperial Bank of Commerce	114 196 406	2	Vancouver City Savings Credit Union	2 267 115	2	Canada Trustco Mortgage Co.	34 593 037
3 Bank of Montreal	87 369 944	3	Credit Union Central of Saskatchewan	1 974 000	3	National Trustco	15 653 350
4 Bank of Nova Scotia	87 226 914	4	British Columbia Central Credit Union	1 732 986	4	Central Guaranty Trustco Ltd.	14 776 103
5 Toronto Dominion Bank	66 900 443	5	Credit Union Central of Ontario	1 257 354	5	Montreal Trustco Inc.	12 383 335
6 National Bank of Canada	35 921 638	6	Surrey Credit Union	903 309	6	General Trustco of Canada	5 929 102
7 Hongkong Bank of Canada	10 231 212	7	Canadian Co-operative Credit Society Ltd.	804 299	7	First City Trustco Inc.	4 053 687
8 Laurentian Bank of Canada	6 059 190	8	Richmond Savings Credit Union	800 408	8	Trustco Desjardins Inc.	3 139 773
9 Citibank Canada	5 533 019	9	Pacific Coast Savings Credit Union	700 681	9	Prenor Trust Co.	1 318 142
10 Barclays Bank of Canada	2 890 338	10	Civil Service Co-operative Credit Society	720 307	10	Municipal Savings & Loan Corp.	1 304 408

SOURCE: *The Financial Post 500*, Summer 1991.

can issue bank notes. How, then, do the banks create money? The answer is through demand deposits, which as we saw are considered money.

Let's examine a number of hypothetical transactions to illustrate the process of money creation. We'll assume that all deposits are demand deposits and that the banks have just enough reserves to meet the requirement (say 10 percent of their demand deposits). Reserves are bank assets held in the form of currency or deposits with the Bank of Canada. This reserve requirement will not vary. We'll also assume that a fixed amount of money is in circulation, so that changes in the money supply are changes in demand deposits. No one withdraws his or her deposit for cash and holds the money.

Transaction #1

Suppose your rich aunt leaves you ten crisp new $100 bills. Being careful with your money, you decide to deposit it all in a chequing account with Bank A. What happens to the balance sheet of Bank A? As we saw in Chapter 6, the balance sheet portrays the financial position of a firm. Transactions balance when assets equal liabilities plus net worth.

Table 19.2 shows Bank A's balance sheet. With your deposit, it has an additional $1000 of currency in its vaults. In other words, it has increased its assets by $1000. At the same time, this deposit is a liability to the bank—it must be prepared to pay you $1000 in currency on your request. Assets and liabilities thus both increase by $1000 and the totals balance.

What happens to the money supply as a result of this transaction? The answer is, nothing. Your original $1000 in currency was part of the money supply. All you have done is change the form in which you hold the money from currency to a chequing account. The money supply has $1000 more in chequing accounts and $1000 less in currency, but the total supply remains unchanged. Remember that currency held in banks is not considered part of the money supply, so the money

Table 19.2 Transaction #1—Bank A's balance sheet

BANK A			
ASSETS		LIABILITIES	
Currency deposit	+ $1000	Chequing deposits	+ $1000
Required reserves	$100		
Excess reserves	$900		
Total	$1000	Total	$1000

When the bank receives your $1000 deposit, its assets and liabilities both increase by $1000. The money supply is unaffected, however, since you have simply converted the $1000 of currency into a chequing deposit of $1000.

Table 19.3 Transaction #2—Bank A loans money

BANK A			
ASSETS		LIABILITIES	
Currency reserves	+ $1000	Chequing deposits:	
		Yours	+ $1000
Loan credited to chequing account	+ $ 900	Mine	+ $ 900
Total	+ $1900	Total	+ $1900

When the bank loans $900, its assets and liabilities both increase by $900. Since the chequing deposits have increased by $900, the net increase in the money supply is $900.

supply does not increase by the $1000 cash in the bank plus the $1000 of your new demand deposit.

Transaction #2

But, the process does not end there. Following your transaction, Bank A's actual reserves increased by $1000—the currency you deposited. Of this, the bank must hold 10 percent ($100) as required reserves, but it also has $900 in excess reserves. With these excess reserves, Bank A is in a position to loan money.

Suppose, then, that I wish to borrow $900 from Bank A. After checking my financial resources, Bank A's loans officer agrees. Bank A then credits my chequing account with $900.

What happens to Bank A's balance sheet as a result of this transaction? As shown in Table 19.3, assets increase by the amount of the loan added to the chequing account—$900. Similarly, liabilities increase by $900 since I can withdraw the amount of the loan from my chequing account at any time. The assets and liabilities both total $1900 and balance.

What happens to the money supply? Bank A's chequing deposits have increased from $1000 to $1900. Since chequing deposits are money, the money supply has also increased by $900. Thus, when a bank makes a loan, the money supply increases.

You might be wondering on what grounds the bank can make the $900 loan in the first place. Apart from the required 10 percent reserve, the bank does not

necessarily have $900 in cash to loan. It creates the money simply by a book entry and runs no great risk since it will almost always have enough people making deposits to cover the demand for cash. So many large transactions are made by cheque, in fact, that banks need not keep large amounts of currency in reserve.

Transaction #3

Since I wish to buy a new stereo system with my bank loan, I make out a cheque for $900 to the Sound Store. The store, in turn, deposits the $900 in a chequing account at Bank B.

What happens to the balance sheets of the two banks now? Table 19.4 shows the results. The deposits at Bank A are reduced by $900, but the $900 loan still remains. I must still repay the bank, and so this $900 still stands as an addition to the money supply. The transfer of the $900 from Bank A to Bank B takes place between the accounts the two banks hold at the Bank of Canada. For Bank B, total reserves and chequing account liabilities both increase by $900. Bank B must hold the required reserves of $90 ($900 x 10 percent), but it now also has excess reserves of $900 - $90 = $810. Can you see how the scenario of money creation is unfolding?

Transaction #4

Now suppose Ms A. Debtor applies and receives a loan from Bank B of $810. This bank loan results in an increase in the money supply of $810, as shown in

Table 19.4 Transactions #3 and #4—Balance sheets of banks A and B and changes in the money supply

TRANSACTION	BANK BALANCE SHEETS			MONEY SUPPLY
BANK A #1	Assets		Liabilities	
	Currency reserves	+ $ 1000	Chequing deposits: Yours + $ 1000	Unchanged
	Required reserves	+ $ 100		
	Excess reserves	+ $ 900		
#2	Loans	+ $ 900	Chequing deposits: Mine + $ 900	+ $ 900
#3	Reserves	– $ 900	Chequing deposits: – $ 900	
BANK B #3	Assets		Liabilities	
	Reserves	+ $ 900	Chequing deposits: + $ 900	Unchanged
	Required reserves	+ $ 90		
	Excess reserves	+ $ 810		
#4	Loans	+ $ 810	Chequing deposits: + $ 810	+ $ 810

When a cheque is written on the $900 loan and the recipient deposits the money in Bank B, that bank then has excess reserves of $810 to loan and the money supply increases by $810.

Table 19.4. So far, then, your initial deposit of $1000 has resulted in a net increase in the money supply of $900 + $810 = $1710. If the process continued through successive transactions, we would have the cancellation of the $810 deposit credited to Ms A. Debtor, but when she writes a cheque or spends the cash, the amount remains with the person who receives the funds and who then could make a deposit that would increase the money supply by $729, and so on. The total possible increase in the money supply that could be created by an initial deposit can be calculated using the deposit multiplier outlined in the Skill Development section on page 408.

□ The Process in Reverse—Money Destruction

Since banks can "create" money, it stands to reason that they can also "destroy" it. In other words, banks can both increase and decrease the money supply.

Suppose you return to Bank A to withdraw $1000 in cash from your account and you decide to keep the money under your mattress at home. What happens to Bank A's balance sheet? Both currency reserve assets and chequing deposit liabilities at the bank will be reduced by $1000. Since we have assumed that the bank has just enough reserves to meet the requirement, required reserves will decrease by $100, but actual reserves will decrease by $1000. The bank will be short $900.

How will Bank A make up this shortfall? As some loans are paid off, the bank will cease to grant new loans until the $900 has been accumulated in required reserves. Table 19.5 shows the results. Where would borrowers from Bank A get the money to pay off their

Table 19.5 Reduction in the money supply

BALANCE SHEETS OF BANK A				
A LOSS OF DEPOSIT			B REDUCTION IN LOANS	
Assets	Liabilities		Assets	Liabilities
Currency reserves – $ 1000	Deposits – $ 1000		Currency reserves + $ 900 Loans – $ 900	
Changes in reserves:			Changes in reserves:	
Actual reserves – $ 1000			Actual reserves + $ 900	
Required reserves – $ 100			Required reserves no change	
Excess reserves – $ 900			Excess reserves + $ 900	
Total - $ 1000	Total - $ 1000		Total no change	Total no change

When Bank A loses a $1000 deposit, its actual reserves fall by $1000 while its required reserves decrease by $100. Thus, total negative excess reserves equal $900. Bank A must then reduce its loans by $900 to make up for the shortfall. In part B of the table, the bank has reduced its loans by $900, thus increasing its reserves by the same amount. This amount cancels the reserve deficiency of $900. As Bank A reduces its loans, however, borrowers would withdraw from their accounts at other banks and thus the process would continue, gradually reducing the money supply.

□ □ □ □ □

Skill Development: Calculating the Deposit or Money Multiplier

The lengthy process of money creation we have described can be calculated by a simple formula. The **deposit** or **money multiplier** is the factor by which bank deposits and the money supply are changed with a $1 change in bank reserves. The deposit multiplier is calculated as the reciprocal of the reserve ratio, that is:

$$\text{Deposit multiplier (D)} = \frac{1}{\text{Required reserve ratio (R)}}$$

$$D = \frac{1}{R}$$

Both the money supply and bank deposits increase together in relation to the reserve ratio. Bank deposits increase as a multiple of the change in reserves, while the money supply increases as a multiple of the change in excess reserves. Let's examine how the deposit or money multiplier can be used to calculate changes both in the money supply and in total demand deposits.

Changes in the Money Supply

A change in the reserve ratio or bank reserves can have a significant impact on the loans banks can make, and thus on the money supply. The change in the money supply is calculated as:

$$\text{Change in money supply} = \frac{1}{R} \times \frac{\text{Change in excess}}{\text{reserves}}$$

Examples:
(a) How much could the money supply increase in total with an initial bank deposit of $1000 and a cash reserve ratio of 10 percent? The excess reserve is $1000 − $100 = $900.

$$D = \frac{1}{.10} \times \$900 = \$9000$$

The money supply would increase by $9000.

(b) How much could the money supply decrease in total with an initial withdrawal of $1000 and a cash reserve ratio

of 20 percent? The (negative) excess reserve is $1000 − $200 = $800.

$$D = \frac{1}{.20} \times -\$800 = -\$4000$$

The money supply would decrease by $4000.

Change in Deposits

Changes in the reserve ratio also affect deposits.

$$\frac{\text{Change in}}{\text{deposits}} \text{(D)} = \frac{1}{\text{Reserve ratio (R)}} \times \frac{\text{Change in}}{\text{reserves}} \text{(C)}$$

Examples:
(a) How much could total deposits increase with an initial deposit of $1000 and a cash reserve ratio of 10 percent?

$$D = \frac{1}{.10} \times \$1000 = \$10\ 000$$

Total deposits may increase by $10 000.

(b) How much could total deposits decrease with an initial withdrawal of $1000 and a cash reserve ratio of 20 percent?

$$D = \frac{1}{.20} \times -\$1000 = -\$5000$$

Total deposits could decrease by $5000.

Applications

1. Suppose the required reserve ratio is 20 percent and I. Spender makes a deposit of $10 000. What is the maximum amount by which the following could increase:
(a) the money supply
(b) demand deposits.
Assume that, initially, the banks have made their maximum number of loans.

2. Suppose that the banks have made their maximum number of loans and the required reserve ratio is 12.5 percent. I make a deposit of $1000. What is the maximum amount by which the money supply can increase?

loans? The answer is probably from their accounts at other banks.

Let's assume all the borrowers make withdrawals from Bank B. Bank B, therefore, loses $9000 in deposits and $9000 in reserves. It will be short $8100 in required reserves and will have to reduce loans by $8100. Other banks will then lose reserves and deposits of $8100. As deposits are withdrawn, the money supply is reduced and the process continues just as it did with money creation. Deposits would fall by a total of $10 000 and the money supply would decrease by $9000.

☐ Some Limitations

It may seem that the banks could go on creating money endlessly. Of course, this is not the case. In our examination of money creation, we made a number of assumptions to simplify the illustration. Now let's consider what happens when we remove these assumptions and examine a more realistic situation.

Currency Leakage

We assumed that all money was in circulation. No one held any currency. Clearly, people do hold money outside bank deposits. Instead of putting all your $1000 inheritance in a chequing account, for example, you may have decided to keep all or some of it under the mattress at home. If you held on to all of it, the entire process we have examined would not even begin, and consequently, no money would be created. If you held on to some of the $1000, the initial deposit would be reduced and so, too, would the total addition to the money supply.

Similarly, suppose one of the borrowers in the process—me, for example—had decided to keep some cash, say $100. Bank B would then have received only $800 as a deposit. The decrease in excess reserves would reduce the banking system's lending potential accordingly.

Excess Reserves

We also assumed originally that the banks would be both willing and able to lend all of their excess cash reserves and that they had no excess cash reserves initially. This, however, is not always the case. For example, suppose Bank A had decided to add $200 to its reserves instead of the required $100 when it received your $1000 deposit because it foresaw a downturn in the economy. The amount the bank could lend would then be reduced to $800 from $900—with a significant reduction in the deposit (or monetary) multiplier. Businesses and households may also be unwilling to borrow money if they anticipate an economic downturn with increased unemployment and business bankruptcies. During the Great Depression of the 1930s, for example, Canadian and US banks held large excess reserves.

Generally, banks have an incentive to hold only small amounts in excess reserves. Loans and investments earn income for banks. Excess reserves do not. Banks, like other enterprises, are in the business of making a profit. They are also sensitive to upswings and downturns in the economy. During periods of expansion, banks are more willing to make loans and expand the money supply than during slowdowns. By expanding the money supply during upswings, however, they contribute to generally rising prices (inflation). By restricting the money supply during downturns, they may aggravate the slowdown and contribute to unemployment. The creation of money, therefore, must be regulated to promote economic stability—the role of the Bank of Canada.

▌ The Bank of Canada

The Bank of Canada is our central bank. It functions in a similar way to central banks in other countries—such as the Federal Reserve in the United States, the Bank of England, or the Banque de France.

The Bank of Canada began operating in 1935 as a private enterprise, but it became a crown corporation in 1938. Its directors are appointed by the federal cabinet, and the directors, in turn, appoint a governor and deputy governor. The Bank is not under the direct jurisdiction of the federal Department of Finance, although the Bank and the federal government have generally co-ordinated their policies. The federal cabinet, however, has the right to veto actions of the Bank and substitute its own policy.

☐ Objectives of the Bank of Canada

The objectives of the Bank of Canada, outlined in the preamble to the Bank Act which established it, are the following:
(i) To regulate credit and currency in the best interests of the economic life of the nation.
(ii) To control and protect the external value of the national monetary unit [i.e., the Canadian dollar].
(iii) To mitigate, by its influence, fluctuations in the general level of production, trade, prices, and employment, so far as may be possible within the scope of the monetary action.
(iv) Generally to promote the economic and financial welfare of the Dominion.

The Bank is, therefore, charged with promoting four of the objectives outlined by the Economic Council of Canada—stable prices, full employment, economic growth, and a viable balance of payments. A 1991 proposal to change the Bank Act—part of the federal government's constitutional reform package—would make price stability the main objective of the Bank's monetary policy. According to John Crow, the Bank's current governor: "Monetary or price stability is the best route for monetary policy to follow in promoting Canada's general economic and financial welfare."

☐ Functions of the Bank of Canada

To achieve its goals, the Bank of Canada performs four main functions. It issues paper currency, acts as the "bankers' bank," serves as the federal government's bank and, most important, controls the money supply. Let's consider these functions in more detail.

Issues Paper Currency
If you look at a Canadian bank note, you will see that it is signed by the governor and deputy governor of the Bank of Canada. The Bank is the only institution authorized to issue paper money and coins. It thus functions as a currency reservoir for the economy.

Acts as the Bankers' Bank
The Bank of Canada functions as the bank for all chartered banks in the country. As such, it holds the chartered banks' deposits, sets the interest rate for loans to chartered banks, settles transactions among banks, and keeps a record of the banks' balance sheets.

(i) Holds chartered bank deposits   Just as you and I may keep deposits in a chartered bank, so too do the chartered banks keep deposits in the Bank of Canada. The chartered banks are required by law to keep 3 percent of notice deposits and 10 percent of demand deposits in cash reserves to back depositors' demands. On average, approximately 4 percent of total deposits are kept in reserve. But not even this amount is held in actual bank notes in the banks' vaults. As much as one half of all banks' reserves are kept as deposits with the Bank of Canada.

(ii) Sets the bank rate   The chartered banks may also borrow from the Bank of Canada. However, the Bank acts only as a "lender of last resort" should a commercial bank not be able to meet its depositors' demands. This occurs only rarely. The Bank prefers not to act as a lender, so it sets its lending rates at a relatively high level. The interest rate charged by the Bank of Canada on loans to chartered banks is known as the **bank rate**.

Changes in the bank rate have a ripple effect on other interest rates in the economy. Consequently, the bank rate is carefully monitored by business people, bankers, and economists. The **prime rate**—the interest rate charged by the chartered banks to their best (or least risky) customers, usually large stable corporations—is often set at about one percent higher than the bank rate.

(iii) Acts as a clearing house for bank transactions   The Bank of Canada is also the final clearing house for the transactions of the banks. Suppose, for example, I owe you $100, which I pay with a cheque drawn on my account in Bank A. You then deposit the money in Bank B. Your account is credited $100 and my account is debited $100. But the transaction means also that Bank A must pay Bank B $100. This payment is made through the Canadian Payments Association (CPA), an

institution established in 1980 to which all chartered banks belong. All the cheques drawn against (debits) and all those drawn in favour (credits) are totalled by the CPA each day for each bank. The Bank of Canada is advised of the net debits and credits and makes the appropriate adjustment to each chartered bank's account. Trust and mortgage companies, caisses populaires, and credit unions may also be members of the Canadian Payments Association if they so choose.

(iv) Collects and publishes information on chartered banks The Bank of Canada also collects and publishes detailed and up-to-date information on the assets and liabilities of the chartered banks. Thus, it should be quickly aware of any unsound banking practices that could have serious effects on the functioning of the financial system and the economy. In the case of the Canadian Commercial Bank's failure in 1985, for example, too many loans were made to risky real estate and energy ventures, and too little was set aside to cover the costs of non-paying loans. Bank failures, however, are relatively rare.

Serves as the Federal Government's Banker

The Bank of Canada performs many of the services you would expect from your bank for the federal government.

(i) Provides expert advice Since the bank is staffed with experts in financial and monetary affairs, it is in a position to advise the federal Department of Finance on economic and financial affairs.

(ii) Holds federal government deposits The Bank of Canada holds some of the federal government's deposits. In early September 1991, for example, the federal government's deposits with the Bank of Canada totalled $11 million. Most of the government's bank deposits, however, are with the chartered banks.

(iii) Issues government bonds The Bank also manages the government's bond issues. It supervises the sale of new bonds and their repayment as they fall due. The sale of bonds to the chartered banks, the general public, and the Bank of Canada is one way the federal government finances its deficit. In other words, it is one way the government borrows money. The total value of Canada Savings Bonds, for example, equalled $33 billion in 1991. Other bond issues (with maturities of up to 10 years and over) totalled $150 billion in 1991. Approximately two-thirds of the value of these bonds was held by the general public in 1991. Managing the sale and repayment of these bonds efficiently and economically is clearly an important activity of the central bank.

(iv) Sells treasury bills Weekly treasury bill sales are also handled by the Bank of Canada. **Treasury bills** are short-term securities (as compared to bonds, which are long-term securities)—the principal amount of which is to be repaid in 91, 182, or 365 days. The federal government uses treasury bills to meet its short-term borrowing requirements.

Treasury bills have no stated rate of interest— instead, they are sold by auction at a price below their face value. The Bank of Canada and the Department of Finance determine the amount to be borrowed, or to put it another way, the number of treasury bills to be sold. If the amount sold is less than is required, the Bank of Canada will buy the remaining bills—that is, loan the money to the federal government. The total value of treasury bills held by the Bank of Canada in June 1991 was over $13 billion. The total value of treasury bills outstanding in June 1991 was approximately $145 billion.

(v) Controls exchange rates The Bank of Canada also acts on behalf of the federal government in foreign exchange markets to control the value of the Canadian dollar. To raise the value of the dollar, the Bank buys Canadian dollars with its reserve of foreign currencies. To lower the value of the dollar, it sells Canadian dollars. We will return to this function of the Bank of Canada in Unit Five on international trade.

Controls the Money Supply

The most important function of the central bank is to control the money supply. In other words, the Bank must ensure that the right amount of money is available to achieve full employment, stable prices, economic growth, and a viable balance of payments. By comparison with this demanding and important task, the other functions of the Bank are relatively routine.

Regulation of the Money Supply

Activities by the Bank of Canada to control the money supply are generally known as **monetary policy**. Policies to increase the money supply are **expansionary monetary policies**. Policies to decrease the money supply are **contractionary monetary policies**. The Bank of Canada can control the money supply by five main means:

(i) open market operations
(ii) transfer of federal government deposits
(iii) changes in the bank rate
(iv) moral suasion
(v) changes in the required reserve ratio.
Of these five techniques, the first three are the most important.

☐ Open Market Operations

Open market operations refer to the buying and selling of bonds and treasury bills by the Bank of Canada in order to control the money supply. The market is described as "open" because anyone who wishes to buy or sell federal bonds or treasury bills may do so—banks or any member of the public.

How then do the purchases and sales of bonds and bills affect the money supply?

Buying Bonds and Bills

Suppose the Bank of Canada buys a $100 000 bond from a Canadian corporation. The Bank gets the bond and the Canadian corporation deposits its cheque in its chequing account at Bank A. As a result, the chequing account of the Canadian corporation increases by $100 000 and the reserves of Bank A increase by $100 000. Initially, then, the money supply increases by $100 000. Table 19.6 shows the balance sheets.

But, this initial increase of $100 000 in the money supply is not all. With a 10-percent reserve ratio, Bank A has excess reserves of $90 000 and, consequently, can make loans of that amount. Thus, based on the deposit multiplier, a whole series of transactions can take place by which a maximum increase of $1 million in demand loans can occur. And, of course, the increase in demand loans means a corresponding increase in the money supply.

We should emphasize, however, that in reality the increase in demand loans will likely not reach the maximum for reasons we have already encountered.

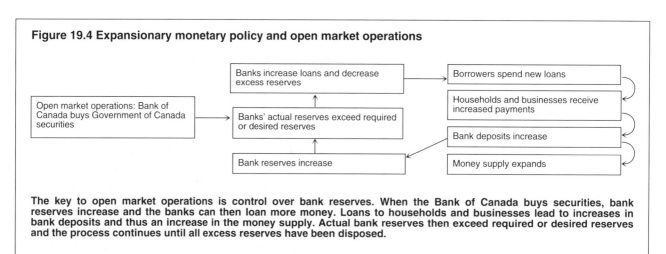

Figure 19.4 Expansionary monetary policy and open market operations

The key to open market operations is control over bank reserves. When the Bank of Canada buys securities, bank reserves increase and the banks can then loan more money. Loans to households and businesses lead to increases in bank deposits and thus an increase in the money supply. Actual bank reserves then exceed required or desired reserves and the process continues until all excess reserves have been disposed.

Table 19.6 Open market operations and expansionary monetary policy (thousands of dollars)

BANK OF CANADA

ASSETS		LIABILITIES	
Federal government bonds	+ $100	Reserve deposits of chartered Bank A	+ $100
Total	$100	Total	$100

CHARTERED BANK A

ASSETS		LIABILITIES	
Reserve deposit in Bank of Canada	+ $100	Chequing deposit with a Canadian corporation	+ $100
Required reserves $10 Excess reserves $90			
Total	$100	Total	$100

When the Bank of Canada buys a $100 000 bond from a Canadian corporation and the corporation deposits the funds in a chequing account with a bank, the demand deposits and reserves of the bank increase by $100 000. The money supply thus also increases by $100 000. With a reserve ratio of 10 percent, the bank has excess reserves of $90 000 and can loan this amount. Based on the deposit multiplier, the total increase in the money supply could be $1 million.

The public may prefer to hold cash rather than make demand deposits. The chartered banks may hold excess reserves, and may be unable or unwilling to lend the maximum amount. Nevertheless, simply by the purchase of a bond, the Bank of Canada can bring about a multiple increase in the country's money supply. Figure 19.4 summarizes the process.

Selling Bonds and Bills

Suppose now the Bank of Canada sells a $100 000 bond to a Canadian corporation. What happens? The Canadian corporation writes a cheque for $100 000 drawn on its chequing account in Bank A to the Bank of Canada in exchange for the bond. Bank A's account with the Bank of Canada is reduced by $100 000 and Bank A reduces the Canadian corporation's account by $100 000. The money supply decreases by $100 000.

But again, the process does not stop there. Bank A's reserves fall by $100 000 and (if we assume a 10-percent cash reserve ratio), only $10 000 is held in reserve for the Canadian corporation's deposit. Bank A must, therefore, reduce its deposits until it has the appropriate cash reserve ratio.

Again, we see that an action by the Bank of Canada has a multiple effect. The sale of a $100 000 government bond can result in a $1 million reduction in deposits (and, therefore, in the money supply) and a reduction of $900 000 in loans—assuming, of course,

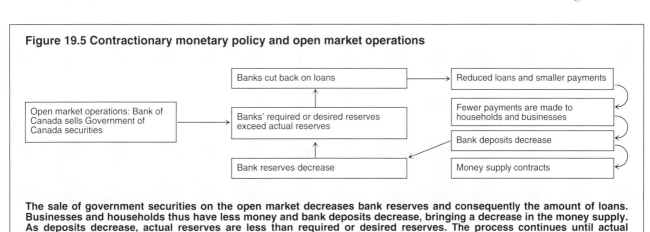

Figure 19.5 Contractionary monetary policy and open market operations

The sale of government securities on the open market decreases bank reserves and consequently the amount of loans. Businesses and households thus have less money and bank deposits decrease, bringing a decrease in the money supply. As deposits decrease, actual reserves are less than required or desired reserves. The process continues until actual reserves once again equal required reserves.

that Bank A has loaned out all of its reserves. Figure 19.5 summarizes the process.

However, since a growing money supply is necessary to increase aggregate demand and promote economic growth, the Bank of Canada usually cuts back on its purchase of bonds and bills rather than actually selling them. This action is generally enough to control the increase in the money supply.

Interest Rates

Open market operations also have a significant impact on interest rates and thus on the amount of money spent and invested in the economy. To illustrate, let's consider the purchase of treasury bills. While government bonds provide for a fixed rate of interest, treasury bills are simply promises by government to pay the face amount, say $100 000, in three months. The interest depends on the price paid by buyers. Suppose I pay $96 000 for a bill and in three months receive $100 000. I gain $4000, or about 4.2 percent interest for the three-month period (16.8 percent per year). If I were to pay $98 000 for a bill and in three months received the $100 000, I would gain only $2000— about 2 percent for the three-month period or 8 percent per year.

If the Bank of Canada starts buying treasury bills, the purchase price will rise. Suppose the price rises from $96 000 to $97 000 for a three-month bill. The interest rate has fallen from 4.2 percent to 3.1 percent over the three months (from 16.8 percent to 12.4 percent per year). Thus, when the Bank of Canada enters the open market by buying government bills, it tends to raise the prices of the bills and thereby lower interest rates.

Moreover, as the Bank of Canada's open market purchases increase the chartered banks' reserves, the banks will increase their lending activities and buy more securities. Both these activities will tend to lower the interest rate.

Changes in interest rates have a considerable impact on the economy. Higher interest rates can reduce consumption spending and investment, and thus help to cool off an overheated economy. Lower interest rates can stimulate consumption spending and investment, and thus help to bring the economy out of a recession. The Bank of Canada's open market operations, therefore, can control the money supply and influence the level of spending and investment by affecting interest rates.

Of the five instruments used to control the money supply, open market operations are the most important. They have the advantage of flexibility and produce relatively immediate results. Government securities can readily be bought or sold in large or small quantities.

☐ Transfer of Federal Government Deposits

Since the Bank of Canada is the government's bank, it can increase the money supply by transferring federal government deposits to the chartered banks. If, for example, it transfers $100 million from the federal government's account into a chartered bank account, then the chartered bank's reserves are increased by $100 million. If the required reserve ratio is 10 percent, then the chartered bank will have excess reserves of $90 million. Thus, the effect is the same as that achieved by open market operations—the chartered banks' cash reserves are increased and more money is available in the economy.

Conversely, the Bank of Canada can contract the money supply by switching government deposits from the chartered banks to the government's account with the Bank of Canada. Chartered banks' reserves are thereby reduced, their ability to lend diminished, and the money supply reduced.

☐ Changes in the Bank Rate

As we have seen, the Bank of Canada acts as a "bankers' bank." In this role, it makes advances (loans of small amounts of money for a short duration—often less than a week) to the chartered banks. The bank rate is the interest rate at which these loans are made.

Before 1980, the bank rate was fixed and the Bank of Canada formally announced increases or decreases. Since March 1980, however, the bank rate has been floating, at 1/4 of a percent above the average rate of interest paid by the federal government on its 91-day treasury bills at each weekly auction. The government finances its immediate cash needs by borrowing large amounts of short-term funds through purchases of treasury bills at these auctions. While it may seem, therefore, that the bank rate can vary independently of the central bank, in fact, the Bank of Canada achieves the bank rate it wants since it decides on the amount of treasury bills to be bought and sold and actually conducts the weekly auction.

The Bank of Canada can influence the amount the chartered banks borrow (and thus their total cash reserves) by changing the bank rate. Since the chartered banks do not often borrow significant amounts from the Bank of Canada, however, changes in the bank rate function primarily as signals of the central bank's policies. An increase in the bank rate tells the chartered banks that the Bank of Canada wants a reduction in loans and higher interest rates to reduce the money supply. A decrease in the bank rate signals that the Bank of Canada wants the chartered banks to loan more at lower rates and thus increase the money supply.

□ Changes in Reserve Requirements

We have seen that the amount of deposits banks can create depends on two factors—the amount of reserves and the reserve ratio. Changes in the reserve ratio can, therefore, significantly affect the money supply. Suppose the reserve ratio is raised from 10 to 12.5 percent with bank reserves at $200 million. The actual maximum amount of deposits would be reduced from $2 billion to $1.6 billion—a drop of $400 million!

Since the Bank of Canada's other monetary tools—particularly open market operations—are more effective, the Bank's power to change the reserve ratio was rarely exercised and was consequently abolished.

Since 1980, required primary reserves have been fixed at 10 percent of demand deposits and 3 percent of notice and term deposits. **Primary** or **cash reserves** take the form of deposits at the Bank of Canada or currency notes at the chartered banks.

In addition to the required cash reserves, the chartered banks must also hold up to 12 percent of their demand deposits in the form of secondary reserves. **Secondary reserves** are the chartered banks' hold-ings in treasury bills, loans to investment dealers, and cash in excess of primary reserves. The secondary reserve ratio has not changed since 1981 when it stood at 4 percent.

What effect will changes in the secondary reserve ratio have on the money supply? The answer is, not much. Changes in the ratio may require banks to rearrange their assets, but little else. With an increase in the ratio, banks may have to increase their holdings of treasury bills, for example, thus raising their secondary assets and reducing their long-term bonds (which do not qualify as secondary assets). But, only the composition of their reserves are affected, not the amount. Thus, the money supply is unaffected.

In 1991, the Bank of Canada announced its intention to eliminate reserve requirements. One reason was that the chartered banks' competitors, the near banks, do not have legal reserve requirements. Nevertheless, the chartered banks will continue to keep reserves to meet the needs of their customers and facilitate payments between banks through the Canadian Payments Association.

□ Moral Suasion

Moral suasion refers to attempts by the Bank of Canada to persuade the chartered banks to act in accordance with a particular policy, though without legal obligation. In the past, for example, the Bank of Canada has persuaded the chartered banks to increase their lending to particular groups (small businesses and less prosperous parts of the country) or to restrict lending to others (finance companies and retail stores offering retail credit). Such selective policies could not be achieved by other techniques, such as open market operations or the transfer of government deposits, which have a more general effect on the economy.

One of the difficulties with moral suasion is that banks are in competition with one another and with other financial intermediaries such as trust and mortgage loan companies. Even if all the chartered banks comply equally with the Bank of Canada's wishes to restrict lending to a particular group, for example, it is probable that other institutions would provide the group with their needs.

Summary

a. Many different commodities considered to have value have been used as money, including cattle, beaver pelts, wampum, cigarettes, and playing cards. Gold and silver became most widely used. From bits carefully weighed out, gold and silver money evolved to coins guaranteed by rulers, paper currency backed by gold and silver, fractionally-backed bank notes, fiat money (legal tender) not backed by any precious metal, and deposit money.

b. Money is anything that is generally accepted as a means of payment for goods and services. Money has four major functions—as a medium of exchange, a measure of value, a store of value, and a standard of deferred payments. It must be generally acceptable as a means of exchange, durable, portable, easily divisible, easily recognizable, of uniform value, difficult to counterfeit, and of stable value.

c. The demand for money is determined by the transactions motive (the need for money to meet immediate expenses), the precautionary motive (the need for money to meet emergencies or deal with unexpected events), and the speculative motive (the need for money to speculate on securities).

The quantity of money demanded varies indirectly with the interest rate. As interest rates rise, the quantity of money demanded declines and *vice versa*. Changes in real GDP and the price level can shift the demand for money. An increase in real GDP or the price level shifts the demand curve for money to the right and a decrease in these factors shifts the demand curve for money to the left.

d. The money supply is the total stock of money available in the economy at any particular time. Definitions of what the money supply includes, however, vary. The narrowest definition, M1, includes only what can be used directly as a means of exchange (i.e., currency outside banks and demand deposits). Other broader definitions include other deposits on which cheques can be written (M1A), savings and term deposits or near money (M2), deposits with financial intermediaries other than chartered banks (M2+), and foreign currency and term deposits (M3). Credit cards are not money.

e. The interest rate or price of money is determined by the supply and demand for money. The supply curve is a straight vertical line because the money supply is fixed at any particular time. The demand curve slopes down to the right. The interest rate is the point at which the two curves intersect. The Bank of Canada can vary the money supply over time, however.

f. The Bank of Canada and the eight domestic chartered banks constitute the banking system in Canada. Other financial intermediaries, or institutions that accept deposits and make loans, include trust and mortgage loan companies, and credit unions and caisses populaires. These are known as near banks.

g. Banks can create money through demand deposits. When deposits are made, the banks are required to keep only a fraction as reserves and can loan the remainder. The loans provide money for households and businesses, some of which will in turn be deposited, thus increasing the money supply. The opposite may also occur.

h. The deposit or money multiplier, which is calculated as the reciprocal of the reserve ratio, can be used to determine how much deposits and the money supply will change with changes in bank reserves.

i. The Bank of Canada is the nation's central bank and a crown corporation. Its objectives are to promote stable prices, full employment, economic growth, and a viable balance of payments. The functions of the Bank include issuing paper currency, acting as the bankers' bank, serving as the federal government's bank, and controlling the money supply.

j. The Bank of Canada controls the money supply through open market operations (buying and selling securities on the open market), transfer of federal government deposits, changes in the bank rate, and moral suasion. Open market operations are the most important monetary policy tool. The Bank's prerogative to change reserve requirements has been virtually abolished.

▮ Review of Key Terms

Define the following key terms introduced in this chapter and provide examples where appropriate.

fiat money
money
barter system
double coincidence of
    wants
transactions motive
precautionary motive
speculative motive
liquidity preference
money supply
currency
cheque
demand deposit
near money
M1
M1A
M2
M2+
M3

financial intermediary
near banks
mortgage
deposit or money
    multiplier
bank rate
prime rate
treasury bill
monetary policy
expansionary
    monetary policy
contractionary
    monetary policy
open market
    operations
primary reserves
secondary reserves
moral suasion

▮ Application and Analysis

1. Assess how well cigarettes, playing cards, cattle, beaver pelts, and the present Canadian currency fulfill the functions of money by completing Table 19.7.

Table 19.7 Assessing forms of money

FUNCTION OF MONEY	CIGARETTES	PLAYING CARDS	CATTLE	BEAVER PELTS	CANADIAN CURRENCY
Medium of exchange					
General acceptability					
Portable					
Divisible					
Durable					
Difficult to counterfeit					
Easily recognizable					
Of uniform value					
Good store of value					
Good standard of deferred payments					

2. Referring to Table 19.8 below, calculate:
(a) the amount of currency in circulation
(b) M1   (c) M2   (d) M2+   (e) M3.

3. Assume that on January 1 last year, you had $1000 that you wished to spend on (or about) January 1 of this year. Use your library to calculate which of the following would be the best store of value over the period.

(a) the Canadian dollar

(b) stocks whose prices vary with the Dow Jones Industrial Average

(c) gold

(d) silver

(e) stocks whose prices vary with the TSE 300 Composite index

Table 19.8 Monetary aggregates, January 1991, seasonally adjusted (millions of dollars)

1 CURRENCY OUTSIDE BANKS	2 DEMAND DEPOSITS	3 PERSONAL SAVINGS DEPOSITS AND NON-PERSONAL NOTICE DEPOSITS	4 NON-PERSONAL FIXED TERM DEPOSITS AND FOREIGN CURRENCY DEPOSITS	5 DEPOSITS AT DEPOSIT-TAKING INSTITUTIONS OTHER THAN BANKS
19 216	19 931	225 929	51 038	188 521

SOURCE: *Bank of Canada Review*, September 1991.

Figure 19.6 A comparison of credit and charge cards

CARD	ANNUAL FEE	ANNUAL INTEREST RATE	GRACE PERIOD	INTEREST FROM:		HOW WIDELY ACCEPTED	OTHER FEATURES
				DATE OF PURCHASE	DATE OF STATEMENT		

VISA

Bank of Nova Scotia

Canadian Imperial Bank of Commerce

Central Guaranty

Centre Desjardins

Laurentian Bank

Montreal Trust

Royal Bank

Toronto Dominion Bank

Vancouver City Savings

MASTERCARD

Bank of Montreal

Canada Trust Super Card

CS Co-op

National Bank

National Trust

Niagara Credit Union

Shell/Royal Trust

OTHER CREDIT CARDS

Canadian Tire

Eaton's

en Route

Home Hardware

Hudson's Bay

Petro-Canada

Sears

Simpsons

Sunoco

Ultramar

Woodward's

Zellers

CHARGE CARDS

American Express

Diners Club

Esso Petroleum of Canada

Husky Oil Ltd.

Irving Oil

Shell Canada Products

Texaco Canada

(f) a one-year Guaranteed Investment Certificate which pays 6 percent

(g) a savings account at 4 percent interest

4. Suppose the Bank of Canada buys a $100 000 bond from a Canadian corporation. Assuming a 20-percent reserve ratio, outline the process of how the money supply is increased.

5. What effect would each of the following have on the money supply? Explain.

(a) a desire by the banks to increase their excess reserves

(b) a decline in the public's confidence in banks

(c) an increase in the use of credit cards

6. The actions of the Bank of Canada to increase the money supply have been described as "pushing on a string." Is this analogy appropriate? Explain.

7. In Table 19.9, explain how the Bank of Canada would use each of the monetary policy instru-

Table 19.9 Monetary policy

MONETARY POLICY INSTRUMENT	CONTRACTIONARY POLICY	EXPANSIONARY POLICY
Open market operations		
Switching federal government deposits		
Varying the bank rate		
Changing the secondary reserve requirement		
Moral suasion		

ments listed to implement a contractionary and an expansionary policy.

8. Compare the Cards

Suppose you have decided to get a credit or charge card. To find out which card will best suit your needs, complete the survey outlined in Figure 19.6 for those cards that most interest you. Credit cards provide revolving credit and require a minimum monthly payment. Charge cards require full payment every month.

CHAPTER TWENTY

Monetary Policy

Objectives

a. Outline and assess the monetary policies appropriate to combat unemployment and inflation in the Keynesian view.

b. Demonstrate the effects of monetary policy on the business cycle.

c. Analyze and assess the advantages and disadvantages of monetary policy in attaining economic stability.

d. Outline the Keynesian view of how fiscal and monetary policies can be used to stabilize the economy.

e. Compare the effects of demand-pull and cost-push inflation.

f. Investigate how economic conditions in the 1960s led economists to postulate a trade-off between inflation and unemployment.

g. Analyze the reasons for and effects of stagflation in the 1970s and early 1980s in Canada.

h. Explain and evaluate the prices and incomes policies instituted by the Canadian government since the late 1970s.

i. Analyze the views of supply-side economists.

j. Assess the main ideas of monetarism, including the velocity of circulation of money, the equation of exchange, and the quantity theory of money.

k. Examine the economic ideas put forth by Milton Friedman.

l. Assess the monetary policies of the Bank of Canada since 1975.

We have examined how the banking system can expand and contract the money supply and how the Bank of Canada controls the total stock of money in the economy. What we have not yet examined is why it is necessary for the Bank of Canada to expand or contract the money supply and when action is appropriate. Monetary policy, like fiscal policy, can be used to control the fluctuations of the business cycle and thus work toward the goal of economic stability.

In this chapter, then, we examine the advantages and limitations of monetary policy in achieving economic stability, both in the Keynesian view and in the view of other schools of thought. We also consider how various monetary policies have been applied in Canada and their effects.

Easy Money and Tight Money

The Bank of Canada can institute either an easy or a tight money policy. With an **easy** or **expansionary money policy**, the Bank acts to increase the money supply, lower interest rates, and thus increase bank loans to consumers and businesses. As consumers spend more and businesses increase investment, real GDP and employment increase. An easy money policy, therefore, can be implemented in a recession to combat unemployment and stimulate the economy.

With a **tight** or **contractionary money policy**, the Bank of Canada acts to decrease the money supply, raise interest rates, and thus discourage bank loans. Consumer spending and business investment decline, real GDP falls, and the price level declines. A tight money policy, therefore, can be implemented to control the rate of inflation.

☐ Monetary Policy During a Recession

Our discussion in the first part of this chapter will focus on the Keynesian view of the economy. Then, we will consider the views of supply-side economists and monetarists.

Suppose the economy is facing widespread unemployment, a decrease in aggregate demand, and a declining GDP—in other words, a recession. The Bank of Canada adopts an easy money policy and decides to purchase bonds on the open market. We can summarize what happens in three steps.

Step 1 Interest rates fall As we saw in the last chapter, the purchase of bonds by the Bank of Canada on the open market means that the chartered banks will have excess reserves. They will, therefore, be able to increase their demand loans and thus the money supply. With an increase in the money supply, interest rates fall and bank credit increases.

Step 2 Investment and consumption increase With lower interest rates, the cost of financing new investment declines and businesses increase their purchases of land, buildings, machinery, equipment, and labour services. Loans will also be more attractive to con-

sumers, particularly for buying homes, automobiles, household appliances, and other "big-ticket" items. Consumption thus also increases.

Step 3 Real GDP increases New investment and increased consumer spending shift the aggregate demand curve to the right, raising real GDP, employment, and incomes. The rise in real GDP is magnified by the multiplier effect. The increased GDP generates further increases in spending, employment, and thus GDP once again.

An easy money policy thus stimulates the economy during a recession. The effects are shown graphically in Figure 20.1. The AD curve shifts to the right from AD_1 to AD_2 and though prices rise slightly, the recessionary gap is significantly reduced.

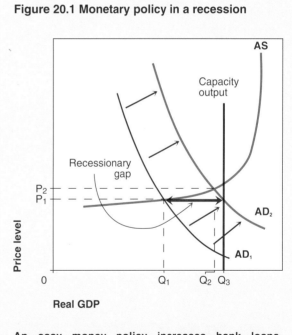

Figure 20.1 Monetary policy in a recession

An easy money policy increases bank loans, investment, and consumption, shifting the aggregate demand curve from AD_1 to AD_2. Though prices rise slightly—from $0P_1$ to $0P_2$—the main effect is an increase in real GDP from $0Q_1$ to $0Q_2$ and along with it, increases in employment and incomes. The recessionary gap between $0Q_1$ and $0Q_3$ is almost closed.

☐ Monetary Policy to Combat Inflation

A restrictive or tight monetary policy works in the opposite way. Let's assume the economy is facing severe inflation. The Bank of Canada acts to reduce the money supply by selling bonds on the open market.

Step 1 Interest rates increase   The sale of bonds decreases the ability of the chartered banks to loan money. As competition for the limited money supply increases, interest rates rise.

Step 2 Investment and consumption decline   With higher interest rates, the cost of financing new investment increases and the total amount of new investment consequently declines. Consumers are also discour-

aged from borrowing money by higher interest rates. Consumers thus have less money to spend and total consumption declines.

Step 3 Real GDP declines   With a decline in new investment and consumer spending, the aggregate demand curve shifts to the left. Real GDP, employment, and incomes decline. Reductions in GDP are again magnified by the multiplier effect. With a lower aggregate demand and real GDP, prices rise less rapidly, slowing the rate of inflation.

Figure 20.2 illustrates the effect of a tight monetary policy to combat inflation. The AD curve shifts to the left from AD_1 to AD_2 and real GDP declines slightly from $0Q_1$ to $0Q_2$, narrowing the inflationary gap. The price level falls from $0P_1$ to $0P_2$.

Of course, the Bank of Canada could use any of the five monetary policy tools discussed in the last chapter to vary the money supply. Open market operations and changing the bank rate, however, are generally considered the most important. Open market operations allow for the greatest flexibility, since government bonds can be bought and sold in large or small amounts and their impact on bank reserves is almost immediate. Changes in the bank rate are effective because they clearly demonstrate the Bank's policy and are often quickly followed by changes in the chartered banks' prime rate and other interest rates.

☐ Effect of Monetary Policy on the Business Cycle

How does monetary policy affect the business cycle? Figure 20.3 illustrates the effects. A tight or contractionary monetary policy helps to cool the economy during an expansionary period by lowering aggregate demand and slowing inflation. Thus, the ascent to the peak of the cycle is not so sharp. Similarly, an easy or expansionary monetary policy smooths the descent toward the trough in a recession by increasing aggregate demand and thus stimulating the economy.

☐ Advantages of Monetary Policy

We saw that fiscal policy had both advantages and disadvantages as a means of combatting inflation and

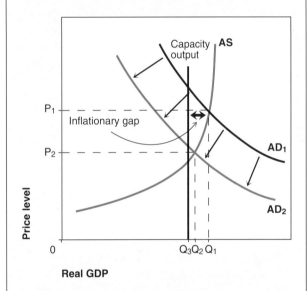

Figure 20.2 Monetary policy to combat inflation

A tight monetary policy reduces bank loans, investment, and consumption, shifting the aggregate demand curve to the left from AD_1 to AD_2. The inflationary gap between $0Q_1$ and $0Q_3$ is narrowed as the equilibrium point moves closer to capacity output. Thus, while real GDP falls slightly from $0Q_1$ to $0Q_2$, the price level falls more rapidly from $0P_1$ to $0P_2$. The main effect of a tight money policy is to decrease the price level and slow the rate of inflation.

unemployment. The same is true of monetary policy. Monetary policy has two main advantages over fiscal policy—political acceptability and speed and flexibility.

Political Acceptability

Fiscal policies, since they constitute changes in government taxation and spending, are usually accompanied by considerable political controversy. No one wants to pay higher taxes. Similarly, spending cuts draw strong opposition from the groups affected. Monetary policy is generally less visible and less controversial, though in the late 1980s and early 1990s, a tight monetary policy with prolonged high interest rates sparked heated debate. Some economists blamed the government's tight monetary policy for the recession of 1990-91.

Speed and Flexibility

Fiscal policy, as we have seen, is subject to decision and implementation lags as government decides exactly what spending and taxing policies to implement and how. Monetary policy, on the other hand, can be implemented relatively quickly. Buying and selling securities or switching the government's bank deposits, for example, can be effected day-by-day as conditions warrant. Similarly, the bank rate is often altered weekly to reflect changing conditions.

☐ Limitations of Monetary Policy

Monetary policy, however, has some basic limitations.

Targetting Limitations

Fiscal policy can be targeted to affect particular regions since each level of government can implement its own taxing and spending measures. In provinces with high unemployment, for example, all levels of government could increase expenditures, and provincial and municipal governments could cut taxes, though such co-ordination is not always feasible. Monetary policy, however, is less flexible in this regard. Its effects are nation-wide.

Recognition Lag

While the decision and implementation lags are likely to be much shorter with monetary policy than with fiscal policy, the recognition lag could be equally lengthy. Current economic conditions may not always be clearly and quickly read. Future trends in the economy are also difficult to predict accurately and in time.

Easy Money Policy May Not Work

While a tight monetary policy can force banks to reduce loans by contracting their excess reserves, an easy money policy can only ensure that the banks have excess reserves and, therefore, the *ability* to grant more loans. If the banks are unwilling to lend or if investors are unwilling to borrow, then the easy money policy could fail. In a severe recession with a poor economic outlook, for example, banks may be reluctant to lend. Investors and consumers may also cut back on borrowing—even though they have access to "easy money." Too great an increase in the money supply and the consequent increase in spending may increase inflation.

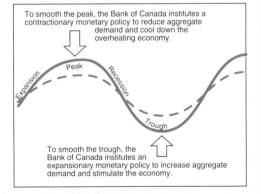

Figure 20.3 Effects of monetary policies on the business cycle

To smooth the peak, the Bank of Canada institutes a contractionary monetary policy to reduce aggregate demand and cool down the overheating economy.

To smooth the trough, the Bank of Canada institutes an expansionary monetary policy to increase aggregate demand and stimulate the economy.

Business conditions

Time

A tight or contractionary monetary policy reduces aggregate demand and smooths the movement to the peak of the cycle so that it is not so sharp. An easy or expansionary monetary policy increases aggregate demand, stimulating the economy and smoothing the descent to the trough.

Conflicts With Management of the Federal Debt

Monetary policies and policies to manage the federal debt may conflict. The best time to refinance the debt is when the interest rate is low—that is, in a recession. Substantial sales of bonds, however, could raise interest rates, discourage investment, and prolong a recession.

Cost-Push Inflation

Tight monetary policy is designed to control inflation resulting from excess aggregate demand—a situation known as demand-pull inflation. It is much less effective, however, in controlling inflation that originates from the supply-side of the market—cost-push inflation. We will return to cost-push inflation later in this chapter.

Transmission Process

In the Keynesian view, a lengthy and uncertain transmission process occurs between the implementation of monetary policy and its impact on GDP. Results, therefore, may be slow and not always as predicted.

☐ Fiscal or Monetary Policy?

In the Keynesian view, the key to stabilization policy—both fiscal and monetary—is in controlling aggregate demand. Fiscal and monetary policy must be coordinated to achieve economic stability. Before we go on to consider other views of stabilization policy, let's review the major components of Keynes's theory.

The basis of Keynes's theory is that levels of output, employment, income, and prices all depend on the level of aggregate demand. As we have seen, aggregate demand consists of four spending components: consumption spending (C), investment spending (I), government spending (G), and net foreign spending (X-M). A change in any of these components can affect aggregate demand.

Consumption Spending (C) The level of consumption spending varies with disposable income, which varies with changes in GDP. Consumption spending, therefore, changes with changes in GDP.

Investment Spending (I) As we have seen, investment spending is the most variable of the four spending flows and is, therefore, the one most likely to cause changes in aggregate demand. Fiscal policy influences the level of investment through changes in taxes and government expenditures on public works, for example. Monetary policy affects investment by varying the money supply and thus influencing interest rates.

Government Spending (G) Government spending is the component of aggregate demand most easily and effectively varied by public policy. While the motive for consumption and investment spending is the private interest of consumers and business people, the motive for government spending is the general interest and the desire to meet national economic goals. Among these goals are growth in real GDP and full employment at stable prices.

Foreign Spending (X-M) The expenditure of non-Canadians on our exports depends mainly on the level of their GDP. Our expenditures on foreign goods and services—our imports—depend mainly on the level of our GDP. The amount of expenditures on exports and imports can, however, be influenced by the trade policy of governments through the use, for example, of tariffs and quotas.

Monetary policy affects aggregate demand by varying the money supply and hence interest rates, which affect investment and consumer expenditures. An easy money policy increases aggregate demand; a tight money policy decreases it.

Fiscal policy most directly affects aggregate demand by varying government expenditures. Taxation affects aggregate demand by influencing consumption and investment. Decreased personal taxes are likely to increase consumption, while increased personal taxes are likely to decrease consumption. Reductions in business taxes are likely to increase investment, and increases in business taxes to reduce investment. An expansionary fiscal policy is designed to combat unemployment by increasing government, consumption, and investment expenditures, and thus aggregate demand. A contractionary policy works in the opposite way and reduces aggregate demand. Figure 20.4 summarizes

Figure 20.4 A summary of Keynesian employment theory and stabilization policy

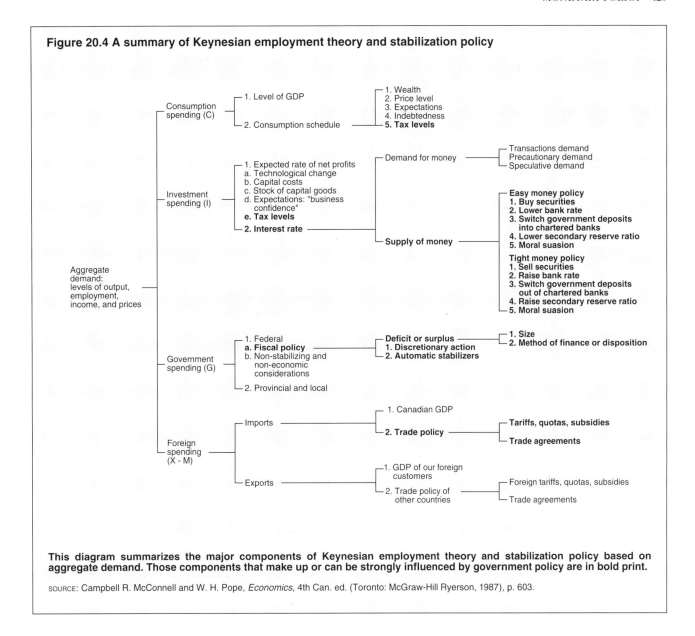

This diagram summarizes the major components of Keynesian employment theory and stabilization policy based on aggregate demand. Those components that make up or can be strongly influenced by government policy are in bold print.

SOURCE: Campbell R. McConnell and W. H. Pope, *Economics*, 4th Can. ed. (Toronto: McGraw-Hill Ryerson, 1987), p. 603.

the main components of Keynes's stabilization theory.

So which can we rely on—fiscal or monetary policy—to control aggregate demand? The answer, not surprisingly, is both. Fiscal policy, however, is the primary tool because monetary policy is limited in some key situations. In the depths of a recession, for ex-

ample, an easy money policy may drive down interest rates, but there is no guarantee that spending will increase. With the bleak economic outlook, banks may not want to loan the new money and if they did, businesses and consumers may not wish to borrow it. In these circumstances, monetary policy has been described as "pushing on a string"—totally ineffectual.

While the Bank of Canada may be able to buy or sell government securities on the open market, adjust the bank rate, or switch federal government deposits quickly, the actual effects of monetary policy on the economy are both slow and unpredictable in the Keynesian view. It takes considerable time for any action by the central bank to work its way through affecting interest rates, influencing the spending and investment decisions of consumers and businesses, and finally affecting GDP. Monetary policy, therefore, is used primarily to support fiscal policy actions in the Keynesian view.

□ Unemployment and Inflation Together

The Keynesian analysis of business cycles implies that the economy will face either unemployment or inflation. During a recession, unemployment is high. Expansionary fiscal and monetary policies are, therefore, most effective. During expansion periods, inflation is high and contractionary policies are most appropriate.

Until the end of the 1960s, many agreed that Keynes had provided an accurate model of how an economy functions. In the 1970s, however, economies began to experience rising inflation and rising unemployment at the same time. The Keynesian model does not explain the simultaneous appearance of these two problems. To understand how they could occur together, we need to examine the nature of inflation.

■ Inflation

We have defined inflation as a persistent rise in the general level of prices. Economists generally identify two types of inflation—demand-pull and cost-push.

□ Demand-Pull Inflation

Demand-pull inflation occurs when aggregate demand exceeds what the economy can produce at full employment. The high demand for a limited supply of goods produced at full employment pushes up prices.

Demand-pull inflation is, therefore, often described as "too many dollars chasing too few goods."

The cause of demand-pull inflation is relatively clear. An increase in spending—whether by businesses, government, or consumers when the economy is at full employment—shifts the aggregate demand curve to the right and thus raises prices. Increased demand thus "pulls up" prices.

Figure 20.5 illustrates this situation. The economy is in equilibrium and at or close to capacity output at E_1, where the aggregate demand and aggregate supply curves intersect. With an increase in aggregate demand from AD_1 to AD_2, the general price level increases from $0P_1$ to $0P_2$ since the economy can produce no more goods and services to meet the increased demand.

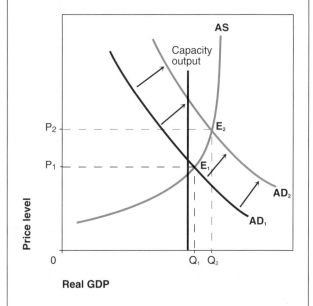

Figure 20.5 Demand-pull inflation

Demand-pull inflation occurs when aggregate demand exceeds the economy's capacity output at full employment. The economy is in equilibrium close to capacity output at E_1. An increase in aggregate demand shifts the aggregate demand curve from AD_1 to AD_2 well beyond capacity output, and the price level thus rises from $0P_1$ to $0P_2$.

☐ Cost-Push Inflation

Demand-pull inflation originates from the demand side of the economy. Cost-push or "sellers'" inflation is generated from the supply side. **Cost-push inflation** occurs when wages or other costs of production rise (such as those of essential raw materials), thus "pushing up" prices. Cost-push inflation can occur even in periods when resources are unemployed, that is, when the economy is not operating at or near capacity.

A glance at the history of prices since 1940 shows that, in general, they increased almost every year. Prices rose during recessions and rose more rapidly during booms.

Figure 20.6 illustrates cost-push inflation graphically. If strong labour unions succeed in pushing up wages ("wage-push" inflation), or if powerful oligopolies increase prices to raise profits ("profit-push" inflation), producers will cut production and the aggregate supply curve will shift to the left from AS_1 to AS_2. The equilibrium point, therefore, moves from E_1 to E_2. With the higher level of aggregate demand at E_2, prices rise and real GDP falls. Thus, we have rising prices and declining employment and output—that is, stagflation. **Stagflation** is economic *stag*nation—little economic growth, high unemployment—and in*flation* together.

☐ The Phillips Curve

In the early 1960s, the British economist A.W. Phillips suggested that there was a link between the rate of inflation and the unemployment rate. Figure 20.7

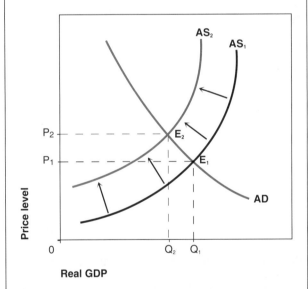

Cost-push inflation occurs when rising wages or other production costs shift the aggregate supply curve to the left, as from AS_1 to AS_2. The equilibrium point, therefore, shifts from E_1 to E_2. The price level increases from $0P_1$ to $0P_2$ and real GDP decreases from $0Q_1$ to $0Q_2$. Cost-push inflation thus leads to stagflation, the combination of inflation and high unemployment or economic stagnation.

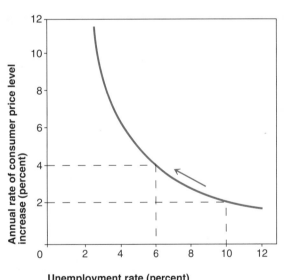

The Phillips curve shows an inverse relationship between inflation and unemployment rates. As unemployment declines from 10 percent to 6 percent, for example, the inflation rate rises from 2 to 4 percent. The converse is also true. The curve presumes a trade-off between inflation and unemployment—the lower the inflation rate, the higher the employment rate, and *vice versa*.

shows a **Phillips curve**, which postulates a stable and predictable inverse relationship between inflation and unemployment rates. If inflation rises, unemployment falls and *vice versa*. If a country implements an easy money policy and an expansionary fiscal policy to lower its unemployment rate, for example, it would have to accept a higher inflation rate. The converse would also be true. A tight money policy and a contractionary fiscal policy might combat inflation, but increase unemployment. This trade-off between inflation and unemployment was believed to exist in both the short and long runs.

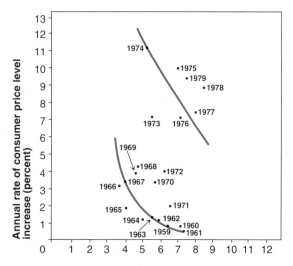

Figure 20.8 The Phillips curve in the 1960s and 1970s

The Phillips curve, based on the unemployment and inflation rate statistics for the 1960s, shows a trade-off between inflation and unemployment. While unemployment rates were relatively high in the early 1960s at an average of between 6 and 7 percent, inflation rates were low at an average of 1 percent. In the mid- and late 1960s when unemployment rates were lower, inflation rates rose to an average of between 3 and 4 percent. In the 1970s, however, the Phillips curve had shifted to the right and become more vertical. The trade-off between inflation and unemployment was not as evident.

As Figure 20.8 shows, the unemployment and inflation rates in the 1960s seemed to support this view of a trade-off between the two. In the early 1960s, when unemployment rates averaged between 6 and 7 percent, inflation rates were low at around 1 percent. In the mid- to late 1960s, as unemployment rates declined, inflation rates rose to an average of between 3 and 4 percent.

The Phillips curve seemed to be consistent not only with the facts of the 1960s, but also with logic. It made sense that as the economy moved closer to full employment, shortages would occur. The supply of certain types of labour would become scarce in some locations, for example. These shortages would bring about wage increases, and thus price increases. Inflation could occur even when the economy was at less than full employment. The Phillips curve was thus consistent with cost-push inflation.

In addition, large labour unions and oligopolistic corporations with a degree of control over the market can demand, and get, higher prices as the economy approaches full employment. Labour unions that negotiate higher wages can generate wage-push inflation. Oligopolies that not only pass along the higher costs to consumers but also raise prices for higher profits, can produce profit-push inflation—both elements of cost-push inflation.

□ Stagflation in the 1970s and 1980s

Economic conditions in the 1970s and 1980s, however, called into question the idea of a consistent, long-run trade-off between inflation and unemployment. As Figure 20.8 shows, the Phillips curve in the 1970s shifted upward and to the right, and was more vertical. The economy experienced higher unemployment and inflation together—stagflation.

What caused this stagflation? The two main factors were supply-side shocks and changes in the labour market.

Supply Shocks

Supply-side shocks shifted the aggregate supply curve to the left, raising both the unemployment rate and the price level. These shocks included soaring oil prices,

□ □ □ □ □ □

The Phillips Curve in the 1980s

What shape did the Phillips curve take in the 1980s? The Consumer Price Index and unemployment rates for 1980-1990 are displayed in Table 20.1 below.

Table 20.1 Consumer Price Index and unemployment rates, 1980-90

	CONSUMER PRICE INDEX ANNUAL CHANGE	UNEMPLOYMENT RATE
1980	10.2	7.5
1981	12.4	7.5
1982	10.9	11.0
1983	5.7	11.8
1984	4.4	11.2
1985	3.9	10.5
1986	4.2	9.5
1987	4.4	8.8
1988	3.9	7.8
1989	5.1	7.5
1990	4.8	7.9
1991 (mid)	5.8	10.5

SOURCE: Statistics Canada.

Applications

1. Graph a Phillips curve using the data in Table 20.1.

2. In what ways do the shape and position of the Phillips curve for the 1980s differ from those of the Phillips curves shown in Figure 20.8 for:
(a) the 1960s
(b) the 1970s?

3. What relationship between unemployment and inflation does the curve for the 1980s suggest?

4. How would you describe economic conditions in the 1980s?

poor agricultural harvests, and the devaluation of the dollar.

In the 1970s and early 1980s, the Organization of Petroleum and Exporting Countries (OPEC), a cartel including many of the world's major oil producers, used its oligopolistic powers to raise oil prices more than eleven-fold, from less than $3 a barrel in 1973 to $34 a barrel in 1982. Then, after falling in the mid-1980s, oil prices began to rise once again at the end of the decade. Since oil is an essential resource for many industries, is used in fuel for transportation, and served to heat many homes and businesses in the 1970s and early 1980s, prices of most goods and services rose sharply.

Poor harvests in the Soviet Union and Asia in the early 1970s contributed to inflation by increasing the prices of agricultural products. The value of both the US and Canadian dollars also declined over the 1970s, pushing up the prices of imported goods and services.

Changes in the Labour Market

Changes in the labour market were mainly the result of the push by labour for higher wages to meet inflation and increased unemployment benefits.

With the accelerating inflation rates of the early 1970s, people expected that prices would continue to rise. Consequently, workers began to push for higher wages and cost of living adjustments in labour contracts. Rising wages increased costs and thus prices. Higher labour costs also meant higher unemployment.

The early 1970s also saw increases in unemployment benefits and easier terms of qualification. Some workers, therefore, were less willing to move to new locations to find work and others took more time to find new jobs. Frictional unemployment, therefore, increased.

These changes in the labour force shifted the aggregate supply curve to the left, increasing the price level and unemployment.

□ Income and Price Policies

Stagflation in the 1970s and 1980s, combined with the shift in the Phillips curve, led governments to look beyond fiscal and monetary policies for ways of stabilizing the economy. Attention turned to policies directed at incomes and prices to control inflation.

Prices and incomes policies represent attempts to control price and wage increases directly. Since 1969, the federal government has instituted controls on wages and/or prices four times.

In 1969, the federal government established the Prices and Incomes Commission headed by the economist, John Young. The Commission sought voluntary agreements with unions and businesses to limit wage and price increases. However, union representatives showed little support for wage restraints and the government made no attempt to enforce specific wage and price controls.

By the mid-1970s, Canada faced double-digit inflation. In the fall of 1975, the federal government instituted compulsory wage and price controls. Under the program, increases in wages and salaries were to be limited to 10 percent in the first year, 8 percent in the second, and 6 percent in the third.

Price increases were to be reviewed by an Anti-Inflation Board, which would allow increases only when higher costs could be proven. Profit statements and collective bargaining agreements were examined by the Board to ensure compliance with the controls.

The effectiveness of the program is a matter of controversy. In the first year, 1976, the inflation rate was significantly below that of 1975. However, when the Board approved of wage increases above the guidelines, those unions that had complied with the limits were embittered. As time went on, fewer unions were willing to stay within the guidelines, so that in 1977 and 1978, the inflation rate rose. By 1978, the inflation rate was at 9 percent—5 percent above the planned rate for that year.

The "Six and Five" Program (1982-1984)
In 1982, the federal government committed itself to limiting wage increases in the federal public sector to 6 percent in 1982/3 and 5 percent in 1983/4. Prices of goods and services subject to government regulation (e.g., agricultural products and transportation) would also be limited. The government appealed to provincial governments to follow its lead. No attempt was made, however, to control prices and wages in the private sector and the program met with opposition from public sector unions.

The success of the Six and Five Program is also subject to debate. The rate of inflation in Canada fell from 10 percent in 1982 to 5 percent in 1984. However, this decline was against an unemployment rate of 10 percent. Critics of the program have argued that with such high rates of unemployment, inflation would probably have fallen even without the controls.

Figure 20.9 The CPI and wage and price controls, 1969-1991

Percentage annual change in CPI

1969
Prices and Incomes Commission voluntary wage and price controls

1975-1978
Compulsory wage and price controls

1982-1984
Six and Five Program

1991-1994
Three-percent wage cap on federal public service employees

Since 1969, the federal government has instituted wage and/or price controls four times. The objective of most programs was to restrain inflation. The 3-percent wage cap, introduced in 1991, was aimed primarily at cutting government spending and reducing the deficit. Success of the programs has been the subject of much debate.

SOURCE: Statistics Canada, *Canadian Economic Observer*, Historical Statistical Supplement 1990/91 and September 1991.

The 3-Percent Annual Wage Cap (1991)

As part of its plan to cut the budget deficit and lower the rate of inflation from 5 percent in 1991 to a target of 2 percent by 1996, the federal government introduced a maximum 3-percent annual limit on federal public service wage increases in 1991. The program was to remain in effect for three years. Public sector unions vowed to fight the controls and went on strike to protest in the fall of 1991. The government passed back-to-work legislation and granted only minor wage concessions.

Figure 20.9 shows the effects of the government's wage and price control programs on the Consumer Price Index from 1969 to 1991.

☐ Problems With Wage and Price Controls

Though it may seem at first glance that wage and price controls should be an effective means of controlling inflation, since 1945 they have been used only infrequently. Why?

Long-Term Ineffectiveness

Experience with wage and price controls suggests that while they may control inflation for a short period, they are much less effective over the long term. While the Anti-Inflation Board was quite successful in its first year, for example, it was less successful in subsequent years and failed to achieve a lasting reduction in the inflation rate.

Lack of Control Over Import Prices

Prices of imports are beyond the control of the Canadian government. Imports make up between one-quarter and one-third of our GDP and their prices thus figure prominently in our cost of living. High prices of imports can raise the inflation rate significantly in Canada. Inflation can be imported. Some would argue that since prices cannot effectively be controlled, it is unreasonable to expect workers to accept wage limits.

Interference with Allocative Efficiency

Price controls interfere with the free operation of the market. As we have seen, prices provide information and rewards to producers. When the demand for goods and services increases, prices rise and producers are encouraged to increase production. Thus, consumer needs and wants are efficiently met. Price controls, however, limit the self-correcting mechanism of the market.

Limits on Economic Freedom

Wage and price controls restrict the economic freedom of individuals and groups. Wage limits work against one of the major reasons for the existence of labour unions—to improve the situation of their members. The freedom of workers to change jobs for better wages and benefits is also limited. Similarly, price controls mean that businesses must accept lower profits and competition is limited.

▌ Supply-Side Economics

As we have seen, fiscal and monetary policies focus on influencing aggregate demand. Some economists, however, appropriately called **supply-siders**, have suggested that economic policy is too demand-oriented. They argue that aggregate supply, and not aggregate demand, is the key force in determining levels of inflation, unemployment, and GDP. Stimulating the supply side of the economy—that is, increasing output—will decrease both inflation and unemployment. Two of the most prominent supply-side economists are Arthur Laffer and Robert Mundell.

We have already noted how supply shocks in the 1970s and 1980s shifted the aggregate supply curve to the left, bringing about stagflation. Supply-siders suggest a number of other reasons for the shift in the aggregate supply curve. Increasing taxes, in their view, reduced incentives to work, invest, and save. Real GDP, therefore, increased only slowly in the 1980s. Individuals and firms became increasingly discouraged as more of their incomes was taken in taxes. As a result, less was produced.

High taxes, the supply-siders argue, are also eventually incorporated into production costs and the burden is passed on to the consumer. Thus, taxes have a cost-push effect on prices. They constitute an artificial wedge between the cost of productive resources and purchase costs. This tax wedge shifts the aggregate supply curve to the left.

In addition, government regulations have discouraged competition and thus the incentives to produce efficiently and innovate. Social security programs, such as welfare and unemployment insurance, have also reduced incentives to work, particularly when the benefits are approximately equal to or higher than what people could earn in a job.

The key for the supply-siders, therefore, is to increase productivity and thus aggregate supply. How? The answer is through lower taxes, deregulation of industries, and lower government deficits. Lower taxes would give those with jobs greater incentives to work longer and harder because less of their incomes would be taken in taxes. The higher take-home pay would also encourage those not in the workforce to find jobs. Rewards for investment and entrepreneurial risk-taking would also be higher, encouraging investment spending and the establishment of new businesses. Deregulation of industries would increase competition and thus productivity. With lower deficits, there would be less competition between governments and businesses in capital markets. Thus interest rates would be lower and investment incentives for businesses would be greater. Businesses would not be "crowded out" of capital markets as much by government.

All of these measures would increase aggregate supply, shifting the aggregate supply curve to the right. Thus, the price level would fall and production and employment would increase.

☐ The Laffer Curve

Moreover, the supply-siders argue, tax cuts do not necessarily mean a significant reduction in tax revenues. Arthur Laffer, a prominent US supply-side economist, has argued that the net effect may actually be an increase in tax revenues.

The **Laffer curve**, shown in Figure 20.10, illustrates this effect. At tax rates of zero percent and 100 percent, the total tax revenue is the same—nothing. It is obvious that a zero tax rate produces no tax revenue, but the revenue is also zero at a tax rate of 100 percent because there is no incentive for anyone to produce.

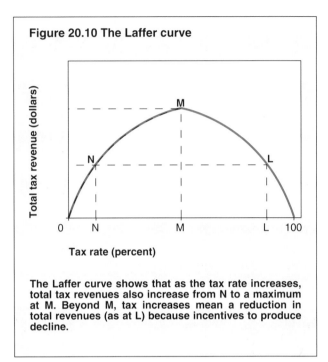

Figure 20.10 The Laffer curve

The Laffer curve shows that as the tax rate increases, total tax revenues also increase from N to a maximum at M. Beyond M, tax increases mean a reduction in total revenues (as at L) because incentives to produce decline.

According to Laffer, as tax rates increase from 0 to 100 percent, total tax revenues rise until they reach a maximum (at M) and then decline to zero. Beyond M, tax revenues decline because higher tax rates then have disincentive effects. In the view of the supply-siders, Canada and the US had moved beyond the maximum in the early 1990s.

An increase in the tax rate above 0M would decrease total tax revenues. Conversely, a decrease in the tax rate from 0M would increase incentives for production and thus increase total tax revenues.

☐ Reaganomics, 1980-1988

The ideas of the supply-siders provided the basis for the economic program introduced by President Reagan in the United States in 1981. This program, called Reaganomics, included the following elements: a reduction in government regulation of business, cuts in personal and corporate income taxes, and an attempt to control government expenditures (except on defence).

The effects of the policy were not exactly as the supply-siders had anticipated—at least in the short term. Consumer demand rose rapidly as the US recovered from the 1981-82 recession. The resulting rise in government revenues was not enough to offset the losses from the tax cuts.

Canadian governments did not adopt supply-side economics. Actions to reduce government ownership and regulation of businesses and to lower income and capital gains taxes, however, may have reflected supply-side policies.

Critics of supply-side economics argue that the impact of supply-side policies on saving, investment, and aggregate supply is likely to be minimal and far in the future. Large tax cuts significantly increase aggregate demand, but they are far less likely to have a major impact on aggregate supply. For example, a series of personal income tax cuts in the US under Reagan (totalling a 25-percent reduction) did not substantially increase saving and employment as the supply-siders had predicted.

■ Monetarism

In the 1960s, the Keynesian view of the economy, which had dominated economic thought since the 1940s, was challenged by another group of economists who reviewed, refined, and updated the ideas of the classical economists. This new group of economists believed that money was of central importance in the operation of the macroeconomy and they became known as monetarists. **Monetarism** asserts that the major cause of fluctuations in the macroeconomy is changes in the money supply. Nobel-prize winner and former professor of economics at the University of Chicago, Milton Friedman, is one of the best-known monetarists.

The Keynesians and monetarists differed on two key points—the basic stability of the economy and the role of government.

The Keynesian View
As we have seen, the Keynesians believe that the macroeconomy is essentially unstable. Prices and wages tend to be inflexible and seldom fall through the free operation of the market. The self-adjusting mechanisms of the market are not particularly effective. There is thus no guarantee that planned saving will equal planned investment at full employment to produce a stable economy, and so government must intervene to ensure economic stability. Fiscal policy is the most useful tool, with monetary policy playing a supporting role.

The Monetarists' View
Monetarists believe that the market system is inherently stable when free from the unwise and often harmful intervention of governments through discretionary fiscal and monetary policies. Government laws establishing rent controls, minimum wages, and price controls, for example, hinder the market's ability to adjust to changes automatically. Monetarists argue that the money supply—not changes in government spending and taxation—is key in the determination of GDP, income, and employment. Stabilization policy should, therefore, focus on control of the money supply.

□ The Velocity of Circulation

In the Keynesian view, total spending or aggregate demand is the sum of its parts: consumption (C), investment (I), government (G), and net foreign expenditures (X-M). However, the monetarists and other modern economists believe total spending can be viewed in another way—as a mass of moving money. This view arose from revisions and refinements of the monetary theories of the classical economists.

If we multiply the total money supply by the average number of times it is used over a particular period, then we can calculate aggregate demand. For example, suppose a particular $10-bill is used to buy cassette tapes in January. The owner of the store that sells the cassette tapes uses the $10 in February to buy gasoline. In July, the service station owner spends it at a summer resort. The resort uses it to pay the wages of a university student in August and finally that year, the $10 is spent by the university student to pay her tuition fees. In that year, the $10-bill has been used five times. The velocity of circulation was, therefore, five. If the bill

□ □ □ □ □ □

Economic Thinkers

Milton Friedman (b. 1912)

Two centuries after Adam Smith, the economist Milton Friedman reiterated Smith's basic message: Free markets, if left to operate without government interference, will largely resolve our economic problems. Milton Friedman is known today as a leader of the monetarist school, which emphasizes the importance of the money supply in the health of the economy.

Friedman worked as an economist for the US federal government in Washington during World War II and then became a professor of economics at the University of Chicago. In 1976, he was awarded the Nobel prize in economics for "his achievements in the field of consumption analysis, monetary history and theory, and for his demonstration of the complexity of stabilization policy." His publications include *Capitalism and Freedom* (1962), *A Monetary History of the US, 1867-1960* with Anna Schwartz (1963), *A Theoretical Framework for Monetary Analysis* (1971), and *Free to Choose* written with his wife, Rose Friedman (1980).

Friedman took his first economics courses at university in 1930 and 1931 in the depths of the Great Depression. Economics was an obvious choice for him since the Depression in Friedman's view was easily the "single most important issue facing the world." Since the 1930s, government involvement in the economic life of the US and other nations has increased tremendously. Friedman views this growing encroachment as unnecessary, wasteful, and dangerous to individual freedoms.

While [Friedman] is a sufficiently brilliant technical economist to have earned the Nobel Prize, he is also an irrepressible public advocate of his libertarian views [a school of thought that emphasizes the importance of individual freedom]. In fact, it is in this latter role. . . that Friedman has received most notice, or notoriety.

SOURCE: William J. Baumol and Alan S. Blinder, *Economics: Principles and Policy*, 4th ed. (New York: Harcourt Brace Jovanovich, 1988), p. 503.

Economic Freedom

The abolition of minimum wage legislation is but one part of a comprehensive and consistent pattern of actions modern capitalist economies should follow in Friedman's view. Tariffs, quotas, subsidies, and much social welfare should also be eliminated. Tariffs, quotas, and subsidies favour special interest groups at the expense of the general population and promote the inefficient allocation of resources. Social welfare legislation requires a large bureaucracy to administer it and provides little incentive for recipients to seek independence. In its stead, Friedman advocates the negative income tax, which has none of these disadvantages.

Friedman would also apply free market principles to the supply of education. Parents could be provided with vouchers equal in value to the cost of a child's education. They could spend the vouchers at any school of their choice. Schools would then develop to meet the demands of parents—who best know the needs of their children. Thus, there would be a variety of schools catering to the varied needs of students. Schools that did not attract sufficient students would go bankrupt and disappear.

Importance of the Money Supply

Friedman's lack of faith in the ability of government to solve economic problems also extends to the management of the macroeconomy. In the view of many economists, Friedman's most important contribution to economics is his views on the money supply. Friedman believes that adjusting the money supply through open market operations or changes in the bank rate will not resolve economic problems. In fact, such policies are more likely to exacerbate the problems. It takes time to recognize the problems and to act. Governments are always under pressure from particular interest groups, so that by the time action is taken, it is too late and often inappropriate. Government should, therefore, follow an invariable rule of raising the money supply by a fixed amount equal to the long-term growth rate of the economy—that is, between 3 and 5 percent.

Friedman views economics as Alfred Marshall viewed it, as "an engine for analyzing concrete problems. In practice, the analysis of economic problems always comes down to understanding the forces of supply and demand—using scarce resources to achieve alternative goals."

FRIEDMAN IN HIS OWN WORDS

The Role of Government

...the Great Depression, like most other periods of severe unemployment, was produced by government mismanagement rather than by any inherent instability of the private economy. A governmentally established agency— the Federal Reserve System [the central bank of the US]—has been assigned responsibility for monetary policy. In 1930 and 1931, it exercised this responsibility so ineptly as to convert what otherwise would have been a moderate contraction into a major catastrophe. Similarly today, governmental measures constitute the major impediments to economic growth in the United States. Tariffs and other restrictions on international trade, high tax burdens and a complex and inequitable tax structure, regulatory commissions, government price and wage fixing, and a host of other measures, give individuals an incentive to misuse and misdirect resources and distort the investment of new savings. What we urgently need, for both economic stability and growth, is a reduction of government intervention not an increase.

Such a reduction would still leave an important role for government in these areas. It is desirable that we use government to provide a stable monetary framework for a free economy—this is part of the function of providing a stable legal framework. It is desirable too that we use government to provide a general legal and economic framework that will enable individuals to produce growth in the economy, if that is in accord with their values.

1. What examples does Friedman give of government intervention in the economy?
2. In Friedman's view, what is the appropriate role of government in the economy? Do you agree? Explain.
3. How do Friedman's views compare with those of Adam Smith?
4. How do Friedman's views on government's role compare with those of J.M. Keynes?

A Monetary Rule

...How can we establish a monetary system that is stable and at the same time free from irresponsible governmental tinkering, a system that will provide the necessary monetary framework for a free enterprise economy yet be incapable of being used as a source of power to threaten economic and political freedom?

The only way that has yet been suggested that offers promise is to try to achieve a government of law instead of men by legislating rules for the conduct of monetary policy that will have the effect of enabling the public to exercise control over monetary policy through its political authorities, while at the same time it will prevent monetary policy from being subject to the day-by-day whim of political authorities....

In the present state of our knowledge, it seems to me desirable to state the rule in terms of the behavior of the stock of money. My choice at the moment would be a legislated rule instructing the monetary authority to achieve a specified rate of growth in the stock of money. For this purpose, I would define the stock of money as including currency outside commercial banks plus all deposits of commercial banks. I would specify that the Reserve System shall see to it that the total stock of money so defined rises month by month, and indeed, so far as possible, day by day, at an annual rate of x percent, where x is some number between 3 and 5. The precise definition of money adopted, or precise rate of growth chosen, makes far less difference than the definite choice of a particular definition and a particular rate of growth....

I should like to emphasize that I do not regard my particular proposal as a be-all and end-all of monetary management, as a rule which is somehow to be written in tablets of stone and enshrined for all future time. It seems to me to be the rule that offers the greatest promise of achieving a reasonable degree of monetary stability in the light of our present knowledge. I would hope that as we operated with it, as we learned more about monetary matters, we might be able to devise still better rules, which would achieve still better results. Such a rule seems to me the only feasible device currently available for converting monetary policy into a pillar of a free society rather than a threat to its foundations.

5. Why does Friedman believe it is necessary to have a rule for monetary policy? What is that rule?
6. How does Friedman view his rule?

SOURCE: Extracts taken from Milton Friedman, *Capitalism and Freedom* (Chicago: University of Chicago Press, 1963), pp. 38, 51, 54-55.

had been spent six times, the velocity of circulation would have been six.

The same concept can be applied to the total money supply in the economy. If the total money supply (M) is $5 billion, for example, and on average it is used to buy final goods and services once a month, the velocity of circulation (V) would be 12. Annual aggregate expenditure, therefore, would be $5 billion x 12 months = $60 billion.

The **velocity of circulation of money (V)** thus refers to the number of times, on average, a unit of money is spent on final goods and services in one year. In other words, it can be seen as the speed at which the stock of money is turned over. Since we cannot track how many billions of transactions occur in the Canadian economy over one year, how can we measure the velocity of circulation? One statistic that can give us some idea of how often transactions take place is GDP in current dollars or nominal GDP. Thus, we can calculate the velocity of circulation as follows:

$$\text{Velocity of circulation (V)} = \frac{\text{Value of transactions}}{\text{Stock of money (M)}}$$

$$V = \frac{\text{Nominal GDP}}{M}$$

or MV = GDP.

The Equation of Exchange

GDP in current dollars, as we have seen, is the total quantity of final goods and services produced in a particular period (Q) times the average price level (P). If MV = GDP, we can rewrite our familiar C + I + G + (X - M) = GDP equation in the following way:

$$MV = PQ$$

This formula is called the **equation of exchange** or the quantity equation of exchange. The equation of exchange is an identity. In effect, we are saying GDP = GDP. The equation relates the quantity of money to the value of goods exchanged, that is, it tells us that the money spent (MV) on the GDP is equal to the total amount of money received (PQ).

☐ The Quantity Theory of Money

The equation of exchange is the basis for the quantity theory of money. The **quantity theory of money** states that a change in the money supply, with a fairly stable velocity of circulation, will bring about a roughly proportional change in nominal GDP. For example, an increase in the money supply (M) of 10 percent will bring about an increase in the nominal GDP (PQ) of approximately 10 percent.

Clearly, if the velocity of money never changes—or changes only slightly—we have a very simple model for determining nominal GDP. The model could be used to predict nominal GDP from changes in the money supply, and nominal GDP could be controlled by simply changing the money supply.

In reality, however, the velocity of circulation does not remain stable, as Figure 20.11 shows. But according to the monetarists, changes are relatively minimal and predictable in the short run since the velocity of circulation is chiefly affected by institutional factors such as the frequency of wage payments. The more frequently wages are paid (weekly rather than monthly, for example), the less the need to hold money. Money consequently circulates more rapidly and the velocity of circulation factor thus increases. But, the frequency of wage payments does not vary considerably in the short run and so the velocity of circulation also does not vary significantly over the short run.

To understand how any action might affect the economy, then, the monetarists ask two main questions: How will the action affect the money supply and how will it affect the velocity of circulation?

In the equation of exchange (MV = PQ), if V is fairly stable over the short run, it is changes in the money supply (M) that will bring about changes in GDP or PQ. Since the monetarists believe the private sector of the economy is also relatively stable, it stands to reason that most fluctuations in nominal GDP are the result of changes in the money supply. Changes in the money supply are brought about by changes in monetary policy. Therefore, to ensure macroeconomic stability, governments should provide a stable money supply. Milton Friedman has suggested that governments adopt a policy rule of increasing the money supply at

Figure 20.11 The velocity of money circulation, 1970-1991

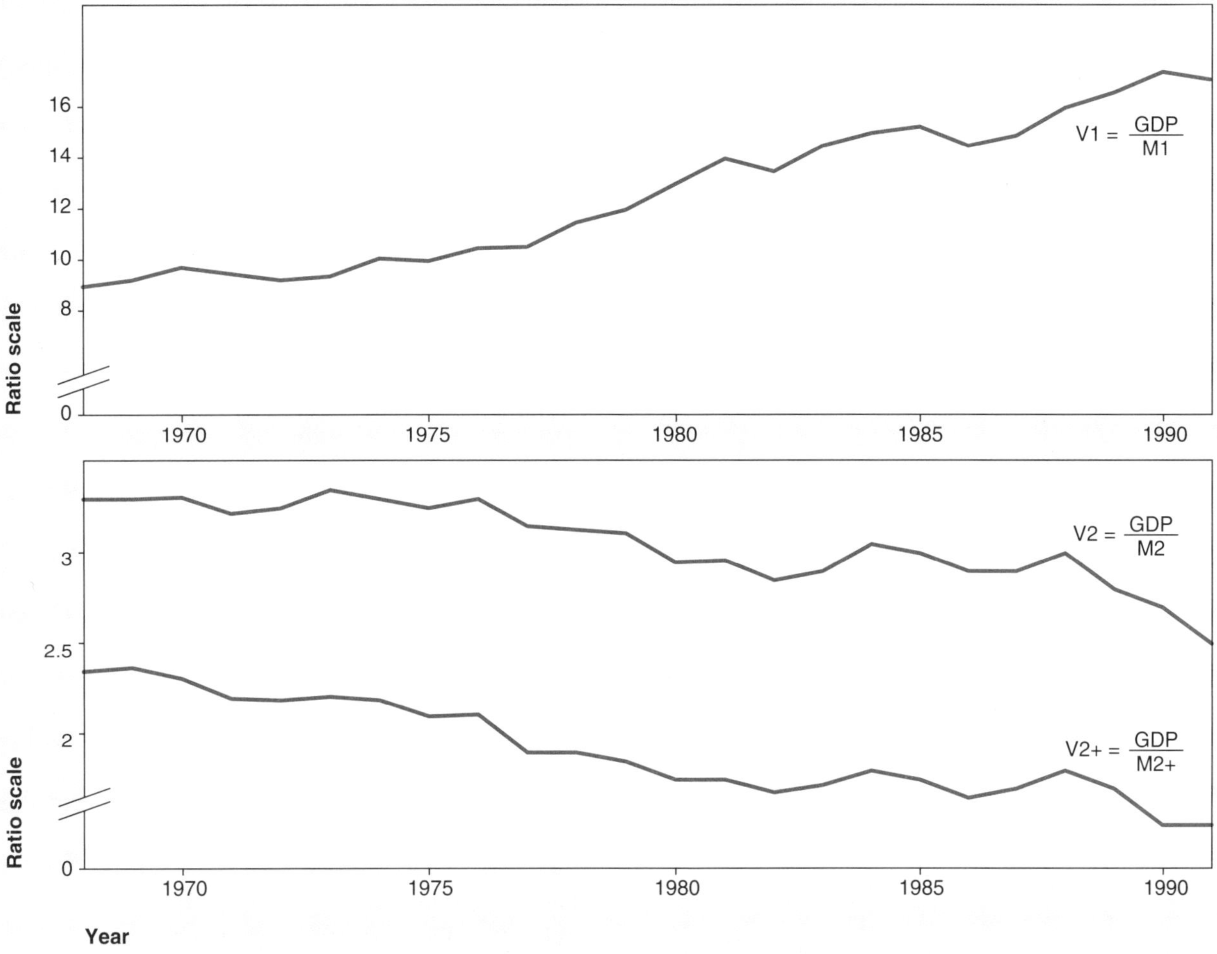

The stability of the velocity of circulation varies with the definition of the money supply. With the money supply defined as M1, the general trend since the mid-1970s has been upward. With the money supply defined as M2 and M2+, the velocity of circulation has been more stable over the period.

SOURCE: Statistics Canada and *Bank of Canada Review*, November 1991.

the rate of between 3 and 5 percent a year—approximately the rate of growth in the economy.

Monetarists do not believe that monetary policy has to go through a lengthy and uncertain transmission process before it affects GDP, as the Keynesians believe. With a fairly stable velocity of circulation, the impact of a change in the money supply on the price level (P), or the total quantity of final goods and services produced (Q), or both, will be direct and relatively quick.

The Experience With Monetary and Fiscal Policy

It would seem that the best way to resolve the debate between the Keynesians and the monetarists would be to look at the past and see what has, in fact, happened. Unfortunately, the real world does not provide us with a clear answer. At times, the facts seem to support the monetarist position and at other times, the Keynesian position.

In the late 1970s and 1980s, monetary policy was favoured by the federal government. Expenditure cuts and/or tax increases proved politically unacceptable with the government's large deficits. Thus, major fiscal policy actions were ruled out and monetary policy became the major means of stabilizing the economy.

☐ Recent Monetary Policy

Since 1975, we can identify four main periods in which the Bank of Canada adopted various policies based on monetarism.

Monetary Gradualism, 1975-1980

By the mid-1970s, the economy was experiencing a rapidly accelerating rate of inflation. The Bank of Canada adopted a policy of "monetary gradualism" to slow the inflation rate. The money supply would be permitted to grow within a predetermined target range. The objective of the policy was to check the growth of the money supply and thus curb the rate of inflation.

Between 1975 and 1980, the Bank was able to keep the growth of the money supply (defined as M1) within the target range. But between 1977 and 1981, though the growth of the money supply had slowed, the inflation rate accelerated. What happened? Clearly, with M1 being carefully controlled, the velocity of circulation increased rapidly (as Figure 20.11 shows). By 1982, the Bank formally abandoned its policy of monetary gradualism, though not its attempts to control aggregate demand through monetary policy.

Contractionary Monetary Policy, 1981-1983

To combat the rising inflation rate, the Bank of Canada followed the example set by the US central bank and imposed severe restraints on the growth of the money supply in 1981. As a result, interest rates rose rapidly in 1981—up to 20 percent for treasury bills. The rate of inflation thus plummeted from a peak of 12.7 percent in the third quarter of 1981 to 4.6 percent two years later. Interest rates were halved by 1983, but the cost was high. Unemployment rose to its highest level since the Great Depression—12.7 percent in early 1983. The economy was in a recession.

Recovery and the "Zero Inflation" Policy, 1983-1990

In the spring of 1983, the economy began to recover from its worst post-war recession. The main problem for the Bank of Canada during this period was to provide enough money to fuel the recovery, but not too much to spark inflation. Until 1987, many felt the Bank had been largely successful.

But by 1988, the Bank determined that inflation must be kept strongly in check and announced its inflation target. The target was to lower the inflation rate to 3 percent by the end of 1992, 2.5 percent by mid-1994, and 2 percent by the end of 1995—within 1 percent. The Bank defines inflation as a year-over-year increase in the CPI, excluding the volatile food and energy components. The Bank began to slow the rate of increase in the money supply and raise interest rates.

Recession and the Beginning of Recovery, 1991-1992

By 1990, the economy was in a recession and unemployment was increasing rapidly—especially in central Canada. With declining GDP, inflation rates began to fall to levels not seen since the 1970s, declining to 1.5 percent in 1992. The rate of increase in the money supply fell in 1991. Interest rates also fell and a weak recovery began in mid-1991 as the bank rate and inflation rate declined.

Summary

a. To combat unemployment during a recession, the Bank of Canada can implement an easy money policy to increase the money supply. As a result, banks could increase loans, lower interest rates, and thus make more money available for investment and consumer spending. Employment and GDP would then increase.

To combat inflation, the Bank of Canada could implement a tight money policy to decrease the money supply. As a result, banks would decrease loans, raise interest rates, and thus make less money available for investment and consumer spending. Prices would, therefore, fall.

b. A tight monetary policy during an inflationary expansion of the economy would reduce aggregate demand and shift the AD curve to the left. With the lower price level and real GDP, the peak of the business cycle would not be so sharp. An easy monetary policy during a recession would increase aggregate demand and shift the AD curve to the right. With the increased employment and real GDP, the economy's descent toward the trough of the business cycle would be smoothed. The overall effect of these monetary policies, therefore, would be to reduce the fluctuations of the business cycle and stabilize the economy.

c. Monetary policy has the advantages of greater political acceptability, speed of implementation, and flexibility over fiscal policy, but it is limited by an inability to target specific regions, a recognition lag, no guarantee that banks will be willing or able to loan more money with an easy money policy, conflicts with the management of the federal debt, ineffectiveness against cost-push inflation (in the Keynesian view), and a lengthy and uncertain transmission process.

d. In the Keynesian view, the key to both fiscal and monetary policy is control over the level of aggregate demand. Fiscal policy is the primary tool because monetary policy is limited by the lengthy transmission process and the possible ineffectiveness of an easy money policy in a recession or depression.

e. Demand-pull inflation occurs when aggregate demand exceeds capacity output at full employment. It originates from the demand side of the economy. Cost-push inflation occurs when suppliers' costs rise, thus pushing up prices. It originates from the supply side of the economy.

f. Economic conditions in the 1960s suggested a trade-off between inflation and unemployment. When inflation was low, unemployment was high. When unemployment was low, inflation was high. The British economist A. W. Phillips suggested an inverse relationship between inflation and unemployment rates, illustrated by the Phillips curve.

g. In the 1970s and 1980s, however, the economy experienced both high unemployment and high inflation together—that is, stagflation. Stagflation was the result of supply-side shocks and changes in the labour force that shifted the aggregate supply curve to the left, raising both unemployment and the price level. The supply shocks included soaring oil prices, poor agricultural harvests, and the devaluation of the dollar. The changes in the labour market included workers' demands for wage increases in line with inflation and higher unemployment benefits.

h. Price and income policies are attempts to control price and wage increases directly. Since 1969, the Canadian government has instituted several price and income policies, including voluntary restraints in 1969, compulsory wage and price controls in 1975, the "Six and Five Program" of wage restraints on federal public sector workers in 1982 (to 1984), and the 3-percent cap on wages of federal public service workers in 1991 (to 1996).

Price and income policies have limited long-term value since they cannot control the prices of imports and interfere with allocative efficiency and economic freedom.

i. Supply-side economists suggest that aggregate supply and not aggregate demand is the key to controlling levels of employment, inflation, income, and GDP. They believe that stimulating the supply side of the economy—or increasing output through lower taxes, deregulation of industries, and decreased social security program spending—will lower both inflation and unemployment. The Laffer curve shows that tax cuts may in fact increase tax revenues by increasing incentives to produce to a particular point. Critics of supply-side economics argue that the effects of such policies on aggregate supply are minimal and slow.

j. Monetarism is a school of economic thought which asserts that the major cause of economic fluctuations is changes in the money supply. Based on the idea that the velocity of circulation of money in the economy is fairly stable over the short term, monetarists believe governments should promote economic stability by maintaining a stable money supply. Other government interference in the market, they feel, is unwise and may be harmful.

k. Milton Friedman, a leading monetarist, believes that markets—if left to function freely without government interference—will largely resolve economic problems. He believes that instead of controlling the money supply to stabilize the economy, governments should adopt a rule to increase the money supply by an amount equal to the rate of economic growth—that is, between 3 and 5 percent.

l. Between 1975 and 1992, four main periods in the Bank of Canada's monetary policy can be identified. Between 1975 and 1980, the Bank allowed the money supply to grow within a limited range to slow the rate of inflation. Between 1981 and 1983, the Bank imposed severe restraints on the increase in the money supply to cut the rapidly rising rate of inflation. From 1983 to 1990, the Bank sought to provide enough money to fuel the economic recovery after the 1982-83 recession, but not too much to feed inflation. With the onset of the 1990-91 recession, interest rates and the inflation rate dropped dramatically.

∎ Review of Key Terms

Define the following key terms introduced in this chapter and provide examples where appropriate.

easy money policy
tight money policy
demand-pull inflation
cost-push inflation
stagflation
Phillips curve
prices and incomes
   policy

supply-side economics
Laffer curve
monetarism
velocity of circulation of
   money
equation of exchange
quantity theory of
   money

∎ Application and Analysis

1. For each situation listed in Figure 20.12, indicate whether the Bank of Canada should act to increase or decrease aggregate demand, increase or decrease the bank rate, and buy or sell government bonds.

Figure 20.12 Monetary action

	AGGREGATE DEMAND (INCREASE OR DECREASE?)	BANK RATE (INCREASE OR DECREASE?)	GOVERNMENT BONDS (BUY OR SELL?)
(a) Unemployment is at the high level of 11 percent and is expected to increase.			
(b) Inflation is at 12 percent and rising.			
(c) Retail sales are falling and inventories are piling up. Consumer confidence is at an all-time low.			
(d) Business investment is increasing and inventories are being rapidly depleted. Business confidence is high.			

2. You are an economic advisor to the prime minister and you have the following statistics on the state of the economy before you.

Table 20.2 Statistics on the state of the economy

	THIS QUARTER LAST YEAR	LAST QUARTER	ESTIMATE FOR QUARTER NOW ENDING
Real GDP (annual rate in billions of constant dollars)	132.75	128.00	126.00
Consumer Price Index	120	124	124.3
Unemployment Rate	5.1	10.2	10.3
Business Fixed Capital Investment (annual rate in billions of constant dollars)	21.35	20.20	20.10
Business Inventories (annual rate in billions of constant dollars)	1.67	0.60	0.63

(a) Based on these statistics, what would you say is the major economic problem?

(b) What economic goals are you most interested in achieving?

(c) What specific monetary policies would you institute to achieve these goals?

(d) What specific fiscal policies would you institute to achieve these goals?

3. In Figure 20.13 below, decide which policy in each pair would be most effective to combat a recession and inflation and explain why in each case.

4. Decide whether an expansionary or contractionary monetary policy would increase or decrease each item listed in Figure 20.14 on page 442.

5. Suppose the Canadian economy is only slowly recovering from a recession, as it was in 1991. The economic outlook is for continuing high unemployment rates above 10 percent, slow growth of less than 2 percent, and a low inflation rate of less than 2 percent. Annual federal budget deficits are expected to rise above the $30.5 billion mark to $32 billion despite an increase in unemployment insurance premiums to pay for increased expenditures on benefits. Over the past seven years, the value of the Canadian dollar increased steadily from 71 to 89 cents US. Consider the following views on what the government should do.

View #1 Finance Minister The finance minister believes any quick-fix schemes are illusory. The government cannot institute increases in expenditures or

Figure 20.13 Fiscal and monetary policies

	COMBAT RECESSION	COMBAT INFLATION
Fiscal policy		
(a) raise income taxes		
(b) lower income taxes		
(a) increase government spending		
(b) decrease government spending		
Monetary policy		
(a) raise the bank rate		
(b) lower the bank rate		
(a) buy government bonds		
(b) sell government bonds		

Figure 20.14 Effects of monetary policies

	EXPANSIONARY MONETARY POLICY	CONTRACTIONARY MONETARY POLICY
(a) consumer spending		
(b) investment in factories and machines		
(c) inventory investment		
(d) inflation		
(e) unemployment		
(f) interest rates		
(g) the money supply		
(h) the rate of economic growth		

tax cuts if it is to reduce its budget deficit. Interest rates should continue their slow decline, but only as the rate of inflation declines.

View #2 University Economist This economist generally agrees with the views of the finance minister, but rejects the government's fiscal policy stance. He believes the government's move to raise unemployment insurance premiums by 30 percent has, in fact, put a tax on employment when there is widespread unemployment. The government should be allowing the automatic stabilization that increased unemployment benefit spending would provide.

View #3 Bank Vice-President and Chief Economist This economist believes the government has few fiscal policy options because of the massive deficit. She recommends cutting interest rates and lowering the value of the Canadian dollar. She also recommends a cut in the GST to 5 percent from 7 percent.

View #4 Canadian Manufacturers Association Economist This economist recommends a reduction in the Canadian dollar to 78 cents US and an investment tax credit.

View #5 University Economist The suggestion from this economist is that the government allow people to take money out of tax-sheltered savings without a tax penalty. For example, people could take $20 000 tax-free out of RRSPs and spend it.

View #6 President of the Canadian Federation of Independent Business This president advocates a 1-percent cut in the GST and provincial sales taxes. This move would boost consumer confidence and perhaps stimulate the economy enough to offset the temporary loss in government tax revenues.

View #7 President of the Atlantic Provinces Economic Council This president affirms that, during recessions, governments should temporarily allow deficits to increase to preserve jobs and keep the economy functioning as smoothly as possible. He cites a proposed four-lane expansion of the Trans-Canada Highway in the Atlantic Provinces as an example of the kind of project governments should undertake immediately.

(a) Assess the pros and cons of each view outlined above.

(b) Which view or views do you support? Explain why.

6. What policies would each of the following have recommended during the 1982-83 recession? Refer to pages 339-41 for information on this recession. Briefly outline the reasoning behind each position.

(a) a Keynesian economist

(b) a monetarist

(c) a supply-side economist

(d) Milton Friedman

Economic Growth and International Trade

Of the six major objectives for the Canadian economy we outlined in Chapter 2, there remain two we have not yet addressed—economic growth and a viable balance of payments. These two objectives are the focus of this final unit. In our examination of economic stability in Unit Four, our focus was primarily on the short run and on aggregate demand. In addressing economic growth in Chapter 21, our focus shifts to the long run and primarily to aggregate supply. We examine growth and productivity in Canada and less developed nations, considering both the costs and benefits of economic progress.

In the final two chapters of this unit, we turn to international trade and the goal of a viable balance of payments. We consider the importance, composition, and direction of Canadian external trade and the arguments for and against trade. Then, we turn to trade policy and the movements toward freer trade—the globalization of national economies—since 1945.

□ □ □ □ □ □

CHAPTER TWENTY-ONE

Economic Growth and Productivity

Few people would argue that Canadians today have a much higher standard of living than they did a century ago. We enjoy a greater variety of food, clothing, and entertainment. Our opportunities for education, travel, and recreation have increased substantially. We have better housing with running hot and cold water, central heating, and a vast array of electrical appliances. Our real income per capita, the statistic economists generally use to measure our standard of living, has increased in 1981 dollars from less than $2000 in 1870 to over $20 000 in 1990. How can we account for this increase in standard of living? Many attribute it to our economic growth.

In this chapter, we examine how we define economic growth, various determinants of growth, its costs and benefits, and its limitations.

Objectives

a. Define economic growth and examine its relationship to standard of living and the productivity of labour.

b. Outline the general trends in Canada's economic growth since Confederation.

c. Apply the rule of 72 to calculations of future economic growth and the accumulation of savings.

d. Examine and assess the ideas of Thomas Malthus on population and economic growth.

e. Analyze and apply the capital accumulation model as a way of explaining economic growth.

f. Assess the major determinants of economic growth.

g. Evaluate the costs and benefits of economic growth and consider its limitations.

h. Analyze the reasons why the economic growth of less developed countries has been hindered.

i. Evaluate the major arguments in the debate over why the less developed countries have not broken out of the poverty cycle and how they might best achieve the benefits of economic growth.

What Is Economic Growth?

How can we define economic growth? In Chapter 2, we noted that economic growth is measured as an increase in real GDP. But an increase in real GDP alone does not mean that a country's people are better off. The population of Canada has risen substantially over the last century. If the percentage increase in real output had been less than the percentage increase in population, the amount of goods and services available per person would have declined. In other words, our real income or GDP per capita would be less and we would not be as well off. **Economic growth**, therefore, is often defined as a sustained increase in real GDP *per capita*.

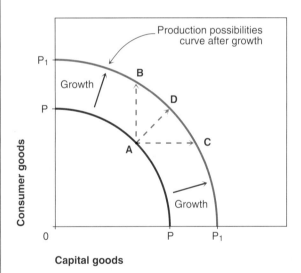

Figure 21.1 Economic growth and the production possibilities curve

Economic growth is shown as the outward movement of the production possibilities curve from PP to P₁P₁. If population has not increased, more consumer and/or capital goods are available per person. If the economy formerly produced at A, it could choose to produce more consumer goods and the same amount of capital goods at B on P₁P₁, more capital goods and the same amount of consumer goods at C, or more consumer and capital goods at D.

Note that this definition also specifies that growth must be sustained. Real GDP per capita is usually measured annually, but only when increases are recorded over a number of years has growth actually taken place.

Economic growth is also associated with an increase in productive capacity. An increase in productive capacity implies an increase in all productive resources—land, labour, and capital—but it most commonly refers to an increase in the productivity of labour. In Canada, we have not only produced more goods and services, but we have produced them with fewer working hours. The **productivity of labour**, or the output per hour of labour, has increased significantly. Since 1926, the average work week in manufacturing has decreased by about 40 percent—from 55 to 35 hours.

Economic growth, therefore, can be illustrated by the outward movement of the production possibilities curve shown in Figure 21.1. With the increase in productive capacity and the new curve P_1P_1, the society can choose to produce more consumer goods with the same amount of capital goods, more capital goods and the same amount of consumer goods, or more consumer and capital goods.

Economic Growth in Canada

Figure 21.2 on page 446 illustrates the path of economic growth in Canada since 1870. While the path has not been smooth, the overall trend has been upward. Periodic downturns are evident primarily with the Great Depression during the 1930s and other recessions, most recently in 1990-1991.

Upswings have occurred with expansions of key export industries in the early 1900s and again in the 1920s, and with surges of immigration to open the West in the early 1900s and again in the late 1950s and early 1960s. Remarkably, the two world wars in the century have also been marked by increases in real GDP per capita. The questions this fact raises we will consider later in this chapter.

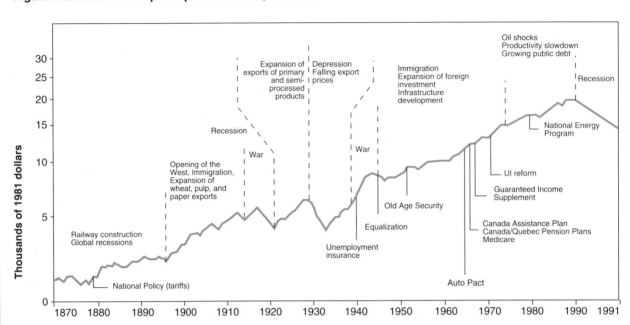

Figure 21.2 Real income per capita in Canada, 1870-1991

The general trend has been an increase in Canadians' real income per capita since 1870. Note that periods of increased exports, higher investment, and war are associated with rising real income per capita. Recessions and depressions are periods of declining real income per capita.

SOURCE: M.C. Urquhart, "Canadian economic growth, 1870-1980," Discussion Paper No. 734, Institute for Economic Research, Queen's University, Kingston, Ont., 1988, and estimates by the Economic Council, based on data from Statistics Canada.

■ Theories of Economic Growth

Thomas Malthus presented one of the earliest theories of economic growth in his book *Essay on the Principle of Population* (1798).

□ Malthus and the Malthusians

Malthus's basic view was that the growth of population far outstrips the earth's capacity to provide food. The best the future can provide, therefore, is a subsistence standard of living. (See pp. 448-49).

During the nineteenth and early twentieth centuries, however, Malthus's predictions began to lose their credibility. The development of new technology, improved agricultural practices, and the application of increasing amounts of capital (labour, machinery, and equipment, for example) enabled food production to increase faster than the increase in population in industrialized nations. In addition, as living standards increased, the birth rate began to fall. The increase in population was checked. With the optimism that accompanied the advances of the nineteenth and early twentieth centuries, it seemed that population expansion posed no threat human ingenuity could not handle.

More recently, however, population growth has again raised concern—particularly in the less developed countries of Africa, Asia, and South America.

□ □ □ □ □ □

Skill Development: The Rule of 72

Some people are astonished that economists (among others) express concern when the rate of economic growth falls by 1 or 2 percent a year. After all, what could a few percentage points matter? The answer is—a great deal over the long run. To you as you grow older and to your children and grandchildren, it could matter very much.

How much? The rule of 72 is one way of finding out. The **rule of 72** is a simple approximation device for calculating how long it takes for a given income to double at various growth rates. The formula is as follows:

$$\frac{72}{\text{Percentage growth rate}} = \begin{array}{c}\text{Number of years for income to}\\\text{double}\end{array}$$

For example, suppose our economy is growing at 2 percent per year. How long, approximately, will it take for our real GDP to double?

$$\frac{72}{2} = 36 \text{ years}$$

The rule of 72 can also be used to calculate how long it takes to double money at various interest rates, assuming no tax payments. For example, if you have $1000 in a chequing-savings account earning 4 percent interest, how long would it take to double your money?

$$\frac{72}{4} = 18 \text{ years}$$

Applications

1. Complete Table 21.1 below.

Table 21.1 Applying the rule of 72

	ANNUAL GROWTH RATES (PERCENT)			
	2	4	6	9
1990 GDP in billions of current dollars	670	670	670	670
Number of years needed to double real GDP	36	18		
GDP in 2026, assuming a constant growth rate	$1340 billion	$2680 billion		
If Canadian population in 2026 is 50 million, real GDP per person in 1990 dollars. In 1990 real GDP per capita was approximately $25 500.	$26 800			

2. Suppose that instead of putting your $1000 in the chequing-savings account at 4 percent interest, you decide to buy a government bond that yields 8 percent interest. Assuming you pay no income tax, how much more would your bond be worth than the chequing-savings deposit in 18 years?

Improved hygiene, better health care (with vaccinations and antibiotics), cleaner drinking water, and other developments have led to a rapidly declining death rate, but no corresponding decline in the birth rate. Consequently, populations in these nations have increased dramatically. While some nations have increased their real GDP, living standards have not improved significantly since much of the increase in real income has been distributed over a larger population.

Neo-Malthusians argue that significant increases in real GDP per capita are only possible when there is a significant reduction in the rate of population growth. Indeed, some have argued that the objective should be zero population growth.

□ **Capital Accumulation Model**

Malthus based his analysis on the scarcity of land. Since 1800, however, economic development has focussed not on land, but primarily on large investments of capital—that is, factories, equipment, and machinery.

☐ ☐ ☐ ☐ ☐ ☐

Economic Thinkers

Thomas Robert Malthus (1766-1834)

Thomas Malthus was an English economist who pioneered the modern study of population and presented one of the first theories related to economic growth. He was a contemporary and very good friend of David Ricardo. Though the two men disagreed constantly, they did not disagree over Malthus's views on population.

Malthus's best-known work, *Essay on the Principle of Population As It Affects the Future Improvement of Society*, was published anonymously in 1798. Malthus chose the ministry as his profession, but in 1805 was appointed professor of history and economics at a college of the East India Company near London. From this appointment, he has a claim to be the first professional economist.

Malthus's thought was influenced by the economic conditions in Britain during the late 1700s and early 1800s. The nation was in the midst of the Industrial Revolution, with workers crowding into the cities and struggling to survive on subsistence wages. A prolonged war with France, which began in the 1790s and ended with the defeat of Napoleon at Waterloo in 1815, aggravated the plight of the people. Poor crops also pushed prices up to near-famine levels, particularly as the population was increasing rapidly. It seemed that the growth of population was outstripping the ability of the land to feed the people.

. . .[Malthus] embodied many contradictions. Physically, he was handsome, known to be generous and kind with a wealth of ideas to share, but he had a speech defect that made him difficult to understand. Personally, he was interested in the tangible world, in mathematics, and in exactness; however, his chosen field was the ministry. And intellectually, Malthus had rather brutal, frightening ideas about the future that fit neither his character nor his original profession.

SOURCE: From ECONOMICS: OUR AMERICAN ECONOMY by E. L. Schwartz. Copyright © 1990 by Longman Publishing Group.

Population Growth and Productivity

Malthus's ideas on population and economics were based on two premises, both of which he regarded as self-evident. The first is that food is necessary for human life and the second that the sexual instinct will continue unchanged in the future.

From these two premises, Malthus deduced that the power of population to grow is much greater than the ability of the earth to provide food. Unchecked, the population would double every generation. It grows in a geometrical progression (1, 2, 4, 8, 16, 32, 64, 128, 256, 512). The best we can expect of food production is that it will increase by the amount of food currently produced in each 25-year period. Food production can be increased only in an arithmetical progression (1, 2, 3, 4, 5, 6, 7, 8, 9, 10).

To feed the growing population, existing agricultural land must be cultivated more intensively and inferior land must be brought into cultivation. As increasing amounts of labour are used to cultivate the fixed stock of land, the productivity of each additional worker declines.

Thus, the natural tendency is for the growth of population to outstrip, by far, the increase in food production. In 225 years the ratio of population to food production would be 512 to 10!

Checks on Population Growth

Obviously then, significant checks must be placed on the growth of population. These Malthus called preventive checks (those which decrease births) and positive checks (those which result in a shorter life). The preventive checks include moral restraints, such as postponement of marriage. The positive checks—which include wars, famine, pestilence, disease, and epidemics—are the ultimate controllers of population increase.

The Future

For Malthus, the future is bleak. If wages rise above the minimal level of subsistence—in other words, if the standard of living should rise—more children will survive to have yet more children. Then, as the growth in population outstrips food production, living standards will fall below subsistence levels. Fewer children will survive to adulthood as positive checks control the population growth. Population will then decline and the standard of living can rise to the minimal level of subsistence once again.

Thus, while the standard of living may for a time rise above (or fall below) the minimum level of subsistence, in the long run it will return to the minimum level. Public welfare would be worse than useless—it would ensure that more children are born and survive and have children—resulting in more misery.

MALTHUS IN HIS OWN WORDS

Scarcity of Land and Population Growth

It may safely be pronounced,...that population, when unchecked, goes on doubling itself every twenty-five years, or increases in a geometrical ratio.

The rate according to which the productions of the earth may be supposed to increase, it will not be so easy to determine. Of this, however, we may be perfectly certain, that the ratio of their increase in a limited territory must be of a totally different nature from the ratio of the increase of population. A thousand millions are just as easily doubled every twenty-five years by the power of population as a thousand. But the food to support the increase from the greater number will by no means be obtained with the same facility. Man is necessarily confined in room.

1. Why does Malthus believe that population growth will outstrip food production on the earth?

An Illustration

Let us suppose...that the produce of this island [Britain] might be increased every twenty-five years by a quantity equal to what it at present produced. The most enthusiastic speculator cannot suppose a greater increase than this. In a few centuries it would make every acre of land in the island like a garden.

If this supposition be applied to the whole earth, and if it be allowed that the subsistence for man which the earth affords might be increased every twenty-five years by a quantity equal to

what it at present produces, this will be supposing a rate of increase much greater than we can imagine that any possible exertion of mankind could make it.

It might be fairly pronounced, therefore, that, considering the present average state of the earth, the means of subsistence, under circumstances the most favourable to human industry, could not possibly be made to increase faster than in an arithmetical ratio.

The necessary effects of these two different rates of increase, when brought together, will be very striking. Let us call the population of this island eleven millions; and suppose the present production equal to the easy support of such a number. In the first twenty-five years the population would be twenty-two millions, and the food being also doubled, the means of subsistence would be equal to this increase. In the next twenty-five years the population would be forty-four millions, and the means of subsistence only equal to the support of thirty-three millions. In the next period the population would be eight-eight millions, and the means of subsistence just equal to the support of half that number. And, at the conclusion of the first century, the means of subsistence only equal to the support of fifty-five millions, leaving a population of a hundred and twenty-one millions totally unprovided for.

Taking the whole earth, instead of this island, emigration would of course be excluded; and, supposing the present population equal to a thousand millions, the human species would increase as the numbers, 1, 2, 3, 8, 16, 128, 256, and subsistence as 1, 2, 3, 4, 5, 6, 7, 8,

9. In two centuries the population would be to the means of subsistence as 256 to 9; in three centuries as 4096 to 13, and in two thousand years the difference would be almost incalculable.

2. (a) Describe the conditions Malthus predicted for the future. Have his predictions been fulfilled? Explain.

(b) What factors have allowed some nations to support substantial population increases?

The Checks on Population Growth

On examining these obstacles to the increase of population which I have classed under the heads of preventive and positive checks, it will appear that they are all resolvable into moral restraint, vice, and misery.

Of the preventive checks, the restraint from marriage which is not followed by irregular gratifications may properly be termed moral restraint.

Promiscuous intercourse [...] is a preventive check that clearly comes under the head of vice.

Of the positive checks, those which appear to arise unavoidably from the laws of nature, may be called exclusively misery; and those which we obviously bring upon ourselves, such as wars, excesses, and many others which it would be in our power to avoid, are of a mixed nature. They are brought upon us by vice, and their consequences are misery.

3. Why does Malthus suggest that the positive checks are the ultimate controllers of population increase?

SOURCE: Extracts taken from Howard D. and Natalie J. Marshall, *The History of Economic Thought: A Book of Readings* (New York: Putnam, 1968), pp. 65, 66-67, 69.

The steam engine revolutionized industrial production and transportation in the nineteenth century—as have gasoline, diesel, and electric engines, computers, and robotics in this century. Some economists, therefore, have attempted to explain economic growth by the **capital accumulation model**.

Let's examine the model in its simplest form first. We start with four assumptions:

(i) Output is produced by labour and capital.
(ii) The main variable is the stock of capital.
(iii) The level of technology remains constant.
(iv) Population and labour are fixed.

Figure 21.3 is a graphical illustration of the model. As increasing amounts of capital are used by the fixed labour force, output increases but at a slower rate than the increase in capital due to diminishing returns. The rate of return on each additional unit of capital, therefore, declines. The rate of return on each additional capital investment is known as the **marginal efficiency of capital (MEC)**. Assuming fixed labour and

technology, the MEC curve slopes down to the right.

Wages, however, increase as each worker has more capital to work with and his or her productivity increases. Thus, the marginal product of labour, or the amount each additional worker can produce, rises.

The Development of Technology

As we know, however, technology does not remain constant. In Europe and North America, a steady flow of inventions—especially over the last two centuries—has led to the outward shift of the MEC curve, as shown in Figure 21.4. Both labour and capital have become more productive. More goods can be produced with the same amount of resources as before. Technological change has largely kept pace with the diminishing returns to capital. As a result, the rate of return to capital has remained fairly constant, while worker productivity and thus real wages have increased. In Europe and North America, the increasing capital to worker ratio and the application of new technologies have led to a higher GDP per person—that is, a higher standard of living.

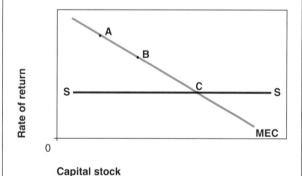

Figure 21.3 Marginal efficiency of capital

As the capital stock increases from A to B to C, the rate of return on capital declines because of the law of diminishing returns. In the absence of technological change, increases in the stock of capital are represented by a movement down along the MEC curve. Eventually, the rate of return may be so low that no further increase in capital takes place—as at C. At this point, growth in output comes to a halt.

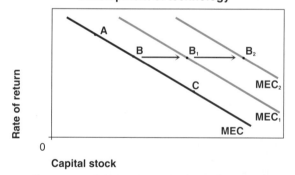

Figure 21.4 Marginal efficiency of capital and the development of technology

Advances in technology shift the MEC curve to the right, to MEC$_1$ and later MEC$_2$ as productivity increases. If technological change keeps pace with diminishing returns to capital, then an economy at B moves to B$_1$ and then B$_2$, rather than down the MEC curve to C. The rate of return remains fairly constant at B$_1$ and B$_2$, while the capital stock increases. Consequently, while real interest rates and profits remain relatively unchanged, labour productivity and thus real wages rise significantly.

Sources of Economic Growth in Canada

What factors, then, contribute to economic growth? The determinants of growth can be classified in two ways: by their quantity and their quality or productivity.

☐ The Quantity of Resources

Clearly, the greater the quantity of resources available, the greater the potential for growth. As we have seen from the example of the capital accumulation model, the more capital available per worker, the greater the potential output per worker. Quantities of three major resources have contributed to economic growth in Canada—our natural resources, labour force, and capital stock.

Growth of the Labour Force

The increase in the labour force has been one of the principal spurs to economic growth. Canada's total labour force grew from 4.5 million in 1945 to 13.8 million in 1991.

The growth of the labour force can be attributed to the natural increase in population, immigration, and increasing participation rates. While birth rates and immigration rates have slowed since the 1950s, this trend has been counterbalanced by the increasing participation of women in the Canadian labour force. In 1946, the female participation rate was 24.7 percent. By 1990, it had more than doubled to 58.4 percent. The net result of the birth, immigration, and changing participation rates is that our total labour force is currently growing by approximately 200 000 workers a year.

Generally, a larger labour force means a higher real output. However, if technology and other productive factors remain unchanged, diminishing returns will set in since the productivity of labour depends in large part on the technology and capital resources with which it works. The quantity and quality of other productive factors, therefore, must keep pace with the increase in the labour force if the economy is to grow. If the labour force grows too quickly, unemployment may result. If it grows too slowly, productive factors will remain unemployed and the economy will be operating below its potential.

Natural Resources

Canada, like Australia and Russia, is richly endowed with natural resources. Minerals, fresh water, productive farmland, and forests, for example, are available in relative abundance. The Canadian economy has relied heavily on its natural resource base in the past for its growth.

But a rich endowment of natural resources does not guarantee economic growth. Indonesia, for example, has a wealth of natural resources, but its economic growth rate has been slow and its per capita income is low. On the other hand, two countries with the highest economic growth rates and incomes per capita in the world are Switzerland and Japan—both of which are relatively poorly endowed with natural resources.

An abundant natural resource base, therefore, is important for economic growth but does not guarantee it.

Capital Resources

Canadian workers enjoy one of the highest ratios of capital to worker in the world. On average, each worker has over $75 000 in capital with which to work and in some industries, the figure is even higher. In the petroleum industry, for example, the ratio is $250 000 in capital for every worker. Since 1945, the amount of capital per worker in Canada has increased three-fold.

Capital investment accounts for approximately one-fifth of Canada's GDP. The main sources of investment funds are personal, business, and foreign savings, and bank credit. Compared with Americans (though not with the Japanese), Canadians save a high proportion of their disposable incomes and these savings are a major source of investment funds. The Canadian personal savings rate for most years between 1975 and 1990 was well above 10 percent (with the exceptions of 1987 and 1988, when it dipped below this figure). In the US, the personal savings rate averages at about 5 percent.

The retained earnings of businesses account for about half of total investment. Much of foreign investment comes from the reinvestment of earnings by foreign-owned corporations in Canada. Banks and other financial intermediaries, such as trust and mortgage loan companies, credit unions, and caisses populaires, provide the fourth source of investment funds.

Over the period 1926 to 1991, annual business fixed capital investment increased from $5.5 billion to $105 billion. The Canadian population increased from 9.5 to 27 million over the same period. Thus, increasing amounts of capital became available per person.

Figure 21.5 shows the trends since 1971 in the major components of capital investment—residential construction, non-residential construction, machinery and equipment, and business inventories. Total investment has shown a significant increase over the period, particularly in the machinery and equipment component, though all four categories registered declines during the recessions of 1974-75, 1982-83, and 1990-91. By encouraging investment during a recession and discouraging it during expansions, government can either promote economic growth or check it.

Figure 21.6 illustrates the impact capital investment can have on economic growth by comparing the capital investment of Canada and Japan since 1965. In 1965, production possibilities per person were much greater in Canada than in Japan. While Canada devoted one-fifth of its productive resources to capital goods after 1965, Japan devoted about one-third. As a result, Japan's production possibilities curve moved outward more rapidly than Canada's, so that by 1991 the curves of the two nations were roughly at the same point. If Japan continues to invest a larger proportion of its resources in capital, its economy will continue to grow more rapidly than Canada's.

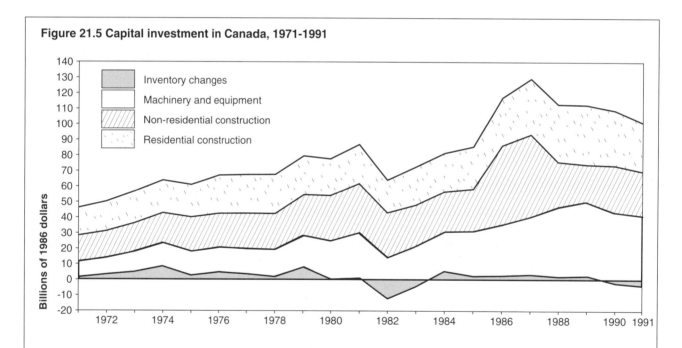

Figure 21.5 Capital investment in Canada, 1971-1991

Since 1971, total investment in Canada has increased significantly. The largest increase has been in machinery and equipment investment. All categories declined during the recessions of 1974-75, 1982-83, and 1990-91, particularly business inventories.

SOURCE: *Bank of Canada Review*, November 1991.

□ The Quality of Resources

Just as the quantity of resources can affect productivity, so too can their quality. The potential for growth increases with increases in the quality of a resource and/or an improvement in its combination with other resources.

Quality of Human Resources

Among the factors affecting the quality of human resources—or human capital—are the health, education, and training of the labour force, and the skills of managers and entrepreneurs.

Improvements in the health and life span of workers are, of course, desirable in themselves. Healthy workers are also less likely to lose time through sickness and absenteeism, and thus are generally more productive.

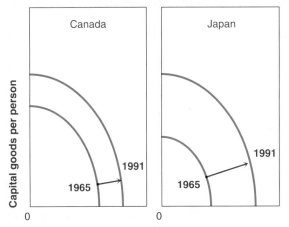

Figure 21.6 A comparison of economic growth in Canada and Japan (production possibilities per person)

Production possibilities per person in 1965 were much greater in Canada than in Japan. However, while Canada invested one-fifth of its productive resources in capital goods, Japan invested one-third. Japan's production possibilities per person curve thus shifted outward more rapidly than Canada's. By 1991, the two curves were approximately at the same point.

Economists are concerned, however, that as the "baby boomers" reach retirement age, an increasingly large group of non-workers will have a legitimate claim on the nation's output and rate of increase in real GDP per person may decline considerably.

Increased knowledge and skills enable workers to perform their tasks more efficiently. Education and training are needed to operate, repair, and invent the machines of a modern economy. The better educated the labour force, the more easily it can adapt to meet the challenges of a modern economic system. The Canadian labour force is highly educated. Over 80 percent of the workforce has attained at least some high school education. Some people have recently expressed concern, however, that Canadian workers are not receiving adequate training in key skills vital to the country's future economic growth—particularly technical and mathematical skills.

Managerial and entrepreneurial skills are needed to bring together the factors of production, innovate and employ the most productive technology, and promote good relations among workers. All are conducive to high productivity.

Stage of the Business Cycle

The productivity of resources also varies with the stage of the business cycle. As an economy goes into a recession, plant and equipment are used at less than capacity. Firms may retain key workers even as output declines. Thus, as the recession deepens, productivity declines. The reverse holds true as the economy pulls out of a recession. Labour, plant, and machinery are used more efficiently and productivity rises.

Technological Progress

Technological progress includes not only new machines and production techniques, but also new ways of organizing and managing economic activity.

The first step in technological progress is invention, which has no direct impact on economic growth. The second step is innovation, when the invention is applied to the production process. The third stage is diffusion, when the innovation spreads through the economy. The new idea thus replaces the old and the real impact on total output is felt.

□ □ □ □ □ □

Research and Development—Has Canada Kept Up?

It is clear that nations are competing ever more vigorously in the world economy. What is Canada's place in the global economy? What must we do to compete effectively? There is concern that the Canadian economy is not keeping up. The following article describes a report tabled in 1991 suggesting that Canada must take action to maintain and improve its competitive position.

Canada's most urgent challenge is to devise an economic strategy to halt the slide in our standard of living and put the country back on the path to strong, productive growth, a report says. The report, *Science and Technology, Innovation and National Prosperity: The Need for Canada to Change Course*, warns that Canada is falling dangerously behind its trading partners, with dire consequences for employment and our ability to maintain or improve our standard of living.

It blames a lack of investment in science and technology, inadequate education and training, business people who don't understand the need for research and development, and a failure by government to provide leadership and policies to make Canadian industry more competitive.

Focussing on the critical importance of the links between science and technology, innovation and productivity, the task force says the "urgent challenge" for Canada "is to bring about a fundamental change of course—from an economy in which the primary source of prosperity has been the exploitation of natural resources to an economy in which prosperity comes primarily from innovation."

This implies a massive national effort to boost the scientific and technological capabilities of Canadian industry and of Canadians themselves if Canada is to remain in the front rank of nations in the world.

The members of the task force contend that Canada cannot rely on market forces alone to overcome the widening technological gap between its industry and that of other, more innovative countries. Massive government intervention isn't the answer either.

But they point to the fact that Canada has successfully employed industrial policies in the past, such as crown corporations to develop Canada's transportation systems, tax policies to build up the resource industries, and procurement policies and monopolies to build up powerful hydro and telecommunications industries.

"Although some of these industrial policies would be inappropriate today, it is nevertheless still the case that competitive advantage can be significantly enhanced through conscious policy," the report says.

The report sets out a highly disturbing picture of how Canada is failing to meet the challenges of the modern world and of "the widening gap between the technological fitness of Canadian industry and that of our competitors."

Among its concerns:

• Canada continues to rely heavily on resource exports to pay for its high-tech imports as well as servicing its high level of foreign debt—but resource exports are declining in value and face intense new competition from other countries and other materials.

• Canada's main manufacturing industry is autos and auto parts. But the assembly of autos relies almost exclusively on imported technology, while auto parts companies lack the technology to compete, as evidenced by Canada's steadily growing trade deficit in auto parts.

• Canada's wages are rising faster than those in the US, which when combined with the increase in the value of the Canadian dollar, means that in US dollars, Canadian manufacturing wages are at least 10 percent higher than those in the US.

• Canadian manufacturing productivity increases in the past decade have lagged "significantly" behind all the other top industrial countries, with the productivity gap between Canada and the US widening in the process.

• The result of faster rising wages, the increase in the value of the dollar, and weaker productivity performance is that unit manufacturing costs rose 31.6 percent in Canada and only 2.4 percent in the US.

• Canada ranks 17th among 23 industrial countries in the ratio of spending on research and development to Gross Domestic Product. Canada spends about 1.3 percent of GDP on R & D, compared to more than 2.5 percent by countries such as the US, Japan, Germany, and Sweden. And while other countries have seen the level of R & D spending rise, Canada's position has been stagnant since the mid-1980s.

• Young Canadians are increasingly reluctant to enrol in courses in science and engineering. This means "young Canadians are choosing not to educate themselves for the jobs of the 21st century" so Canada will lack the skills to run a modern economy.

• Shortcomings in Canadian education are not being offset by workplace training. The average Canadian worker receives about seven hours of training a year, compared to 200 hours for the average Japanese and almost 170 for the average Swede.

While much of the effort to overhaul and reorient the Canadian economy must be made by companies and individuals, "there is nevertheless an essential role for government to establish the most favourable possible conditions to encourage innovation and productivity," the task force stresses.

SOURCE: Adapted from David Crane, "Our economy sinks as other nations soar," *The Toronto Star*, April 28, 1991. Reprinted with permission—The Toronto Star Syndicate.

Applications

1. Why is investment in research and development of particular concern at this point in Canada's economic development?

2. What role does the report suggest for government?

3. What specific actions do you think should be taken by both private businesses and government to ensure Canada maintains its position in the top ranks of developed nations?

Technological progress is promoted by investments in research and development (R & D). Canadian expenditures on R & D in the 1980s and 1990s averaged approximately 1.3 percent of GDP. However, twice that percentage was devoted to research and development in other industrialized nations such as Japan, Sweden, the United States, and Germany. There is real concern that Canada is not keeping up.

Structural Change
Shifts in an economy's structure can significantly affect productivity. For example, in this century there has been a significant shift of labour out of agriculture and into manufacturing. While 50 percent of the workforce was employed in agriculture in 1900, the figure was less than 5 percent in 1990. This shift accounted for a considerable increase in the country's productivity.

More recently, employment has shifted from the manufacturing to the service industries. Between 1965 and 1990, the percentage of the labour force employed in the service industries increased by 25 percent. Approximately 70 percent of the workforce is now engaged in the service industries. This trend is reflected in the economies of other industrialized nations.

Economies of Scale
The larger and more specialized the plant (up to a certain point), the better able it is to take advantage of the economies of scale. High production runs can bring per unit costs down. Many economists believe that one of the reasons Canadian productivity is below that of the United States is that Canadian plants typically are smaller and produce a greater diversity of products. Access to the larger American market and the ability, therefore, to take advantage of the economies of scale was one of the major arguments for the Free Trade Agreement with the United States.

Economic Growth—An Evaluation

Economic growth has long been considered a positive goal. But after the rapid growth of the past decades, people have become increasingly concerned about the negative effects and have indeed questioned the possibility of persistent growth in a finite world. Do the benefits outweigh the costs?

☐ Benefits of Growth

The primary reason economic growth is considered desirable is that it promotes the key economic objectives we outlined in Chapter 2—economic efficiency, economic stability, an equitable distribution of incomes, and a higher standard of living.

Higher Living Standards
A major benefit of economic growth is that it has raised the material standard of living in many countries. Between 1926 and 1990, the population of Canada increased from about 9.5 million to approximately 26.5 million. If the growth in GDP had not kept pace with the population growth, Canadian living standards would have declined.

In fact, GDP at 1986 prices rose from approximately $38.5 billion in 1926 to $568 billion in 1990. Therefore, while population grew less than three times, GDP in real terms increased more than 15 times. Real GDP per capita increased five times. This increase has meant both more goods and services and more leisure time as increases in productivity have reduced the average work week.

Income Distribution
The gains from growth are not distributed equitably throughout society. Many of the poor are not employed, and hence do not benefit from the higher wages that come from economic growth. Policies to ensure a more equitable distribution of income are, therefore, necessary.

Nevertheless, income is likely to be distributed more equitably in a growing than in a stagnant economy. Social security programs are more affordable and generally receive less criticism in prosperous than in difficult times.

Stability
Economic growth promotes economic stability. Higher growth rates are associated with lower unemployment. In the 1960s and early 1970s, for example, GDP in real terms increased at an average rate of 5 percent and unemployment rates averaged below 5 percent. After 1973, growth rates fell to an annual average of 3 percent and unemployment rose to about 7 percent. With a growing economy, an expanding labour force can be more rapidly and more fully employed.

Efficiency
As we have seen, increases in productivity mean increases in efficiency—getting more from the same amount of resources. Canadians today, for example, get more kilometres from a litre of gasoline than they did in the past. In 1975, the average passenger car in Ontario burned 18.6 L of fuel to travel 100 km. By 1989, this figure was almost halved to 9.6 L per 100 km. Not only do cars use fuel more efficiently, they emit fewer pollutants than older models.

☐ Costs of Growth

What, then, are the opportunity costs of growth?

Environmental Pollution
Increasingly, critics have voiced their concerns about the impact of growth on the environment. Rapid industrial expansion and urbanization have contributed to serious pollution problems as accumulating waste products are dumped into the air, water, and on land. Pollution controls have not kept pace.

Pollution—a negative externality—results in part from a failure in the price system. Damage to the environment occurs because the cost of the damage is not borne by the producer (and not passed on in the price of products to the consumer). Industries can dump their wastes in the water or air because no one owns the water and the air. They are available to all at no charge.

Growth and pollution, however, are not necessarily synonymous. If we were to cut growth completely, we would still face pollution from current production. Some argue that without economic growth, the costs of dealing with pollution can be met only by a reduction in current living standards. With growth, we can continue to enjoy our current living standards and set aside resources to deal with pollution.

Dislocation of Workers

As an economy grows, it changes and renders obsolete some of the skills workers have acquired. Workers, therefore, must learn new skills and continually adjust to changing conditions. These demands can cause much distress and dislocation in peoples' lives.

Losses in Current Consumption

Allocating resources to investment in capital or human development means that these resources are not available to produce goods and services for current consumption. Thus, the immediate opportunity cost of growth is foregone current consumption.

Suppose, for example, an economy is at full employment and is growing at a rate of 2 percent per year. To sustain this growth, let's assume 15 percent of GDP must be invested—which leaves 85 percent for consumption. However, if investment and saving are increased to 23 percent, the people can increase their growth rate to 3 percent per year. Should they do it?

Table 21.2 outlines the options. If GDP in 1992 is $600 billion in 1986 dollars, it is not until the 2002th year that the 3 percent solution equals the 2 percent solution in terms of annual consumption. The cumulative consumption losses of the higher investment rate are not made up until 2011—the nineteenth year. Sacrificing current consumption for benefits so far in the future is not likely to appeal to the middle-aged and elderly. Only the very young are likely to benefit.

☐ Limits to Growth

While opponents of economic growth argue that it is undesirable, others doubt that sustained economic growth is possible. The world's population has increased from 2.5 billion in the mid-1940s to 5.2

Table 21.2 Opportunity costs of growth (billions of dollars)

1 YEAR	2 CONSUMPTION WITH A 2 PERCENT GROWTH RATE AND 15 PERCENT OF GDP INVESTED	3 CONSUMPTION WITH A 3 PERCENT GROWTH RATE AND 23 PERCENT OF GDP INVESTED	4 CUMULATIVE (LOSS) OR GAIN IN CONSUMPTION WITH A 3 PERCENT GROWTH RATE COMPARED TO A 2 PERCENT RATE
1992	510	462	(48)
1993	520	476	(92)
1994	531	491	(133)
1995	541	505	(169)
1996	552	521	(201)
1997	563	537	(227)
1998	575	557	(245)
1999	587	570	(262)
2000	598	587	(272)
2001	611	605	(278)
2002	623	623	(277)
2007	688	725	(172)
2012	761	842	118
2022	929	1164	1506
2032	1135	1534	4475

SOURCE: Adapted from Economics 5/ed. by Richard Lipsey *et al.* Copyright © 1978 by Lipsey, Purvis, and Steiner. Reprinted by permission of HarperCollins Publishers.

Current consumption is lowered when more resources are invested to promote economic growth. When the growth rate is increased from 2 to 3 percent, future consumption is raised substantially. However, for ten years, annual consumption is less than in 1992. It is not until 20 years have elapsed that the cumulative consumption with a 3 percent growth rate exceeds that with a 2 percent growth rate.

billion in 1990. It is expected to continue to grow by an astonishing 1.6 percent to reach 6.2 billion by the year 2000 and 8.5 billion by 2025. But the quantity of natural resources in the world (water, land, minerals, etc.) is finite. Since World War II, these resources have been consumed at a rapidly increasing rate. At some point, they will run out. Furthermore, it is argued, the increasing amount of pollution generated by our economy is likely to overwhelm the ability of the world's ecological system to deal with it. Thus, even renewable resources, such as our forests, will be consumed.

□ □ □ □ □ □

The Debate Over Economic Growth

"Growth Must Be Curtailed"

David Suzuki is a geneticist, broadcaster, writer, and analyst of social and environmental issues. In the following article, he argues that increased consumption and economic growth are not essential to quality of life and indeed cannot be sustained in our finite world.

Exponential growth is a mathematical expression describing the steady increase over time of anything such as pollution, population, disease, resource use, manufactured products, and so on.

The necessity to do everything possible to maintain a steady increase in the economy is an unquestioned assumption by politicians and the business community. But the economy is ultimately based on the finite resources of the planet—air, water, soil, living things.

University of Colorado physicist Albert Bartlett has pointed out that it is impossible to maintain exponential growth of anything indefinitely because we live within real limits of the finite physical world and to think otherwise is a destructive mindset.

Anything growing exponentially will double within predictable intervals: a 1 percent annual growth will double in 70 years, 2 percent in 35 years, 3 percent in 23 years, and so on.

Bartlett illustrates the impossibility of maintaining endless growth using the example of an imaginary test-tube culture of bacteria.

At 11 o'clock, we inoculate a test tube of culture medium with a single bacterial cell that will undergo exponential growth by doubling every minute. So at 11 the test tube contains one cell, at 11:01 there are two, at 11:02 there are four, and so on. The culture is on a 60-minute cycle, so at 12 the tube is full and the food depleted.

When is the test tube only half full (or half empty, depending on whether you are an optimist or pessimist)? The answer, of course, is at 11:59. If you were a bacterium in that culture, when would you sense a space or overpopulation problem?

At 11:58 the tube would be 25 percent full, at 11:57 it would be 12.5 percent full, and so on. If a bacterium were to say to its mates at 11:55, "I think we're running out of space," chances are it would be laughed out of the tube. Any sensible bacterium could see 97 percent of the tube was empty, and besides, they had already been around for 55 minutes. Yet they'd only be five minutes from filling the test tube.

Suppose bacteria, like people, only acknowledge an impending crisis at 11:59. So, like humans, they desperately fund scientific megaprojects to come up with a solution. And suppose the bacterial experts deliver; in less than a minute, they synthesize three test tubes of food.

That is a phenomenal achievement—three times the previously existing supply! (Can you imagine how reassured we'd be if we made such a find of oil or food in the ocean?)

How much time would the bacteria now have? At 12, the first tube would be filled, at 12:01, the second would be occupied and at 12:02, all four would be packed.

Quadrupling the amount of food and space would only buy two more minutes if growth continues at the same rate. In our world, no amount of scientific mega-effort will be able to add more than a few percentage points of increase in food production, land, and resources. And many scientists believe we are well past the 59th minute.

Within the lifetimes of our children, the fate of our species will have been decided.

Plots of curves over the entire period of our species' existence of human activity such as our population, destruction of soil and forests, pollution, are virtually flat for 99.9 percent of that time.

But in the past few decades, the lines leap straight up off the page. That cannot continue and they will level off and turn downward. The only question is whether we will bring them down deliberately or let nature do it for us.

It is remarkable how deeply we have come to believe that greater consumption and economic growth are absolutely essential to maintain our "quality of life."

So to speak of aiming for zero growth, to say nothing of

cutting back, is regarded as an outrageous heresy or an impractical urge to turn back the clock and live more "primitively."

Yet in my childhood during the 1940s we had far less of everything (my family of six lived on less than $1500 a year) while our lives were rich and rewarding. And we had central heating, running water, and electricity.

The consequences of relentless exponential growth are undeniable. Bartlett warns us that we will get off our destructive rampage only when we recognize the folly of the worship of mindless growth. It is nonsense to think that our current rate of consumption cannot be reduced; it has to be.

Indeed, I believe our excesses have contributed to the breakdown in our society, minds, and bodies; and the quality of life will improve when we make do with less.

Growth has become the reason governments and societies exist, so there can be no end to it. But when will we ever have enough?

SOURCE: David Suzuki, "The grim arithmetic of mindless growth," *The Toronto Star*, July 27, 1991. Copyright David Suzuki, Southam Syndicate.

"Growth Is Good"

The following extracts present the other side of the debate, that economic growth and private enterprise can, in fact, work to preserve the environment and allow for a more equitable distribution of incomes, health care, education, leisure, and other amenities of life.

An Open Letter to the Ordinary Citizen from a Supporter of the "Growth Is Good" School

Dear Ordinary Citizen:

You live in the world's first civilization that is devoted principally to satisfying *your* needs rather than those of a privileged minority. Past civilizations have always been based on leisure and high consumption for a tiny upper class, a reasonable standard for a small middle class, and hard work with little more than subsistence consumption for the great mass of people.

The continuing Industrial Revolution is based on mass-produced goods for you, the ordinary citizen. It ushered in a period of sustained economic growth that has dramatically raised consumption standards of ordinary citizens. Reflect on a few examples: travel, live and recorded music, art, good food, inexpensive books, universal literacy, and a genuine chance to be educated. Most important, there is leisure to provide time and energy to enjoy these and thousands of other products of the modern industrial economy.

Would any ordinary family seriously prefer to go back to the world of 150 or 500 years ago in its same relative social and economic position? Surely the answer is no. However, for those with incomes in the top 1 or 2 percent of the income distribution, economic growth has destroyed much of their privileged consumption position. They must now vie with the masses when they visit the world's beauty spots and be annoyed, while lounging on the terrace of a palatial mansion, by the sound of charter flights carrying ordinary people to inexpensive holidays in far places. Many of the rich complain bitterly about the loss of exclusive rights to luxury consumption, and it is not surprising that they find their intellectual apologists.

Whether they know it or not, the antigrowth economists are not the social revolutionaries that they think they are. They say that growth has produced pollution and wasteful consumption of all kinds of frivolous products that add nothing to human happiness. However, the democratic solution to pollution is not to go back to where so few people consume luxuries that pollution is trivial, but rather to learn to control pollution that mass consumption tends to create.

It is only through further growth that the average citizen can enjoy consumption standards (of travel, culture, medical and health care, etc.) now available only to people in the top 25 percent of the income distribution—which includes the intellectuals who earn large royalties from the books that they write in which they denounce growth. If you think that extra income confers little real benefit, just ask those in the top 25 percent to trade incomes with average citizens.

Ordinary citizens, do not be deceived by disguised

elitist doctrines. Remember that the very rich and the elite have much to gain by stopping growth and even more by rolling it back, but you have everything to gain by letting it go forward.

Onward!   *A.N. Optimist*

Walter Block is an economist with the Fraser Institute in Vancouver, an educational and economic research institution which promotes the idea that free markets can make a substantial contribution to our economic well-being.

. . .Most people see an unbridgeable chasm between the desire of ecologists and environmentalists to have clean air and water and to control toxic wastes, on the one hand, and the pursuits of economists and business people concerned with economic development and prosperity, on the other hand. These two views are seen as impossible to reconcile, and the attitude of most people is that one of them has to give way to the other. I suggest that it is possible to reconcile the two—a reconciliation that upholds the goals of environmentalists but not necessarily their means. . . .

The first principle [that guides this analysis] is that of private property and the incentives engendered thereby. . . .

[Take]. . .the case of agriculture [in the former Soviet Union]. In the pre-*perestroika* days. . .on the 98 percent of the land that was communally owned, only 75 percent of the crops were produced. On the 2 percent of the land that was privately owned in the form of small gardens around workers' houses, fully 25 percent of the crops were grown. This illustrates the difference in incentives that operates when something is privately owned versus when it is publicly owned. . . .

The second principle is the tragedy of the commons. One way to illustrate this is to suppose that we are all shepherds, grazing our sheep on a common meadow. Some public-spirited citizen decides that the grass is being grazed too closely by the sheep. He takes his sheep elsewhere, at some expense, in order to preserve the meadow. But what typically happens is that other people

then allow their sheep to graze on the meadow that has just been vacated by this public-spirited citizen, and the grass is not saved. As you can see, there is very little incentive to act in a public-spirited way in a common meadow. If you owned the entire meadow and saw that it was becoming overgrazed, you would stop the sheep from grazing there and let that grass build up while they grazed elsewhere. That you will not do so under the institution of public property is the tragedy of the commons.

Let us now consider species extinction. Thanks to the modern miracle of television we have all seen the results of actions of poachers in Africa, the herds of elephants left to die with their tusks cut off with a chain saw. Pregnant cows are killed, the meat and leather go to waste, and the tusks don't get their true market value but only their black market value. Entire herds of elephants have been killed in this fashion.

Here we have the tragedy of the commons and a lack of the incentives that only private ownership can supply. The poachers are aided and abetted in their activities by the villagers because these elephants are not privately owned. . .The elephants destroy the crops of the villagers.

Several African countries have. . .allowed privatization of the animals. Hunting rights are sold to the native peoples, who can then rent them out to people who want to join safaris. These countries have given an incentive to their people to protect the elephants because now they have a value to them. Under such conditions, elephant herds are actually increasing. . . .

One proposed solution to the greenhouse effect is to maintain large acreages devoted to forests because trees take in carbon dioxide and give off oxygen. This raises the question of why our forests are disappearing. I think the culprit is government ownership of forest preserves, not greed and profits, as people like David Suzuki maintain. . . .

If a forestry company owns a hundred square miles of forest and cuts it all down without replanting, the present discounted value of that land plummets. If a company does that once too often, it risks courting bankruptcy. In sharp contrast, suppose the government owns the land and gives the company a contract to do with that land as it wishes for six months. In this situation it is in the best interests of the company to clear cut, and the economic incentives to reforest are greatly attenuated. . . .

There are many serious environmental groups with impeccable credentials that have seen that the best way to preserve woodlands is to buy them and administer them. The Audubon Society has a vast holding in Alabama and oil was discovered on it. Instead of saying that oil is evil and we're not going to have anything to do with it, they made a deal with an oil company to exploit this resource, in a very clean way, so they could buy more property for wildlife preserves. People open to the evidence will eventually be convinced that there is a case to be made for employing tools and analysis of economics in the marketplace to preserve these holdings.

SOURCE: Walter E. Block, "Environment Problems, Free Market Solutions," *Fraser Forum* (February 1990), pp. 4-17. By permission of the Fraser Institute.

Barber Conable, the president of the World Bank, an organization that provides loans to developing nations said in a speech in London in 1991:

Why is growth essential? Because more than one billion people live on a dollar a day or less. Because rising incomes can fuel environmental investment. And because it is unreasonable to expect developing countries, which already consume so few of the world's resources, to consume even less.

Applications

1. Outline the costs and benefits of growth discussed in the above extracts.

2. Which point of view comes closest to your position? Explain your reasoning.

Estimates indicate that the richest sixth of the world's population (which would include most of the population of Canada) consumes more than 15 times as much oil and more than 5 times as much of the earth's resources per person as the less fortunate five-sixths. If the "poor" five-sixths continue to push for a higher standard of living through economic growth, the pressure on the world's natural resources will only increase even more.

□ **Future Prospects**

The Club of Rome—a group of 100 scientists, business executives, and academics—predicted in 1972 that the world's economic system would collapse before the end of the twenty-first century because of the increase in pollution, population, and production.

This doomsday scenario was echoed in a report to the US president in 1980. Critics of this doomsday scenario, however, point out that the assumptions of population growth, fixed resources, and technological change that cannot keep pace are probably unfounded. Malthus made similar predictions two centuries ago based on the arithmetical increase in the supply of food and the geometrical increase in population.

Malthus's predictions have not been borne out by events.

The Club of Rome failed, the critics argue, to consider the role of the price system in allocating scarce resources. When resources are in short supply, prices rise, encouraging research and development of new and less expensive products or processes. Similarly, if consumer demand shifts toward environment-saving products, industries will move to meet the demand. The recent surge of recycling industries is an example. The question is whether the new developments will be enough.

Growth and the Less Developed Countries

We have already noted that one-sixth of the world's population consumes the lion's share of the world's resources. Much of the world, therefore, has not shared in the benefits of economic growth (or its costs). This part of the world is largely made up of the **less developed countries (LDCs)**—countries which have a relatively low per capita income and are less industrialized than Canada. Most LDC nations are in

Africa, Asia, and Central and South America. Much of the population in many of these countries is faced with problems of ill-health, illiteracy, malnourishment, limited life spans, and poor cramped housing conditions with few prospects for improvement.

Table 21.3 displays some key facts by which the world's economies can be compared. Generally, countries are divided into the three broad categories described below.

(i) Low-income economies (Less Developed Countries)
In the low-income economies—which comprise over

half the world's population and include such countries as China, India, Bangladesh, and Ethiopia—population growth rates are relatively high (averaging around 2 percent per year), growth rates of GDP/GNP are very low (although China is a notable exception), life expectancy at birth averages less than 60 years, illiteracy rates are high, and the ratio of physicians to the population is low.

(ii) Middle-income economies   This category includes two very different groups. One group comprises less developed countries (such as Brazil and Mexico),

Table 21.3 A comparison of economies

1 COUNTRIES	2 POPULATION (MILLIONS) MID-1989	3 AVERAGE ANNUAL GROWTH OF POPULATION (PERCENT) 1989-2000	4 AVERAGE ANNUAL GROWTH IN GNP/GDP PER CAPITA (PERCENT) 1965-1989	5 AVERAGE ANNUAL GROWTH IN GNP/GDP (PERCENT) 1980-1989	6 GNP/GDP (MILLIONS OF US DOLLARS)	7 AVERAGE ANNUAL RATE OF INFLATION (PERCENT) 1980-1989	8 LIFE EXPECTANCY AT BIRTH (YEARS) 1989	9 POPULATION PER PHYSICIAN 1984	10 DAILY CALORIE SUPPLY (PER CAPITA) 1988	11 ADULT ILLITERACY (PERCENT) 1985	12 TOTAL EXTERNAL DEBT (MILLIONS OF DOLLARS) 1989	13 TOTAL DEBT SERVICE AS A PERCENTAGE OF EXPORTS 1989
LOW-INCOME ECONOMIES												
Bangladesh	110.7	2.1	0.4	3.5	20 240	10.6	51	6 730	1 925	38	10 712	19.9
Bolivia	7.1	2.8	−0.8	−0.9	4 520	391.9	54	1 540	2 086	26	48 799	31.3
China	1 113.9	1.4	5.7	9.7	417 830	5.8	70	1 010	2 632	31	44 857	9.8
Ethiopia	49.5	3.4	−0.1	1.9	5 420	2.0	48	78 770	1 658	38	3 013	38.7
India	832.5	1.7	1.8	5.3	235 220	7.7	59	2 520	2 104	57	62 509	26.4
MIDDLE-INCOME ECONOMIES												
Brazil	147.3	1.7	3.5	3.0	319 150	227.8	66	1 080	2 709	22	111 290	31.3
Czechoslovakia	15.6	0.3	..	1.7	50 470	1.6	72	280	3 564	..	..	..
Hungary	10.6	−0.1	..	1.6	29 060	7.5	71	310	3 601	under 5	20 605	26.3
Jamaica	2.4	0.5	−1.3	1.2	3 880	18.5	73	2 050	2 572	..	4 322	26.41
Mexico	84.6	1.8	3.0	0.7	200 730	72.7	69	242	3 135	..	95 642	39.6
Poland	37.9	0.4	..	2.5	68 290	38.1	71	490	3 451	10	43 324	9.4
HIGH-INCOME ECONOMIES												
Canada	26.2	0.8	4.0	..	488 590	4.6	77	510	3 447	under 5		
France	56.2	0.4	2.3	2.1	955 790	6.5	77	320	3 310	under 5		
Japan	123.1	0.4	4.3	4.0	2 818 520	1.3	79	660	2 848	under 5		
United Kingdom	57.2	0.3	2.0	2.6	717 870	6.1	76	..	3 252	under 5		
United States	248.8	0.8	1.6	3.3	5 156 440	4.0	76	470	3 666	under 5		

SOURCE: The World Bank, *World Development Report 1991* (Oxford: Oxford University Press, 1991).

The data indicate the wide disparity that exists between the high- and low-income economies of the world. The low-income economies are characterized primarily by relatively high population growth rates, low GNP/GDP per capita, low growth rates in GNP/GDP, and high debt levels. The middle-income economies include both less developed nations with substantial GNP/GDP levels but high population growth rates, and the countries of the former communist block. The high-income economies are dominated by the industrialized nations which have low population growth rates and high GNP/GDP per capita.

which have achieved a substantial GNP/GDP per capita, but which have high rates of population increase, high inflation rates, large external debts, and significantly lower life expectancy and literacy rates than those of other middle-income economies.

The second group includes those countries once part of the communist block—many, if not all of which are in the process of moving toward a market economy—such as Czechoslovakia, Poland, and Hungary. China and Cuba are also sometimes included in this group, but are more often considered as low-income economies. These middle-income nations have relatively low rates of population increase, and higher literacy rates, physician to population ratios, life expectancies, and daily calorie intakes than low-income economies.

(iii) High-income economies This group includes the industrialized market economies dominated by the United States, Japan, and the European Economic Community (which includes Germany, France, Italy, Spain, and the United Kingdom). Canada also fits into this category. As Table 21.3 shows, these countries have low population growth rates, a comparatively high GNP/GDP per capita, a high life expectancy at birth averaging over 76 years, little or no illiteracy, a high physician to population ratio, and a daily calorie intake averaging over 3000.

☐ Problems of Less Developed Countries

Why is it difficult for the less developed countries to grow rapidly? We'll examine three cycles that help to explain why poverty is self-perpetuating.

Cycle #1 As Figure 21.7 illustrates, this cycle begins with low incomes which mean low savings, low investment, limited use of technology, low increases in productivity, and thus low incomes once again. With low incomes, people can save very little since most or all of their incomes are needed to buy the basic necessities of food, clothing, and shelter. Limited savings mean little money is available for investment and the accumulation of capital—one of the essentials for economic growth—is, therefore, slow. With little capital invest-

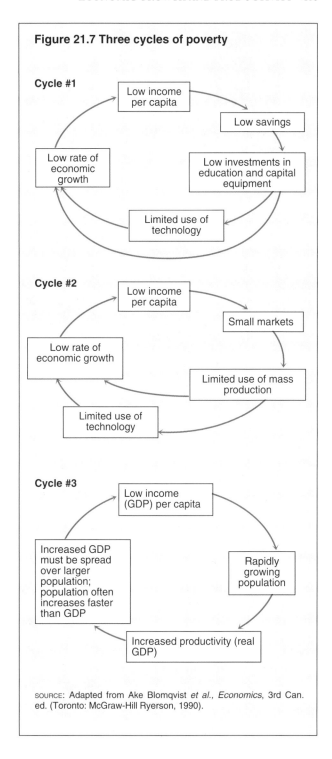

Figure 21.7 Three cycles of poverty

Cycle #1

Low income per capita → Low savings → Low investments in education and capital equipment → Limited use of technology → Low rate of economic growth → Low income per capita

Cycle #2

Low income per capita → Small markets → Limited use of mass production → Limited use of technology → Low rate of economic growth → Low income per capita

Cycle #3

Low income (GDP) per capita → Rapidly growing population → Increased productivity (real GDP) → Increased GDP must be spread over larger population; population often increases faster than GDP → Low income (GDP) per capita

SOURCE: Adapted from Ake Blomqvist *et al.*, *Economics*, 3rd Can. ed. (Toronto: McGraw-Hill Ryerson, 1990).

ment, technological advancements are limited and growth rates remain low. Incomes, therefore, cannot increase and the poverty cycle is perpetuated.

Cycle #2 The second cycle shown in Figure 21.7 illustrates that with low incomes, markets for goods are likely to be small. People have little disposable income and, therefore, demand for goods and services is low. Businesses are unable to sell in large volumes and take advantage of the economies of scale. The rate of growth thus remains low and incomes do not rise. The circle is complete again—low incomes lead to low incomes.

Cycle #3 The third cycle moves from low incomes through rapid population growth to low incomes once again. Less developed nations have experienced rapid population growth since the 1960s. Any small increase in capital must, therefore, be spread among more workers. Increases in productivity can then only be low and income per capita does not increase.

Population growth in some LDCs, in fact, is in excess of 3 percent, which means that total population will double in 24 years. Any gains in real GDP must be spread over a larger and larger population. This rapid population increase also means a rise in the dependent/worker ratio. In Canada, our rate of population increase is less than 1 percent and only 1 in 5 persons is less than 15 years of age. In Ethiopia, with a population increase rate of 3 percent, 50 percent of the population is under 15. Each adult worker has to support many more children.

The combined effect of the three poverty cycles makes it difficult for the LDCs to achieve higher standards of living. It seems that the poor are poor because they are poor. There are other obstacles as well. These include some social and cultural attitudes that discourage growth, wars and political instability, population growth, and the burden of international debts.

Social and Institutional Factors

Economic growth entails fundamental changes in the social and political life of a community. Many long-lived traditions and customs must be set aside and such change is profoundly unsettling. It can take place only very slowly. In some communities, for example, custom may inhibit the flow of workers from one occupation to another. Similarly, land passed down over many generations has sometimes been divided into tiny plots too small for the use of modern technology.

Some countries are struggling to co-ordinate a truly national economy. The legacies of colonialism have placed formidable barriers in the path of economic development, however. National boundaries set by colonial powers often did not make economic or political sense for the indigenous peoples. Economies were geared to provide the imperial powers with raw materials, markets, and places for capital investment. Today, tribal group and community loyalties are often stronger than national loyalties and conflicts break out among groups. Local conflicts have sometimes been exacerbated by rivalries among superpowers and turned into long-running and devastating civil wars—as has been the case in Ethiopia, Mozambique, Angola, and El Salvador.

In countries where only the wealthy few still own the majority of land, social unrest is not uncommon and poverty is widespread. With few resources or prospects for the future, incentives for workers to save and invest are low.

Rapid Population Growth

As we have seen, the population in many less developed nations is increasing at an astounding rate—as high as 3 percent per annum. If, as Mao Tse Tung once said, with every mouth comes a pair of hands, why is this rapid population increase a barrier to economic growth? One reason is that each worker must support a greater number of dependents. Second, capital resources are directed into providing housing, roads, and other basic facilities rather than into increasing the nation's productive capacity. Third, with a fixed supply of land and scarce capital, labour productivity falls and with it, real wages.

In an effort to break out of the poverty cycle, almost all less developed nations have turned to population control measures. These measures have included encouraging people to have fewer children, discouraging people from having children, and the provision of inexpensive or free methods of birth control.

China has one of the most widely-known programs of population control. The nation has 22 percent of the world's population but only 7 percent of the arable land. The government population control plan calls for "only one child per couple, strict limitation on second births, and resolute prevention of third births" in an attempt to reach zero population growth by 2010.

To implement the policy, the government uses a combination of propaganda, community pressure, and material incentives. Billboards nation-wide proclaim "Have one child for a beautiful tomorrow" and "Increased production in one field means nothing if you have more than one baby." Neighbourhood committees pay visits to families to ensure they are not proceeding with any unauthorized pregnancy.

Women who give birth to unauthorized children face stiff penalties. They may lose their jobs or be fined up to 15 percent of the couple's combined salary for the next 14 years. In rural areas, parents are informed that unauthorized children will not be allotted farmland. Couples who agree to have only one child and sign a contract with the state can receive cash bonuses, tax deductions, improved housing opportunities, and more farmland. Some experts, however, are skeptical about the success of these measures.

The Burden of Debt

Less developed nations have often borrowed from foreign banks, governments, and international organizations. Countries borrowing for projects with a rate of return that exceeds the interest rate will not be overburdened with debt. But, if interest rates increase and the return on investment falls, or if the debt is incurred for unproductive purposes, then the debt can become a serious burden. Payments of interest on debts and the repayment of capital can be made only when the nation has a surplus of exports over imports. Few nations have enjoyed this situation in recent decades.

In the 1980s, the foreign debt of many less developed nations became a serious concern. Many debts were incurred in the 1970s when the prices of raw materials exported by these nations (such as copper and oil) were rising and interest rates were low. In the 1980s, the prices of many raw materials declined, while interest rates rose.

By 1989, the total external debt of Brazil, the most indebted developing nation, reached CDN$139 billion. Mexico's total debt reached $113 billion; Argentina's $75 billion; India's $74 billion; and Egypt's $57 billion. Simply to pay the interest on the debt proved overwhelming and placed a brake on investment.

In the early 1990s, some actions were taken to ease the international debt crisis. Negotiations between debtor nations (such as Brazil and Argentina) and bankers helped to reduce the debts. The World Bank, a Washington-based organization owned by 150 nations, also acted by providing low-interest loans and technical assistance to many nations. Falling interest rates in the early 1990s also aided the cause, but the crisis for many nations has not yet been overcome.

□ Breaking the Poverty Cycle

How can the less developed countries break their low productivity cycle? There are several recurring themes in the debate. These concern the choices between industrial development and the green revolution, the development of domestic products or exports, and the merits of central plans *vs.* the market system.

Agricultural Development or Industrial Development?

Because those who work in industry are better paid and because many rich nations are industrialized, some think that to industrialize is to develop and become affluent. However, industrialization is capital-intensive and concentrates workers in already crowded cities. The less developed nations do not have large capital resources and the rapid growth of large cities has created hundreds of impoverished shantytowns.

Some suggest the solution is not in industrial development, but in the **green revolution**. Agriculture is the mainstay of many less developed nations and outputs could be increased by investing in more productive seeds and fertilizers. The nations could then feed their own people, avoid the industrial pollution and massive migration of workers to the already overcrowded cities, and produce food for export.

□ □ □ □ □ □

Sylvia Ostry on Global Economic Equity

Sylvia Ostry is a world-renowned Canadian economist. Born in Winnipeg, she studied economics at McGill University and Cambridge University in England, and completed her PhD in 1954. After teaching and conducting research at a number of universities, she joined the federal government in 1964. She has held a number of positions including chief statistician at Statistics Canada, deputy minister of consumer and corporate affairs, chair of the Economic Council of Canada, deputy minister of international trade, and ambassador for multilateral trade negotiations. She also served as head of the department of economics and statistics for the Paris-based Organization for Economic Cooperation and Development—an organization promoting economic co-operation among developed nations.

In the following extract from her paper "Economic Justice: Reality or Illusion?" Dr Ostry examines the question of economic justice in global terms. As you read the extract, consider the extent of poverty in the world and the strategies that may be used to combat the problem.

Economic Justice: Reality or Illusion?

There is no definition of *economic* justice. The market is a device—the most efficient device—for securing economic growth. Justice, however we define it, concerns the *distribution* of the benefits of this growth. How best to combine these twin objectives of all societies—efficiency and equity, the market *and* justice—has been the subject of an unending and unsettled debate since the Industrial Revolution. The Marxist answer—get rid of the market—has now been revealed as a lengthy and painful diversion in that discourse. What I want to do is provide some insight into this policy debate in *global* terms because today, more than ever in history, the concern with distributional equity extends beyond the borders of the nation state. The role of the media and especially television in arousing the awareness and the conscience of the citizens of the rich countries has, of course, been a primary force in this development.

The Profile of Poverty

I want to focus on only one aspect of economic justice—of distributional equity, if you'll permit the economists' term. That aspect is *poverty*...Poverty is the most fundamental constraint on human well-being, as is shown by a range of social indicators such as the life expectancy, child mortality, and educational attainment of the poor.

The recent *World Bank Development Report* provides a comprehensive overview of the profile of world poverty. The data are stark and revealing. The policy implications are significant and compelling.

More than one billion people in the developing world are living in poverty, defined by the World Bank as an income of less than $370 a year. These are the poorest of the poor. The struggle to survive means high infant mortality: in South Asia 170 deaths per thousand; in Sweden fewer than 10. It means a life expectancy in Sub-Saharan Africa of 50 years: in Japan almost 80. It means 110 million children without access even to a primary education, promising a continuing toll of deprivation.

In one sense your chance of being poor depends mainly on the region where you're born. Nearly half of the world's poor live in South Asia, a region that accounts for about 30 percent of the world's population. A quarter of the poor live in East Asia, which is home to 40 percent of the people of this earth. Sub-Saharan Africa, with only 11 percent of world population, constitutes 16 percent of the poverty group.

But these figures tell only part of the story. They capture a snapshot of the poverty profile. They can only be correctly interpreted in the light of history and future trends.

During the past three decades, many countries in the developing world have grown at rates much faster than did the developed countries and the incidence of poverty has diminished, often dramatically. This is true of both East Asia, and to a lesser extent, South Asia. Both domestic policies and international factors were essential ingredients in their superior performance. In Latin America, in contrast, both these pre-conditions were negative, especially in the 1980s, and the living standards of millions of Latin Americans are now lower than at the outset of the decade.

But economic performance was weakest by far in Sub-Saharan Africa. This dismal situation was compounded by rapid population growth and, as a result, poverty has steadily increased. Living standards have fallen to levels last seen in the 1960s.

Policy Strategy to Combat Poverty

An effective co-ordinated policy to combat poverty will have to include action by both developing and developed countries. Most important of all, and this requires underlining, it would require that rich and poor countries alike make the war on poverty a priority of the highest order. Without such commitment, inequality in the world will likely significantly increase. More than ever today both North and South have a mutual interest in reducing economic deprivation, not only for humanitarian reasons, but also because of broader international objectives such as reducing environmental degradation, stemming the drug trade, and other threats to international security such as terrorism.

The policy elements are trade, debt, and aid. In all three areas the issues are complex. On the trade front the key is a successful conclusion to the Uruguay Round [a series of trade negotiations begun in 1986 and continuing to 1992, aimed at reducing restrictions on international trade] and, at the present time, the outlook is uncertain. The outcome of the Uruguay Round will determine the future of the multilateral trading system and will, therefore, fundamentally affect the prospects of all developing countries.

Debt policy is also important, especially for the severely indebted low-income countries—heavily concentrated in Sub-Saharan Africa. Although a number of international initiatives for dealing with their debt burdens (which are largely official rather than private, as in the case of Latin America) have been instituted, the combined impact has been small. If the low-income nations are to both invest more and increase the consumption of their poor, further efforts by the international community will be needed both to reduce their debts and to increase aid. In both instances, these efforts should be conditional on appropriate domestic policy reform.

Public Education and the Policy Process

Joseph Schumpeter, the eminent German economist who emigrated to Harvard at the end of the 1930s, remarked that policy was a product of politics. My own long experience as a government official has taught me how perceptive this observation was. And it also convinced me that the most difficult challenge confronting policy-makers is how to make good *policy* good *politics*. One route, too little expected, is to use information dissemination to enhance public understanding and, therefore, commitment.

In the developed world, a major problem is to secure broad public support for the anti-poverty objective. There are so many high profile international issues today that the plight of the world's poor only captures attention when a crisis—like the Kurdish refugees or the Ethiopian or Sudanese famine victims—flashes on our TV screens or grabs a newspaper headline. Because the war on poverty—even under the rosy scenario I've outlined—will be a long and difficult battle, the crafting of a sophisticated and sustained information strategy stressing the mutual interest of North and South will present a formidable challenge. In any such, the strategy of the private sector is crucial. If we are to come to grips with the issue of economic justice in this last decade of the twentieth century it will take the combined efforts and commitment of all the key actors in the global economy today. Whether that is forthcoming will resolve the implied contradiction in the title of this essay "Economic Justice: Reality or Illusion?"

Applications

1. Why does Dr Ostry feel that it is necessary to consider economic justice in global terms?

2. Why does she concentrate on poverty in her discussion?

3. (a) What policy strategies does she suggest to combat global poverty?

(b) Which do you think has the greatest chance of success? Explain.

Import Substitution or Export Promotion?

If the decision is made to support industrialization, should the emphasis be on supplying the local market with locally-produced import substitutes, or should the emphasis be on developing goods for an export market? The advantages of specialization are achieved by concentrating on world markets and export-oriented industries. But will other countries—especially the developed nations—allow the challenge to their own industries? China, India, and Sri Lanka have export-oriented textile industries, but Canada and the United States, for example, have placed import restrictions on textiles. Other developing countries have used tariffs to protect local industries—but this results in higher costs for domestic products and short production runs. Mexico, for example, has an automobile industry protected against imports from Japan. Critics of import substitution policies point out that they are likely to keep local standards of living low.

Monoculture

Another danger the less developed nations face is that of over-specialization—sometimes in only one product. Variations in the world price for the good then have a dramatic impact on earnings from foreign trade and thus on real incomes in the country. Saudi Arabia, Iraq, Iran, and Kuwait are heavily dependent on oil; Columbia, Tanzania, and Costa Rica are dependent on coffee, for example. Developed countries suffer less from price swings in individual products because their economies are more diversified. The less developed nations must avoid the dependency on only one or a few major export products and diversify their economies.

Planning vs. the Market

In the years of decolonization after 1945, there was almost universal acceptance among less developed nations that central planning was the best way to achieve economic growth. It was argued that the market would be unable to send the appropriate signals for the efficient allocation of scarce resources. The socially low-priority demands of the rich would receive higher priority in a market system than the essential needs of the poor. Moreover, planning could mobilize the will and imagination of the people to meet the established objectives. A plan was also often an essential prerequisite for foreign aid.

By the beginning of the 1980s, however, the results of years of planning were disappointing. Real income per person had increased little in many less developed nations. Reasons included overambitious plans with competing or even conflicting objectives in some cases. Plans were also often developed on the basis of unreliable or insufficient data. Many plans relied on foreign aid, trade, and investment, which were continually changing. Plans also sometimes relied on inefficient and cumbersome bureaucracies for their implementation.

In the 1980s, with the popularity of conservatism under Margaret Thatcher in Britain and Ronald Reagan in the United States, and with the adoption of more market-oriented policies in developed nations, government planning as a major means of promoting economic growth came under close scrutiny. Supply-side economists argued that the weak economic growth of less developed nations was the result of excessive state intervention, and not of actions by developed nations to rig international markets in their favour.

What was needed, the supply-siders argued, was not the dismantling of the current international trade system or better state planning, but rather the elimination of state intervention in less developed nations. Poor resource allocation, ineffective pricing policies, and a lack of economic incentives had hindered economic growth. The invisible hand of the market, and not the overly visible hand of government, should be allowed to kick start the economies. Tax policies could be used to encourage saving and capital accumulation by replacing income taxes with taxes on consumption.

Supply-siders pointed to the limited growth of the Latin American economies burdened by government intervention and the success of the market economies in Taiwan, Singapore, South Korea, and Hong Kong.

More recently, emphasis has been placed on the removal of international trade barriers, which should open new opportunities for many less developed nations. We will consider some of these developments over the next two chapters.

Summary

a. Economic growth is defined as a sustained increase in real GDP per capita. It is also often expressed as an increase in productivity, particularly in the productivity or output per hour of labour. It can be illustrated by the outward shift of the production possibilities curve. Since economic growth means more goods and services, higher real incomes per person, and more leisure time, it is also often associated with a higher standard of living.

b. Since Confederation, the general trend in real income per capita has been upward in Canada, increasing ten-fold from $2000 in 1981 dollars to over $20 000 in 1990. The most notable downturn in economic growth occurred during the Great Depression of the 1930s. Upturns have been associated with the expansion of domestic and export industries, immigration, and war.

c. The rule of 72 is a simple approximation device for calculating the time it takes to double a given income at various growth rates. It can be used to estimate how long it would take for real GDP per capita to double at various growth rates or for the amount of an investment to double at various interest rates.

d. Thomas Malthus developed one of the earliest theories of the relationship between population growth and economic development. He suggested that since population grows exponentially, while food production can increase only arithmetically because the total supply of land is fixed, the best that the population can expect over the long term is a subsistence standard of living. While positive checks such as wars, famine, and disease are the ultimate controllers of population growth, preventive checks such as late marriages should also be encouraged.

e. The capital accumulation model suggests that as investments in capital increase, output increases though at a slower rate because of the law of diminishing returns. If technological change keeps pace with the rate of diminishing returns to capital, output will increase at a steady rate. The accumulation of capital then increases productivity and real wages, and hence raises the standard of living.

f. Factors determining economic growth can be considered in terms of both the quantity and quality of resources. The quantity of natural resources available, the size of the labour force, and the amount of capital investment can all contribute to economic growth. Factors affecting the quality or productivity of resources include the health, training, and education of the labour force; the phase of the business cycle and the efficiency with which resources are used; technological development; structural changes in the economy; and economies of scale.

g. The major benefits of economic growth include higher living standards as measured by real income per capita, the opportunity for a more equitable distribution of income, economic stability, and economic efficiency. The costs include environmental pollution, dislocation of workers, and losses in current consumption. It is also argued that the goal of persistent economic growth cannot be sustained since the earth's resources are finite.

h. Economic growth in less developed countries has been hindered by social traditions, the legacies of colonialism, social unrest and sometimes civil wars, debt burdens, and rapid population growth (which has meant that increases in real GDP must be spread among many more people). The difficulties are also illustrated by the three cycles of poverty, which indicate that low income breeds low income.

i. Suggestions for how the less developed countries could achieve the benefits of economic growth include an emphasis on agricultural development with the help of new technologies provided by the green revolution, a strategy of import substitution or export promotion, a shift away from central planning toward the free market system, and economic diversification away from dependencies on only one or a few export products.

■ Review of Key Terms

Define the following key terms introduced in this chapter and provide examples where appropriate.

economic growth
productivity of labour
rule of 72
capital accumulation model

marginal efficiency of
  capital (MEC)
less developed country
green revolution

■ Application and Analysis

1. If GDP in money terms increases by $100 billion next year, has there been growth? Explain.

2. As an economy recovers from a recession, its productivity generally rises. During recessions, productivity generally falls. Explain why.

3. "Our prime national goal...should be to reach a zero growth rate as soon as possible. Zero growth in people, in GDP, and in our consumption. That is the only hope of attaining a stable economy; that is, of halting the deterioration of the environment on which our lives depend."

(a) What effect would such a policy have in Canada, if adopted?

(b) What specific programs and policies would be necessary to achieve zero growth?

(c) Do you believe such a policy should be implemented? Explain your position.

4. Suppose a decree allowing the unrestricted migration of people among nations were instituted. What effect would it likely have on:

(a) economic efficiency

(b) world-wide distribution of income?

5. What are the vicious cycles of poverty? How can nations escape from them?

6. It is 1902 and you are a successful buggy-whip manufacturer. But the advent of the horseless carriage has begun to cut into your market. You are considering the following options.

Option #1 Have the Canadian Buggy-Whip Manufacturing Association lobby Ottawa for a countervailing duty on imported automobiles and research and development support to develop a better buggy whip.

Option #2 Downsize and go for a niche market, such as high-end users who like to use their buggies for Sunday outings or the folks who drive the Royal Coach in coronation processions.

Option #3 Rationalize. Make a takeover bid for your biggest competitor.

Option #4 Try the high-tech route. Start making your buggy whips out of teflon. Introduce robotics to your manufacturing process.

Option #5 Give up now, move to New York, and sell Model Ts.
In 1902, which option might appear to you as the best? Why?

7. In 1991, the Swedish government introduced a tax on the carbon dioxide emissions of commercial aircraft, energy companies, and land-based transportation in a bid to reduce pollution and combat the greenhouse effect. The Swedish government had already imposed taxes on emissions of nitrogen oxides and hydrocarbons from aircraft in 1989 to fight acid rain. Some aircraft companies responded by retooling the engines of their aircraft and hydrocarbon emissions were reduced by as much as 90 percent on one domestic carrier plane. Other nations are seriously considering similar measures.

(a) "Such a tax on polluters compensates for one of the failings of the price system." Explain this statement.

(b) "Such government intervention in the market system seriously hinders the self-correcting mechanisms of the market." Do you agree or disagree with this statement? Explain your position.

(c) "Such measures can actually increase productivity by encouraging innovation and the more efficient use of resources." Explain this statement. Do you agree or disagree? Why?

8. Issue—Revisionist View of Scrooge

In the following extract, Michael Walker, director of the Fraser Institute, suggests that the view of the oppressed working class presented in the books of Charles Dickens is one-sided. Wasn't Scrooge really the Cratchits' beneficent provider? Consider Michael Walker's arguments.

After reading Dickens, we will come away with a reinforcement of a very common notion about the 19th century in Britain and the onset of the Industrial Revolution—namely that its consequences were chiefly to reduce the already low standard of living of working people who were forced by a heartless capitalist class into working in the horrifying surroundings of the industrial factory.

My favorite example of these depictions, because it also excoriates economists, is Dickens's novel *Hard Times*, written in 1854. What *Hard Times* shares with other Dickensian epics such as *A Christmas Carol* is his depiction of the harsh life which was the lot of the average person.

The horror of workhouses, the prisons and indeed even the conditions of work endured by the likes of Bob Cratchit working in the office of investment banker Ebenezer Scrooge, are the only historical notions that many people have about these earlier times. Not infrequently when people discuss laissez-faire capitalism, it is Dickensian characters who inform their judgement.

The mischief which these images conjure up is the notion that poverty, misery, and degradation are a historical phenomenon imposed by the capitalist class on the workers.

As a matter of fact, there's nothing historic about their circumstance at all and indeed it is descriptive of the condition of most human beings even today. It is a condition which is imposed on humankind because of the low productivity of raw human effort.

A crucial ingredient in boosting the productivity of labour then and now is the acquisition of capital, both in the form of machinery and equipment and in the form of knowledge and skills. Both forms of capital require saving and the accumulation of financial capital on the part of the population. That is to say, the increase in productivity that eradicated widespread poverty in Britain in the 1850s required at least the accumulation of capital, if not the existence of a capitalist class.

The Industrial Revolution as it unfolded in Britain was one of the first occasions upon which there was a successful linkage of savings and investment in the creation of the industrial infrastructure, which in its infancy Dickens was so prone to castigate. It was, in turn, the advent of industrial machinery that boosted the productivity of the wretched masses.

Industrialism has been highly favorable to labour's real wage. As a distinguished economist and Nobel-prize winner Sir John Hicks has written: "There is no doubt at all that industrialism in the end has been highly favorable to the real wage of labour. Real wages have risen enormously in all industrialized countries over the last century and it is surely evident that without the increase in productive power that is due to industrialization, the rise in real wages could not possibly have occurred."

The curious thing about all of this is that Bob Cratchit, Scrooge's clerk, undoubtedly had a much higher standard of living than his grandfather, largely because people like Ebenezer Scrooge mobilized and invested savings in activities that produced a positive rate of return.

In real life, as in *A Christmas Carol*, it was the savings and investment in capital equipment by the likes of Scrooge and Jacob Marley that ultimately raised the income of the Bob Cratchits and made for a happy holiday.

And so, the ultimate profile of Scrooge as the beneficent provider for the Cratchits is closer to reality than the miserable image which first confronts the ghosts of Christmas past.

SOURCE: Adapted from *The Financial Post*, December 21, 1990. Reprinted with permission of the Fraser Institute.

(a) Briefly summarize Michael Walker's argument that Scrooge was really the Cratchits' beneficent provider.
(b) Do you agree with his argument? Explain.

CHAPTER TWENTY-TWO

International Trade

Objectives

a. Assess the importance of international trade to the Canadian economy.

b. Demonstrate, using the circular flow model, the role of international trade in an economy.

c. Outline and assess the benefits of trade with reference to absolute and comparative advantage.

d. Examine and assess the costs of trade.

e. Determine Canada's major merchandise trading partners and the nature of its major merchandise imports and exports.

f. Outline the nature of Canada's invisible or non-merchandise trade and its balance of trade on current account.

g. Investigate the components of Canada's capital account.

h. Examine and evaluate Canada's balance of payments record.

i. Calculate foreign currency exchanges and recognize the applications of this skill.

j. Demonstrate, using graphs, how the exchange rate of the Canadian dollar is determined and the factors affecting it.

k. Analyze the fixed, floating, and managed float exchange rate policies of the Canadian government.

l. Examine the international exchange rate systems used since the early 1900s.

International trade is of vital importance to the Canadian economy. Even a quick glance around the parking lot of a local supermarket will reveal Volkswagens from Germany, Hyundais from South Korea, and Toyotas, Nissans, and Mazdas from Japan—in addition to North American-made cars. Inside the supermarket are products from the world over: oranges and orange juice from Florida and California, grapes from Chile, bananas from Costa Rica, sugar from Jamaica, cookies from the United Kingdom and the Netherlands, ham from Poland, lamb from New Zealand, and so on.

We are all largely dependent on **imports**—goods and services bought from other nations—for much of what we buy. In 1990, Canada imported a total of $204 billion in goods and services. In turn, Canadians sell a large number of goods and services around the world. Goods and services sold to foreign nationals—our **exports**—typically account for almost 25 percent of our GDP ($188 billion in 1990) and one in five jobs in Canada is directly dependent on exports. Exports account for only about 9 percent of GDP in the United States and approximately 20 percent of GDP in the United Kingdom and Italy. Trade is clearly of great importance to the Canadian economy.

In this chapter, we examine the benefits and costs of trade, Canada's international trade in merchandise and non-merchandise goods and services, and the importance of currency exchange rates.

International Trade and the Circular Flow

How does international trade fit into the circular flow model of the economy we have developed? As Figure 22.1 illustrates, Canadian households, businesses, and governments buy goods and services from other countries through the products markets. In return for this real flow of imports from other countries, a money flow of payments goes from Canadian households, businesses, and governments to other countries through the products markets.

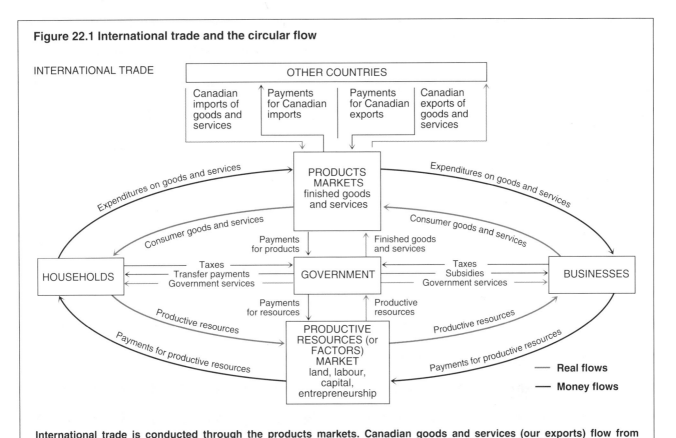

Figure 22.1 International trade and the circular flow

International trade is conducted through the products markets. Canadian goods and services (our exports) flow from businesses to foreign nations through the products markets. A parallel flow of goods and services from foreign nations (imports) goes through the products markets to Canadian households, businesses, and governments. These two flows are matched by flows of payments from Canada to other nations in return for imports and from other nations to Canada in return for exports.

The flows also go in the opposite direction. Foreign nations buy goods and services from Canadian businesses (exports) through the products markets and in return provide payments.

Why Trade?

Why do nations trade? Instead of relying on imports of food and manufactured goods, why does not Canada simply produce these goods for itself? Nations buy goods and services from other nations for the same reasons that individuals buy from other individuals. No individual or nation can be totally self-reliant. You cannot produce all of the food, clothing, medicines, entertainment, information, construction materials, etc., that you need alone. Your standard of living is much higher and your needs are more efficiently met if you can specialize in what you do best and buy the rest of what you need from others—who are specialists in their products or services. Trade, therefore, allows nations to specialize and thus achieve greater economic efficiency and a higher standard of living for their peoples.

Let's examine how international trade affords these benefits. Some key factors are increased competition, economies of scale, and specialization.

Increased Competition
Many people argue that exposing industries to the larger international marketplace forces them to become more competitive and thus more efficient. The Canadian auto industry is a case in point. Increased competition from German, Japanese, and South Korean automakers has put pressure on domestic producers to keep prices down, improve quality and productive efficiency, and produce smaller, more fuel-efficient cars. Canadian consumers thus gain from international trade.

Economies of Scale
Industries with access to large international markets can increase production runs and gain from economies of scale. As output increases, the average cost of pro-

duction falls. Production is thus more efficient and prices for the products go down. One of the arguments in favour of free trade between Canada and the US was that elimination of trade barriers between the two countries would give Canadian manufacturers access to a market ten times the size of Canada's, and they could then take advantage of much better economies of scale.

Specialization
International trade allows countries to specialize—concentrating on activities in which they have the necessary resources and can use them most efficiently. To understand exactly how this works, we need to examine the concepts of absolute and comparative advantage.

□ Absolute Advantage

Suppose I am a naturally skilled, highly trained, and practised word processor who can input 100 words a minute without error. It takes me half an hour, however, to change a tire. You, on the other hand, are a skilled, highly trained, and experienced garage worker who can change a car tire in five minutes. It takes you a minute to process a single sentence, however. In this case, I have an absolute advantage in word processing and you in changing tires. I need far less time and resources to perform my word processing tasks than you do, and you require less time and resources than I to change a tire. We can accomplish more with greater efficiency if I specialize in word processing and pay you to change my tire, and *vice versa*.

Absolute advantage, therefore, is the ability of an individual, region, or country to produce a good or service with fewer resources (and thus more efficiently) than other individuals, regions, or countries. Saskatchewan has an absolute advantage over Newfoundland and Labrador in the production of wheat, for example. Newfoundland and Labrador have an absolute advantage over Saskatchewan in the production of cod. Brazil has an absolute advantage over Canada in the production of coffee, while Canada has an absolute advantage over Brazil in the production of wheat. Thus, it is to Canada's advantage to specialize in wheat production and sell the surplus to Brazil in exchange for Brazil's surplus coffee, and *vice versa*.

☐ Comparative Advantage

Assuming a country produces only two products, what happens when it has an absolute advantage in the production of both goods? Is it still advantageous for the country to trade?

To answer this question, let's consider a simple model similar to one outlined by David Ricardo nearly two centuries ago. Our model has only two countries (let's say Canada and a hypothetical country called Tradia) producing only two products at constant cost. We assume no transportation costs and no government restrictions on trade.

As Table 22.1 shows, Canada can produce more wheat and machinery than Tradia with the same resources. It, therefore, has an absolute advantage in both products. But let's consider the opportunity costs involved in the production of the two commodities. In other words, how much machinery must Canada and Tradia give up to produce 1 unit of wheat, and how much wheat must they give up to produce 1 unit of machinery. The opportunity costs are summarized in Part B of Table 22.1.

Table 22.1 Production of machinery and wheat in Canada and Tradia (hypothetical data)

A. OUTPUT PER WORKER

	Machinery		Wheat
In Canada	6 units	or	3 units
In Tradia	4 units	or	1 unit

B. OPPORTUNITY COSTS

	For 1 unit of wheat	For 1 unit of machinery
Canada	2 units of machinery	0.5 units of wheat
Tradia	4 units of machinery	0.25 units of wheat

Canada has an absolute advantage in the production of both machinery and wheat, as Canadian workers out-produce Tradian workers in both products. When the opportunity costs of production are considered, however, it is clear that Canada has a comparative advantage in wheat production and Tradia in machinery production. The countries can benefit by specializing in the product for which they have a comparative advantage and trading to obtain the other product.

The opportunity cost of 1 unit of wheat is 2 units of machinery in Canada and 4 units of machinery in Tradia. For 1 unit of machinery, the opportunity cost is 0.5 units of wheat in Canada and 0.25 units of wheat in Tradia. Canada, therefore, has a comparative advantage in wheat production (it costs less machinery to produce per unit than in Tradia) and Tradia has a comparative advantage in machinery production (it costs less wheat to produce per unit than in Canada).

Comparative advantage, therefore, is the ability of an individual, region, or country to produce a good or service relatively more efficiently (at a lower opportunity cost) than another individual, region, or country. Both countries will benefit from trade when they specialize in the good for which they have a comparative advantage.

☐ Terms of Trade

How do the countries benefit? Before trade, Canadians would exchange 1 unit of wheat for 2 units of machinery in Canada. Tradians would exchange 1 unit of wheat for 4 units of machinery in Tradia.

When the countries engage in trade, the exchange rate will logically settle somewhere between the rates or price structures in the two countries, that is, between 1:2 and 1:4. Let's suppose it settles at the midpoint between the two ratios—at 1 unit of wheat for 3 units of machinery. This rate of exchange, the rate at which a country's exports are exchanged for its imports, is known as the **terms of trade**.

With an exchange rate of 1:3, how would Canada benefit from trade and specialization? For each Canadian worker who moved out of machinery production and into wheat production, we would lose 6 units of machinery and gain 3 units of wheat. With the terms of trade at 1:3, we can exchange our 3 units of wheat for 9 units of machinery. Thus, by trade, we gain 9 − 6 = 3 units of machinery.

How would the Tradians fare? For each Tradian worker who left wheat production to manufacture machinery, the Tradians would lose 1 unit of wheat, but gain 4 units of machinery. The 4 units of machinery could be exchanged for 1 1/3 units of wheat. Thus, by trade and specialization, Tradia gains 1/3 unit of wheat.

Clearly, both countries gain by trade and specialization in the products for which they have a comparative advantage. In fact, the total output of both countries increases by trade. The following analysis shows how.

1. Before trade and specialization
Let's suppose that Canada has two workers and Tradia four. Each country allocates an equal amount of resources to the production of each good.
Canada will produce 6 units of machinery and 3 units of wheat. Tradia will produce 8 units of machinery and 2 units of wheat. Total Production: 14 units of machinery and 5 units of wheat.

2. After trade and with specialization
Suppose, now, we have free trade and the countries have specialized.
Canada will produce 0 units of machinery and 6 units of wheat. Tradia will produce 16 units of machinery and 0 units of wheat. Total Production: 16 units of machinery and 6 units of wheat.

By comparing the total production before and after trade, we can see that through specialization (while using the same amount of labour), total production increases by 2 units of machinery and 1 unit of wheat.

Several factors can affect the terms of trade. As we saw, the cost structures of the countries engaging in trade is one factor. Demand also plays a significant part. Suppose, for example, the staple food product in Tradia became bread rather than rice or potatoes. The demand for wheat would rise and so would the price. More units of machinery would be required for each unit of wheat. A higher price for wheat in Tradia would change the rate of exchange in trade.

☐ Sources of Comparative Advantage

The sources of comparative advantage are primarily different endowments of necessary productive resources. Canada has vast areas of forest, which give it a comparative advantage in the production of timber, wood pulp, and paper. China has a large pool of semi-skilled workers, which provides a comparative advantage in the production of inexpensive clothing, for example. Japan has a highly skilled and hard-working workforce with advanced technology at its disposal, which gives it a comparative advantage in the production of electronics equipment. With each country specializing in those products for which it has the comparative advantage, total world production increases and all nations can gain through a higher standard of living for their peoples.

█ Trade—Who Wins and Who Loses?

However, while there are winners who gain by international trade, there are also losers. If we look at our earlier example of trade between Canada and Tradia from a different perspective, we see that before trade 1 unit of wheat exchanged for 2 units of machinery in Canada. After trade, the price of 1 unit of wheat rose to 3 units of machinery. Consumers of wheat in Canada lose because prices rise, though wheat producers gain by achieving higher profits.

With Canadian imports of machinery, the picture is reversed. Consumers benefit because prices decline, but domestic producers lose because they face increased competition and lower profits.

There are a number of real and current examples of how imports have affected various businesses in Canada. Imports of shoes, textiles, clothing, and bicycles have pushed down Canadian prices and limited sales of domestically-manufactured products. Thus, Canadian consumers have benefitted, but domestic industries have suffered. Factories have closed and workers have lost their jobs.

But, some would argue that while increased trade may lead to increased employment and output in the exporting industries and corresponding declines in the importing industries, large overall losses or gains in employment are unlikely. Immediately following the introduction of imports, many people in the domestic industry may be unemployed, but they will eventually move into another industry. The main purpose of trade, it is argued, is to increase the efficiency of factors of production and thereby raise incomes. It is not to increase employment.

■ Patterns of Trade

What, then, is Canada's trade position and how do we benefit from trade? Trade occurs in goods, services, and financial assets. The exchange of goods is generally referred to as **merchandise** or **visible trade**. The exchange of services, as well as investment incomes or payments and transfers of immigrants' funds, is known as **invisible** or **non-merchandise trade**. Let's consider Canada's merchandise trade patterns first.

□ Canada's Major Merchandise Trading Partners

Figure 22.2 shows Canada's major merchandise trading partners. Clearly, the United States is Canada's most important partner, buying over 75 percent of Canadian exports and accounting for almost 69 percent of imports in 1990. More surprisingly, Canada is also the United States's main trading partner. The proximity of the United States to Canada's major population centres means that transportation costs are low. The Free Trade Agreement between the two countries, which came into effect on January 1, 1989, is also strengthening trade ties. Japan and the major countries of the European Economic Community (which includes among others Germany, Italy, France, the United Kingdom, and Spain) are Canada's other most important international markets.

Table 22.2 on page 478 provides data on Canadian trade (total import and export dollar values) with its major partners from 1971 to 1990. Efforts were made in the 1970s to promote trade with European countries and diversify Canada's trading base away from the heavy dependence on the US, but the United States nonetheless remained Canada's dominant trading partner and Canada-US trade actually increased in the 1980s. The near doubling of the export value to the US was a result of the upswing in the US economy after the recession of the early 1980s. Exports to and imports from the United Kingdom declined significantly between 1971 and 1990 as Britain joined the European Economic Community. Over the same period, however, Canada's percentage trade with Japan increased.

Figure 22.2 Canada's major merchandise trading partners, 1990 (millions of dollars)

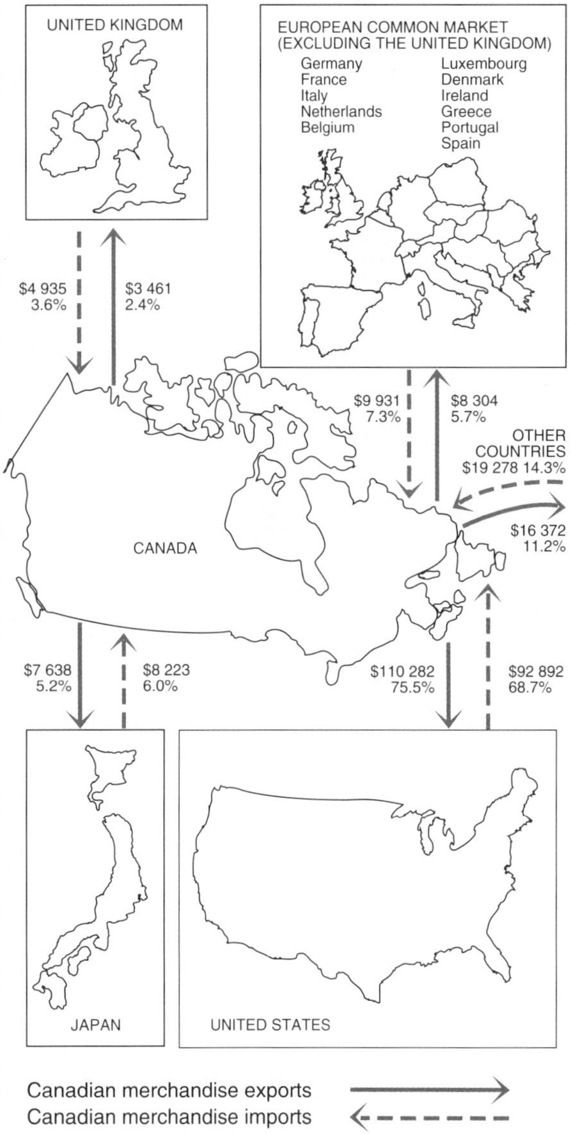

UNITED KINGDOM

EUROPEAN COMMON MARKET (EXCLUDING THE UNITED KINGDOM)
Germany   Luxembourg
France   Denmark
Italy   Ireland
Netherlands   Greece
Belgium   Portugal
                 Spain

$4 935 $3 461
3.6%   2.4%

$9 931 $8 304
7.3%   5.7%

OTHER COUNTRIES
$19 278 14.3%

$16 372
11.2%

CANADA

$7 638 $8 223 $110 282 $92 892
5.2%   6.0%   75.5%   68.7%

JAPAN   UNITED STATES

Canadian merchandise exports ———→
Canadian merchandise imports ←– – – –

The United States is Canada's major merchandise trading partner, followed by the European Community and Japan.

SOURCE: Statistics Canada, *Canadian Economic Observer*, April 1991.

Table 22.2 Canadian merchandise trade, 1971-1990

EXPORTS

	UNITED STATES		UNITED KINGDOM		OTHER EEC		JAPAN		OTHER COUNTRIES		TOTAL	
	$ MILLION	PERCENT	$ MILLION	PERCENT	$ MILLION	PERCENT	$ MILLION	PERCENT	$ MILLION	PERCENT	$ MILLION	PERCENT
1971	12 066	56.1	1 379	7.8	1 133	5.6	831	4.7	2 373	13.3	17 782	100.0
1975	22 059	65.6	1 889	5.6	2 323	6.9	2 140	6.4	4 321	12.8	33 616	100.0
1980	48 975	63.9	3 221	4.2	6 295	8.2	4 275	5.6	13 554	17.7	76 681	100.0
1985	93 793	78.8	2 456	2.0	4 486	3.8	5 597	4.7	12 730	10.7	119 061	100.0
1990	110 282	75.5	3 461	2.4	8 304	5.7	7 638	5.2	16 372	11.2	146 057	100.0

IMPORTS

	UNITED STATES		UNITED KINGDOM		OTHER EEC		JAPAN		OTHER COUNTRIES		TOTAL	
1971	10 727	70.0	877	5.7	972	6.3	803	5.2	1 934	12.6	15 314	100.0
1975	23 058	67.9	1 244	3.3	2 046	6.0	1 189	3.5	6 446	19.0	33 962	100.0
1980	47 343	69.7	1 942	2.8	3 740	5.5	2 810	4.1	12 068	17.8	67 903	100.0
1985	73 406	71.5	3 104	3.0	7 469	7.3	6 063	5.9	12 627	12.2	102 669	100.0
1990	92 892	68.7	4 935	3.6	9 931	7.3	8 223	6.0	19 278	14.3	135 259	100.0

SOURCE: Statistics Canada, *Canadian Economic Observer*, Historical Supplement 1989/90 and April 1991.

The United States has remained Canada's major merchandise trading partner despite some efforts to increase trade with other nations in the 1970s. Trade with the United States and Japan increased most significantly in the 1980s.

□ □ □ □ □ □

New York Diary

Out of my bed and into the shower: it's another day on the job in New York. Read *The New York Times*—printed on Canadian newsprint. . . .

Into the subway. Fight my way into one of the new Bombardier cars—so clean, quiet, and quick. And no graffiti. . . .

Working in New York means a dress-for-success business suit—where else but Brooks Brothers. . .now owned by Canadians.*

Downtown. Maybe I should go to work for Olympia & York: they seem to own every building down here. Perhaps then I could find an apartment in O&Y's Battery Park City— certainly the *in* place to live.

Time for lunch. Whet my appetite with a Molson Golden—or maybe a Moosehead. . .Buy a copy of *The Globe and Mail* on the corner. . . .

What's on for tonight? Movie on the West Side, at one of Cineplex Odeon's palaces. . . .

The television news says that 10 percent of our electricity in New York now comes from Canada. . . .Home with a good book. Margaret Atwood sells well here.

Settle down for the night. An elegant night cap: eggs and Canadian bacon and a glass of Canada Dry ginger ale—the only things I know with Canada in the name— and they're not Canadian.

*now not owned by Canadians.
SOURCE: *The Globe and Mail*, March 3, 1988.

Applications

1. We often think that Canada is affected much more by the dominance of the US in its trading relations than the other way around. How does this article suggest a different point of view?

2. List the types of Canadian exports to the US mentioned in the article. Note other examples of goods and services that Canada might typically export to the US.

☐ Canadian Merchandise Imports and Exports

If we look at the major categories of Canada's imports and exports, illustrated in Figure 22.3 for 1990, we can see that roughly half of our exports to other countries were natural resource products and the other half manufactured goods. Table 22.3 on page 480 outlines the specific products in these categories and their dollar values. Forest products (primarily newsprint, wood pulp, and lumber) and metals and minerals account for the major portion of our natural resource exports, followed by energy materials (oil, natural gas, and coal), and food products (including wheat, other grains, and fish products). Motor vehicles and parts constitute a large portion of our manufactured exports. Other manufactured exports include aircraft and parts, communications and electronics equipment, and agricultural and industrial machinery.

Traditionally, our principal exports have been natural resource products. Canada is a nation richly endowed with forests, minerals, and other natural resources. In the nineteenth century, farm, fish, and forest products dominated our trade. With the discovery and development of minerals in the late nineteenth and early twentieth centuries, minerals became an important export. In the early twentieth century, the emphasis shifted somewhat to the export of manufactured products as the nation industrialized, our workforce became more highly skilled, and trade agreements with the United States were instituted (e.g., the Auto Pact).

The majority of our imports in 1990, as shown in Figure 22.3, were manufactured goods—principally machinery (industrial and agricultural) and equipment (communications and transportation). Motor vehicles and parts constituted another major portion of imports (almost one-quarter) followed by industrial materials. Food imports were primarily fresh fruits and vegetables from southern climates, and imports of energy goods included principally crude petroleum and coal. The reason for the prominence of motor vehicles and parts in our exports and imports will become clearer when we examine the Canada-US Auto Pact in the next chapter.

Figure 22.3 Canadian merchandise trade, 1990 (millions of dollars and percentages)

EXPORTS

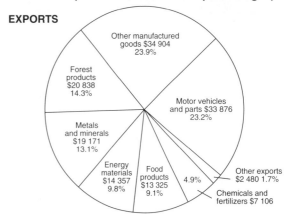

TOTAL 1990 EXPORTS $146 057 million

Approximately half of Canada's merchandise exports in 1990 were resource-based products, including forest products, metals and minerals, energy goods, and food products. The other half were manufactured goods, such as motor vehicles and parts, aircraft, and communications and electronics equipment.

IMPORTS

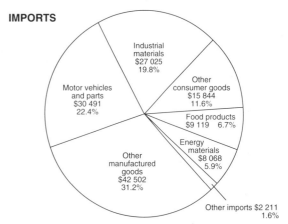

TOTAL 1990 IMPORTS $135 259 million

Most Canadian merchandise imports in 1990 consisted of manufactured goods, including motor vehicles and parts, machinery, aircraft, and industrial and energy materials.

Note: Figures have been rounded so they may not add to 100 percent.

SOURCE: *Bank of Canada Review*, March 1991.

Table 22.3 Canada's merchandise imports and exports, 1990 (millions of dollars)

EXPORTS

Food Products

Wheat	3 383
Other grains	1 650
Fish and fish products	2 619
Other farm products	5 673
Total	13 325

Energy Materials

Crude petroleum	5 689
Natural gas	3 189
Coal	1 659
Petroleum and coal products	3 282
Electricity	538
Total	14 357

Forest Products

Lumber	5 192
Other sawmill products	1 375
Wood pulp	5 924
Newsprint	6 201
Other paper	2 147
Total	20 838

Metals and Minerals

Ores and concentrates	5 441
Iron, steel, and alloys	2 454
Precious metals and alloys	3 061
Aluminium and alloys	2 949
Copper, nickel, and alloys	2 259
Other metals and alloys	1 141
Non-metallic minerals	1 866
Total	19 171

Chemicals and Fertilizers

Fertilizers	1 360
Other chemicals	5 746
Total	7 106

Motor Vehicles and Parts

Motor vehicles	24 366
Parts	9 510
Total	33 876

Other Manufactured Goods

Aircraft and parts	4 623
Other transportation equipment	1 905
Agricultural machinery	922
Communications and electronic equipment	8 779
Industrial machinery	5 120
Other manufactured goods	13 556
Total	34 904

Other Exports	2 480
Total Merchandise Exports	146 057

IMPORTS

Food	9 119

Energy Materials

Crude petroleum	5 381
Coal and petroleum and coal products	2 687
Total	8 068

Industrial Materials

Construction materials	2 511
Industrial metals (iron, etc.)	7 597
Chemical plastics, cotton, and other industrial materials	16 919
Total	27 025

Motor Vehicles and Parts	30 491

Other Manufactured Goods

Aircraft and parts	2 762
Other transport equipment	1 958
Agricultural machinery	1 542
Communications and electronic equipment	13 656
Industrial machinery	11 037
Other equipment and tools	11 548
Total	42 502

Other Consumer Goods	15 844
Other Imports	2 211
Total Merchandise Imports	135 259

SOURCE: *Bank of Canada Review*, March 1991.   Note: Numbers may not sum due to rounding.

A nation's imports, exports, and trade patterns are determined largely by its climate, location, resources, and the qualities of its population—the elements that provide it with absolute or comparative advantages in trade. Canada's rich endowment of natural resources and our expertise in transportation, communication, and electronics technology account for the dominance of these elements in our trade.

Nations differently endowed have different trade patterns. Japan, for example, is natural-resource poor, but has a highly educated and technologically sophisticated population. It, therefore, exports a diversity of sophisticated and high-quality manufactured products and imports the food, fuel, and raw materials it needs. Table 22.4 illustrates the contrast between Canada's and Japan's major imports and exports.

During the 1980s, Canadian exports of goods and services increased by approximately 60 percent in real terms and imports increased by about 70 percent. In terms of current dollars, both approximately doubled: exports from about $88 billion in 1980 to $169 billion in 1990 and imports from $82 billion in 1980 to $167

billion in 1990. The major increase in exports came in motor vehicles and parts, aircraft and parts, and communications equipment. Wheat exports declined during the decade in money terms with competition from heavily-subsidized US and European Common Market wheat. Sales of lumber to the US declined from the 1987 level as the US insisted Canada place a levy on lumber exports to the US.

☐ The Balance of Merchandise Trade

The **balance of trade** is the difference between the value of merchandise exports and imports. Our balance of trade is favourable if the value of our exports is greater than the value of our imports, and unfavourable if the value of imports is greater than that of exports.

From Figure 22.4, we can see that in 1990 our merchandise exports totalled $146 057 million and our merchandise imports $135 259 million. In 1990 then, we had a favourable balance of trade of $10 798 million. Since 1971, Canada has had only one year, 1975, with an unfavourable trade balance.

Our trade balance with the United States is also generally favourable, with the exception of one year since 1971. In 1990, our favourable trade balance with the US registered $17 billion. Since the mid-1980s, however, Canada has had an unfavourable balance of trade with its other principal trading partners.

Table 22.4 Japan's trade by category, 1990 (billions of US dollars)

	EXPORTS	IMPORTS
Foodstuffs	1.6	31.6
Raw materials	1.9	28.5
Fuels	1.3	56.7
Chemical products	15.9	16.0
Motor vehicles	51.0	6.4
Other machinery and transport equipment	150.3	31.5
Other manufactures	60.3	57.9
Miscellaneous	4.6	6.2

SOURCE: OECD; Japanese Ministry of Finance.

Japan is a natural-resource poor country with an industrious and highly-educated population. As a result, its main imports are foodstuffs, raw materials, and fuels, while its main exports are manufactured goods.

Figure 22.4 Canada's balance of merchandise trade, 1990 (millions of dollars)

Total merchandise exports $146 057 − Total merchandise imports $135 259 =

Balance of merchandise trade $10 798

The balance of merchandise trade is the difference between the total values of merchandise exports and imports.

☐ Canadian Invisible Trade

How does Canada's invisible trade fit into the picture? Our invisible exports and imports, as we noted earlier, can be divided into three categories—services, investment income or payments, and transfers. Canada's invisible trade in 1990 is illustrated in Figure 22.5. Since it may not be clear how trade in these categories occurs, let's examine them in a little more detail and consider examples.

Services

Payments by non-nationals for Canadian services are considered Canadian exports, since just as with exported goods, money from foreign sources comes into Canadian hands. Thus, when foreign tourists travel in Canada, their expenditures on services such as hotel accommodations and restaurant meals are Canadian exports. Similarly, when Americans, for example, use Canadian freight trains or Great Lakes ships to transport their goods, they are availing themselves of Canadian services. These services are thus exported.

On the other hand, payments made by Canadians for foreign services are considered invisible imports. Again, as with imported goods, money is passing from Canadian into foreign hands. The plane or train fares, meals, etc., Canadians buy in foreign countries, therefore, are service imports.

Investment Payments

Invisible exports include interest payments on loans made by Canadians to foreign corporations and governments, and dividends paid to Canadian shareholders of foreign corporations. Invisible imports incorporate interest payments to non-Canadians on money borrowed by Canadians, and dividends paid to foreign shareholders in Canadian corporations. These transactions are imports since Canadian funds must be converted into foreign funds.

Transfers

The invisible export of transfer payments consists primarily of the funds immigrants bring to Canada and payments made to Canadians from foreign inheritances. Imported transfers include funds Canadians

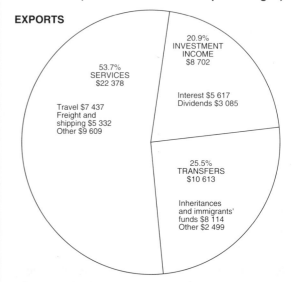

Figure 22.5 Canadian invisible trade, 1990 (millions of dollars and percentages)

EXPORTS

53.7% SERVICES $22 378
Travel $7 437
Freight and shipping $5 332
Other $9 609

20.9% INVESTMENT INCOME $8 702
Interest $5 617
Dividends $3 085

25.5% TRANSFERS $10 613
Inheritances and immigrants' funds $8 114
Other $2 499

TOTAL INVISIBLE EXPORTS 1990 $41 692 million

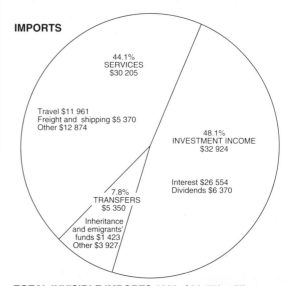

IMPORTS

44.1% SERVICES $30 205
Travel $11 961
Freight and shipping $5 370
Other $12 874

48.1% INVESTMENT INCOME $32 924
Interest $26 554
Dividends $6 370

7.8% TRANSFERS $5 350
Inheritance and emigrants' funds $1 423
Other $3 927

TOTAL INVISIBLE IMPORTS 1990 $68 478 million

Canada's invisible or non-merchandise trade consists primarily of services, investment income, and transfers. In 1990, Canada had a non-merchandise trade deficit of $26 786 million.

SOURCE: *Bank of Canada Review*, March 1991.

take with them when they emigrate and money inherited in Canada by non-residents.

☐ The Balance of Non-merchandise Trade

Typically, Canada has a negative balance on non-merchandise trade. Since 1965, for example, the balance has been negative every year and the deficit has increased steadily. In 1990, Canada had a non-merchandise trade deficit of $26 786 million, as shown in Figure 22.6.

Figure 22.6 also shows that our income from investment, services, and transfer exports is far below our expenditures on comparable invisible imports. Interest payments alone exceeded our interest income by almost $20 million. Dividend payments were more

than twice the receipts. Obviously, we are very dependent on external capital. We will return to this issue when we examine the foreign ownership of Canadian industry in the next chapter. Our expenditures on travel exceeded our income from that source by 50 percent.

☐ The Balance of Trade on Current Account

The **balance of trade on current account** is the difference between the money value of our visible and invisible exports and the money value of our visible and invisible imports. From Figure 22.7, we can see that our visible and invisible exports equalled $187 749 million in 1990, while our visible and invisible exports totalled $203 737 million. Thus, in 1990, we had an unfavourable current account balance of –$15 989 million.

Since 1965, Canada has had a current account surplus on only six occasions. The major reason for the deficit is that the favourable balance of merchandise trade has not made up for the consistently negative balance on non-merchandise trade, which increased over 20 times from 1965 to 1990. A significant component of this negative balance in service trade is the growth in interest payments on the Canadian debt held in other countries—from less than half a billion dollars in 1965 to $26.5 billion annually in 1990. Figure 22.8 on page 484 summarizes Canada's current account balance from 1965 to 1990.

☐ Canada's Capital Account

There is one other aspect of international trade we have not yet examined—the exchange of capital.

Figure 22.6 Balance of non-merchandise trade, 1990 (millions of dollars)

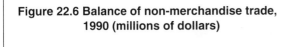

| Total non-merchandise exports $41 692 | − | Total non-merchandise imports $68 478 | = |

Balance of non-merchandise trade –$26 786

The balance of non-merchandise trade is the difference between the total value of non-merchandise exports and imports.

Figure 22.7 Canadian current account balance, 1990 (millions of dollars)

| Merchandise exports $146 057 | + | Invisible exports $41 692 | − | Merchandise imports $135 259 | + | Invisible imports $68 478 | = | Current account balance –$15 989 |

$187 749 $203 737

The current account balance is the difference between the merchandise and invisible exports and the merchandise and invisible imports. In 1990, Canada had a current account deficit of –$15 989 million.

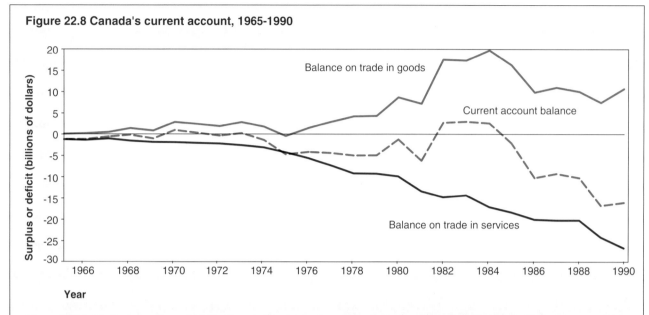

Figure 22.8 Canada's current account, 1965-1990

Since 1965 (with the exception of 1975), Canada has had a favourable balance of merchandise trade. This has been offset by an almost consistent and increasing negative balance on non-merchandise trade due largely to the burgeoning increase in interest payments on the Canadian debt held in other countries.

SOURCE: *Bank of Canada Review*, March 1991.

Table 22.5 Canada's capital account, 1990 (millions of dollars)

CANADIAN CLAIMS ON NON-RESIDENTS (PAYMENTS)		CANADIAN LIABILITIES TO NON-RESIDENTS (RECEIPTS)	
Direct investment abroad	−1 422	Foreign direct investment in Canada	5 729
Portfolio investment abroad	−1 150	Foreign portfolio investment in Canada	11 688
Other claims	−6 075	Other liabilities	12 838
Total	−8 647	Total	30 255
Official international reserves	− 649		
Total	−9 296		

The capital account is a summary of investment capital flows into and out of the country and changes in international reserves. In 1990, total payments exceeded total receipts on capital investments by $20 969 million. International reserves increased by $649 million, shown as a negative number because Canadian dollars are exchanged into a foreign currency to record the increase.

Suppose you buy American stocks on the New York Stock Exchange, purchase US government bonds, or decide to make a deposit in a foreign bank. These three transactions are similar to Canadian imports of goods in that they provide non-Canadians with Canadian dollars. In return for these payments, Canadian investors and creditors *import* securities—bonds, stocks, and claims against foreign banks, for example.

Non-Canadians can also engage in similar transactions in Canada. They can hold Canadian stocks or bonds or have accounts in Canadian banks. In these cases, Canada *exports* the stocks, bonds, and claims on Canadian banks, and—just like exports of goods or services—receives foreign currency in exchange.

Table 22.5 shows Canada's **capital account**—that is, the flows of investment capital into and out of the country for 1990. Purchases by Canadians of foreign capital (stocks, bonds, etc.) are categorized under the heading "Canadian claims on non-residents" and are shown as minus values (money paid out). Purchases by non-Canadians of Canadian capital are listed under the heading "Canadian liabilities to non-residents" and are shown as positive values (money received). The difference between the total exported investment capital and the total imported investment capital gives the net capital flow—$20 969 million in 1990. In other words, foreign investment in Canada was greater than Canadian investment abroad.

Table 22.5 also shows that investment capital may take the form of direct investment, portfolio investment, or deposits in banks. Changes in official international reserve holdings are also an important category of the Canadian capital account.

Direct Investment

Direct investment is investment made to achieve direct control over a company. Non-residents who establish companies in Canada or increase their ownership shares so that control of the company passes out of Canadian hands are making direct investments in Canada.

Canadians, too, can establish corporations or gain control of existing corporations in other countries. From Table 22.5, we can see that foreign direct investment in Canada exceeded Canadian direct investment abroad by $4307 million.

Portfolio Investment

Portfolio investment occurs when investors buy stocks or bonds for capital gains or interest and dividend income. Thus, non-residents who buy stocks or bonds of Canadian-controlled corporations, or bonds of provincial or federal governments, are making portfolio investments in Canada. Canadians can do likewise in other countries. In 1990, non-residents bought $10 538 million more in Canadian securities than Canadians bought elsewhere.

Other Claims and Liabilities

Other claims include short-term international transactions, such as changes in Canadian-held bank account balances abroad or in Canadian federal government loans. Similar transactions are included under "other liabilities," but for non-residents and foreign governments.

Official International Reserves

Canada's official international reserves, managed by the Bank of Canada for the federal government, are composed mainly of US dollars ($9.5 billion in 1991) and other foreign currencies ($4.5 billion in 1991). Canada also has reserves in gold, which could be sold for US$650 million in 1991. Other reserves include Special Drawing Rights (usually called SDRs) with the International Monetary Fund (IMF), which can be used to settle international debts. Canada can also borrow money from the IMF up to US$600 million by supplying Canadian dollars as collateral.

Canada's official international reserves are similar to the bank account of an individual. If the total you earn is greater than what you spend, you will have a surplus and you will probably add it to your bank account. If what you earn is less than what you spend, you will probably make up the difference from your bank account. Your account is a cushion to help you through financially difficult times. Similarly, our official international reserves are our national cushion. When we buy more goods, services, and securities than we sell, we sell some of our foreign reserves for Canadian dollars to make up the shortfall. When we sell more goods, services, and securities than we buy, our foreign reserves increase.

As Table 22.5 shows, Canada's international reserves increased by $649 million in 1990. In other words, inflows of money to buy Canadian exports, bonds, etc., exceeded money outflows for Canadian imports, foreign stocks, etc., by $649 million. This figure is shown as a negative number because for our international reserves to increase, Canadian dollars must be exchanged into a foreign currency—just as when we purchase imports.

☐ The Balance of Payments

We have considered each facet of Canada's international trade—merchandise, invisible, and capital exchanges. For a complete picture of Canada's trade performance, however, we need to consider them all together. In other words, we must examine Canada's balance of payments. The **balance of payments** is the summary of all visible, invisible, and capital transac-

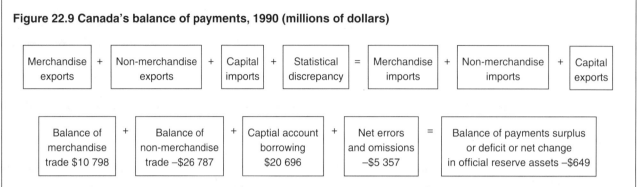

Figure 22.9 Canada's balance of payments, 1990 (millions of dollars)

The balance of payments is the summary of all merchandise, non-merchandise, and capital transactions between one nation and the rest of the world in a given year. All money received from exports must equal all money paid out for imports. However, in 1990, Canada had a balance of payments surplus of $649 million, shown as a negative number because for an increase in international reserves, Canadian dollars must be changed into a foreign currency.

tions between one country and the rest of the world over a period of time—usually one year.

Figure 22.9 illustrates Canada's balance of payments for 1990. If all the measurements in the balance of payments were both complete and completely accurate (that is, error free), then the addition of Canadian visible and invisible exports and capital imports would exactly equal Canadian visible and invisible imports and capital exports. The international payments would exactly balance. However, as we can see from Figure 22.9, there is a $5357 million discrepancy between the two, which according to Statistics Canada is an indicator of errors and unrecorded transactions. Errors or omissions can occur in the collection, sampling, and estimation of data.

Figure 22.9, however, also shows that Canada had a balance of payments surplus of $649 million in 1990. If all money received from exports must equal all money paid out for imports, how can we have a balance of payments surplus or deficit? The answer is that the official international reserves are not calculated into the balance of payments. The surplus in 1990 is shown as a negative number because an increase in the international reserves means that Canadian dollars must be changed into a foreign currency.

■ Exchange Rates

An **exchange rate** is the price at which one currency is exchanged for another. On January 24, 1992, for example, the exchange rate of the Canadian dollar was 85.46 cents American.

The value of the Canadian dollar is of great importance to many people. If you are taking a holiday outside Canada, for example, the exchange rate in part determines how much you will have to pay for the goods and services you buy. If you travel in France and the exchange rate is 5 francs to the dollar, you will pay half as much as if the exchange rate were 2.5 francs to the dollar. Within Canada, the exchange rate influences the price of all imported goods and services. The higher the value of the Canadian dollar, the less expensive are the imports.

The exchange value of the Canadian dollar also affects the prices of our exports. The lower the value of the dollar, the cheaper are our exports. Cheaper exports mean that demand for them will be greater and so will the demand for Canadian workers to produce them. The exchange rate thus has a significant effect on Canadian trade, our employment rate, and the health of our economy as a whole.

□ □ □ □ □ □

Skill Development: Calculating Foreign Currency Exchanges

Foreign currency exchanges are an important part of international trade transactions, but they are also important for many of us as individuals. Suppose you have decided to take a shopping trip to the United States. Millions of Canadians make trips to the US by car for less than 24 hours every year and buy US goods and services while they are there. One question you would certainly want to answer is how Canadian prices compare to US prices for the goods you want to buy. Knowing the Canadian prices and the US prices is not enough, however. You also need to know how much the Canadian dollar is worth in terms of the US dollar.

Four Baskets of Border Buys

BASKET #1	BRITISH COLUMBIA (CANADIAN DOLLARS)	WASHINGTON STATE (US DOLLARS)	BASKET #2	MANITOBA (CANADIAN DOLLARS)	NORTH DAKOTA (US DOLLARS)
Sony compact disc player	504.45	403.81	Sanyo 25" Television	569.99	364.64
Sony Trinitron 28" television	1 129.95	991.48	Women's casual canvas shoes	17.09	4.30
Oshkosh girls overalls	34.23	18.68	10-cup coffee maker	33.05	16.78
Homogenized milk (4L)	3.59	2.76	Latex paint (5 L)	19.35	7.04
Fresh turkey (450 g)	1.99	0.93	Butter (450 g)	2.39	1.10
Medium cheddar cheese (450 g)	4.50	1.76	Package of cream cheese	2.39	0.89

BASKET #3	ONTARIO (CANADIAN DOLLARS)	NEW YORK STATE (US DOLLARS)	BASKET #4	NEW BRUNSWICK (CANADIAN DOLLARS)	MAINE (US DOLLARS)
Sony 8-mm video camera	1 264.95	1 030.47	Compact disc player	235.95	133.74
Men's Sperry Topsider deck shoes	103.38	79.62	Kenmore one cubit foot microwave oven	249.99	207.85
Oshkosh infant's denim overalls	36.38	17.21	Woman's unlined coat	182.25	63.72
2 percent milk (4 L)	4.69	1.90	Fresh chicken per 450 g	2.00	0.63
4 AA Energizer batteries	5.73	2.77	2 percent milk (4 L)	5.03	2.26
President's Choice Chocolate Chip Cookies	3.69	2.51	Medium cheddar cheese	4.50	3.32

NOTE: Prices include GST, state, and provincial taxes. Prices of American goods also include Canadian duties and taxes to be paid at the Canadian border. Comparisons are of exactly the same or similar goods.

SOURCE: *Maclean's*, April 29, 1991.

Calculating the Exchange

(a) To change Canadian dollars into US dollars (or any other currency).

Example: Suppose a litre of regular unleaded gasoline in New Brunswick costs 58.8 cents. What would it cost in US currency to a visitor from nearby Maine? We'll assume the current exchange rate is $1.00 Canadian equals $1.17 American.

$$58.8 \text{ cents Canadian} = \frac{58.8}{1.17} = 50.3 \text{ cents American}$$

(b) To change US dollars into Canadian dollars.

Example: Suppose a litre of regular unleaded gasoline in Maine costs 29.5 cents. What would it cost in Canadian currency to a visitor from nearby New Brunswick?

29.5 cents American = 29.5 x 1.17 = 34.5 cents Canadian

Applications

1. In 1991, the price of a litre of regular unleaded gasoline was 56.4 cents in Ontario, 48.9 cents in Manitoba, and 54.9 cents in British Columbia. In the neighbouring US states, a litre of gasoline cost US26.5 cents in New York, 25.6 cents in North Dakota, and 29.1 cents in Washington. What are the price differences for a litre of gasoline between each province and its neighbouring state in US currency?

2. In the early 1990s, cross-border shopping became a major concern for Canadian retailers. Canadian consumers were finding prices for many goods in the United States significantly lower than those in Canada. How much lower? For two of the baskets of "border buys" outlined on page 487, calculate how much Canadians would save in Canadian dollars on each good by shopping in the neighbouring US state.

German auto manufacturers who want to sell cars in Canada, Americans who want to buy Canadian bonds, Canadians who want to buy shares in British corporations, and the Canadian aircraft manufacturer who hopes to sell Canadian waterbombers to the Spanish government are all concerned with the exchange value of the Canadian dollar.

For transactions within a country, usually only one currency is involved. However, since we are so close to the US and so familiar with its currency, many stores and restaurants in Canada will readily accept US dollars at a posted exchange rate in payment for their goods and services.

In international trade, however, two currencies are involved. When you buy a meal in a restaurant in France or take a trip on the Paris subway, you will pay in French francs. To buy the French francs, you will sell your Canadian-dollar travellers' cheques. Similarly, when German auto manufacturers sell their cars in Canada, they receive Canadian dollars. But Canadian dollars are of little use to German workers or auto parts suppliers. The German auto manufacturer, therefore, has to change the Canadian dollars into Deutsche Marks. The same is true of Americans who wish to buy Canadian bonds. They, too, have to exchange their US dollars into Canadian dollars, and so on.

□ Demand for Canadian Dollars

How is the exchange value of the Canadian dollar determined? The answer by now will be obvious to you—by supply and demand. Let's start by examining the demand for Canadian dollars from those who hold US dollars. The demand for Canadian dollars in this case comes from three main sources.

(i) US imports of Canadian goods or, to put it another way, Canadian exports to the US   When an American company buys Canadian lumber, for example, a demand for Canadian dollars is created.

(ii) US imports of Canadian services   When a US citizen dines in a Canadian restaurant or stays in a Canadian hotel, for example, a demand for Canadian dollars is also created.

(iii) US purchases of Canadian bonds or companies
To complete the purchase of Canadian bonds or businesses, a payment has to be made to Canadian bondholders or owners of the business in Canadian dollars. Thus, these transactions also create demand for Canadian dollars.

The quantity of Canadian dollars demanded—just like the demand for any other good or service—depends on the price. Suppose, for example, the price of the Canadian dollar in terms of the US dollar falls (depreciates) from 80 cents to 75 cents. What effect will this have on the quantity of Canadian dollars demanded? With a cheaper Canadian dollar for Americans, it means that they will be paying much less for Canadian goods, services, and assets. For example, before the depreciation, a meal that cost an American tourist CDN$10 would cost $10 × 0.80 = US$8.00. With the depreciation, the price in US dollars falls to $10 × 0.75 = $7.50. Therefore, with a cheaper Canadian dollar, more American tourists are likely to come to Canada and more American companies are likely to buy Canadian goods and services and invest in the country. With a decline or a depreciation in the value of the Canadian dollar, the quantity of Canadian dollars demanded increases.

Similarly, if the value of the Canadian dollar in terms of the US dollar increases (appreciates), then the quantity of Canadian dollars demanded will decrease. With an increase in the price of the Canadian dollar from US80 cents to US$1.00, the price of the $10 Canadian meal for the American tourist increases from US$8.00 (0.80 × $10) to US$10.00 (1.00 × $10). Therefore, fewer Americans are likely to visit Canada. The price of US imports from Canada will also increase and American companies will be less likely to buy from Canada.

Thus, as the price of the Canadian dollar appreciates, the quantity demanded decreases. As the price of the dollar depreciates, the quantity demanded increases.

☐ Supply of Canadian Dollars

When Canadians wish to buy US goods, services, or assets, a payment has to be made in US dollars. Cana-

dian dollars are, therefore, exchanged for US dollars and a supply of Canadian dollars is created.

The supply of Canadian dollars depends on the amount of goods and services Canadians import and the amount they invest. The supply also depends on the price of Canadian dollars. If the Canadian dollar increases in value, Canadians can buy more US goods with the same expenditure. For example, suppose you wish to buy a US-made CD player that costs US$1000. If the exchange rate is at US$0.80 = CDN$1.00, then you would pay CDN$1.20 for each US dollar. For US$1000, you would pay 1000 × CDN$1.25 = CDN$1200.

Suppose now the value of the Canadian dollar appreciates, so that the rate is US$1.00 = CDN$1.00. Now you would pay 1000 × $1.00 = CDN$1000. With lower prices, Canadians will tend to buy more US goods and services. Thus, as the value of the Canadian dollars appreciates, more dollars will be supplied.

A depreciation in the value of the Canadian dollar has the opposite effect. US goods will cost Canadians more and we will tend to buy fewer of them. As the value of the Canadian dollar depreciates, fewer dollars will be supplied.

☐ Exchange Market for the Canadian Dollar

We have considered only the market in which Canadian dollars are exchanged for US dollars. There are, clearly, many other markets in which the Canadian dollar is exchanged for the Japanese yen, the British pound, and so on. The market that is most important to us is the Canadian-US dollar market, however, since it is in this market that most of our international transactions take place.

The exchange rate or value of the Canadian dollar is, of course, determined by the point at which supply and demand are in equilibrium. As shown in Figure 22.10, the exchange rate is the price at which the supply and demand curves intersect, in this example at US$0.80. If the exchange rate falls below US$0.80 to US$0.75, more Canadian dollars are demanded than are supplied and the market has a shortage. Competition among buyers of Canadian exports for the dollars will push the price up again until it reaches equilibrium at US$0.80.

Similarly, if the exchange rate is above US$0.80 at US$1.00, more Canadian dollars will be supplied than are demanded and the market has a surplus. Competition among suppliers will push the rate down until it again reaches equilibrium at US$0.80.

☐ Determination of Exchange Rates

Exchange rates may be determined by supply and demand or they may be influenced by government. If the exchange rate is determined by the unregulated market forces of supply and demand, it is said to be floating or flexible. If government establishes the exchange rate, it is said to be pegged or fixed. The exchange rate may also be determined by a combination of these two methods, a system known as a managed float.

Floating (Flexible) Exchange Rates
Freely floating or **flexible exchange rates** are determined by the forces of supply and demand. Figure 22.10 shows how supply and demand operate to

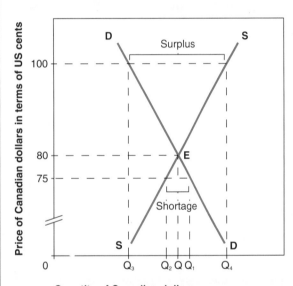

Figure 22.10 Demand and supply of Canadian dollars

The exchange rate or equilibrium price of the Canadian dollar is the point at which the supply and demand curves intersect—at US$0.80 in this example. If the exchange rate is US$0.75, the quantity of Canadian dollars demanded is 0Q₁ and the quantity supplied is 0Q₂. The market has a shortage. Competition among buyers of Canadian exports for the limited number of Canadian dollars will push the exchange rate up to US$0.80 once again. If the exchange rate is US$1.00, the quantity demanded is 0Q₃ and the quantity supplied is 0Q₄. The market has a surplus and competition among suppliers will push the exchange rate down to US$0.80 once again.

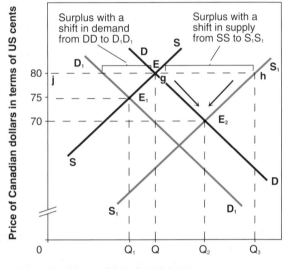

Figure 22.11 Shifts in the supply and demand for Canadian dollars

With supply initially at SS and demand at DD, equilibrium is at E and the exchange rate is US$0.80 = CDN$1.00. If demand shifts from DD to D₁D₁, there is a surplus of Canadian dollars. With flexible exchange rates, the value of the Canadian dollar will fall until a new equilibrium is reached at E₁ where US$0.75 = CDN$1.00. Similarly, a surplus of Canadian dollars is also created when supply increases to S₁S₁. The exchange rate will fall to a new equilibrium at E₂, where CDN$1.00 = US$0.70. With a fixed exchange rate, however, the dollar is not permitted to fall. The Bank of Canada buys the surplus dollars to keep the exchange rate at US$0.80.

determine the value of the Canadian dollar, at US$0.80 in the example illustrated. However, both supply and demand curves are subject to change. The demand for Canadian dollars may decrease if fewer Americans spend money on Canadian vacations, buy Canadian bonds, or buy Canadian goods such as newspapers made from Canadian-made paper. As a result, the demand curve would shift to the left from DD to $D_1 D_1$, as shown in Figure 22.11.

Under a floating exchange rate policy, government simply allows the value of the Canadian dollar to adjust to the changed conditions. In this case, the value of the Canadian dollar would fall from US$0.80 to US$0.75.

Similarly, if the supply of Canadian dollars increases (as a result, for example, of Air Canada buying more US aircraft, more Canadians travelling on Miami-based cruise ships, or Canadians buying more US stocks), then the supply curve would shift to the right from SS to $S_1 S_1$ and the equilibrium would shift from E to E_2. Again, under a floating exchange rate policy, government simply allows the dollar to depreciate, in this case from US$0.80 to US$0.70.

How does the new equilibrium come about? With the exchange rate at CDN$1.00 = US$0.80 and the increased supply of Canadian dollars, the market has a surplus of Canadian dollars shown as gh in Figure 22.11. Only jg Canadian dollars are demanded to pay for US imports from Canada, while jh dollars are supplied. There is, then, a balance of payments deficit. The surplus of Canadian dollars means that the price of the dollar will fall until it reaches a new equilibrium at US$0.70.

A change in the exchange rate of the Canadian dollar changes the prices of all Canadian goods bought by Americans and all American goods bought by Canadians. As the value of the Canadian dollar depreciates from US$0.80 to US$0.70, the price of Canadian imports from the US increases and the price of Canadian exports to the US decreases.

Suppose you wanted to buy a $1000 US CD player when the exchange rate is CDN$1.00 = US$0.80. It would cost you 1000 × 100/80 = CDN$1250. With the exchange rate at US$0.70, it would cost you 1000 × 100/70 = CDN$1428.57. At the higher price, you are less likely to buy the American product and more likely to buy Canadian. Thus, the supply of Canadian dollars in foreign exchange markets is likely to diminish as the exchange rate falls.

At the same time, with the depreciation of the Canadian dollar, the price of Canadian exports to the US decreases and the quantity demanded increases. Suppose an American corporation had decided to buy a Canadian-made corporate jet for CDN$10 million. At the rate of CDN$1.00 = US$0.80, the price would be US$8 million. At the new exchange rate of CDN$1.00 = US$0.70, the price would be US$7 million. At lower prices, Americans would demand more Canadian goods. Thus, as the value of the Canadian dollar depreciates from US$0.80 to US$0.70, the quantity demanded increases and the quantity supplied decreases until a new equilibrium is reached.

Similarly, when there is a balance of payments surplus as a result of a shortage of Canadian dollars in foreign exchange markets, the value of the Canadian dollar will appreciate. Canadian exports will increase in price and sales will decline. Canadian imports will decrease in price and purchases will increase. As Canadian imports increase and exports decrease, the balance of payments surplus will diminish until a new equilibrium is achieved.

The adjustments necessary to correct the surplus of Canadian dollars in foreign exchange markets—the increase in Canadian exports and the decrease in Canadian imports—are precisely those necessary to correct the situation. These adjustments take place automatically without government intervention.

Fixed (or Pegged) Exchange Rates
Instead of allowing exchange rates to float freely, Canadian governments may institute a **fixed exchange rate** policy, by which the Canadian dollar is fixed at a particular value. During most of the 1960s, for example, the Canadian dollar was fixed at 92.5 cents American. However, even while the value of the dollar is fixed, the supply and demand for the dollar will vary over time. Indeed, under a fixed exchange rate system, government must continually intervene to influence the supply and demand for Canadian dollars. How? It may buy or sell foreign currency, regulate imports and exports, and/or adjust the interest rate.

(i) Buying and selling foreign currency Suppose the Canadian government has fixed the exchange rate of the Canadian dollar at US$0.80. At this exchange rate, the demand for Canadian goods and services in the US decreases and the demand for US goods and services in Canada increases. These shifts in supply and demand bring an increase in the supply of Canadian dollars in foreign exchange markets and a decrease in demand for the dollars. By buying Canadian dollars using the official international reserves available in the Exchange Fund Account, the Bank of Canada can bring the supply and demand for Canadian dollars back to equilibrium at the desired exchange rate of US$0.80.

Conversely, if the demand in the US for Canadian goods increases and/or US imports to Canada decrease, then there will be pressure on the Canadian dollar to rise in value. In this situation, the Bank of Canada sells Canadian dollars for foreign currencies. The increased supply of Canadian dollars will thus bring supply and demand back into equilibrium at the fixed exchange rate.

This method of intervening in foreign exchange markets to keep the value of the dollar fixed works if the dollar is pegged at about its equilibrium value. In this case, over time, balance of payments surpluses and deficits are roughly equal. Prolonged and substantial balance of payments deficits, however, could bankrupt the Exchange Fund Account and force the abandonment of the fixed exchange rate policy.

(ii) Regulating imports and exports If there is a balance of payments deficit—which would result in pressure to lower the value of the Canadian dollar—the Canadian government can discourage imports by imposing higher tariffs and lower quotas. It could also encourage exports by the provision of subsidies. Thus, the supply of Canadian dollars would be diminished and the demand increased, bringing the two forces closer to equilibrium at the fixed exchange rate.

(iii) Adjusting the interest rate By increasing short-term interest rates, the Bank of Canada can make Canada a more attractive place for Canadians and non-Canadians to invest their funds. An inflow of funds increases the demand for Canadian dollars and thus helps to stem or reverse a decline in its value. Conversely, short-term decreases in interest rates will tend to make Canada a less attractive location for investments and thus stem or reverse an increase in the value of the Canadian dollar.

Of the three ways to fix the exchange value of the dollar, the preferred method is the sale and purchase of foreign funds. The imposition of tariffs and quotas results in higher prices for imports and the use of subsidies to promote exports results in higher taxes. Changing interest rates are likely to have an impact on aggregate investment and aggregate demand. High interest rates, for example, may result in declining investment, declining aggregate demand, declining employment, and declining income.

The advantage of the floating exchange rate system is that the rate adjusts automatically to day-by-day changes in the supply and demand for international currencies without the intervention of the central bank. The advantage of the fixed exchange rate system is that the rate of exchange is known in advance, thus removing one source of risk for importers and exporters—that of changes in the value of the currency.

The Managed Float

The **managed float** is a combination of the fixed and floating exchange rate systems. It is like the fixed exchange rate system in that the central bank intervenes from time to time in foreign exchange markets to buy and sell currencies and control the fluctuations in exchange rates. But it is like the floating exchange rate system in that the exchange rate is left to a considerable extent to fluctuate according to market forces. There is usually no "official" exchange rate.

The managed float is the system that has been used by successive Canadian governments since 1970. The Bank of Canada has intervened in foreign exchange markets to buy foreign currencies and hold down the exchange rate (as it did, for example, in 1987-88 when the economy was booming) and to sell foreign currencies to buttress the value of the Canadian dollar (as it did in April 1991 when the economy was in a recession).

☐ Aims of Exchange Rate Policy

We have examined three exchange rate systems— fixed, floating, and managed floating. But what is the major objective of the Bank of Canada's policy? Should it attempt—as far as it can—to raise the value of the Canadian dollar? Clearly, a highly valued Canadian dollar in terms of foreign currencies would be to the advantage of Canadian consumers. Imports would be cheaper and holidays in other countries less expensive. For Canadian producers that export goods and services or compete with imports, however, an increase in the value of the dollar is disadvantageous. Canadian exports will be more expensive for foreign nations to buy and imports will be cheaper for Canadians. Both effects would cut into the profits of domestic producers.

A lower-priced dollar, on the other hand, would benefit producers but disadvantage Canadian consumers. Canadian consumers would have to pay more for imports and trips abroad, but producers' exports would be cheaper and since imports would be more expensive, they would be better able to compete in Canada.

Changes in the value of the Canadian dollar have wide-ranging effects on the economy. Reductions in the value of the dollar stimulate employment and incomes in export-oriented industries and in Canadian industries that compete with foreign imports in Canada. Thus aggregate demand, employment, and GDP increase—but at a price. The prices of imports also increase and because imports are an important part of our GDP, the general price level will tend to rise. Thus, a decrease in the value of the Canadian dollar is likely to increase employment, inflation, and the balance of payments.

An increase in the value of the dollar is likely to have the opposite effect. Since Canadian exporters will find it more difficult to compete in foreign markets and Canadian producers will find it harder to compete with imports from other countries, employment, inflation, and GDP are likely to decline along with the balance of payments.

Thus, in choosing the appropriate exchange rate policy, the Bank of Canada must balance the objectives of reduced inflation and unemployment with that of a viable balance of payments.

☐ Exchange Rates 1945-1992

Since 1945, Canada has had periods of fixed exchange rates and of floating rates. Exchange rates have fluctuated widely—between a low of US$0.69 in 1986 and a high of US$1.04 in 1957.

The 1940s and 1950s

During World War II (1939-1945), the value of the dollar was fixed at US90.9 cents, as shown in Figure 22.12. The International Monetary Fund (IMF) was established at the end of World War II to monitor balance of payments and exchange rates, and to help countries with exchange rate problems by providing them with loans. These loans were designed to avoid the destructive devaluations of currencies experienced during the Great Depression of the 1930s. Currencies were pegged to the US dollar at a fixed rate and the US dollar was fixed at US$35.00 for one ounce of gold.

In 1946, the pegged value of the Canadian dollar was raised to par—that is, CDN$1.00 = US$1.00. In 1949, following the devaluation of the British pound, the value of the Canadian dollar was reduced to US90.9 cents. This devaluation was followed by a large inflow of capital, which despite a current account deficit with the end of the fixed exchange rate, resulted in an increase in the value of the Canadian dollar. Throughout much of the 1950s, the dollar floated above par with the US dollar.

The 1960s and 1970s

Through much of the 1960s, the dollar was fixed at US92.5 cents. In the 1970s, Canada returned to a flexible exchange rate system as increases in foreign reserves resulting from trade surpluses showed the dollar was fixed too low. Interventions in the foreign exchange market by the Bank of Canada meant that we had a managed float. In the first half of the decade, the dollar rose above par with the US dollar. In the 1970s, most countries left the fixed exchange rate system under the IMF and allowed their currencies to float.

The function of the IMF also changed. Now it provides loans to less developed countries to ease their balance of payments problems and the loans are usually conditional on the country adopting economic policies specified by the IMF. Toward the end of the decade, declining short-term interest rates in Canada reduced short-term capital inflows from the US, resulting in a decline in the value of the dollar.

The 1980s and Early 1990s

In the 1980s, the exchange rate continued to fall until the dollar reached a record low of US$0.69 in 1986. Higher inflation rates in Canada than in the US and the continuing recession in Canada helped bring about the decline. After 1987, continuing high interest rates in Canada helped push the dollar up to US$0.87 by the end of 1991. Interventions by the Bank of Canada in the foreign exchange market meant that we continued to have a managed float.

☐ International Exchange Rate Systems

In the twentieth century, three international exchange rate systems have been used. These include the gold standard, pegged exchanged rates, and most recently managed floating rates.

The Gold Standard

The gold standard prevailed until the 1930s (with the exception of the years 1914-1918 during World War I). Under this system, each nation defined its currency in terms of a certain amount of gold—and thus defined the exchange rate with other currencies. With these stable exchange rates, risks and uncertainties of varying exchange rates were eliminated and international trade was stimulated. However, this system largely broke down during the Great Depression of the 1930s as currency devaluations by many countries undermined one of its principal benefits.

Pegged Exchange Rates (1945-1973)

Between 1945 and 1973, most countries adhered to a system of fixed exchange rates supervised by the International Monetary Fund. Currencies were defined in terms of gold or US dollars. Each nation was obligated to keep its currency stable in relation to that of other countries. In the event of a fundamental imbalance in a nation's external trade, it was permitted to alter its currency value by 10 percent without the permission of the IMF.

This system functioned well until the 1970s when the US suspended the convertibility of the US dollar into gold because of persistent and growing trade deficits. The US dollar was unpegged and its value determined by market forces.

Managed Floating Exchange Rates (1973 to Present)

Since 1973, most countries have adopted a managed floating exchange rate system. Exchange rates are allowed to float to meet persistent and long-term shifts in supply and demand. Short-term fluctuations, on the other hand, are controlled by central banks.

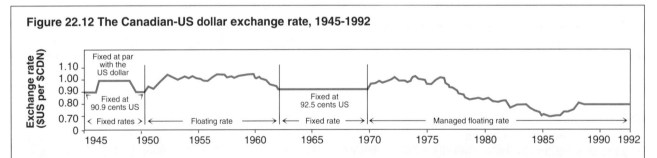

Figure 22.12 The Canadian-US dollar exchange rate, 1945-1992

During World War II (1939-1945), the Canadian dollar was fixed at US90.9 cents. In 1946, it was fixed at par with the US dollar. Between 1950 and 1962, the Canadian dollar was allowed to float and reached a post-war high of US$1.06 in 1957. In 1962, it was pegged at US92.5 cents. After 1970, the dollar was allowed to float, though the Bank of Canada intervened from time to time to influence the exchange rate. The Canadian dollar reached a low of US$0.69 in 1985. Since then, the dollar has tended to increase in value, reaching a high of US$0.87 in mid-1991.

SOURCE: Computed from data in Statistics Canada, *CANSIM Databank* and *Bank of Canada Review*, December 1991 and January 1992.

Summary

a. Trade is of vital importance to the Canadian economy since we depend on imports for many of our goods and services and exports account for approximately 25 percent of our GDP and one in five jobs.

b. International trade is conducted through the products markets. Goods and services flow from Canadian businesses through the products markets to foreign nations (real flow of exports). Goods and services also flow from foreign nations to Canadian households, businesses, and governments through the products markets (real flow of imports). In return for these real flows, money flows from foreign nations to Canadian businesses as payments for exports and from Canadian households, businesses, and governments to foreign nations for imports.

c. International trade allows nations to increase productivity through increased competition, economies of scale, and specialization in products for which they have an absolute or comparative advantage. Absolute advantage refers to a nation's ability to produce a good or service with fewer resources (and more efficiently) than any other nation. Comparative advantage refers to a nation's ability to produce a good or service with relatively fewer resources than other nations. By specializing in products for which they have absolute or comparative advantages, all nations can increase total production and the standard of living for their peoples.

d. Disadvantages of trade include higher prices for some products depending on the terms of trade (rate of exchange for products), displacement of workers when imports are cheaper than domestically-produced goods, and dependency on foreign nations for some goods and services.

e. Canada's major merchandise trading partner is the United States. Japan and the countries of the European Economic Community are Canada's other major foreign markets. Approximately half of Canada's merchandise exports are natural resource products (particularly forest products, wheat and other grains, metals and minerals). The other half are manufactured goods, primarily automobiles and auto parts, aircraft and parts, and communications and electronics equipment. Since 1971, Canada has had a favourable balance of merchandise trade (with the exception of 1975).

f. Invisible or non-merchandise trade is the exchange of services, investment income and payments, and transfers of immigrants' funds and inheritances by Canadians. Canada has had a negative balance on its non-merchandise trade consistently since 1965 and the deficit is growing largely as a result of increasing interest payments on the debt Canadians hold in foreign nations. Canada's balance of trade on current account—the difference between visible and invisible exports and visible and invisible imports—has also been consistently negative since 1965.

g. Capital account summarizes the flows of investment capital into and out of the country. It includes direct investment (control of corporations), portfolio investment (the purchase and sale of stocks and bonds), short-term investment (deposits and loans), and changes in official international reserves.

h. The balance of payments is the summary of all international transactions (merchandise, non-merchandise, and capital) over a period of time, usually a year. All payments for imports from foreign nations must equal all receipts from exports—thus the term "balance of payments." Merchandise exports + non-merchandise exports + capital imports + statistical discrepancy = Merchandise imports + non-merchandise imports + capital exports. However, since the changes in official international reserves are not calculated in the balance of payments, we may have a balance of payments surplus or deficit.

i. The exchange rate of the Canadian dollar is its value in terms of other currencies. It is important because it affects the price of our exports and imports.

j. The exchange rate is shown as the point at which the demand and supply curves for Canadian dollars intersect. The quantity of Canadian dollars demanded depends on the amount of Canadian exports and the purchases of Canadian assets by non-Canadians. The greater is the value of these transactions, the greater is the quantity of dollars demanded (and *vice versa*). The quantity of Canadian dollars supplied depends on the amount of Canadian imports and the purchases of foreign assets by Canadians. The greater is the value of these transactions, the greater is the quantity of Canadian dollars supplied.

k. Exchange rates may be determined by supply and demand (floating or flexible exchange rate), by government (fixed or pegged exchange rate), or by a combination of the two (managed floating exchange rate). With a floating dollar, the exchange rate fluctuates according to changes in supply and demand without any government intervention. A shortage of dollars will create a balance of payments surplus and put pressure on the dollar to rise. A surplus of dollars will cause a balance of payments defict and put

pressure on the dollar to decline.

With a fixed exchange rate system, government pegs the value of the dollar at a specific rate and intervenes in the market to maintain this rate by either buying or selling foreign currency, regulating imports or exports, and/or adjusting the interest rate. Under a managed float system, the dollar is allowed to float but the central bank intervenes from time to time to smooth the fluctuations in the exchange rate.

l. In the nineteenth and early twentieth century, the international exchange rate system used was the gold standard. After World War II, most countries adhered to a system of fixed exchange rates supervised by the International Monetary Fund. Currencies were defined in terms of gold or the US dollar. In the 1970s, the US suspended the convertability of the US dollar into gold and most nations have since adopted a managed float system.

■ Review of Key Terms

Define each of the following key terms introduced in this chapter and provide examples where appropriate.

export
import
absolute advantage
comparative advantage
terms of trade
merchandise or visible trade
non-merchandise or
   invisible trade
balance of trade
balance of trade on current
   account

capital account
direct investment
portfolio investment
balance of payments
exchange rate
floating exchange rate
fixed exchange rate
managed float system

■ Application and Analysis

1. Suppose that two countries, Economia and Tradia, produce two goods only as outlined in Table 22.6.

Table 22.6 Output per worker in units for Economia and Tradia

	AUTOMOBILES	BREAD
Economia	5	3
Tradia	4	1

(a) Which country has an absolute advantage in the production of which good(s)?

(b) What is the opportunity cost of each product for each country?

(c) Which country has a comparative advantage in the production of which good?

2. Classify each of the following according to whether it is a Canadian visible or invisible export, or a visible or invisible Canadian import.

(a) the sale of Canadian aircraft in the US

(b) the sale of the British weekly magazine, *The Economist*, in Canada

(c) the purchase of a ticket on Singapore Airlines by a Canadian business woman

(d) the purchase of a hotel room in St John's, Newfoundland, by an American business woman

(e) your purchase of postcards of Notre Dame Cathedral in Paris

(f) your purchase of a ticket on the London subway

3. Referring to Table 22.7, calculate:

(a) the balance of trade

(b) the balance on non-merchandise trade

(c) the current account balance

(d) the balance of payments

(e) the change in international reserves.

4. What effect might each of the following have on the exchange rate of the Canadian dollar in terms of the US dollar? Explain why in each case.

(a) Canadian exports of automobiles to the US increase

(b) Canadian interest rates fall sharply as the Bank of Canada pursues an expansionary monetary policy

(c) Canadian inflation rates fall well below those in the United States

(d) Canadians flee south in record numbers this winter to escape a record cold winter

(e) US housing starts reach record numbers as the Federal Reserve (the US central bank) cuts interest rates to an all-time low

(f) Foreign borrowing by the Canadian federal government reaches an all-time high

5. As an importer, which would you prefer—a strong dollar or a weak dollar? Why?

Table 22.7 Canadian balance of payments, 1979 and 1989 (millions of dollars)

	1979	1989
I Merchandise trade		
Exports	65 581	141 768
Imports	61 158	134 673
II Non-merchandise trade		
Services		
Receipts	9 493	21 509
Payments	12 120	28 492
Investment income		
Receipts	2 648	9 836
Payments	9 803	30 980
Transfers		
Receipts	2 003	3 877
Payments	1 509	3 568
III Capital Flows		
Direct investment abroad	2 550	4 900
Portfolio investment abroad	582	2 324
Other claims on non-residents	2 470	4 078
Foreign direct investment in Canada	750	4 200
Foreign portfolio investment in Canada	3 874	21 087
Other liabilities	8 350	8 913
Statistical discrepancy	2 507	4 365

SOURCE: *Bank of Canada Review*, October 1991.

6. Suppose you export Canadian goods for sale in the US. As an exporter, you know that the values of currencies vary considerably over time. Complete Table 22.8 on page 498 by calculating the effect changes in the exchange rate have on the prices of the goods you export using the information given.

Exchange rate 1   CDN$1.00 = US$0.80

Exchange rate 2   CDN$1.00 = US$0.85

Exchange rate 3   CDN$1.00 = US$0.75

Table 22.8 Prices for exports

EXPORT	PRICE IN US DOLLARS PER UNIT	TOTAL PRICE IN CANADIAN DOLLARS		
		EXCHANGE RATE 1	EXCHANGE RATE 2	EXCHANGE RATE 3
1000 copies of a novel	$20			
100 snowmobiles	$5000			
100 kg of beef	$5			

Table 22.9 Prices for imports

PRODUCT	PRICE IN ANOTHER CURRENCY	PRICE IN CANADIAN DOLLARS		
		SITUATION 1	SITUATION 2	SITUATION 3
Personal computer	US$600			
CD player	30 000 Y			
Automobile	30 000 DM			

7. Suppose you import goods for sale in Canada from the United States, Japan, and Germany. As an importer, you know that the values of currencies vary on a day-to-day basis.

(a) Complete Table 22.9 by calculating the effect of changes in the exchange rate on the prices you pay for imports using the information given.

Situation 1   CDN$1.00 = US$0.80 = 175 yen (Y) = 2 German Marks (DM)

Situation 2   CDN$1.00 = US$0.70 = 150 Y = 1.75 DM

Situation 3   CDN$1.00 = US$0.90 = 200 Y = 2.25 DM

(b) In which situation are you likely to import most goods? In which situation are you likely to import fewest goods? Explain why in each case.

(c) A "weak dollar" is one that exchanges for smaller amounts of foreign currency than a "strong dollar." In which of the three situations were the prices highest?

(d) In which situation are you likely to export most goods? Explain why.

(e) A weak dollar is one whose value is low and is expected to decline. As an exporter, would you prefer a weak or a strong dollar? Explain.

CHAPTER TWENTY-THREE

Trade and Investment Policy

Objectives

a. Examine the means governments use to control trade with other countries, including both tariffs and non-tariff barriers.

b. Demonstrate, using a graph, the economic effects of a protective tariff.

c. Outline and evaluate the major arguments for protection.

d. Examine the development of Canadian trade policy since Confederation.

e. Analyze and assess the costs and benefits of the major bilateral trade agreements between Canada and the United States, including the Auto Pact and the Canada-US Free Trade Agreement.

f. Assess the advantages and disadvantages of a North American free trade area including Canada, the US, and Mexico from the perspective of all three nations.

g. Analyze the growth and potential of the European Economic Community.

h. Assess the foreign control of Canadian industry.

"Globalization" has become a catchword for the late twentieth century. What does it mean? Certainly, in one aspect, it describes the movement toward new international economic relationships among nations, particularly relationships centring on trade and investment. In recent years, we have seen such developments as the emergence of the European Economic Community intent on breaking down old internal trade barriers and establishing new links. We have witnessed the Canada-US Free Trade Agreement and negotiations for a North American free trade area including Mexico. International trade talks have focussed on reducing barriers to trade among nations.

In this chapter, we consider trade and investment policies in the past, as well as new developments and some of the motivations behind them. We examine the effects recent developments may have on Canada's trading position in the world and on our domestic economy.

◼ Trade Barriers

Though trade offers substantial benefits, as we saw in the last chapter, governments are swayed by a number of arguments to control trade with other countries. Controls are mainly exercised on imports—either by changing their price or the quantity imported. Two main means of control are tariffs and non-tariff barriers (NTBs).

☐ Tariffs

Tariffs are taxes levied on imported goods. Revenue tariffs are imposed to provide a return to the federal government. Protective tariffs, on the other hand, are designed to shield domestic industry from foreign competition by raising the prices of imports.

Tariffs are costs to the consumer since they raise the prices of imported goods. The prices of comparable domestically-produced goods also usually rise to equal the prices of the imports. Thus, the costs of domestic goods may be higher when they are protected by tariffs.

Let's consider a hypothetical example—say the clothing market in Canada. Figure 23.1 illustrates the effects on the Canadian clothing market of a protective tariff.

(i) Under free trade   Under free trade, before the imposition of a tariff, Canada imports 400 units of clothing and produces 200 units, for a total supply of 600 units at a price of $10 per unit. At this price, total demand is also 600 units. The domestic price equals the world price under free trade.

(ii) Imposition of a moderate tariff   After the imposition of a moderate tariff of $5 per unit, the price rises to $15 per unit, domestic production increases to 300 units, and imports decline to 200 units. Total demand

at $15 per unit is 500 units. The imposition of the tariff, therefore, raises prices by $5 per unit, reduces imports by 200 units, raises domestic production by 100 units, and lowers domestic consumption by 100 units.

(iii) Imposition of a very high tariff   If tariffs are raised to $10 per unit or more, then all imports are eliminated. With a world price of $10 per unit and a tariff of $10 or more, it will not pay importers to bring in clothing since they can get no more than $20 per unit—the price at which the domestic demand and supply curves intersect. A very high tariff that drastically reduces or eliminates any profit importers can make thus has the effect of eliminating imports.

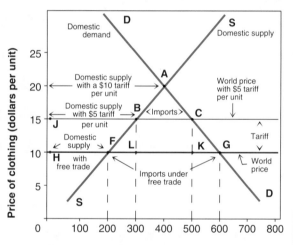

Figure 23.1 Economic effects of a protective tariff

Under free trade, the Canadian price is equal to the world price of $10 per unit. Domestic production is 200 units (HF) and imports equal 400 units (FG) for a total supply of 600 units (HG). With a tariff of $5 per unit, the price rises to $15 a unit, domestic supply increases from 200 to 300 units (JB), and imports are reduced from 400 to 200 units (BC). The amount of the tariff paid by Canadian consumers is shown by the shaded area, BCKL. With a very high tariff of $10 per unit, price rises to $20 a unit, where the domestic supply and demand curves intersect at 400 units (A). Importers are thus effectively shut out of the market.

☐ Non-Tariff Barriers (NTBs)

Non-tariff barriers include quotas, voluntary export restraints, licensing requirements, red tape in customs procedures and safety standards and procedures, government procurement policies, and subsidies. With the recent general decline in tariffs, many countries have come to rely more on NTBs.

Probably the best-known NTB to Canadians is the quota. A **quota** is a restriction on the quantity of particular products that may be imported over a given period. In the past, Canadian governments have imposed quotas on imports of shoes and clothing from some less developed nations and eggs from the United States, for example, to protect these industries from foreign competition. The quotas were meant to secure the jobs and incomes of the domestic workers in these industries.

Nations may also turn to **voluntary export restraints (VERs)**, persuading an exporter to limit its exports into the country "voluntarily." The Canadian and US governments have made agreements with Japan, for example, to restrict Japanese imports of automobiles into the two countries and thus protect the jobs of Canadian and American auto and auto parts manufacturers.

Japan and some European nations have required importers to obtain licences. By limiting the number of licences issued, imports can be effectively controlled. The United Kingdom controls imports of coal in this fashion.

Administrative delays and red tape can also be used to put pressure on exporters. The Canadian government used this method to tie up Japanese cars in the port of Vancouver in 1986, for example, "persuading" the Japanese manufacturers to accept lower "voluntary" export quotas to Canada.

Health and safety standards set by the importing country may also be so detailed and exacting that the exporting country cannot meet them. The Japanese, in the past, have effectively banned the import of the natural sparkling water Perrier exported from France by requiring that it be boiled.

Government procurement policies have been used to favour domestic trade. The United States federal and state governments frequently have "buy American" clauses in contracts with suppliers, strongly encouraging or requiring the purchase of US goods over those of other countries.

Subsidies may also be granted to domestic industries so that they are better able to compete with foreign companies. Canadian governments, for example, have granted subsidies to aircraft manufacturers in Canada to develop new aircraft.

☐ Arguments for Protection

Why do governments implement these protectionist measures? Indeed, why do citizens, industry representatives, and other interest groups lobby for trade barriers when, as we have seen, they may mean higher domestic prices, reduced economies of scale, fewer opportunities for specialization, and perhaps a lower general standard of living?

The arguments for trade restrictions can be seen to fall into three categories—non-economic arguments, arguments based on faulty economic analysis, and valid economic arguments.

Non-Economic Arguments

These arguments suggest that we must sacrifice some trade to achieve other key national objectives. The non-economic objectives most frequently cited are military self-sufficiency and the preservation of Canadian culture.

(i) Military self-sufficiency Proponents of this argument state that certain industries key to our defence—such as shipbuilding and aircraft construction—should receive protection by the Canadian government from foreign competition. In our uncertain world, they argue, it is essential that we do not depend on others for the means to defend ourselves. Defence industries must be protected and maintained.

One of the problems with this argument is that almost all industries could claim that, in some way, they are essential for our national defence. It is difficult to think of an industry that was not in some way essential to the war effort during World War II, for example.

(ii) Preservation of Canadian culture and identity
Since the vast majority of our population lives within 100 km of the US border, we are subject to the influence of US print and electronic media. To preserve and nurture our own culture, it is argued, the government should protect and promote key cultural industries, such as publishing, broadcasting, and the arts.

These non-economic objectives may indeed have merit. However, protecting these industries with tariffs is usually less efficient than providing them with subsidies. The amount and the beneficiaries of the subsidies are known and the assistance is periodically reviewed in parliament. The costs and the beneficiaries of tariffs, however, are less visible and are only infrequently subject to scrutiny.

Arguments Based on Faulty Economic Analysis

Arguments in this category may have considerable appeal and a superficial plausibility. They are often quoted, but they are based on faulty economic analysis.

(i) "Spend the money at home."   This common argument goes something like this: "When I buy a Japanese car, I get the car and Japan gets the money. When I buy a Canadian-made car, I get the car and Canada gets the money. Therefore, I should buy only Canadian-made cars."

This argument confuses the ends and the means of economic activity. Money is not an end in itself. We generally acquire money only for what it will buy. The Japanese sell their cars to other countries so that they can buy goods with the money they earn from the sales—such as Canadian wheat or newsprint.

(ii) "We can't compete with cheap foreign labour."
This argument suggests that if we import lower-priced goods produced in countries where labour is relatively inexpensive, such as in China or Mexico, Canadian workers' wages will fall and the higher living standards of Canadians will be eroded.

This argument ignores the reason for Canada's relatively high wages. Canadian wages are higher than those in China or Mexico because Canadian workers are more productive, not because Canadian industry is

protected from foreign competition. High wages are, therefore, not a handicap to Canadian industry.

The cheap foreign labour argument also ignores comparative advantage. Let's return to our example of Canada and Tradia outlined on pp. 475-76 in the last chapter for a moment. We saw that Canada had an absolute advantage in the production of both machinery and wheat. The Canadian labour force was more productive than Tradia's in both industries and we can reasonably expect, therefore, that Canadian wages would also be higher. Nevertheless, it is beneficial for Canada to trade with Tradia based on its comparative advantage in wheat production and Tradia's comparative advantage in machinery production. Shutting out imports from Tradia, even though wages there may be lower, would mean that Canadian workers in the comparatively efficient wheat industry would move into the relatively inefficient machinery industry. Productivity would decline, and so would wages and the standard of living. In fact, living standards in both countries would fall if trade were blocked since total output in both countries was lower without trade.

Arguments That Have Economic Merit

Some arguments are based on sound economic analysis. However, raising tariffs or implementing other protectionist means may not be the most efficient way of combatting the problem.

(i) "If we buy autos from Canada rather than Japan, employment in Canada will increase at the expense of Japan."   In the past, one of the strongest reasons for raising tariffs or imposing quotas has been to create or preserve jobs. The tariff or quota raises the domestic demand for the product. It thus also raises aggregate demand, income, and GDP. Such a "beggar my neighbour" policy was common during the Great Depression, when nations were faced with massive unemployment. The measures may work—at least until other countries retaliate. In the 1930s, for example, US attempts to protect its industries and workers led to retaliation from other countries such as Canada, which in turn imposed tariffs.

Expansionary monetary and fiscal policies, such as lowering taxes and interest rates to raise employment

□ □ □ □ □ □

The Petition of the Candlemakers

Frédéric Bastiat (1801-1850), a French economist and a staunch supporter of free trade, was incensed by the arguments of the protectionists. In his *Sophisms of Protection*, he overstated the case for protection so as to make it appear ridiculous. This is his satirical description of a fictitious request by French candlemakers for protection from the sunlight that is ruining their business.

Petition of the Candlemakers to the French Parliament (1845)

We are subjected to the intolerable competition of a foreign rival, who enjoys, it would seem, such superior facilities for the production of light, that he is enabled to inundate our national market at so exceedingly reduced a price, that, the moment he makes his appearance, draws off all custom from us; and thus an important branch of French industry, with all its innumerable ramifications, is suddenly reduced to a state of complete stagnation. This rival is no other than the sun. Our petition is, that it would please your honourable body to pass a law whereby shall be directed the shutting up of all windows, dormers, skylights, shutters, curtains, in a word, all openings, holes, chinks, and fissures through which the light of the sun is used to penetrate into our dwellings, to the prejudice of the profitable manufactures which we flatter ourselves we have been able to bestow upon the country; which country cannot, therefore, without ingratitude, leave us now to struggle unprotected through so unequal a contest. . . .

Does it not argue the greatest inconsistency to check as you do the importation of coal, iron, cheese, and goods of foreign manufacture, merely because...their price approaches zero, while at the same time you freely admit, and without limitation, the light of the sun, whose price is during the whole day a zero?

We, if you confer upon us the monopoly of furnishing light during the day, will as a first consequence buy large quantities of tallow, coals, oil, resin, wax, alcohol, silver, iron, bronze, crystal, for the supply of our business; and then we and our numerous contractors having become rich, our consumption will be great, and will become a means of contributing to the comfort and competency of the workers in every branch of national labour.

SOURCE: Arthur MacEwan and Thomas Weisskopf, *Perspectives on the Economic Problem* (Englewood Cliffs, New Jersey: Prentice-Hall, 1970), pp. 253-54.

Applications

1. Identify the argument(s) in favour of protection that Bastiat is ridiculing.

2. If such a petition were to be adopted, what effect would it have on candlemakers? What effects would it have on the economy of the country?

3. Should Canadian industries suffering from foreign competition be protected? Support your point of view.

---

and GDP, may be more efficient. With macroeconomic policies, workers move to better jobs in industries with comparative advantage rather than to the less efficient, tariff-sheltered industries.

(ii) "We should protect and nurture our infant industries until they are able to stand on their own." This argument is based on the premise that an industry may be unable to grow and take advantage of economies of scale until it is well established. In the interim, it needs

protection from competitors that enjoy lower costs and can produce higher volumes. When the industry has grown to maturity, the protective measures can be lifted. Canada and Mexico have used tariff protection in the past to help the development of their manufacturing industries and to move away from a dependence on raw materials.

While this argument has much to recommend it, how are governments to determine which industries will grow and mature and which will not? Which should be given protection and when can the measures safely be lifted? Once provided with protection in the form of tariffs or quotas, infant industries often lobby governments hard to retain them. They do not easily give up protection and may, therefore, be slow to mature. Tariffs may protect the industry too long from the competition that would compel it to become more efficient.

Moreover, foreign industries that wished to produce for the Canadian market got around tariffs in the past by establishing branch plants in Canada. While these branch plants provided jobs for Canadians, they were small-scale and thus less efficient than other more internationally competitive firms that could take advantage of economies of scale.

☐ **A Summary**

We have considered many arguments for protectionism—some of which have merit in economic, military, political, or cultural terms. However, while we might agree that an industry needs protection, a tariff or quota may not be the best means. As we have seen, tariffs often mean higher prices for consumers and protection of some inefficient industries. Tariffs and

quotas also tend to stick around a long time, even after they have outlived their original purpose. Many people, such as those employed in the protected industry, have a vested interest in their continuance and may oppose any attempt to remove them. While protectionism has some merits, therefore, there are trade-offs.

Development of Canadian Trade Policy

Throughout our history, average tariff rates have varied considerably. As Figure 23.2 shows, the history of Canadian tariff policy can be summarized in four periods: a rapid rise in tariffs from 1867 to 1890; a slow decline from the 1890s to the 1920s; an increase during the Great Depression of the 1930s; and finally a gradual decline since the 1930s. By 1990, tariff rates averaged less than 5 percent. Let's consider these four periods and the reasons for the trends.

Period One: Rapidly Rising Tariffs, 1867-1890
Between 1854 and 1866, British North America (as Canada was then called) participated in a limited free

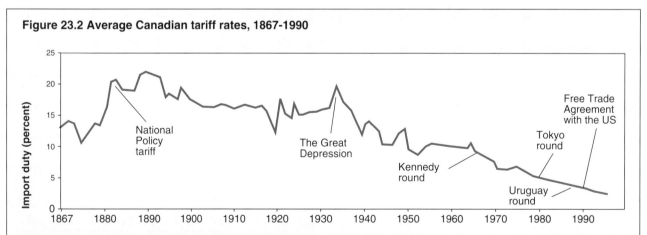

Figure 23.2 Average Canadian tariff rates, 1867-1990

Average Canadian tariff rates have varied considerably since 1870. Following Sir John A. Macdonald's National Policy (1879), they peaked around 1890, reached another high point during the Great Depression, but gradually declined thereafter to an average of less than 5 percent in 1990.

SOURCE: 1968-1975: *Historical Statistics of Canada* and 1976-1988: *Bank of Canada Review*.

trade agreement with the United States. The agreement ended in 1866 and after Confederation in 1867, there seemed little possibility that the agreement could be revived. Canada embraced Sir John A. Macdonald's three-pronged National Policy in the late 1870s. The main points of the policy were:

(i) High tariffs on imported manufactured goods. This part of the policy was meant to help develop manufacturing industries in Canada. It was especially favourable to southern Quebec and Ontario, where the majority of manufacturing industries were located.

(ii) The building of the Canadian Pacific Railway to open the Prairies to settlement and to trade with central Canada. The CPR was meant to promote a strong east-west trading pattern, rather than a north-south one with the United States. There were some fears that too close economic ties with our southern neighbour might lead to a takeover of Canada by the US.

(iii) The promotion of Prairie settlement through the provision of cheap land for settlers. The CPR would provide transportation for the settlers, and Quebec and Ontario would provide a market for their products and a major source of manufactured goods.

Period Two: Slow Decline in Tariffs, 1890-1930

After 1890, the prevailing trend was one of slowly declining tariffs in Canada. The period was one of general prosperity. Governments are more likely to lower tariffs during prosperous periods than during recessions or depressions. A Liberal government was also in power for more of the period 1890-1930 than 1867-1890, and the Liberals favoured free trade more so than the Conservatives.

Period Three: Tariff Increases in the 1930s

During the Great Depression of the 1930s, nations attempted to increase employment by raising tariffs. Rising protectionism in the US in response to the miseries of the Great Depression, for example, brought similar policies in Canada and elsewhere. The results, however, were decreased efficiency, less trade, and little increase in employment as industries dependent on trade were disrupted.

Period Four: Gradual Decrease in Tariffs Since the 1930s

Since the failure of protectionist trade policies in the 1930s, the prevailing trend has been toward lower tariffs. In 1947, 23 nations including Canada and the United States signed the **General Agreement on Tariffs and Trade (GATT)**, an international agreement designed to reduce trade barriers among nations.

General Agreement On Tariffs and Trade (GATT)

The GATT is based on three main principles:
(i) equal treatment for members
(ii) the elimination of import quotas, and
(iii) reduction of tariffs by multilateral negotiations.

Multilateral tariff and trade negotiations involve agreements among a number of nations. Bilateral negotiations are conducted between two countries.

Agreements under GATT, which now has more than 100 member countries, have led to substantial reductions in trade barriers among participants. In the Kennedy Round of negotiations lasting from 1964 to 1967, members agreed to lower the average level of tariffs by a third within five years. In the Tokyo Round of negotiations, conducted from 1973 to 1979, agreement was reached to cut tariffs about another third between 1980 and 1987. The most recent round of GATT negotiations began in Uruguay in 1986. The objectives of these talks were to reduce not only tariffs, but also the non-tariff barriers which had become more common after the Kennedy Round and the 1982 recession. Slower economic growth and higher unemployment had led many nations toward increased protectionism through non-tariff barriers.

Three particularly difficult problems in the negotiations are subsidies to agriculture, restrictions on the trade in services, and government purchasing policies. Subsidies to farmers has been the most contentious issue. The US, Canada, Australia, and other nations sought a cut in farm subsidies by 90 percent over 10 years. European nations offered to cut subsidies by only 30 percent. The US also wanted controls on imports by Canadian agricultural marketing boards replaced by gradually diminishing tariffs. Talks also centred around liberalizing trade in services (such as banking, insurance, engineering, and computer services), long protected by most countries. Governments found preferential buying from their own national suppliers difficult to give up as well, particularly with the recession of the early 1990s.

The increased number of nations attending the talks has also made the negotiating process more complex. Some observers believe the trend may be toward more specialized trade agreements between smaller groups of countries, such as the Auto Pact and the Free Trade Agreement between Canada and the US. These special trade agreements between groups of nations negotiated outside of GATT are known as **trading blocs**.

Bilateral Agreements Between Canada and the US Since 1945

The two most important bilateral trade agreements between the United States and Canada since 1945 are the Canada-US Automotive Agreement of 1965 (commonly called the Auto Pact) and the Free Trade Agreement, which took effect on January 1, 1989.

☐ The Auto Pact (1965)

Before 1965, a 15-percent tariff was imposed on US automobiles imported into Canada. To get around the tariff, US automakers established branch plants in Canada. With the large number of different models to be produced and the relatively small size of the protected domestic market, Canadian plants were unable to take advantage of economies of scale. As a result, production was inefficient, automobile prices were much higher than those in the US, and Canadian autoworkers' wages were lower than those in the US.

The agreement signed in 1965 was composed of two parts. The first part established free trade in automotive vehicles, parts, and products between the two countries. Both countries removed tariffs on automotive imports from the other nation. The Auto Pact

thus made the integration and rationalization of the Canadian and US auto industries possible. The objective was increased efficiency.

The second part of the agreement was between the Canadian government and Canadian auto manufacturers and was intended to guarantee Canadian jobs. The number of Canadian jobs in the automotive industry was to be proportional to the volume of sales in the country.

In many respects, the Pact was a success. The efficiency of the Canadian auto industry improved as fewer models were made for a vastly expanded market. Thus, the Canadian industry was able to achieve economies of scale. Canadian autoworkers' wages rose and the relative price of automobiles declined.

☐ The Canada-US Free Trade Agreement (1989)

Traditionally, Canadian manufacturers have opposed any Canada-US free trade agreement. In the 1980s, however, that opposition turned to support in the face of stiff competition from abroad. Canadians had a tariff-free and widely dispersed market of only 25 million people. By comparison, the American, Japanese, and Western European producers had an internal tariff-free market of at least 100 million people. In addition, the rising tide of protectionism in the US threatened to restrict Canadian exports to its major market. How, then, could Canadian producers maintain, or better yet, improve their access to the US market? The response from the Canadian government was to negotiate a free trade agreement with the US.

What is a Free Trade Area?

There are three main free trade arrangements—a common market, a customs union, and a free trade area. The one that allows the freest movement of goods and services is the common market. A **common market** has the following characteristics:

(i) No tariffs or other barriers on goods produced by member countries.

(ii) Common tariff rates and non-tariff barriers on goods entering member countries from non-member nations.

(iii) No restrictions on the movement of capital and workers among member countries.

The European Economic Community is perhaps the best-known example of a common market. It is currently composed of 12 European nations, including Germany, France, Italy, Spain, and the United Kingdom.

The Parti Québécois's proposal for sovereignty association with Canada also involves a common market. The Parti's definition of sovereignty provides that Quebecers would be governed only by laws passed by the National Assembly in Quebec City, not by laws passed in Ottawa. Quebec would receive no intergovernmental transfers or equalization payments and individual Quebecers would receive no federal transfers, such as family allowances or Canada pension benefits. The province would receive its share of federal assets, however, and be responsible for a portion of the federal debt.

But, the proposal also suggests *association* with the rest of Canada in the form of a common market and monetary union. A common market means that workers and capital goods could move freely between Canada and Quebec and they would have common rules governing imports from other nations. Under a monetary union, the Canadian dollar would remain the official currency of Quebec and the Bank of Canada would continue to control monetary policy within the framework of an agreement between Quebec and the rest of Canada.

The **customs union** has no internal tariff and non-tariff barriers. Common tariff rates and non-tariff barriers are applied to goods and services imported from non-members. However, restrictions on the movement of capital and workers among member countries remain.

A free trade area—such as the one negotiated by Canada and the United States—is the least comprehensive of the three arrangements. A **free trade area** covers only the elimination of tariffs and other barriers to trade among the countries in the agreement. No common tariff rates or non-tariff barriers exist on imports from other nations. Each nation applies its own restrictions on trade with non-member nations and national restrictions on the movement of capital and workers also remain in place.

Provisions of the Free Trade Agreement

In 1988, after a hard-fought election campaign in which both opposition parties opposed the Free Trade Agreement, the Progressive Conservatives prevailed and the Agreement came into effect on January 1, 1989.

The main provisions of the Agreement are:

1. Tariffs and most (but not all) trade barriers are to be phased out by January 1, 1998.

2. Trade in services will be largely freed from restraints. Architects, for example, will be able to sell their services in both countries.

3. A binding mechanism with Canadian and US representatives will exist to settle trade disputes between the two countries.

4. The provisions of the Auto Pact will be retained. Restrictions on the import of used cars into Canada will be eliminated. Tariffs on automobile parts will be eliminated over 10 years.

5. No export subsidies will be permitted on trade between Canada and the US.

6. Both sides will eliminate restrictions on energy imports and exports.

7. Restrictions on US investment in Canada (except in "cultural" industries, such as the media and publishing) will be eased. US takeovers of Canadian firms with assets less than $150 million will not be subject to Canadian approval.

Benefits and Costs of the Agreement

What are the main benefits that can be expected from the Free Trade Agreement?

(i) Removal of Canadian barriers to US imports Canadian consumers should benefit from the removal of barriers to US imports. More US goods and services will enter the country and their prices should be lower.

(ii) Removal of US barriers to Canadian exports
With the removal of barriers on Canadian exports to the US, Canadian manufacturers gain freer access to the much larger US market. They can specialize in a smaller range of products, produce them in higher volume, and therefore at lower cost. With lower costs, Canadian producers can reduce domestic prices and/or pay higher wages.

(iii) More secure access to the US market   In the 1980s, US protectionist sentiment grew and resulted in action to restrict imports of Canadian shakes and shingles, steel, softwood lumber, and potash. One of the advantages of the Free Trade Agreement is that the future form of US trade policy on Canadian exports should be clearer. Uncertainty should be reduced.

Clearly, then, the Free Trade Agreement with the United States offers economic advantages. Nevertheless, Canadians have voiced a number of concerns about the possible impact of the deal. What are the costs?

(i) Job losses   Even if the net impact of the Agreement is an increase in employment opportunities (as some studies have suggested), it is clear that some jobs will be lost. These job losses will be especially evident in US branch plants and subsidiaries, which were established in Canada to avoid protective tariffs. Many of the branch plants in the tire, chemical, and plastics industries, for example, will become redundant with free trade and close down. Workers will have to move into new industries, acquire new skills, and/or move to different communities. The amount of such adjustment unemployment may be small, however, since the Agreement is being phased in over a long period.

Tariff rates in many cases were also not high, so that their removal may not have a great impact in some industries. It is important to recognize also that some unemployment will be the result of other economic changes, such as domestic technological changes, competition from other countries, changes in the value of the Canadian dollar, or the fluctuations of the business cycle.

(ii) Threat to Canadian sovereignty and independence
Probably the most frequently stated potential cost of

the Agreement is the threat it may pose to Canadian sovereignty and independence. Groups have expressed concern that Canadian social programs, such as medicare, regional development policies, and unemployment insurance, may be at risk. Americans have argued that since medicare is provided by the provincial and federal governments in Canada, while medical insurance is typically paid for in part by individual firms in the US, medicare is an unfair subsidy to Canadian firms and should be abolished in the interests of fair competition. Similarly, unemployment insurance benefits to Canadians in the fishing industry, it is argued, subsidize incomes and allow Canadians to sell their fish at lower prices than would otherwise be the case.

Canadian cultural programs, such as subsidies and protection for Canadian media and publishing industries, have also been points of contention under the Agreement. Americans have argued that in a free trade deal, all Canadian industries should be subject to competition from the US.

Furthermore, some Canadians fear that since the US is the dominant partner in the Agreement, it will determine trade policy for both countries, thus limiting Canadian sovereignty. Supporters of the Agreement, however, point to the examples of the smaller countries in the European Common Market—such as Belgium and the Netherlands—which have retained their cultural identity despite their small size. Opponents of the Agreement contend that the relationship between Canada and the US cannot be compared to the European situation, pointing out Canada's heavy economic dependence on its larger neighbour.

(iii) Loss of control over foreign investment   The Agreement specifies that restrictions on US investment in Canada will be eased and that takeovers of Canadian companies with assets less than $150 million do not require Canadian approval. Some fear that Canada will lose control over foreign investment in its economy. Supporters of the Agreement argue that this clause permits new investment in Canada and allows opportunities for Canadian investment in the US.

(iv) Loss of control over domestic energy   The energy clause allows Canada to restrict its sale of oil and gas to

□ □ □ □ □ □

The Level Playing Field

Trade negotiations between Canada and the US often seemed to hinge on the concept of a level playing field. What does this mean? The following article by Walter Block, an economist with the Fraser Institute in Vancouver, offers an explanation and provides his point of view on the "benefits" of a level playing field. Consider his views as you read the article.

A new phrase has entered the common lexicon: "the level playing field." It sounds like sports jargon, but it is not. Instead, it refers to a rather technical aspect of the international trade negotiations between Canada and the US.

The level playing field alludes to a situation in which the citizens of neither country have an unfair competitive advantage over the other. If trade between nations can be represented by a playing field, then it should tilt neither one way nor the other, nor should the wind be at the back of either team, nor the sun more in the eyes of one side than the other.

The practice of particular concern to advocates of the level playing field is that of subsidizing exports. The Americans, for example, are worried about the cheap fish sent to their country. This is a result, they contend, of our unemployment insurance scheme, which pays people all winter for what is in effect only a seasonal summer job.

In the view of the Americans, this is only a thinly disguised form of subsidy for our Atlantic fishery, one that harms their own maritime industry. For without this advantage, our fishing industry would not be able to compete so efficiently. Instead, they want a "level playing field," where the Canadian government does not help its citizens to compete "unfairly" against Americans.

In a superficial analysis, this point of view makes sense. After all, there are specific losers—the New England fishermen—who suffer directly from Canadian unemployment insurance. But if we look a little deeper, we can see that insisting on a "level playing field" makes no economic sense at all.

To prove this, let us consider an extreme hypothetical case where the Canadian government encourages us to give away our goods to them for free. For example, suppose that a law were passed tomorrow permanently subsidizing to the rate of 110 percent all free gifts of lumber to the US. That is, for every $100 worth of wood products we sent across the border at a zero price, our government would give us $110. We pass lightly over the objection that this would bankrupt Canada even faster than at the present furious pace, and ask only what effect this would have on the economy of the US.

Here, it is easy to see that although this policy would drive into bankruptcy the entire American forest industry, it would be a boon to their economy as a whole. They could have just as much wood as before, while freeing up large numbers of workers and whatever capital could be transferred to other occupations. In this way, their standard of living would rise, with no additional inputs.

This is all that an "uneven" playing field consists of: an offer from one country to subsidize the economy of another. Instead of objecting to other nations pursuing such policies, each should encourage others to tilt the playing field in the direction of subsidizing exports. And yet, the economic level of sophistication that commonly prevails in North America holds the very opposite—that each nation should protest when its neighbours subsidize it.

SOURCE: Walter Block, "Export subsidy helps economy of importer," *The Financial Post*, October 5, 1988. With permission of the Fraser Institute.

Applications

1. What does the phrase "level playing field" mean in international trade jargon?

2. Why might the US object to Canadian subsidies on goods sold in the American market?

3. (a) What is Walter Block's opinion of the "uneven playing field?"

(b) Do you agree with him? Explain your point of view.

the US in the event of a domestic shortage, but only when Canadians make "a proportional sacrifice." The clause prevents Canadians from setting lower prices on energy than those charged Americans. Supporters of the Agreement, however, point out that access to the US market is important.

The North American Free Trade Area (NAFTA) Negotiations

In February 1991, Canadian Prime Minister Brian Mulroney, US President George Bush, and Mexican President Carlos Salinas de Gortari announced that formal negotiations to create a North American Free Trade Area would begin. The proposed North American Free Trade Area (NAFTA), with 360 million people and a combined output of US$6 trillion, would rival the European Common Market with its 326 million people and $US5 trillion output.

☐ Characteristics of the Three Economies

Some major characteristics of the three nations are outlined in Table 23.1. The US and Canada are comparable in terms of GNP per capita, inflation rate, infant death rates, literacy rates, and percentage of the labour force in the service industries. The major difference is in the size of the two economies. The population, total GNP, and size of the labour force in the US are about ten times those of Canada.

Mexico, however, provides a very different picture. Mexican GNP per person is about one-tenth that of the US and Canada. Its inflation rate and infant mortality rate are both about five times those of the other two countries. The total number of college graduates is also low compared to that of Canada and the United States. With a population more than three times Canada's, fewer students graduate from college.

Mexico also has a potentially crippling foreign debt of some US$97 billion—the second largest after Brazil in Latin America. It is recovering from the 1980s—a decade of economic decline. Mexican wages in 1991, for example, were well below those in 1978 in real

terms. Economic growth in the 1980s was stagnant, but in 1990 there were signs of a turnaround with growth at 3.8 percent. Mexico's labour force is also growing rapidly—an estimated one million new jobs will be created by the end of the decade.

In the mid-1980s, Mexico began a vigorous campaign to restructure its economy. The government slashed maximum tariff rates from 100 percent to 20 percent and average tariff rates from 25 percent to 10 percent. Many other non-tariff barriers were eliminated and Mexico joined GATT. Many of the 1155 government-owned and often inefficient industries in the country were put up for sale. Mexico's import-substitution strategy for economic growth was largely scrapped and stiff foreign investment rules were also relaxed. High tariffs and quotas had been placed on some imported manufactured goods (such as automobiles, radios, bicycles, and household electrical appliances) to encourage the establishment of local indus-

Table 23.1 Characteristics of the three North American economies

	CANADA	UNITED STATES	MEXICO
Population (millions)			
1989	26	246	84
2000 (est.)	29	272	103
2025 (est.)	32	309	142
GNP 1989 (billions)	$522	$5 816	$212
GNP per person 1989	$20 352	$23 808	$2 212
Inflation rate (1990 est.)	5.2	5.5	27
Growth rate per capita 1965-1989	3.0	1.6	3.0
Infant deaths (per 1000 live births)	7	10	46
Life expectancy at birth	77	76	69
Literacy rate	99	99	88
Labour force (millions)	13.4	122.0	26.1
Percentage of labour force in service occupations	75	75	31

SOURCES: The Royal Bank of Canada, *World Bank Development Report*, Informetrica Ltd., *World Almanac 1990*, Canadian Institute for International Affairs.

Figure 23.3 A profile of North American trade

CANADA
Exports to US $89.3
Exports to Mexico $0.51
Imports from US $78.9
Imports from Mexico $1.43

UNITED STATES
Exports to Canada $78.9
Exports to Mexico $17.5
Imports from Canada $89.3
Imports from Mexico $18.1

(US BILLIONS
OF DOLLARS)

MEXICO
Exports to Canada $1.43
Exports to US $18.1
Imports from Canada $0.51
Imports from US $17.5

CHEAP LABOUR IN MEXICO'S *MAQUILADORA* SECTOR

Customs-bonded assembly plants along the US border handle labour-intensive work for US manufacturers. Workers in such plants appear to earn roughly half as much as Mexican manufacturing workers in general.

Hourly labour costs, 1988, in US dollars, for *maquiladora* production workers

Industry	Wages	Benefits	Total
Total food and related products	$0.62	$0.13	$0.75
Apparel and textiles	0.60	0.16	0.76
Footwear and leather	0.68	0.21	0.89
Chemicals, chemical products	0.78	0.20	0.98
Furniture and fixtures	0.77	0.24	1.01
Electrical and electronic	0.75	0.27	1.02
Transportation equipment	0.84	0.25	1.09
Toys and sporting goods	0.81	0.31	1.12
Machinery and equipment	0.93	0.22	1.15
Maquiladora average	0.74	0.24	0.98

SOURCE: *US Bureau of Labor Statistics.*

CANADA'S TOP EXPORTS TO MEXICO, 1989

Rank	Commodity	Million dollars	Percentage of total
1	Vehicle parts, except engines	74.4	12.3
2	Rapeseed	59.3	9.8
3	Steel plate, sheet, and strip	58.9	9.5
4	Dairy products, eggs, and honey	46.4	7.7
5	Aircraft	39.9	6.6
6	Telecommunications equipment	30.8	5.1
7	Sulphur	30.3	3.9
8	Pulp	23.5	3.9
9	Vehicle engines and parts	18.8	3.1
10	Meat	17.6	2.9
	All exports	$604.0	100.0

CANADA'S TOP IMPORTS FROM MEXICO, 1989

Rank	Commodity	Million dollars	Percentage of total
1	Vehicle parts, except engines	347.2	20.4
2	Vehicle engines	217.7	12.8
3	Precious metals	182.6	10.7
4	Computers	146.9	8.6
5	Television sets, radios, phonographs	81.1	4.8
6	Telecommunications equipment	77.2	4.5
7	Passenger cars and chassis	73.3	4.3
8	Crude oil	49.9	2.9
9	General industrial machinery	37.5	2.2
10	Vehicle engine parts	29.4	1.7
	All imports	$1 704.8	100.0

SOURCE: Statistics Canada.

NORTH AMERICAN BLOC	EUROPEAN COMMUNITY
360 million people	326 million people
US $6 trillion annual production	US $5 trillion annual production

SOURCE: *The Financial Post*, Feb. 6, 1991.

A TALE OF THREE COUNTRIES

Hourly labour costs, including fringe benefits, for production workers in manufacturing

Year	$CDN Canada	$US Canada	$US United States	$US Mexico
1989	$17.43	$14.72	$14.31	$2.32
1988	16.65	13.53	13.85	1.99
1987	15.85	11.95	13.40	1.57
1986	15.28	11.00	13.21	1.50
1985	14.75	10.80	12.96	2.09

SOURCE: *US Bureau of Labor Statistics.*

tries. It was hoped that these industries would be able to achieve economies of scale and improve the nation's balance of payments as fewer imports were needed. In many cases, however, these new industries were unable to survive without tariff and quota protection.

Politically, a North American Free Trade Agreement might bolster the sagging popularity of Mexico's Institutional Revolutionary Party, which has ruled the country without interruption for more than 60 years.

□ Perspectives on a North American Free Trade Agreement

In each of the three countries, there are supporters and opponents of the negotiations. Let's consider the perspectives of the three nations.

The Mexican Perspective

The United States is Mexico's principal trading partner. A free trade deal would grant Mexico many advantages. The elimination of US and Canadian tariffs would increase Mexican competitiveness in those markets. Mexican products and services would be more competitive with both US and Canadian domestic products and other products imported from Mexico's competitors, such as Brazil, Taiwan, and South Korea.

However, the advantages to be gained from a reduction in tariffs should not be overstated. The average American tariff on Mexican imports in 1989 was only 3.4 percent. Mexicans hope, however, that the US will invest $25 billion in the country by 1994, thus creating new jobs, raising wages, increasing the standard of living, and bringing in more US technology.

A free trade zone of a kind already exists along the 3000-km US-Mexico border. Since 1965, US companies have been establishing border factories (called *maquiladoras*), which import raw materials duty-free and export their products to the US with tariffs paid only on the value-added in Mexico. These labour-intensive factories employ about 400 000 workers. In 1990, it was estimated that the *maquiladoras* earned Mexico $3.5 billion in foreign exchange.

Many Mexicans are concerned about the costs of a free trade agreement, however. One long-standing fear concerns the threat to Mexican culture that greater exposure to the US may pose. This concern was expressed long ago by one of Mexico's nineteenth century presidents in the following lament: "Pity poor Mexico, so far from God—and so close to the United States."

Another concern is that US investment will flood the country and take control of much of Mexico's economy. In this view, Mexicans would provide the unskilled and semi-skilled labour, while the Americans and Canadians would provide the skilled managers, researchers, expertise, and capital. Thus, the Mexicans would be, in a phrase familiar to Canadians, "the hewers of wood and the drawers of water."

The United States' Perspective

For the US, as for Mexico, both politics and economics are the driving forces behind the negotiations for a North American Free Trade Area. A free trade agreement with Mexico is a way to enhance the political stability and economic prosperity of a neighbour and diminish the distrust which has disturbed dialogue between the two nations for over a century and a half.

Mexico is also the United States' third most important trading partner—after Canada and Japan. It supplies the US with approximately 6 percent of its imports. Renewed economic growth and reduced tariffs led to a more than doubling of US exports to Mexico between 1986 and 1990 (from $12.4 billion to $28.4 billion). A free trade agreement could open the Mexican market even more to US capital equipment, appliances, plastics, rubber, chemicals, and food—products in which the US has a comparative advantage. A more prosperous Mexico could also stem the flood of illegal Mexican immigrants to the southwestern US—estimated to be in the millions.

But, the US would also face costs from a North American free trade area. If tariffs and quotas are eliminated, US labour unions fear that many US jobs will be lost. Wages in the US are seven or more times higher than those in Mexico. Labour-intensive industries such as clothing, construction, parts of the fruit and vegetable industries, furniture, leather, and glass (in which Mexico has a comparative advantage) could suffer considerably from Mexican competition. US manufacturers in these industries may move their

☐ ☐ ☐ ☐ ☐ ☐

Judith Maxwell on Economics and International Trade

Judith Maxwell earned her BComm from Dalhousie University and then went to the London School of Economics for graduate work. She has had a distinguished career as a journalist (for *The Financial Times of Canada*), a researcher, and a director of research. From 1985 to 1992, she has chaired the Economic Council of Canada. The following is the text of an interview with Judith Maxwell about her career and the economic challenges confronting Canada in the global economy of the 1990s. Judith Maxwell was interviewed by Michael Parkin, professor of economics at the University of Western Ontario.

INTERVIEWER: Ms Maxwell, when did you decide to become an economist?

MAXWELL: When I went to university, I didn't want to take science because that meant standing in labs all day, and I didn't want to take arts because that meant writing too many essays. So I took a BComm. The fact that economics was part of that degree was an accident. But I got very engaged with the subject. Then I kept on learning as a journalist. Having to write every week about, say, why the unemployment rate had gone up or the inflation rate wouldn't move meant that I learned from the real world almost as much economics as I had from a textbook.

INTERVIEWER: Why don't more women work as economists?

MAXWELL: I don't know. Women have a lot to bring to economics. Given their interest in the other social sciences, it's surprising that more of them are not drawn to the subject. Actually, there are quite a few women— Caroline Pestieau, Wendy Dobson, Maureen Farrow, Gail Cook, and Sylvia Ostry—in the forefront of public policy debates and economics. But there are too few women behind them. It's not the usual pyramid.

INTERVIEWER: What excites you about economics?

MAXWELL: For me economics is about the well-being of real people. I always feel most comfortable when I connect economic analysis to policy decisions that influence the distribution of income or the quality of life of real individuals.

INTERVIEWER: How do you see the world economy of the 1990s and Canada's place in it?

MAXWELL: What's emerging are three big trading areas: North America, the Pacific Rim, and Europe. Canada fits into this global economy as a highly developed but slow-growing, middle-sized power that's going to have to adapt to competition of new types and from new sources. It's going to be a testing but exciting decade for Canadians.

INTERVIEWER: What's your assessment of the first year of the operation of the Canada-United States Free Trade Agreement?

MAXWELL: The Council's projection was that free trade would bring a small but significant increase in living standards for Canadians. But it's hard to figure out what's been going on in the past year because we've had not only the new trading structure but also a high exchange rate, high interest rates, and a high degree of capacity utilization. There is no question that a lot of new investment and restructuring is going on. We just don't know how much of it can be attributed to the free trade agreement.

INTERVIEWER: What are the implications for Canada of a trade agreement between the United States and Mexico? Should Canada be a player in the discussions?

MAXWELL: Canada and the United States together will be neither the largest nor the most diversified of the three big trading areas. So they should certainly be looking at Latin America for a wider trading area in this hemisphere. But building a formal trade area with such diverse countries is no easy matter. The Canada-United States trade agreement is a consolidation of a relationship that evolved over 50 years. In the case of Mexico I suspect that what we're talking about is the gradual construction of a more intimate relationship among the three countries. I don't think Canada should leave that purely to the United States. There are all kinds of potential Canada-Mexico linkages. So I think we should be a player, either on our own or in conjunction with the US-Mexico discussions.

INTERVIEWER: What about the rest of this hemisphere?

MAXWELL: Think of what would happen if Brazil or Mexico takes off. Both were looking very promising in the 1970s. Debt burdens held them back through the 1980s, but they have tremendous potential. Mexico has been getting its house in order, and Brazil recently took some important initiatives that could make a big difference to its capacity to grow internally and play internationally.

INTERVIEWER: What are the implications for Canada of Europe's 1992 economic unification?

MAXWELL: Production systems in Europe are being integrated through a tremendous wave of merger and acquisition activity. Large companies are being organized, and cross-border alliances are being forged. To compete, Canadians are going to need production facilities inside Europe in many industries. The process of integration will make a faster-growing market, creating more opportunities for Canadians. But the Europeans will end up with a lot of stronger companies. As they reach out to compete inside the North American market, there may be stronger competition in certain areas.

INTERVIEWER: What about developments in Eastern Europe?

MAXWELL: What's interesting is whether the deepening of the European common market through the 1992 process is compatible with the broadening of the market, which is where the Eastern European countries come in. Some people argue that the opening of Eastern Europe will accelerate integration in Western Europe. But others argue that the process of unifying Germany and building links between Western and Eastern Europe will be a distraction that's destabilizing for Europe in the short run. The European economy is relatively fully utilized, so shifting resources into Eastern Europe will mean that something has to be given up. Whether that's going to be managed in a way that is not inflationary and not destabilizing to European currency arrangements is an open question.

INTERVIEWER: How will these developments affect Canada?

MAXWELL: The first impact, which appears to be unavoidable, is that world demand for saving will increase, and therefore, world interest rates will be higher in the 1990s than they would otherwise have been. As a debtor country, Canada will therefore face higher debt service costs. Another impact will be a sort of trade creation effect on specific markets. For example, all the countries of Eastern Europe have to modernize their telephone systems. Canada has a very well-developed communications system, and one of our most successful exporting companies is

Northern Telecom. There are great opportunities there. But also there's potential trade diversion effects. The Soviet Union [sic] exports grain, oil, and natural gas, which are two of our key products, and so its entry into the world market may well be unfavourable for Canada.

INTERVIEWER: Let's turn to the Pacific. Postwar Japan has been amazingly successful. What lessons does it offer us?

MAXWELL: Canada cannot transplant Japanese institutions, but we should try to develop Japan's capacity for consensus and its social cohesion. These areas have been our stumbling blocks for decades. Given the frictions that we now see on the federal-provincial front and that are emerging in management-labour relationships, during the 1990s we have to try to build stronger institutions in Canada for the resolution of conflicts and for reaching consensus before conflicts emerge.

INTERVIEWER: You've had a very distinguished career, doing economics and communicating it to the general public and to policymakers. Many students would love to pursue such a career. What advice can you give?

MAXWELL: Get a really solid degree in economics, and make sure you have strong computer and writing skills. The best way to hone all these skills is to work in economics with researchers or other users of economics. When you are applying for jobs later, you should be able to demonstrate that you've used economics in a project situation, either during your summers or in a couple of selected areas immediately after you finish your degree. I hope that we will generate more and more economists who have all the technical skills, which are important, but who also see economics as a means to understanding people and who understand that the end result is the quality of life and the well-being of individuals in society.

INTERVIEWER: Unlike you, few people are good economics writers. Is there something a student can do to develop good writing skills, other than just practice?

MAXWELL: Writing was an acquired skill for me. I got a job as a research assistant at a newspaper and gradually moved into writing. I kept getting stuff thrown back on me, all marked up. Eventually I got the hang of it. There's no substitute for deliberate effort. Take a course in how to structure your message. Also, let's face it: what makes a good writer is being a clear thinker.

SOURCE: Michael Parkin and Robin Bade, *Economics: Canada in the Global Environment* (Don Mills: Addison-Wesley, 1991).

Applications

1. Judith Maxwell notes that Canada will have to adapt to new competition from new sources in the next decade. What forms will this new competition take and how might Canada respond to it?

2. Why does Maxwell believe it is difficult to assess the real impact of the Canada-US Free Trade Agreement at this point? Do you agree? Explain.

3. Why should Canada be involved in the talks with the US and Mexico over a North American free trade area?

4. How does Maxwell suggest Europe's 1992 economic unification will affect Canada? Suggest what Canada can do to meet this new competition.

5. What problems and opportunities do the developments in Eastern Europe pose for Canada?

6. Do you agree that Canada has been held back by internal conflicts and could learn some lessons about consensus from Japan? Support your view.

7. What does Judith Maxwell see as the real goal of economics? Do you agree? Explain.

operations south of the border to take advantage of the relatively low wage rates.

A US government study found that employment in the US furniture industry dropped 10 percent in 1990. Most of those jobs were lost when 28 furniture manufacturers moved to Mexico in search of cheaper labour. Florida fruit and vegetable growers fear that free trade would destroy their industry and put 8700 out of work. According to the United Automobile Workers, 75 000 jobs have already been lost to Mexico.

The impact free trade will have on US and Canadian workers, critics argue, can be seen by the *maquiladoras* along the US-Mexico border. The half-million *maquiladora* workers represent US and Canadian jobs that have been lost to Mexico. With free trade, more jobs may be lost.

In addition to the job losses, critics point to the ecological impact. The *maquiladoras* have a poor environmental record and the enforcement of Mexican environmental laws is lax. The result is the massive pollution of rivers and the atmosphere along the US-Mexico border. With free trade and tougher environmental protection laws north of the Rio Grande, more Canadian and US firms are likely to move to Mexico. Mexico may be exporting not only its goods, but also its pollution to its northern neighbours.

The Canadian Perspective

The issue of free trade with Mexico is highly contentious in Canada. In general, the organized labour movement opposes a North American free trade area,

as it did free trade with the US. Indeed, the opposition to free trade with Mexico may be even stronger. Foremost among the concerns of many Canadians (as among Americans) are the low wages and weak environmental protection laws in Mexico. With free trade, it is feared that more Canadian industries will move to Mexico to take advantage of the lower labour costs. Labour leaders suggest that the agreement should include a harmonization of standards ("a level playing field"), so that no one country has an unfair advantage over the others. Suggestions have also been made for the inclusion of a social charter guaranteeing minimum standards for wages, working conditions, and the environment in all three countries.

Supporters of the NAFTA argue that, for many reasons, the Canadian government has made the right decision in agreeing to participate in the trade talks. While Mexico is not one of Canada's major trading partners, Canada can obtain improved access to the Mexican market through the agreement. In addition, Canadians will benefit from low-cost, duty-free imports from Mexico. Participation in the talks is also necessary to ensure that Canada's interests are protected and that the gains made under the US-Canada Free Trade Agreement are preserved. Concerns about the *maquiladoras'* pollution performance can perhaps also be addressed in the new agreement.

One aspect of the agreement that will significantly affect Canada is the competition from Mexico in the US market. Canada and Mexico compete directly in 2500 goods imported into the US. These 2500 goods account for about 60 percent of the products Canada exports to the US and 75 percent of the goods exported by Mexico. The total value of the trade for which the two countries compete is $80 billion—some 40 times the direct trade between Canada and Mexico. Thus, if there is a deal between Mexico and the US, Mexican exports are likely to become more competitive in the US market. And, of course, we cannot prevent a US-Mexico deal.

■ The European Common Market

Another development that has led to the reduction of trade barriers is the formation of the European Community (EC), formerly known as the European Economic Community (EEC).

Established in 1958, the European Community originally had six members—France, Germany, Italy, Netherlands, Belgium, and Luxembourg. Since then, the Community has expanded to include six more nations—United Kingdom, Ireland, Denmark, Greece, Spain, and Portugal. East Germany entered the Community when it was reunited with West Germany.

The objectives of the Community are both political and economic. The original objective was to integrate the economies of western Europe (and especially of France and Germany), and thereby reduce or eliminate the possibility of war between the nations. At the same time, the Community sought to secure the advantages of free trade among the members.

Project 1992, agreed on by the leaders of the EC in 1986, seeks to establish a frontier-free market for the 350 million people of the 12-nation Community. It aims to sweep away all remaining obstacles to the free movement of people, capital, goods, and services within the Community, so that by the end of 1992, a single, integrated market will be in place.

□ The European Community—An Assessment

How successful has the European Community been in achieving its goals? The GDP and living standards of member nations have risen considerably since the Community was formed. How far these achievements are due to the formation of the Common Market and how far they are due to other factors is difficult to assess.

The effects of Project 1992 may be even more difficult to gauge. Economists are divided over whether the impact will be a once-and-for-all increase of 2.5 to 6 percent in GDP, or whether it will result in growth over the long-term and perhaps at a higher rate. One indicator of the success of the market is that other European nations such as Sweden and Austria (both members of the six-nation European Free Trade Association), and other former Comecon (the communist equivalent of the EC) nations such as Hungary and Czechoslovakia, are considering applying for membership in the organization.

The impact of the Community on nations outside it—such as Canada—is also uncertain. The growing and prosperous European market has created increased opportunities for sales and investment by non-member countries. This is counterbalanced, however, by the fact that non-members have a competitive disadvantage inside the market. For example, before the establishment of the EC, Canadian exports to the Netherlands faced the same trade barriers as those from France, Germany, Italy, and Britain. But with the Common Market, the trade barriers on French, German, Italian, and British goods are eliminated, while barriers to Canadian goods remain in place.

■ Foreign Investment and Control of Canadian Corporations

In the 1970s and early 1980s, one of the most controversial issues in Canada centred around the foreign ownership and control of Canadian industry. Foreign funds in Canada are invested in two ways. Direct investment occurs when non-nationals acquire control of Canadian corporations or when they establish or expand corporations they already control. Fifty-one percent ownership of stocks is defined as clear control. However, since shares are often widely held, control can be achieved with a much lower ownership percentage. In Canada, many subsidiaries—such as Ford Canada—are 100 percent owned by the parent corporation.

Portfolio investment occurs when non-nationals buy bonds or stocks of Canadian corporations or bonds issued by Canadian federal or provincial governments. Portfolio investment differs from direct investment in that control of Canadian corporations does not pass into foreign hands, though non-Canadians may have substantial investments in the companies.

Canada continues to be heavily reliant on foreign investment. As shown in Figure 23.4, total foreign investment in Canada was approximately $35 billion in 1965. Since then, the total has increased more than 13 times, reaching $456 billion in 1990. Over the same period, Canadian investment in other countries increased 15 times from $13 billion to $197 billion. Direct investment in Canada totalled $127 billion in 1990, while Canadian direct investment in other countries totalled $85 billion. Since 1965, Canadian direct investment in other countries has grown more rapidly than foreign direct investment in Canada.

Most foreign direct investment in Canada has come from the US, as shown in Figure 23.5. Typically, the US has accounted for about 75 percent of foreign direct investment. However, this proportion is declining as direct investment by the Japanese and members of the European Community increases.

The amount of foreign control varies considerably

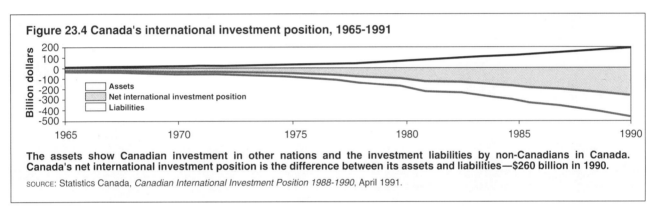

Figure 23.4 Canada's international investment position, 1965-1991

Legend: Assets / Net international investment position / Liabilities

The assets show Canadian investment in other nations and the investment liabilities by non-Canadians in Canada. Canada's net international investment position is the difference between its assets and liabilities—$260 billion in 1990.

SOURCE: Statistics Canada, *Canadian International Investment Position 1988-1990*, April 1991.

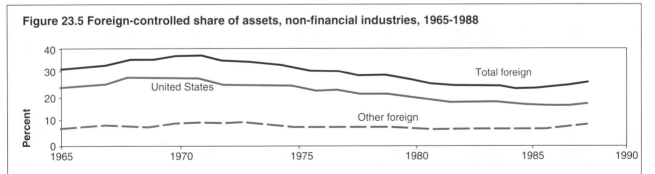

Figure 23.5 Foreign-controlled share of assets, non-financial industries, 1965-1988

Total foreign
United States
Other foreign

Foreign control of Canadian industries reached a peak in 1970 at about 37 percent of total Canadian assets, declined to about 25 percent by 1985, and then began to increase again. US control of non-financial industry assets followed a similar trend, but has declined from about 75 percent of foreign-controlled assets in the 1960s and 1970s to about 66 percent in the 1980s.

SOURCE: Statistics Canada, *CALURA*, October 1991.

among industries, however. Measured by control of assets in 1988, it was highest in manufacturing (44 percent), followed by mining (42 percent), and wholesale trade (34 percent), as shown in Figure 23.6. The lowest levels were recorded in agriculture and utilities (3 percent). These figures represent significant declines since the late 1970s, when 54 percent of manufacturing, 51 percent of mining, 8 percent of agriculture, and 7 percent of utilities were under foreign control. Only the wholesale trade has registered an increase since the late 1970s.

Significant variations also occur within the manufacturing sector, as shown in Figure 23.7. Foreign control of assets in the manufacture of tobacco products is almost 100 percent. In the manufacture of rubber products, transportation equipment, petroleum and coal products, and in chemicals, the percentage of assets under foreign control is well above 60 percent. In other industries—such as knitting and clothing mills—the proportion is well below 10 percent.

Table 23.2 outlines the 25 largest foreign-owned companies in Canada. As you can see, some of Canada's

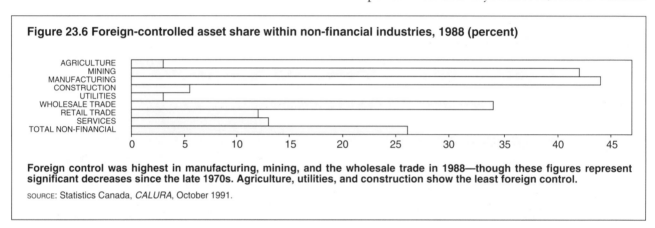

Figure 23.6 Foreign-controlled asset share within non-financial industries, 1988 (percent)

Foreign control was highest in manufacturing, mining, and the wholesale trade in 1988—though these figures represent significant decreases since the late 1970s. Agriculture, utilities, and construction show the least foreign control.

SOURCE: Statistics Canada, *CALURA*, October 1991.

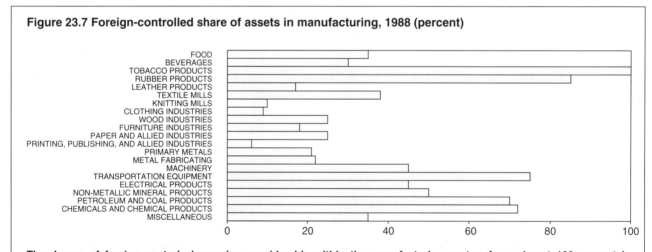

Figure 23.7 Foreign-controlled share of assets in manufacturing, 1988 (percent)

The degree of foreign control also varies considerably within the manufacturing sector, from almost 100 percent in tobacco products to less than 10 percent in textile and knitting mills and printing and publishing industries.

SOURCE: Statistics Canada, *CALURA*, October 1991.

Table 23.2 Largest foreign-owned companies in Canada

RANK	COMPANY	1990 SALES (THOUSANDS OF DOLLARS)	PERCENTAGE OF FOREIGN OWNERSHIP	PARENT
1	General Motors of Canada	18 458 171	100	General Motors (US)
2	Ford Motor of Canada	13 706 200	94	Ford Motor (US)
3	Imperial Oil	10 223 000	70	Exxon (US)
4	Chrysler Canada	7 067 000	100	Chrysler (US)
5	Shell Canada	5 508 000	78	Shell Petroleum (Netherlands/Britain)
6	IBM Canada	4 578 000	100	IBM (US)
7	Sears Canada	4 571 000	61	Sears Roebuck (US)
8	Amoco Canada Petroleum	4 444 000	100	Amoco (US)
9	Canada Safeway	4 317 951	100	Safeway (US)
10	Total Petroleum	3 179 929	52	Total Compagnie Française des Petroles (France)
11	Canada Packers	3 092 238	56	Hillsdown Holdings (Britain)
12	Mitsui & Co. (Canada)	2 728 680	100	Mitsui (Japan)
13	United Westburne	2 563 522	69	Dumez (France)
14	Honda Canada	2 454 476	100	Honda/American Honda (Japan/US)
15	F.W. Woolworth	2 321 791	100	Woolworth (US)
16	Great Atlantic & Pacific	2 299 881	100	Great Atlantic & Pacific Tea (US)
17	Falconbridge	2 032 483	50	Trelleborg (Sweden)
18	Mobil Oil Canada	1 869 685	85	Mobil Investments (US)
19	Canadian Ultramar	1 798 232	100	Ultramar (Britain)
20	Consumers' Gas	1 771 963	100	British Gas (Britain)
21	Dow Chemical of Canada	1 629 856	100	Dow Chemical (US)
22	Cargill	1 612 000	100	Cargill (US)
23	Pratt & Whitney Canada	1 583 589	98	United Technologies (US)
24	General Electric Canada	1 580 965	100	General Electric (US)
25	Kraft General Foods Canada	1 550 139	100	Philip Morris (US)

SOURCE: *The Financial Post 500*, 1991.

Some of Canada's best-known and successful companies are 100 percent foreign owned.

best-known corporations are foreign-owned, including General Motors, Ford, Imperial Oil, and IBM. In most cases, the corporations listed are 100 percent foreign-owned.

Of the top 100 companies in Canada by sales in 1990, 35 were foreign-owned. In most cases, foreign ownership of the Canadian plant is well above 51 percent. While British and Japanese corporations control a significant number of the foreign-owned companies, the majority are subsidiaries of US corporations. Foreign-owned corporations control much of the Canadian oil, gas, and automobile industries.

In most cases, the corporations are owned by US **transnational corporations (TNCs)**. TNCs (sometimes called multinational enterprises) are corporations with locations in more than one country. British and Japanese TNCs also have a significant number of subsidiaries in Canada. TNCs control much of the Canadian automobile, oil, and chemical industries.

☐ Benefits of Foreign Investment

Many economists have argued that foreign investment is advantageous to Canada. Foreign investment brings additional capital into the country and with more capital at their disposal, Canadian workers can be more productive. In addition, TNCs established in Canada bring new products and new business expertise. The foreign competition also compels existing firms in Canada to be more competitive.

The growth of world competition, world production, and world markets has sparked an increase in transnational corporations—which can take advantage of the world-wide division of labour and thus produce goods and services with increased efficiency. Most TNCs are owned by the three economic superpowers—Japan, the US, and the members of the European Community. Restricting investment by TNCs would mean that Canada would lose the benefits of a world-wide division of labour.

Costs of Foreign Investment

The benefits, however, come with certain costs. Profits earned by TNCs accrue to foreign rather than domestic capitalists. Thus, it is argued, foreign investment may present a future balance of payments problem for Canada if it continues to increase.

A second frequently expressed objection to TNCs in Canada is that they represent a loss of Canadian control over industry. Canadian law does, however, regulate TNCs in Canada just as it does Canadian corporations. Laws governing rates and methods of natural resource extraction, pollution, and worker safety, for example, apply to TNCs in Canada just as they do to Canadian-owned corporations.

In the past, TNCs in Canada have posed the problem of extraterritoriality. **Extraterritoriality** is the extension of the laws of the country where the TNC is owned to its operations in another country. For example, the US attempted to force American-owned TNCs operating in Canada to obey US laws restricting trade with China and Cuba in the past. This clearly represents an intrusion of US law on Canadian sovereignty. Canadian and other governments strongly objected to the practice.

A third frequently voiced objection to TNCs is that research and development jobs tend to be located in the country where the corporation is owned. Thus the higher-paid, more prestigious jobs are concentrated in the home country, while the lower-paid production jobs are located in other countries.

☐ Canadian Government Policy on Foreign Ownership and Control

Until the 1960s, successive Canadian governments had welcomed foreign investment—seeing it as a means of promoting economic growth. In the 1960s and 1970s, however, more people began to question the value of foreign investment. In response to this increasing concern, the federal government established the **Foreign Investment Review Agency (FIRA)** in 1974. The purpose of FIRA was to screen new foreign investment in Canada and all foreign takeovers of Canadian corporations to ensure that they would bring "significant benefit to Canada" in terms of increased employment, investment, and productivity. FIRA rejected about 5 percent of the applications it received. On many of the applications it did accept, it imposed requirements in the form of increased domestic employment, production, and exports.

Ten years after the establishment of FIRA, faced with a decline in Canadian economic nationalism and a sluggish economy, the government replaced FIRA with a new agency called **Investment Canada**. While foreign takeovers of major Canadian firms were still to be reviewed, it was to be done on a much reduced level. Foreign investment in Canada that created new businesses would not be subject to review. Since its inception, Investment Canada has turned down no applications, though it has insisted on conditions before approving some takeovers.

Summary

a. Tariffs are taxes levied on imported goods either to increase government revenues or to shield domestic industries from foreign competition. Non-tariff barriers to trade include quotas (restrictions on the quantity of imports), voluntary export restraints, licensing requirements, red tape in customs procedures and safety standards and procedures, government procurement policies favouring domestic suppliers, and subsidies for domestic industries.

b. Tariffs represent costs to consumers since they raise the prices of imported goods and thus generally also the prices of domestic goods. Tariffs may also reduce total production and eliminate some advantages of economies of scale. Very high tariffs can effectively shut out imports.

c. Arguments for protection include non-economic arguments such as the need to sacrifice some trade for military self-sufficiency and the preservation of Canadian culture and identity. Faulty arguments include the beliefs that Canadians can gain by spending their money at home and that we cannot compete with cheap foreign labour. Arguments that tariffs can help to create or preserve Canadian jobs and that we should protect infant industries until they can stand on their own have some economic merit, but are not without drawbacks.

d. Canadian tariffs were highest around 1890 after Sir John A. Macdonald's National Policy (1879) took effect. While they declined during the prosperous period from 1890 to 1930, they rose again during the Great Depression of the 1930s as nations attempted to increase employment through protectionist measures. Since the 1930s, however, tariffs have generally declined and Canada has signed the General Agreement on Tariffs and Trade (GATT) designed to eliminate import quotas and reduce tariffs through multilateral negotiations.

e. The Auto Pact signed in 1965 established free trade between Canada and the United States in automotive vehicles, parts, and products. The integration of the auto industry increased economies of scale and the wages of Canadian autoworkers, and decreased the prices of automobiles.

The Canada-US Free Trade Agreement took effect on January 1, 1989. Its provisions include the gradual phasing out of tariffs and most trade barriers by 1998, the elimination of export subsidies and restrictions on energy imports and exports, and the easing of restrictions on US investment in Canada. Benefits include lower prices for US imports and freer access for Canadian industry to the large US market, allowing for greater specialization and economies of scale. Costs include job losses, particularly in branch plants and subsidiaries, the threat to Canadian sovereignty, and the loss of control over foreign investment and domestic energy supplies.

f. A North American free trade area would create a trading bloc that could rival the European Community. For Mexico, the free trade area could increase the competitiveness of Mexican products in the US and Canada, increase investment and the level of technology in Mexican industries, create new jobs, raise wages, and increase the standard of living. Some Mexicans are concerned about the threat to their culture and the loss of control of their economy.

For the United States, the free trade area would enhance the stability and prosperity of its southern neighbour and third most important trading partner. It would stem the illegal immigration of Mexicans to the southwestern US and open the door for US exports to Mexico. Some fear job losses, as US industries are forced to compete with cheaper Mexican products and labour. The spread of pollution from Mexican industries is also a concern.

Canada would gain free access to the Mexican market and consumers would benefit from low-priced Mexican imports. Job losses, pollution, and increased competition from Mexican products in the US are concerns, however.

g. The European Community, established in 1958, plans

to eliminate all remaining obstacles to the free movement of people, capital, goods, and services among its members by the end of 1992. The common market is expected to raise the GDP of all member nations, but non-member nations such as Canada will face barriers to trade with the Community.

h. Canada relies heavily on foreign investment. Total foreign investment in Canada has increased 13-fold since 1965, reaching $456 billion in 1990. Most direct foreign investment comes from the US, though the percentage of total foreign-owned assets held by US nationals in non-financial industries has declined from 75 percent to 66 percent in the 1980s. Most foreign control is centred in the manufacturing, mining, and wholesale trade industries. Economists argue that foreign investment brings additional capital, products, and technology into Canada, allowing workers to increase productivity. Foreign competition also compels existing firms in Canada to be more competitive. Transnational corporations also take advantage of the world-wide division of labour, increasing efficiency.

Objections to direct foreign investment include the fact that profits accrue to foreign and not domestic capitalists, Canadians may lose control over their industries, extraterritoriality may pose threats to Canadian sovereignty, and the most prestigious jobs may remain in the owner nation rather than coming to Canada.

▊ Review of Key Terms

Define each of the following key terms introduced in this chapter and provide examples where appropriate.

tariff
non-tariff barrier
quota
voluntary export restraint
General Agreement on Tariffs and Trade (GATT)
trading bloc
common market
customs union
free trade area
Auto Pact

Canada-US Free Trade Agreement
North American Free Trade Area
European Community (EC)
transnational corporation (TNC)
extraterritoriality
Foreign Investment Review Agency (FIRA)
Investment Canada

▊ Application and Analysis

1. Suppose that Canada has been experiencing a balance of payments deficit. What effect would each of the following have on the deficit? Explain why.

(a) an increase in tariffs on imports of German automobiles

(b) a reduction in the duty-free exemptions for Canadian tourists when they return to Canada

(c) subsidies for Canadian exports

(d) the imposition of a 15-percent federal tax on Canadian softwood lumber exported to the US

(e) the imposition of reduced quotas on imports of Japanese cars

(f) the reduction of subsidies to American and European grain farmers

2. What effect would each of the following probably have on (i) inflation (ii) employment and (iii) the balance of payments—assuming no other changes? Explain why in each case.

(a) an increase in interest rates

(b) an expansionary monetary policy

(c) a contractionary fiscal policy

(d) an expansionary fiscal policy

(e) a reduction in the exchange rate of the Canadian dollar

(f) an increase in the inflow of capital from other countries

3. Refer to Figure 23.8 below.

(a) If the world price of corn is $2.20 a bushel, how much will Myopia demand and supply assuming free trade?

(b) With a tariff of $1.00 a bushel, how much corn will Myopia demand and supply?

(c) With a tariff of $2.00 a bushel, how much corn will Myopia supply and demand?

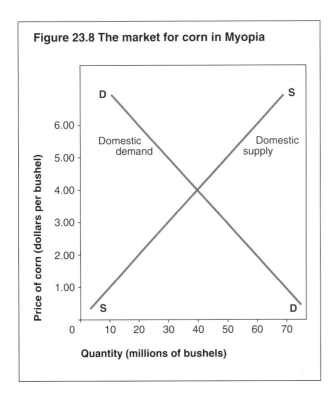

Figure 23.8 The market for corn in Myopia

4. Since 1981, imports of Japanese cars into Canada have been significantly limited by "voluntary" export quotas. What effect might such quotas have on each of the following? Explain why in each case.

(a) the profits of automobile firms in Canada

(b) employment in Canadian automobile plants

(c) prices of automobiles in Canada

(d) the standard of living of Canadians

5. To pull Canada out of the recession of 1990-1991, several members of the opposition parties suggested cutting the bank rate to less than 8 percent and lowering the value of the Canadian dollar from US$0.85 to US$0.80. What would some of the probable consequences of such actions be? Explain.

6. Assuming no other changes and a freely floating exchange rate, what effect would each of the following have on the exchange value of the Canadian dollar?

(a) increased tariffs on the import of Canadian-produced aircraft and parts

(b) a significant upturn in the US economy following a deep recession

(c) an increase in Canadian interest rates

(d) the federal government's adoption of an expansionary fiscal policy

7. Debate the following: "Resolved that free trade among Canada, the US, and Mexico would be beneficial to Canada."

8. Should the Canadian government require all foreign-controlled corporations to sell 51 percent of their stock to Canadians within a particular time period—say 10 years? Outline your arguments for or against.

GLOSSARY

Absolute advantage The ability of an individual, region, or country to produce a good or service with fewer resources (and thus more efficiently) than other individuals, regions, or countries. Canada has an absolute advantage over Brazil in the production of wheat, for example, while Brazil has an absolute advantage over Canada in the production of coffee.

Accelerator The process by which changes in consumer demand cause magnified changes in the rate of capital investment by businesses, and thus fluctuations in national income.

Acid test ratio See Quick ratio.

Aggregate demand (AD) The total amounts of goods and services that would be bought in an economy at various price levels over a particular period of time.

Aggregate supply (AS) The total amounts of final goods and services that would be offered for sale in an economy at various price levels over a particular period of time.

Allocative efficiency The production of the best combination of goods and services to meet consumer needs and wants.

Arbitration An arrangement, such as that in a labour/management dispute, by which both sides agree to accept the ruling of a third party (an arbitrator). The arbitrator's decision is binding on both parties.

Assets Anything that is owned by individuals, companies, or governments.

Automatic stabilizers Government programs which act to stabilize economic fluctuations without any specific action on the part of the government. Unemployment insurance payments, for example, increase during an economic slowdown and decrease as economic activity picks up.

Average A single number that is typical of a set of numbers. The mode, median, and mean are examples of averages.

Average fixed cost Total fixed cost divided by output. Since total fixed cost is constant, dividing it by the quantity produced gives a steadily falling average fixed cost curve as production increases.

Average product The total product per worker (or per unit of the variable factor).

Average revenue The total revenue from the sale of a product divided by the quantity sold. For a perfectly competitive firm, average revenue is the same as price.

Average total cost The sum of average variable cost and average fixed cost at each level of output, or total cost divided by output.

Average variable cost Total variable cost divided by output.

Balance of payments The summary of all visible, invisible, and capital transactions between one country and the rest of the world over a period of time—usually one year.

Balance of trade The difference between the value of a country's merchandise exports and the value of its merchandise imports.

Balance of trade on current account The difference between the money value of a country's visible and invisible exports and the money value of its visible and invisible imports.

Balance sheet One of the two most important financial statements for investors, which provides a picture of a company's financial status at a particular point in time—usually at the close of business on December 31st, the last day of the year. It includes a statement of the firm's assets, liabilities or debts, and shareholders' equity.

Balanced budget A budget with revenues equal to expenditures.

Bank rate The interest rate charged by the Bank of Canada on its loans to chartered banks.

Barter system A system of exchange in which goods and services are exchanged for other goods and services without the use of money.

Base year Starting or reference year that is given the value of 100 when constructing a price index.

Benefits-received principle A principle based on the concept that taxes should be paid in proportion to the benefits taxpayers receive. For example, air travellers pay an excise tax on airline tickets to help pay for airport security.

Black market The buying and selling of a good at a price above the ceiling or maximum legal price.

Boycott A campaign to encourage consumers not to buy a firm's products. California farm workers, for example, have organized boycotts of some of the state's agricultural products.

Break-even point The level of output at which total revenue equals total cost and thus total profits (and total losses) are zero.

Budget deficit A budget in which expenditures exceed revenues.

Budget surplus A budget in which revenues exceed expenditures.

Business cycles Fluctuations in economic activity between expansion and recession which occur over a period of years.

Business plan A written outline of the management, financing, operating, and marketing plans of a business.

Businesses Economic units involved in the production, distribution, and sale of goods and services. They may be very small operations, such as a corner store, or very large enterprises, such as a steel or automobile corporation.

Capital Human-made resources, such as factories, machines, and tools, used in the production of goods and services. Human capital includes the training and education that make people more productive.

Capital account The account in a country's balance of payments that records the flows of capital.

Cash-flow forecast A monthly statement of a firm's projected receipts and expenditures. It outlines how much a business expects to receive in cash and from whom, and when funds must be spent to pay the bills.

Ceiling price The maximum legal price that may be charged for a good or service. Rent controls are an example.

Cheque An order to pay an individual or group a specified sum of money from an account.

Closed shop A term in an agreement between a union and the management of a firm specifying that only union members may be employed.

Collective bargaining The process of negotiation between representatives of a union and management, the object of which is to establish terms and conditions of employment acceptable to both sides.

Collusion A covert agreement between or among firms to reduce or eliminate competition and/or control output. The collusion may be informal, such as by verbal agreement, or formal, such as by the firms' agreement to establish their own marketing organization.

Common market A free trade arrangement that includes no tariffs or other barriers on goods produced by member countries, common tariff rates and non-tariff barriers on goods entering member countries from non-member nations, and no restrictions on the movement of capital and workers among member countries. The European Community is an example.

Common stocks or shares Part ownership of a corporation. The ownership of 2 percent of the common stock entitles the owner to 2 percent of the issued dividends (profits), 2 percent of the vote at annual meetings, and 2 percent of the net assets if the corporation closes down.

Comparative advantage The ability of an individual, region, or country to produce a good or service relatively more efficiently (at a lower opportunity cost) than another individual, region, or country.

Competition The continuing search by consumers for lowest prices and greatest satisfaction, and by owners of productive resources for highest returns. The unco-ordinated actions of competing buyers and sellers determine what will be produced, how it will be produced, and for whom in a free market economy.

Competition Act An act passed in 1986 (replacing the Combines Investigation Act) designed to maintain and encourage competition in Canadian industry. A Competition Tribunal was established under the Act to review any possible violations.

Complementary goods Pairs of goods that "go together" or complement each other in the sense that the consumption of one involves the consumption of the other. Oil and gasoline are an example.

Compulsory check-off A term in an agreement between a union and management whereby union dues are deducted from the pay cheques of all employees in the bargaining unit.

Concentration ratio The percentage of total market sales for the four (or eight) largest firms in an industry.

Conciliation A situation in a labour/management dispute, for example, where both sides agree to submit their proposals to a third party (a conciliator or mediator). The conciliator attempts to bring the two sides to an agreement, but neither side is obliged to accept the conciliator's recommendations.

Conglomerate merger When firms in unrelated industries combine. A conglomerate could include firms from as widely different industries as mining, insurance, and retailing. Conglomerate mergers are less likely to reduce competition substantially than are either vertical or horizontal mergers.

Consumer Price Index (CPI) A measure of the average price of goods and services bought by representative urban Canadian households. It is often thought of as the cost of a "basket" of goods and services bought by a typical urban Canadian household.

Consumer sovereignty The dominant role consumers play

in a market economy by determining through their expenditures what, how, and for whom goods and services are to be produced.

Consumer surplus The difference between what a consumer is willing to pay for each unit of a good or service and what he or she actually pays (i.e., the market price).

Consumption spending That part of personal disposable income which is spent.

Contractionary fiscal policy Government spending and taxing policies to decrease aggregate demand.

Contractionary monetary policy Policies, such as increasing the bank rate or selling government bonds, designed to decrease the money supply.

Co-operative A form of business organization jointly owned by a group of people and in which benefits are distributed according to member patronage. Co-operatives are usually formed by people in the same industry or occupation and are run democratically, with everyone sharing in the profits or surpluses. Farmers have established agricultural co-operatives to market their products, for example, and workers in unions have established credit unions to supply them with credit.

Corporate bonds Bonds sold or issued by corporations in order to borrow funds. Corporate bonds represent the corporation's debt, which it is obliged to pay at some time in the future (as well as periodic interest payments) whether it makes a profit or not. Corporate bonds are generally long-term, and may fall due 10, 15, or more years from the date of issue. A bondholder is the creditor of the corporation and is entitled to receive payment prior to the shareholders on dissolution of the corporation.

Corporation A form of business organization that has a legal existence of its own, separate from that of those who created or own it. Corporations include many of the large firms people are familiar with, such as Air Canada, Canadian Pacific, Bell Canada, Alcan Aluminium, and Shell Canada.

Cost-pull inflation A situation in which wages or other costs of production rise (such as those of essential raw materials), thus "pushing up" the general level of prices.

Craft union A recognized association of workers practising a particular trade or craft, such as the United Brotherhood of Carpenters and Joiners of America.

Crowding out The displacement of private investment by government expenditure. Private investment is thus "crowded out."

Crown corporations Government-owned corporations that are expected to draw revenues from the sale of their goods and services. Examples include Canada Post and Canadian National Railways.

Customs duties See Tariffs.

Customs union An agreement among countries to eliminate trade barriers (such as tariffs or quotas) among them and to establish common tariff barriers on non-members.

Cut-throat competition The sale of goods at prices below the cost of production in order to drive rivals out of business.

Cyclical deficit That part of a budget deficit incurred by government during a recession to stimulate the economy.

Cyclical (or inadequate demand) unemployment Unemployment caused by the reduction of economic activity during downturns in business cycles.

Debits (or liabilities) What is owed by an individual, company, or government.

Decision lag The time that passes between recognizing that a problem exists (e.g., a recession) and deciding what to do about it.

Demand The quantities of a good or service consumers are willing and able to buy at various prices over a period of time.

Demand curve A graphic representation of the quantities of a good or service buyers are willing and able to purchase at various prices over a period of time.

Demand deposits Bank deposits on which the depositor can, without giving the bank advance notice, withdraw or transfer money. Personal chequing accounts are an example since money can be withdrawn on demand.

Demand schedule A table showing the quantities of a good or service consumers are willing and able to buy at various prices over a particular time.

Demand-pull inflation Inflation caused by excess aggregate demand. The excess demand "pulls up" the general level of prices. Demand-pull inflation is often described as "too many dollars chasing too few goods."

Depreciation An estimate of the loss in value of capital goods, such as machinery or buildings, through wear and obsolescence over time.

Depression A prolonged period of significantly reduced economic activity characterized by widespread unemployment, declining prices, declining output, little capital investment, and many business failures.

Derived demand Demand for a factor of production that results from, or is derived from, the demand for the product it is used to make. The demand for workers who make shirts, for example, is derived from the demand for shirts.

Direct foreign investment Foreign investment made to achieve control over a company.

Direct tax A tax that cannot be transferred or passed on to someone else. Federal and provincial income taxes are an example.

Discouraged workers Those who would like to work, but have stopped looking because they believe no work is available for them. Once they stop looking, they are no longer considered part of the labour force and are not included among the unemployed.

Discretionary fiscal policy Any deliberate government actions to alter spending or taxation policies in order to influence the level of output, employment, economic growth, or balance of payments.

Discretionary income That part of personal disposable income left after essentials, such as food and clothing, have been paid for. Discretionary income can be saved or spent according to the wishes and tastes of the household.

Diseconomies of scale A situation where increases in inputs bring a less than proportional increase in output.

Domestic income The sum of incomes earned by all factors of production in a country.

Dow Jones Industrial Average The best-known and most widely quoted daily index of stock market prices on the New York Stock Exchange.

Earnings per common share The net earnings of a firm divided by the number of outstanding shares.

Economics The science that studies human behaviour as a relationship between ends and scarce means which have alternative uses.

Economic Council of Canada (ECC) An advisory body established by the federal government in 1963 (and dismantled in 1992) to study the future prospects of the economy, to advise government about appropriate economic policies, and to inform the Canadian public. The Council reports to parliament through the prime minister.

Economic efficiency The goal of realizing the most effective use of productive resources by producing a given output with the minimum amount of resources.

Economic goods Concrete, tangible items that satisfy human wants and have value, such as automobiles and shirts.

Economic growth A sustained increase in real GDP, often adjusted on a per capita (per person) basis.

Economic models Simplified representations of an economy or part of an economy and expressed verbally, graphically, or mathematically.

Economic system The set of laws, institutions, and customs by which a society determines how to use its scarce resources to meet the needs and wants of its members.

Economic theory A generalization or set of generalizations about how an economic system, or part of it, functions.

Economies of scale A situation where an increase in inputs results in a more than proportional increase in output. In other words, the long-run average cost curve decreases as output increases.

Elasticity of demand The responsiveness of buyers to changes in price. Demand is elastic if buyers respond strongly to changes in price and inelastic if buyers respond weakly to changes in price.

Elasticity of supply The responsiveness of producers to changes in price. Supply is elastic if suppliers respond strongly to small changes in price and inelastic if they respond weakly to large changes in price.

Employed Those who did any work at all—part-time or full-time—during the month in which Statistics Canada does its survey of Canadian households, including those who had a job but did not work because of labour disputes, vacations, or illness.

Entrepreneurs Individuals who start their own businesses or who aggressively expand existing ones. They organize natural, human, and capital resources to produce goods and services.

Equalization payments Transfer payments made by the federal government to the "have-not" provinces with a small tax base to ensure that they can provide reasonably comparable levels of public services without resorting to high levels of taxation. Equalization payments are made with no strings attached.

Equilibrium A situation in which change is unlikely to occur. In other words, a stable or balanced situation.

Equilibrium price The price at which quantity demanded equals quantity supplied.

Excess supply See Surplus.

Exchange rate The price of one currency in terms of another.

Excise taxes Those federal or provincial taxes levied on specific goods—such as tobacco, beer, gasoline, cosmetics, and liquor.

Expansionary fiscal policy Government spending and taxing policies designed to increase aggregate demand.

Expansionary monetary policy Policies, such as decreasing the bank rate or buying government bonds, designed to increase the money supply.

Expenditure approach A method of determining GDP by calculating the total amount spent on all final goods and services over a period of time—usually a year.

Explicit costs A firm's direct (or out-of-pocket) expenditures on such things as labour, rent, materials, transportation, and electricity.

Exports Goods and services sold to foreign nationals.

Externality A beneficial or harmful side effect (or spillover) of production or consumption. Pollution of the air and water, for example, is a negative externality of some industrial production. The costs are borne by the people who depend on and enjoy the clean air and water. A well-kept garden, on the other hand, is a positive externality, providing pleasure to passers-by and increasing the value of neighbours' homes.

Extraterritoriality The extension of the laws of the country where a transnational corporation is owned to its operations in another country. For example, the US has attempted to force American-owned TNCs operating in Canada to obey US laws restricting trade with China and Cuba in the past.

Federal debt The total amount owed by the federal government to households, businesses, and non-Canadians.

Fiat money Money declared by government order (or fiat) to be legal tender. It is not defined in terms of a particular amount of gold or silver and its value is not backed by any precious metal.

Final goods Products that have been bought by the last user and are not for resale or further processing.

Financial intermediaries All institutions that accept deposits from individuals, businesses, and governments and loan funds to borrowers. They include banks, trust and mortgage loan companies, credit unions, and caisses populaires.

Fiscal policy Changes in government spending and taxing programs that influence the level of aggregate demand and thus the levels of income, output, prices, and employment.

Fixed exchange rate An exchange rate that is fixed at a specific level by the monetary authorities of a nation.

Fixed resources Resources, such as buildings and equipment or "plant," that do not change as output increases.

Floor price A minimum price below which it is illegal to buy or sell a good or service. The minimum wage is an example.

Foreign Investment Review Agency (FIRA) An agency, established in 1974, which screened new foreign investment in Canada and all foreign takeovers of Canadian corporations to ensure that they would bring "significant benefit to Canada" in terms of increased employment, investment, and productivity. In the mid-1980s, foreign investment policy became less restrictive and FIRA was renamed Investment Canada.

Franchise A contractual arrangement under which a person or company (the franchisor) grants another person or company (the franchisee) the right to produce or sell a product or service in a specified area under the franchisor's name.

Free goods Those goods that exist in sufficient quantities to satisfy everyone's wants, even at no cost.

Free riders Those who benefit from a good or service, just as well as those who pay, but who do not pay.

Free trade area A free trade arrangement that covers only the elimination of tariffs and other barriers to trade among the countries in the agreement. No common tariff rates or non-tariff barriers exist on imports from other nations. Each nation applies its own restrictions on trade with non-member nations and national restrictions on the movement of capital and workers remain in place.

Freely floating or flexible exchange rate An exchange rate determined by the forces of supply and demand and left to fluctuate freely as the market for it determines.

Frictional unemployment The short-term unemployment of those who are "between jobs," or who are just entering or re-entering the labour market.

Full employment A situation where all those who wish to work can find a job relatively rapidly. Full employment, however, is not 100 percent employment since some unemployment (frictional, for example) is considered inevitable.

GDP deflator A measurement of the price changes of all final goods and services produced in an economy.

GDP gap The difference between the potential GDP, which the country could produce at full employment, and the actual GDP. The GDP gap is, therefore, one measure of the economic costs of unemployment.

General Agreement on Tariffs and Trade (GATT) An international agreement, reached in 1947 by 23 nations including Canada, to reduce trade barriers among nations. In 1992, some 140 nations were members.

Goods The concrete, physical products we produce, such as wheat and automobiles.

Graph A diagram or illustration that shows how two or more sets of data are related.

Green revolution The revolution in grain production associated with new hybrid seed varieties of corn, wheat, and rice which has helped bring about high farm yields in many developing countries.

Greenhouse effect The gradual warming of the world's climate due to the release of sulphur dioxide, carbon dioxide, and other gases into the planet's atmosphere.

Gross Domestic Product (GDP) The value, at market prices, of all final goods and services produced in Canada over a period of time—usually one year.

Gross National Product (GNP) The value, at market prices, of all final goods and services produced by all Canadian-owned factors of production over a period of time—usually one year.

Horizontal merger The union of two or more firms in the same industry. The union of Canadian Airlines International Ltd. and Wardair in 1989 is an example.

Horizontal tax equity An approach to fairness in taxation which states that taxpayers with the same ability to pay should pay the same amount of taxes.

Household Any person or group of persons living together and functioning as an economic unit. A household may be a family, single individual, or group of unrelated individuals. Through their needs and wants for goods and services and their expenditures (dollar votes), households represent the demand or consumer side of the economy. They also supply factors of production to businesses and governments.

Human capital See Capital.

Human resources (also called labour) The human services (manual and non-manual) used in the production of goods and services.

Hyperinflation Rapidly rising inflation, such as that suffered by Germany in the early 1920s.

Hypothesis An explanation for the relationship between two or more variables, which can be tested by reference to facts.

Imperfect competition Market structures that are not perfectly competitive, particularly monopolistic competition (imperfect competition among the many) and oligopoly (imperfect competition among the few).

Implementation lag The delay between the time a policy has been approved and the time it takes to have an effect.

Implicit costs Estimated payments for resources that a firm already owns, such as the owner's salary and interest on money the owner has invested in the firm.

Imports Goods and services bought from other countries.

Income approach One method of measuring GDP by totalling the incomes of all factors of production.

Income effect The change in the quantity of a good demanded resulting from a change in real income. The income effect of a price change will depend on how much the price is changed and the proportion of total expenditure made on the good.

Income statement A record of the flow of a company's earnings and expenditures over a period of time, such as a year.

Indirect tax A tax that can be transferred or passed along to someone else. Customs duties levied on imported goods and paid by the importer, for example, usually result in higher prices which are ultimately passed on to the consumer.

Induced investment Investment that results from increased domestic product.

Industrial union A recognized organization of many different kinds of workers—including skilled, semi-skilled, and unskilled—usually all employed in the same industry. The National Automobile, Aerospace, and Agricultural Implement Workers Union of Canada is an example.

Inferior goods Commodities for which demand varies inversely (in the opposite direction) with income. Cabbage and potatoes are examples. When incomes rise beyond a certain point, the demand for these goods tends to decline because people switch to "higher grade" food products, such as meat and fruit.

Inflation A general increase in the prices of goods and services over time.

Inflationary gap The decrease in the level of aggregate demand required to bring equilibrium GDP down to the level of the full employment GDP.

Injection An expenditure other than consumption put into the circular flow that raises domestic income. Investment, exports, and government expenditures are injections.

Interest The payment made to (or the income earned by) a lender for the use of money over a period of time.

Intermediate goods Goods that are bought for further processing or sale.

Inventory The stock of goods—including raw materials, semifinished, and finished goods—held for future sale or production by businesses and governments.

Investment Canada The federal agency which replaced FIRA in the mid-1980s and which reviews foreign takeovers of Canadian firms.

Invisible or non-merchandise trade The exchange of services, investment incomes or payments, and transfers of immigrants' funds.

Keynesian economics The major macroeconomic theory as described by J.M. Keynes in his book *The General Theory of Employment, Interest and Money*. Keynes believed an economy could reach equilibrium below full employment and that government action—especially fiscal policy—was therefore necessary to move the economy to full employment.

Kinked demand curve A demand curve used to explain price stickiness in oligopoly markets. The kink in the curve is at the existing price.

Labour force That part of the population 15 years of age and over, which is both willing and able to work for a wage or salary. It includes both the employed and unemployed.

Labour union A certified organization of workers that negotiates with employers on matters of pay, benefits, working conditions, and other issues. The Canadian Union of Public Employees and the United Steelworkers of America are two of the largest unions with members in Canada.

Laffer curve A graph showing the relationship between changes in the tax rate and changes in tax revenue.

Law of demand The law stating that as the price of a good falls the quantity purchased increases, providing all other things remain the same. Conversely, as the price rises, the quantity purchased decreases.

Law of diminishing marginal utility The law stating that each additional unit consumed in any given time yields less utility or satisfaction than the one previously consumed, all other things being equal.

Law of diminishing returns Also called the law of diminishing marginal product, states that as additional units of a variable resource are added to a fixed resource, beyond some point the marginal product attributable to each additional unit of the variable resource will decline.

Law of supply The law stating that for most goods, the higher their prices, the greater will be the quantity supplied. Conversely, the lower their prices, the lower will be the quantity supplied, assuming no other changes.

Leading indicators Data used to predict emerging trends in the business cycle. They help to predict when changes will take place, whether from trough to recovery or peak to recession, for example, and basically signal the short-term developments in the economy because they reflect what businesses and consumers have actually begun to produce and spend.

Leakage A withdrawal from the income-expenditure stream of the economy. The major leakages are savings, taxes, and imports.

Less developed countries (LDCs) Countries which have a relatively low per capita income and are less industrialized than nations such as Canada. Most LDC nations are in Africa, Asia, and Central and South America.

Limited liability The principle that the risk or liability of a corporation's owners is limited to the amount they have invested.

Liquidity preference The demand for money.

Lockout A bargaining tool used by management which involves the temporary closing of a plant or business thus "locking out" workers and taking away their jobs. It is the employer's equivalent of a strike.

Long-run costs The period in which all factors and costs are variable. In the long run, the firm can change not only the amount of labour and raw materials (variable resources), but also its plant size and the amount and type of equipment it uses (fixed resources). The number of firms in the industry may also vary, as some new firms start production and others shut down.

Lorenz curve A curve showing the extent to which the actual distribution of income differs from perfect equality.

M1 The narrowest definition of the money supply that includes only what can be used as a direct medium of exchange—that is, currency outside banks and demand deposits in chartered banks.

M1A M1 plus daily interest chequable savings accounts and those non-personal savings accounts that are connected to chequing accounts.

M2 M1A plus savings and term deposits—what is known as "near money".

M2+ M2 plus deposits at institutions other than banks, such as trust and mortgage loan companies, credit unions, and caisses populaires.

M3 M2 plus foreign currency deposits held in Canada by Canadian residents and large term deposits (over $100 000) held by businesses, often in the form of certificates of deposit (CDs).

Macroeconomics The study of the economy as a whole, including investigations of such questions as the overall level of consumption, investment, government spending, prices, employment, and output.

Managed float A combination of the fixed and floating exchange rate systems. It is like the fixed exchange rate system in that the central bank intervenes from time to time in foreign exchange markets to buy and sell currencies and control the fluctuations in exchange rates, but it is like the floating exchange rate system in that the exchange rate is left to a considerable extent to fluctuate according to market forces. There is usually no "official" exchange rate.

Marginal cost The extra or additional cost of producing one more unit of output.

Marginal efficiency of capital The marginal rate of return on a country's capital stock.

Marginal efficiency of investment A curve or schedule showing the relationship between the amount of investment and the rate of interest.

Marginal product The additional output that comes from each addition of a variable resource (such as labour).

Marginal productivity theory of wages The theory which states that in a competitive market, a firm will hire workers to the point where the wage rate equals the marginal revenue product.

Marginal propensity to consume (MPC) The proportion of any increase in disposable income that a family or a community would spend on additional consumption.

Marginal propensity to save (MPS) The proportion of any

increase in disposable income that a household or a community would save.

Marginal resource cost The amount each additional worker adds to the total cost of a firm.

Marginal revenue The change in a firm's total revenue that results from the sale of one additional unit.

Marginal revenue product (MRP) The addition to the firm's total revenue resulting from each additional worker.

Marginal tax rate The fraction of extra income that would be paid in taxes.

Market A network that keeps buyers and sellers in contact for the purpose of exchanging goods and services and determining prices.

Market failure An imperfection in the price system that results in an inefficient allocation of productive resources. Examples include public goods, merit goods, externalities, and the breakdown of perfect competition.

Marketing boards Government-sanctioned organizations of farmers. Some, such as those for milk and eggs, have the legal power to fix prices and limit production.

Mean The sum of a group of scores divided by the total number of scores.

Median The middle number in a range of values that divides the group of numbers into two equal parts—just as a median strip divides a highway in two.

Mediation See Conciliation.

Merchandise or visible trade Trade between countries in goods.

Merger The joining or combination of two or more firms into a single firm.

Merit goods Goods or services that governments consider to be particularly desirable and that they, therefore, support through subsidies and/or regulations. The education of children is an example.

Microeconomics The study of the roles and behaviour of individual units in the economy, such as that of households and firms.

Mixed economy An economy in which some decisions are made by households and firms and others are made by government. The former USSR had a mixed command economy. Canada has a mixed market economy.

Mode The most frequent value of a set of numbers.

Monetarism A term describing the economic theories of a group of economists who reject much of Keynesian economic thought and believe that the economy is essentially stable if the money supply is stable and that government generally plays far too great a role in the economy. The most famous contemporary monetarist is Milton Friedman.

Monetary policy Policies of the government, working through the central bank (in Canada, the Bank of Canada), to control the money supply and thus achieve economic stability and a viable balance of payments.

Money Anything that is generally accepted as a means of payment for goods and services.

Money supply The total stock of money available in a country at any particular time.

Monopolistic competition A market situation in which a large number of sellers provide similar, but not identical products. Different hamburger restaurants, for example, offer similar, but not identical hamburgers.

Monopoly See Pure monopoly.

Monopsony A market situation with only one buyer of a good or service. A monopsony employer, therefore, would have monopoly power in hiring workers.

Moral suasion Attempts by the Bank of Canada to persuade the chartered banks to act in accordance with a particular policy, though without legal obligation.

Mortgage A loan secured by the value of land and buildings.

Multiplier The factor by which initial changes in spending change the level of total spending. The size of the multiplier varies with the MPC.

Natural monopolies Monopolies which occur when a single firm can supply the entire market with lower average total costs, and thus a lower price, than can two or more firms. Many of the services provided by public utilities—such as natural gas, electricity, water, telephone, and urban transportation—fall into this category.

Natural resources (sometimes called land) All the resources in nature that have value, including land, minerals, fresh water, and forests.

Near banks Trust and mortgage loan companies, credit unions, and caisses populaires which function much as do the chartered banks.

Near money Savings (or notice) and term deposits, and Canada Savings Bonds, that cannot be used directly to make payments, but which can be converted into cash (through withdrawals) or transferred to chequing accounts.

Needs The basic human physical requirements necessary to sustain life, such as food, clothing, and shelter.

Net Domestic Income (NDI) Income-based GDP minus depreciation, indirect taxes less subsidies, and the statistical discrepancy. These components are deducted because they are not part of the income that goes to owners of productive resources. NDI is the total income earned by Canadian-owned factors of production.

Net Economic Welfare (NEW) A single comprehensive measure of economic welfare including not only GDP, but also additions for leisure time and subtractions for urbanization (pollution, overcrowding of cities, etc.).

Net (after-tax) profit margin ratio A ratio that measures a firm's profitability and is useful for comparing the company's performance year-to-year and the performances of various companies in the same industry.

Net worth (or equity) Total assets minus total liabilities.

Neutrality principle A principle which affirms that taxes should have a neutral effect on the operation of the market system and on individual decision making. Thus, for example, taxes on income should not dissuade people from working or investing.

Nominal GDP GDP at market prices.

Non-tariff barriers Barriers to international trade other than tariffs, including quotas, voluntary export restraints, licensing requirements, red tape in customs procedures and safety standards and procedures, government procurement policies, and subsidies.

Normal profit The minimum profit necessary to keep a business producing a particular good or service.

Normative (or policy) economics Economics concerned with what *should* or *ought to be*. Normative statements cannot be settled solely by reference to facts. They are value judgements.

North American Free Trade Area (NAFTA) A proposed free trade agreement between Canada, the US, and Mexico.

Okun's law The observation that a 2 percent change in real GDP is associated with a 1 percent change in the unemployment rate in the opposite direction. Thus, if actual GDP declines 2 percent, the unemployment rate increases 1 percent.

Oligopoly A market structure in which a few large firms provide most of the goods or services. Imperial Oil, Shell, and PetroCanada, for example, provide most of the gasoline Canadians use.

Open market operations The buying and selling of bonds and treasury bills by the Bank of Canada in order to control the money supply.

Open shop A firm in which union membership is voluntary.

Opportunity cost The cost of all that is lost from taking one course of action over another.

Paradox of thrift The possibility that a community, by attempting to save more (i.e., be more thrifty), may actually save less.

Paradox of value The seeming contradiction that water, which is so essential to us, has such a low price while diamonds, which are inessential, command such a high price.

Participation rate The percentage of the population of working age that is in the workforce.

Partnership A form of business organization in which two or more individuals enter a business as owners and share the profits and losses. Partnerships are common in service industries, such as small stores and restaurants, and in the professions, such as accounting and law.

Patent Exclusive ownership of a product or technique for a period of years granted to firms or individuals which have invented it.

Peak One of the four phases of the business cycle where economic activity is at its greatest. The turning point from expansion to recession.

Perfectly competitive market A market with many buyers and sellers, and in which no individual buyer or seller is able to influence price.

Personal Disposable Income (PDI) Personal income minus personal income taxes.

Personal Income (PI) Income received by households, both earned and unearned, thus including transfer payments.

Phillips curve A curve showing the relationship between the rate of inflation and the rate of unemployment.

Picket line A line of striking union members across the entrance to their work place, with the purpose of informing people that a strike is in progress.

Poor Those whose income is inadequate to pay for the basic necessities of life. In Canada, a family is defined as poor if it must spend more than 58.5 percent of its income on the basic necessities of life (food, clothing, and shelter).

Portfolio investment Purchases by foreign investors of stocks or bonds in corporations under Canadian control.

Positive (or analytical) economics Economics concerned with the way things are.

Potential or full-employment output The level of GDP that an economy would produce if there were full employment.

Poverty line An estimate of the income needed to be just above the level of poverty. The line varies with family size and area of residence.

Precautionary demand for money The desire to hold money to meet emergencies or deal with unexpected events.

Preferred (or preference) shares Shares in a company that entitle the owner to a fixed return on investment before profits are distributed to common shareholders. In the event that the corporation is liquidated, preferred shareholders are entitled to an amount equal to the face value of their shares before any payment is made to common shareholders.

Price The exchange value of goods and services expressed in money terms.

Price discrimination A practice of monopolists by which prices are varied to different consumers—though the costs of production are unchanged.

Price-earnings ratio (or PE multiple) A ratio obtained by dividing the current market price of a share by the annual earnings per share.

Price elastic See Elasticity of demand and Elasticity of supply.

Price index A number that shows the average percentage change in the prices of a collection of goods and/or services over a period of time.

Prices and incomes policies Attempts by governments to control inflation by controlling prices and wages directly.

Primary (or cash) reserves Deposits at the Bank of Canada or currency notes at the chartered banks.

Prime rate The interest rate charged by the chartered banks to their best (or least risky) customers, usually large stable corporations. The prime rate is often set at about one percent higher than the bank rate.

Production function The relationship between a firm's inputs (or factors of production) and its output.

Production possibilities curve or schedule A curve or schedule showing the different combinations of outputs possible with the full employment of resources.

Productive resources or factors market The market in which productive resources or factors (land, labour, capital, entrepreneurship) are sold.

Productivity Total output per unit of input over a period of time.

Profit The return to the entrepreneur and/or capital once all costs—including opportunity costs and normal profit—have been met.

Progressive tax A tax that takes a larger proportion of income as income rises.

Proportional tax A tax that remains unchanged with changes in income. The tax takes a constant percentage no matter what the level of income.

Proxy A document signed by a shareholder appointing someone other than the shareholder (often the management of the corporation) the right to vote at the annual or other meetings of the corporation.

Public good A good or service that benefits the general public, no matter who pays for it. National defence is an example.

Pure command economy An economy in which the answers to the what, how, and for whom questions are provided by a government or other central authority. Natural and capital resources are owned by the state.

Pure market economy An economy in which the actions of individual buyers and sellers operating through a system of prices and markets co-ordinate economic activity. Natural and capital resources are privately owned.

Pure monopoly A market structure with only one producer of a good or service, for which there are no close substitutes and many buyers. Electric power is an example.

Pure traditional economy An economy in which the traditions or past practices of the society provide the answers to the three main economic questions: What to produce? How to produce? For whom to produce?

Quantity theory of money A theory which states that a change in the money supply, with a fairly stable velocity of circulation, will bring about a roughly proportional change in nominal GDP. For example, an increase in the money supply of 10 percent will bring about an increase in the nominal GDP of approximately 10 percent.

Quick ratio (or acid test) A stringent test of a firm's ability to pay its debts, calculated by dividing a company's current assets minus inventories by its current liabilities.

Quota A restriction placed on the quantity of a product that may be bought, produced, imported, or exported.

Real capital The tangible assets of a firm, such as buildings and machinery, etc. Financial (money) and real capital are closely related since the main purpose of raising money capital is to invest in real capital.

Real flow In the circular flow model, the flow of goods and services from businesses through the products markets to households and of resources from households through the productive resources market to businesses.

Real GDP GDP adjusted to take into account changes in the general price level (inflation).

Real interest rate The nominal rate of interest minus the rate of inflation.

Recession A phase of the business cycle when the seasonally adjusted real GDP declines for two or more quarters (three-month periods) in succession.

Recessionary gap The gap between equilibrium real GDP and capacity GDP.

Recognition lag A delay between the onset of recession or inflation and the recognition of the extent and nature of the problem.

Regressive tax A tax that regresses or declines as income increases. Provincial sales taxes are an example.

Rent Payment made to the owner of a resource, such as land.

Resources Those inputs used in the production of goods and services—land, labour, capital, and entrepreneurial skill.

Rotating strike A strike whereby workers in various parts of a corporation or industry go on strike in turn. In this way, the union can cause considerable disruption, while limiting the cost in lost pay to workers and strike pay it must provide, and reducing the prospect of back-to-work legislation in some cases.

Sales taxes Taxes levied on the sale of goods and services.

Scarcity A situation in which only a limited amount of resources is available to produce a limited number of goods and services to meet relatively unlimited human wants.

Scientific method The basic method scientists follow in their investigations, including four main steps: observation, collection, explanation, and verification.

Seasonal unemployment Unemployment that occurs as a result of the change in seasons. The lumbering, fishing, and construction industries, for example, experience seasonal fluctuations in employment.

Self-interest The pursuit of one's own advantage.

Services Those intangible things or actions that satisfy human wants and needs, such as medical care and retail services.

Shortage (or excess demand) The amount by which quantity demanded exceeds quantity supplied at a particular price.

Shut-down point The price below which the firm cannot cover its variable costs and must therefore shut down.

Sole (or single) proprietorship A form of business organization wholly owned by one person.

Speculative demand for money The desire to hold money in bank accounts waiting for an advantageous time to buy stocks or bonds for profit.

Spillover See Externality.

Stabilization policy Deliberate actions taken by governments to smooth the fluctuations of the economy. Stabilization policy includes both fiscal and monetary policies.

Stagflation A situation of rising prices and declining employment and output: economic *stag*nation—little economic growth, high unemployment—and in*flation* together.

Stockbroker A member of a stock exchange who buys and sells stocks for investors.

Stock exchange A building where stocks of major corporations are bought and sold by traders employed by stockbrokers.

Stock market An organized market, at which listed stocks can be bought and sold.

Strike The temporary withholding of labour services by a union to compel management into modifying its collective bargaining position.

Structural deficit The amount above the cyclical deficit that would continue to exist even if the economy were at full employment without inflation.

Structural unemployment Unemployment that occurs when the skills and/or locations of workers do not match those of the jobs available.

Substitute (or competing) goods Those goods that can be interchanged for one another, such as cassette tapes for compact discs, or apple for orange juice.

Substitution effect The tendency of buyers to purchase more of a good when its price falls and to purchase less of a good when its price rises. For example, reduction in the price of compact discs means that we are likely to buy more compact discs rather than tapes. In other words, we *substitute* compact discs for tapes.

Superior (or normal) goods Commodities for which demand varies directly (in the same direction) with income. Steak is one of the most commonly cited examples, since with a rise in incomes, people will tend to buy more steak.

Supply The various amounts of a good or service producers are willing and able to produce and sell at various prices over a period of time.

Supply curve A graphic representation of the quantities of a good or service producers are willing and able to supply at various prices over a period of time.

Supply schedule A table showing the quantities of a good or service producers are willing and able to supply at various prices over a period of time.

Supply-siders Economists who suggest that economic policy is too demand-oriented and argue that aggregate supply, and not aggregate demand, is the key force in determining levels of inflation, unemployment, and GDP. Stimulating the supply side of the economy—that is, increasing output, they argue—will decrease both inflation and unemployment and promote economic growth. Two of the most prominent supply-side economists are Arthur Laffer and Robert Mundell.

Surplus The amount by which the quantity supplied is greater than the quantity demanded at the existing price.

Tariff A tax imposed on imported goods. Tariffs may be levied to raise revenues or to protect domestic industry.

Tax An obligatory payment made by individuals and corporations to governments.

Technological efficiency The production of the maximum amount of goods and services with the available resources while working at a sensible pace.

Terms of trade The rate of exchange at which a country's exports are exchanged for its imports.

Theory A hypothesis which accounts satisfactorily for the facts on which it is based, and more importantly, explains new data or predicts events.

Total cost The sum of fixed and variable costs. Since fixed costs remain unchanged in the short run, total costs increase as variable costs increase.

Total fixed costs Those costs that do not change in total with changes in output. They include the costs of insurance, rent, depreciation on capital equipment, interest on debt, and management salaries.

Total product Total quantity produced.

Total revenue The total receipts from the sale of a product, calculated as price times quantity sold.

Total revenue-total cost approach An approach which holds that a firm maximizes profit when total revenue exceeds total cost by the maximum amount.

Total variable costs Those costs that vary directly as output varies—that is, as output increases, total variable costs also increase, and as output decreases, total variable costs also decrease. Examples of variable costs include materials, fuel, power, and labour.

Transactions demand for money The desire to hold money to finance immediate purchases.

Transfer payments Payments made by one level of government to another level of government, individual, or business, for which no good or service is provided in return. Family allowances, federal payments to provincial governments, Canada pension benefits, and unemployment insurance payments are examples.

Transnational corporations (TNCs) TNCs (sometimes called multinational enterprises) are corporations with locations in more than one country.

Treasury bills Short-term securities (as compared to bonds, which are long-term securities), the principal amount of which is to be repaid in 91, 182, or 365 days. The federal government uses treasury bills to meet its short-term borrowing requirements.

Trough The low point of the business cycle between recession and recovery.

TSE 300 Composite Index Canada's leading stock market indicator, which since its inception on January 3, 1977, tracks approximately three-quarters of the dollar value of Canadian stock trades.

Unemployed Those over the age of fifteen who are actively seeking work and have no employment. Excluded are those who, though not working, are not actively seeking work. Thus full-time high school, college, and university students, those who have given up hope of finding a job, retirees, and prison inmates are not considered "unemployed."

Unemployment equilibrium The point at which the macroeconomic equilibrium real GDP is less than capacity real GDP.

Unemployment rate The percentage of the labour force that is unemployed.

Union See Labour union.

Union shop A firm which requires that all new employees become members of the union within a short time—usually a month.

Unitary elasticity When a price increase or decrease will have no effect on total revenue. The loss in revenue due to a reduction in price is exactly balanced by the increase in sales. Conversely, the increase in revenue due to an increase in price is exactly balanced by the reduction in sales.

Universality The principle by which social security payments are paid to everyone—rich or poor, whether needy or not. Examples of universal social insurance programs include the Canada (or Quebec) Pension Plan, unemployment insurance, and medical insurance.

Unlimited liability The principle by which an individual is accountable for all debts without limit.

Utility The pleasure, satisfaction, or usefulness derived from the consumption of a good or service.

Utility maximizing rule A rule which states that to obtain the maximum utility, the consumer should spend total income in such a way that the marginal utility from a dollar spent on one good is equal to the marginal utility of every dollar spent on every other good.

Value-added The amount added to the value of a product at each stage of the production process. It is calculated by subtracting the value of intermediate goods received from other firms from the selling price.

Variable A factor that can take on different values.

Variable resources Resources that can be increased or decreased by the firm in the short run.

Velocity of circulation of money The number of times, on average, a unit of money is spent on final goods and services in one year. In other words, it can be seen as the speed at which the stock of money is turned over.

Vertical equity Fairness in taxation for people with different incomes.

Vertical merger The merger of two or more firms engaged in different stages of the production of a good.

Voluntary export restraint (VER) An agreement by an exporting country to restrict, voluntarily, its exports of a particular good to another country. Canadian and US governments have made agreements with Japan, for example, to restrict Japanese imports of automobiles into the two countries and thus protect the jobs of Canadian and American auto and auto parts manufacturers.

Wages Regular payments and other benefits, such as holidays with pay, paid leave for sickness, and insurance payments to employees for labour services.

Wants The desire for goods or services not essential to sustain human life, such as stylish clothing or luxury travel.

Welfare state An industrial capitalist society that seeks to ensure the health, education, and economic prosperity of its citizens by means of government-operated social programs.

Canada, along with most other western mixed market economies, is a welfare state.

Working capital ratio (or current ratio) A ratio used as a measure of a corporation's liquidity, and calculated by dividing current assets by current liabilities.

Working poor Those who work full time and whose wages are below the poverty line.

Work-to-rule Action taken by workers to put pressure on management during a dispute. The workers perform their duties strictly according to their job descriptions, without shortcuts they may have found and without any additional effort.

BIBLIOGRAPHY

General

Archer, Maurice. *Introduction to Economics: A Canadian Analysis*. 2nd edition. Oakville: Maurice Archer Enterprises, Inc., 1984.

Baumol, William J., Alan S. Blinder, and William M. Scarth. *Economics: Principles and Policy*. 3rd Canadian edition. Toronto: Harcourt Brace Jovanovich, 1991.

Blomqvist, Ake, Paul Wonnacott, and Ronald Wonnacott. *Economics*. 2nd Canadian edition. Toronto: McGraw-Hill Ryerson, 1987.

Brue, Stanley L., and Donald R. Wentworth. *Economic Scenes: Theory in Today's World*. Englewood Cliffs: Prentice-Hall, 1988.

Lipsey, Richard G., Douglas D. Purvis, and Peter O. Steiner. *Economics*. 7th edition. New York: Harper and Row, 1991.

McConnell, Campbell R., Stanley L. Brue, and William Henry Pope. *Economics*. 5th Canadian edition. Toronto: McGraw-Hill Ryerson, 1990.

Parkin, Michael, and Robin Bade. *Economics: Canada in the Global Environment*. Don Mills: Addison-Wesley, 1991.

Samuelson, Paul, William D. Nordhaus, and John McCallum. *Economics*. 6th Canadian edition. Toronto: McGraw-Hill Ryerson, 1988.

Stager, David. *Economic Analysis and Canadian Policy*. 6th edition. Toronto: Butterworths, 1988.

The History of Economic Thought

Barber, William J. *A History of Economic Thought*. Harmondsworth: Penguin, 1991.

Galbraith, John Kenneth. *The Age of Uncertainty*. Boston: Houghton-Mifflin, 1977.

Heilbroner, Robert. *The Worldly Philosophers*. 6th edition. New York: Simon and Schuster, 1986.

Marshall, Howard D., and Natalie J. Marshall. *The History of Economic Thought: A Book of Readings*. New York: Pitman, 1968.

Soule, George. *Ideas of the Great Economists*. New York: Mentor, 1955.

Dictionaries

Bannock, Graham, R.E. Baxter, and Evan Davis. *The Penguin Dictionary of Economics*. 5th edition. London: Penguin, 1992.

Crane, David. *A Dictionary of Canadian Economics*. Edmonton: Hurtig, 1980.

Statistics

Bank of Canada. *Bank of Canada Review*. Ottawa: Bank of Canada, monthly.

Statistics Canada. *Canadian Economic Observer*. Ottawa: Statistics Canada, monthly.

————*Canadian Economic Observer: Historical Statistical Supplement*. Ottawa: Statistics Canada, annually.

————*Perspectives Canada*. Ottawa: Statistics Canada, annually.

————*Canada Yearbook*. Ottawa: Statistics Canada, annually.

Urquhart, M.C., and K.A.H. Buckley. *Historical Statistics of Canada*. 2nd edition. Ottawa: Statistics Canada, 1983.

World Bank. *Economic Development Report 1991: The Challenge of Development*. Oxford: Oxford University Press, annually.

Recent Economic Developments

Canadian News Facts

Financial Post Corporation Service Cards. Index of Publicly-Held Canadian Companies. Toronto: Financial Post.

The following newspapers:
Financial Post
Financial Times
The Globe and Mail

The following periodicals:
The Economist
Maclean's
Canadian Business
Fortune
Profit

Unit One Economics Is...

Heilbroner, Robert L. *The Making of Economic Society*. 6th edition. Englewood Cliffs: Prentice-Hall, 1980.

Heyne, Paul. *The Economic Way of Thinking*. 6th edition. New York: Macmillan, 1991.

Leblanc, Ronald C. *Values, Value Clarification and Economic Understanding*. Toronto: Canadian Foundation for Economic Education, 1986.

Marx, Karl. *Capital*. Volumes 1 and 2. Introduction by G.D.H. Cole and translated by Eden and Cedar Paul. London: Dent, 1930.

———and Friedrich Engels. *The Communist Manifesto*. In Raymond Postgate. *Revolution from 1789-1906*. New York: Harper Torchbooks, 1962.

Robinson, Marshall A. *An Introduction to Economic Reasoning*. New York: Anchor Books, 1980.

Schmelev, Nicholai, and Vladimir Popov. *The Turning Point: Revitalizing the Soviet Economy*. New York: Doubleday, 1989.

Smith, Adam. *An Inquiry into the Nature and Causes of the Wealth of Nations*. Edited by Edward Cannan. London: Methuen, 1951.

Unit Two Efficient Use of Resources

Cheveldayoff, Wayne. *The Business Page: How to read it and understand the economy*. New edition. Ottawa: Deneau, 1981.

De Jordy, Herve. *On Your Own: Successful Entrepreneurship in the '90s*. Toronto: McGraw-Hill Ryerson, 1990.

Financial Post 500. Summer 1992. Toronto: Maclean Hunter, 1992.

Frank, Robert H. *Microeconomics and Behaviour*. New York: McGraw-Hill, 1991.

Fry, Joseph N., *et al*. *Business Policy: A Canadian Casebook*. 2nd edition. Scarborough: Prentice-Hall, 1989.

Fuhrman, Peter H. *Business in the Canadian Environment*. 3rd edition. Scarborough: Prentice-Hall, 1989.

Heyne, Paul. *Microeconomics*. Chicago: SRA, 1988.

Jennings, William E. *Entrepreneurship: A Primer for Canadians*. Toronto: Canadian Foundation for Economic Education, 1985.

Pindyck, Robert S., and Daniel L. Rubinfeld. *Microeconomics*. New York: Macmillan, 1989.

Ruggieri, G.C. *The Canadian Economy: Problems and Policies*. 3rd edition. Toronto: Gage, 1987.

Vogt, Roy, and Edwin Dolan. *Microeconomics*. 3rd Canadian edition. Toronto: Holt, Rinehart, and Winston, 1988.

White, Jerry S. *The Art and Science of Small Business Management*. Markham: Penguin, 1989.

Unit Three Equitable Distribution of Income

Auld, D.A.L., and F.C. Miller. *Principles of Public Finance: A Canadian Text*. Toronto: Methuen, 1977.

Block, Walter E., ed. *Economics and the Environment: A Reconciliation*. Vancouver: The Fraser Institute, 1990.

Department of Finance, Canada. *Goods and Services Tax: A Summary*. Ottawa: 1990.

Galbraith, John Kenneth. *The Affluent Society*. New York: Mentor, 1958.

Gunderson, Morley, and W. Craig Riddell. *Labour Market Economics: Theory, Evidence and Policy in Canada*. 2nd edition. Toronto: McGraw-Hill Ryerson, 1988.

Leblanc, Ronald C. *Values, Value Clarification, and Economic Understanding*. Toronto: Canadian Foundation for Economic Education, 1986.

Minister of Supply and Services. *Current Year Estimates. Part 1: The Government Expenditure Plan*. Minister of Supply and Services Canada.

Morton, Desmond, with Terry Copp. *Working People: An Illustrated History of the Canadian Labour Movement*. Revised edition. Ottawa: Deneau, 1984.

Rabbior, Gary. *An Overview of the Goods and Services Tax*. Economic Bulletin #3. Toronto: Canadian Foundation for Economic Education, 1990.

Smith, Larry. *Canada's Charitable Economy: Its Role and Contribution*. Toronto: Canadian Foundation for Economic Education, 1992.

Statistics Canada. *Women in Canada: A Statistical Report*. 2nd edition. Ottawa: Minister of Supply, 1990.

———*Canadian Social Trends*. Ottawa: Minister of Supply, various issues.

Strick, J.C. *Canadian Public Finance*. 3rd edition. Toronto: Holt, Rinehart and Winston, 1985.

Unit Four Economic Stability

Berton, Pierre. *The Great Depression, 1929-1939*. Toronto: McClelland and Stewart, 1990.

Binhammer, H.H. *Money, Banking and the Canadian Financial System*. 5th edition. Scarborough: Nelson, 1988.

Courchene, Thomas J. *In Praise of Renewed Federalism*. Toronto: C.D. Howe Institute, 1991.

Friedman, Milton. *Capitalism and Freedom*. Chicago: University of Chicago Press, 1962.

Friedman, Milton and Rose. *Free to Choose: A Personal Statement*. New York: Harcourt, Brace, Jovanovich, 1980.

———*Tyranny of the Status Quo*. New York: Harcourt, Brace, Jovanovich, 1984.

Galbraith, John Kenneth. *Money: Whence it came, where it went*. New York: Bantam, 1976.

Grant, John. *A Handbook of Economic Indicators*. Toronto: University of Toronto Press, 1992.

Lipsey, Richard G., ed. *Zero Inflation: The Goal of Price Stability*. Toronto: C.D. Howe Institute, 1990.

Rabbior, Gary. *The "Macro" Economy: An Introduction to How It Works*. Toronto: Canadian Foundation for Economic Education, 1989.

Rugman, Alan M., and Joseph R. D'Cruz. *Fast Forward: Improving Canada's International Competitiveness*. Kodak Inc., 1991.

Vogt, Roy, and Edwin G. Dolan. *Macroeconomics*. 3rd Canadian edition. Toronto: Holt, Rinehart and Winston, 1988.

Unit Five Economic Growth and International Trade

Block, Walter E., ed. *Economics and the Environment: A Reconciliation*. Vancouver: The Fraser Institute, 1990.

Economic Council of Canada. *Pulling Together, Productivity, Innovation and Trade: A Summary*. Ottawa, 1992.

————*A Joint Venture: The Economics of Constitutional Options*. Summary of the 28th annual review. Ottawa, 1991.

Price, Victoria Curzon. *Free Trade Areas, The European Experience: What Lessons for Canadian-U.S. Trade Liberalization?* Toronto: C.D. Howe Institute, 1987.

Rabbior, Gary. *The Canadian Economy: Adjusting to Global Change*. Toronto: Canadian Foundation for Economic Education, 1990.

Smith, Murray G., and Frank Stone, eds. *Assessing the Canada-U.S. Free Trade Agreement*. Halifax: Institute for Research on Policy Debates, 1987.

Stanford, Quentin. *The Global Challenge: A Study of World Issues*. Toronto: Oxford, 1990.

Todaro, Michael P. *Economic Development in the Third World*. 4th edition. New York: Longman, 1989.

Wonnacott, Ronald J. *The Economics of Overlapping Free Trade Areas and the Mexican Challenge*. Toronto: C.D. Howe Institute, 1991.

World Bank. *World Development Report 1991: The Challenge of Development*. Oxford: Oxford University Press, 1991.

World Resources Institute. *World Resources 1990-91*. New York: Oxford University Press, 1990.

INDEX

Absolute advantage, 474-75
Accelerator, 358-60
  and interaction with the multiplier, 360
  characteristics of, 360
Accounting profit, 145-46
Acid rain, 87
Acid test, 131
Advertising, 89, 182, 196, 201
  and the market system, 89
  in monopoly, 182, 201
  in oligopoly, 196, 201
Aggregate demand, 364-67, 369-73, 377-80, 421-22
  and aggregate supply, 369-73
  and consumption, 365-66
  and equilibrium, 369-72
  and fiscal policy, 377-80
  and foreign trade, 366, 367
  and government spending, 366-67
  and investment, 365-66
  and monetary policy, 421-22
  shape of curve, 365
  shifts in, 366-67
Aggregate supply, 367-69, 371-73, 424-25, 428-29, 431-32
  and aggregate demand, 369-73
  and equilibrium, 369-72
  and fiscal policy, 371-73
  and monetary policy, 421-22
  and supply-side economics, 431-32
  shape of curve, 367-68
  shifts in, 368-69
  supply shocks and, 368-69, 428-29
Agriculture, 92-93, 465, 468, 505-6
  and farm incomes, 93
  and marketing boards, 92-93
  government policies toward, 92
  in less developed countries, 465, 468

trade negotiations affecting, 505-6
Alias Research Inc., 100-101
Arbitration (of contract disputes), 233
Assets, 128, 129
Average, 285-86
Average costs, 147-49
  fixed, 147, 148, 149
  long-run, 150-51
  short-run, 146-51
  total, 147, 148, 149
  variable, 147-48, 149
Average product, 142-43, 144
Auto Pact, 506
Automatic stabilizers, 380
Ayre's Ltd., 113

Balance of merchandise trade, 481
Balance of payments, 34, 481-93
  and exchange rate, 486-93
  capital account, 483-85
  current account, 483
Balance sheet, 128-29
Balance sheet ratios, 131
Balanced budget, 383
Bank of Canada, 409-15, 420-38
  and changes in the bank rate, 414-15
  and changes in the required reserve ratio, 415
  and moral suasion, 415
  and open market operations, 412-14
  and transfer of federal government deposits, 414
  functions of, 410-15
    banker's bank, 410-11
    control of money supply, 411-15, 420-38
    federal government's banker, 411
    issue of paper currency, 410
  objectives of, 410

Bank of Nova Scotia, 116
Bank rate, 410, 414-15
Bankruptcies, in Canada, 1981-1991, 340
Banks, 404, 405, 409-15. *See also* Bank of Canada; Money
  branch banking, 404
  chartered banks, 404, 405
  near banks, 404
Barrier Technology Inc., 101-2
Barter, 395
Baseball salaries, 223
Bastiat, Frédéric, 503
Benefits-received principle, of taxation, 276, 278
Bid rigging, 200
Bingham, Stephen, 100-1
Black markets, 90, 91
Block, Walter, 460-61, 509
  on economic growth, 460-61
  on the level playing field, 509
Boycotts, 233
Break-even point, 167
British Columbia Hydro and Power Authority, 117
Budget deficit, 376-80, 383-84, 385-88
  and federal debt, 384-88
  and fiscal policy, 376-80
  control of, 389
  financing of, 384
  in Canada, 1967-1991, 385-87
  problems of, 388
  real *vs.* nominal, 387-89
  three views on, 383
Budget surplus, 376-80, 383, 385-87
  and fiscal policy, 376-80
  in Canada, 1967-1991, 385-87
  three views on, 383
Business cycle, 338-60, 377-80, 420-37

542 INDEX

and fiscal policy, 377-80
and income and price policies, 429-31
and monetary policy, 420-28, 431-37
causes of, 342-47, 350-53, 356-60
expansions and contractions of, 1952-1991, 338
in Canada, 339-41, 342
phases of, 338, 341-42
Business failures, 106-8
Business finance. *See* Business organization and finance
Business fluctuations. *See* Business cycle
Business organization and finance, 115-36
co-operatives, 116-17, 127-28
corporations, 116-22
government enterprises, 117, 133, 134, 135-36
partnerships, 116
sole proprietorships, 116
Business plan, 104-6, 110-11

Canada Assistance Plan, 265, 296
Canada Labour Relations Board, 231
Canada Pension Plan, 296
Canada Post, 117
Canada-US Free Trade Agreement, 506-10, 513
benefits and costs of, 507-8, 509
provisions of, 507
Canadian Airlines International Limited, 204
Canadian banking system, 403-15
and money creation, 404-9
Bank of Canada, 409-15
branch banking, 404
chartered banks, 404, 405
near banks, 404
Canadian economic system
and three major economic questions, 29
characteristics of, 29-31
objectives of, 31-35
role of government in, 23, 28-29
Canadian Federation of Labour, 239
Canadian Labour Congress, 238-39
Canadian Pacific Limited, 116, 209-10
Canadian Radio-Television and

Telecommunications Commission, 206
Canadian Transport Commission, 206
Canadian Wheat Board, 92
Cappit, 104-6
Careers, in economics, 17, 514
Cartel, 200. *See also* Organization of Petroleum Exporting Countries (OPEC)
Cash-flow forecast, 110-11
Cashless society, 401-2
Ceiling Doctor International, 109-10
Cement industry, 203-4
Central labour organizations, 238-39
Chatham Run Inc., 107-8
Circular flow model, 45, 213, 261-62, 307, 343, 346, 350, 473-74
and measuring GDP, 307
with government, 261-62, 350
with international trade, 473-74
with productive resources market, 213
with saving and investment, 346
Clipping coinage, 394
Closed shop, 231
Club of Rome, 461
Collective bargaining, 231-32
Collusion, 176, 199-200
Combined ratios, 132
Common market, 506. *See also* European Community
Common stock (or shares), 119
Commonwealth of Independent States, 38
Comparative advantage, 475-76
Competition, 31
Adam Smith's views on, 24
and international trade, 474, 475, 476, 508, 509, 512, 515
and the market system, 31
and monopolistic competition, 190-93
and oligopoly, 195-201
and perfect competition, 158-70
in competitive markets, 73-77, 86, 89
in the German auto industry, 40-41
legislation to promote, 204-6
Competition Act, 204-6, 210
Competition Bureau, 205
Competition Tribunal, 204-6
Composite Index of Leading Indicators

(Statistics Canada), 381, 382
Compulsory check-off, 232
Conable, Barber, 461
Concentration, in Canadian industry, 193-94
Conciliation (to resolve contract disputes), 233
Confederation of National Trade Unions, 238-39
Consumer Price Index (CPI), 324-25, 327, 330, 429, 430-31
and wage and price controls, 430-31
changes in, 325
in Canada, 1980-1990, 429
increases in components of, 1961-1991, 325
limitations of, 325, 327, 330
weights of major components, 324
Consumer sovereignty, 31
Consumer spending, 311, 313, 343-44
and availability of credit, 343
and current disposable income, 343
and expectations of future income, 343
and expectations of future price levels, 344
and interest rates, 343-44
and wealth, 344
as a component of GDP, 311
Consumer surplus, 56-57
Consumers Association of Canada, 205
Contracts, labour, 231-32
Co-operatives, 127-28, 134
advantages of, 128
disadvantages of, 128
in Canada, 127
principles of, 127-28
Co-op Fédérée du Québec, 116-17
Corporate bonds, 121
Corporation profits, 254-55, 309, 310
as a proportion of domestic income, 254-55
in GDP, 309, 310
Corporation income tax, 271, 275
Corporations, 116, 119, 120-22, 434. *See also* Crown corporations
advantages of, 121
and limited liability, 119
Canada's top 30, 120

characteristics of, 119
control of, 121
disadvantages of, 121-22
examples of, 116, 120
financing of, 119, 121
Costs, of the firm, 144-51
  average fixed, variable, and total, 147-49
  explicit, 145-46
  fixed, 146
  implicit, 145-46
  long-run, 150-51
  marginal, 149, 150
  short-run, 146-51
  total, 146-49, 150
  variable, 146, 147-48
Court injunction, 236
Craft union, 231
Credit cards, 401, 403
Credit unions, 404, 405
Cross, Steve, 107-8
Crown corporations, 133, 134, 135-36, 259
  advantages of, 135-36
  disadvantages of, 135-36
  federal, 133, 135
  provincial, 133, 135
Currency, 397
Custom duties, 273
Customs union, 507
Cut-throat competition, 200

Debasement, 394
De Beers, 182-83
Debit cards, 401-2
Decision making, 4-5
Decreasing returns to scale, 152-53
Deficits. See Budget deficits
Demand, 44-57, 60-62, 74-76, 92. See also Aggregate demand; Demand curve
  and prices, 74-75
  changes (shifts) in, 48-50, 60-62
  changes in and equilibrium, 76
  elasticity of, 50-55, 78-79
  for agricultural products, 92
  law of, 46
  market, 47
  utility and, 55-57

Demand curve, 46-50, 159-62, 178, 190-91, 196-99. See also Demand
  in monopolistic competition, 190-91
  in monopoly, 178
  in oligopoly, 196-99
  in perfect competition, 159-62
Demand deposits, 399
Demand for Canadian dollars, in foreign trade, 488-89
Demand for labour, 214-20
  elasticity of, 219-20
  derived demand, 215
  market demand for labour, 218
  of competitive firm, 215-16
  of imperfectly competitive firm, 216-18
  shifts in, 218, 221
Demand for loans, 250
Demand for money
  and money market, 403
  factors influencing, 398
  liquidity preference, 398
  precautionary motive, 397
  speculative motive, 397
  transactions motive, 397-98
Deposits, 395, 399-401
  daily interest chequable savings, 399, 400, 401
  demand deposits, 399, 400, 401
  multiplier, 408
  non-personal savings or notice, 399, 400, 401
  savings or notice, 399, 400, 401
  term, 399, 400, 401
Depreciation, 129, 130
  and GDP, 310, 312
Depression, 338, 341, 342
Diamonds, 182-83
Direct investment, 516-19, 484
Discouraged workers, 318
Discretionary fiscal policy, 377-79
Discretionary income, 313
Diseconomies of scale, 152-53
Distribution of income. See Income distribution
Distribution of wealth, in Canada, 288-89
Dividend, 119, 128
Domestic income, 254-55, 312-13

components of, 254-55
Double coincidence of wants, 395
Dow Jones Industrial Average, 123-25

Earnings per common share ratio, 132
Easy money policy. See Monetary policy
Economic Council of Canada, 31-32, 322, 513
Economic efficiency, 32, 43-210
  allocative, 32, 169-70
  in competitive markets, 168-71
  in monopolistically competitive markets, 193
  in monopoly markets, 181, 184
  in oligopoly markets, 202
  of the tax system, 278
  productive, 169, 170
  technological, 32
Economic forecasting, 380-83
  Help-wanted Index, 382
  leading indicators and, 381
  statistical models for, 380-81
Economic growth, 33-34, 444-68
  definition of, 445
  and capital accumulation model, 447, 450
  and less developed countries, 461-68
  and production possibilities, 445
  and Thomas Malthus, 446-47, 448-49
  benefits of, 456, 458-60
  costs of, 456-57, 459-61
  in Canada, 445-46, 452, 453
  in Canada vs. Japan, 452, 453
  sources of, 451-53, 455
  theories of, 446-50
Economic profit, 145-46
Economic reasoning, 10-11
  assumptions, 9
  cause-and-effect fallacy, 10
  fallacy of composition, 11
  loaded terminology, 10-11
  personification of a problem, 11
  single causation fallacy, 10
  subjectivity, 10
  wishful thinking, 10
Economic systems, 20-38
  and the three basic economic questions, 21
  types of

mixed market
  (Canada), 23, 28-35
  mixed command (former Soviet
    Union), 35-38
  pure command, 22
  pure market, 22-23, 85-86, 89
  traditional, 21
Economics
  definition of, 5
  and scientific method, 5, 7, 8
  as a science, 5, 7-9
  laws, principles, models, and theories
    in, 9
  normative, 8-9
  positive, 8-9
Economies of scale, 152-53, 184, 195,
  455, 474
  and economic growth, 455
  and international trade, 474
  in monopolies, 184
  in oligopolies, 195
Efficiency. See Economic efficiency
Elasticity. See Elasticity of demand;
  Elasticity of supply
Elasticity of demand, 50-55, 63-65, 78-
  79
  and income and substitution effects,
    78-79
  applications of, 53
  calculation of, 51, 63-65
  examples of, 65
  factors affecting, 52
  unitary, 50
Elasticity of supply, 62-67, 82-83
  and market equilibrium, 82-83
  and time, 82-83
  calculation of, 64
  factors affecting, 62-67
Employment, 317-20. See also Unemployment
  definition of employed, 317
  employment record, Canada, 318
  limitations of statistics, 318
  participation rate, 317
  trends in Canada, 1951-1990, 228, 230
  unemployment rate, 318-20
Energy taxes, 273
Entrepreneur, 98-112
  case studies of, 99-102, 107-8, 109-
    110, 113-14

characteristics of, 102-3
  functions of, 99
Equal pay for work of equal value,
  294-95
Equation of exchange, 436
Equilibrium, of market, 74-79, 82-83,
  90-91
  Alfred Marshall on, 81
Equilibrium level of income, 346-47,
  350-52
Equitable distribution of income. See
  Domestic income; Lorenz curve;
  Income distribution; Income
  inequality
Equity, of tax system, 276-78
Exchange rates, 486-94
  calculating, 487-88
  fixed, 491-92, 494
  floating (flexible), 490-91, 494
  international systems of, 494
  managed floating, 492, 494
  of Canadian dollar since 1945, 493-94
  policy, 493-94
Excise taxes, 271
Expansion (phase of the business
  cycle), 338, 342
Expenditure approach, to measuring
  GDP, 311-12, 313
Exports, 312, 353, 424, 473, 477-83. See
  also International trade
  as a component of GDP, 312
  Canadian, 477-83
  fluctuations in, 353
Externalities, 86, 87-88, 170, 260. See
  also Pollution
Extraterritoriality, 520
European (Economic) Community,
  507, 514, 516

Factors market. See Productive
  resources market
Family Allowance, 296
Federal debt, 384-89
  growth of, 385-86
  policies concerning, 389
  problems associated with, 388
  real vs. nominal, 386-88
Federal expenditures. See Government
  spending
Federal revenues. See Revenues

Federal Sales Tax, 271, 273
Fiat money, 395
Final goods, and GDP, 308-9
Financial statements, assessments of,
  128-33
First come, first served, 90, 91
Fiscal policy, 376-80, 383
  and the budget, 383
  and the business cycle, 379
  contractionary, 378-79
  discretionary, 377-79
  expansionary, 377-78
  limitations of, 379-80
Fixed costs, 146-47
Fixed exchange rates, 491-92
Floating exchange rates, 490-91, 494
Floor prices, 90
Flour bid riggers, 200
Ford Motor Company of Canada, 116
Forecasting. See Economic forecasting
Foreign exchange rates. See Exchange
  rates
Foreign investment and control, in
  Canada, 516-20
  benefits of, 520
  costs of, 520
  direct investment, 516-19
  government policy concerning, 520
  portfolio investment, 517
Foreign Investment Review Agency,
  520
Forever Green, 113-14
Franchise, 108-10
  advantages and disadvantages of, 109
  case study of, 109-10
  contract terms of, 109
  kinds of, in Canada, 109
Free riders, 86, 87
Free trade. See European Community;
  Free Trade Agreement, Canada and
  US; North American free trade area
  negotiations (NAFTA)
Free Trade Agreement, Canada and
  US, 1989, 506-8, 510
  benefits of, 507-8
  costs of, 508, 510
  provisions of, 507
Free trade area, 507
Friedman, Milton, 433, 434-35
  on economic freedom, 434

on importance of money supply, 434
on the monetary rule, 435
on the role of government, 435
Full employment, 32-33, 322. *See also*
Employment, Unemployment

Galbraith, John Kenneth, 266-67
GDP deflator, 327-28
General Agreement on Tariffs and
Trade (GATT), 505-6
*General Theory of Employment, Inter-
est, and Money*, 342, 348, 349
George, Henry, 247
Gold standard, 494
Goods and Services Tax (GST), 271-73,
277-78, 281
and the Federal Sales Tax, 271, 273
assessment of, 273, 277-78
how it works, 272
Gorbachev, Mikhail, 37
Government, 23, 28-29, 90-93, 133,
134, 135-36, 258-80, 293-301, 376-80,
384-89, 422-38. *See also* Bank of Canada; Budget; Fiscal policy; International trade; Monetary policy; Revenues; Taxes; Unemployment
and circular flow, 261-62
and efficient allocation of resources,
260-61
and equitable distribution of income,
261, 293-301
and legal framework of society, 259
and market, 90-93
and prices, 90
Crown corporations of, 133, 134, 135-
36, 259
economic functions of, 259-61
expenditures of, 259, 264-68
federal debt, 384-89
regulations of, 259
role in mixed market economy, 23, 24,
28-29, 259-61
Government spending, 262-65, 266-68
federal, 264-65, 267
federal transfers and, 264-65
growth of, in Canada since 1926, 262-
63
in Canada, compared with other
countries, 262-63
incomes and prices policy and, 429-31

local, 267-68
monetary policy and, 422-29, 433-38
provincial, 267, 268
public debt and, 267, 384-89
transfer payments and, 264-65
Graphing, 12-14
Green revolution, 465
Gross Domestic Product (GDP), 33,
307-12, 314-15, 329, 330, 339
definition of, 307
and distribution of income, 314-15
and environmental pollution, 315
and final goods, 308-9
and kinds of goods produced, 315
and leisure, 315
and market prices, 307-8
and population increases, 314
and price increases, 314
compared to GNP, 309
criticism of, by David Suzuki, 316-17
in Canada, 1980-1991, 339
limitations of, as a measure of economic well-being, 314-15
measurement of, expenditure
approach, 311-12
measurement of, income approach,
309-11
statistical discrepancy and, 310-11
underground economy and, 315
Gross National Product (GNP), 309
compared to Gross Domestic Product,
309
Growth. *See* Economic growth
Guaranteed Income Supplement, 296

Health insurance, 296
Help-wanted Index, 382
Horizontal equity, of tax system, 276
Hyperinflation, 33
Hypothesis, 7

Imperfect competition, 189. *See also*
Monopolistic competition; Oligopoly
Imperial Oil, 205
Import substitution, and economic
growth, 465
Imports, 312, 472, 477-82, 511-12,
515-16
as a component of GDP, 312
in Canada, 479-82

barriers to, 500-01
Income and price policies, 429-31
effectiveness of, 431
Prices and Incomes Commission, 430
Six and Five Program, 430
Three-Percent Annual Wage Cap, 431
Income approach, to measuring GDP,
309-11, 313
Income distribution, 282-301. *See also*
Lorenz curve
after taxes and transfers, 297-98
in other countries, 298-300
of families, 283-84
of unattached individuals, 284
trends in, 298
Income inequality, 283-87. *See also*
Lorenz curve
causes of, 287-90
trends in, 284
Income tax, 270-71, 274, 275
corporation, 271, 275
personal, 270-71, 274
Income of self-employed persons, in
GDP, 310
Income statement, 128, 130
Income statement ratios, 131-32
Increasing returns to scale, 152
Indirect taxes, 269, 275
in GDP, 310
Industrial union, 231
Inflation
definition of, 33
AD curve, equilibrium, and, 378-79
and automatic stabilizers, 380
and interest rates, 251
and fiscal policy, 378-79, 379-80
and income and price policies, 429-31
and monetarism, 433, 436-37
and monetary policy, 422-29, 433-38
and Phillips curve, 427-28, 429
and supply-side economics, 431-33
measurements of
Consumer Price Index, 324-37, 330
Consumer Price Index, in Canada,
1961-1991, 325
GDP deflator, 327-28
GDP deflator, in Canada, 1971-1991,
328
types of
cost-push, 424, 427

demand-pull, 424, 426
Inflationary gap, 370
Injections
    exports, 351-52
    government expenditures, 350-51, 352
    investment, 344, 351, 352
Injections and leakages approach, 342-47, 350-52
Interest, 249, 255, 309, 310
    as a proportion of domestic income, 255
    and GDP, 309, 310
Interest rates, 249-51
    and balance of payments, 492, 494
    and easy money policy, 421, 424-25
    and open market operations, 414
    and tight money policy, 422, 424-25
    determination of, 250-51
    factors influencing, 251
Intermediate goods, and GDP, 308
International trade, 472-94, 499-520.
    See also Exports; Imports; Injections;
    Leakages; Trade policy
    balance of merchandise trade, 481
    balance of non-merchandise trade, 483
    balance of payments, 485-86
    balance of trade on current account, 483
    capital account, 483-85
    invisible trade, 482-83
    merchandise imports and exports, 479-81
    policy concerning, 499-520
    reasons for, 474-75
    trade partners, Canada, 477-78
International unions, 238
Inventories
    and the business cycle, 344
    and GDP, 310
Investment
    and acceleration effect, 358-60
    and multiplier effect, 356-58
    and business cycles, 344-46, 353, 356
    and expectations about the future, 345-46
    and interest rates, 344, 345, 346
    and rates of return, 345

as a component of GDP, 311
    fluctuations in, 353, 356
    inventories and, 344
    in plant and equipment, 345-46
    in residential construction, 345
Investment Canada, 520
Invisible trade, 482-83
Ismail, Raghib (Rocket), 248-49, 283

Japan
    Canadian trade policy toward, 501, 502
    economic growth in, 452, 453, 514
    investment in Canada, 519-20
    trade with Canada, 477, 478, 481
Job prospects, in the 1990s, 229
Jones, Sonia, 99-100

Kelesi, Helen, 283
Keynes, John Maynard, 342, 348-49, 424-26, 433, 437
    and classical thought, 348, 349
    and Say's law, 348, 349
    on consumption, 349
    on employment, 349
    on equilibrium, 349
    on investment, 349
    stabilization policy of, 424-26
    vs. Monetarists, 433, 437
Kolker, William, 101-2

Labour force, 225-28, 317
    growth of, since 1945 (Canada), 225
    participation rates in, 225-26
    trends in, 226, 228-30
    women in, 227-28
Labour legislation, in Canada, 230
Labour markets, 224-25. *See also*
    Demand for labour; Supply of labour
Labour unions, 230-39
    and collective bargaining, 231-33
    and contracts, 232
    development of, in Canada, 237
    impact of, on wages, 239
    strikes and lockouts, 233, 236
    structure of, in Canada, 237-39
    types of, in Canada, 231

Laffer, Arthur, 431, 432
Laffer curve, 432
Law of diminishing returns, 143-44
Leading economic indicators, 381-82
Leakages
    imports, 351-52
    savings, 344, 352
    taxation, 350-51, 352
Less developed countries, 461-68
    and economic equity, 466-67
    and economic growth strategies, 465, 468
    characteristics of, 462
    problems of, 463-65
Liabilities, 128, 129
Limited liability, 119
Lindros, Eric, 223
Local government expenditures, 267-68
Local unions, 237
Lockouts, 233, 236
Long-run costs, 150-51
Long-run equilibrium, in competitive markets, 168
Lorenz curve, 284, 287, 297-99
    after taxes and transfers, in Canada, 297-98
    before taxes and transfers, in Canada, 284, 285, 286
    comparisons among countries, 299

M1, 381, 399, 400, 401
MIA, 399, 400
M2, 399, 400, 401
M2+, 399, 400, 401
M3, 399, 400, 401
MR = MC rule
    and monopolistic competition, 191-92
    and oligopoly, 198, 200-01
    and pure competition, 163-66
    and pure monopoly, 180-81
Macroeconomics, definition of, 43
Macroeconomic equilibrium, 369-72
    and changes in aggregate demand, 371
    and employment, 370
    and changes in aggregate supply, 371
    in the Canadian economy, 372
Malthus, Thomas, 446-47, 448-49, 461

on population growth, 446-47, 448, 449

on production growth, 446, 448, 449

on the future, 448-49

Managed floating exchange rates, 492, 494

Manufacturing capacity utilization rate, in Canada, 1981-1990, 339

Maquiladora, 513, 515

Marginal cost, 149, 150. *See also* MR = MC rule

Marginal efficiency of investment, 249-50, 345

Marginal product, 142-43, 144

Marginal productivity theory of wages, 216

Marginal propensity to consume, 354
  and the multiplier, 356-57
  calculation of, 354

Marginal propensity to save, 354
  and the multiplier, 356-57, 358
  calculation of, 354

Marginal revenue, 161-62. *See also* MR = MC rule

Marginal revenue product, 215-18

Marginal tax rate, 271

Marginal utility, 55-56

Market system, 24, 25, 26, 85-89
  advantages of, 85-86
  disadvantages of, 86-89
  views of Adam Smith on, 24, 25, 26

Market, 30, 73-93
  definition of, 30, 73
  agricultural, 92-93
  black, 90, 91
  competitive, 74-93
  demand and, 45-57
  equilibrium, 74-79
  labour, 224-25
  monopolistic, 175-84
  monopolistically competitive, 189-93
  oligopolistic, 195-206
  supply and, 57-67

Market failure, 260

Market structures, 158-59, 201. *See also* Monopoly; Oligopoly; Monopolistic competition; Perfect competition

Marketing boards, 92-93

Marshall, Alfred, 80-82
  definition of economics, 80
  on demand, 80-83
  on equilibrium, 80, 81
  on supply, 80-83
  on time and equilibrium, 80, 81
  on value, 80, 81-82

Marx, Karl, 26-28, 35
  labour theory of value, 27
  on capitalism, 27-28
  program, 28
  theory of labour, 26

Maxwell, Judith, 513-14

Mean, 285

Measure of value, 396

Median, 285

Mediation, of labour disputes. *See* Conciliation

Merchandise trade, 479-81

Mergers, 176, 204-6
  conglomerate, 205-6
  horizontal, 204
  vertical, 204-5

Merit goods, 260

Mexico, 510-12, 513-14
  and NAFTA negotiations, 512
  characteristics of, compared with Canada and US, 510-12

Microeconomics, definition of, 43

Minimum wage, 90, 242-44
  arguments against, 243-44
  arguments for, 244
  rates in Canada, 243

Mode, 286

Monetarism, 433-37
  and equation of exchange, 436
  and Milton Friedman, 434-35
  and quantity theory of money, 436-37
  and velocity of circulation, 433-34

Monetary policy, 420-38
  advantages of, 422-23
  and business cycle, 422, 423
  and fiscal policy, 424-26, 438
  and inflation, 422, 424
  and recession, 421
  easy (or expansionary), 421, 438
  Keynesian view of, 424-26, 433
  limitations of, 423-24

Monetarists' view of, 433-37
  recent, in Canada, 438
  tight (or contractionary), 421, 438

Money, 393-403
  definition of, 395
  characteristics of, 397
  demand for, 397-98
  evolution of, 394-95
  fiat money, 395
  fractionally-backed bank notes, 394
  functions of, 395-97
  market for, 403
  multiplier, 408
  near, 399
  paper, 394
  supply of, 399-401

Money creation, 403-9
  and currency leakage, 409
  and excess reserves, 409

Money destruction, 407-8

Money supply, 399-401, 403, 411-15

Monoculture, 468

Monopolistic competition, 158, 189-93
  characteristics of, 190
  demand curve of firms under, 190-91
  efficiency of, 193
  non-price competition under, 192-93
  price determination under, 190-91
  profit-maximizing output of, 191-92
  short-run equilibrium of, 190-92

Monopoly, 158, 175-84
  characteristics of, 176
  combinations and collusion, 176
  comparison with perfect competition, 181, 184
  De Beers, 182-83
  demand curve of, 178-79
  economic impact of, 181, 184
  government policy toward, 202-6
  legal, 176
  natural, 176, 206
  on Aspartame, 177
  profit-maximization under, 180-81
  revenues of, 179-81

Monopsony, 222, 223

Montreal Expos, 283

Moral suasion, 415

Mortgage, 404

Multiplier, 356-58
  and the accelerator, 358
  calculation of, 358
  in Canada, 357-58
Mundell, Robert, 431
Myrias Research, 107

National debt. *See* Federal debt
National Energy Board, 206
National unions, 238
Natural monopolies, 206
Natural resources, 3, 246-49
  and rent, 246-49
Needs, 3
Negative income tax, 303-4
Net Economic Welfare, 315
Net profit margin ratio, 131-32
Net worth, 128, 129
Neutrality principle, of taxation, 278-79
Non-tariff barriers, 501
Normative economics, 8-9, 234-35
North American Free Trade Area
  (NAFTA) negotiations, 510-16
  characteristics of the three economies,
    510-12
  Canadian perspective on, 515-16
  Mexican perspective on, 512
  US perspective on, 512, 515

Objectives, of the Canadian economy,
  31-35
Official International Reserves, 485
Okun's Law, 322-23
Old Age Security pension, 296
Oligopoly, 158, 195-206
  characteristics of, 195
  collusion in, 199-200
  differentiated, 195
  efficiency of, 202
  government policy toward, 202-6
  homogeneous, 195
  kinked demand curve of, 197
  price and output decisions under,
    196-97
  profit-maximization under, 198-99
  reasons for existence of, 195-96
  tacit agreement under, 202
Open market operations, 412-14
Open shop, 232

Opportunity cost, 5, 7, 15, 456-57, 475
Organization of Petroleum Exporting
  Countries (OPEC), 199, 371
Ostry, Sylvia, 466-67
  on global economic equity, 466-67
  on policies to combat poverty, 467
  on poverty, 466-67
  on poverty and public education,
    466-67
Ozone layer, 87

PE multiple, 132
Paper money, 394
Paradox of thrift, 352
Paradox of value, 58
Participation rates, 225, 226, 317
Partnerships, 116, 118-19, 134
  advantages of, 118
  characteristics of, 118
  disadvantages of, 118-19
  examples of, 116
Patent, 176
Pay equity, 295-96
Peak (of the business cycle), 338, 341
Peninsula Farms Ltd., 99-100
Perestroika, 37, 460
Perfect (or pure) competition, 157,
  159-70
  conditions necessary for, 159
  firm's demand curve under, 159-62
  market demand curve under, 159-60
  profit-maximization under, 162,
    163-66
  revenue curves under, 160-62
Personal disposable income, 313
Personal income, 313
Personal income tax, 270-71, 274
  federal rates, 271
  marginal rate, 271
  provincial, 274
  taxable income, 270
Phillips curve, 427-29
Picketing, 233
Planned investment, 346-47
Planned saving, 346-47
Pocket calculators, 78
Pollution, 86, 87-89, 260, 456-57,
  460-61
  acid rain, 87

and economic growth, 456-57, 460-61
  and government, 460
  decay of ozone layer, 87
  global warming, 87
  measures to control, 88-89
Portfolio investment, 485, 517
Positive checks, on population, 449
Positive economics, 8-9
Poverty, 290-96, 300-1
  definition of, 290
  and the welfare state in the 1980s and
    1990s, 300-1
  in less developed countries, 463-68
  incidence of, in Canada, 291-93
  programs to alleviate, 294-96
  programs to reduce, 293, 294
Poverty cycles, 463-65
Poverty line, 290-91
Precautionary motive, for holding
  money, 397
Predatory pricing, 206
Preferred shares, 119
Preventive checks, on population, 449
Price, 30-31
  definition of, 30
  Alfred Marshall's views on, 80-82
  and elasticity of demand, 78-79
  and elasticity of supply, 82-83
  and marketing boards, 92-93
  and monopolistic competition, 190-91
  and monopoly, 176-81
  and natural monopolies, 206
  and oligopoly, 195-202
  and shifts in demand, 76
  and shifts in supply, 77
  and the Competition Act, 204, 206
  and the competitive firm, 159-70
  competitive *vs.* monopolistic, 181, 184
  competitive *vs.* monopolistically com-
    petitive, 192-93
  competitive *vs.* oligopolistic, 202
  in a market system, 30-31, 85-86
  in the former Soviet economy, 36, 37
  maintenance, 206
  predatory, 206
  stickiness of, under oligopolies, 196-99
Price and income policies, 429-31
  Prices and Incomes Commission, 430
  problems of, 431

"Six and Five" Program, 430
  Three Percent Annual Wage Cap, 431
Price ceilings, 90-91
Price collusion, 199-200
Price discrimination, 184, 206
Price-earnings ratio, 132
Price floor, 90
Price index, 326-27. *See also* Consumer
  Price Index; GDP deflator
Price leadership, 200-2
Price level
  and aggregate supply and demand,
    369, 371-72
  and fiscal policy, 378-79
  and income and price policies, 429-31
  and monetary policy, 422
  and shifts in AD and AS, 371-72
  and supply-side economics, 431
  and supply shocks, 368
  and the equation of exchange, 436
  and the quantity theory of money,
    436-37
Product differentiation
  and monopolistic competition, 190,
    192
Production, 141-44
  average product, 142-43, 144
  law of diminishing returns, 143-44
  marginal product, 141-43, 144
  total product, 141-43, 144
Production costs, 144-51. *See also*
  Costs, of the firm
Production function, 141-53
Production possibilities curve, 13-16,
  445, 453
  and economic growth, 445, 453
  and opportunity cost, 15-16
Productive resources market, 213
Productivity, 92, 444-45, 453, 455
  and standard of living, 444
  in agriculture, 42
  marginal, 142-43, 144
  marginal productivity theory of wages,
    216
  of labour, 215, 445, 453
Profit, 22, 24, 31, 85, 86, 118, 120, 127,
  145-46, 251, 254-55, 309, 340, 345-46
  accounting, 145-46
  and Canadian business organizations,

116-17, 120, 127
  and domestic income, 254-55
  and investment, 345-46
  and the entrepreneur, 99
  and the market system, 85, 86
  as a characteristic of the Canadian
    economic system, 31
  as a percentage of GDP, 1982-1991,
    340
  corporation, as part of GDP, 309
  economic, 145-46
Profit maximization, 162-66, 180-81,
  191-92, 196-97
  in monopolistic competition, 191-92
  in oligopoly, 196-97
  in pure competition, 162-66
  in pure monopoly, 180-81
Profit-maximizing assumption, 141
Property taxes, 275-76
Provincial government revenues, 274-
  75
Provincial government expenditures,
  267, 268
Proxy, 121
Public goods, 260

Quantity theory of money, 436-37
Quebec Pension Plan, 296
Quick ratio, 131
Quotas, 91, 500

Rationing, 90, 91
Reaganomics, 432-33
Recession, 338, 341
  automatic stabilizers and, 380
  characteristics of, 339-41
  fiscal policy and, 377-78
  monetary policy and, 420, 438
  unemployment and, 321-22
Recessionary gap, 370
Recognition lag, 423
Rent, 246-49, 252, 253
  and GDP, 309, 310
  as a proportion of domestic income,
    255
  David Ricardo's views on, 252, 253
  determination of, 246-47
  economic rent and salaries, 248-49
  factors affecting, 247-48

Henry George's views on, 247
Research and development, 454-55
Reserve ratios, 415
Resources, 3, 141, 246-49, 451-53
  capital, 3, 451-52
  fixed, 141
  human, 3, 451, 453
  natural, 3, 246-49, 451
  variable, 141
Retail sale price maintenance, 206
Revenues
  in monopolistic competition, 191-92
  in monopoly, 178-81
  in oligopoly 197-98
  in perfect competition, 160-66
  of federal government, 270-74
  of local governments, 275-76
  of provincial governments, 274-75
Reynolds International Pen Company,
  187
Ricardo, David
  on conflict between workers and capi-
    talists, 253
  on distribution of income, 252
  on rent, 252, 253
  on wages, 252, 253-54
Rule of 72, 447

Sales taxes, 271, 275
Saving, 119, 249-51, 313, 343-47, 350-
  52, 366, 451, 471
  and aggregate demand, 366
  and circular flow, 343, 344, 346
  and economic growth, 451, 471
  and GDP, 313
  and interest rates, 249-51
  and investment, 346-47
  and spending, 344
  as a leakage, 346-47, 350-52
  business, 119, 346
  in less developed countries, 463
Say's law, 348, 349
Scarcity, 3, 5, 6, 14-16
  and agricultural land, 6
  and the production possibilities curve,
    14-16
Schatten, Kaaydah, 109-10
Scientific method, 7-8
Secondary reserve ratio, 415

Self-employed persons' income, 255
  as a proportion of domestic income,
  255
Self-interest, 24, 25, 29
  Adam Smith's views on, 24, 25
Share. See Stock
Shareholders, 119, 121, 129
Shareholder's equity, 129
Shatalin, Stanislav, 37
Shortages, in competitive markets, 75
Shut-down point, 167-68
Smith, Adam, 24-26
  on competition, 24
  on division of labour, 24, 25-26
  on self-interest, 24, 25
  on "the invisible hand", 25
Sobey's Inc., 100
Social balance, 266-67
Sole proprietorships, 116, 117-18, 134
  advantages of, 117
  characteristics of, 118
  disadvantages of, 117
  examples of, 116, 117
Sovereignty association, 507
Soviet economy, 22, 35-38
Soviet Union, 22, 35-38
Speculative motive (for holding
  money), 397-98
Spillovers, 86, 87-88
Stabilization policy, 261, 376-80, 420-
  27, 429-31. See also Fiscal policy;
  Monetary policy; Income and price
  policies
Stagflation, 427-31
  and changes in the labour market, 429
  and income and price policies, 429-31
  and supply shocks, 428-29
Standard of deferred payments, 397
Standard of living, 283, 456, 458, 459,
  461-63, 465-68
  Canadian, 283, 456, 458, 459, 462, 463
  in less developed nations, 463-65
  in low-income countries, 462
  in middle-income countries, 462-63
  in high-income countries, 462-63
  strategies for raising, 465-68
Statistical discrepancy, in GDP, 310-11
Stieb, Dave, 283
Stock, 119-20. See also Stock market
Stock market, 122-26

characteristics of, 122
  Dow Jones Industrial Average, 123-25
  quotations and indicators, 122-25
  TSE 300 Composite Index, 125-26
Store of value, 396-97
Strikes, 233, 234-35, 236
  Manitoba nurses strike, 1991, 234-35
  rotating, 233
Subsidy, 93, 260, 265, 501, 505, 508
Supply, 57-67, 74-77, 82-83. See also
  Aggregate supply
  and demand in competitive markets,
  74-77
  and price, 74
  changes in, 58-62
  changes in and equilibrium, 77
  elasticity of, 62-67, 82-83
  law of, 57-58, 74
  of labour, 220, 221, 225-26, 231
    and craft unions, 231
    and growth in Canadian labour force,
    225-26
    shifts in, 221
  of loans, 250-51
  shocks, 428
Supply-side economics, 431-33, 468
  and economic growth, 468
  and Laffer curve, 432
  and Reaganomics, 432-33
Surplus, in competitive markets, 75
Suzuki, David, 316-17, 458-59
  criticism of GNP and GDP, 316-17
  on economic growth, 458-59

Tacit agreement, 202
Tariffs, 273, 492, 500, 504-12, 515-16
  and Canada-US Free Trade Agreement, 506-8, 510
  and European Community, 516
  and federal government revenues, 273
  and fixed exchange rates, 492
  and GATT, 505-6
  and NAFTA negotiations, 510-12,
  515-16
  and the Auto Pact, 506
  arguments for, 501-4
  effects on prices, 500
  history since 1867, in Canada, 504-5
Tax, 269-73. See also Tariffs
  corporation income tax, 271

customs duties, 273
  direct, 269
  energy, 273
  excise, 271
  Federal Sales Tax, 271, 273
  Goods and Services Tax, 271-73,
  277-78
  indirect, 269, 275, 310
  personal income tax, 270-71, 274
  progressive, 269
  property, 275-76
  proportional, 269
  regressive, 269
  sales, 271
Tax system, 276-79
  criteria to evaluate, 276-79
  efficiency of, 278
  equity of, 276
  neutrality of, 278-79
Technological progress, 453, 455
Terms of trade, 475-76
Texaco, 205
Tight money policy. See Monetary
  policy
Toronto Blue Jays, 283
Toronto Stock Exchange, 300
  composite index, 125-26
Toronto Transit Commission, 117
Total costs, 146-47, 150
Total product, 142-43, 144
Total revenue minus total cost approach
  (TR-TC)
  applied under pure competition, 162,
  163, 164
  applied under pure monopoly, 180
Trade, international. See International
  trade
Trade policy, 499-516. See also Interna-
  tional trade; Tariffs
  arguments for protection, 501-4
  barriers to trade, 500-1
  Canada-US trade agreements, 506-8,
  510-12, 515-16
  development of, Canadian, 504-5
Traditional economic system, 21
Transactions motive (for holding
  money), 397
Transfer payments, 264-65, 275-76
  federal, to other levels of government,
  265

federal, to persons, 264-65
to local governments, 276
to provincial governments, 275
Transmission process, 424
Treasury bills, 414-15
Trough, of business cycle, 338, 341
Trust companies, 404, 405

Underemployment, 318
Underground economy, 315
Unemployment, 32-33, 317, 321-23,
341, 347, 350-52, 370-72, 377-78, 380,
421-23, 427-31, 476, 502-3, 508. *See
also* Unemployment rate
definition of (Statistics Canada), 317,
330
and aggregate demand-aggregate supply, 347, 370-72, 377-78
and automatic stabilizers, 380
and fiscal policy, 377, 380
and inflation, 426-29
and injections and leakages, 347, 350-
52
and international trade, 476, 502-3,
508
and monetary policy, 421-23, 438
and objectives of the Canadian economy, 32-33
and Phillips curve, 427-29
and price and income policy, 430-31
and stagflation, 428-31
costs of, 322-23
economic, 322-23
social, 323
equilibrium, 370
in depression, 341, 435
in recession, 341
types of, 321-22
cyclical, 321-22
frictional, 321
seasonal, 321
structural, 321
Unemployment Insurance, 271, 296

Unemployment rate, 318-20, 340
by age and sex in Canada, 1966-1990,
320
by region in Canada, 1977-1991,
319-20
in Canada, 1966-1991, 319
in the Great Depression, 338
of selected industrialized nations,
1987-1991, 320
Union federations, 238-39
Union locals, 237
Union shop, 232
Unions. *See* Labour unions
United States
and Auto Pact, 506
and free trade with Canada, 506-8,
510
and NAFTA negotiations, 512,
514
characteristics of, compared with
Mexico and Canada, 510-12
income distribution in, 298-300
investment in Canada, 516-20
Universality, 296
Utility, 55-57
and consumer decisions, 56
and consumer surplus, 56-57
and demand, 55
diminishing marginal utility, 55-56

Value
labour theory of (Marx), 27
paradox of, 58
Value-added, and GDP, 308-9
Value ratios, 132
Vancity Savings Credit Union, 117
Variable costs, 146-47
Velocity of circulation, 433, 436, 437
Vertical equity, of tax system, 276
Voluntary export restraints, 500

Wage and price controls. *See* Income
and price policies

Wages, 213, 215-16, 224-25, 252-55
as a proportion of domestic income,
254, 255, 309
David Ricardo's views on, 252, 253-54
determination of, in competitive
markets, 220-21
determination of, in imperfectly competitive markets, 222
differentials, 224-25
marginal productivity theory of, 216
Walker, Michael, 96-97, 471
Wants, 3
Wardair, 204
Welfare state, 293, 295-98, 300-1
criticism of, 300-1
in the 1980s and 1990s, 300
programs of, 293, 295-96
Women
entrepreneurs, 102. *See also* Jones,
Sonia; Schatten, Kaaydah
in economics, 513. *See also* Maxwell,
Judith; Ostry, Sylvia
in the labour force, 227, 228
Work-to-rule, 233
Working capital ratio, 131
Working poor, 301

Zero inflation policy, 438

Every reasonable effort has been made
to trace the original source of reprinted
material in this book. Where the
attempt has been unsuccessful, the
publisher would be pleased to hear
from copyright holders to rectify any
omission.

Quotations from **Karl Marx**'s work on
pages 27-28 are reprinted with the permission of A.P. Watt Ltd. on behalf of
Professor J. Postgate.